Contemporary Controversy

Contemporary
Controversy SECOND EDITION

Morris Freedman University of Maryland

Paul B. Davis University of New Mexico

The Macmillan Company, New York

PE 1417
F69
1973

The Macmillan Company
866 Third Avenue, New York, New York 10022

Collier-Macmillan Canada, Ltd., Toronto, Ontario

Library of Congress catalog card number: 78–190667

Printing: 1 2 3 4 5 6 7 8   Year: 3 4 5 6 7 8 9

Preface

William Hazlitt's contention that "when a thing ceases to be a subject of controversy, it ceases to be a subject of interest" is particularly appropriate in the classroom. We have found that in reading, writing, and discussion, students respond more intensely and perform more capably when stimulated and engaged by the controversial. This anthology is designed to provide such stimulation and engagement. It ranges from disputes about the right to bear arms to disagreements about the virtues of population control, from essays of vigorous polemic to ones of gentle persuasion. All the topics have two things in common: each is both a significant issue and the subject of controversy.

In our questions and assignments we have tried to emphasize narrower problems of composition and rhetoric as well as broader aesthetic, humanistic, social, and scientific issues. These broader issues are bound to overlap from one section to the next. We have noted some of these interrelationships, but we urge instructors to point out others and to concentrate on those aspects of the anthology that best suit their own inclinations and best serve their own purposes.

Some of the issues are represented by diametric oppositions, like the confrontation between Vice President Agnew and CBS President Stanton on television news or the debate between Doctors Szasz and Thorne on mental illness. Other issues are treated in a selective and analytical, rather than polemical, way; still other sections contain several differing, though not mutually exclusive, views of the chosen issues, as, for example, in the discussions of sex education and gun control. In nearly all the sections we have provided "objective" material, so that the opinions in the arguments may be judged against the "facts." In other controversies, the evidence emerges in the course of debate, as in the television play *The Pill Man*, from *The Defenders* series, in which the substantiation for the pro and con arguments is educed in the course of the trial.

The suggestions for additional reading serve to make a small casebook of each section. By pursuing these readings, a student can delve in depth into particular aspects of broad issues, like those in "Soul Language and Standard English," or go into broader questions from sections with a more specific focus, like those on Lawrence's Christology or the literary selections in "Studies in Black and White." Teachers may wish to place certain books on reserve in their campus libraries since they directly supplement our text: "The Pentagon Papers," for example, in any one of the several published versions, and D. H. Lawrence's *The Man Who Died*.

The controversies we have chosen illustrate different kinds of written

English, from the technical, precise language of the scientific report to the evocative rhetoric of a lawyer's defense in a capital case. In using the book the student will be confronted by widely varying degrees of concern for documentation, by different styles of footnoting and punctuation, and even by variations in spelling. Although the most obvious differences may be those observed between British and American usage in vocabulary, idiom, and spelling, more basic and general differences can be noted between legal or scientific prose, with its requirements for precision, and prose that is intended for the general reader. We have not standardized the texts or tried to eliminate these differences. Rather, we hope that the variety will give the student a more realistic view of the written language than is provided by more conventional essay texts. Effective writing depends upon the recognition of many kinds of English style and the development of the capacity to discriminate among them.

We owe many debts in compiling this book, to our colleagues, family, friends, students, and editors, among whom we wish especially to thank George Arms, Carolyn Banks, Jackson Bryer, Molly G. Emler, Mary Davis, Bess Earp, Charlotte K. Freedman, Nathan Glazer, Pamela Hill, Klara Kelly, Susan Kornit, Susan Nippes, Ralph Norman, Pamela Riepe, Susan Robinson, Almira Saffle, Don Schlegel, Alvin L. Schorr, Murray Stein, Martin Steinmann, E. W. Tedlock, and David Vernon. All mistakes and shortcomings are, of course, our own.

M. F.

P. B. D.

Contents

SECTION FOUR *Method and Madness*

SECTION FIVE *Drug Addiction: Family Illness or Social Crime?*

SECTION SIX *Christ and the Body*

SECTION SEVEN *Population Control
Begins at Home*

SECTION EIGHT *Sex and the School Child*

SECTION TWELVE *Women as Professors*

SECTION THIRTEEN *The Death Sentence*

SECTION FOURTEEN *When Does Life End?*

SECTION ONE *Channeling*

Opinion

You can fool all of the people some of the time, and
some of the people all the time, but you cannot
fool all the people all of the time.
ABRAHAM LINCOLN

Remarks of the President on Vietnam, November 3, 1969

Richard M. Nixon

Good evening, my fellow Americans:

Tonight I want to talk to you on a subject of deep concern to all Americans and to many people in all parts of the world—the war in Vietnam.

I believe that one of the reasons for the deep division about Vietnam is that many Americans have lost confidence in what their government has told them about our policy. The American people cannot and should not be asked to support a policy which involves the overriding issues of war and peace unless they know the truth about that policy.

Tonight, therefore, I would like to answer some of the questions that I know are on the minds of many of you listening to me.

How and why did America get involved in Vietnam in the first place?

How has this Administration changed the policy of the previous Administration?

What has really happened in the negotiations in Paris and on the battlefront in Vietnam?

What choices do we have if we are to end the war?

What are the prospects for peace?

Let me begin by describing the situation I found when I was inaugurated on January 20.

- The war had been going on for four years.
- 31,000 Americans had been killed in action.
- The training program for the South Vietnamese was behind schedule.
- 540,000 Americans were in Vietnam with no plans to reduce the number.
- No progress had been made at the negotiations in Paris and the United States had not put forth a comprehensive peace proposal.
- The war was causing deep division at home and criticism from many of our friends as well as our enemies abroad.

In view of these circumstances there were some who urged I end the war at once by ordering the immediate withdrawal of all American forces.

From a political standpoint this would have been a popular and easy course to follow. After all, we became invoved in the war while my predecessor was in office. I could blame the defeat which would be the result of my action on him and come out as the peacemaker. Some put it quite bluntly: This was the only way to avoid allowing Johnson's war to become Nixon's war.

But I had a greater obligation than to think only of the years of my Administration and the next election. I had to think of the effect of my decision on the next generation and on the future of peace and freedom in America and in the world.

Let us all understand that the question before us is not whether some Americans are for peace and some Americans are against peace. The question at issue is not whether Johnson's war becomes Nixon's war.

The great question is: How can we win America's peace?

Let us turn now to the fundamental issue. Why and how did the United States become involved in Vietnam in the first place?

Fifteen years ago North Vietnam, with the logistical support of Communist China and the Soviet Union, launched a campaign to impose a Communist government on South Vietnam by instigating and supporting a revolution.

In response to the request of the government of South Vietnam, President Eisenhower sent economic aid and military equipment to assist the people of South Vietnam in their efforts to prevent a Communist takeover. Seven years ago, President Kennedy sent 16,000 military personnel to Vietnam as combat advisors. Four years ago, President Johnson sent American combat forces to South Vietnam.

Now, many believe that President Johnson's decision to send American combat forces to South Vietnam was wrong. And many others—I among them—have been strongly critical of the way the war has been conducted.

But the question facing us today is—now that we are in the war what is the best way to end it?

In January I could only conclude that the precipitate withdrawal of American forces from Vietnam would be a disaster not only for South Vietnam but for the United States and for the cause of peace.

For the South Vietnamese, our precipitate withdrawal would inevitably allow the Communists to repeat the massacres which followed their takeover in the North 15 years before.

They then murdered more than 50,000 people and hundreds of thousands more died in slave labor camps.

We saw a prelude of what would happen in South Vietnam when the Communists entered the city of Hue last year. During their brief rule, there was a bloody reign of terror in which 3,000 civilians were clubbed, shot to death, and buried in mass graves.

With the sudden collapse of our support, these atrocities of Hue would become the nightmare of the entire nation—and particularly for the million and a half Catholic refugees who fled to South Vietnam when the Communists took over in the North.

For the United States, this first defeat in our nation's history would result in a collapse of confidence in American leadership, not only in Asia but throughout the world.

Three American Presidents have recognized the great stakes involved in Vietnam and understood what had to be done.

In 1963, President Kennedy, with his characteristic eloquence and clarity, said, "we want to see a stable government there carrying on the struggle to maintain its national independence. We believe strongly in that. We're not going to withdraw from that effort. In my opinion for us to withdraw from that effort would mean a collapse not only of South Vietnam, but Southeast Asia, so we're going to stay there."

President Eisenhower and President Johnson expressed the same conclusion during their terms of office.

For the future of peace, precipitate withdrawal would thus be a disaster of immense magnitude.

- A nation cannot remain great if it betrays its allies and lets down its friends.
- Our defeat and humiliation in South Vietnam would without question promote recklessness in the councils of those great powers who have not yet abandoned their goals of world conquest.
- This would spark violence wherever our commitments help maintain peace—in the Middle East, in Berlin, eventually even in the Western Hemisphere.

Ultimately, this would cost more lives.

It would not bring peace but more war.

For these reasons, I rejected the recommendation that I should end the war by immediately withdrawing all our forces. I chose instead to change American policy on both the negotiating front and the battlefront.

In order to end a war fought on many fronts, I initiated a pursuit for peace on many fronts.

In a television speech on May 14, in a speech before the United Nations, and on a number of other occasions I set forth our peace proposals in great detail.

- We have offered the complete withdrawal of all outside forces within one year.
- We have proposed a cease-fire under international supervision.
- We have offered free elections under international supervision with the Communists participating in the organization and conduct of the elections as an organized political force. The Saigon Government has pledged to accept the result of the elections.

We have not put forth our proposals on a take-it-or-leave-it basis. We have indicated that we are willing to discuss the proposals that have been put forth by the other side. We have declared that anything is negotiable except the right of the people of South Vietnam to determine their own future. At the Paris peace conference, Ambassador Lodge has demonstrated our flexibility and good faith in 40 public meetings.

Hanoi has refused even to discuss our proposals. They demand our unconditional acceptance of their terms, which are that we withdraw all American forces immediately and unconditionally and that we overthrow the government of South Vietnam as we leave.

We have not limited our peace initiatives to public forums and public statements. I recognized, in January, that a long and bitter war like this usually cannot be settled in a public forum. That is why in addition to the public statements and negotiations I have explored every possible private avenue that might lead to a settlement.

Tonight I am taking the unprecedented step of disclosing to you some of our other initiatives for peace—initiatives we undertook privately and secretly because we thought that we thereby might open a door which publicly would be closed.

I did not wait for my inauguration to begin my quest for peace.

- Soon after my election through an individual who is directly in contact on a personal basis with the leaders of North Vietnam I made two private offers for a rapid, comprehensive settlement. Hanoi's replies called in effect for our surrender before negotiations.
- Since the Soviet Union furnishes most of the military equipment for North Vietnam, Secretary of State Rogers, my Assistant for National Security Affairs, Dr. Kissinger, Ambassador Lodge, and I, personally, have met on a number of occasions with representatives of the Soviet Government to enlist their assistance in getting meaningful negotiations started. In addition we have had extended discussions directed toward that same end with representatives of other governments which have diplomatic relations with North Vietnam. None of these initiatives have to date produced results.
- In mid-July, I became convinced that it was necessary to make a major move to break the deadlock in Paris talks. I spoke directly in this office, where I am now sitting, with an individual who had known Ho Chi Minh on a personal basis for 25 years. Through him I sent a letter to Ho Chi Minh.

I did this outside of the usual diplomatic channels with the hope that with the necessity of making statements for propaganda removed, there might be constructive progress toward bringing the war to an end. Let me read from that letter:

Dear Mr. President:

I realize that it is difficult to communicate meaningfully across the gulf of four years of war. But precisely because of this gulf, I wanted to take this opportunity to reaffirm in all solemnity my desire to work for a just peace. I deeply believe that the war in Vietnam has gone on too long and delay in bringing it to an end can benefit no one—least of all the people of Vietnam. . . .

The time has come to move forward at the conference table toward an early resolution of this tragic war. You will find us forthcoming and open-minded in a common effort to bring the blessing of peace to the brave people of Vietnam. Let history record that at this critical juncture, both sides turned their face toward peace rather than toward conflict and war.

I received Ho Chi Minh's reply on August 30, three days before his death. It simply reiterated the public position North Vietnam had taken in the Paris talks and flatly rejected my initiative.

The full text of both letters is being released to the press.

- In addition to the public meetings I referred to, Ambassador Lodge has met with Vietnam's chief negotiator in Paris in 11 private meetings.
- We have taken other significant initiatives which must remain secret to keep open some channels of communication which may still prove to be productive.

But the effect of all the public, private, and secret negotiations which have been undertaken since the bombing halt a year ago and since this Administration came into office on January 20, can be summed up in one sentence—

No progress whatever has been made except agreement on the shape of the bargaining table. Now who is at fault?

It has become clear that the obstacle in negotiating an end to the war is not the President of the United States. And it is not the South Vietnamese.

The obstacle is the other side's absolute refusal to show the least willingness to join us in seeking a just peace. It will not do so while it is convinced that all it has to do is to wait for our next concession, and the next until it gets everything it wants.

There can now be no longer any question that progress in negotiation depends only on Hanoi's deciding to negotiate, to negotiate seriously.

I realize that this report on our efforts on the diplomatic fronts is discouraging to the American people, but the American people are entitled to know the truth—the bad news as well as the good news, where the lives of our young men are involved.

Now let me turn, however, to a more encouraging report on another front.

At the time we launched our search for peace I recognized we might not succeed in bringing an end to the war through negotiation. I, therefore, put into effect another plan to bring peace—a plan which will bring the war to an end regardless of what happens on the negotiating front.

It is in line with a major shift which I described in my press conference at Guam on July 25. Let me briefly explain what has been described as the Nixon Doctrine—a policy which not only will help end the war in Vietnam, but which is an essential element of our program to prevent future Vietnams.

We Americans are a do-it-yourself people. We are an impatient people. Instead of teaching someone else to do a job, we like to do it ourselves. And this trait has been carried over into our foreign policy.

In Korea and again in Vietnam, the United States furnished most of the money, most of the arms, and most of the men to help the people of those countries defend their freedom against the Communist aggression.

Before any American troops were committed to Vietnam, a leader of another Asian country expressed this opinion to me when I was traveling in Asia as a private citizen. He said, "When you are trying to assist another nation defend its freedom, U.S. policy should be to help them fight the war but not to fight the war for them."

Well, in accordance with this wise counsel, I laid down in Guam three principles as guidelines for future American policy toward Asia:

First, the United States will keep all of its treaty commitments.

Second, we shall provide a shield if a nuclear power threatens the freedom of a nation allied with us or of a nation whose survival we consider vital to our security.

Third, in cases involving other types of aggression, we shall furnish military and economic assistance when requested in accordance with our treaty commitments. But we shall look to the nation directly threatened to assume the primary responsibility of providing the manpower for its defense.

After I announced this policy, I found that the leaders of the Philippines, Thailand, Vietnam, South Korea, and other nations which might be threatened by Communist aggression, welcomed this new direction in American foreign policy.

The defense of freedom is everybody's business—not just America's business. And it is particularly the responsibility of the people whose freedom is threatened. In the previous Administration, we Americanized the war in Vietnam. In this Administration, we are Vietnamizing the search for peace.

The policy of the previous Administration not only resulted in our assuming the primary responsibility for fighting the war but, even more significantly, did not adequately stress the goal of strengthening the South Vietnamese so that they could defend themselves when we left.

The Vietnamization Plan was launched following Secretary Laird's visit to Vietnam in March. Under the plan, I ordered first a substantial increase in the training and equipment of South Vietnamese forces.

In July, on my visit to Vietnam, I changed General Abrams' orders so that they were consistent with the objectives of our new policies. Under the new orders, the primary mission of our troops is to enable the South

Vietnamese forces to assume the full responsibility for the security of South Vietnam.

Our air operations have been reduced by over 20 percent.

And now we have begun to see the results of this long-overdue change in American policy in Vietnam.

- After five years of Americans going into Vietnam, we are finally bring-American men home. By December 15, over 60,000 men will have been withdrawn from South Vietnam—including 20 percent of all of our combat forces.
- The South Vietnamese have continued to gain in strength. As a result they have been able to take over combat responsibilities from our American troops.

Two other significant developments have occurred since this Administration took office.

- Enemy infiltration, infiltration which is essential if they are to launch a major attack, over the last three months is less than 20 percent of what it was over the same period last year.
- Most important—United States casualties have declined during the last two months to the lowest point in three years.

Let me now turn to our program for the future.

We have adopted a plan which we have worked out in cooperation with the South Vietnamese for the complete withdrawal of all U.S. combat ground forces, and their replacement by South Vietnamese forces on an orderly scheduled timetable. This withdrawal will be made from strength and not from weakness. As South Vietnamese forces become stronger, the rate of American withdrawal can become greater.

I have not and do not intend to announce the timetable for our program. There are obvious reasons for this decision which I am sure you will understand. As I have indicated on several occasions, the rate of withdrawal will depend on developments on three fronts.

One of these is the progress which can be or might be made in the Paris talks. An announcement of a fixed timetable for our withdrawal would completely remove any incentive for the enemy to negotiate an agreement.

They would simply wait until our forces had withdrawn and then move in.

The other two factors on which we will base our withdrawal decisions are the level of enemy activity and the progress of the training program of the South Vietnamese forces. I am glad to be able to report tonight progress on both of these fronts has been greater than we anticipated when we started the program in June for withdrawal. As a result, our timetable for withdrawal is more optimistic now than when we made our first estimates in June. This clearly demonstrates why it is not wise to be frozen in on a fixed timetable.

We must retain the flexibility to base each withdrawal decision on the situation as it is at that time rather than on estimates that are no longer valid.

Along with this optimistic estimate, I must—in all candor—leave one note of caution.

If the level of enemy activity significantly increases we might have to adjust our timetable accordingly.

However, I want the record to be completely clear on one point.

At the time of the bombing halt just a year ago, there was some confusion as to whether there was an understanding on the part of the enemy that if we stopped the bombing of North Vietnam they would stop the shelling of cities in South Vietnam. I want to be sure that there is no misunderstanding on the part of the enemy with regard to our withdrawal program.

We have noted the reduced level of infiltration, the reduction of our casualties, and are basing our withdrawal decisions partially on those factors.

If the level of infiltration or our casualties increase while we are trying to scale down the fighting, it will be the result of a conscious decision by the enemy.

Hanoi could make no greater mistake than to assume that an increase in violence will be to its advantage. If I conclude that increased enemy action jeopardizes our remaining forces in Vietnam, I shall not hesitate to take strong and effective measures to deal with that situation.

This is not a threat. This is a statement of policy which as Commander-in-Chief of our Armed Forces I am making in meeting my responsibility for the protection of American fighting men wherever they may be.

My fellow Americans, I am sure you recognize from what I have said that we really only have two choices open to us if we want to end this war.

- I can order an immediate, precipitate withdrawal of all Americans from Vietnam without regard to the effects of that action.
- Or we can persist in our search for a just peace through a negotiated settlement if possible, or through continued implementation of our plan for Vietnamization if necessary—a plan in which we will withdraw all of our forces from Vietnam on a schedule in accordance with our program, as the South Vietnamese become strong enough to defend their own freedom.

I have chosen the second course.
It is not the easy way.
It is the right way.

It is a plan which will end the war and serve the cause of peace—not just in Vietnam but in the Pacific and in the world.

In speaking of the consequences of a precipitate withdrawal, I mentioned that our allies would lose confidence in America.

Far more dangerous, we would lose confidence in ourselves. The immediate reaction would be a sense of relief that our men were coming home. But as we saw the consequences of what we had done, inevitable remorse and divisive recrimination would scar our spirit as a people.

We have faced other crises in our history and have become stronger by rejecting the easy way out and taking the right way in meeting our challenges. Our greatness as a nation has been our capacity to do what had to be done when we knew our course was right.

I recognize that some of my fellow citizens disagree with the plan for peace I have chosen. Honest and patriotic Americans have reached different conclusions as to how peace should be achieved.

In San Francisco a few weeks ago, I saw demonstrators carrying signs reading: "Lose in Vietnam, bring the boys home."

Well, one of the strengths of our free society is that any American has a right to reach that conclusion and to advocate that point of view. But as President of the United States, I would be untrue to my oath of office if I allowed the policy of this nation to be dictated by the minority who hold that point of view and who try to impose it on the nation by mounting demonstrations in the street.

For almost 200 years, the policy of this nation has been made under our Constitution by those leaders in the Congress and in the White House selected by all of the people. If a vocal minority, however fervent its cause, prevails over reason and the will of the majority this nation has no future as a free society.

And now I would like to address a word if I may to the young people of this nation who are particularly concerned, and I understand why they are concerned about this war.

I respect your idealism.

I share your concern for peace.

I want peace as much as you do.

There are powerful personal reasons I want to end this war. This week I will have to sign 83 letters to mothers, fathers, wives and loved ones of men who have given their lives for America in Vietnam. It is very little satisfaction to me that this is only one-third as many letters as I signed the first week in office. There is nothing I want more than to see the day come when I do not have to write any of those letters.

I want to end the war to save the lives of those brave young men in Vietnam.

But I want to end it in a way which will increase the chance that their younger brothers and their sons will not have to fight in some future Vietnam someplace in the world.

And I want to end the war for another reason. I want to end it so that the energy and dedication of you, our young people, now too often directed into bitter hatred against those responsible for the war, can be turned to the great challenges of peace, a better life for all Americans, a better life for all people on this earth.

I have chosen a plan for peace. I believe it will succeed.

If it does not succeed, what the critics say now won't matter. Or, if it does succeed, what the critics say now won't matter. If it does not succeed, anything I say then won't matter.

I know it may not be fashionable to speak of patriotism or national destiny these days. But I feel it is appropriate to do so on this occasion.

Two hundred years ago this nation was weak and poor. But even then, America was the hope of millions in the world. Today we have become the strongest and richest nation in the world. The wheel of destiny has turned so that any hope the world has for the survival of peace and freedom will be determined by whether the American people have the moral stamina and the courage to meet the challenge of free world leadership.

Let historians not record that when America was the most powerful nation in the world we passed on the other side of the road and allowed the last hopes for peace and freedom of millions of people to be suffocated by the forces of totalitarianism.

And so tonight—to you, the great silent majority of my fellow Americans—I ask for your support.

I pledged in my campaign for the Presidency to end the war in a way that we could win the peace. I have initiated a plan of action which will enable me to keep that pledge.

The more support I can have from the American people, the sooner that pledge can be redeemed; for the more divided we are at home, the less likely the enemy is to negotiate at Paris.

Let us be united for peace. Let us also be united against defeat. Because let us understand: North Vietnam cannot defeat or humiliate the United States. Only Americans can do that.

Fifty years ago, in this room and at this very desk, President Woodrow Wilson spoke words which caught the imagination of a war-weary world. He said, "This is the war to end wars." His dream for peace after World War I was shattered on the hard realities of great power politics and Woodrow Wilson died a broken man.

Tonight I do not tell you that the war in Vietnam is the war to end wars. But I do say this:

I have initiated a plan which will end this war in a way that will bring us closer to that great goal to which Woodrow Wilson and every American President in our history has been dedicated—the goal of a just and lasting peace.

As President I hold the responsibility for choosing the best path to that goal and then leading the nation along it.

I pledge to you tonight that I shall meet this responsibility with all of the strength and wisdom I can command in accordance with your hopes, mindful of your concerns, sustained by your prayers.

Thank you and good night.

Transcripts of the Analyses Broadcast by the Three Commercial Television Networks

ABC Television Network

REYNOLDS: Back at our studios in Washington we propose to spend the next 25 minutes or so in a discussion of President Nixon's speech tonight on the war in Vietnam and his hopes of bringing it to an early end. I want to call first on our White House Correspondent Tom Jarriel who has tried to keep track of the President's preparation of the speech. And Tom, I'd like to ask you—we've all had a chance now not only to hear the President's speech but to read it just before he went on—did Mr. Nixon hope to mute the voices of dissent in this country, or was his primary goal really to rally the silent majority to his side?

JARRIEL: Frank, I don't think there's any question at all about it that his speech tonight was to the silent majority. He feels that these are the people who elected him, and these are the people who tonight he was reporting to. And his remarks were directed certainly to them and not to those who are the so-called peace groups in the country or those who are opposed to his administration. Tonight, perhaps, he has given the silent majority in the country a brief history lesson on Vietnam, explaining how we got there. He has restated his determination to continue exactly where we are and to firm that determination up and he projected a certain degree of optimism over it. He also feels perhaps that he has tonight better armed the silent majority with more information about Vietnam; given them some moral leadership against the opposing forces in the country who are opposing his course in Vietnam. He has, of course, offered no quick solutions, pulled no rabbits from hats, and those who

FROM the special ABC program as broadcast on ABC-TV, November 3, 1969. Reprinted with the permission of ABC. Participants are Frank Reynolds, Tom Jarriel, Averill Harriman, John Scali, William Lawrence, Robert Clark, and Bill Downs.

were looking for that certainly would be disappointed. The President tonight perhaps has polarized attitude in the country more than it ever has been into groups who are either for him or are against him.

REYNOLDS: And he's confident, no doubt, that those who are for him will perhaps not be quite so silent in the near future. Tom, why was there really nothing new; nothing substantively new in this speech? Why the big build-up for it? Why were we told 21 days ago that this speech was going to be given at this time tonight?

JARRIEL: Certainly that is a very good question, and I still haven't seen the answer from the White House. They say that the President periodically wants to report to the people on the situation in Vietnam. They say this speech was scheduled long before the October 15 Moratorium and it is a routinely scheduled affair not having anything to do with tomorrow's elections. Certainly, he did feel, I'm sure, that the time had come to restate his position, and we were warned repeatedly against speculation at the White House; against going out on a limb saying that there might be massive troop withdrawals or perhaps a standstill cease-fire, and tonight after seeing the speech we certainly know why we were warned against speculation.

REYNOLDS: The warnings against speculation, however, did not, I suggest, dampen the expectations of a great many people who did possibly anticipate something tonight. Thank you, Tom.

One of the men most qualified, certainly, the most qualified to speculate on North Vietnam's reaction to the speech is Governor Harriman. For some nine months, of course, he was our chief negotiator in Paris, face to face with the North Vietnamese across the conference table. He is now here in Washington face to face with our State Department Correspondent John Scali.

SCALI: Governor, could you tell us what is your immediate reaction to Mr. Nixon's address?

HARRIMAN: Well, John, I'm sure you know I wouldn't be presumptuous to give a complete analysis of a very carefully thought-out speech by the President of the United States. I'm sure he wants to end this war and no one wishes him well any more than I do. But since I'm here, I've got to answer your question. He approaches the subject quite differently from the manner in which I approach it. Let me first say, though, that I'm utterly opposed to these people who are talking about cutting and running. I'm against the Republican Senator from New York's proposal, Senator Goodell, to get out our troops in a year willy-nilly. I think we should have a responsible withdrawal. But my emphasis has been, and I think it should be, on winning the peaceful contest that will come after the fighting stops. The first thing we must do is do everything we can to end the fighting and I think we could have made more progress in that direction. As far as winning the peaceful contest, we've got to look at who this government is—President Thieu. He is not representative of the people by my opinion from all that I've heard. Today, you've probably noticed that the most popular man in South Vietnam, General Duong Van Minh (Big Minh) proposed that there be a national convention to consider the future. He didn't define what it should be but it should combine what I've been saying—all of the non-Communist groups. This is a very small group that are in the government—we've been talking to him for two years about expanding his base and he's contracted it this last time he was there. There's nothing said in this speech about that, which to me is the all-important question. I don't think we can be successful in Vietnamizing the war, because I don't think they can carry the weight. People should consider that. We can reduce our forces, no doubt, we can take it down to a couple of hundred-thousand troops, but we will have to leave, probably, for many years, a very large force. If we attempt to reduce the fighting earnestly and reduce the fighting, we can possibly get the South Vietnamese to expand the base of their government and to bring together, rally all of the non-Communist forces.

SCALI: President Nixon, Governor, says nothing at all about the advisability of some kind of cease-fire. Do you favor this as a step?

HARRIMAN: Well, I have said that I thought we ought to have taken that up in early November. You know, the trouble also, something he leaves out, was that we expected President Thieu to have his representative in Paris on November 2. And then progress would have been made. The North Vietnamese had disengaged in the northern two provinces where the toughest fighting had been. Ninety percent of their troops were taken out, half of those had gone to 200 miles north of the DMZ, and we never had a chance to talk about it. They have stated, of course, that the February and March offensive were counter-offensive to our pressures. Now, whether that's true, whether it isn't, one can't judge, but they did give us to understand that if we wanted to accept the status quo then that we could make progress. If we tried to improve our position militarily, then there would be—go on and talk. Now, even after this table question was settled, which I thought was a stall so as to wait until President Nixon was in. Maybe I was wrong, but President Thieu said he wouldn't sit down privately. Now, all these things have been left out and I think this should be very carefully debated by the Congress, particularly by the Foreign Relations Committee and take a look at where we're going.

SCALI: But do you think one of the prompt steps should be to initiate a cease-fire—to propose a cease-fire?

HARRIMAN: Well, I think the first thing we should do is to begin to work right away to freeze the reduction in the fighting; to announce that we're going to keep this fighting down. To insist that the South Vietnamese do the same and demand the same thing of the other side—working toward the cease-fire.

SCALI: Right.

HARRIMAN: Cy Vance wants to have a cease-fire called for now. If that is what the President proposes, I would certainly support it.

SCALI: Do you agree that there would be a blood bath in South Vietnam if the North Vietnamese were to take over?

HARRIMAN: Well, you know, I may be entirely wrong, but I don't think from the talks we've had that either the North Vietnamese nor their colleagues the VC-NLF want to have a military takeover. They want to see a settlement. I think they assume that over a period of years they can win out. But I'm sure they'd agree to having the South independent from the North for five or ten years. They've already proposed that it not be what they call a Communist society.

SCALI: Do you see a reign of terror there?

HARRIMAN: No. Well, there might well be a reign of terror if there was a complete pullout, but there's no need for a cease-fire—for a pullout—if we sit down with these people and try to work out the details. Now, of course, the President gives us some inkling that he's had private talks. I found Mr. L. Duc Tho, the North Vietnamese representative in Paris, a very reasonable man. He's a member of the Politburo, and I would have liked to have seen some talks with him, to explore with him before we make proposals what proposition they have to make to us. I think we could have gotten more out of that than our making formal proposals. Now these things—perhaps I'm wrong, but this is my first reaction, and my first reaction is that we ought to give more thought to whom we're supporting, whom President Thieu represents, how much political influence he has in the country and how this group could win the political contest which is going to come after the fighting stops.

SCALI: Governor, you've had a distinguished career as politician in the United States. You're a [former] Governor of New York, so I don't hesitate to ask you a question of this kind. Do you think that the silent majority in the United States will rally behind the President as a result of his speech?

HARRIMAN: I don't know whether it's a silent majority or not or whether it's a silent minority. I just don't know. You can pick any poll you want. There were 57 per cent for the Goodell resolution in one poll. There's another poll which shows that 64 per cent of the people want to see the goverment in Saigon changed. There are other polls which show the President has the support of the people. I think he's got the full support of the people. He certainly has got my support in hoping he will develop a program for peace. But I think we've gone so far in Vietnam that this has to be discussed but cannot be accepted without more explanation and it seems to me the Senate Foreign Relations Committee would be a very fine, place for that discussion.

SCALI: I gather, then, Governor, you were somewhat disappointed in the President's approach.

HARRIMAN: Well, I wouldn't say I was disappointed. I was not surprised. Because this is about what I thought he would say from the positions he had previously taken. He's followed the advice of many people who believe this, many people who advised President Johnson—which wasn't successful—and I'm not sure that this advice would be successful in the future. We heard here this evening accurately reported saying the war is being won now—anyone who is a neutralist is stupid. Has the President abandoned the end of a military—or he ruled out on May 14 a military solution. There are so many things we've got to know about this, but I want to end this by saying I wish the President well, I hope he can lead us to peace. But this is not the whole story that we've heard tonight.

SCALI: Governor Harriman, thank you very much. Frank?

REYNOLDS: Thank you, Governor. Thank you, John. Now I want to turn to some of my colleagues who are here with me . . . Bill Lawrence, our National Affairs Editor, Bob Clark, our Capitol Hill Correspondent, and our Pentagon Correspondent, Bill Downs. Bill, it's your job to take the temperature of the country. Tell me, how's the country going to react to this speech?

LAWRENCE: Well, Frank, it is fair to talk about this speech politically because Mr. Nixon was out on a stump in New Jersey last week inviting people to listen in. Politically, I'm not sure why he did it, because there was nothing new in it politically, and its impact will be on those who are moved by words, not by deeds. His appeal was not to the youth who've been raising trouble, but rather to the silent majority, if they are a majority, who presumably have been with him all along. But there wasn't a thing new in this speech that would influence anybody to vote tomorrow or six months from now in a different way than his mood was, set. Now the Democrats engaged in a little one-upmanship on this speech, after the White House announced it three weeks ago. They started very vigorously to build up hope about what the speech might contain in the way of some new move towards substantively winning the war sooner. They talked about a cease-fire; they talked about greater reduction in troops. Nothing happened.

REYNOLDS: Do you think they were mousetrapping him?

LAWRENCE: Well, I think that was their purpose, perhaps, and I think to that extent this speech certainly did not meet the expectations of those who turned on their television or radio sets tonight and expected to learn some big new move in Vietnam. Because it just wasn't there.

REYNOLDS: Bob Clark, I have the impression that the cease-fire that has been observed on Capitol Hill of late might well be shattered as a result of the President's speech tonight because he did not announce any major changes in policy. Do you agree?

CLARK: Well, I would be very much surprised if it isn't shattered resoundingly tomorrow, Frank. I think, at the very least, tonight too, the President passed a flaming torch to Fulbright, who can be expected to go galloping off with it, with new hearings on Vietnam before his Foreign Relations Committee. Those hearings, of course, were announced for last month and were postponed by Senator Fulbright to give the President a chance to give his speech tonight. Obviously now they will be rescheduled and they are designed as specific hearings on specific proposals for bringing the war to an end, and on the Goodell proposal, among others, to get American troops out by a specified date. So, it's very clear tonight that the gantlet will be flung down to the President at those new hearings before the Foreign Relations Committee.

REYNOLDS: Well, there seems to be a note of combativeness in the President's speech tonight too, calling on the silent majority to rally around the flag or stand with him.

CLARK: Well, I think undoubtedly, Frank, that is true but there will be plenty of takers on the Hill and you'll hear them tomorrow morning. Not only from what we might call the militant doves, the ones who have been in the forefront for years of efforts to end the war but there's a growing impatience in Congress, just as there is across the country—this cuts across party lines—there are many who have been moderates on the

Vietnam war in the past who now feel more and more urgently about the need to set a termination date on the war. That, of course, is what the President failed tonight to do.

REYNOLDS: Well, Bill Downs, you cover the Pentagon. What do you think the reaction there is? They probably are not too unhappy about this speech tonight, are they?

DOWNS: Well, I think the Pentagon has come off pretty good in this. If there's been any wonder about the influence of Secretary of Defense Laird in the Administration and whether the State Department or Dr. Kissinger or who else is shaping the President's thoughts, why, I think Mr. Laird comes out pretty well. I think the sort of key from the military viewpoint, the Pentagon viewpoint, the key statement was that our defeat or humiliation in South Vietnam would purport recklessness among the great powers who have not yet abandoned their goals of world conquest. Now, this is the Joint Chiefs of Staffs' argument, the Pentagon line, if you will, that in a world of nations in a state of international anarchy, military power is the only answer to our security and to our freedom and the way we want to shape this world.

REYNOLDS: It is not really the domino theory all over again, but it reminds me of what Dean Rusk used to talk about—the credibility of the American commitment. It must be honored. We simply cannot back out on an American commitment.

DOWNS: This is strictly Rusk's policy, the way I see it, and McNamara policy. Although they won't like that down on 1600 Pennsylvania Avenue, it does one thing. It allays any fears that people might have had round the world that the Nixon Administration might be heading us toward a neutralist or isolationist course, but it's certainly not in this speech.

REYNOLDS: Bill Lawrence, I want to put this to you. Mr. Nixon is an extremely skillful politician. I don't think there's any doubt about that. Do you believe that there is possibly a full appreciation in the White House now of the depth of the discontent in the country or of the disenchantment with the war, the weariness of the war?

LAWRENCE: Well, Frank, I don't know whether understanding is the right word. I don't believe the White House believes that there is this deep discontent. I'm not, you know, really sure despite Mr. Nixon's victory for the Presidency last time that he is so big a politician as you suggest.

REYNOLDS: Well, he's come a long way . . .

LAWRENCE: Well, true, but he lost for the Presidency once, he lost for Governor, but he hasn't followed up. He hasn't used the powers of the Presidency. A good politician would have taken the momentum of the election and inauguration and come forward with a program of some kind. You would not be explaining Vietnam now, you would have done that in February. He had this time to think these things . . . everybody knew he was going to be elected.

CLARK: Bill, in fairness to the President, could you say he said what he did tonight because there simply is no program that he would not regard as a cut-and-run program; that that is his basic dilemma.

LAWRENCE: Yes, but in his campaign, he said he had a plan that would end the war and win the peace.

CLARK: He said that again tonight.

LAWRENCE: He says it again tonight.

DOWNS: Can I interrupt both you gentlemen. I happen to disagree with Bill. I think Mr. Nixon is a consummate politician. I think that around Christmas time he's going to announce the withdrawal of possibly more than 40 or 50,000 in a third slice cut and I think that Vice President Ky, whose crystal ball has been pretty good, said that by the end of 1970 there would be 180,000 Americans out of Vietnam. I think that if you're building toward the 1970 election, you don't blow your game all in one speech and that's what I think. . . .

REYNOLDS: That's true . . .

LAWRENCE: The President said he wasn't playing that game.

REYNOLDS: Well, yes, and we must also recognize that this speech tonight was given 10 days or so before another great big demonstration and they'll be all over this town, you know. Apparently, Mr. Nixon has decided not to be influenced by that, and it may well be that he feels there is more political advantage in giving the back of his hand to the demonstrators and standing up there with him as the embattled President, holding firm against the onslaughts of public opinion.

CLARK: Frank, I would think that one immediate spin-off of the President's speech tonight is that you can now expect substantially more congressional participation in that November 15 Moratorium. Many members of Congress who have been reluctant to involve themselves in what is shaping up as a more violent demonstration or a demonstration that may produce some serious violence will now feel obligated to just reply to the President.

REYNOLDS: Well, thank you very much, gentlemen. History, of course, will give us the proper perspective with which to view Mr. Nixon's speech tonight. Earlier this evening on the ABC Evening News, Howard K. Smith referred to it as a battle, a battle for public opinion. Well, Howard, how do you think the President fought the battle tonight?

SMITH: Frank, you're talking about history—the most impressive thought that came to me from this speech was how much alike all Presidents who have had to deal with Vietnam have thought about it. I was looking through President Truman's memoirs today, and I ran across a prediction by him that if Indochina, which Vietnam is a part of, were to fall, other countries would soon follow, and therefore he was not willing to see it fall. Truman and Eisenhower, who disagreed on many things, joined together to sponsor a citizens' committee supporting President Johnson's intervention in Vietnam. And I recall a news conference in March before his death when President Kennedy was asked a question about it and he said if the Communists took South Vietnam, their rift would soon run all the way to India, and who knows, perhaps all the way to the Middle East, so he said, "I can't agree to it." Up until now, Mr. Nixon has not endorsed the action of his predecessor and even tonight he disagreed with the tactics and the way it's been handled, but he did endorse the general goal of not yielding to the opposing side and seemed even unperturbed at the thought, which he mentioned himself, that people are now calling Johnson's war Nixon's war. I think for the first time I have a strong impression, which I didn't have a couple of weeks ago when the Senators who had criticized him had begun to support him. I, for the first time, have the impression he's not going to be hustled or yield to anything but a negotiated settlement involving free elections which probably the Communists couldn't win. I would guess that by his speech tonight he's let himself in for some very rough handling in that next Moratorium demonstration that's coming. I would guess with Bob Clark that a topic grown dormant will now come aflame in Senator Fulbright's committee and possibly on the floor of the Senate. He got his message across to the people he's counting on, called the silent majority, but what matters is whether he got his point across to Hanoi; that there will be no surrender in any guise, and that they will have to negotiate. And, as has been so often said tonight, we'll just have to wait and see.

REYNOLDS: Thank you, Howard. And thank you all, gentlemen. The President said tonight, and I think perhaps this certainly expresses his view with respect to the Moratorium upcoming and the past demonstrations, that if a vocal minority, however fervent its cause, prevails over reason and the will of the majority, this nation has no future as a free society. That, apparently, is the guide that is going to guide the President as he tries to end this war and also deal with the dissent at home. This is Frank Reynolds in Washington. Good night.

CBS Television Network

DAN RATHER: The President of the United States has just addressed the nation live, direct from the White House. These appeared to be the major points of his approximately 32-minute address:

President Nixon said he has adopted a plan for withdrawing all United States ground troops from Vietnam; however, he said he would not, could not, commit himself to a fixed timetable for troop reductions. President Nixon said his secret plan for complete withdrawal has been worked out in conjunction with the Saigon government. He made no mention of any further troop withdrawals after the current pullout of 60,000 men by December 15.

He flatly rejected demands that he should end the war at once by ordering an immediate and complete withdrawal. The President listed several heretofore secret attempts at peace. He said he had tried, since being elected President, including one personal letter to Ho Chi Minh, a letter which President Nixon said was answered only three days before Ho's death, and the answer was, in the President's opinion, discouraging.

Those are the highlights. Next, an effort to put those highlights in perspective. A brief CBS News examination of the President's speech.

With me in our CBS studios are my colleagues CBS Diplomatic Correspondent Marvin Kalb and our National Correspondent Eric Sevareid.

Marvin Kalb, in your judgment, and let's preface this by saying, as always, this is a difficult bit of guesswork to immediately follow a Presidential address—what in your judgment is going to be the reaction in this country to the President's speech and, after dealing with that, then overseas?

MARVIN KALB: Well, first, Dan, I'm not sure, but it seemed to me first that the speech cut no new ground. It seemed a soft-spoken straight-in-the-eye restatement of policy that clearly is not aimed at that group of Americans dubbed by Vice President Agnew as "an effete corps of impudent snobs."

Rather it was aimed, as the President put it, at you, the great silent majority of my fellow Americans. Presumably those who do not demonstrate; those who want an honorable end to the war but have difficulty defining what an honorable end is and are willing to trust the President to get it.

FROM the CBS News broadcast, November 3, 1969. Reprinted with the permission of CBS.

Those who are not so willing will point to the absence of a new announcement on troop withdrawals or a definite timetable for the total withdrawal of U.S. forces and they may disagree with the President's judgment that the Ho Chi Minh letter was a flat rejection of his own letter. The Ho Chi Minh letter contained, it seems, some of the softest, most accommodating language found in a Communist document concerning the war in Vietnam in recent years.

The President's policy is best summed up in one of his phrases—a negotiated settlement, presumably in Paris, if possible; Vietnamization if necessary. Tonight a White House source issued what seemed like a veiled threat to change the character of the Paris talks, perhaps even to break them up, if the Communists, he said, continue to refuse to negotiate seriously.

RATHER: Eric Sevareid, this speech was widely anticipated to be something of a watershed for the Nixon Administration. What is your gut reaction to it?

ERIC SEVAREID: Well, Dan, this, it seems to me, is an appeal to the American people for unity and for support of their President, done in a low-keyed but very fervent manner. As you've said, or Marvin said, nothing of a substantial nature or dramatic nature that is new; he is standing his ground; he is offering no cease-fire, no public fixed timetable for withdrawal, no announcement of a new contingent of troop withdrawals. He is asking for trust to let him have flexibility and a free hand.

I would think that on its face this speech would not draw the fangs of some of the leading critics, particularly here in the capital, some like Senator Fulbright and others, who were ready, if there was something given them of a definite nature in this speech, to cease their criticism and to support the President. I would doubt now that they would do any thing but keep on with the attack.

It may give a little more strength to that demonstration scheduled for the middle of the month. But I can't escape the feeling—and it's only a feeling—that this is not all we're going to get this fall. That there may well be an announcement of a quite sizable troop withdrawal and fairly soon, possibly before these mid-November demonstrations. I have no evidence for this at all except the feeling that it cannot rest where he has left it.

I think it indicates that he believes the majority of opinion in this country is still riding with him, and that he does have more time. And I would think that if there is to be another announcement of a troop withdrawal with numbers, that that may tell us a good deal more about the time scale in which he is thinking, the magnitudes of his thought about winding down the war.

Philosophically, where this war is concerned he doesn't seem to be any different from Mr. Johnson or Secretary Rusk. He adopts the notion that on a worldwide basis freedom is indivisible, the notion that an American pullout would collapse confidence in American leadership all over the world. It's the test-case idea that failure there would set Communists into action in many other areas, even in the Western Hemisphere, he says.

This, of course, is hotly debated by philosophers of foreign policy, and has been for a long time. And one would think if all that were true, if this war and our presence there was of this cosmic and universal importance then the war should be won.

But he has said it is not to be—a military victory is not to be sought. And in that, it seems to me, there lies a profound illogic; that it's over the dam, he is trying to get us out.

RATHER: Eric, in your judgment is the President going to win this gamble that he can hold a majority of American public opinion behind him for this policy of winding down the war slowly, deliberately, orderly, and, as he sees it, honorably?

SEVAREID: I personally hope he can. I don't know that he can. I think this speech would have been effective last spring, but it's late in the day; and this is why I think something else is going to come and very soon. I do not believe it can rest here. But this is only my horseback opinion of one man. And I could be wrong.

RATHER: Marvin Kalb, a horseback opinion of one man on what the effect is going to be on the North Vietnamese and the Viet Cong?

KALB: Well, it seems to me that what they could say, and they may not be too far off base in this kind of judgment, is that the President has not given them anything terribly new to chew on; but I don't really feel that the President was talking to them.

As he pointed out, he was talking very much to the great, silent majority of the American people, and the North Vietnamese haven't been given anything, really, in this speech to chew on, not at all. It seems to me, if anything, it's going to be somewhat negative in terms of the President's judgment of the Ho Chi Minh letter. Ho Chi Minh is now dead; he is a god in North Vietnam at least, and certainly has a good deal of strength elsewhere in the Communist world.

The President defines this [Ho's letter] as a flat rejection, and yet you have a number of statements in here which suggest considerable flexibility in negotiating posture. This may not yet be apparent in Paris, but it certainly is there in the language of this Ho Chi Minh letter.

RATHER: Gentlemen, we're running short on time, but very briefly, do you see this speech as an indication that President Nixon and those around him still feel that the war is winnable in the sense that we can keep from losing? Do you agree, Eric?

SEVAREID: Yes, I think that's what he's trying to do, to keep from an outright open humiliating loss.

RATHER: Marvin?

KALB: Very much. I agree with that completely. He apparently feels the great effect that this might have on domestic life in this country; and he fears that almost as much as he does the implications abroad.

RATHER: It may be, then, that the pertinent section of this speech was when the President said: "Let us understand North Vietnam cannot humiliate or defeat the United States, only Americans can do that." Gentlemen, thank you very much. Good night.

NBC Television Network

JOHN CHANCELLOR: And so President Nixon, having spoken a little more than a half an hour from the Oval Office in the White House on Vietnam, says that he will not be bound by a specific timetable for troop withdrawal from Vietnam, but that he has plans for the complete withdrawal of all United States ground combat forces from that country, the withdrawal to be based on the increasing ability of the South Vietnamese to defend themselves and the lower level of enemy actions against American forces.

The President said that they had done a number of private things that had not been announced until tonight, asking the Russians to help us with the Vietnam situation and sending a personal letter to Ho Chi Minh, and Ho replying three days before his death was announced.

The President said that a "precipitate withdrawal," his term, would bring more war to Vietnam and not more peace. And he asked for the support of the great silent majority of the American people to support him in his peace plan.

He said that the air war in Vietnam was down 20 percent, that he had given orders to General Abrams, our commander there, in July, to change the nature of the fighting; that enemy infiltration since July was less than 20 percent of the similar period last year; that American casualties in this period were the lowest in three years.

The President used some hard language, apparently directed against the anti-war demonstrators who demonstrated last month and will demon-

FROM the NBC News broadcast, November 3, 1969. Reprinted with the permission of NBC News.

strate this month. He was not opposing the cease-fire which Hugh Scott, his man in the Senate, and Mike Mansfield, the head of the Senate Democrats, had proposed. But a precipitate withdrawal, in the President's words, would be a disaster; it would lead to defeat and humiliation for the U.S. It would be a betrayal.

There has been a pause in the criticism of the President in the days preceding this address, particularly in the Congress. It seems certain now that that criticism will begin again, probably tomorrow. The essence of the speech has been a defense of his plan to end the war, which he thinks is working. His critics think it's not working and it's making the war go on longer, and they will be after him again.

With me, with us, this evening here at our studio in Washington is Mr. Richard Scammon, who advises and consults NBC News on public opinion.

I have talked about the Congress, Mr. Scammon. What do you think this did to that great silent majority of Americans the President spoke of?

RICHARD SCAMMON: Well, I think the President represented the viewpoint of the majority. There is no question but that there is a very substantial minority who want an immediate withdrawal from Vietnam. But I think he is correct in referring to it as a minority. As you know, in the weeks since the Moratorium, the support for President Nixon's policies in Vietnam has gone up, not down.

And I think if you could really summarize the attitude of the American people, at least as far as public-opinion polls are concerned, they are saying, in effect: "Mr. President, we want you to get us out of Vietnam. We're willing to let you do it; get on with the job. We recognize the validity of the very kind of points that you are making here tonight."

This is the majority view. But there is of course a strong minority, as you have pointed out, John, which in the Congress and outside will oppose his proposals.

CHANCELLOR: Do you suppose that the way in which it was presented tonight, as a direct appeal to people, is a successful device? We have seen other politicians do it from time to time, going directly to the populace and saying: "I am right." Does that work?

SCAMMON: I think that it does tend to bridge over whatever kind of a credibility gap there may be.

In the final analysis, of course, it really depends on whether the argument is a sound one, because the people, the voters, the electorate, the citizenry, are usually a good deal more perceptive about these things than many people give them credit for. And if the argument is basically sound, I think you'd find that there would be support for it, while there always will be a minority on both sides, you know, who will oppose any middle-of-the-road policy, which is what I think you would call this, which does not go either far to the left or far to the right.

But I think that when he speaks of the great silent majority that he's right, and the polls would indicate he does have support, at least for the time being, for this policy.

CHANCELLOR: Let me ask you just one temporary question here. The polls went up after the demonstrators marched on the 15th of October.

SCAMMON: Yes.

CHANCELLOR: They'll be marching again in about another 10 or 12 days. Would you guess that the President's support in the polls would rise after the November Moratoriums?

SCAMMON: I think that might depend a good deal on the nature of the Moratorium demonstration in November. If they are essentially decent as they were in October, I'm not sure. If they became violent, it's quite possible it would go up.

CHANCELLOR: Herbert Kaplow, our NBC News White House Correspondent, is standing by at the White House. He was there. Herb, I'd like to put a question to you, as an old President-watcher, and a man who has been watching President Nixon for some time. How did he appear to you tonight?

HEBERT KAPLOW: He doesn't normally like to read speeches, but obviously, because of the delicacy of this issue, he chose not to take any chances.

As a scripted performance, it was a pretty good Nixon performance. Obviously, he had exercised great care in writing it. I think this is probably one of the few speeches that the President probably read a few times before, in a sense rehearsed. He doesn't like to rehearse them.

But the image that came across tonight was that of a man who was familiar with what he had written and what he was reading, obviously designed to counter the—activating the silent majority into support for him, to maybe overwhelming, in a sense, by their expressions, the people who had been marching around the fences of the White House on October 15 and are supposed to be back here on November 15.

CHANCELLOR: Herb, let me ask you. He said that we were going to take out all the U.S. ground combat forces, and I have seen various estimates of that. If they were taken out, given our present strength level, force level, in Vietnam, that would leave 270,000 Americans there.

What can you tell us about whatever that number may be, of American troops, not ground combat troops, who may have to stay for some time in Vietnam?

KAPLOW: Well, the people here are very careful not to talk any numbers. And so I'm afraid I can't tell you very much about that. They just don't like to talk about numbers because they feel that, in a sense, you are tipping your hand to the other side, which would just then sit and wait.

CHANCELLOR: Well, going beyond the numbers involved, just the pure numbers, Herb, whatever number of—"X" number of American troops being left there in support of Vietnamese combat troops—do you have any idea under what standards they would be withdrawn? Have you learned anything tonight about that?

KAPLOW: Only in a sense that it is the continuation of this policy of Vietnamization. When our people are satisfied that the Vietnamese soldier can do his job, and that enough of them can do their jobs, we will pull our people out accordingly. That applies also to, obviously, the support troops.

CHANCELLOR: Herb, did you get an impression tonight at the White House, and with your sources there, that of the three standards for pulling out of Vietnam the President had articulated—more ability on the South Vietnamese part; some progress in Paris; and lower American casualties, a lower level of enemy fighting—that the Paris part now is becoming a standard they don't much talk about?

KAPLOW: I agree, yes. I don't think they think anything—there has been any progress at all, to speak of, in Paris, and the only thing they really are basing their decisions on troop withdrawals on now is how the South Vietnamese army is strengthened, and also the level of fighting, and probably the level of fighting more than anything else. We've had this two months' lull.

CHANCELLOR: Well, with that, Herb, I'm looking at the copy of the speech we have. The President said tonight something that seemed to me to be singularly important.
He said: "I therefore put into effect a plan to bring peace, a plan which will bring the war to an end, regardless of what happens on the negotiating front." And as we saw just a few days ago, Ambassador Henry Cabot Lodge, our negotiator at the Paris peace talks, said to the other side, in effect, stop propagandizing or stop talking with us.
And the President says this isn't a threat, his attitude toward that. But it just seems to me that Paris is being regarded as less important.

And Richard Scammon, again in your role as a public opinion consultant for NBC, what about Paris, in terms of the response of the American people? Do you suppose they would rather just get out, in terms of Vietnam, turn it over to the Vietnamese, even with the perils involved in that, than go on with a long negotiation in Paris?

SCAMMON: I think actually for most people Paris, Vietnam, all of these things, are just sort of mixed in together. I think there were great expectations when Paris opened, and these have been pretty well disappointed for the people as well as for the President.

I would think myself that, you know, American public opinion has been very ambivalent about Vietnam. It has wanted to get out, it has wanted a Vietnamese war. On the other hand, it has wanted to get a settlement which did not permit the Communists to take over. And even though the American public says get out of Vietnam, Mr. President, they also say if you get out of Vietnam and lose, two thirds of us are going to be against you.

CHANCELLOR: It's not easy to have that job.

Thank you very much for watching.

Address by the Vice President

Spiro T. Agnew

Tonight I want to discuss the importance of the television news medium to the American people. No nation depends more on the intelligent judgment of its citizens. No medium has a more profound influence over public opinion. Nowhere in our system are there fewer checks on vast power. So, nowhere should there be more conscientious responsibility exercised than by the news media. The question is . . . are we demanding enough of our television news presentations? . . . And, are the men of this medium demanding enough of themselves?

Monday night, a week ago, President Nixon delivered the most important address of his Administration, one of the most important of our decade. His subject was Vietnam. His hope was to rally the American people to see the conflict through to a lasting and just peace in the Pacific. For thirty-two minutes, he reasoned with a nation that has suffered almost a third of a million casualties in the longest war in its history.

An address by the Vice President before the Midwest Regional Republican Meeting, Des Moines, Iowa, November 13, 1969.

When the President completed his address—an address that he spent weeks in preparing—his words and policies were subjected to instant analysis and querulous criticism. The audience of seventy million Americans—gathered to hear the President of the United States—was inherited by a small band of network commentators and self-appointed analysts, the *majority* of whom expressed, in one way or another, their hostility to what he had to say.

It was obvious that their minds were made up in advance. Those who recall the fumbling and groping that followed President Johnson's dramatic disclosure of his intention not to seek reelection have seen these men in a genuine state of non-preparedness. This was not it.

One commentator twice contradicted the President's statement about the exchange of correspondence with Ho Chi Minh. Another challenged the President's abilities as a politician. A third asserted that the President was now "following the Pentagon line." Others, by the expressions on their faces, the tone of their questions, and the sarcasm of their responses, made clear their sharp disapproval.

To guarantee in advance that the President's plea for national unity would be challenged, one network trotted out Averell Harriman for the occasion. Throughout the President's address he waited in the wings. When the President concluded, Mr. Harriman recited perfectly. He attacked the Thieu Government as unrepresentative; he criticized the President's speech for various deficiencies; he twice issued a call to the Senate Foreign Relations Committee to debate Vietnam once again; he stated his belief that the Viet Cong or North Vietnamese did not really want a military take-over of South Vietnam; he told a little anecdote about a "very, very responsible" fellow he had met in the North Vietnamese delegation.

All in all, Mr. Harriman offered a broad range of gratuitous advice— challenging and contradicting the policies outlined by the President of the United States. Where the President had issued a call for unity, Mr. Harriman was encouraging the country not to listen to him.

A word about Mr. Harriman. For ten months he was America's chief negotiator at the Paris Peace Talks—a period in which the United States swapped some of the greatest military concessions in the history of warfare for an enemy agreement on the shape of a bargaining table. Like Coleridge's Ancient Mariner, Mr. Harriman seems to be under some heavy compulsion to justify his failures to anyone who will listen. The networks have shown themselves willing to give him all the air time he desires.

Every American has a right to disagree with the President of the United States, and to express publicly that disagreement.

But the President of the United States has a right to communicate directly with the people who elected him, and the people of this country have the right to make up their own minds and form their own opinions about a Presidential address without having the President's words and thoughts characterized through the prejudices of hostile critics before they can even be digested.

When Winston Churchill rallied public opinion to stay the course against Hitler's Germany, he did not have to contend with a gaggle of commentators raising doubts about whether he was reading public opinion right, or whether Britain had the stamina to see the war through. When President Kennedy rallied the Nation in the Cuban Missile Crisis, his address to the people was not chewed over by a roundtable of critics who disparaged the course of action he had asked America to follow.

The purpose of my remarks tonight is to focus your attention on this little group of men who not only enjoy a right of instant rebuttal to every Presidential address, but more importantly, wield a free hand in selecting, presenting and interpreting the great issues of our Nation.

First, let us define that power. At least forty million Americans each night, it is estimated, watch the network news. Seven million of them view ABC; the remainder being divided between NBC and CBS. According to Harris polls and other studies, for millions of Americans the networks are the sole source of national and world news.

In Will Rogers' observation, what you knew was what you read in the newspaper. Today, for growing millions of Americans, it is what they see and hear on their television sets.

How is this network news determined? A small group of men, numbering perhaps no more than a dozen "anchormen," commentators and executive producers, settle upon the 20 minutes or so of film and commentary that is to reach the public. This selection is made from the 90 to 180 minutes that may be available. Their powers of choice are broad. They decide what forty to fifty million Americans will learn of the day's events in the Nation and the world.

We cannot measure this power and influence by traditional democratic standards, for these men can create national issues overnight. They can make or break—by their coverage and commentary—a Moratorium on the war. They can elevate men from local obscurity to national prominence within a week. They can reward some politicians with national exposure and ignore others. For millions of Americans, the network reporter who covers a continuing issue, like ABM or Civil Rights, becomes, in effect, the presiding judge in a national trial by jury.

It must be recognized that the networks have made important contributions to the national knowledge. Through news, documentaries, and specials, they have often used their power constructively and creatively to awaken the public conscience to critical problems.

The networks made "hunger" and "black lung" disease national issues overnight. The TV networks have done what no other medium could have done in terms of dramatizing the horrors of war. The networks have tackled our most difficult social problems with a directness and immediacy that is the gift of their medium. They have focused the nation's attention on its environmental abuses . . . on pollution in the Great Lakes and the threatened ecology of the Everglades.

But it was also the networks that elevated Stokely Carmichael and George Lincoln Rockwell from obscurity to national prominence . . . nor is their power confined to the substantive.

A raised eyebrow, an inflection of the voice, a caustic remark dropped in the middle of a broadcast can raise doubts in a million minds about the veracity of a public official or the wisdom of a government policy.

One Federal Communications Commissioner considers the power of the networks equal to that of local, state and federal governments combined. Certainly, it represents a concentration of power over American public opinion unknown in history.

What do Americans know of the men who wield this power? Of the men who produce and direct the network news—the nation knows practically nothing. Of the commentators, most Americans know little, other than that they reflect an urbane and assured presence, seemingly well informed on every important matter.

We do know that, to a man, these commentators and producers live and work in the geographical and intellectual confines of Washington, D.C., or New York City—the latter of which James Reston terms the "most unrepresentative community in the entire United States." Both communities bask in their own provincialism, their own parochialism. We can deduce that these men thus read the same newspapers, and draw their political and social views from the same sources. Worse, they talk constantly to one another, thereby providing artificial reinforcement to their shared viewpoints.

Do they allow their biases to influence the selection and presentation of the news? David Brinkley states, "objectivity is impossible to normal human behavior." Rather, he says, we should strive for "fairness."

Another anchorman on a network news show contends: "You can't expunge all your private convictions just because you sit in a seat like this and a camera starts to stare at you. . . . I think your program has to reflect what your basic feelings are. I'll plead guilty to that."

Less than a week before the 1968 election, this same commentator charged that President Nixon's campaign commitments were no more durable than campaign balloons. He claimed that, were it not for fear of a hostile reaction, Richard Nixon would be giving into—and I quote the commentator—"His natural instinct to smash the enemy with a club or go after him with a meat ax."

Had this slander been made by one political candidate about another, it would have been dismissed by most commentators as a partisan assault. But this attack emanated from the privileged sanctuary of a network studio and therefore had the apparent dignity of an objective statement.

The American people would rightly not tolerate this kind of concentration of power in government. It is not fair and relevant to question its concentration in the hands of a tiny and closed fraternity of privileged men, elected by no one, and enjoying a monopoly sanctioned and licensed by government?

The views of this fraternity do *not* represent the views of America. That is why such a great gulf existed between how the nation received the President's address—and how the networks reviewed it.

As with other American institutions, perhaps it is time that the networks were made more responsive to the views of the nation and more responsible to the people they serve.

I am not asking for government censorship or any other kind of censorship. I am asking whether a form of censorship already exists when the news that forty million Americans receive each night is determined by a handful of men responsible only to their corporate employers and filtered through a handful of commentators who admit to their own set of biases.

The questions I am raising here tonight should have been raised by others long ago. They should have been raised by those Americans who have traditionally considered the preservation of freedom of speech and freedom of the press their special provinces of responsibility and concern. They should have been raised by those Americans who share the view of the late Justice Learned Hand that "right conclusions are more likely to be gathered out of a multitude of tongues than through any kind of authoritative selection."

Advocates for the networks have claimed a First Amendment right to the same unlimited freedoms held by the great newspapers of America.

The situations are not identical. Where the *New York Times* reaches 800,000 people, NBC reaches twenty times that number with its evening news. Nor can the tremendous impact of seeing television film and hearing commentary be compared with reading the printed page.

A decade ago, before the network news acquired such dominance over public opinion, Walter Lippmann spoke to the issue: "There is an essential and radical difference," he stated, "between television and printing . . . the three or four competing television stations control virtually all that can be received over the air by ordinary television sets. But, besides the mass circulation dailies, there are the weeklies, the monthlies, the out-of-town newspapers, and books. If a man does not like his newspaper, he can read another from out of town, or wait for a weekly news magazine. It is not ideal. But it is infinitely better than the situation in television. There, if a man does not like what the networks offer him, all he can do is turn them off, and listen to a phonograph."

"Networks," he stated, "which are few in number, have a virtual monopoly of a whole medium of communication." The newspapers of mass circulation have no monopoly of the medium of print.

"A virtual monopoly of a whole medium of communication" is not something a democratic people should blithely ignore.

And we are not going to cut off our television sets and listen to the phonograph because the air waves do not belong to the networks; they belong to the people.

As Justice Byron White wrote in his landmark opinion six months ago, "It is the right of the viewers and listeners, not the right of the broadcasters, which is paramount."

It is argued that this power presents no danger in the hands of those who have used it responsibly.

But as to whether or not the networks have abused the power they enjoy, let us call as our first witness, former Vice President Humphrey and the City of Chicago.

According to Theodore H. White, television's intercutting of the film from the streets of Chicago with the "current proceedings on the floor of the convention created the most striking and *false* political picture of 1968—the nomination of a man for the American Presidency by the brutality and violence of merciless police."

If we are to believe a recent report of the House Commerce Committee, then television's presentation of the violence in the streets worked an injustice on the reputation of the Chicago police.

According to the Committee findings, one network in particular presented "a one-sided picture which in large measure exonerates the demonstrators and protestors." Film of provocations of police that was available never saw the light of day, while the film of the police response which the protestors provoked was shown to millions.

Another network showed virtually the same scene of violence—from three separate angles—without making clear it was the same scene.

While the full report is reticent in drawing conclusions, it is not a document to inspire confidence in the fairness of the network news.

Our knowledge of the impact of network news on the national mind is far from complete. But some early returns are available. Again, we have enough information to raise serious questions about its effect on a democratic society.

Several years ago, Fred Friendly, one of the pioneers of network news, wrote that its missing ingredients were "conviction, controversy, and a point of view." The networks have compensated with a vengeance.

And in the networks' endless pursuit of controversy, we should ask what is the end value . . . to enlighten or to profit? What is the end result . . . to inform or to confuse? How does the on-going exploration for more action, more excitement, more drama, serve our national search for internal peace and stability?

Gresham's law seems to be operating in the network news.

Bad news drives out good news. The irrational is more controversial than the rational. Concurrence can no longer compete with dissent. One minute of Eldridge Cleaver is worth ten minutes of Roy Wilkins. The labor crisis settled at the negotiating table is nothing compared to the confrontation that results in a strike—or, better yet, violence along the picket line. Normality has become the nemesis of the evening news.

The upshot of all this controversy is that a narrow and distorted picture of America often emerges from the televised news. A single dramatic piece of the mosaic becomes, in the minds of millions, the whole picture. The American who relies upon television for his news might conclude that the majority of American students are embittered radicals, that the majority of black Americans feel no regard for their country; that violence and lawlessness are the rule, rather than the exception, on the American campus. None of these conclusions is true.

Television may have destroyed the old stereotypes—but has it not created new ones in their place?

What has this passionate pursuit of "controversy" done to the politics of progress through logical compromise, essential to the functioning of a democratic society?

The members of Congress or the Senate who follow their principles and philosophy quietly in a spirit of compromise are unknown to many Americans—while the loudest and most extreme dissenters on every issue are known to every man in the street.

How many marches and demonstrations would we have if the marchers did not know that the ever-faithful TV cameras would be there to record their antics for the next news show?

We have heard demands that Senators and Congressmen and Judges make known all their financial connections—so that the public will know who and what influences their decisions or votes. Strong arguments can be made for that view. But when a single commentator or producer, night after night, determines for millions of people how much of each side of a great issue they are going to see and hear; should he not first disclose his personal views on the issue as well?

In this search for excitement and controversy, has more than equal time gone to that minority of Americans who specialize in attacking the United States, its institutions, and its citizens?

Tonight, I have raised questions. I have made no attempt to suggest answers. These answers must come from the media men. They are challenged to turn their critical powers on themselves. They are challenged to direct their energy, talent, and conviction toward improving the quality and objectivity of news presentation. They are challenged to structure their own civic ethics to relate their great freedom with their great responsibility.

And the people of America are challenged too . . . challenged to press for responsible news presentations. The people can let the networks know that they want their news straight and objective. The people can register their complaints on bias through mail to the networks and phone calls to local stations. This is one case where the people must defend themselves . . . where the citizen—not government—must be the reformer . . . where the consumer can be the most effective crusader.

By way of conclusion, let me say that every elected leader in the United States depends on these men of the media. Whether what I have said tonight will be heard and seen at all by the nation is not *my* decision; it is not *your* decision; it is *their* decision.

In tomorrow's edition of the *Des Moines Register* you will be able to read a news story detailing what I said tonight; editorial comment will be reserved for the editorial page, where it belongs. Should not the same wall of separation exist between news and comment on the nation's networks?

We would never trust such power over public opinion in the hands of an elected government—it is time we questioned it in the hands of a small and un-elected elite. The great networks have dominated America's air waves for decades; the people are entitled to a full accounting of their stewardship.

Address

Frank Stanton

I am not here to defend broadcast journalism as being beyond all criticism. No one could have worked as long as I have in radio and television without realizing that we are far from perfect in carrying out our enormous responsibilities in broadcast journalism. We have never been satisfied with the job we are doing. We are not satisfied now. It is our continuing hope and our continuing effort to do better. We are concerned with what the press says of us. We are concerned with what our audiences write us. We are concerned with what our affiliates tell us. We do strive for objectivity, although it is not always easy to achieve. While freedom of the press is meaningless without the freedom to be wrong, we do try to be right. And I think that in the vast majority of cases we have succeeded.

Let me turn now to the events of the past few weeks that have commanded the attention of many of us. On November 3, the President of the United States delivered a much-publicized and eagerly awaited speech presenting the Administration's position and plans on the war in Vietnam.

An address given by Frank Stanton, President, Columbia Broadcasting System, Inc., before the International Radio and Television Society, Inc., New York, November 25, 1969.

That war has been the subject of one of the longest and most fervent public debates in all American history. Good, conscionable and dedicated men and women, from all sections of our society, have earnest and deeply felt differences as to its meaning, its conduct and its prospects. Fundamental questions of rightness and wrongness have disturbed our people as no other issue has in this century.

The President spoke for 32 minutes on all four nationwide television networks, four nationwide radio networks and scores of independent stations. Some 88 million people heard his words as they were conveyed, uninterrupted and in a place and under conditions of his own choosing. Following the President's address, each of the television networks provided comments by professionals analyzing the content of the speech. Participating were experienced newsmen, most of whom have performed similar functions for many years following the live broadcast of special events of outstanding significance. Since the participants were different on the four television networks, the comments of none of them were heard by the same huge audience that heard the President. One of the networks added to the expertise by presenting the views of a distinguished diplomat and public servant, who had held high posts in nine Presidential terms, of both parties, prior to the present Administration. Another presented the comments of two United States senators, who took divergent views of the policy advocated in the speech.

In all this, nothing unprecedented had happened. Such comments have customarily been offered after most significant Presidential appearances—State of the Union, Inaugurals, United Nations addresses, press conferences, for example. And they usually have been more than mere bland recapitulations, which would serve little purpose, and have frequently called attention to emphases, omissions, unexpected matters of substance, long-anticipated attitudes, changes of views, methods of advocacy or any other aspect of the speech. Such comments have been offered by enterprising news organizations since the dawn of the modern press and continued into the era of radio and television.

Following the President's speech and following the relatively brief comments made directly after it, the White House was deluged with telegrams and letters approving the President's speech, the White House reported, by an overwhelming margin. Two days later, the Gallup Survey reported that nearly 4 out of every 5 of those who heard it approved the President's speech and the course that it advocated with regard to Vietnam.

Ten days after the President's speech, the second highest official in the Administration launched an attack on the television networks on the grounds that critical comments on government policy as enunciated in a Presidential address might unduly influence the American people—even though, following such comments, the President received a 77 percent vote of confidence from those who heard him on the issue discussed.

The Vice President also censured television network news for covering events and personalities that are jolting to many of us but that nevertheless document the kind of polarized society—not just here but throughout the world, whether or not there is television and whether it is controlled or free—in which, for better or worse, we are living. It is not a consensus society. It is a questioning, searching society—unsure, groping, running to extremes, abrasive, often violent even in its reactions to the violence of others. Students and faculties are challenging time-honored traditions in the universities. Young clergy are challenging ancient practices and even dogma of the churches. Labor union members are challenging their leaderships. Scientists, artists, businessmen, politicians—all are drawn into the fray. Frequently, because everyone is clamoring for attention, views are set forth in extreme terms.

As we do not propose to leave unreported the voice of the Vice President, we cannot in good conscience leave unreported any other significant voice or happening—whether or not it supports government policy, whether or not it conforms with our own views, whether or not it disturbs the persuasions of any political party or bloc. But no healthy society and no governing authorities worth their salt have to fear the reporting of dissenting or even of hostile voices. What a healthy society and a self-respecting government do have to fear—at the price of their vitality if not of their life—is the suppression of such reporting.

To strengthen the delusion that, as a news medium, television is plunging the nation into collapse and can be deterred only by suppressing criticisms and by either withholding bad news or contriving a formula to balance it with good news, the Vice President's speech was replete with misinformation, inaccuracies and contradictions. To deal adequately with all of these on this occasion would take us through the afternoon, but let me note some of them by way of example, then move on to consider with you the context of the Vice President's speech so far as the actions and statements of other Administration officials are concerned and, finally, make some observations on the significance of this unhappy affair.

The Vice President began his indictment of November 13 with a monstrous contradiction. He asserted flatly that "no medium has a more profound influence over public opinion" than television. And yet he also claimed that the views of America have been very little affected by this "profound influence," when he said, "The views of the majority of this fraternity [i.e., television network news executives and editors] do not—and I repeat, not—represent the views of America." The Vice President can't have it both ways. If the views of the American people show "a great gulf" between how a speech is received by them and how it is treated in a broadcast, obviously the treatment of it has no material effect upon their opinion. Even the premise of the Vice President's claim is proved wrong by the Gallup findings already mentioned.

The Vice President objected to the subjection of the words and policies of the President to "instant analysis and querulous criticism." The analysis, whatever its merits or failings, was hardly instant. Highly informed speculation about the content of the speech had gone on for days and even weeks. Copies were made available at least two hours in advance of the analysis, allowing at least as much time as most morning newspapers had before press time. If a professional reporter could not arrive at some meaningful observations under those circumstances, we would question his competence.

The Vice President took care—and the point should not be lost on us —to remind us that television is "enjoying a monopoly sanctioned and licensed by government." A monopoly, by any definition I know, is the exclusive control of a product or a service by a single entity. Television news is broadcast in this country by four networks, all with different and fiercely competitive managements, producers, editors and reporters, involving hundreds of strongly individualistic people; by a dozen station groups, initiating and producing their own news broadcasts, and by hundreds of stations, producing their own news broadcasts wholly independent and distinct from those of any network they may otherwise be associated with. Moreover, it is estimated that, on the average day, 65 percent more hours of viewing are devoted to station-originated news broadcasts than to network news broadcasts. In addition, there are 6717 radio stations in this country—the overwhelming majority without network affiliations.

All this hardly represents monopolistic control.

The Vice President seems to maintain that the First Amendment applies differently to NBC from the way it does to the *New York Times*, because NBC's audience is bigger and because television has more impact. That the First Amendment is quantitative in its applicability is a chilling innovation from a responsible officer of the government. By this standard, the *Times* is less entitled to the protection of the Bill of Rights than the *Des Moines Register*, with a third of its circulation, and twice as entitled to it as the *New York Daily News*, which has double the *Times'* circulation. As for the impact of the television medium, it may be true that combined picture and voice give television a special force. On the other hand, print can be reread, it can be lingered over, it can be spread around, it can be consulted over and over again. Should, on the grounds of these advantages over television, the print media have less freedom?

The Vice President asked how many "marches and demonstrations" there would be if there were no television cameras. An elementary textbook in American history might prove instructive. There was no television to record the demonstrations against slavery; demonstrations against the Mexican War; demonstrations against the Civil War draft; demonstrations for women's suffrage; demonstrations for Prohibition; demonstrations for the League of Nations; demonstrations against child labor; demonstrations for economic justice. That there would be no disturbing news except for television is a canard as dangerous as it is egregious.

Now let us turn to the crucial issue raised by the Vice President.

Despite his complaints about how and what we report, the Vice President protested that he was not advocating censorship. He found it necessary, a week later, to repeat his protest three times in one paragraph. It is far more shocking to me that the utterances of the second-ranking official of the United States government require such repeated assurances that he had in mind no violation of the Constitution than it is comforting to have them at all. Of course, neither he nor any of his associates are advocating censorship—which would never survive judicial scrutiny. But it does not take overt censorship to cripple the free flow of ideas. Was the Vice President's reference to television's being "sanctioned and licensed by government" accidental and devoid of any point or meaning? Was his suggestion that "it is time that the networks were *made* [emphasis added] more responsive to the views of the nation" merely sloppy semantics and devoid of any notion of coercion?

Perhaps the Vice President, in his November 20 follow-up speech, was not referring to government action, but only to a dialogue among citizens when he said, "When they [network commentators and some gentlemen of the *New York Times*] go beyond fair comment and criticism they will be called upon to defend their statements and their positions just as we must defend ours. And when their criticism becomes excessive or unjust, we shall invite them down from their ivory towers to enjoy the rough and tumble of public debate." Who, in those sentences, will do the calling of these men to defend themselves, and before whom? Who is the "we" who shall do the inviting? And by whose standards will the limits of "fair comment" and "just criticism" be judged and who shall be the judges?

The ominous character of the Vice President's attack derives directly from the fact that it is made upon the journalism of a medium licensed by the government of which he is a high-ranking officer. This is a new relationship in government-press relations. From George Washington on, every Administration has had disputes with the press, but the First Amendment assured the press that such disputes were between equals, with the press beyond the reach of the government. This all-important fact of the licensing power of life and death over the broadcast press brings an implicit threat to a government official's attacks on it, whether or not that is the intention and whether or not the official says he is speaking only as an individual.

But the Vice President does not seem to have been walking a lonely path in the direction of suppression and harassment:

Herbert G. Klein, the Administration's Director of Communications, revealed that, on November 4, the day after the President's speech, calls from White House offices went out to broadcast stations asking whether editorials were planned and, in Mr. Klein's words, "to ask them what they would say in their editorial comment."

In Washington, D.C., television stations were called by a member of the Subversive Activities Control Board, Paul O'Neil, requesting logs of news coverage devoted to support of and in opposition to the Administration's Vietnam policy. His wife, a Dade County official of the Republican Party, who specified her husband's official position, made the same request of Miami, Florida, stations.

On November 4, ,the Chairman of the Federal Communications Commission, in unprecedented calls to the presidents of the three broadcasting companies with national television networks, requested transcripts of the remarks of their reporters and others who had commented on the speech, saying there had been complaints, the source of which he failed to specify—although two weeks later on sober second thought, he seemed to reverse himself when he signed a letter adopted by the full Commission finding that the comments made on the networks after the speech in no way violated its doctrine of fairness.

A special counsel to the President, Clark R. Mollenhoff, said that the speech "was developed by various White House aides," adding "if you are asking me, 'does it reflect the Administration's views,' the evidence is abundant that it does." The President's press secretary, Ronald Ziegler, agreed that a White House special assistant, Patrick J. Buchanan, "very well could have contributed some thoughts to the speech."

Mr. Klein, on November 16, said, "I think that any time any industry— and I include newspapers very thoroughly in this, as well as the networks—if you look at the problems you have today and you fail to continue to examine them, you do invite the government to come in."

In my judgment, the whole tone, the whole content and the whole pattern of this government intrusion into the substance and methods of the broadcast press, and indeed of all journalism, have the gravest implications. Because a Federally licensed medium is involved, no more serious episode has occurred in government-press relationships since the dark days in the fumbling infancy of this republic when the ill-fated Alien and Sedition Acts forbade criticism of the government and its policies on pain of exile or imprisonment.

In the context of this intimidation, self-serving disavowals of censorship, no matter how often repeated, are meaningless. Reprisals no less damaging to the media and no less dangerous to our fundamental freedoms than censorship are readily available to the government—economic, legal and psychological. Nor is their actual employment necessary to achieve their ends; to have them dangling like swords over the media can do harm even more irreparable than overt action. If these threats implicit in the developments of the past week are not openly recognized, unequivocally denounced and firmly resisted, freedom of communications in this country will suffer a setback that will not be limited to checking the freedom of television or to barring critical comment on government policy. It will precipitate an erosion that will inevitably destroy the most powerful safeguard of a free society—free, unhampered and unharassed news media.

This does not have to be the resolute intention of any person or group, any party or government. We can wander unintentionally—all of us—into a lethal trap if we let our dissatisfaction with the handling of specific issues, which are variable, and of events, which are transitory, compromise our adherence to basic principles, which are constant. No permanent freedom was ever wisely exchanged for temporary popularity, for the popularity can be gone with changing political or social cycles and the freedom can be regained, if ever, only at fearful cost. And this is a truth that should be remembered by those who demand that our freedoms be preserved only when they agree with us, but who have been eager to restrict them whenever they disagree with us. You cannot side with restrictions or with bullying or with recriminations when they support your views and then oppose them when they differ, for they will rise up and haunt you long after your cause is lost or won.

The issue here is simple. Dwight D. Eisenhower said, "I believe the United States is strong enough to expose to the world its differing viewpoints. . . ." His successor, John F. Kennedy, said, "The men who create power make an indispensable contribution to the nation's greatness, but the men who question power make a contribution just as indispensable."

Criticism is an essential ingredient in that mix. It is central, not tangential, to a free society. It is always a free society's strength and often its salvation. Television itself is not and should not be immune to such criticism. As a matter of fact, it is the most criticized medium in the history of communications. Newspapers, magazines, academic groups, learned societies—who wouldn't dream of criticizing each other—criticize us every single day. Everyone has free access to what we do, and everyone sees us do it. We are *not* unaccountable. We are *not* clandestine. We have *no* end product that is not seen and judged by everyone. But such open criticism is a far cry from sharp reminders from high official quarters that we are licensed or that if we don't examine ourselves, we in common with other media "invite" the government to move in.

The troubled pages of this country's history are writ dark with the death of liberty in those nations where the first fatal symptom of political decay was an effort to control the news media. Seldom has it been called censorship. Seldom is the word used except in denials. Always it has been "guidelines" in the name of national unity. And we might well ponder the fate of the unhappy roll of nations that had no regard for their freedoms or took them for granted or held them lightly.

As we meet here, 39 nations in the world have a controlled press or a press that wavers uncertainly between control and freedom. This melancholy statistic might well be borne in mind by those of our own countrymen who, as the Vice President descends upon one part of the country to attack the journalists of another part, are moved by their temporary irritations to applaud their own ensnarement. In his speech of November 13, the Vice President turned to Learned Hand to support a proposition that would have been total anathema to the great judge. Let me, in conclusion, invoke Hand in more revealing words:

Our democracy rests upon the assumption that, set free, the common man can manage his own fate; that errors will cancel each other by open discussion; that the interests of each when unguided from above, will not diverge too radically from the interests of all. . . .

I appreciate having had this opportunity to speak to you today in what all thoughtful people must regard as a critical period in the life of a free society and of the free communications without which it cannot exist.

Questions

1. What are the principal charges that Vice President Spiro T. Agnew makes against the television news medium? Might the same charges be made against the newspapers and radio? What about magazines? What would be the differences in the nature and in the forcefulness of the charges made against other news media?

2. How do you think some of the Vice President's objections to television might be countered? Would you argue that they ought not to be countered? Why?

3. What are the defenses made against the Vice President's speech by Frank Stanton, president of the Columbia Broadcasting System? How valid do you think they are? Do they respond point for point to the Vice President's attack?

4. Leonard H. Goldenson, president of the American Broadcasting Company, commented on Vice President Agnew's speech as follows:

As I said last week after the Vice President's first speech, I firmly believe that in our free society the ultimate judges of the reliability of our news presentation will be the viewing public.

Again I leave it to the public to determine whether the Vice President's renewed attack today (Nov. 20) is an attempt to intimidate and discredit not only television news reporting, but other major news media. Personally, I believe it is.

I hope we are not facing a period in the history of our nation when high government officials try to act both as judge and jury on the issue of a free press.

How valid do you consider the point that the public should be left to determine whether the Vice President's attack on television is "an attempt to intimidate and discredit"?

5. Among the reactions to the Vice President's speech were some of the following, as quoted by the Vice President himself in a later speech: the speech was "disgraceful, ignorant and base"; it "leads us as a nation into an ugly era of the most fearsome suppression and intimidation"; one national commentator said, "I hesitate to get into the gutter with this guy"; another commentator called the Vice President's speech "one of the most sinister speeches I have ever heard made by a public official"; the president of a network said it was "an unprecedented attempt to intimidate a news medium which depends for its existence upon Government licenses"; the president of another network charged the Vice President with "an appeal to prejudice." In what ways might these comments be described as "overreaction"? In what ways might they be justified?

6. Why does the issue arouse such emotional reaction and overreaction? Does it indeed relate to freedom of thought and expression in this country? In what particular ways? How are the issues here related to those discussed by the Justices of the Supreme Court in regard to the Pentagon Papers (Section Two)?

Assignments

1. Analyze the tone and the rhetoric of Mr. Agnew's speech and Mr. Stanton's response. Try to account for the differences. Keep in mind the different audiences being addressed.

2. The *New Republic* in its issue of November 29, 1969, page 6, reports that the *New York Post* reprinted all the comments that the Vice President refers to, which were made on the TV networks immediately after President Nixon's speech on Vietnam. The *New Republic* describes the commentary by the several network specialists as "a good, balanced extemporaneous job." Argue either that there should have been no comment at all, because the President's words spoke for themselves, or that the comment should have been more supportive of the President's position than a merely "balanced" comment could be. In your discussion you might take up the question of whether it is at all necessary to comment or condense or summarize a speech by a public official after he has just made it on television.

3. Without reference to the particular issues involved in the Agnew-Stanton exchange, discuss what you consider to be the important effect, good or bad, of television on American life. Take into account the possibility that the effect of television has sometimes been exaggerated.

Additional Reading

The Vice President's rebuttal to his critics, delivered November 20, 1969, and reprinted in whole or in part in newspapers a day later is an extended commentary on the reaction to his original speech. Specific references should be available in your library in the usual periodical and newspaper guides. The general question of the influence of television in shaping the image of a public figure is discussed at length in a book by Joe McGinnis, called *The Selling of the President, 1968*, a section of which, with the same title, appeared in *Harper's Magazine* for August, 1969. Extended thoughtful analyses of the issues raised by Vice President Agnew have appeared and will continue to appear in journals of opinion for some time. Again, specific references to these may be found in the usual reader's guides.

SECTION TWO *The Public's*

Right to Know: The Pentagon

Papers and the Supreme Court

Congress shall make no law respecting an establishment
of religion, or prohibiting the free exercise thereof;
or abridging the freedom of speech, or of the press;
or the right of the people peaceably to assemble, and
to petition the Government for a redress of grievances

Article I of the U.S. Constitution

The Court which wrote the decision on the Pentagon Papers. From left to right: *sitting:* Mr. Justice Harlan, Mr. Justice Black, Mr. Chief Justice Burger, Mr. Justice Douglas, Mr. Justice Brennan; *standing:* Mr. Justice Marshall, Mr. Justice Stewart, Mr. Justice White, Mr. Justice Blackmun.

The Decision of the Court

Supreme Court of the United States

Nos. 1873 and 1885.—October Term, 1970

New York Times Company, Petitioner,

1873   *v.*

United States.

On Writ of Certiorari to the United States Court of Appeals for the Second Circuit.

United States, Petitioner,

1885   *v.*

The Washington Post Company et al.

On Writ of Certiorari to the United States Court of Appeals for the District of Columbia Circuit.

[June 30, 1971]

PER CURIAM.

We granted certiorari in these cases in which the United States seeks to enjoin the New York Times and the Washington Post from publishing the contents of a classified study entitled "History of U. S. Decision-Making Process on Viet Nam Policy." —— U. S. —— (1971).

"Any system of prior restraints of expression comes to this Court bearing a heavy presumption against its constitutional validity." *Bantam Books, Inc.*, v. *Sullivan*, 372 U. S. 58, 70 (1963); see also *Near* v. *Minnesota*, 283 U. S. 697 (1931). The Government "thus carries a heavy burden of showing justification for the enforcement of such a restraint." *Organization for a Better Austin* v. *Keefe*, —— U. S. —— (1971). The District Court for the Southern District of New York in the *New York Times* case and the District Court for the District of Columbia and the Court of Appeals for the District of Columbia Circuit in the *Washington Post* case held that the Government had not met that burden. We agree.

The judgment of the Court of Appeals for the District of Columbia Circuit is therefore affirmed. The order of the Court of Appeals for the Second Circuit is reversed and the case is remanded with directions to enter a judgment affirming the judgment of the District Court for the Southern District of New York. The stays entered June 25, 1971, by the Court are vacated. The judgments shall issue forthwith.

So ordered.

Mr. Justice Black, Concurring

Nos. 1873 and 1885.—October Term, 1970

New York Times Company, Petitioner, 1873 *v.* United States.	On Writ of Certiorari to the United States Court of Appeals for the Second Circuit.
United States, Petitioner, 1885 *v.* The Washington Post Company et al.	On Writ of Certiorari to the United States Court of Appeals for the District of Columbia Circuit.

[June 30, 1971]

MR. JUSTICE BLACK, with whom MR. JUSTICE DOUGLAS joins, concurring.

I adhere to the view that the Government's case against the *Washington Post* should have been dismissed and that the injunction against the *New York Times* should have been vacated without oral argument when the cases were first presented to this Court. I believe that every moment's continuance of the injunctions against these newspapers amounts to a flagrant, indefensible, and continuing violation of the First Amendment. Furthermore, after oral arguments, I agree completely that we must affirm the judgment of the Court of Appeals for the District of Columbia and reverse the judgment of the Court of Appeals for the Second Circuit for the reasons stated by my Brothers DOUGLAS and BRENNAN. In my view it is unfortunate that some of my Brethren are apparently willing to hold that the publication of news may sometimes be enjoined. Such a holding would make a shambles of the First Amendment.

Our Government was launched in 1789 with the adoption of the Constitution. The Bill of Rights, including the first Amendment, followed in 1971. Now, for the first time in the 182 years since the founding of the Republic, the federal courts are asked to hold that the First Amendment does not mean what it says, but rather means that the Government can halt the publication of current news of vital importance to the people of this country.

In seeking injunctions against these newspapers and in its presentation to the Court, the Executive Branch seems to have forgotten the essential purpose and history of the First Amendment. When the Constitution was adopted, many people strongly opposed it because the document contained no Bill of Rights to safeguard certain basic freedoms.[1] They especially feared that the new powers granted to a central government might be interpreted to permit the government to curtail freedom of religion, press, assembly, and speech. In response to an overwhelming public clamor, James Madison offered a series of amendments to satisfy citizens that these great liberties would remain safe and beyond the power of government to abridge. Madison proposed what later became the First Amendment in three parts, two of which are set out below, and one of which proclaimed: "The people shall not be deprived or abridged of their right to speak, to write, or to publish their sentiments; *and the freedom of the press, as one of the great bulwarks of liberty, shall be inviolable.*" [2] The amendments were offered to *curtail* and *restrict* the general powers

---

[1] Introducing the Bill of Rights in the House of Representatives, Madison said: "[B]ut I believe that the great mass of the people who opposed [the Constitution], disliked it because it did not contain effectual provisions against the encroachments on particular rights. . . ." 1 Annals of Congress 433 (1834). Congressman Goodhue added: "[I]t is the wish of many of our constituents, that something should be added to the Constitution, to secure in a stronger manner their liberties from the inroads of power." *Id.*, at 426.

[2] The other parts were:
"The civil rights of none shall be abridged on account of religious belief or worship, nor shall any national religion be established, nor shall the full and equal rights of conscience be in any manner, or on any pretext, infringed.
"The people shall not be restrained from peaceably assembling and consulting for their common good; nor from applying to the Legislature by petitions, or remonstrances, for redress of their grievances." 1 Annals of Congress 434 (1834). (Emphasis added.)

granted to the Executive, Legislative, and Judicial Branches two years before in the original Constitution. The Bill of Rights changed the original Constitution into a new charter under which no branch of government could abridge the people's freedoms of press, speech, religion, and assembly. Yet the Solicitor General argues and some members of the Court appear to agree that the general powers of the Government adopted in the original Constitution should be interpreted to limit and restrict the specific and emphatic guarantees of the Bill of Rights adopted later. I can imagine no greater perversion of history. Madison and the other Framers of the First Amendment, able men that they were, wrote in language they earnestly believed could never be misunderstood: "Congress shall make no law . . . abridging the freedom of the press. . . ." Both the history and language of the First Amendment support the view that the press must be left free to publish news, whatever the source, without censorship, injunctions, or prior restraints.

In the First Amendment the Founding Fathers gave the free press the protection it must have to fulfill its essential role in our democracy. The press was to serve the governed, not the governors. The Government's power to censor the press was abolished so that the press would remain forever free to censure the Government. The press was protected so that it could bare the secrets of government and inform the people. Only a free and unrestrained press can effectively expose deception in government. And paramount among the responsibilities of a free press is the duty to prevent any part of the government from deceiving the people and sending them off to distant lands to die of foreign fevers and foreign shot and shell. In my view, far from deserving condemnation for their courageous reporting, the *New York Times*, the *Washington Post*, and other newspapers should be commended for serving the purpose that the Founding Fathers saw so clearly. In revealing the workings of government that led to the Vietnam War, the newspapers nobly did precisely that which the Founders hoped and trusted they would do.

The Government's case here is based on premises entirely different from those that guided the Framers of the First Amendment. The Solicitor General has carefully and emphatically stated:

Now, Mr. Justice [BLACK],your construction of . . . [the First Admendment] is well known, and I certainly respect it. You say that no law means no law, and that should be obvious. I can only say, Mr. Justice, that to me it is equally obvious that 'no law' does not mean 'no law,' and would seek to persuade the Court that that is true. . . . [T]here are other parts of the Constitution that grant power and responsibilities to the Executive and . . . the First Amendment was not intended to make it impossible for the Executive to function or to protect the security of the United States.[3]

And the Government argues in its brief that in spite of the First Amend-

[3] Transcript of Oral Argument, at 76.

ment, "[t]he authority of the Executive Department to protect the nation against publication of information whose disclosure would endanger the national security stems from two interrelated sources: the constitutional power of the President over the conduct of foreign affairs and his authority as Commander-in-Chief." [4]

In other words, we are asked to hold that despite the First Amendment's emphatic command, the Executive Branch, the Congress, and the Judiciary can make laws enjoining publication of current news and abridging freedom of the press in the name of "national security." The Government does not even attempt to rely on any act of Congress. Instead it makes the bold and dangerously far-reaching contention that the courts should take it upon themselves to "make" a law abridging freedom of the press in the name of equity, presidential power and national security, even when the representatives of the people in Congress have adhered to the command of the First Amendment and refused to make such a law.[5] See concurring opinion of MR. JUSTICE DOUGLAS, *post*, at ——. To find that the President has "inherent power" to halt the publication of news by resort to the courts would wipe out the First Amendment and destroy the fundamental liberty and security of the very people the Government hopes to make "secure." No one can read the history of the adoption of the First Amendment without being convinced beyond any doubt that it was injunctions like those sought here that Madison and his collaborators intended to outlaw in this Nation for all time.

The word "security" is a broad, vague generality whose contours should not be invoked to abrogate the fundamental law embodied in the First Amendment. The guarding of military and diplomatic secrets at the expense of informed representative government provides no real security for our Republic. The Framers of the First Amendment, fully aware of both the need to defend a new nation and the abuses of the English and Colonial governments, sought to give this new society strength and security by providing that freedom of speech, press, religion, and assembly should not be abridged. This thought was eloquently expressed in 1937 by Mr. Chief Justice Hughes—great man and great Chief Justice that he was—when the Court held a man could not be punished for attending a meeting run by Communists.

The greater the importance of safeguarding the community from incitements to the overthrow of our institutions by force and violence, the more imperative is the need to preserve inviolate the constitutional rights of free speech, free press and free assembly in order to maintain the opportunity for free political discussion, to the end that government may be responsive to the will of the people

---

[4] Brief for United States, at 12.

[5] Compare the views of the Solicitor General with those of James Madison, the author of the First Amendment. When speaking of the Bill of Rights in the House

and that changes, if desired, may be obtained by peaceful means. Therein lies the security of the Republic, the very foundation of constitutional government.[6]

Mr. Justice Douglas, Concurring

Nos. 1873 and 1885.—October Term, 1970

New York Times Company, Petitioner, 1873 *v.* United States.	On Writ of Certiorari to the United States Court of Appeals for the Second Circuit.

United States, Petitioner, 1885 *v.* The Washington Post Company et al.	On Writ of Certiorari to the United States Court of Appeals for the District of Columbia Circuit.

[June 30, 1971]

MR. JUSTICE DOUGLAS, with whom MR. JUSTICE BLACK joins, concurring.

While I join the opinion of the Court I believe it necessary to express my views more fully.

It should be noted at the outset that the First Amendment provides that "Congress shall make no law . . . abridging the freedom of speech or of the press." That leaves, in my view, no room for governmental restraint on the press.[1]

There is, moreover, no statute barring the publication by the press of the material which the *Times* and *Post* seek to use. 18 U.S.C. § 793(e) provides that "whoever having unauthorized possession of, access to, or control over any document, writing, . . . or information relating to the national defense which information the possessor has reason to believe could be used to the injury of the United States or to the advantage of

---

of Representatives, Madison said: "If they [the first ten amendments] are incorporated into the Constitution, independent tribunals of justice will consider themselves in a peculiar manner the guardians of those rights; they will be an impenetrable bulwark against every assumption of power in the Legislative or Executive; they will be naturally led to resist every encroachment upon rights expressly stipulated for in the Constitution by the declaration of rights." 1 Annals of Congress 439 (1834).

[6] *DeJonge v. Oregon,* 299 U. S. 353, 365 (1937).

[1] See *Beauharnais v. Illinois,* 343 U. S. 250, 267 (dissenting opinion of MR. JUSTICE BLACK), 284 (my dissenting opinion); *Roth v. United States,* 354 U. S. 476, 508 (my dissenting opinion which MR. JUSTICE BLACK joined); *Yates v. United States,* 354 U. S. 298, 339 (separate opinion of MR. JUSTICE BLACK which I joined); *New York Times v. Sullivan,* 376 U. S. 254, 293 (concurring opinion of MR. JUSTICE BLACK which I joined); *Garrison v. Louisiana,* 379 U. S. 64, 80 (my concurring opinion which MR. JUSTICE BLACK joined).

any foreign nation, wilfully communicates . . . the same to any person not entitled to receive it . . . shall be fined not more than $10,000 or imprisoned not more than ten years or both."

The Government suggests that the word "communicates" is broad enough to encompass publication.

There are eight sections in the chapter on espionage and censorship, §§ 792–799. In three of those eight "publish" is specifically mentioned: § 794(b) provides "Whoever in time of war, with the intent that the same shall be communicated to the enemy, collects records, *publishes*, or communicates . . . [the disposition of armed forces]."

Section 797 prohibits "reproduces, *publishes*, sells, or gives away" photos of defense installations.

Section 798 relating to cryptography prohibits: "communicates, furnishes, transmits, or otherwise makes available . . . *or publishes*." [2]

Thus it is apparent that Congress was capable of and did distinguish between publishing and communication in the various sections of the Espionage Act.

The other evidence that § 793 does not apply to the press is a rejected version of § 793. That version read: "During any national emergency resulting from a war to which the U. S. is a party or from threat of such a war, the President may, by proclamation, prohibit the publishing or communicating of, or the attempting to publish or communicate any information relating to the national defense, which in his judgment is of such character that it is or might be useful to the enemy." During the debates in the Senate the First Amendment was specifically cited and that provision was defeated. 55 Cong. Rec. 2166.

Judge Gurfein's holding in the *Times* case that this Act does not apply to this case was therefore pre-eminently sound. Moreover, the Act of September 23, 1950, in amending 18 U. S. C. § 793 states in § 1(b) that:

> Nothing in this Act shall be construed to authorize, require, or establish military or civilian censorship or in any way to limit or infringe upon freedom of the press or of speech as guaranteed by the Constitution of the United States and no regulation shall be promulgated hereunder having that effect. 64 Stat. 987.

Thus Congress has been faithful to the command of the First Amendment in this area.

So any power that the Government possesses must come from its "inherent power."

The power to wage war is "the power to wage war successfully." See *Hirabayashi* v. *United States*, 320 U.S. 81, 93. But the war power stems from a declaration of war. The Constitution by Article I, § 8, gives Congress, not the President, power "to declare war." Nowhere are presidential

---

[2] These papers contain data concerning the communications system of the United States, the publication of which is made a crime. But the criminal sanction is not urged by the United States as basis of equity power.

wars authorized. We need not decide therefore what leveling effect the war power of Congress might have.

These disclosures [3] may have a serious impact. But that is no basis for sanctioning a previous restraint on the press. As stated by Chief Justice Hughes in *Near* v. *Minnesota,* 283 U. S. 697, 719–720:

> . . . While reckless assaults upon public men, and efforts to bring obloquy upon those who are endeavoring faithfully to discharge official duties, exert a baleful influence and deserve the severest condemnation in public opinion, it cannot be said that this abuse is greater, and it is believed to be less, than that which characterized the period in which our institutions took shape. Meanwhile, the administration of government has become more complex, the opportunities for malfeasance and corruption have multiplied, crime has grown to most serious proportions, and the danger of its protection by unfaithful officials and of the impairment of the fundamental security of life and property by criminal alliances and official neglect, emphasizes the primary need of a vigilant and courageous press, especially in great cities. The fact that the liberty of the press may be abused by miscreant purveyors of scandal does not make any the less necessary the immunity of the press from previous restraint in dealing with official misconduct.

As we stated only the other day in *Organization for a Better Austin* v. *Keefe,* —— U. S. ——, "any prior restraint on expression comes to this Court with a 'heavy presumption' against its constitutional validity."

The Government says that it has inherent powers to go into court and obtain an injunction to protect that national interest, which in this case is alleged to be national security.

Near v. *Minnesota,* 283 U. S. 697, repudiated that expansive doctrine in no uncertain terms.

The dominant purpose of the First Amendment was to prohibit the widespread practice of governmental suppression of embarrassing information. It is common knowledge that the First Amendment was adopted against the widespread use of the common law of seditious libel to punish the dissemination of material that is embarrassing to the powers-that-be. See Emerson, The System of Free Expressions, c. V (1970); Chafee, Free Speech in the United States, c. XIII (1941). The present cases will, I think, go down in history as the most dramatic illustration of that principle. A debate of large proportions goes on in the Nation over our posture in Vietnam. That debate antedated the disclosure of the contents of the present documents. The latter are highly relevant to the debate in progress.

Secrecy in government is fundamentally anti-democratic, perpetuating bureaucratic errors. Open debate and discussion of public issues are vital

---

[3] There are numerous sets of this material in existence and they apparently are not under any controlled custody. Moreover, the President has sent a set to the Congress. We start then with a case where there already is rather wide distribution of the material that is destined for publicity, not secrecy. I have gone over the material listed in the *in camera* brief of the United States. It is all history, not future events. None of it is more recent than 1968.

to our national health. On public questions there should be "open and robust debate." *New York Times, Inc.* v. *Sullivan,* 376 U. S. 254, 269–270.

I would affirm the judgment of the Court of Appeals in the *Post* case, vacate the stay of the Court of Appeals in the *Times* case and direct that it affirm the District Court.

The stays in these cases that have been in effect for more than a week constitute a flouting of the principles of the First Amendment as interpreted in *Near* v. *Minnesota.*

Mr. Justice Brennan, Concurring

Nos. 1873 and 1885.—October Term, 1970

New York Times Company, Petitioner, 1873 *v.* United States.	On Writ of Certiorari to the United States Court of Appeals for the Second Circuit.
United States, Petitioner, 1885 *v.* The Washington Post Company et al.	On Writ of Certiorari to the United States Court of Appeals for the District of Columbia Circuit.

[June 30, 1971]

MR. JUSTICE BRENNAN, concurring.

I

I write separately in these cases only to emphasize what should be apparent: that our judgment in the present cases may not be taken to indicate the propriety, in the future, of issuing temporary stays and restraining orders to block the publication of material sought to be suppressed by the Government. So far as I can determine, never before has the United States sought to enjoin a newspaper from publishing information in its possession. The relative novelty of the questions presented, the necessary haste with which decisions were reached, the magnitude of the interests asserted, and the fact that all the parties have concentrated their arguments upon the question whether permanent restraints were proper may have justified at least some of the restraints heretofore imposed in these cases. Certainly it is difficult to fault the several courts below for seeking to assure that the issues here involved were preserved for ultimate review by this Court. But even if it be assumed that some of the interim restraints were proper in the two cases before us, that assumption has no bearing upon the propriety of similar judicial action in the future. To begin with, there has now been ample time for reflection and judgment; whatever values there may be in the preservation of novel questions for appellate review may not support any restraints in the future. More important, the First Amendment stands as an absolute bar to the imposition of judical restraints in circumstances of the kind presented by these cases.

II

The error which has pervaded these cases from the outset was the granting of any injunctive relief whatsoever, interim or otherwise. The entire thrust of the Government's claim throughout these cases has been that publication of the material sought to be enjoined "could," or "might," or "may" prejudice the national interest in various ways. But the First Amendment tolerates absolutely no prior judicial restraints of the press predicated upon surmise or conjecture that untoward consequences may result.* Our cases, it is true, have indicated that there is a single, extremely narrow class of cases in which the First Amendment's ban on prior judicial restraint may be overridden. Our cases have thus far indicated that such cases may arise only when the Nation "is at war," *Schenck* v. *United States,* 249 U. S. 47, 52 (1919), during which times "no one would question but that a Government might prevent actual obstruction to its recruiting service or the publication of the sailing dates of transports or the number and location of troops." *Near* v. *Minnesota,* 283 U. S. 697, 716 (1931). Even if the present world situation were assumed to be tantamount to a time of war, or if the power of presently available armaments would justify even in peacetime the suppression of information that would set in motion a nuclear holocaust, in neither of these actions has the Government presented or even alleged that publication of items from or based upon the material at issue would cause the happening of an event of that nature. "The chief purpose of [the First Amendment's] guarantee [is] to prevent previous restraints upon publication." *Near* v. *Minnesota, supra,* at 713. Thus, only governmental allegation and proof that publication must inevitably, directly and immediately cause the occurrence of an event kindred to imperiling the safety of a transport already at sea can support even the issuance of an interim restraining order. In no event may mere conclusions be sufficient: for if the Executive Branch seeks judicial aid in preventing publication, it must inevitably submit the basis upon which that aid is sought to scrutiny by the judiciary. And therefore, every restraint issued in this case, whatever its form, has violated the First Amendment—and none the less so because that restraint was justified as necessary to afford the court an opportunity to examine the claim more thoroughly. Unless and until the Government has clearly made out its case, the First Amendment commands that no injunction may issue.

---

* *Freedman* v. *Maryland,* 380 U. S. 51 (1965), and similar cases regarding temporary restraints of allegedly obscene materials are not in point. For those cases rest upon the proposition that "obscenity is not protected by the freedoms

Mr. Justice Stewart, Concurring

Nos. 1873 and 1885.—October Term, 1970

New York Times Company, Petitioner, 1873 *v.* United States.	On Writ of Certiorari to the United States Court of Appeals for the Second Circuit.

United States, Petitioner, 1885 *v.* The Washington Post Company et al.	On Writ of Certiorari to the United States Court of Appeals for the District of Columbia Circuit.

[June 30, 1971]

MR. JUSTICE STEWART, with whom MR. JUSTICE WHITE joins, concurring.

In the governmental structure created by our Constitution, the Executive is endowed with enormous power in the two related areas of national defense and international relations. This power, largely unchecked by the Legislative [1] and Judicial [2] branches, has been pressed to the very hilt since the advent of the nuclear missile age. For better or for worse, the simple fact is that a President of the United States possesses vastly greater constitutional independence in these two vital areas of power than does, say, a prime minister of a country with a parliamentary form of government.

In the absence of the governmental checks and balances present in

---

of speech and press." *Roth* v. *United States,* 354 U. S. 476 (1957). Here there is no question but that the material sought to be suppressed is within the protection of the First Amendment; the only question is whether, notwithstanding that fact, its publication may be enjoined for a time because of the presence of an overwhelming national interest. Similarly, copyright cases have no pertinence here: the Government is not asserting an interest in the particular form of words chosen in the documents, but is seeking to suppress the ideas expressed therein. And the copyright laws, of course, protect only the form of expression and not the ideas expressed.

[1] The President's power to make treaties and to appoint ambassadors is of course limited by the requirement of Article II, § 1, of the Constitution that he obtain the advice and consent of the Senate. Article I, § 8, empowers Congress to "raise and support Armies," and "provide and maintain a Navy." And, of course, Congress alone can declare war. This power was last exercised almost 30 years ago at the inception of World War II. Since the end of that war in 1945, the Armed Forces of the United States have suffered approximately half a million casualties in various parts of the world.

[2] See *Chicago & Southern Air Lines* v. *Waterman Steamship Corp.,* 333 U. S. 103; *Hirabayashi* v. *United States,* 320 U. S. 81; *United States* v. *Curtiss-Wright Export Corp.,* 299 U. S. 304; cf. *Mora* v. *McNamara,* cert. denied 389 U. S. 934.

other areas of our national life, the only effective restraint upon executive policy and power in the areas of national defense and international affairs may lie in an enlightened citizenry—in an informed and critical public opinion which alone can here protect the values of democratic government. For this reason, it is perhaps here that a press that is alert, aware, and free most vitally serves the basic purpose of the First Amendment. For without an informed and free press there cannot be an enlightened people.

Yet it is elementary that the successful conduct of international diplomacy and the maintenance of an effective national defense require both confidentiality and secrecy. Other nations can hardly deal with this Nation in an atmosphere of mutual trust unless they can be assured that their confidences will be kept. And within our own executive departments, the development of considered and intelligent international policies would be impossible if those charged with their formulation could not communicate with each other freely, frankly, and in confidence. In the area of basic national defense the frequent need for absolute secrecy is, of course, self-evident.

I think there can be but one answer to this dilemma, if dilemma it be. The responsibility must be where the power is.[3] If the Constitution gives the Executive a large degree of unshared power in the conduct of foreign affairs and the maintenance of our national defense, then under the Constitution the Executive must have the largely unshared duty to determine and preserve the degree of internal security necessary to exercise that power successfully. It is an awesome responsibility, requiring judgment and wisdom of a high order. I should suppose that moral, political, and practical considerations would dictate that a very first principle of that wisdom would be an insistence upon avoiding secrecy for its own sake. For when everything is classified, then nothing is classified, and the system becomes one to be disregarded by the cynical or the careless, and to be manipulated by those intent on self-protection or self-promotion. I should suppose, in short, that the hallmark of a truly effective internal security system would be the maximum possible disclosure, recognizing

[3] "It is quite apparent that if, in the maintenance of our international relations, embarrassment—perhaps serious embarrassment—is to be avoided and success for our aims achieved, congressional legislation which is to be made effective through negotiation and inquiry within the international field must often accord to the President a degree of discretion and freedom from statutory restriction which would not be admissible were domestic affairs alone involved. Moreover, he, not Congress, has the better opportunity of knowing the conditions which prevail in foreign countries, and especially is this true in time of war. He has his confidential sources of information. He has his agents in the form of diplomatic, consular and other officials. Secrecy in respect of information gathered by them may be highly necessary, and the premature disclosure of it productive of harmful results. Indeed, so clearly is this true that the first President refused to accede to a request to lay before the House of Representatives the instructions, correspondence and documents relating to the negotiation of the Jay Treaty—a refusal the wisdom of which was recognized by the House itself and has never since been doubted. . . ." *United States* v. *Curtiss-Wright Corp.*, 299 U. S. 304, at 320.

that secrecy can best be preserved only when credibility is truly maintained. But be that as it may, it is clear to me that it is the constitutional duty of the Executive—as a matter of sovereign prerogative and not as a matter of law as the courts know law—through the promulgation and enforcement of executive regulations, to protect the confidentiality necessary to carry out its responsibilities in the fields of international relations and national defense.

This is not to say that Congress and the courts have no role to play. Undoubtedly Congress has the power to enact specific and appropriate criminal laws to protect government property and preserve government secrets. Congress has passed such laws, and several of them are of very colorable relevance to the apparent circumstances of these cases. And if a criminal prosecution is instituted, it will be the responsibility of the courts to decide the applicability of the criminal law under which the charge is brought. Moreover, if Congress should pass a specific law authorizing civil proceedings in this field, the courts would likewise have the duty to decide the constitutionality of such a law as well as its applicability to the facts proved.

But in the cases before us we are asked neither to construe specific regulations nor to apply specific laws. We are asked, instead, to perform a function that the Constitution gave to the Executive, not the Judiciary. We are asked, quite simply, to prevent the publication by two newspapers of material that the Executive Branch insists should not, in the national interest, be published. I am convinced that the Executive is correct with respect to some of the documents involved. But I cannot say that disclosure of any of them will surely result in direct, immediate, and irreparable damage to our Nation or its people. That being so, there can under the First Amendment be but one judicial resolution of the issues before us. I join the judgments of the Court.

Mr. Justice White, Concurring

Nos. 1873 and 1885.—October Term, 1970

New York Times Company, Petitioner, 1873 *v.* United States.	On Writ of Certiorari to the United States Court of Appeals for the Second Circuit.
United States, Petitioner, 1885 *v.* The Washington Post Company et al.	On Writ of Certiorari to the United States Court of Appeals for the District of Columbia Circuit.

[June 30, 1971]

MR. JUSTICE WHITE, with whom MR. JUSTICE STEWART joins, concurring.

I concur in today's judgments, but only because of the concededly extraordinary protection against prior restraints enjoyed by the press under our constitutional system. I do not say that in no circumstances would the First Amendment permit an injunction against publishing information about government plans or operations.[1] Nor, after examining the materials the Government characterizes as the most sensitive and destructive, can I deny that revelation of these documents will do substantial damage to public interests. Indeed, I am confident that their disclosure will have that result. But I nevertheless agree that the United States has not satisfied the very heavy burden which it must meet to warrant an injunction against publication in these cases, at least in the absence of express and appropriately limited congressional authorization for prior restraints in circumstances such as these.

The Government's position is simply stated: The responsibility of the Executive for the conduct of the foreign affairs and for the security of the Nation is so basic that the President is entitled to an injunction against publication of a newspaper story whenever he can convince a court that the information to be revealed threatens "grave and irreparable" injury to the public interest;[2] and the injunction should issue whether or not the material to be published is classified, whether or not publication would be lawful under relevant criminal statutes enacted by Congress and regardless of the circumstances by which the newspaper came into possession of the information.

[1] The Congress has authorized a strain of prior restraints against private parties in certain instances. The National Labor Relations Board routinely issues cease-and-desist orders against employers whom it finds have threatened or coerced employees in the exercise of protected rights. See 29 U. S. C. § 160(c). Similarly, the Federal Trade Commission is empowered to impose cease-and-desist orders against unfair methods of competition. 15 U. S. C. § 45(b). Such orders can, and quite often do, restrict what may be spoken or written under certain circumstances. See, e.g., *NLRB* v. *Gissel Packing Co.*, 395 U. S. 575, 616–620 (1969). Art. I, § 8 of the Constitution authorizes Congress to secure the "exclusive right" of authors to their writings, and no one denies that a newspaper can properly be enjoined from publishing the copyrighted works of another. See *Westermann Co.* v. *Dispatch Co.*, 249 U. S. 100 (1919). Newspapers do themselves rely from time to time on the copyright as a means of protecting their accounts of important events. However, those enjoined under the statutes relating to the National Labor Relations Board and the Federal Commission are private parties, not the press; and when the press is enjoined under the copyright laws the complainant is a private copyright holder enforcing a private right. These situations are quite distinct from the Government's request for an injunction against publishing information about the affairs of government, a request admittedly not based on any statute.

[2] The "grave and irreparable danger" standard is that asserted by the Government in this Court. In remanding to Judge Gurfein for further hearings in the *Times* litigation, five members of the Court of Appeals for Second Circuit directed him to determine whether disclosure of certain items specified with particularity by the Government would "pose such grave and immediate danger to the security of the United States as to warrant their publication being enjoined."

At least in the absence of legislation by Congress, based on its own investigations and findings, I am quite unable to agree that the inherent powers of the Executive and the courts reach so far as to authorize remedies having such sweeping potential for inhibiting publications by the press. Much of the difficulty inheres in the "grave and irreparable danger" standard suggested by the United States. If the United States were to have judgment under such a standard in these cases, our decision would be of little guidance to other courts in other cases, for the material at issue here would not be available from the Court's opinion or from public records, nor would it be published by the press. Indeed, even today where we hold that the United States has not met its burden, the material remains sealed in court records and it is properly not discussed in today's opinions. Moreover, because the material poses substantial dangers to national interests and because of the hazards of criminal sanctions, a responsible press may choose never to publish the more sensitive materials. To sustain the Government in these cases would start the courts down a long and hazardous road that I am not willing to travel, at least without congressional guidance and direction.

It is not easy to reject the proposition urged by the United States and to deny relief on its good-faith claims in these cases that publication will work serious damage to the country. But that discomfiture is considerably dispelled by the infrequency of prior restraint cases. Normally, publication will occur and the damage be done before the Government has either opportunity or grounds for suppression. So here, publication has already begun and a substantial part of the threatened damage has already occurred. The fact of a massive breakdown in security is known, access to the documents by many unauthorized people is undeniable and the efficacy of equitable relief against these or other newspapers to avert anticipated damage is doubtful at best.

What is more, terminating the ban on publication of the relatively few sensitive documents the Government now seeks to suppress does not mean that the law either requires or invites newspapers or others to publish them or that they will be immune from criminal action if they do. Prior restraints require an unusually heavy justification under the First Amendment; but failure by the Government to justify prior restraints does not measure its constitutional entitlement to a conviction for criminal publication. That the Government mistakenly chose to proceed by injunction does not mean that it could not successfully proceed in another way.

When the Espionage Act was under consideration in 1917, Congress eliminated from the bill a provision that would have given the President broad powers in time of war to proscribe, under threat of criminal penalty, the publication of various categories of information related to the national defense.[3] Congress at that time was unwilling to clothe the President with

---

[3] "Whoever, in time of war, in violation of reasonable regulations to be prescribed by the President, which he is hereby authorized to make and promulgate,

such far-reaching powers to monitor the press, and those opposed to this part of the legislation assumed that a necessary concomitant of such power was the power to "filter out the news to the people through some man." 55 Cong. Rec. 2008 (1917) (remarks of Senator Ashurst). However, these same members of Congress appeared to have little doubt that newspapers would be subject to criminal prosecution if they insisted on publishing information of the type Congress had itself determined should not be revealed. Senator Ashurst, for example, was quite sure that the editor of such a newspaper "should be punished if he did publish information as to the movements of the fleet, the troops, the aircraft, the location of powder factories, the location of defense works, and all that sort of thing." 55 Cong. Rec. 2009 (1917).[4]

The criminal code contains numerous provisions potentially relevant to these cases. Section 797[5] makes it a crime to publish certain photographs or drawings of military installations. Section 798,[6] also in precise

---

shall publish any information with respect to the movement, numbers, description, condition, or disposition of any of the armed forces, ships, aircraft, or war materials of the United States, or with respect to the plans or conduct of any naval or military operations, or with respect to any works or measures undertaken for or connected with, or intended for the fortification or defense of any place, or any other information relating to the public defense calculated to be useful to the enemy, shall be punished by a fine . . . or by imprisonment. . . ." 55 Cong. Rec. 2100 (1917).

[4] Senator Ashurst also urged that ". . . 'freedom of the press' means freedom from the restraints of a censor, means the absolute liberty and right to publish whatever you wish; but you take your chances of punishment in the courts of your country for the violation of the laws of libel, slander and treason." 55 Cong. Rec. 2005 (1917).

[5] Section 797, 18 U. S. C., provides:

"On and after thirty days from the date upon which the President defines any vital military or naval installation or equipment as being within the category contemplated under section 795 of this title, whoever reproduces, publishes, sells, or gives away any photograph, sketch, picture, drawing, map, or graphical representation of the vital military or naval installations or equipment so defined, without first obtaining permission of the commanding officer of the military or naval post, camp, or station concerned, or higher authority, unless such photograph, sketch, picture, drawing, map, or graphical representation has clearly indicated thereon that it has been censored by the proper military or naval authority, shall be fined not more than $1,000 or imprisoned not more than one year, or both."

[6] In relevant part 18 U.S. C. § 798 provides:

"(a) Whoever knowingly and willfully communicates, furnishes, transmits, or otherwise makes available to an unauthorized person, or publishes, or uses in any manner prejudicial to the safety or interest of the United States or for the benefit of any foreign government to the detriment of the United States any classified information—

"(1) concerning the nature, preparation, or use of any code, cipher, or cryptographic system of the United States or any foreign government; or

"(2) concerning the design, construction, use, maintenance, or repair of any device, apparatus, or appliance used or prepared or planned for use by the United States or any foreign government for cryptographic or communication intelligence purposes; or

"(3) concerning the communication intelligence activities of the United States or any foreign government; or

"(4) obtained by the processes of communication intelligence from the com-

language, proscribes knowing and willful publications of any classified information concerning the cryptographic systems or communication intelligence activities of the United States as well as any information obtained from communication intelligence operations.[7] If any of the material here at issue is of this nature, the newspapers are presumably now on full notice of the position of the United States and must face the consequences if they publish. I would have no difficulty in sustaining convictions under these sections on facts that would not justify the intervention of equity and the imposition of a prior restraint.

The same would be true under those sections of the criminal code casting a wider net to protect the national defense. Section 793(e) [8] makes it

---

munications of any foreign government, knowing the same to have been obtained by such processes—
"Shall be fined not more than $10,000 or imprisoned not more than ten years, or both."
[7] The purport of 18 U. S. C. § 798 is clear. Both the House and Senate Reports on the bill, in identical terms, speak of furthering the security of the United States by preventing disclosure of information concerning the cryptographic systems and the communication intelligence systems of the United States, and explaining that "[t]his bill makes it a crime to reveal the methods, techniques, and matériel used in the transmission by this Nation of enciphered or coded messages. . . . Further, it makes it a crime to reveal methods used by this Nation in breaking the secret codes of a foreign nation. It also prohibits under certain penalties the divulging of any information which may have come into this Government's hands as a result of such a code-breaking." H. R. Rep. No. 1895, 81st Cong., 2d Sess., 1 (1950). The narrow reach of the statute was explained as covering "only a small category of classified matter, a category which is both vital and vulnerable to an almost unique degree." *Id.*, at 2. Existing legislation was deemed inadequate.
"At present two other acts protect this information, but only in a limited way. These are the Espionage Act of 1917 (40 Stat. 217) and the act of June 10, 1933 (48 Stat. 122). Under the first, unauthorized revelation of information of this kind can be penalized only if it can be proved that the person making the revelation did so with an intent to injure the United States. Under the second, only diplomatic codes and messages transmitted in diplomatic codes are protected. The present bill is designed to protect against knowing and willful publication or any other revelation of all important information affecting the United States communication intelligence operations and all direct information about all United Sates codes and ciphers." *Ibid.*
Section 798 obviously was intended to cover publications by non-employees of the Government and to ease the Government's burden in obtaining convictions. See H. R. Rep. No. 1895, *supra*, at 2–5. The identical Senate Report, not cited in parallel in the text of this footnote, is S. Rep. No. 111, 81st Cong., 1st Sess. (1949).
[8] Section 793(e) of 18 U. S. C. provides that:
"(e) Whoever having unauthorized possession of, access to, or control over any document, writing, code book, signal book, sketch, photograph, photographic negative, blueprint, plan, map, model, instrument, appliance, or note relating to the national defense, or information relating to the national defense which information the possessor has reason to believe could be used to the injury of the United States or to the advantage of any foreign nation, willfully communicates, delivers, transmits or causes to be communicated, delivered, or transmitted, or attempts to communicate, deliver, transmit or cause to be communicated, delivered, or transmitted the same to any person not entitled to receive it, or willfully retains the same and fails to deliver it to the officer or employee of the United States entitled to receive it;"

a criminal act for any unauthorized possessor of a document "relating to national defense" either (1) willfully to communicate or cause to be communicated that document to any person not entitled to receive it or (2) willfully to retain the document and fail to deliver it to an officer of the United States entitled to receive it. The subsection was added in 1950 because pre-existing law provided no penalty for the unauthorized possessor unless demand for the documents was made.[9] "The dangers

---

is guilty of an offense punishable by 10 years in prison, a $10,000 fine, or both. It should also be noted that 18 U.S. C. § 793(g), added in 1950, see 64 Stat. 1004–1005 (1950); S. Rep. No. 2369, 81st Cong., 2d Sess., 9 (1950), provides that "[i]f two or more persons conspire to violate any of the foregoing provisions of this section, and one or more of such persons do any act to effect the objective of the conspiracy, each of the parties to such conspiracy shall be subject to the punishment provided for the offense which is the object of such conspiracy."

[9] The amendment of § 793 that added subsection (e) was part of the Subversive Activities Control Act of 1950, which was in turn Title I of the Internal Security Act of 1950. See 64 Stat. 987 (1950). The report of the Senate Judiciary Committee best explains the purposes of the amendment:

"Section 18 of the bill amends section 793 of title 18 of the United States Code (espionage statute). The several paragraphs of section 793 of title 18 are designated as subsections (a) through (g) for purposes of convenient reference. The significant changes which would be made in section 793 of title 18 are as follows:

"(1) Amends the fourth paragraph of section 793, title 18 (subsec. (d)), to cover the unlawful dissemination of 'information relating to the national defense which information the possessor has reason to believe could be used to the injury of the United States or to the advantage of any foreign nation.' *The phrase 'which information the possessor has reason to believe could be used to the injury of the United States or to the advantage of any foreign nation' would modify only 'information relating to the national defense' and not the other items enumerated in the subsection.* The fourth paragraph of section 793 is also amended to provide that only those with lawful possession of the items relating to national defense enumerated therein may retain them subject to demand therefor. Those who have unauthorized possession of such items are treated in a separate subsection.

"(2) Amends section 793, title 18 (subsec. (e)), to provide that unauthorized possessors of items enumerated in paragraph 4 of section 793 must surrender possession thereof to the proper authorities without demand. Existing law provides no penalty for the unauthorized possession of such items unless a demand for them is made by the person entitled to receive them. The dangers surrounding the unauthorized possession of such items are self-evident, and it is deemed advisable to require their surrender in such a case, regardless of demand, especially since their unauthorized possession may be unknown to the authorities who would otherwise make the demand. The only difference between subsection (d) and subsection (e) of section 793 is that a demand by the person entitled to receive the items would be a necessary element of an offense under subsection (d) where the possession is lawful, whereas such a demand would not be a necessary element of an offense under subsection (e) where the possession is unauthorized." S. Rep. No. 2369, 81st Cong., 2d Sess., 8–9 (1950) (emphasis added).

It seems clear from the foregoing, contrary to the intimations of the District Court for the Southern District of New York in this case, that in prosecuting for communicating or withholding a "document" as contrasted with similar action with respect to "information" the Government need not prove an intent to injure the United States or to benefit a foreign nation but only willful and knowing conduct. The District Court relied on *Gorin* v. *United States*, 312 U.S. 19 (1941). But that case arose under other parts of the predecessor to § 793, see 312 U.S., at 21–22—

surrounding the unauthorized possession of such items are self-evident, and it is deemed advisable to require their surrender in such a case, regardless of demand, especially since their unauthorized possession may be unknown to the authorities who would otherwise make the demand." S. Rep. No. 2369, 81st Cong., 2d Sess., 9 (1950). Of course, in the cases before us, the unpublished documents have been demanded by the United States and their import has been made known at least to counsel for the newspapers involved. In *Gorin* v. *United States*, 312 U. S. 19, 28 (1941), the words "national defense" as used in a predecessor of § 793 were held by a unanimous court to have "a well understood connotation"—a "generic concept of broad connotations, referring to the military and naval establishments and the related activities of national preparedness"—and to be "sufficiently definite to apprise the public of prohibited activities" and to be consonant with due process. 312 U. S., at 28. Also, as construed by the Court in *Gorin*, information "connected with the national defense" is obviously not limited to that threatening "grave and irreparable" injury to the United States.[10]

It is thus clear that Congress has addressed itself to the problems of protecting the security of the country and the national defense from unauthorized disclosure of potentially damaging information. Cf. *Youngstown Sheet & Tube Co.* v. *Sawyer*, 343 U. S. 579, 585–586 (1952); see also *id.,* at 593–628 (Frankfurter, J., concurring). It has not, however, authorized the injunctive remedy against threatened publication. It has apparently been satisfied to rely on criminal sanctions and their deterrent effect on the responsible as well as the irresponsible press. I am not, of course, saying that either of these newspapers has yet committed a crime or that either would commit a crime if they published all the material now in their possession. That matter must await resolution in the context of a criminal proceeding if one is instituted by the United States. In that event, the issue of guilt or innocence would be determined by procedures and standards quite different from those that have purported to govern these injunctive proceedings.

---

parts that imposed different intent standards not repeated in § 793(d) or § 793(e). Cf. 18 U. S. C. §§ 793(a), (b), and (c). Also, from the face of subsection (e) and from the context of the act of which it was a part, it seems undeniable that a newspaper, as well as others unconnected with the Government, are vulnerable to prosecution under § 793(e) if they communicate or withhold the materials covered by that section. The District Court ruled that "communication" did not reach publication by a newspaper of documents relating to the national defense. I intimate no views on the correctness of that conclusion. But neither communication nor publication is necessary to violate the subsection.

[10] Also relevant is 18 U. S. C. § 794. Subsection (b) thereof forbids in time of war the collection or publication, with intent that it shall be communicated to the enemy, any information with respect to the movements of military forces, "or with respect to the plans or conduct . . . of any naval or military operations . . . or any other information relating to the public defense, which might be useful to the enemy. . . ."

Mr. Justice Marshall, Concurring

Nos. 1873 and 1885.—October Term, 1970

New York Times Company, Petitioner, 1873 *v.* United States.	On Writ of Certiorari to the United States Court of Appeals for the Second Circuit.
United States, Petitioner, 1885 *v.* The Washington Post Company et al.	On Writ of Certiorari to the United States Court of Appeals for the District of Columbia Circuit.

[June 30, 1971]

MR. JUSTICE MARSHALL, concurring.

The Government contends that the only issue in this case is whether in a suit by the United States, "the First Amendment bars a court from prohibiting a newspaper from publishing material whose disclosure would pose a grave and immediate danger to the security of the United States." Brief of the Government, at 6. With all due respect, I believe the ultimate issue in this case is even more basic than the one posed by the Solicitor General. The issue is whether this Court or the Congress has the power to make law.

In this case there is no problem concerning the President's power to classify information as "secret" or "top secret." Congress has specifically recognized Presidential authority, which has been formally exercised in Executive Order 10501, to classify documents and information. See, e.g., 18 U. S. C. § 798; 50 U. S. C. § 783.[1] Nor is there any issue here regarding the President's power as Chief Executive and Commander-in-Chief to protect national security by disciplining employees who disclose information and by taking precautions to prevent leaks.

The problem here is whether in this particular case the Executive Branch has authority to invoke the equity jurisdiction of the courts to protect what it believes to be the national interest. See *In re Debs*, 158 U. S. 564, 584 (1895). The Government argues that in addition to the inherent power of any government to protect itself, the President's power to conduct foreign affairs and his position as Commander-in-Chief give him authority to impose censorship on the press to protect his ability to deal effectively with foreign nations and to conduct the military affairs

---

[1] See n. 3, *infra.*

of the country. Of course, it is beyond cavil that the President has broad powers by virtue of his primary responsibility for the conduct of our foreign affairs and his position as Commander-in-Chief. *Chicago & Southern Air Lines, Inc.* v. *Waterman Corp.,* 333 U. S. 103 (1948); *Hirabayashi* v. *United States,* 320 U. S. 81, 93 (1943); *United States* v. *Curtiss-Wright Export Co.,* 299 U. S. 304 (1936).[2] And in some situations it may be that under whatever inherent powers the Government may have, as well as the implicit authority derived from the President's mandate to conduct foreign affairs and to act as Commander-in-Chief there is a basis for the invocation of the equity jurisdiction of this Court as an aid to prevent the publication of material damaging to "national security," however that term may be defined.

It would, however, be utterly inconsistent with the concept of separation of power for this Court to use its power of contempt to prevent behavior that Congress has specifically declined to prohibit. There would be a similar damage to the basic concept of these coequal branches of Government if when the Executive has adequate authority granted by Congress to protect "national security" it can choose instead to invoke the contempt power of a court to enjoin the threatened conduct. The Constitution provides that Congress shall make laws, the President execute laws, and courts interpret law. *Youngstown Sheet & Tube Co.* v. *Sawyer,* 343 U. S. 579 (1952). It did not provide for government by injunction in which the courts and the Executive can "make law" without regard to the action of Congress. It may be more convenient for the Executive if it need only convince a judge to prohibit conduct rather than to ask the Congress to pass a law and it may be more convenient to enforce a contempt order than seek a criminal conviction in a jury trial. Moreover, it may be considered politically wise to get a court to share the responsibility for arresting those who the Executive has probable cause to believe are violating the law. But convenience and political considerations of the moment do not justify a basic departure from the principles of our system of government.

In this case we are not faced with a situation where Congress has failed to provide the Executive with broad power to protect the Nation from disclosure of damaging state secrets. Congress has on several occasions given extensive consideration to the problem of protecting the military and strategic secrets of the United States. This consideration has resulted in the enactment of statutes making it a crime to receive, disclose, communicate, withhold, and publish certain documents, photographs, instruments, appliances, and information. The bulk of these statutes are found in chapter 37 of U. S. C., Title 18, entitled Espionage and Censorship.[3] In

[2] But see *Kent* v. *Dulles,* 357 U. S. 116 (1958); *Youngstown Sheet & Tube Co.* v. *Sawyer,* 343 U. S. 579 (1952).
[3] There are several other statutory provisions prohibiting and punishing the dissemination of information, the disclosure of which Congress thought sufficiently

that chapter, Congress has provided penalties ranging from a $10,000 fine to death for violating the various statutes.

Thus it would seem that in order for this Court to issue an injunction it would require a showing that such an injunction would enhance the already existing power of the Government to act. See *Bennett* v. *Laman*, 277 N. Y. 368, 14 N. E. 2d 439 (1938). It is a traditional axiom of equity that a court of equity will not do a useless thing just as it is a traditional axiom that equity will not enjoin the commission of a crime. See Z. Chaffe & E. Re, Equity 935–954 (5th ed. 1967); 1 H. Joyce, Injunctions §§ 58–60a (1909). Here there has been no attempt to make such a showing. The Solicitor General does not even mention in his brief whether the Government considers there to be probable cause to believe a crime has been committed or whether there is a conspiracy to commit future crimes.

If the Government had attempted to show that there was no effective remedy under traditional criminal law, it would have had to show that there is no arguably applicable statute. Of course, at this stage this Court could not and cannot determine whether there has been a violation of a particular statute nor decide the constitutionality of any statute. Whether a good-faith prosecution could have been instituted under any statute could, however, be determined.

At least one of the many statutes in this area seems relevant to this case. Congress has provided in 18 U. S. C. § 793(e) that whoever "having unauthorized possession of, access to, or control over any document, writing, code book, signal book . . . or note relating to the national de-

imperiled national security to warrant that result. These include 42 U. S. C. §§ 2161 through 2166 relating to the authority of the Atomic Energy Commission to classify and declassify "Restricted Data" ["Restricted Data" is a term of art employed uniquely by the Atomic Energy Act]. Specifically, 42 U. S. C. § 2162 authorizes the Atomic Energy Commission to classify certain information. 42 U. S. C. § 2274, subsection (a) provides penalties for a person who "communicates, transmits, or discloses . . . with intent to injure the United States or an intent to secure an advantage to any foreign nation. . . ." "Restricted Data." Subsection (b) of § 2274 provides lesser penalties for one who "communicates, transmits, or discloses" such information "with reason to believe such data will be utilized to injure the United States or to secure an advantage to any foreign nation. . . ." Other sections of Title 42 of the U. S. C. dealing with atomic energy prohibit and punish acquisition, removal, concealment, tampering with, alteration, mutilation, or destruction of documents incorporating "Restricted Data" and provide penalties for employees and former employees of the Atomic Energy Commission, the armed services, contractors and licensees of the Atomic Energy Commission. 42 U. S. C. §§ 2276, 2277. Title 50 U. S. C. Appendix § 781 (part of the National Defense Act of 1941, as amended, 55 Stat. 236) prohibits the making of any sketch or other representation of military installations or any military equipment located on any military installation, as specified; and indeed Congress in the National Defense Act conferred jurisdiction on federal district courts over civil actions "to enjoin any violation" thereof. 50 U. S. C. App. § 1152. 50 U. S. C. § 783(b) makes it unlawful for any officers or employees of the United States or any corporation which is owned by the United States to communicate material which has been "classified" by the President to any person whom that governmental employee knows or has reason to believe is an agent or representative of any foreign government or any Communist organization.

fense, or information relating to the national defense which information the possessor has reason to believe could be used to the injury of the United States or to the advantage of any foreign nation, willfully communicates, delivers, transmits . . . the same to any person not entitled to receive it, or willfully retains the same and fails to deliver it to the officer or employee of the United States entitled to receive it . . . shall be fined not more than $10,000 or imprisoned not more than ten years, or both." 18 U. S. C. § 793(e). Congress has also made it a crime to conspire to commit any of the offenses listed in 18 U. S. C. § 793(e).

It is true that Judge Gurfein found that Congress had not made it a crime to publish the items and material specified in § 793(e): He found that the words "communicates, delivers, transmits . . ." did not refer to publication of newspaper stories. And that view has some support in the legislative history and conforms with the past practice of using the statute only to prosecute those charged with ordinary espionage. But see 103 Cong. Rec. 10449 (remarks of Sen. Humphrey). Judge Gurfein's view of the statute is not, however, the only plausible construction that could be given. See my Brother WHITE's concurring opinion.

Even if it is determined that the Government could not in good faith bring criminal prosecutions against the *New York Times* and the *Washington Post,* it is clear that Congress has specifically rejected passing legislation that would have clearly given the President the power he seeks here and made the current activity of the newspapers unlawful. When Congress specifically declines to make conduct unlawful it is not for this Court to redecide those issues—to overrule Congress. See *Youngstown Sheet & Tube* v. *Sawyer,* 345 U. S. 579 (1952).

On at least two occasions Congress has refused to enact legislation that would have made the conduct engaged in here unlawful and given the President the power that he seeks in this case. In 1917 during the debate over the original Espionage Act, still the basic provisions of § 793, Congress rejected a proposal to give the President in time of war or threat of war authority to directly prohibit by proclamation the publication of information relating to national defense that might be useful to the enemy. The proposal provided that:

During any national emergency resulting from a war to which the United States is a party, or from threat of such a war, the President may, by proclamation, prohibit the publishing or communicating of, or the attempting to publish or communicate any information relating to the national defense which, in his judgment, is of such character that it is or might be useful to the enemy. Whoever violates any such prohibition shall be punished by a fine of not more than $10,000 or by imprisonment for not more than 10 years, or both: *Provided,* That nothing in this section shall be construed to limit or restrict any discussion, comment, or criticism of the acts or policies of the Government or its representatives or the publication of the same. 55 Cong. Rec. 1763.

Congress rejected this proposal after war against Germany had been declared even though many believed that there was a grave national emergency and that the threat of security leaks and espionage were serious. The Executive has not gone to Congress and requested that the decision to provide such power be reconsidered. Instead, the Executive comes to this Court and asks that it be granted the power Congress refused to give.

In 1957 the United States Commission on Government Security found that "[a]irplane journals, scientific periodicals, and even the daily newspaper have featured articles containing information and other data which should have been deleted in whole or in part for security reasons." In response to this problem the Commission, which was chaired by Senator Cotton, proposed that "Congress enact legislation making it a crime for any person willfully to disclose without proper authorization, for any purpose whatever, information classified 'secret' or 'top secret,' knowing, or having reasonable grounds to believe, such information to have been so classified." Report of Commission on Government Security 619–620 (1957). After substantial floor discussion on the proposal, it was rejected. See 103 Cong. Rec. 10447–10450. If the proposal that Senator Cotton championed on the floor had been enacted, the publication of the documents involved here would certainly have been a crime. Congress refused, however, to make it a crime. The Government is here asking this Court to remake that decision. This Court has no such power.

Either the Government has the power under statutory grant to use traditional criminal law to protect the country or, if there is no basis for arguing that Congress has made the activity a crime, it is plain that Congress has specifically refused to grant the authority the Government seeks from this Court. In either case this Court does not have authority to grant the requested relief. It is not for this Court to fling itself into every breach perceived by some Government official nor is it for this Court to take on itself the burden of enacting law, especially law that Congress has refused to pass.

I believe that the judgment of the United States Court of Appeals for the District of Columbia should be affirmed and the judgment of the United States Court of Appeals for the Second Circuit should be reversed insofar as it remands the case for further hearings.

Mr. Chief Justice Burger, Dissenting

Nos. 1873 and 1885.—October Term, 1970

New York Times Company, Petitioner,
1873   *v.*
United States.

On Writ of Certiorari to the United States Court of Appeals for the Second Circuit.

United States, Petitioner,
1885   *v.*
The Washington Post Company et al.

On Writ of Certiorari to the United States Court of Appeals for the District of Columbia Circuit.

[June 30, 1971]

MR. CHIEF JUSTICE BURGER, dissenting.

So clear are the constitutional limitations on prior restraint against expression, that from the time of *Near* v. *Minnesota,* 283 U. S. 697 (1931), until recently in *Organization for a Better Austin* v. *Keefe,* —— U. S. —— (1971), we have had little occasion to be concerned with cases involving prior restraints against news reporting on matters of public interest. There is, therefore, little variation among the members of the Court in terms of resistance to prior restraints against publication. Adherence to this basic constitutional principle, however, does not make this case a simple one. In this case, the imperative of a free and unfettered press comes into collision with another imperative, the effective functioning of a complex modern government and specifically the effective exercise of certain constitutional powers of the Executive. Only those who view the First Amendment as an absolute in all circumstances—a view I respect, but reject—can find such a case as this to be simple and easy.

This case is not simple for another and more immediate reason. We do not know the facts of the case. No District Judge knew all the facts. No Court of Appeals judge knew all the facts. No member of this Court knows all the facts.

Why are we in this posture, in which only those judges to whom the First Amendment is absolute and permits of no restraint in any circumstances or for any reason, are really in a position to act?

I suggest we are in this posture because these cases have been conducted in unseemly haste. MR. JUSTICE HARLAN covers the chronology of events demonstrating the hectic pressures under which these cases have been processed and I need not restate them. The prompt setting of these cases reflects our universal abhorrence of prior restraint. But prompt judicial action does not mean unjudicial haste.

Here, moreover, the frenetic haste is due in large part to the manner in which the *Times* proceeded from the date it obtained the purloined documents. It seems reasonably clear now that the haste precluded reasonable and deliberate judicial treatment of these cases and was not warranted. The precipitous action of this Court aborting a trial not yet completed is not the kind of judicial conduct which ought to attend the disposition of a great issue.

The newspapers make a derivative claim under the First Amendment; they denominate this right as the public right-to-know; by implication, the *Times* asserts a sole trusteeship of that right by virtue of its journalist "scoop." The right is asserted as an absolute. Of course, the First Amendment right itself is not an absolute, as Justice Holmes so long ago pointed out in his aphorism concerning the right to shout of fire in a crowded theater. There are other exceptions, some of which Chief Justice Hughes mentioned by way of example in *Near* v. *Minnesota.* There are no doubt other exceptions no one has had occasion to describe or discuss. Conceivably such exceptions may be lurking in these cases and would have been flushed had they been properly considered in the trial courts, free from unwarranted deadlines and frenetic pressures. A great issue of this kind should be tried in a judicial atmosphere conducive to thoughtful, reflective deliberation, especially when haste, in terms of hours, is unwarranted in light of the long period the *Times,* by its own choice, deferred publication.

It is not disputed that the *Times* has had unauthorized possession of the documents for three to four months, during which it has had its expert analysts studying them, presumably digesting them and preparing the material for publication. During all of this time, the *Times,* presumably in its capacity as trustee of the public's "right to know," has held up publication for purposes it considered proper and thus public knowledge was delayed. No doubt this was for a good reason; the analysis of 7,000 pages of complex material drawn from a vastly greater volume of material would inevitably take time and the writing of good news stories takes time. But why should the United States Government, from whom this information was illegally acquired by someone, along with all the counsel, trial judges, and appellate judges be placed under needless pressure? After these months of deferral, the alleged right-to-know has somehow and suddenly become a right that must be vindicated instanter.

Would it have been unreasonable, since the newspaper could anticipate the government's objections to release of secret material, to give the government an opportunity to review the entire collection and determine whether agreement could be reached on publication? Stolen or not, if security was not in fact jeopardized, much of the material could no doubt have been declassified, since it spans a period ending in 1968. With such an approach—one that great newspapers have in the past practiced and stated editorially to be the duty of an honorable press—the newspapers and government might well have narrowed the area of disagreement as to what was and was not publishable, leaving the remainder to be resolved in orderly litigation if necessary. To me it is hardly believable that a newspaper long regarded as a great institution in American life would fail to perform one of the basic and simple duties of every citizen with respect to the discovery or possession of stolen property or secret government documents. That duty, I had thought—perhaps naively—was to report forthwith, to responsible public officers. This duty rests on taxi drivers, Justices and the *New York Times.* The course followed by the *Times,* whether so calculated or not, removed any possibility of orderly litigation of the issues. If the action of the judges up to now has been correct, that result is sheer happenstance.[1]

Our grant of the writ before final judgment in the *Times* case aborted the trial in the District Court before it had made a complete record pursuant to the mandate of the Court of Appeals, Second Circuit.

The consequence of all this melancholy series of events is that we literally do not know what we are acting on. As I see it we have been forced to deal with litigation concerning rights of great magnitude without an adequate record, and surely without time for adequate treatment either in the prior proceedings or in this Court. It is interesting to note that counsel in oral argument before this Court were frequently unable to respond to questions on factual points. Not surprisingly they pointed out that they had been working literally "around the clock" and simply were unable to review the documents that give rise to these cases and were not familiar with them. This Court is in no better posture. I agree with MR. JUSTICE HARLAN and MR. JUSTICE BLACKMUN but I am not prepared to reach the merits.[2]

I would affirm the Court of Appeals for the Second Circuit and allow the District Court to complete the trial aborted by our grant of certiorari meanwhile preserving the *status quo* in the *Post* case. I would direct that the District Court on remand give priority to the *Times* case to the exclusion of all other business of that court but I would not set arbitrary deadlines.

I should add that I am in general agreement with much of what MR.

---

[1] Interestingly the *Times* explained its refusal to allow the government to examine its own purloined documents by saying in substance this might compromise *their* sources and informants! The *Times* thus asserts a right to guard the secrecy of its sources while denying that the Government of the United States has that power.

[2] With respect to the question of inherent power of the Executive to classify papers, records and documents as secret, or otherwise unavailable for public exposure, and to secure aid of the courts for enforcement, there may be an analogy with respect to this Court. No statute gives this Court express power to establish and enforce the utmost security measures for the secrecy of our deliberations and records. Yet I have little doubt as to the inherent power of the Court to protect the confidentiality of its internal operations by whatever judicial measures may be required.

JUSTICE WHITE has expressed with respect to penal sanctions concerning communication or retention of documents or information relating to the national defense.

We all crave speedier judicial processes but when judges are pressured as in these cases the result is a parody of the judicial process.

Mr. Justice Harlan, Dissenting

Nos. 1873 and 1885.—October Term, 1970

New York Times Company, Petitioner, 1873 *v.* United States.	On Writ of Certiorari to the United States Court of Appeals for the Second Circuit.

United States, Petitioner, 1885 *v.* The Washington Post Company et al.	On Writ of Certiorari to the United States Court of Appeals for the District of Columbia Circuit.

[June 30, 1971]

MR. JUSTICE HARLAN, with whom THE CHIEF JUSTICE and MR. JUSTICE BLACKMUN join, dissenting.

These cases forcefully call to mind the wise admonition of Mr. Justice Holmes, dissenting in *Northern Securities Co.* v. *United States,* 193 U. S. 197, 400–401 (1904):

> Great cases like hard cases make bad law. For great cases are called great, not by reason of their real importance in shaping the law of the future, but because of some accident of immediate overwhelming interest which appeals to the feelings and distorts the judgment. These immediate interests exercise a kind of hydraulic pressure which makes what previously was clear seem doubtful, and before which even well settled principles of law will bend.

With all respect, I consider that the Court has been almost irresponsibly feverish in dealing with these cases.

Both the Court of Appeals for the Second Circuit and the Court of Appeals for the District of Columbia Circuit rendered judgment on June 23. The *New York Times'* petition for certiorari, its motion for accelerated consideration thereof, and its application for interim relief were filed in this Court on June 24 at about 11 A.M. The application of the United States for interim relief in the *Post* case was also filed here on June 24, at about 7:15 P.M. This Court's order setting a hearing before us on June 26 at 11 A.M., a course which I joined only to avoid the possibility of even more peremptory action by the Court, was issued less than 24 hours before. The record in the *Post* case was filed with the Clerk shortly before 1 P.M. on June 25; the record in the *Times* case did not arrive until 7 or 8 o'clock that same night. The briefs of the parties were received less than two hours before argument on June 26.

This frenzied train of events took place in the name of the presumption against prior restraints created by the First Amendment. Due regard for the extraordinarily important and difficult questions involved in these litigations should have led the Court to shun such a precipitate timetable. In order to decide the merits of these cases properly, some or all of the following questions should have been faced:

1. Whether the Attorney General is authorized to bring these suits in the name of the United States. Compare *In re Debs,* 158 U. S. 564 (1895), with *Youngstown Sheet & Tube Co.* v. *Sawyer,* 343 U. S. 579 (1952). This question involves as well the construction and validity of a singularly opaque statute—the Espionage Act, 18 U. S. C. § 793(e).

2. Whether the First Amendment permits the federal courts to enjoin publication of stories which would present a serious threat to national security. See *Near* v. *Minnesota,* 283 U. S. 697, 716 (1931) (dictum).

3. Whether the threat to publish highly secret documents is of itself a sufficient implication of national security to justify an injunction on the theory that regardless of the contents of the documents, harm enough results simply from the demonstration of such a breach of secrecy.

4. Whether the unauthorized disclosure of any of these particular documents would seriously impair the national security.

5. What weight should be given to the opinion of high officers in the Executive Branch of the Government with respect to questions 3 and 4.

6. Whether the newspapers are entitled to retain and use the documents notwithstanding the seemingly uncontested facts that the documents, or the originals of which they are duplicates, were purloined from the Government's possession and that the newspapers received them with knowledge that they had been feloniously acquired. Cf. *Liberty Lobby, Inc.* v. *Pearson,* 390 F.2d 489 (CADC 1968).

7. Whether the threatened harm to the national security or the Government's possessory interest in the documents justifies the issuance of an injunction against publication in light of—

a. The strong First Amendment policy against prior restraints on publication;

b. The doctrine against enjoining conduct in violation of criminal statutes; and

c. The extent to which the materials at issue have apparently already been otherwise disseminated.

These are difficult questions of fact, of law, and of judgment; the potential consequences of erroneous decision are enormous. The time which has been available to us, to the lower courts,* and to the parties has been wholly inadequate for giving these cases the kind of consideration they deserve. It is a reflection on the stability of the judicial process that these great issues—as important as any that have arisen during my time on the Court—should have been decided under the pressures engendered by the torrent of publicity that has attended these litigations from their inception.

Forced as I am to reach the merits of these cases, I dissent from the opinion and judgments of the Court. Within the severe limitations imposed by the time constraints under which I have been required to operate, I can only state my reasons in telescoped form, even though in different circumstances I would have felt constrained to deal with the cases in the fuller sweep indicated above.

It is a sufficient basis for affirming the Court of Appeals for the Second Circuit in the *Times* litigation to observe that its order must rest on the conclusion that because of the time elements the Government had not been given an adequate opportunity to present its case to the District Court. At the least this conclusion was not an abuse of discretion.

In the *Post* litigation the Government had more time to prepare; this was apparently the basis for the refusal of the Court of Appeals for the District Court of Columbia Circuit on rehearing to conform its judgment to that of the Second Circuit. But I think there is another and more fundamental reason why this judgment cannot stand—a reason which also furnishes an additional ground for not reinstating the judgment of the District Court in the *Times* litigation, set aside by the Court of Appeals. It is plain to me that the scope of the judicial function in passing upon the activities of the Executive Branch of the Government in the field of foreign affairs is very narrowly restricted. This view is, I think dictated by the concept of separation of powers upon which our constitutional system rests.

In a speech on the floor of the House of Representatives, Chief Justice John Marshall, then a member of that body, stated:

The President is the sole organ of the nation in its external relations, and its sole representative with foreign nations. Annals, 6th Cong., col. 613 (1800).

From that time, shortly after the founding the Nation, to this, there has been no substantial challenge to this description of the scope of executive

---

* The hearing in the *Post* case before Judge Gesell began at 8 A.M. on June 21, and his decision was rendered, under the hammer of a deadline imposed by the Court of Appeals, shortly before 5 P.M. on the same day. The hearing in the *Times* case before Judge Gurfein was held on June 18 and his decision was rendered on June 19. The Government's appeals in the two cases were heard by the Courts of Appeals for the District of Columbia and Second Circuits, each court sitting *en banc*, on June 22. Each court rendered its decision on the following afternoon.

power. See *United States* v. *Curtiss-Wright Export Corp.*, 299 U. S. 304, 319–321 (1936), collecting authorities.

From this constitutional primacy in the field of foreign affairs, it seems to me that certain conclusions necessarily follow. Some of these were stated concisely by President Washington, declining the request of the House of Representatives for the papers leading up to the negotiation of the Jay Treaty:

> The nature of foreign negotiations requires caution, and their success must often depend on secrecy; and even when brought to a conclusion a full disclosure of all the measures, demands, or eventual concessions which may have been proposed or contemplated would be extremely impolitic; for this might have a pernicious influence on future negotiations, or produce immediate inconveniences, perhaps danger and mischief, in relation to other powers. 1 J. Richardson, Messages and Papers of the Presidents 194–195 (1899).

The power to evaluate the "pernicious influence" of premature disclosure is not, however, lodged in the Executive alone. I agree that, in performance of its duty to protect the values of the First Amendment against political pressures, the judiciary must review the initial Executive determination to the point of satisfying itself that the subject matter of the dispute does lie within the proper compass of the President's foreign relations power. Constitutional considerations forbid "a complete abandonment of judicial control." Cf. *United States* v. *Reynolds*, 345 U. S. 1, 8 (1953). Moreover, the judiciary may properly insist that the determination that disclosure of the subject matter would irreparably impair the national security be made by the head of the Executive Department concerned—here the Secretary of State or the Secretary of Defense—after actual personal consideration by that officer. This safeguard is required in the analogous area of executive claims of privilege for secrets of state. See *United States* v. *Reynolds, supra,* at 8 and n. 20; *Duncan* v. *Cammell, Laird & Co.*, [1942] A. C. 624, 638 (House of Lords).

But in my judgment the judiciary may not properly go beyond these two inquiries and redetermine for itself the probable impact of disclosure on the national security.

[T]he very nature of executive decisions as to foreign policy is political, not judicial. Such decisions are wholly confided by our Constitution to the political departments of the government, Executive and Legislative. They are delicate, complex, and involve large elements of prophecy. They are and should be undertaken only by those directly responsible to the people whose welfare they advance or imperil. They are decisions of a kind for which the Judiciary has neither aptitude, facilities nor responsibility and which has long been held to belong in the domain of political power not subject to judicial intrusion or inquiry. *Chicago & Southern Air Lines* v. *Waterman Steamship Corp.*, 333 U. S. 103, 111 (1948) (Jackson, J.).

Even if there is some room for the judiciary to override the executive determination, it is plain that the scope of review must be exceedingly narrow. I can see no indication in the opinions of either the District Court or the Court of Appeals in the *Post* litigation that the conclusions of the Executive were given even the deference owing to an administrative agency, much less that owing to a co-equal branch of the Government operating within the field of its constitutional prerogative.

Accordingly, I would vacate the judgment of the Court of Appeals for the District of Columbia Circuit on this ground and remand the case for further proceedings in the District Court. Before the commencement of such further proceedings, due opportunity should be afforded the Government for procuring from the Secretary of State or the Secretary of Defense or both an expression of their views on the issue of national security. The ensuing review by the District Court should be in accordance with the views expressed in this opinion. And for the reasons stated above I would affirm the judgment of the Court of Appeals for the Second Circuit.

Pending further hearings in each case conducted under the appropriate ground rules, I would continue the restraints on publication. I cannot believe that the doctrine prohibiting prior restraints reaches to the point of preventing courts from maintaining the *status quo* long enough to act responsibly in matters of such national importance as those involved here.

Mr. Justice Blackmun, Dissenting

Nos. 1873 and 1885.—October Term, 1970

New York Times Company, Petitioner, 1873 *v.* United States.	On Writ of Certiorari to the United States Court of Appeals for the Second Circuit.
United States, Petitioner, 1885 *v.* The Washington Post Company et al.	On Writ of Certiorari to the United States Court of Appeals for the District of Columbia Circuit.

[June 30, 1971]

MR. JUSTICE BLACKMUN.

I join MR. JUSTICE HARLAN in his dissent. I also am in substantial accord with much that MR. JUSTICE WHITE says, by way of admonition, in the latter part of his opinion.

At this point the focus is on *only* the comparatively few documents specified by the Government as critical. So far as the other material—

vast in amount—is concerned, let it be published and published forthwith if the newspapers, once the strain is gone and the sensationalism is eased, still feel the urge so to do.

But we are concerned here with the few documents specified from the 47 volumes. Almost 70 years ago Mr. Justice Holmes, dissenting in a celebrated case, observed:

Great cases like hard cases make bad law. For great cases are called great, not by reason of their real importance in shaping the law of the future, but because of some accident of immediate overwhelming interest which appeals to the feelings and distorts the judgment. These immediate interests exercise a kind of hydraulic pressure. . . . *Northern Securities Co.* v. *United States*, 193 U.S. 197, 400–401 (1904).

The present cases, if not great, are at least unusual in their posture and implications, and the Holmes observation certainly has pertinent application.

The *New York Times* clandestinely devoted a period of three months examining the 47 volumes that came into its unauthorized possession. Once it had begun publication of material from those volumes, the New York case now before us emerged. It immediately assumed, and ever since has maintained, a frenetic pace and character. Seemingly, once publication started, the material could not be made public fast enough. Seemingly, from then on, every deferral or delay, by restraint or otherwise, was abhorrent and was to be deemed violative of the First Amendment and of the public's "right immediately to know." Yet that newspaper stood before us at oral argument and professed criticism of the Government for not lodging its protest earlier than by a Monday telegram following the initial Sunday publication.

The District of Columbia case is much the same.

Two federal district courts, two United States courts of appeals, and this Court—within a period of less than three weeks from inception until today—have been pressed into hurried decision of profound constitutional issues on inadequately developed and largely assumed facts without the careful deliberation that, hopefully, should characterize the American judicial process. There has been much writing about the law and little knowledge and less digestion of the facts. In the New York case the judges, both trial and appellate, had not yet examined the basic material when the case was brought here. In the District of Columbia case, little more was done, and what was accomplished in this respect was only on required remand, with the *Washington Post*, on the excuse that it was trying to protect its source of information, initially refusing to reveal what material it actually possessed, and with the district court forced to make assumptions as to that possession.

With such respect as may be due to the contrary view, this, in my opinion, is not the way to try a law suit of this magnitude and asserted importance. It is not the way for federal courts to adjudicate, and to be required to adjudicate, issues that allegedly concern the Nation's vital welfare. The country would be none the worse off were the cases tried quickly, to be sure, but in the customary and properly deliberative manner. The most recent of the material, it is said, dates no later than 1968, already about three years ago, and the *Times* itself took three months to formulate its plan of procedure and, thus, deprived its public for that period.

The First Amendment, after all, is only one part of an entire Constitution. Article II of the great document vests in the Executive Branch primary power over the conduct of foreign affairs and places in that branch the responsibility for the Nation's safety. Each provision of the Constitution is important, and I cannot subscribe to a doctrine of unlimited absolutism for the First Amendment at the cost of downgrading other provisions. First Amendment absolutism has never commanded a majority of this Court. See, for example, *Near* v. *Minnesota*, 283 U. S. 697, 708 (1931), and *Schenck* v. *United States*, 249 U. S. 47, 52 (1919). What is needed here is a weighing, upon properly developed standards, of the broad right of the press to print and of the very narrow right of the Government to prevent. Such standards are not yet developed. The parties here are in disagreement as to what those standards should be. But even the newspapers concede that there are situations where restraint is in order and is constitutional. Mr. Justice Holmes gave us a suggestion when he said in *Schenck*,

It is a question of proximity and degree. When a nation is at war many things that might be said in time of peace are such a hindrance to its effort that their utterance will not be endured so long as men fight and that no Court could regard them as protected by any constitutional right. 249 U. S., at 52.

I therefore would remand these cases to be developed expeditiously, of course, but on a schedule permitting the orderly presentation of evidence from both sides, with the use of discovery, if necessary, as authorized by the rules, and with the preparation of briefs, oral argument and court opinions of a quality better than has been seen to this point. In making this last statement, I criticize no lawyer or judge. I know from past personal experience the agony of time pressure in the preparation of litigation. But these cases and the issues involved and the courts, including this one, deserve better than has been produced thus far.

It may well be that if these cases were allowed to develop as they should be developed, and to be tried as lawyers should try them and as courts should hear them, free of pressure and panic and sensationalism, other light would be shed on the situation and contrary considerations, for me, might prevail. But this is not the present posture of the litigation.

The Court, however, decides the cases today the other way. I therefore add one final comment.

I strongly urge, and sincerely hope, that these two newspapers will be fully aware of their ultimate responsibilities to the United States of America. Judge Wilkey, dissenting in the District of Columbia case, after a review of only the affidavits before his court (the basic papers had not then been made available by either party), concluded that there were a number of examples of documents that, if in the possession of the *Post*, and if published, "could clearly result in great harm to the nation," and he defined "harm" to mean "the death of soldiers, the destruction of alliances, the greatly increased difficulty of negotiation with our enemies, the inability of our diplomats to negotiate. . . ." I, for one, have now been able to give at least some cursory study not only to the affidavits, but to the material itself. I regret to say that from this examination I fear that Judge Wilkey's statements have possible foundation. I therefore share his concern. I hope that damage already has not been done. If, however, damage has been done, and if, with the Court's action today, these newspapers proceed to publish the critical documents and there results therefrom "the death of soldiers, the destruction of alliances, the greatly increased difficulty of negotiation with our enemies, the inability of our diplomats to negotiate," to which list I might add the factors of prolongation of the war and of further delay in the freeing of United States prisoners, then the Nation's people will know where the responsibility for these sad consequences rests.

Questions

1. What are the differences among the justices concurring in the majority decision? How do they agree? Answer the same questions about the justices who dissent.

2. How would you argue that freedom of speech is not an *absolute* freedom? What arguments have these justices who support freedom of the press neglected? Which arguments do they seem to have overstressed? What do you think of Justice Blackmun's comment at the end of his dissent that the people of the United States will know who to blame if the majority opinion should cause harm to American soldiers?

3. What is the relationship of the government's need to conduct some of its diplomatic and military affairs in absolute secrecy to the question of the public's right to know? How would someone argue that *all* government affairs, since they involve the welfare of the people, should be conducted *entirely* in public?

4. How would you argue that there are certain times when it is necessary to abridge certain freedoms? You might want to consider the arguments put forth by the Vice President in Section One on the question of "instant analysis" of Presidential speeches.

5. Why do some of the justices make their own statements and also join in concurring with the statements made by other justices? How would you separate the statements made by a justice, first, when he gives his own opinion and second, when he joins in the opinion of another justice? Why do you suppose a justice chooses to take this way of expressing his opinion?

6. What seem to you to be the most extreme positions in the majority opinions favoring freedom of the press? What are the extreme positions among the three justices offering the dissenting opinion? What are the two extremes represented in the majority and in the minority opinions? Which of these is most congenial to your own point of view? Why? What is meant by "burden of proof"? Why is this concept so important in this case?

7. What common areas of concern can you find in this section and the preceding one on Channeling Opinion? Just how free is it possible for either newspapers or television to be in a democratic society without hurting important segments of the population?

Assignments

1. Pretend that you are a justice of the Supreme Court. Write your own decision, emphasizing general positions regarding freedom of the press and the government's right to declare documents secret whose publication may affect the public welfare. You do not need to refer to the substance of the Pentagon Papers themselves.

2. List in summary form the arguments for and against the publication of the Pentagon Papers. You need not confine yourself to finding negative arguments only among the dissenting justices or positive ones among the majority. For example, some of the justices in the majority express reservations about the publication of the papers.

3. Address yourself to the issue that the decision had to be made in great haste. That is, argue that the requirement to make the decision in speedy fashion really did not affect its outcome, or that it did affect the outcome. Supreme Court decisions are widely available in any library.

4. Expand the arguments made by any of the justices either that newspapers should *never* reprint materials the government says should not be made public, *or* that newspapers *always* have a right to the public to make available all materials that come to its attention, of any sort whatsoever. Remember that you are taking an *extreme* position. (You might wish to consider Chief Justice Burger's contention that "stolen" materials should always be reported to the police.)

5. Differentiate between the style of the decision you like most in terms of its making its points most effectively and the one that you like least, without regard if possible to the substance of the argument. Explain why you like one and not the other.

6. Justices of the Supreme Court have often been described as "strict constructionists" or "liberal constructionists." Explain in what ways Justices Black and Douglas are "liberal" in their interpretation of the First Amendment and in what ways Justices Burger, Harlan, and Blackmun are "strict." You might wish to justify the use of the terms *strict* and *liberal*, or to attack their applicability.

7. A number of the justices refer to the "separation of powers." Write a composition arguing that it is more important to keep the powers of the judicial, the legislative, and the executive branches of the government separate than it is to allow any one of them to assume importance over the others. Conversely, you might wish to argue that the most important branch of the government, the executive, must have powers that are superior to those exercised by the judicial or the legislative branches.

Additional Reading

Many articles and books have come out in recent years about the character of Supreme Court decisions and their effect on American life. With particular reference to the issue of the Pentagon Papers, you might wish to look at the paperback edition reprinting the articles of the *New York Times* which used secret materials prepared by the Department of Defense in several administrations regarding the war in Vietnam. General studies of American participation in the Vietnam War as well as of the French involvement in it should also prove useful.

SECTION THREE *Bearing Arms:*

Liberty or License

A well regulated Militia, being necessary to the security of a free State, the right of the people to keep and bear Arms, shall not be infringed.

Article II of the U.S. Constitution

From *Straight Herblock* (Simon & Schuster, 1964).

Gun Curbs Are Stricter in Many Nations Than in U.S.

The United States is not unique in the world community for its lack of effective nationwide controls over ownership and use of guns.

In Africa, wars and guerrilla movements make gun control impossible in several nations; in parts of Latin America, political assassination by gunfire has been recurrent for generations; in Australia there are so many loopholes to the laws of the various states—and no federal law—that a would-be murderer or assassin would have no trouble obtaining a weapon for himself; in West Germany there is no federal gun control, although the eleven states have strict laws which are very similar.

But, according to a survey by *Washington Post* Foreign Service correspondents and special correspondents, in most of the world's technologically advanced nations and where there is no international tension or civil war, gun control is far stricter than in America. This is particularly true in Japan, the Soviet Union and throughout Europe.

Guns a Privilege. Other aspects of gun control found in the *Washington Post* survey were:

• Constitutions and laws in the countries surveyed are aimed generally at regulatory control of all firearms—both rifles and hand guns. In some countries police or military forces are not able to enforce strict laws.

• Ownership and use of guns is treated as a privilege granted to citizens for a specific reason—most often for hunting. In Japan, whalers and athletic umpires may be given gun permits, as well as policemen, hunters (rifles only) and researchers. In Britain, there are exceptions for dealers, auctioneers, theaters and shooting galleries.

• In none of the countries surveyed was there an attitude among citizens that they should have the right to bear arms, and there was no evidence of popular resentment against gun control laws.

Arms Smuggling

• Restrictions on the availability of firearms tends to save lives.
• The availability and the smuggling of arms—which are manufactured chiefly in the United States, Czechoslovakia and the Soviet Union—makes gun control difficult in areas of unrest.

from the *Washington Post*, June 23, 1968. Reprinted with the permission of the *Washington Post*.

In many countries, national gun control has been built up amid frequent periods of political instability and military dictatorship—as in the case of Peru, for example—and it therefore has historically been in the interest of the government to know who has guns and where they are, John M. Goshko reported from Lima.

Gun control in Britain dates back a century, and the last piece of gun legislation in The Netherlands was passed in 1919. It strictly forbade Dutchmen to possess, import, export, or transport weapons—with exceptions, including sportsmen.

Soviet Union. In the Soviet Union and the East European countries the police strictly control all concealable guns while hunting rifles are restricted to sportsmen enrolled in appropriate organizations. In the vast rural areas of the Soviet Union there are doubtless many peasants and hunters who own rifles illegally, many of the weapons dating from prewar and wartime days.

But, reported Anatole Shub from Moscow, the lack of political assassinations or famous private crimes of violence and bank robberies during the last 20 years indicates that arms in urban areas are under the tightest controls.

Japan. The microscopic amount of crime committed with guns in Japan must be the envy of the world, Richard Halloran reported from Tokyo. Pistols are forbidden, except to police and marksmen under strict supervision, rifles and shotguns are allowed for hunting and target shooting, but again under rigid controls. In 1967, there were only seven murders committed with pistols and 38 with rifles or shotguns.

Most of Japan's 2111 murders that year were crimes of passion committed by hand or with clubs or knives. There were only 11 armed robberies in 1967 for the entire nation.

Even in areas of war or great tension—Cyprus, Israel, Panama and France during the workers' and students' uprising—there was no evidence of enthusiasm by the people to bear and use arms except in actual battle.

Cyprus. Alfred Friendly reported from the Cypriot capital of Nicosia that the island is "stiff with musketry," probably a higher per capita rate than any other place on earth—attributable mainly to the bitter intercommunal struggle between Greek and Turkish Cypriots.

Experts estimate that there are enough small arms in Cyprus to equip every able-bodied man on the island, Friendly reported. Shootings—almost all of them intercommunal—have been chronic and constant since 1963.

And yet, Friendly adds, excluding the intercommunal fighting, shootings (as well as knifings) are rare to the point of nonexistence.

The situation in Cyprus also emphasizes another aspect of worldwide gun control. Gun laws, mostly dating from the British colonial period, are strict. A person may import and possess pistols only on showing an express need and only when a license is granted, which assertedly is seldom. Shotguns must also be licensed.

In fact, however, the United Nations has noted 1025 shooting incidents during the last 24 months, almost all "random or accidental discharges of weapons." The guns pour into the island, despite the laws, from Greek and Turkish army forces. In addition a large gun supply was amassed during the anti-British liberation period of the 1950s.

There are other nations where huge arms supplies are available, contrary to strict laws on the books.

PANAMA. Panama has a turbulent history with many political shootings. The newly elected President, Arnulfo Arias, has himself been shot four times. Though gun carrying laws are strict, reported special correspondent Maryann Gorishek from Panama City, there are so many exceptions to the rules that it is relatively easy to get a permit to carry a gun and many private citizens have them.

Many politicians carry guns at all times, and one newsman is often seen carrying a briefcase which holds a folding-stock carbine.

But, she reports, gun felonies and shootings are relatively rare except in riots or in election years. Most violent crimes in Panama are carried out with machetes, knives and clubs.

Goshko reported from Lima that the use of knives is fairly common throughout South America.

In recent years, the rise of guerrilla activity has been accompanied by a sizeable quantity of automatic weapons being illegally brought into Latin America.

In Africa, almost every country requires licensing or registration of guns, but the regulations are ignored in many rural areas. In the Congo's interior, parts of Ethiopia, in war-torn areas of Nigeria and in the Sudan guns are uncontrolled, Anthony Astrachan reported from Nairobi, Kenya.

KENYA. Wherever governments are firmly in control, he reported, guns are regulated—nowhere more stringently than in East Africa.

Kenya's firearms regulations were passed in 1953 while still a British Colony at the beginning of the Mau Mau emergency, and there have been no substantive changes since independence. Nobody may have firearms or ammunition in Kenya without a valid certificate.

Permits are not granted to anyone of "intemperate habits or unsound mind, or to be for any reason unfitted to be entrusted with such a firearm." In 1967 Kenya had 508 murders and attempted murders and seven manslaughter cases—roughly one homicide for every 20,000 of Kenya's 10 million citizens. There were also 2347 robberies.

The government refuses to say how many of these crimes involved firearms, but it is known to be less than 1 per cent of the total. Gun control laws in Tanzania and Uganda are as tough or tougher than in Kenya.

SCANDINAVIA. In the Scandinavian countries the only interest in firearms is a sporting one. For this reason, reported special correspondent Roland Huntford from Stockholm, licensing regulations—while strict—are not considered irksome.

Firearms regulations are broadly similar in Norway, Sweden and Finland. Hunting and target shooting alone are recognized as grounds for possession of firearms. The only pistols available to the general public are specialized long-barreled single-shot types used in olympic competitions. Revolvers and automatic pistols are virtually unobtainable.

Even if a Swede has a gun, he prefers to do murder with some other instrument. In 1966 there were 65 convictions for murder and manslaughter in the country. Of these, nine were for crimes using firearms and dynamite. The annual murder rate is about 0.9 per thousand people. In Finland, with a population of 4.5 million, there are about 800 homicides of all descriptions per year. In Norway, there are about 50 murders and manslaughters annually among a population of 3.9 million, with not more than four or five carried out by firearms.

Hunting is popular in other European countries. A survey last year indicated that two million hunting rifles and shotguns were registered in France, one million in Italy, and 25,000 weapons each in Belgium and The Netherlands. In Germany it is a sport of the upper class.

FRANCE. Control of firearms is fairly strict in France—very tight on pistols and revolvers but more relaxed for rifles, with hunting one of the favorite national pastimes, Donald H. Louchheim reported from Paris. According to the Interior Ministry, permission to carry firearms is restricted at the moment to less than 10,000 non-government employes (out of a population of 50 million).

The penalty for carrying an unauthorized handgun or for being in possession of an unauthorized firearm of any kind in France is one to three years in prison and a maximum fine of $720. Anyone over 21 years of age can buy a rifle or shotgun, but only to keep in his home. If he wants to hunt, he must get a license. Foreign residents in France have great difficulty obtaining such licenses.

Deaths by shooting average about 500 a year, or one per 100,000 people. Death by stabbing is at approximately the same rate.

However, in the recent rioting in Paris which lasted more than a month, only two shots were fired. An irate resident tired of the noisy demonstrations outside his window and fired off two rounds from his hunting rifle. Two demonstrators were injured.

WEST GERMANY. In West Germany, a law is being drafted for submission to the eleven state legislatures, which would provide uniform gun control throughout the Federal Republic. Already the states' laws are similar, and no weapons can be purchased without a permit from local police. Purchase of weapons by mail order is impossible. A person may be granted a gun permit only if he is reliable, legally accountable for his actions, not previously convicted and can prove need of a weapon.

As a result of strict laws only 32 persons received weapons purchase licenses, and only 84 were given weapons permits in the Bonn area in 1967. Murder by gunshot in West Germany is negligible.

HOLLAND. In Holland, with a population of 12.5 million, only 15 crimes were recorded last year in which a shooting took place.

BELGIUM. Hunting guns and the .22 rifle are responsible for most murders by shooting in Belgium, and periodic attempts have been made by some members in Parliament to subject the sale of these weapons to stricter control. But their efforts have met with failure, reported special correspondent Robert Mauthner from Brussels. Latest statistics show there were 71 murders in Belgium in 1965 in a population of 9.5 million, but there were no statistics on types of weapons used.

Arms manufacturers and rifle clubs do exercise a certain amount of pressure on Parliament in Belgium. The Fabrique Nationale, in particular, has a considerable influence because of its importance to the Belgain economy as a major exporter of arms and war matérial. All efforts to impose legal restrictions on the sale of its .22 rifle have proved unsuccessful. Laws covering pistols and revolvers, however, are very strict.

ITALY. In Italy, gun control laws forbid the selling or otherwise turning over of firearms to anybody without a license or a special purchase permit granted by local police. Regulations apply to all weapons, including hunting rifles.

According to Prof. Franco Ferrarotti, who teaches sociology at the University of Rome, the existing legislation "has a remarkable deterrent effect on the average citizen, who dislikes going through the procedure required for legally purchasing a gun and does not know how to get it through illegal channels."

The overall violent death figure in Italy was just over 4 per thousand population in 1967. More detailed information from 1964 shows there were 319 murders by gunshot that year. Taking into consideration non-deadly attacks and other acts of personal violence, however, it appears that the Italians' favorite weapon is still the "arma bianca" (the "white weapon," a term encompassing knives, axes and other cutting weapons), reported special correspondent Leo J. Wollemborg from Rome.

BRITAIN. The basic law covering firearms in Britain, passed in 1937, consolidated other regulations dating back a century. The firearms act was amended last year to include shotguns, which as of May 1, 1968, also had to be registered.

The British law makes no distinction between rifles and pistols, although it does make it easier to own shotguns. The burden of proof for showing a need for firearms rests on the citizen for pistols and rifles, but in the case of shotguns the police must show why a shotgun should not be permitted, Karl E. Mayer reported from London.

The best estimate is that there are about 220,000 licensed weapons in Britain. Provisional figures for England and Wales (population 48 million) for 1967 showed a total of 2,331 indictable offenses involving firearms. Of the total, 791 involved cases in which firearms actually were fired or used to threaten a victim, 351 involve wounding by shooting, and 45 involve killing by shooting.

All British police are unarmed, except in very rare cases—such as pursuit of armed men. Because the police are unarmed criminals are generally unarmed.

GREECE. In Greece, the law permits general ownership of hunting guns without permits, but requires an annual or semi-annual license. The owner must be a member of a gun club, and cannot carry a gun during closed hunting seasons nor outside hunting areas. Hand guns are permitted under strict control of local police. They are in practical terms limited to night watchmen, guards, payroll custodians and persons whose lives or families have been threatened.

The latest figures for murders in Greece—the great majority by firearms—are 101 in 1960, 113 in 1961, 95 in 1962, and 91 in 1963. Most are crimes of passion and armed robberies are very rare. The Greek population is about 8.5 million.

One problem in Greece, reported Friendly from Athens, is that plenty of guns are probably stashed away in the country—acquired during the civil war in the late 1940s. The government claims these weapons were surrendered, but observers expect there are many secret arsenals.

ISRAEL. Political tension and communal warfare in Palestine even before the establishment of the state of Israel led to the imposition of strict controls on the sale of firearms and other weapons there. Some laws restricting the carrying of guns were in effect 50 years ago under the Ottoman Empire.

Many Israeli civilians have obtained permits to carry pistols, because of the many border incidents. In addition, since most Israelis are in the reserves, there is widespread knowledge of the use of firearms. However, the Israelis do not take their guns home with them and must return weapons to their army units when they are released from service. More than 40,000 licenses for hand guns and shotguns are issued annually by Israeli officials for self-defense and hunting purposes. Permits have to be renewed each year.

In a population of about 2.6 million (not including occupied areas) in 1967 there were 29 murder cases, of which ten involved firearms, special correspondent Yuval Elizur reported from Jerusalem.

CANADA. Canadians are heavily armed with hunting weapons but not with sidearms, special correspondent Gerald Waring reported from Ottawa. There were 281 murders in Canada last year, giving a rate of 1.6 per 100,000 persons over seven years old. Of the total, 140 murders were committed by firearms, for a shooting murder rate of 0.8 per 100,000.

All guns must be registered in Canada, and as of last year registrations totaled 513,176, including the armed forces and police.

Prime Minister Pierre Elliott Trudeau has been heavily guarded during the present election campaign. The Liberal government introduced a bill in the last Parliament to increase gun controls, and presumably the bill would be introduced if the Liberals win the June 25 election.

INTERNATIONAL TRAFFIC. As for international gun traffic, the Soviet Union is the world's largest arms supplier, responsible—according to one estimate—for 40 per cent of the total international arms trade, with Eastern Europe and North Vietnam its main customers.

Sue Masterman reported from The Hague that the Dutch are responsible for the bulk of actual weapons transportation around the world. Little Dutch coasters do most of the gun running from Europe to Asia and Africa, she reported.

Guns in circulation in South America are of European manufacture primarily, according to police. The Italian Beretta seems to be an especially favored gun in Peru, for example. Some of the guns in Latin America are of U.S. manufacture (acquired through surplus channels), but most apparently come from Czechoslovakia. This is largely because Cuba, which does most of the arms smuggling for the growing guerrilla operations in Latin America, can obtain Czech weapons easily, Goshko reported from Lima. In addition, he reported, the Latin guerrillas think that the Czech automatic weapons are the best there are—particularly light submachine guns.

Meet the Press, June 9, 1968 *

MR. SPIVAK: The House of Representatives passed and sent to the President this week an omnibus anti-crime bill. President Johnson criticized its gun control provision as a half-way measure and called upon Congress to give the country the gun control law it needs.

Our guest today on Meet the Press is Senator Joseph D. Tydings, Democrat of Maryland, a leading advocate of strong gun control legislation.

Senator Tydings is a member of the Senate Judiciary Committee and former U. S. Attorney for the District of Maryland.

We will have the first questions from Carl Stern of NBC News.

MR. STERN: Senator, despite the alleged half-way gun control measures in the Crime Control Bill, plus whatever constitutional infirmities it might have, would you recommend the President sign it?

SENATOR TYDINGS: Yes, I would. I didn't support all measures of the bill, but I think he should sign it.

MR. STERN: Additional gun control measures reaching to long guns are to be introduced in the Congress this week, but how could any of these proposed gun limits have helped to avoid the shooting of Senator Kennedy?

SENATOR TYDINGS: The specific legislation, which would be a mail order ban on long guns, which the President has proposed, which we tried to amend to Title IV in the Senate, wouldn't go far enough in my judgment. I think that we need a responsible, sane gun policy in this country which would require the registration of all guns, just as automobiles, and which would require a license to purchase a gun, preferably issued by your local law enforcement officer. It is just tragic that in all of the Western civilization the United States is the one country with an insane gun policy. Our gun murder death is 54 times as great as Great Britain, 67 times as great as Japan. In 1962 there were almost 5,000 gun murders in the United States and less than 30 in Great Britain. It just doesn't make sense.

MR. STERN: This is also a country, though, that has had big city dis-

NBC's *Meet the Press*, June 9, 1968. Reprinted with the permission of *Meet the Press*.

* Those present were the following: Guest: Senator Joseph D. Tydings (D. Md.); Moderator: Lawrence E. Spivak; Panel: Alan Barth (*Washington Post*), Max Frankel (*New York Times*), Donn Downing (*Time Magazine*), Carl Stern (NBC News).

orders. This has produced a desire in many people to obtain a gun. Has this hurt efforts to curb guns?

SENATOR TYDINGS:I don't think so. I think—a responsible licensing provision where your local police chief would have to approve your license first; a license could be issued for legitimate supporting purpose, for home protection, a legitimate purpose. That is all we ask. A responsible gun law. I don't think it would bother the persons who want to protect their home.

MR. STERN: Does not the Defense Department, with the authorization of Congress, still sell surplus guns and ammunition at bargain prices?

SENATOR TYDINGS: They did until three months ago, and it was a national disgrace. Now the Pentagon has finally stopped selling surplus guns. In Detroit last summer 400 police officers couldn't buy surplus carbines until they joined the NRA at $5 a year. Fortunately, I think the Pentagon has come to their senses.

MR. STERN: Has the criticism of the NRA been fair? Have you personally been under any harassment from the NRA?

SENATOR TYDINGS: The NRA is the National Rifle Association. As you know, they don't pay taxes. They have income of some $5 million a year, and 25 per cent of that income comes from advertisements sold in their magazine, most of which are purchased by munitions makers and so forth. Ostensibly they represent the sportsmen, but actually they are the voice of the munitions makers and the gun sellers in the United States. They have a tremendous amount of power in the Congress, unfortunately, in state legislatures. They have always opposed any type of responsible, effective gun legislation.

It is interesting to note that in the past three decades only one state, New Jersey, has ever been able to pass a strong gun control measure over NRA opposition. Of course, one of the unfortunate aspects, by-products, is that many conservation organizations don't really look into the matter themselves and just blindly follow the lead of the NRA in gun regulation matters.

MR. DOWNING: Senator Tydings, public sentiment over the years has favored strong gun control legislation. I believe a poll in the thirties showed that 84 per cent of the people favored a strong bill, and last year another poll showed that 73 per cent favored guns and shotguns being registered. The National Association of Police Chiefs has supported strong legislation, as has F.B.I. Director Hoover.

With all this apparent support, how is it possible for the Congress to ignore?

SENATOR TYDINGS: The National Rifle Association and the other fronts for the various gun makers have been able to confuse sportsmen. And let me say here that I learned to shoot ducks at my father's knee. I still have the shotgun my father gave me on my 21st birthday. I love to shoot ducks and geese. I shoot all over Maryland. But the average sportsman or hunter has been so confused and misled by the National Rifle Association and their various propaganda missiles that they violently react against any type of responsible or sane gun legislation without even realizing what is in it. They have been able to—the NRA and the various gun lobbies—have been able to control state legislatures and to in effect control really the national Congress so that it has been impossible to get responsible or sane gun legislation through any legislative body, with a few exceptions, in his country.

MR. DOWNING: The President of the NRA, Harold Glassen, is recently quoted as saying that the Association is not a lobby and that it has not spent a single dollar over the years for lobbying operations.

SENATOR TYDINGS: The Association has, as I have indicated, over $5 million in revenue. They keep a tremendous bureaucracy or hierarchy, the NRA, working here in Congress. As far as I am concerned, their principal job is to conduct surveillance on all responsible gun legislation and to do whatever they can to defeat it. They spend millions of dollars on their magazine and their various mailings they send out to hunters across the United States, many of which are primarily directed at efforts to kill legislation. I consider them, and I think most responsible legislators, despite the fact that they don't register under the Lobbying Act, to be one of the most powerful lobbies in the United States.

MR. FRANKEL: Senator, I'd like to ask you about the nature of this lobbying, but, first, are you saying that your fellow Senators, like the sportsmen, are also confused, or are they just timid?

SENATOR TYDINGS: I think many of them are actually confused. Of course, bear in mind that Congressmen and legislators represent their constituency, and if the great majority of your constituents who support sane gun legislation remain silent and only your very vocal sportsmen write in, call in and talk to you, you are likely to be responsive to your vocal constitutents.

MR. FRANKEL: Tell us about this lobbying. How does it really work in terms of pressure—

SENATOR TYDINGS: I'll give you the specifics:

The way it would work, the minute a bill is introduced—for instance, both Senator Kennedys, myself and others, have introduced each year responsible gun legislation, mail order ban on sale of pistols and rifles. The minute that bill is introduced, they send a bulletin to all their some 900,000 members giving the bill and giving their views on it and what ought to be done, and the way I know the response is because the NRA misspelled my name. They put it T-i-d-i-n-g-s, instead of "Ty," and I got literally thousands of letters and postcards from my constituents all misspelling my name and all giving the line that was in the propaganda issued by the NRA. And this is done with every state legislator, every city councilman and every congressman across the nation, and meanwhile your average taxpaying moderate citizen sits back and does nothing.

MR. FRANKEL: But is it the function of—let's say Senator Mike Mansfield, a national figure, the Majority Leader of your party—is it his function merely to respond to a volume of mail, especially if he should recognize it as being essentially organized? Does his thinking on an issue stop at that point?

SENATOR TYDINGS: Of course not, but it is bound to be an influence, particularly if you are a state which is small in population, and if a great majority of the people are misled in that state, or some of them, or the leaders, you are bound to be affected by it.

MR. FRANKEL: Even if, as the polls suggest, four out of five voters feel the other way?

SENATOR TYDINGS: Unfortunately it is not the polls that count; it is the constituents or your people back home who take the trouble to contact you.

MR. BARTH: Senator, just following up Max Frankel's question, would it be useful to Congress to have some mail from people who aren't members of the National Rifle Association? Would that be an effective thing?

SENATOR TYDINGS: I think absolutely. It is high time. Particularly in the southern states and in the western states where your NRA is so powerful or your right-wing extremists which oppose any type of sane gun law are strong. I think it is absolutely mandatory that we get some support at the grass roots level.

MR. BARTH: You know that there are something like 100 million guns in private possession, in private hands in the United States?

SENATOR TYDINGS: That is a conservative figure.

MR. BARTH: Can anything effective be done about the gun problem without some measures designed to dry up the availability of guns in private hands?

SENATOR TYDINGS: As I indicated earlier, Mr. Barth, I think the legislation which we passed and which the President proposes, which we tried to pass, is a minimal step. I think to have responsible, sane gun legislation, we have to do what the rest of the civilized Western nations do, have gun registration laws and require a license for the purchase of a firearm.

You notice yesterday when they picked up the assassin of Martin Luther King, or at least a man accused of being involved with Martin Luther King, they picked him up on the charge of possessing an uncertificated, unregistered firearm. I think that is the least we can do in this country.

MR. BARTH: Registration, it seems to me, is fairly minimal too.

SENATOR TYDINGS: Plus licensing.

MR. BARTH: What do you think about confiscation of available firearms, particularly pistols, and a pistol permit program under which these deadly weapons would be allowed in the hands only of military personnel and police authorities and citizens who are determined to have a need of them, say for self-protection?

SENATOR TYDINGS: Mr. Barth, the Japanese have a law which prohibits anyone owning a pistol except a police officer. I wouldn't propose to go that far. What I would propose—and incidentally, I am drafting legislation which I intend to introduce next week, sane gun legislation, which would require a license. It would give a period of time for the states to set up their own enabling legislation, because the states should do it, but if they don't, would require each person to register his firearm and to secure a license for it.

In the case of a hand gun, the license would have to be issued by your local law enforcement officer, and you would have to use it either for a hunting purpose or you would need it to protect your house or your property. You couldn't have a criminal record, and the police would have a chance to check it out.

I think that is a minimum step, a responsible step, and if you couldn't meet those requirements, then I think that the government should pay you just compensation and you should turn it in. A person, say, who is an alcoholic, who has a record of conviction involved in riots or a felony, they shouldn't be permitted to own a gun. The gun should be turned in and confiscated.

MR. SPIVAK: Senator, may I ask you a question? If you are against the gun control provisions of this anti-crime bill, why do you want the President to sign the bill? Why doesn't—

SENATOR TYDINGS: I am not against it. I fought for them, Mr. Spivak. I was one of the floor leaders. I fight for every step I can get.

MR. SPIVAK: You think they are not strong enough?

SENATOR TYDINGS: Definitely they are not strong enough, but I think they are much better than nothing. I fought too long in the Senate trying to get just this minimal safeguard for the American people to want the President to veto it. I think we need all the protection we can get, and I urge him to sign it.

MR. SPIVAK: But the state of public opinion today being what it is, if you started all over again, wouldn't you be more likely to get a strong bill if he vetoed it and you started all over again?

SENATOR TYDINGS: I don't know, Mr. Spivak. That is always a possibility, but that is a little illusory and I just don't want to take the chance. I would rather try to strengthen what we have got rather than lose that minimal safeguard, as minimal as it is.

MR. STERN: A criminal by definition is someone who breaks the law. It is said, of what value would more laws be if in fact criminals will continue to get guns anyway?

SENATOR TYDINGS: It is not a question of more laws. It is keeping a pistol or a deadly weapon out of the hands of a criminal.

Take Detroit last summer. Michigan has a law which says you can't sell a pistol to a convicted felon, and yet all they had to do in Detroit— and the weapons confiscated after the riots showed that, I think—70 or 80 per cent of the individuals involved had prior criminal records, couldn't purchase a weapon in Michigan, so they hopped in their car, sped over the state line into Ohio, bought a Saturday night special for eight or ten bucks at the store down there in Toledo, Ohio, and came back in and used it for whatever purpose they wanted.

We have got to try to keep the guns out of the hands of individuals.

You hear the argument, the NRA and the gun lobby say, well, just make the penalty greater on the possession of guns. That is a lot of baloney. We have the toughest penalties in the world for guns involved in a murder or robbery or anything, and yet we have 67 times the rate of gun murder deaths here that they do in Japan, where they keep the guns out of the hands of criminals, or 54 times as great a murder rate as they do in Great Britain. I mean, the answer is to limit the possession of fire-arms, to stop them from getting into the hands of criminals, narcotics addicts, alcoholics, before—

MR. STERN: Last July during hearings of the Senate Subcommittee on Juvenile Delinquency, Senator Hruska of Nebraska pointed out that only 17,000 New Yorkers, for example, have guns legally. He said, "The intruder breaking into an apartment has it made because he knows there is no one to shoot back." In essence, he is saying restrictions on guns encourage crime. What is your response to that?

SENATOR TYDINGS: Well, that is a misleading argument.

First of all, in New York, with the Sullivan law, you are permitted to have a pistol for the safety of your home or your store, so that wipes that argument right out.

In New York they say you can't purchase a pistol if you have a criminal record, and they give the police an opportunity to check your criminal record and the background. I might point out that in New York both the murder rate and the gun murder rate are far below that of western states and southern states that don't have any responsible gun regulation.

Last year in the United States, I think there were 335 police officers murdered; 96 per cent of them were shot down with guns. In all of the eastern states, all of the northeastern states, there were less than 60 police officers killed. In the southern states, where they have little or no gun regulation, 151 police officers were killed, shot down with guns.

I mean it shows that where you even take minimal efforts—and certainly the northeastern states have a long way to go, but even minimal efforts help.

MR. DOWNING: Senator, opponents also maintain that there is no relationship between the gun control laws and the level of crime. They say the target is wrong, that the real causes are social and economic, so why pick on them?

SENATOR TYDINGS: Let me say this, no one, least of all myself, would advocate that gun law is the answer to crime. It is a tremendous first step. It has been requested, as a matter of fact begged for, by police chiefs from all over the country. I do think that if we are going to meet the problems of crime, in addition to responsible gun legislation we have got to pay decent salaries to our law enforcement officials, give them decent education and back them up. And in the long run if we are going to do anything we have got to try to do something about the environment which makes it so likely that crime is going to take place.

A little more long-winded answer to your question: We have a great quarterback with the Baltimore Colts, John Unitas. If John Unitas in the first play of a practice game were to have his arm broken, a compound fracture, with bones sticking out in three places, the first thing we would have to do, or the trainer would do, is try to get him some sedative or novocaine to deaden the pain. That is the immediate problem with crime. We have got to beef up the police force, do something about the law enforcement officer on the beat, help him, pay him. But if they ignore the broken arm, if the doctor didn't come in and set that bone, put it in a cast, John Unitas could never play football again. And if we sit back and don't do anything about the conditions in the cities, about job opportunities, about providing a decent education for the children in the ghettoes, about providing decent housing, we are never going to solve the problem of crime, and of course I think that is in the long run. That is of course the major approach we have to make.

MR. FRANKEL: Senator, the things you just said were reminiscent, of course, of Senator Robert Kennedy and the things he was saying, and I am sure that is no accident because you were close to him. Is it too soon to ask what happens now to the people who were allied with him and who felt that he stood for things that other people in the Party did not?

SENATOR TYDINGS: I don't know that anyone at this particular time, any of us who were close to Senator Kennedy, really knows what we are thinking, what we are doing. Yesterday, as you know, was just too much. But I do know this: I don't see how we can just go back to politics as usual, how we can just support somebody or anybody who is not willing to speak up courageously as he did about the problems which divide our society, about the problems of racial hatred, of black against white, about the disaffected groups within our society, about the problem of this ghastly war in Vietnam. I just don't see how we can go back to that "politics as usual."

MR. FRANKEL: Are you suggesting that neither the President in his way or the Vice President in his—that they are politics as usual?

SENATOR TYDINGS: I am not suggesting anything, Mr. Frankel. I am just telling you how one man who was inspired by Robert Kennedy and his brother feels, and it is difficult to say anything today, particularly after yesterday.

MR. FRANKEL: Let me ask you: the President seemed to feel that the horror of this shooting at least might galvanize the Congress, at least in this small respect, on beefing up the gun bill. Is it your judgment after the fights that you have been through in this same cause in the Senate—and that you lost, really, on the way to moving this bill through—that the shooting was enough to change enough votes?

SENATOR TYDINGS: No, I think the President was wrong. Nothing is going to move the Congress, nothing is going to move the state legislatures across the country except a most tremendous outpouring of demands from the citizens of this country. It is only the people who are going to do it. The Congress is not going to change; we are not going to get a bill through the Senate unless the people themselves get on the telephone and get hold of their Senators and say, "We demand action." I think the President is dead wrong.

MR. FRANKEL: Do you think the Administration and the President may have done enough to arouse that kind of support?

SENATOR TYDINGS: I think—I am delighted with the statement that the President made yesterday but generally the leadership—and I might say the Republican leadership—has not met its responsibilities. Richard Nixon just several weeks ago issued a white paper on crime. It took six pages of fine print in the Congressional Record. He talked about everything, and he conspicuously avoided any mention whatsoever of gun control.

If we have that kind of leadership and timidity and fear of the gun lobbies, we are never going to get a responsible legislative program.

MR. SPIVAK: Gentlemen, we have less than two minutes.

MR. BARTH: I'd like to ask something about the legal problems involved in gun legislation.

You spoke earlier of a permit system for the possession of pistols and the registration of firearms. Can the Federal Government, under the commerce power, I suppose, act effectively in this field, or must a part of the control be left to local legislation?

SENATOR TYDINGS: No, we can constitutionally act. It has been passed by the Supreme Court, the Federal Firearms Act of 1934 and again in 1938. My proposal would be to give the states a period of time to act. Hopefully they would, but if they didn't, then we have a responsibility to act.

MR. BARTH: Could the Federal Government confiscate guns, take them away from people who ought not to have them?

SENATOR TYDINGS: Oh, I think they could, yes.

MR. SPIVAK: Senator, the United States has been called the most lawless nation in the world. Do you think that is so?

SENATOR TYDINGS: I don't know all the statistics, but insofar as gun murders are concerned, I would have to answer, that is correct.

MR. SPIVAK: Gentlemen, on that note, I am afraid we must end.

I am sorry to interrupt, but our time is up.

Thank you, Senator Tydings, for being with us today on Meet the Press.

Lost Art

The Washington Post

What in the world is American youth coming to? There was a time—and not many years ago, either—when one could pick up his newspaper almost any day and find in it a fascinating story about some enterprising young sportsman who had, unfortunately, blown his brains out with a six-shooter in the course of a happy-go-lucky game of Russian Roulette. The sport got a bad name, unhappily, because the newspapers seemed always to publicize the cases in which a fellow lost and never to give any space at all to accounts of those who won. That's American journalism for you, always accenting the negative.

The fast draw is another form of sport which seems virtually to have been abandoned. Just because some of the plucky chaps practicing fast draws shot their legs off or killed someone else when the hammer of the revolver got snagged while it was being pulled out of its holster, the game suddenly became unpopular, as though there were something to be ashamed of in a good, clean bullet wound. Have all the kids these days turned chicken, or something? You can hardly see a fast draw anywhere anymore except on one of those antique TV Westerns.

The National Rifle Association and particularly its younger members had better bear in mind that the future of Russian Roulette and the fast draw rests with them. No one else is going to keep these delightful folk pastimes alive if they don't. There is, to be sure, nothing in the current anti-gun legislation specifically forbidding such games. The truth of the matter, nevertheless, is that the Government is trying to curb them. You can't very well shoot yourself, can you, if you can't get hold of a gun and one or two cartridges?

FROM the *Washington Post,* June 28, 1968. Reprinted with the permission of the *Washington Post.*

Statistics on Firearms in Accidents and Crimes

National Rifle Association

Notable Facts

In 1966, there were 113,000 deaths resulting from all accidents for a rate of 57.7 per 100,000 persons. A rise of 5 per cent over 1965.

In 1966, the number of motor vehicle accident deaths was 53,000 for a rate of 27.1 per 100,000 population; a rise of 8 per cent over 1965. More people have been killed in auto accidents in the last two years than have been killed in firearms accidents over the last 30 years.

In 1966, there were 2,600 firearms accident fatalities, for a rate of 1.3 per 100,000 population. The greatest increase was noted in the 15 to 24 age group, predictably, since this age group is now more numerous than at any other time in our history (post-war baby boom, etc.).

In 1966, the number of public accident deaths (accidents in public places or places used in a public way) was 19,500, an increase of 7 per cent over 1965, for a rate of 10.0 per 100,000 persons. Of this number, firearms accounted for only 1,000 deaths for a rate of 0.5 per 100,000 population.

The Travelers Company, one of the nation's largest insurance companies, rated hunting as 15th on the list of dangerous sports in a recent five-year report of the causes of accidents in sport and recreation.

Of the 29,500 deaths from home accidents in 1966, firearms accounted for slightly more than 1,500, for a rate of 0.8 per 100,000 persons.

The FBI reports that 3,243,000 serious crimes were committed in the United States in 1966. The total number of crimes of violence committed with firearms (on available figures) was approximately 109,500 or 3.4 per cent.

In 1966, there was one hunting fatality for every 14,352 hunters. In the same period of time, there was one driving fatality for every 1,925 drivers.

Over the past 30 years (1936–1966), some 1,136,928 people have been killed in U.S. auto accidents. That is as many people as are presently living in the cities of Indianapolis, Ind., and St. Louis, Mo.

Compiled by the Legislative Service of the National Rifle Association of America, Washington, D.C. Reprinted with permission.

Dr. Donald B. Louria, associate professor at Cornell University and president of the New York State Council of Drug Addiction, has estimated that there are about 98,000 drug addicts in the U.S., about half of whom live in New York City. He estimates that about 1 per cent of those in New York die each year from an overdose of their narcotics. That's about 490 each year, at least two and a half times as many as are murdered in the city each year with firearms.

New York City is second only to Los Angeles in major crime rate per 100,000 population. (N.Y.: 3,208.1; L.A.: 3,780.2.) Even with the Sullivan Law, its homicide rate is about 12 per cent above the national average (6.4 *vs.* 5.7). In addition, its homicide *per capita* rate is higher than those of the following cities: Boston, Buffalo, Columbus, Ohio, Denver, Indianapolis, Los Angeles, Milwaukee, Minneapolis, Newark, Omaha, Philadelphia, Pittsburgh, San Francisco, and Seattle, to name only a few.

More children under the age of 5 died from an overdose of *aspirin* in the years 1961–1965 than did from firearms accidents. An average of 125 by aspirin, average of roughly 100 from firearms.

According to the statistics of the National Safety Council, more people are killed in their homes each year from household poisons than from firearms accidents. The household poisons are such common articles as aspirin and other drugs, bleaches, lye, cosmetics, insecticides, turpentine and kerosene.

The volume of crime is up approximately 62 per cent since 1960, outdistancing our population growth by nearly 7 to 1. Eighty-three per cent of those persons acquitted or whose cases were dismissed in 1963 were rearrested for new crimes within 30 months.

Statistics on Firearms in Accidents and Crime

The statistics listed below have been gathered from publications of the National Safety Council; the U.S. Bureau of the Census; the U.S. Public Health Service; the U.S. Fish and Wildlife Service; the Travelers Insurance Company; the Federal Bureau of Investigation; and the records of the National Rifle Association.

I. Total Accidents Statistics—1966

In 1966, there were 113,000 deaths resulting from accidents of all types, for a rate of 57.7 per 100,000 persons. In 1965, there were 107,000 deaths, for a rate of 55.2 per 100,000 persons.

Motor vehicles	53,000 or 27.1 per 100,000 population
Falls	20,000 or 10.2 per 100,000 population
Fire, burns, etc.	7,900 or 4.0 per 100,000 population

Drowning	7,000 or	3.6 per 100,000 population
Firearms *	2,600 or	1.3 per 100,000 population
Machinery accidents	2,100 or	1.1 per 100,000 population
Poisoning by solids and liquids	2,100 or	1.1 per 100,000 population
All other types	16,800 or	8.6 per 100,000 population

The total number of accidents from all causes in 1966 increased 5 per cent over 1965. Most categories of accidents experienced an increase in percentage of total accidents, as well as number per 100,000 population. The category of firearms experienced an increase of 11 per cent (400 more deaths).

Since 1903, there have been approximately 159,547 accidental deaths caused by the use of firearms, for an annual average since that year of 2,493. In 1903 there were 2,100 such accidents; 2,600 in 1966. However, the death rate per 100,000 population has fallen from 2.3 in 1903 to 1.3 in 1966, despite a population increase during that period from 80 million to 196 million.

II. Public Accidents (Hunting)—1966

These accidents include deaths in public places or places used in a public way, not involving vehicles. Most sports and recreational deaths are included. Deaths in the course of employment are excluded. Of the 19,500 deaths in this category, firearms accounted for 1,000.

According to the U.S. Fish and Wildlife Service, in 1966 (fiscal year— July to July) there were 14,351,768 paid hunting license holders in the United States. The National Safety Council states that there were only 900 accidental deaths resulting from firearms accidents and a few deaths (less than 3 per cent) from accidents involving explosives (dynamite, etc.). The exact number of fatal hunting accidents is not known. However, using the Council's figure of 1,000, there was 1 hunting death for every 14,352 hunters. In all likelihood, the exact figures would reveal much less of a ratio of hunting deaths attributable to firearms.

III. Uniform Hunter Casualty Reports—(1951–1960)

Of the hunters involved in the casualties during that period, almost all were male. About 80 per cent had hunting licenses. The majority were 20 years of age or older. Nearly 75 per cent had hunted in 3 or more previous years, and not more than 1 per cent were reported as being under the apparent influence of intoxicants or drugs.

Forty percent of the casualties took place while the shooter was hunt-

* Includes deaths in firearms accidents in recreational activities or on home premises and a small number (less than 3 per cent) from explosions of dynamite, bombs, grenades, etc. These figures do not include suicides, murders, or deaths resulting from war operations.

ing small game. Most casualties occurred while hunting with a shotgun.

Over half of the casualties occurred while the shooter did not intend to discharge his firearm. "Unintentional discharge" covers such circumstances as these:

The shooter stumbled and fell.
The trigger caught on brush (or some other object).
The shooter inadvertently pulled the trigger while seeking game.
The shooter was removing a firearm from, or placing it in a vehicle.
The shooter was crossing a fence with a loaded weapon.

In "intentional discharge" casualties, between 60 per cent and 70 per cent occurred with visibility "clear." Between 55 per cent and 65 per cent occurred with "light" or "open" cover. About 40 per cent of the victims were wearing bright-colored clothes, and in about 50 per cent the victim was within 11–50 yards from the shooter.

During that time period, approximately 18 per cent of all hunter casualties ended in death to the victim.

The Travelers Company, one of the nation's largest insurance companies, rates hunting as 15th on the list of dangerous sports in their recent 5-year report on the causes of accidents in sport and recreation for which they have paid out claims. Those sports that produce more accidents than hunting are:

Football	7,481
Baseball	3,228
Winter sports	2,860
Bathing and swimming	2,743
Basketball	2,448
In country or at beach	2,194
Skating	1,899
Bicycle	1,717
At parks, picnics, outings	1,480
Boating and canoeing	1,477
Golf	1,448
Gymnasium	1,129
Fishing	1,052
Hunting	731

Closely following hunting are tennis and squash (726); attendance at theaters, churches, concerts (723); bowling (625); athletic games (336) and dancing (331).

The Travelers Company reports that of the 731 hunting accidents listed, "most of them are sprains or fractures resulting from stepping in holes, tripping and so on." Therefore, a small minority of the total figure for hunting accidents was actually caused by the discharge of firearms.

IV. Home Accidents—1966

These accidents include deaths in the home and on home premises to occupants, guests and trespassers. Also included are domestic servants but excluded are other persons working on home premises. Of the 29,500 deaths from home accidents in 1966, firearms accounted for slightly more than 1,500.

The 1965 figures for deaths in this category are as follows:

Falls	11,800 or 6.0 per 100,000 population
Fires, burns, etc.	6,800 or 3.5 per 100,000 population
Poisoning by solids and liquids	1,700 or 0.9 per 100,000 population
Suffocation	1,300 or 0.7 per 100,000 population
Firearms	1,500 or 0.8 per 100,000 population
Poisoning by gases and vapors	1,100 or 0.6 per 100,000 population
All others	4,400 or 2.1 per 100,000 population

Deaths by firearms accidents in the home have never risen above 3,000 (1923–1932 average). This rate has never exceeded 2.5 deaths per 100,000 population (1923–1932 average).

Noteworthy is the fact that almost half of the 1,500 annual fatalities in the home are under 20 years of age.

FIREARMS FATALITIES (NUMERICAL)

1923–1932 (average)	1966	Reduction
3,000	2,600	13.3%

The rate of deaths from firearms accidents has declined during the last 35 years although the population has increased by 75 million persons.

FIREARMS FATALITIES (RATE PER 100,000)

1923–1932 (average)	1966	Reduction
2.5	1.3	48%

V. Firearms and Crime

In approaching the matter of comparative crime statistics, a person is advised to keep the following cautionary notes by the Federal Bureau of Investigation in mind. For many years, the FBI in its *Uniform Crime Reports* has cautioned readers of that publication from "drawing conclusions from direct comparisons of crime figures between individual communities without first considering the factors involved." The FBI further states that "crime is a social problem and the concern of the entire community," and that "the law enforcement effort is limited to factors within its control." The type of crime that occurs from place to place:

Density and size of the community population and the metropolitan area of which it is a part.

Composition of the population with reference particularly to age, sex and race.

Economic status and mores of the population.

Relative stability of the population, including commuters, seasonal, and other transient types.

Climate, including seasonal weather condition.

Educational, recreational, and religious characteristics.

Effective strength of the police force.

Policies of the prosecuting officials and the courts.

Attitude of the public toward law enforcement problems.

The administrative and investigative efficiency of the local law enforcement agency.

Firearms were used as fatal weapons in 60 per cent of the criminal homicides committed in 1966. The total number of murder victims by firearms was 6,552 (based on an estimated population of 195,857,000). There were slightly more than 3.3 murders with a firearm per 100,000 population. Seventy-three per cent of these murders were committed with a hand gun, 15 per cent by the use of a shotgun, and 12 per cent with a rifle or other firearm:

Hand guns	4,804 or 44%
Rifles	764 or 7%
Shotguns	982 or 9%
Cutting and stabbing	2,511 or 23%
Personal weapons (hands, fists, feet, etc.)	982 or 9%
Other weapon (club, poison, etc.)	873 or 8%

In 1966 the Federal Bureau of Investigation revealed the following information concerning the weapons used in the total number of aggravated assaults (231,800) committed during that year. (Aggravated assault is defined in part as "assault with intent to kill or for the purpose of inflicting severe bodily injury. . . .")

Cutting or stabbing	78,812 or 34%
Personal weapon (hands, fists, feet)	57,950 or 25%
Blunt object	50,996 or 22%
Firearms	44,042 or 19%

During the 3-year period, 1964–1966, assaults with a firearm were up 36 per cent, assaults with a knife or other cutting instrument rose 4 per cent, those where blunt objects or other dangerous weapons were used increased 17 per cent and the crimes where personal weapons were employed witnessed an 11 per cent rise.

VI. Homicides and Firearms

	1930	1966
Population	123,077,000	194,583,000
Homicides by use of firearms and explosives	10,473	6,552
Rate per 100,000 population	5.7	2.9

The number of homicides with firearms decreased from 1930 to 1966, as did the rate per 100,000 population (5.7 to 3.4). The percentage of homicides with firearms also decreased approximately 50 per cent.

VII. Suicides and Firearms

	1930	1965
Population	123,077,000	193,800,000
Suicides by all means	18,323	21,507
Rate per 100,000	14.9	11.1
Suicides by firearms and explosives	6,735	9,898
Rate per 100,000	5.5	5.1

The number of suicides with firearms increased from 1930 to 1965, as did the rate of population. The rate per 100,000 population decreased (from 5.5 to 5.1) for a percentage decrease of 7.3 per cent.

In listing the number of homicides and suicides committed with firearms, the figures include not only firearms, but explosives as well. If firearms were listed separately, the results would indicate a more definite decline in the use of firearms proportionate to the increase in population.

The contents of this compilation are taken from a number of sources. The National Rifle Association cannot accept the responsibility for the accuracy or limitation of the data presented here, other than for those which it collects. The responsibility for the selection of the material and for method of presentation, however, rests with NRA.

ANTI GUN BILL

MINUTE-MAN 1966!

Reprinted by permission of Charles G. Werner, copyright 1966, *The Indianapolis Star*.

Statement Before Senate Subcommittee
on Juvenile Delinquency

Franklin L. Orth

Mr. Chairman:

My name is Franklin L. Orth. I am the Executive Vice President of the National Rifle Association of America. Thank you for granting me the

Statement of Franklin L. Orth, Executive Vice President, National Rifle Association of America, before Subcommittee on Juvenile Delinquency of the Judiciary Committee, United States Senate, July 24, 1969. Reprinted with the permission of the National Rifle Association of America, Washington, D.C.

opportunity to speak on the subject of firearms legislation. The courtesy extended by this Subcommittee on all previous occasions is most deeply appreciated.

Last year, after much debate, Congress enacted far-reaching controls on interstate commerce in firearms and ammunition. The basic thrust of the legislation, Public Law 90–618, was to prohibit all interstate shipments of firearms, ammunition and ammunition components except between federal firearms license holders.

The philosophy of the Gun Control Act of 1968 is, however, as significant as the principal effect. The Congress has gone on record as supporting the concept that none except those engaged in a strictly controlled commercial venture should be permitted to receive a firearm or ammunition directly in interstate commerce. In adopting the provisions of the Gun Control Act, Congress chose an approach of absolute denial as opposed to one of control by regulation as reflected in bills supported by the NRA. The central feature of the NRA approach would have required a certified statement system for the receipt of a hand gun in commerce.

There were very practical reasons for the approach supported by the NRA. Unfortunately, in the emotional period during which most of the final discussion of the legislation was held, the pressures of the moment were such as to prevent adequate consideration of the merits of the proposals and objections thereto.

It goes without saying that one of the major considerations of any approach to the question of firearms control should be the effect such legislation will have on the law-abiding legitimate user and owner of firearms. An examination of the record discloses many interesting facts in this connection. For instance, it is estimated that close to 99 per cent of the firearms owners in this country are law-abiding sportsmen. Further, of the firearms used in crimes, approximately 80 per cent are hand guns. Less than 4 per cent of all reported serious crime involves a firearm. Crime itself is largely an urban problem.

Awareness of these facts, coupled with a realization that the subject of firearms control can be discussed largely in terms of the rural-urban division of our population, provokes many thoughts. The most obvious is that federal firearms laws require 100 per cent observance by 99 per cent of the firearms owners in order to control the 1 per cent or less who misuse firearms and who will ignore any firearms laws. Further, the hand gun is the firearm most often used by criminals, while rifles and shotguns remain the firearms of sportsmen. Any additional federal legislation should address itself directly to consideration of this fact, rather than lumping all firearms and all firearms owners in the same category. Sportsmen are tired of being considered and treated the same as criminals simply because of their interest in shooting.

One of the main arguments against a federal firearms registration and licensing system has been the fact that the cost of administering such a program, together with the administrative red tape, would be grossly disproportionate to any possible benefit to be derived from such a system. For these and other worthwhile reasons, the Congress last year voted overwhelmingly against registration bills. My colleague, Mr. Scott, voiced opposition to registration and licensing measures in his testimony.

A basic element of NRA policy regarding firearms legislation is that a person who uses firearms in the commission of a crime, or who is not qualified to possess a firearm, should be subject to strict control and penalty. The NRA has consistently supported legislation reflecting this approach, for it accomplishes most directly the purpose of added firearms controls, without unduly infringing upon legitimate sporting interests. S. 849, by Senator Mansfield of Montana, and S. 2667, by Senator Dominick of Colorado, to impose a mandatory penalty for the possession or use of a firearm in the commission of a crime, deserve favorable consideration by this Committee on the grounds that such legislation will act to deter armed crimes as much as it is possible to do so.

Considering the nature and scope of last year's enactment, passage of a law requiring a minimum mandatory sentence for commission of an armed crime would be highly desirable as it is aimed directly at the criminal. The fact is that the American people have lost faith in the present permissive system of administration of justice and demand that adequate assurance be given that criminals will receive punishment to match their crimes. The present number of recidivists points out a need for stronger punishment and improved methods of rehabilitation. At any rate, existing conditions demand that our citizens be granted the security of knowing that criminals will be punished, and further, that if efforts at rehabilitation fail, the criminal will remain incarcerated, unable to continue to prey on society.

There is rapidly increasing support for some form of the mandatory-penalty approach on both the federal and state levels. At the moment, in the Congress 30 bills, seven of which are restricted to the District of Columbia, call for a special penalty for the possession or use of a firearm in crime. In 1968 and 1969, at least a dozen states enacted some kind of mandatory-penalty statute, while many others considered such a law.

I should like to say a word about the exemption of ammunition from the Gun Control Act, even though this question is not now before this Subcommittee. The National Rifle Association is in full accord and energetically supports legislation to remove ammunition and ammunition components from the Act.

It is common knowledge that the implementation and administration of certain aspects of the Gun Control Act have caused considerable concern and criticism among legitimate firearms owners throughout the nation. One of the principal complaints has been the record-keeping requirements imposed by administrative regulation for all sales of ammunition. Many facts and compelling arguments—statutory, administrative and day-to-day operational—militate against the ammunition record-keeping requirements imposed by administrative fiat. An indication of the reaction against these requirements is the introduction of 65 bills in this session of the Congress to remove ammunition from the Act. Further, the great number of resolutions and individual communications sent to the Congress on this subject is additional evidence of the vast popular support for the removal of small-arms ammunition and ammunition components from the 1968 federal gun law.

The National Rifle Association fervently hopes that this Subcommittee will favorably consider the Mansfield-Dominick proposals and will reject the registration-licensing measures as an undue burden on the American people.

Statement on Firearms and Violence

National Commission on the Causes and

Prevention of Violence

Whether guns cause violence, contribute to it, or are merely coincidental to it has long been debated. After extensive study we find that the availability of guns contributes substantially to violence in American society. Firearms, particularly handguns, facilitate the commission and increase the danger of the most violent crimes—assassination, murder, robbery and assault. The widespread availability of guns can also increase the level of violence associated with civil disorder. Firearms accidents, while they account for only a small percentage of all accidents, cause thousands of deaths and injuries each year.

This relationship between firearms and violence tends to obscure two other important facts bearing on the firearms question. First, the vast majority of gun owners do not misuse firearms. Millions of Americans are hunters, target shooters, and collectors, who use their guns safely and responsibly and who, perhaps more than many of their fellow citizens, deplore the criminal use of firearms. Second, in attending to the firearms problem, we must not forget that the root causes of American violence go much deeper than widespread gun ownership. Firearms generally facilitate, rather than cause, violence.

The challenge for this Commission—and for the nation as a whole—is

Statement by the Commission on Firearms and Violence, July 28, 1969. Reprinted with the permission of the National Commission on the Causes and Prevention of Violence.

to find ways to cope with illegitimate uses of guns without at the same time placing undue restrictions on legitimate uses. We believe this is possible if both the advocates and the opponents of gun control legislation will put aside their suspicions and preconceptions, accept the fact of a common danger without exaggerating its dimensions, and act for the common good.

1. The Domestic Arms Buildup

We find that the United States is in the midst of a period of increasing firearms ownership.

Our Task Force on Firearms estimates that there are now about ninety million firearms in the United States. Half of the nation's sixty million households possess at least one gun, and the number of guns owned by private citizens is rising rapidly.

During the first half of this century, about ten million firearms on the average were added to the civilian firearms supply in each decade. In the decade since 1958, however, nearly thirty million guns have been added to the civilian stockpile. Moreover, the sharpest increases have occurred in the last five years—a period of urban riots and sharply rising crime rates. Annual rifle and shotgun sales have doubled since 1963. Annual handgun sales have quadrupled.

Some of the increased gun sales in recent years have resulted from an increase in hunting and sport shooting, a fact consistent with the rising amount of money being spent on leisure time activities. But these predictable increases in sales of sporting arms cannot explain the much larger increases in the sales of handguns. With a few scattered exceptions, handguns are not sporting guns.

A substantial part of the rapidly increasing gun sales, particularly handgun sales, must be attributed to the rising fear of violence that the United States has recently experienced. Studies by our Task Force on Firearms, as well as by the Stanford Research Institute and the Senate Subcommittee on Juvenile Delinquency, show that gun sales in a particular area tend to increase sharply during and after a period of disorder. After the 1967 Detroit riot, for example, gun sales skyrocketed: Detroit issued four times as many handgun permits in 1968 as it did in 1965, and a nearby, predominantly white surburb issued five times as many permits.

Lending impetus to the arms buildup are the exhortations of extremist groups, both black and white. In their speeches and publications, leaders of these groups urge their members to buy firearms and be prepared to use them against "the enemy." Neighborhood protective associations have proliferated and have sometimes come to share the fears of the right-wing paramilitary groups, with the result that firearms are now being stock-piled in homes as well as "in the hills." A new wave of American vigilan-tism could result from these activities. Further, black extremist organiza-tions urge their members to obtain firearms for neighborhood and home defense, and sometimes for guerrilla warfare and terrorist activities as well. Ironically, extremist groups, regardless of race, are remarkably alike in their attitudes toward firearms and their opposition to firearms control.[1]

Quite apart from civil disorders, the urban arms buildup has increased the role of firearms in accidents and violent crime. Our Task Force has found that in Detroit accidental firearms deaths were three times greater in 1968, the year after the riot, than in 1966, the year before the riot. Between 1965 and 1968, homicides in Detroit committed with firearms increased 400 per cent while homicides committed with other weapons increased only 30 per cent; firearms robberies increased twice as fast as robberies committed without firearms. (These rates of increase are much higher than for the nation as a whole.)

Other studies confirm our finding that the proportion of gun use in violence rises and falls with gun ownership. The urban arms buildup threatens not only to escalate future civil disorders, but also to bring with it greater misuse of firearms in crimes and accidents.

2. Firearms and Violent Crime

We find that firearms, particularly handguns, play a major role in the commission of homicide, aggravated assault, and armed robbery, and that they are being used in greater percentages of these violent crimes.

Many Americans are alarmed by the rise of violent crime in the United States, and not without reason. Personal injury and death from crime occur more often in the United States than in any other industrial nation of the world.

Firearms are a primary instrument of injury and death in American crime. Two out of every three homicides are committed with guns. Since 1963 the number of homicides involving firearms has increased 48 per cent in the United States while the number of homicides committed with other weapons has risen only 10 per cent.

The circumstances of most homicides suggest that a person without ready access to a gun would not inevitably kill with another weapon. Studies show that most persons who commit homicide are not relentless, determined killers, but rather are persons likely to act on impulse in a moment of rage or passion and without a plan or determined intent to

---

[1] This is not to imply that all persons who oppose additional controls are extremists.

kill. There is no hard evidence to prove or disprove the thesis that lacking a gun, an enraged person will resort to a knife or other weapon. But there is evidence demonstrating that the fatality rate of firearms attacks is more than four times greater than the fatality rate of knife attacks (knives being the next most frequent and lethal weapon used in homicides). Thus, even if the number of violent attacks did not go down, the number of fatalities resulting from violent attacks would be substantially reduced if the attackers did not have guns.

The deadliness of firearms is perhaps best illustrated by the fact that they are virtually the only weapons used in killing police officers. Policemen are armed. They are trained in the skills of self-defense. They expect trouble and are prepared for it. Yet, from 1960 through 1967, 411 police officers were killed in the course of their official duties—76 of them in 1967 alone. Guns were used in 96 per cent of these fatal attacks on police.

In assassinations, guns play a crucial role because they extend the deadliness and the effectiveness of the assassin. Of the nine assassination attempts on American presidents or presidential candidates, all involved firearms. All, except the assassination of President Kennedy, involved handguns.

Guns also play an increasingly deadly role in aggravated assault and robbery. In 1968, 23 per cent of all aggravated assaults were committed with guns, as opposed to only 13 per cent in 1963. One out of every three robberies (two out of every three *armed* robberies) is committed with a gun, and the fatality rate for victims of firearms robberies is almost four times as great as for victims of other armed robberies.

In all these violent crimes, handguns are the weapon predominantly used. Although only slightly more than one-fourth (or 24 million) of the firearms in the nation are handguns, they account for about half of all homicides and three-fourths of all firearms homicides. When firearms are involved in aggravated assaults and robberies in large cities, the handgun is almost invariably the weapon used.

3. Firearms and Self-defense

> *We find that firearms in the home are probably of less value than commonly thought in defending the householder's life against intruders, but that firearms in business establishments may sometimes be effective in defending against robberies.*

It may seem incongruous that in our advanced and civilized society individual citizens should feel the need to keep a gun for self-protection. Yet a 1966 public opinion survey, conducted for the President's Commission on Law Enforcement and the Administration of Justice, disclosed that more than 22 million households (37 per cent of the total and 66 per cent of the households with guns) include self-defense as one reason, among others, for owning a firearm. Since many owners keep their guns in the home for protection against intruders, it is important to assess, to the extent possible, the nature of the threat from intruders and the chances of gun owners to defend themselves successfully with their weapons.

What is the nature of the threat in the home? The number of killings in the home by burglars and robbers [2] is not large relative to the total number of homicides. Burglars usually try to avoid contact with the home-owner: they rely on stealth and are more likely to flee than fight when discovered. The robber poses a much greater threat to the personal safety of the occupant of the house, but robberies occur in the home far less often than in other places.[3] Because of these factors, studies in several cities indicate that killings in the home by robbers and burglars account for no more than 2 per cent or 3 per cent of all criminal homicides.[4]

What are the householder's chances of successfully defending himself with a gun? In only a relatively small number of instances do home robberies or burglaries result in the death of the victim. Examination shows that in the great majority of the cases, the householder had no warning and thus no chance to arm himself with a gun. Studies in Los Angeles and Detroit indicate that only about two per cent of home robberies, and two-tenths of one per cent of home burglaries, result in the firearms death or injury of the intruder at the hands of the householder.[5] Moreover, in considering the value of handguns, or firearms generally, for self-defense in the home, one must also take into account the risks associated with home possession of a gun. A substantial number of the 23,000 annual firearms accidents occur in the home. Of the 8,000 annual firearms homicides, a large percentage occur among family members or acquaintances, and many of these also occur in the home.

From the standpoint of the individual householder, then, the self-defense firearm appears to be a dangerous investment. The existence of guns in one-half of America's homes may deter intruders. One may assume a robber is reluctant to ply his trade in homes rather than on the street

[2] Robbery involves taking property by force; burglary involves illegal entry without force against the person.

[3] The 17-city victim-offender survey conducted by our Task Force on Individual Acts of Violence shows an average of 6 percent of armed robberies occurring in the home.

[4] Home intrusions resulting in sexual attacks are also a threat, but they occur much less frequently than commonly believed. Our victim-offender survey suggests that substantially less than one-fourth of the 27,000 rapes or rape attempts reported in the United States each year are committed by intruding strangers in the home. Since about 20,000 robberies (armed and unarmed) and 800,000 burglaries occur annually in the home, not more than three-quarters of one percent of home intrusions result in an attempted rape.

[5] No data are available on how frequently robberies and burglaries are foiled by the householder's display of a gun that is not fired. Nor are data available on use of guns by women to prevent attempted rapes; presumably this occurs extremely infrequently.

because of the possibility that he may encounter an alert, armed house-holder. Our Task Force made an effort to study the extent of this deter-rence, but was unable to arrive at any firm conclusion. The evidence is convincing, however, that the home robber most often has the advantage of surprise, and the armed segment of our population is paying a heavy price in accidents and in the shooting of family members, friends and acquaintances for whatever deterrent effect their possession of self-defense firearms may be providing. In a more rational world, home intrusion would be deterred by other means—such as non-lethal weapons, alarm systems, and other security arrangements—that are less dangerous to the occupants of the home.

Burglars and robbers also threaten businesses, and firearms are fre-quently kept in places of business for protection. Such firearms are useful primarily against robbers, since burglars usually break and enter after the business has closed. Research to date does not permit us to draw firm conclusions as to the net usefulness of self-defense firearms possessed by storeowners and other businessmen. We do know, however, that business self-defense firearms do *not* cause the great number of accidents caused by home firearms or involve the same risk of homicide to family members and friends. Thus, the home and the business establishment must be clearly distinguished from each other when considering the usefulness of firearms for self-defense.

4. Firearms Control in the United States

A national firearms policy which significantly reduces the availability of handguns will reduce the amount of firearms violence.

The United States still does not have an effective national firearms policy. Federal gun laws have been passed largely in response to sensa-tional episodes of gun violence. In general the approach of these laws has been to use federal power merely to curtail interstate movements of firearms, leaving each of the states free to adopt the degree and kind of internal control it wished. Moreover, even this limited policy objective was not effectively implemented. It was perfectly legal, until the passage of the Gun Control Act of 1968, to sell or ship weapons from a state which had little or no firearms control to persons in a state with a stricter system. Since attempts to establish uniform state and local firearms laws never succeeded, the few serious efforts at state and local regulation (as in Massachusetts and New York) have been consistently frustrated by the flow of firearms from jurisdictions with looser or no controls.

Under this patchwork statutory regime, our firearms population has grown to the point where guns are readily available to everyone—legally in most cases, illegally in the rest. The Gun Control Act of 1968 does curtail imports of cheap foreign firearms; it significantly restricts mail order and interstate gun shipments to individuals; and it forbids the possession of handguns by convicted felons and other dangerous classes. But the 1968 Act is not designed to affect either the overall size of the tremendous United States gun population which is the legacy of past firearms policies, or the hand-to-hand or "street" sales of second-hand guns. Yet such sales appear to be the major source of the firearms used in crime. We have learned that almost half of all rifles and shotguns and more than half of all handguns are acquired second-hand—usually from a friend or other private party.

Our lack of an effective national firearms policy is primarily the result of our culture's casual attitude toward firearms and its heritage of the armed, self-reliant citizen. These are the factors that have prevented passage of effective gun regulation legislation in the United States. Guns are routinely carried in pockets and left in closets, corners, and bureau drawers. In many parts of the country, they are standard equipment in pickup trucks and small businesses. Nearly 15 million licensed hunters make extensive use of firearms for sporting purposes. The hero of American movies and television is the man with a gun—the soldier, cowboy, spy, sheriff, or criminal—and our children accumulate an arsenal of toy guns. Accustomed to firearms, convinced that they are household necessities, entertained by fiction and drama that portray the gun as a glamorous instrument of personal justice, many Americans underestimate the consequences of widespread firearms availability.

Despite the acceptance of guns as a common part of everyday American life, there is also a growing realization in the United States of the social costs of ineffective gun control. On the one hand, firearms manufacturers are on record as favoring the requirement of an identification card for firearms owners and denying gun ownership to felons and mental and physical incompetents. On the other hand, advocates of strict gun control are increasingly inclined to acknowledge the legitimate use of guns by sportsmen. Both the President's Commission on Law Enforcement and the Administration of Justice in 1967 and the National Advisory Commission on Civil Disorders in 1968 recommend that the federal government and the states should act to strengthen the presently inadequate firearms control laws.

In determining what our national firearms policy should be, it is necessary to keep clearly in mind that just as the term "firearms" includes different kinds of weapons which contribute unequally to violence, so also does the phrase "gun control" comprise a number of quite separate ideas. Four different strategies of gun control can be identified, though in legislative measures the strategies are often found in various combinations.

1. REGISTRATION OF FIREARMS. Registration is designed to provide a record of all persons who own firearms as well as the firearms they own. Proponents point out that registration would help police trace weapons and thus deter a registered owner from criminal use or illegal transfer of his firearm. Opponents of registration reply that criminals will not register firearms and that the registration process is costly.

2. PROHIBITION OF GUN OWNERSHIP BY CERTAIN CLASSES OF PERSONS (FELONS, ADDICTS, ETC.). This type of control is put forward as making it more difficult for poor gun risks to obtain firearms from legitimate sources. Licensing and investigation of applicants are often utilized as part of this strategy. Opponents argue that the prohibited class can still obtain guns by theft or in the hand-to-hand market, while legitimate users are caused added inconvenience.

3. INCREASED CRIMINAL PENALTIES FOR THE USE OF GUNS IN CRIME. Increased penalties are urged as a means to deter criminals from using firearms. Opponents point out that existing penalties for violent crime are already severe and that an extra measure of punishment will have little additional deterrent effect.

4. RESTRICTIVE LICENSING. This method requires all persons seeking to buy a particular type of firearm, typically a handgun, to demonstrate to the authorities an affirmative need to own the firearm. Its proponents urge that alone among the four control strategies, restrictive licensing is designed to reduce substantially the number of handguns in circulation. Its opponents note that restrictive licensing systems require the surrender of many previously lawful firearms, and amount to "confiscation."

Can any of these systems of firearms control be expected to reduce firearms violence? Some argue that with 90 million firearms in our country, no system of control will prevent persons from obtaining guns and using them illegally. The criminal, they declare, can always get a gun. The argument is not without merit, for it points the way to the steps which must be taken.

Our studies have convinced us that the heart of any effective national firearms policy for the United States must be to reduce the availability of the firearm that contributes the most to violence. *This means restrictive licensing of the handgun.* We believe, on the basis of all the evidence before us, that reducing the availability of the handgun *will* reduce firearms violence.

Although no other nation in history has ever attempted to institute firearms control with so many guns already dispersed throughout all segments of the population, foreign crime statistics provide some encouraging insights into the possible results of stricter control of the handgun in the

United States. Thus in England and Wales, with restrictive licensing systems and with much lower rates of violent crime than the United States, only 18 per cent of homicides in 1967 were committed with firearms weapons, as compared to 64 per cent in the United States. Only 6 per cent of all robberies in England and Wales in 1967 involved guns, as compared to 36 per cent in the United States. These lower rates of homicides and armed robberies and, more importantly, of firearms usage in such crimes suggest that a system which makes it substantially more difficult to obtain firearms can reduce the use of firearms in violent behavior and consequently can reduce both the frequency and the dangerousness of such behavior. In England and Wales the criminal cannot—or at least does not—always get a gun, and the public safety is much improved as a result.[6]

5. Recommendations for a National Firearms Policy

The Commission offers the following recommendations to reduce the role which firearms play in violence in the United States.

Public Education

- We urge a public education campaign, aided by the National Rifle Association and other private organizations devoted to hunting and sport shooting, to stress the duties and responsibilities of firearms ownership so that a new awareness of the proper role of firearms in American life can prevail in the more than 30 million homes which possess firearms. In particular, we urge the nation's gun manufacturers to issue safety booklets with each gun that they sell and to administer safety tests by mail to purchasers, based upon these booklets.
- We urge individual citizens—particularly on the basis of the statistics on firearms accidents—to reflect carefully before deciding that loaded firearms are necessary or desirable for self-defense in their homes.

Research

- We urge that further research be undertaken on the relationships between firearms and violence and on the measures that can reduce firearms violence. Further work should especially be done on how firearms accidents occur and can be prevented and on the psychological impact of guns on criminals.

[6] Comparison of firearms crimes in cities within the United States, although complicated by the problem of "leakage" across state lines, also shows that rates of firearm use in violence are lowest in the Northeast where firearms possession rates are the lowest.

- Further research is also needed as part of the effort to design firearm control systems that are no more restrictive than necessary and which minimize costs to firearms users and to the community as a whole.
- Scientific research should be intensified on devices to assist law enforcement personnel in detecting the presence of concealed firearms on the person.
- The Federal Government should join with private industry to speed the development of an effective non-lethal weapon. We consider this recommendation to be of the utmost importance. So long as crime rates mount in this nation and civil disorders threaten, law-abiding Americans understandably fear for their safety. An effective non-lethal weapon could serve defensive needs without risk to human life.

Legislation

We conclude that the rising tide of firearms violence in this country merits further legislative action at the present time.

It is the ready availability of the handgun, so often a weapon of crime and so infrequently a sporting arm, that is the most serious part of the current firearms problem in this country. The time has come to bring the handgun under reasonable control.

A restrictive licensing system for handguns is needed. State governments should be given the first opportunity to establish such systems in conformity with minimum federal standards that afford considerable discretion to each state to adopt a system suitable to its own needs. Accordingly—

- We recommend federal legislation to encourage the establishment of state licensing systems for handguns. The federal legislation would introduce a federal system of handgun licensing, applicable only to those states which within a four-year period fail to enact a state law that (1) establishes a standard for determining an individual's need for a handgun and for the licensing of an individual who shows such a need and (2) prohibits all others from possessing handguns or buying handgun ammunition.

We propose that the states be permitted to determine for themselves what constitutes "need" to own a handgun. For the federal system applicable to states which fail to enact their own licensing systems, we recommend that determinations of need be limited to police officers and security guards, small businesses in high crime areas, and others with a special need for self-protection. At least in major metropolitan areas, the federal system should *not* consider normal household self-protection a sufficient showing of need to have a handgun.

We also recommend that a system of federal administrative or judi-

cial review be established to assure that each state system is administered fairly and does not discriminate on the basis of race, religion,
national origin, or other unconstitutional grounds.

We note that it will be necessary to compensate those handgun owners
who are required to give up previously lawful firearms; this cost,
which should be borne by the Federal Government, could amount
to $500 million.

Finally, we emphasize that laws controlling handguns should provide serious penalties for the possession of such guns by unlicensed
persons. The apprehension of such persons should in time greatly
reduce the rate of violent crime in the United States.

SHOTGUNS AND RIFLES. These are far less of a threat than handguns, particularly in the area of violent crime. At the same time, legitimate use of
the long gun is widespread. The significant differences between handguns
and long guns call for substantially different control strategies. We can
make substantial inroads on firearms violence without imposing major
inconveniences on hunters and skeet and trap shooters, and without im-
peding other legitimate activities of millions of long gun owners. Accordingly—

• We recommend federal legislation to establish minimum standards for
state regulation of long guns under which (1) an identification card
would be required for long gun owners and purchasers of long gun
ammunition (a system similar to that recommended by gun manufacturers) and (2) any person 18 and over would be entitled to such a
card, except certain classes of criminals and adjudicated incompetents.
For states which do not adopt such regulations within four years, a
federal regulatory system would be established.

• We do *not* recommend federal legislation to require nationwide registration of existing long guns. Substantially the same benefits could be
obtained from less costly and burdensome control strategies.

• We *do* recommend that persons who *transfer* long guns be required
to fill out a single card giving the serial number, type, make, and model
of the weapon, the transferee's social security and firearms identification card numbers, the transferor's name and social security number,
and the date of the transaction.

Supplementary Measures

Restrictive licensing of handguns and the simple identification card
system for long guns represent the key legislative recommendations of
this Commission in the area of gun control. There are, however, a number
of other important goals which uniform and effective gun control legisla-

tion should accomplish. We urge the nation's lawmakers to consider them.

First, the Gun Control Act of 1968, which is intended to curtail the import of firearms unsuitable for sporting use, should be extended to prohibit domestic production and sale of "junk guns." Second, a federal firearms information center should be established to accumulate and store information on firearms and owners received from state agencies; this information would be available to state and federal law enforcement agencies. Third, licensed gun dealers should be required by federal statute to adopt and maintain security procedures to minimize theft of firearms.

6. Conclusion

An effective national firearms policy would help to reduce gun violence in the United States. It would also have a significance beyond the question of firearms. In comparison with most of the causes of violence in America, the firearms problem is concrete and manageable. But it is also complex and emotion-laden. For the United States to move effectively toward its solution would signify a new ability to transcend our violent past.

Separate Statement

Four members of the Commission (Senator Roman L. Hruska, Judge Ernest W. McFarland, Congressman Hale Boggs, and Leon Jaworski) state that there is a great deal with which they agree in the report on "Firearms and Violence." They feel, however, that the needs are not the same in the various States, or, for that matter, in all parts of a State. It is their opinion that each State should be permitted to determine for itself without additional restrictions from the Federal Government the system which best meets its needs to control the use of both the handguns and the long guns. They are unable, therefore, to concur fully in the report of the Commission.

STATISTICAL APPENDIX

1. Total number of firearms in civilian hands (U.S., 1968):

Rifles:	35 million.
Shotguns:	31 million.
Handguns:	24 million.
Total:	90 million.

Source: Task Force Report, *Firearms and Violence in American Life* (National Commission on the Causes and Prevention of Violence. July, 1969).

2. Annual increase in number of firearms in civilian hands (U.S., 1962 vs. 1968):

Rifles:	1962, 0.7 million	1968, 1.4 million.
Shotguns:	1962, 0.7 million	1968, 1.4 million.
Handguns:	1962, 0.6 million	1968, 2.5 million.
Total:	1962, 2.1 million	1968, 5.3 million.

3. Mode of acquisition of firearms (U.S., 1968):

Rifles:	New, 56%	Used, 44%.
Shotguns:	New, 54%	Used, 46%.
Handguns:	New, 46%	Used, 54%.

Note: More than 50% of all acquisitions of used firearms are from private parties, rather than from stores.

4. Accidental deaths of civilians from firearms and other causes (U.S., 1967):

Motor Vehicles:	53,100
Falls:	19,800
Fires:	7,700
Drowning:	6,800
Firearms:	*2,800*
Poisons:	2,400
Machinery:	2,100

5. Total number of major violent offenses (U.S., 1964 vs. 1967):

Homicides:	1964, 9,250	1967, 12,100.
Aggravated Assaults:	1964, 200,000	1967, 253,300.
Robberies:	1964, 129,830	1967, 202,050.

6. Criminal uses of firearms (U.S., 1964 vs. 1967):

Homicides:	1967, 63% with firearms.	1964, 55% with firearms
Aggravated Assaults:	1967, 21% with firearms.	1964, 15% with firearms
Robberies:	1967, 37% with firearms.	1964, not available

7. Deadliness of firearms attacks vs. knife attacks (U.S., 1967):

Percentage of firearms attacks resulting in death: 12.8.
Percentage of knife attacks resulting in death: 2.9.

(Firearms attacks are thus 4.4 times as deadly as knife attacks.)

8. Type of gun used in crimes committed with firearms (large U.S. cities, 1967):

Homicide:	Long guns, 8%	Handguns, 92%.
Aggravated Assault:	Long guns, 14%	Handguns, 86%.
Robbery:	Long guns, 4%	Handguns, 96%.

Note: Handguns were used in 76% of gun homicides throughout the United States in 1967.

A Crash Program for Right to Drive

Art Buchwald

"The Committee to Abolish the Registration of Automobiles and the Licensing of Drivers" has just opened up a lobby in Washington and I was happy to visit with Roger Crash, their spokesman.

Mr. Crash said, "We have formed this organization because the constitutional rights of all automobile drivers are at stake. There is no reason why anybody should not be allowed to own and drive an automobile in this country without his rights being infringed by local, state and Federal authorities."

"Obviously you're against registration of vehicles, then?"

"We certainly are. Most people who drive should not be inconvenienced by some bureaucrat who wants to know what they intend to use a car for. There is a conspiracy in this country to get everyone to register their automobiles, so they eventually can be taken away from them."

"Who is behind the conspiracy?"

"The Communists. They know that America would collapse overnight if their automobiles were confiscated. This country is going through an hysterical period right now. They blame all the automobile deaths and accidents on the drivers. But you're not going to prevent accidents by asking people to register their vehicles. If somebody wants a car to kill somebody, he'll find it, no matter how many laws you have."

"You're also against driver's tests, aren't you?"

"We certainly are. Why should you penalize the law-abiding average driver by making him take a driver's test just to catch a few nuts who are outside the law?

"By asking someone to take a driver's test, you are subjecting him to indignity and guilt by association. You cannot punish the car-loving citizen who only uses his automobile for pleasure, in order to prevent accidents caused by lawless elements of our society."

"Mr. Crash, one of the arguments for registering automobiles and making people take driver's test is that it prevents the vehicles from getting into the hands of children, criminals, and unstable people who might cause accidents."

"The bleeding hearts and do-gooders use this argument all the time. But the automobile is part of our American birthright. Has it ever occurred

FROM the *Washington Post*, June 27, 1968. © 1968, The Washington Post Co. Reprinted by permission of the author.

to you that in every police state the dictators make their people register their automobiles and take driver's tests?"

"Is your society for doing away with traffic laws as well?"

"We are against anything that would inconvenience a driver in any way. People must be free to do what they want with their automobiles. Our economy depends on motor vehicles. Every time you pass a traffic law you discourage someone from buying a car. Traffic laws do not prevent accidents, people prevent accidents."

"How do you propose to repeal the registration and driving test laws that are now on the books?"

"By launching a mammoth letter campaign. We're going to ask everyone who owns a car to write his Congressman and Senator demanding the repeal of all laws having to do with motor vehicles. This is an election year and I assure you, our legislators are paying attention to their mail."

"I must admit you make a strong case against automobile controls. Do you think you have a chance?"

Mr. Crash replied, "there is now a big hue and cry about automobile accidents in this country, but it will die down soon. And then our lobby will really be able to go into action. We're tax-free, you know."

Questions

1. What kinds of arguments are made for and against the freedom to bear arms in this country? Which arguments seem to you the most successful, those based on statistics or those based on what are considered rational statements about "human nature"? Can you cite statistical arguments for and against the same point?

2. Which seem to you the most emotional arguments in this section? Which the most rational? Compare the two articles from the *Washington Post* as to detachment and objectivity.

3. What are the main arguments presented by Senator Tydings for gun control laws? What arguments against such laws are implied by the questions put to him?

4. Who seems in your opinion to present the strongest argument on either side of the debate? Can you explain why this argument carries so much weight for you?

5. How many different rhetorical positions are presented in this section? What is the difference in effect among news stories, editorials, interviews, arguments, and statistics?

6. How are the arguments by the officials of the National Rifle Association related to the arguments made by Senator Tydings and in the *Washington Post* editorial?

7. What is the point of the elaborate statistics on firearms in accidents and crime as collected by the National Rifle Association? Do you suppose that another organization gathering the same kinds of statistics might come up with different figures?

8. How do the points made in the statement of the official Commission on the Causes and Prevention of Violence, chaired by Dr. Milton Eisenhower,

differ from the points made by Mr. Orth? How is it that the statistics offered as an appendix by the Commission's statement differ from those offered by the National Rifle Association?

9. Do any of the arguments seem to be self-serving? In what ways? Does it really matter whether the National Rifle Association, dedicated to the promotion of the use of firearms in this country, makes a particularly compelling statistical argument against the regulation of firearms? Can you read its statistics without being troubled by their source?

10. Why do some persons argue that control of firearms is "communistic"? Why do some persons argue that the lack of control of firearms is "fascistic"? Do you see the justice in either of these arguments? Do you see where these arguments may fall short of persuasiveness or plausibility? Are some of the arguments against gun control laws similar to those used against sex education in the schools (see Section Eight)? How does the United States differ from other countries on the matter of firearms?

11. What are the principal differences between laws governing firearms and those governing switchblade knives or other weapons that can be used to attack people? What do you think are the arguments for not licensing all objects that can be used as weapons, such as knives, clubs, pieces of wood, stones, razor blades, and the like? Is this question a kind of reduction to absurdity? On which side of which argument? How does Art Buchwald's column contribute to the discussion?

Assignments

1. In parallel columns classify the arguments for and against licensing the possession of firearms.

2. Analyze the fine distinctions made by the various arguments. For example, what are the arguments against long guns as opposed to handguns?

3. Write a letter to your congressman or senator arguing for or against federal control of firearms in any form. Cite the statistics and arguments presented in this section.

4. Write an editorial similar in length and in tone to the one in the *Washington Post* arguing against gun control laws. Try to analyze the character of your argument.

5. Write an essay discussing the relationship between arguments against gun control laws and arguments in favor of the death penalty (Section Thirteen).

Additional Reading

The most extensive literature opposing gun control legislation may be obtained upon request from the National Rifle Association, 1600 Rhode Island Avenue, N.W., Washington, D.C. 20036. The usual reader's guides in libraries will contain specific magazine articles. One of the more interesting is that by Mayor John V. Lindsay of New York in the *Saturday Evening Post* for February 1, 1964, "Too Many People Have Guns."

Method

and Madness

Mental Illness Is a Myth

Thomas S. Szasz

On Feb. 28, 1966, the United States Court of Appeals for the Second Circuit handed down a decision which displaced the time-honored M'Naghten Rule as a test of criminal insanity, and substituted for it a new rule recommended by the American Law Institute.

The M'Naghten Rule dates from 1843, when one Daniel M'Naghten shot and killed a man named Drummond, the private secretary of Sir Robert Peel, whom M'Naghten had intended to kill. At M'Naghten's trial, evidence was introduced showing that he "was laboring under an insane delusion" of being hounded by enemies, among them Peel. The jury found him "not guilty, on the ground of insanity."

De jure, M'Naghten was acquitted; *de facto,* he was sentenced to life imprisonment in an insane asylum. He died in 1865, having been incarcerated for the last 22 years of his life.

The new ruling (binding on Federal courts in New York, Connecticut and Vermont) provides that: "A person is not responsible for criminal conduct if at the time of such conduct as a result of mental disease or defect he lacks substantial capacity either to appreciate the wrongfulness of his conduct or to conform his conduct to the requirements of law."

Both of these tests—and others, whatever their semantic differences— rest on the premise that the human mind may become "diseased," and that a person who has a "diseased mind" may, because of it, commit criminal acts unintentionally, not know the difference between right and wrong, or be unable to restrain himself from engaging in conduct prohibited by law. The value of all psychiatric tests of criminal responsibility thus hinges on the soundness of this underlying concept of "mental disease."

But what exactly is mental disease? If it is an illness, what kind is it? And if it is not an illness, what is it and why is it called an illness? Because of the frequency with which issues of mental health and illness arise not only in criminal cases but in matters of everyday life, it is important that we ask these questions and intelligently debate various possible answers to them.

I submit that mental illness is a myth. Bodies are physical objects;

FROM *The New York Times Magazine,* June 12, 1966. © 1966 by The New York Times Company. Reprinted with the permission of *The New York Times* and Thomas S. Szasz.

minds, whatever they may be, are not physical objects. Accordingly, mental diseases (such as depression or schizophrenia) cannot exist in the sense in which bodily diseases (such as broken bones or ulcerated skins) exist.

My disbelief in mental illness does not mean that I reject any facts of human behavior. "A myth," says the British philosopher Gilbert Ryle, "is not a fairy story. It is the presentation of facts belonging in one category in the idiom belonging to another. To explode a myth is accordingly not to deny facts, but to reallocate them." To say that mental illness is a myth is therefore not to *deny* facts (such as sadness or fear) but to *reallocate* them (from the category of mental illness to the category of personal conduct). Insofar as men are human beings, not machines, they always have some choice in how they act—hence, they are always responsible for their conduct. There is method in madness, no less than in sanity.

As long ago as the early nineteen-twenties, George H. Mead formulated the thesis that social situations—and human behavior in them—are analogous to games which must be played by certain "rules." In life, the games are infinite. As social conditions undergo rapid change, old games are constantly scrapped and new ones started. But most people are totally unprepared to shift from one type of game playing to another. They have early in life learned one set of rules—or, at most, a few—and find themselves forced to play new games by the old rules. This fundamental conflict leads to various problems in living—some severe enough to be commonly diagnosed as "mental illness" or "disease." It is these problems in living that the psychiatrist is usually called on to treat.

"But surely," someone might say, "a dope fiend, a rapist, or a Lee Harvey Oswald is not a *normal* person. What difference does it make whether we call him sick or something else?"

It makes, of course, all the difference in the world, for what we call things, and especially people, will shape our attitudes and justify our actions toward them. For example, when socially threatening behavior is called "witchcraft," it is handled by means of theological sanctions; when it is called "crime," it is handled by means of judicial sanctions; and when it is called "mental illness," it is handled by means of psychiatric sanctions.

The practices of modern American psychiatrists originate from two principal sources: hospital psychiatry and psychoanalysis.

Institutions for the care of the insane have existed since antiquity. However, the systematic confinement of madmen in buildings labeled "hospitals" did not begin until the middle of the 17th century. For about 250 years, from 1650 to 1900, the psychiatrist worked almost exclusively in the mental hospital. The alienist, as he was then called, was employed by an institution—a private or, more often, a public insane asylum.

The historical model and social prototype of the modern mental hospital is the French Hôpital Général. According to the distinguished medical historian George Rosen, the purposes of this institutional system were three-fold: "In part they were economic: to increase [the] manufacture [of goods], provide productive work for the able-bodied, and to end unemployment; in part social: to punish willful idleness, restore public order, and rid Paris of beggars; and in part, religious and moral: to relieve the needy, the ill and suffering, to deal with immorality and antisocial behavior, and to provide Christian instruction."

A few years after its foundation, the Hôpital Général of Paris alone contained 6,000 persons, or about 1 per cent of the population. Who were these "mentally ill" people? According to regulations issued in 1680, "children of artisans and other poor inhabitants of Paris up to the age of 25 . . . girls who were debauched or in evident danger of being debauched . . . [and] wayward children . . ." were among those listed as proper subjects for confinement. In addition, old people, persons with venereal diseases, epileptics, vagrants, prostitutes—in brief, all of society's *"misérables"*—were incarcerated in the Hôpital Général. Michel Foucault, a French student of psychiatric history, thus concludes: "The Hôpital Général is not a medical establishment. It is rather a sort of semijudicial structure, an administrative entity which, along with already constituted powers, and outside the courts, decides, judges and executes."

The facts I have cited are important in showing us one of the roles of the psychiatrist—indeed, his traditional role: He is a physician working in a mental hospital, employed, as a rule, by the state, and charged with the task of confining and "treating" people who are considered "insane." Although some of his methods have changed, the social role of the institutional psychiatrist has remained what it has always been.

Nor is its importance diminished. At the present time in the United States, approximately 750,000 persons are incarcerated in mental hospitals —90 per cent of them against their will. This is about three times the number of persons imprisoned in jails.

The mental hospital is also important for the psychiatrist: Of 15,200 practicing psychiatrists in the United States, approximately 50 per cent are in institutional practice, most of them in mental hospitals, or in related administrative positions.

I do not imply that the hospital psychiatrist does not try to help his patient, but rather that his interpretation of "helping" is different from the patient's. If one person has the power to confine another, and uses it, it seems inevitable that the confined person will consider the other his jailer. This point of view, often held by mental patients, was expressed by Valentine Alamazov, the protagonist of Valeriy Tarsis's autobiographical novel *Ward 7*. Finding himself incarcerated in a mental hospital, Alamazov had this to say to his psychiatrist:

"I don't regard you as a doctor. You call this a hospital, I call it a prison. . . . So, now, let's get everything straight. I am your prisoner, you are my jailer, and there isn't going to be any nonsense about my health . . . or about examination and treatment."

It was Sigmund Freud who created the second major form of contemporary American psychiatric practice—psychoanalysis.

In the eighteen-eighties, when Freud was a young physician, to be a psychiatrist was to be an alienist or hospital psychiatrist. Traditionally, the psychiatrist was called in by a "mentally healthy" member of the family to treat one of its "mentally sick" members; often this meant removing the sick member from the family and putting him in a mental hospital as a "patient."

Freud departed from this traditional approach. Instead of acting as the agent of the family—ostensibly caring for the patient, but actually protecting the family from him—Freud created a new professional role—the agent of the patient.

He did not accept the situation as it was presented to him, usually by the patient's family. Instead, he listened at length to the patient to ascertain how he perceived his problem; and he tried to help him realize his own aspirations and goals, even if these brought the patient, or Freud himself, into even greater conflict with the family or with society.

Thus, ethically, Freud acted like other physicians, but unlike other psychiatrists: He tried to help his patient, not someone else. By systematically refusing to "treat" patients who did not want to be treated by him, Freud departed from the accepted psychiatric methods of his day. Many psychoanalysts still adhere to this principle in treating patients. Most hospital psychiatrists do not.

It is important to note also that Freud characterized psychoanalytic treatment in humanistic and pedagogic terms and did not regard his work as medical. Psychoanalysis was never intended to make "sick" people "well" again. The analyst's task, in Freud's words, was "to serve the patient . . . as a teacher and educator."

Freud was emphatic that the analyst—and hence also the psychotherapist who only listens and talks and uses no "medical" methods—does not cure disease. Indeed, although the three great pioneers of psychoanalysis—Freud, Adler and Jung—had little good to say about one another's doctrines and methods in later years, they all agreed on one thing: that psychological methods of therapy are *not* medical procedures.

We are now ready to reconsider the question: What is mental illness? In order to do this, it is necessary to understand the principal uses of the concept of mental illness and their social consequences.

First, the term "mental illness" is used to refer to certain types of bodily diseases—that is, to diseases of the brain whose predominant symptoms are abnormalities of behavior (for example, neurosyphilis). According to one school of psychiatric thought, all mental diseases are of this type. Those who hold this view assume that some metabolic, genetic or neurological defect—perhaps a very subtle one—will ultimately be found to explain all disorders of thinking and behavior now called "mental illness."

No one would deny that, like any other part of the body, the brain may be injured or become diseased. Nor are there, to my knowledge, any psychiatrists who would deny that some of the people nowadays diagnosed as mentally ill (and free of demonstrable organic disease) might actually be suffering from the effects of as yet undiscovered neurologic or metabolic disease processes. But for those who regard mental illness as a type of brain disease, the concept of mental illness is unnecessary and misleading. If they mean that people labeled mentally ill suffer from diseases of the brain, it would seem better for the sake of clarity to say that and not something else.

The second major use of the term "mental illness" is to denote a "functional" or "psychological" disorder. Proponents of this view admit that patients called "mentally ill" do not suffer from bodily diseases, but they maintain that such individuals exhibit defects or deformations of their personalities so severe as to justify calling them "ill."

When physicians (or others) label people as "sick" merely because their actions differ from those of their fellows, they speak metaphorically —as poets, not scientists. To be sure, this kind of metaphoric use of the term "sick" is not limited to psychiatry: People also say that our economy is "sick," that a joke is "sick" or that someone they dislike makes them "sick." Yet only in connection with mental illness do we systematically act as if figure of speech were fact. No one believes that "sick economies" require medical help, but nearly everyone believes that "sick minds" do.

The power to name, or to classify, is the basis for the third use of the term "mental illness"—that is, to denote a deviant social role. For our purposes it is necessary only to distinguish between two types of social roles: those that are assumed voluntarily, such as husband or graduate student, and those that are ascribed to a person against his will, such as draftee or convicted criminal.

Roles are social artifacts. Role deviance, therefore, has meaning only in the context of specific social customs and laws. The criminal is deviant because he breaks the law; the homosexual because most people are heterosexuals; the atheist because most people believe—or say they believe —in God. In the same way, the so-called "potential killer" (who, however, has not yet killed anyone) is considered deviant because he appears to be more dangerous than most people; and so is the chronically withdrawn mental-hospital patient, because most people are—and are expected to be—socially more responsive. (I shall say more about the problems that such persons pose for those about them, and for society in general, later on.)

But which kinds of social deviance constitute "mental illness"? The answer is: that conduct which deviates from psychiatrically defined rules for mental health.

However obvious this may be, its implications for our understanding of mental illness seem to be vastly unappreciated. The fact is that every time psychiatrists formulate a new rule of mental health they create a new class of mentally sick individuals. For example, the proposition that prejudice against Jews or Negroes is a manifestation of psycho-pathology —one of many instances in the contemporary inflation of the concept of mental illness—is nothing but an attempt to expand the category of people who can be legitimately classified as psychologically sick.

Since the consequences of being labeled mentally ill include such penalties as personal degradation, loss of employment, loss of the right to drive a car, to vote, to make valid contracts or to stand trial—and, last but not least, incarceration in a mental hospital, possibly for life—the expansion of the category of people who can be so designated is useful for the increased employment of psychiatric methods of social control.

Labeling someone mentally ill is a special kind of name-calling. In other fields name-calling may constitute libel, but calling someone "mentally sick" does not. The main reason for this is that the psychiatrist who makes a diagnosis of mental illness (especially on an involuntary patient) has more social power than the person he diagnoses.

The role of power in the psychiatric diagnostic process becomes obvious only when the potential patient is a Very Important Person. When someone like Secretary of Defense Forrestal disturbs people by his ideas and actions, it is difficult to get a psychiatrist to label him mentally ill. The reason for this is that by casting the individual in a socially deviant role the psychiatric diagnostician imparts a negative, debased identity to that person. This he cannot do if his intended "patient" is socially more powerful than he is. When a mental-hospital superintendent in Louisiana tried to incarcerate and "treat" Governor Earl Long, the Governor fired the doctor—and walked out of the hospital.

One of the traditional problems of legal psychiatry, as we saw at the outset, is the determination of criminal insanity. Lawyers and psychiatrists persist in trying to distinguish between "sane" and "insane" criminals, and in finding a "scientific" basis for determining which offenders ought to be "punished" with imprisonment and which "treated" with involuntary mental hospitalization.

I submit that criminal insanity is a metaphorical and strategic concept just as civil insanity is. The effort to distinguish, by psychiatric methods, among different classes of criminals is really an exercise in second-order classification: Having labeled some persons as "criminals," we have the option of labeling them also as "mentally healthy," and dealing with them by means of penal sanctions, or as "mentally ill" (that is, as "criminally insane"), and dealing with them by means of psychiatric sanctions.

I do not believe that insanity should be an "excusing condition" for crime. Lawbreakers, irrespective of their "mental health" ought to be treated as offenders.

Another classic dilemma of psychiatry is the problem of what society should do with its "insane" citizens who, while having committed no crime, lack "insight" into their "illness" and hence do not seek "treatment." Here we should distinguish between two fundamentally different types of psychiatric practice. The person who decides to consult a psychiatrist and pays him for his services is like a graduate student pursuing a course of study: he assumes the role of mental patient (if we wish so to label his role) *voluntarily* and is free to cast it off. By contrast, the person who is coerced into psychiatric treatment by his relatives or by the law, and who does not pay the psychiatrist for his services, is like a prisoner sentenced to a term of servitude; he is placed in the role of mental patient *against his will* and is not free to cast it off.

The psychiatrist thus has a choice between doing something *to* his patient and doing something *for* him. One of the things the psychiatrist can do to his patient is to prescribe certain life games, with the expectation that these will pacify the patient's family and social environment— and perhaps also "help" the patient. Since this kind of treatment is carried out against the wishes of the patient, it requires coercion.

One of the things the psychiatrist can do for his patient is to analyze his life games, with the expectation that this understanding will help the client to lead a life more free and responsible. To do this, however, requires a voluntary, cooperating client. Coercion has no place whatever in this type of psychiatric work. Such a psychiatrist aspires to be on tap, not on top.

The reader who finds this thesis persuasive might wonder about its practical application. If we look upon mental illness as a metaphor and a social role, rather than as a disease, how will this affect what we *do*?

For work with voluntary clients the consequence would be mainly professional and economic: The humanistic view of mental illness would open opportunities for training nonmedical persons (psychologists, social workers and others) in psychotherapy and psychoanalysis, and would eliminate the rationale for preventing such persons from engaging in the independent practice of these skills.

For work with involuntary clients the consequences would be mainly legal and social: The humanistic view of mental illness would remove the justification for involuntary mental hospitalization and treatment; accordingly, it would require the mobilization of fresh personal efforts and social resources to cope with problems now dealt with by means of traditional psychiatric methods.

It would be impossible suddenly to empty out our mental hospitals and to stop all commitments—though, to be sure, I consider these desirable goals. To attain them, however, we must provide suitable alternatives to the present social functions of involuntary mental hospitalization. I must limit myself here to mentioning only a few such alternatives, each directed toward ameliorating a specific type of human problem.

The usual justification for commitment is that the person whose confinement is sought is "dangerous to himself or others." My position is based on a principle enunciated more than 100 years ago by John Stuart Mill: "The only purpose for which power can be rightfully exercised over any member of a civilized community, against his will, is to prevent harm to others. His own good, either physical or moral, is not sufficient warranty."

Suicide, for example, should be recognized as a basic human right. The threat of suicide, or an attempt at suicide, should not be ground for involuntary mental hospitalization. (This does not mean that a physician should not treat a person who, say, is unconscious as a result of an overdose of barbiturates. It does mean that, after the patient has regained consciousness he should not be confined in a hospital against his will.)

While being "dangerous to oneself" should never be considered a legitimate reason for depriving a person of his liberty, being "dangerous to others"—if it involves breaking the law—is the best reason for doing so. One of the main functions of society is to prevent violence among its members. Thus, if individuals commit violence, or threaten to do so, they should be treated for what they are—lawbreakers.

Judicial sentencing of lawbreakers does not deprive us of the opportunity of also trying to help them. If we truly believe that some lawbreakers are "mentally ill," we could offer them psychiatric help in prison. As always, the clients ought to be free to accept or reject such help.

The social control, by means of psychiatric sanctions, of dangerous behavior is complicated by the fact that people often disagree on what constitutes "dangerousness," and, even if they agree on it, on how such "dangerousness" is to be established. Thus, one group of persons now often committed is composed of individuals who manage their lives more or less adequately, but who break certain laws or social customs, and are therefore considered "dangerous" and treated as involuntary patients.

If we wish to avoid using coercive psychiatric measures against persons of this type, we have two basic options. Instead of constantly proliferating legislation prohibiting various kinds of personal conduct not directly injurious to others (as we now do), we might consider repealing and eschewing such legislation. We would thereby eliminate many types of "crime," and hence the need to define such criminals (as "dope addicts," "homosexuals" and so forth) as mentally sick. Or, if we wish to persist in our efforts to control private behavior by means of criminal sanctions, we might decide that it is more humane to punish persons who transgress these prohibitions by means of penal rather than psychiatric sanctions; the result would be the jailing of many individuals now committed to mental hospitals. (The desirability of confining lawbreakers in mental hospitals rather than in prisons is sometimes advocated on the allegedly humanitarian ground that conditions in mental hospitals are better than in jails.

Even if this were true—and as a rule it is not—it would not justify re-defining lawbreakers as patients. The proper remedy for inadequate prisons is prison reform.)

In addition to persons whose dangerousness is actual, established by what they have done, there are those whose dangerousness is potential, who are feared for what they might do. We often hear of "potential trouble-makers" who, however, have broken no laws, and hence could not be convicted of crime, but whom many would like to "diagnose" as "deranged" and restrain in mental hospitals.

We cannot eat our cake and have it, too: we cannot have a free society and imprison—in jails or mental hospitals—people who have broken no law. This does not mean that some people might not be "potentially" dangerous to others (indeed, many, like drunken drivers, are very danger-ous); it means only that we cannot restrain such people through our mental-hygiene laws without gravely injuring the entire fabric of our society.

Another large group of persons confined involuntarily in mental hospitals is the aged; in some public mental hospitals as many as one-third of the inmates fall into this group. Yet, even hospital psychiatrists admit that many of these patients do not need mental-hospital care. "Only 50 per cent of the [elderly] patients . . . hospitalized required hospitali-zation in a mental institution," testified Dr. Dale C. Cameron, superin-tendent of St. Elizabeth's Hospital in Washington, before a House committee. "For many older patients," he added, "the primary need was found to be for physical rather than psychiatric care."

The fact that public mental hospitals accept geriatric patients—whose "mental illness" is so clearly a strategic concept designed to justify their forcible removal to places of custody—diminishes the pressure of society to provide suitable accommodations for them.

Still another group of involuntarily hospitalized patients is composed of individuals who present so-called psychiatric emergencies. Examples are the young man who becomes uncommunicative, does not leave his room, refuses to eat, perhaps even soils himself; or the young woman who faints and thereafter remains unresponsive and acts as if she were un-conscious.

Patients of this type do not object to being hospitalized or to receiving medical care. Moreover, some of them suffer from bodily illness—brain tumor, head injury, uncontrolled diabetes. Others develop medical prob-lems as a result of their behavior—severe dehydration because of failure to eat and drink, for example. Such patients should therefore be hos-pitalized in medical, not mental, hospitals, and should be treated as medical emergencies. Consent for hospitalization and treatment should be given by relatives, and confinement should last only until the patient has regained his powers.

The application of these principles to the care of chronic mental patients would help us to avoid coercion in their care as well. Regardless of the cause—subtle malfunctions of the brain, the effect of prolonged institutionalization or flight from communal existence into a world of private dreams—people who are almost completely unable to cope with their problems of living will no doubt always be with us. Such "non-dangerous" but gravely disabled individuals could be dealt with by offering them care—good and attractive enough so that they would willingly accept it—while leaving them free to make other choices.

In short, the abolition of involuntary mental hospitalization and treatment would mean that psychiatric help, like medical, would (on the whole) have to be restricted to voluntary clients. Furthermore, some persons who áre now cast in the role of involuntary mental patients would, if they broke laws, have to be dealt with as offenders, not as patients.

The nominal aim of psychiatry is the study and treatment of mental disorders. The consequences of subscribing to this apparently harmless, conventional definition of "mental health" work are, in our present age, momentous. Accepting the existence of a class of phenomena called "mental diseases," rather than inquiring into the conditions under which some persons may designate others as "mentally ill," has been the decisive step in embracing what I call the mental-health ethic. In so doing, the study of a large part of human behavior is subtly transferred from ethics to psychiatry, from the free marketplace of ideas to the closed wards of the mental hospital.

The psychiatrist deals with moral and social problems, not with medical diseases. Hence he cannot help being embroiled in the moral conflicts of his patient and of his society. The psychiatrist's role as moral legislator and social engineer is obscured, however, by the rhetoric of mental health and illness which makes his work appear as a species of medical therapy. This evasion of ethical judgments and choices may be reassuring to the laity and comforting to the profession. But can we, as individuals, afford it?

The individual can never escape the moral burden of his existence. He must choose between obedience to authority and responsibility to himself. Moral decisions are often hard and painful to make. The temptation to delegate this burden to others is therefore ever-present. Yet, as all history teaches us, those who would take from man his moral burdens— be they priests or warlords, politicians or psychiatrists—must also take from him his liberty and hence his very humanity.

A humanistic psychiatry must, therefore, repudiate its seemingly therapeutic mandate, the pursuit of which often results, intentionally or unwittingly, in moral tranquility gained at the expense of freedom and responsibility. Instead of trying to diminish man's moral burdens, such a psychiatry must aim at increasing his powers and so making him equal to his task.

And what is this task? No one has stated it better than Albert Camus when he wrote: "The aim of life can only be to increase the sum of freedom and responsibility to be found in every man and in the world. It cannot, under any circumstances, be to reduce or suppress that freedom, even temporarily."

An Analysis of Szasz'
"Myth of Mental Illness"

Frederick C. Thorne

Thomas S. Szasz has recently created a great deal of public confusion concerning the concept of mental health by his contention that mental illness is a myth and, by implication, the claim that current psychiatric practices infringe on human rights by committing mental patients to hospitals against their will. Szasz has taken his arguments to the general public in popular articles and books, writing in a superficially convincing style which, however, involves serious untruths and distortions of facts.

Because Szasz' arguments might well set back the evolution of modern psychiatry and clinical psychology at a time when a huge national mental health program is just starting, it behooved the author to make an ideological analysis of his latest claims.

Following is an analysis of Szasz' claims in a *New York Times Magazine* article of June 12, 1966, entitled "The Myth of Mental Illness." [1]

1. Mental illness is a myth because minds are not physical objects and consequently are not subject to physical disease in the medical sense.

Rebuttal: While mental disorder may have different causes than physical diseases, the functional effects are comparably disabling. "Illness" as a generic term refers to disablement rather than to any specific physical or psychological cause.

2. Insofar as men are human beings, they always have some choice in how they act—hence they are always responsible for their conduct.

Rebuttal: Not psychiatrically true. All mental disorder involves loss of self-control in some manner. The greater the impairment of self-control, the less a man is volitionally responsible for his conduct.

3. There is method in madness. . . .

FROM the *American Journal of Psychiatry*, CXXIII, pp. 652–656, 1966. Copyright 1966, the American Psychiatric Association. Reprinted with the permission of the *American Journal of Psychiatry* and Frederick C. Thorne.
[1] Szasz, T. S., "The Myth of Mental Illness," *New York Times Magazine*, June 12, 1966, pp. 30–31, 90–92.

Rebuttal: An overgeneralization implying that deliberate motives determine all symptomatology.

4. Social situations and human behavior in them are analogous to games. Confusion over changing rules for playing games results in conflict in trying to solve problems of living—some severe enough to be diagnosed as "mental illness" or "disease." This is invalid because we are dealing with disordered human relations.

Rebuttal: Not psychiatrically true. At best an oversimplification applicable only to limited cases. Mental disorder is more than just poor gamesmanship, as Szasz implies. There is a hen-egg problem here which Szasz does not realize. Are human relations disordered inevitably because of conflicting life or "game" styles? Or because either or all participants in a situation may be psychologically ill? Either may be true.

5. The historical model of mental hospitals is to serve as a place for institutionalizing many types of persons not adapting to society, including many others besides the overtly mentally ill.

Rebuttal: While it is true that the role of mental hospitals has been gradually extended to serve many clinical types other than the classically mentally disordered, the decision to admit other types of cases was made deliberately because better facilities were not available at the time and place.

6. Even though current laws authorize the involuntary commitment of psychotic persons to mental hospitals, such deprivations of human rights are not validly applicable to the aged, epileptics, alcoholics, etc., who do not have any mental disease. In fact, since there is no such thing as mental disease, the whole commitment system is unconstitutional and undemocratic.

Rebuttal: Practices regarding commitment of other groups besides the psychotic evolved as social expedients at a time when more specialized facilities were not economically feasible or professionally possible.

7. Intolerable abuses have occurred when persons have been committed against their will by psychiatrists who were reacting more to the demands of third persons or social authorities than to the needs of the patient, to whom he is first obligated.

Rebuttal: Abuses are possible in any situation involving humans. However, most civilized societies have recognized the physician as the one most able to diagnose and treat conduct disorders with an understanding, healing manner. Historically, greater abuses have occurred with nonpsychiatric case handling.

8. The social role of the psychiatrist is determined by the nature of the institutions in which he works. This role is determined by the "disease" concept and gives the psychiatrist directive, authoritative, controlling powers over unwilling patients, who actually have no "disease" but are only maladapted.

Rebuttal: A great step forward was taken when the old jungle-rule, "eye-for-an-eye" punitive system for discouraging conduct problems was replaced by the healing methods of the physician and hospital. In general, no widespread abuses have occurred under psychiatric management, which represents an evolutionary step forward until society develops something better.

9. Too often, "mental patients" are institutionalized for the convenience of others, with the psychiatrist representing the interests of third parties rather than the primary interest of the patient. Too often, commitment only protects the family or society at the expense of the civil rights of the patient.

Rebuttal: While such complaints occasionally are justified, this argument is an overstatement and overgeneralized. The ethical psychiatrist tries not to be unduly influenced by complaints of third parties against the patient. Moreover, too often third parties and society do need to be protected from the patient.

10. Szasz admits that in the organic psychoses there do occur lesions in the central nervous system such as those which underlie classical physical diseases. However, he claims that "functional" or "psychological" disorders involve conditions manifested chiefly by the person's behaving "differently" from usual social expectations. He contends that it is semantically invalid to categorize persons as "sick" just because they are different.

Rebuttal: Szasz minimizes the psychophysiological dysfunctions underlying all the psychoses, the severe psychoneuroses, epilepsy, alcoholism, addictions, and other conditions involving greater or lesser loss of self-control. The important differentiation is not between being "different" but in being "disabled" and partially out of control.

11. It is invalid to classify a person as "ill" because of behavior expressing deviant social roles. Roles are social artifacts, and deviance has meaning only in terms of social customs or laws.

Rebuttal: An overgeneralization. Only when deviant behavior is dangerous or disabling does it command a psychiatric diagnosis or labeling.

12. Psychiatric opinion concerning the criteria of mental health determines the kinds of deviance regarded as "mental illness." Psychiatric opinion may be fallible, prejudiced by irrelevant factors, or even by ulterior motivations. Constitutional protection should be given against psychiatric invasion of the human rights of freedom and privacy.

Rebuttal: Theoretically true but practically unjustified. No type of clinical practice can be more perfect than what is scientifically known at the time and place. Well trained and competent psychiatric specialists are presumably wiser and more trustworthy in their decisions than are less qualified personnel.

13. Psychiatry creates new classes of mental illness every time it formulates new rules for mental health . . . (constantly expanding) the category of people who can be legitimately classified as psychologically sick. Labeling people as mentally ill is a special kind of name-calling . . .

by a psychiatrist who makes a diagnosis (especially of an involuntary patient) and has more social power than the person he diagnoses.

Rebuttal: These arguments involve a cynical and perverse distortion of the whole process of diagnosis by a qualified specialist. Progress in all clinical sciences occurs by the progressive differentiation of previously unrecognized etiology and patterns of disorder. It is not name-calling to devise more refined diagnoses. Szasz provides no evidence of any widespread name-calling on the part of psychiatrists, the overwhelming majority of whom use diagnosis scientifically and not to discriminate against anybody.

14. Criminal insanity is a metaphorical and strategic concept, just as civil insanity is. . . . Insanity should (not) be an "excusing condition" for crime. Lawbreakers, irrespective of their "mental health," ought to be treated as offenders.

Rebuttal: This argument represents a regression to a prescientific failure to discriminate between the normal and the disabled. In general, hospitalization is more humane than penal incarceration. Penal systems do not provide adequate resources for disposing of many categories of psychiatric cases.

15: Many patients do not seek psychiatric treatment voluntarily and are coerced by relatives or authorities into a role not of their own choosing . . . like a prisoner sentenced to a term of servitude. Coercion has no place in psychiatric treatment, which requires a cooperative client.

Rebuttal: A classical symptom of many mental conditions is lack of insight, i.e., the person does not recognize the degree of his disability or impairment of judgment. In general, the greater the loss of insight and of self-control, the more dangerous the person becomes.

16. The humanistic view of denying the existence of mental illness would remove the justification for involuntary hospitalization and treatment. We should empty out all our mental hospitals and provide more humane alternatives, including the use of non-medical personnel such as clinical psychologists, social workers, ministers, educators, etc.

Rebuttal: This viewpoint does not give proper weight to the fact that psychiatry and our mental hospital and clinic resources represent the best that society has yet been able to devise. Szasz has no evidence that anything currently available would be any better.

17. Even the usual justification for committing persons on the grounds that they are dangerous to self or others is both illogical and unconstitutional.

Rebuttal: This argument seems to be leaning over backwards in protection of the disordered person at the expense of the rights of society, which also deserves protection.

18. Suicide should be recognized as a basic human right. The threat or attempt at suicide should not be made the basis for involuntary hospitalization.

Rebuttal: This view is contrary to established public mores based on Judeo-Christian morality. It disregards the fact that most suicides occur in depressive states which react well to therapy. It is logical that a completely normal person might be regarded as having the right to end his own life but not humane that a curable disordered person should be allowed to do so.

19. The social control of dangerous behavior is complicated by the fact that people disagree as to what is dangerous and also on how such control is to be established. Many persons now committed are dangerous only by "fiat" or in terms of some purely relative standard. This is dangerous to civil liberties and should be unconstitutional.

Rebuttal: Legal status in any era is always relative to the level of enlightenment of time and place. Legal codes and psychiatric standards are not whimsical judgments by irresponsible personnel but rather the best decisions which can be reached by the fairest and best qualified specialists in society.

20. Szasz makes an impassioned appeal for a new humanistic psychiatry which will rethink its social obligations. The nominal aim of studying and treating mental disorders, implying the existence of a class of phenomena called "mental diseases" and embodying classical coercive methods of institutionalization and treatment, should be replaced by inquiries into the conditions under which some persons may designate others as mentally ill and by a more free-thinking consideration of the games which people (including psychiatrists) play on each other.

Rebuttal: Szasz does not have a monopoly on humanistic wishes for the future. He portrays psychiatrists as a group as being nonperceptive of what they are actually doing, responsive to ulterior motivations secondary to the primary goal of satisfying the needs of the patient, heartless in their disregard of the need to be free and uncoerced, and slaves to an authoritarian tradition which gives them total control over the lives and destinies of other humans. While Szasz might gather instances of isolated abuses of clinical authority, he cannot marshal evidence of such an indictment of psychiatry in particular or society in general. He is simply jousting against straw men for the large part of his arguments.

21. The psychiatrist deals with moral and social problems rather than mental disease, hence he cannot keep from becoming embroiled in the moral conflicts of his patient and of society. The individual man can never escape the moral burden of his existence, and any (including psychiatrists) who attempt to take from him his moral burden must also take from him his liberty and hence his very humanity.

Rebuttal: Szasz is behind the times in not recognizing that many social psychiatrists have long been working in the humanistic direction which Szasz recommends. Carl R. Rogers recommended such ideals more than 25 years ago, as did many other pioneers in changing psychiatric practice and hospitals into genuinely humanistic ventures.

22. A humanistic psychiatry must repudiate its seemingly therapeutic mandate and goals of social control, and instead of trying to diminish man's moral burdens, should attempt to increase his powers and so make him equal to his task. Szasz endorses the statement of Camus that "The aim of life can only be to increase the sum of freedom and responsibility to be found in every man and in the world. It cannot, under any circumstances, be to reduce or suppress that freedom, even temporarily."

Rebuttal: This argument is very appealing and is valid as far as it goes. Certainly no responsible authority in society, much less psychiatrists, knowingly works to deprive anyone of civil liberties. The crucial question concerns persons who are too disabled or out of control to be able to utilize freedom responsibly. The uncontrolled, violently dangerous person requires external controls and institutionalization as long as he remains in such a state. The issue is not one of denying freedoms but of withholding them until the person is able to handle them responsibly.

Discussion

Szasz's arguments contain a modicum of truth and of deserved criticism for psychiatric practices at their worst. Undoubtedly many abuses, injustices, and clinical errors have occurred during the growing up of a young clinical science whose personnel consist of fallible humans. However, it is unfair and irresponsible to criticize or categorize the entire profession of psychiatry as inhumane on the basis of isolated examples of malpractice. The profession of clinical psychology (and psychiatry to a lesser degree) has been its own worst critic in scientifically evaluating its clinical results to determine their validity and how they can be improved.

Many of the Szasz arguments are seen to be exaggerated, biased, alarmist, impractical, and even erroneous. This is the kind of harangue which would be expected from a demagogue rather than a responsible scientist. Does Szasz really believe that such immoderate attacks on his own profession will improve public confidence in the mental health movement? To the contrary, there already exist many intemperate groups who are actively lobbying against the mental health movement and whose misguided efforts are encouraged by such specious arguments as Szasz offers.

Szasz's role as an idealistic, liberal reformer would be considerably brighter if his efforts were more constructively directed. The issues he raises should be debated within scientific and professional councils rather than being broadcast to a public which does not have the background to judge the arguments. Szasz is grandiose in depicting himself as the savior of modern psychiatry at a time when a host of devoted colleagues are working with comparably high ideals.

One practical effect of Szasz's arguments has been to confuse the outlook of students, interns, residents, and young psychiatrists who do not have the experience to judge their validity. Perhaps the most important truth in the whole field of psychiatry relates to the refractoriness and difficulty in treating serious psychiatric conditions. In spite of recent progress with drugs, many psychiatric conditions do not respond to any known kind of therapy. Such cases do not respond even to the most humanitarian case handling, including a surfeit of love, everything that money can buy, kindness, warmth, acceptance, and nonjudgmental attitudes. In fact, some very experienced psychiatrists have stated that the most curative influence of the mental hospital was the unpleasantness of the situation, which stimulated the patient to mobilize all his forces to get out. And whether we wish to call severe psychiatric disorders "diseases," "illness," "disorders," "disturbed human relations," "disabilities," or "social deviance," the fact remains that we are dealing with something more malignant than a game.

While everyone wishes to do his utmost for all types of unfortunates, the fact remains that any one group cannot command more than its share of social resources, and the law of diminishing returns limits what can be invested in any single case, no matter how piteous. I suppose if nobody had anything with higher priority to do, one half of society could devote all its time to taking care of the less fortunate. Unfortunately, the work of the world must be done before such surplus resources as are available can be allocated to underprivileged groups, of which the psychiatrically disabled are only one.

Questions

1. What is the tone of Dr. Szasz's essay? What audience does he seem to be addressing?
2. Define the term *games* as Szasz uses it.
3. What factual evidence does Szasz provide to support his arguments? How is it sufficient or insufficient?
4. Summarize Szasz's argument against the concept of criminal insanity.
5. Dr. Szasz describes his point of view as a "humanistic view of mental illness." What does he mean by *humanistic?* How would you define the term?
6. Is the format of Dr. Thorne's article effective? What advantages does it have? What disadvantages?
7. For what audience is Thorne's article written? Is it the same group that Szasz was addressing?
8. How does Thorne refute the significant points made by Szasz?

Assignments

1. Define *mental illness.*
2. Write an essay defending or opposing the proposition that suicide is a basic human right.

3. Consider the relationship between legal and medical issues. Can these issues be clearly separated? *The Pill Man* (Section Five) treats this question from another perspective.

4. Choose a legal case in which mental illness was used as a defense. After reading the records of the case, write an essay discussing the appropriateness of Dr. Szasz's criticisms.

Additional Reading

Dr. Szasz has written several books treating the issues raised in this section, among them: *The Myth of Mental Illness* (New York, 1961); *Ethics of Psychoanalysis: The Theory and Method of Autonomous Psychotherapy* (New York, 1965); *Law, Liberty and Psychiatry* (New York, 1963); and *Ideology and Insanity—Essays on the Psychiatric Dehumanization of Man* (New York, 1969). R. D. Laing's *Politics of Experience* (New York, 1967) raises similar questions about the psychiatric definition of insanity. The Proceedings of the American Psychopathological Association for 1955 on *Psychiatry and the Law*, edited by Paul H. Hook and Joseph Zabin, provides further discussion of these issues.

Among the works of Sigmund Freud, *Civilization and Its Discontents* is probably the most relevant to the questions raised here.

Modern novelists have been concerned about the use of psychological knowledge and treatment to effect social control. Two noteworthy novels which approach these issues from different perspectives are George Orwell's *1984* (1949) and Ken Kesey's *One Flew over the Cuckoo's Nest* (1962).

SECTION FIVE

Drug Addiction:
Family Illness or Social Crime?

Kubla Khan; or, a Vision in a Dream

Samuel Taylor Coleridge

In the summer of the year 1797, the author, then in ill health, had retired to a lonely farmhouse between Porlock and Lynton, on the Exmoor confines of Somerset and Devonshire. In consequence of a slight indisposition, an anodyne had been prescribed, from the effects of which he fell asleep in his chair at the moment he was reading the following sentence, or words of the same substance, in *Purchas's Pilgrimage:* "Here the Khan Kubla commanded a palace to be built, and a stately garden thereunto. And thus ten miles of fertile ground were inclosed with a wall." The author continued for about three hours in a profound sleep, at least of the external senses, during which time he has the most vivid confidence that he could not have composed less than from two to three hundred lines; if that indeed can be called composition in which all the images rose up before him as *things*, with a parallel production of the correspondent expressions, without any sensation or consciousness of effort. On awaking he appeared to himself to have distinct recollection of the whole, and taking his pen, ink, and paper, instantly and eagerly wrote down the lines that are here preserved. At this moment he was unfortunately called out by a person on business from Porlock, and detained by him above an hour, and on his return to his room, found, to his no small surprise and mortification, that though he still retained some vague and dim recollection of the general purport of the vision, yet, with the exception of some eight or ten scattered lines and images, all the rest had passed away like the images on the surface of a stream into which a stone had been cast, but, alas! without the after restoration of the latter! [From Coleridge's preface to *Kubla Khan.*—Ed.]

In Xanadu did Kubla Khan
A stately pleasure dome decree:
Where Alph, the sacred river, ran
Through caverns measureless to man
   Down to a sunless sea.
So twice five miles of fertile ground
With walls and towers were girdled round:
And there were gardens bright with sinuous rills,
Where blossomed many an incense-bearing tree;
And here were forests ancient as the hills,
Enfolding sunny spots of greenery.

But oh! that deep romantic chasm which slanted
Down the green hill athwart a cedarn cover!
A savage place! as holy and enchanted
As e'er beneath a waning moon was haunted
By woman wailing for her demon lover!

And from this chasm, with ceaseless turmoil seething,
As if this earth in fast thick pants were breathing,
A mighty fountain momently was forced:
Amid whose swift half-intermitted burst
Huge fragments vaulted like rebounding hail,
Or chaffy grain beneath the thresher's flail:
And 'mid these dancing rocks at once and ever
It flung up momently the sacred river.
Five miles meandering with a mazy motion
Through wood and dale the sacred river ran,
Then reached the caverns measureless to man,
And sank in tumult to a lifeless ocean:
And 'mid this tumult Kubla heard from far
Ancestral voices prophesying war!

The shadow of the dome of pleasure
Floated midway on the waves;
Where was heard the mingled measure
From the fountain and the caves.
It was a miracle of rare device,
A sunny pleasure dome with caves of ice!

A damsel with a dulcimer
In a vision once I saw:
It was an Abyssinian maid,
And on her dulcimer she played,
Singing of Mount Abora.
Could I revive within me
Her symphony and song,
To such a deep delight 'twould win me,
That with music loud and long,
I would build that dome in air,
That sunny dome! those caves of ice!
And all who heard should see them there,
And all should cry, Beware! Beware!
His flashing eyes, his floating hair!
Weave a circle round him thrice,
And close your eyes with holy dread,
For he on honey-dew hath fed,
And drunk the milk of Paradise.

The Pill Man

Albert Ruben and Charles Eckert

Cast of Characters

Lawrence Preston	Dr. Robert Hartog
Kenneth Preston	Detective Ross
Eddie Clark	Woman Detective
Anne Clark	Judge
Tom Grafton	Dr. William Nelson
Asst. D. A. Sam Wolfe	Stanley
Phil Macy	Foreman
Detective Dewey	

Prologue

(*Interior drugstore. Night.* TOM GRAFTON *enters. Seventeen, ivy league, quick movements. He moves directly to the back counter where* EDDIE CLARK *is finishing waiting on a customer. En route, he passes a* WOMAN, *her hair in curlers under a scarf, examining some shelves at the front of the store.* TOM *waits until* EDDIE *gives the customer her change.*)

EDDIE (*to customer*): Thank you. Call again, please. (*Customer leaves.*)

TOM: Hello, Mr. Clark.

EDDIE: Hello, Tom.

TOM: My prescription ready?

EDDIE (*nodding toward woman*): That lady is next.

TOM: Oh—sorry.

WOMAN: There's no rush . . . you go ahead and finish what you're doing. I don't know what I want yet. Some kind of hand lotion.

EDDIE (*eyeing the woman, to* TOM): I'm afraid I haven't quite finished making up your prescription yet. Could you come back in a—

TOM (*tensely*): I'd rather wait . . . (*under his breath*) Please.

(EDDIE *studies him closely, sees the boy's desperation, leaves for the prescription counter in back.* TOM—*beginning to wander about nervously. Seeing the soda fountain . . .*)

TOM: Mr. Clark, can I have a soda?

Production #88 of *The Defenders*, created by Reginald Rose. Reprinted with the permission of the authors.

EDDIE (*offstage*): I'll be right out.

TOM: I can fix it myself. (*He waits for an answer.*) Okay?

EDDIE (*offstage*): Okay.

(TOM *goes behind the soda fountain. Fixes himself a drink.*)

TOM: By the way, my father said to send his regards. He and I were away, you know. Two-week fishing trip . . . he's still away. I had to come back, though. (*He carries the drink with him as he emerges from behind the counter. He sips his drink nervously*). How's Mrs. Clark?

EDDIE (*off stage*): Fine, thank you.

TOM: Give her my regards, will you?

EDDIE: I will.

(TOM *moves around the store, getting more jittery than ever. He moves close to the* WOMAN *scrutinizing the shelves.*)

TOM (*trying to be jocular but not quite succeeding*): Out of all those hand lotions, can't you find one?

WOMAN: That's what's so confusing. There are so many to choose from.

(TOM *downs the soda in long nervous gulps, walks to the counter with the glass, shaking so he has difficulty putting the glass down without rattling it. He looks around at the* WOMAN, *but she's paying no attention to him. He wipes his mouth with the back of his hand.* EDDIE—*entering from back of store with package.* TOM's *face lightens as he hurries toward him.*)

EDDIE: Here you are, Tom.

TOM: Thanks. Put it on our bill. Thanks, Mr. Clark.

(*Beyond them, the* WOMAN *adjusts her scarf.* TOM *starts toward the front door and is met by two detectives,* DEWEY *and* ROSS, *as they enter.*)

DEWEY: We're police officers. We want to see what's in that package.

TOM (*almost shaking by now as he tries to keep the package*): Nothing— just some medicine. Honestly.

DEWEY: We'd like to see it, please.

TOM: Look. Please. Someone in my family's very sick. They're waiting for this. They need it very badly . . . (TOM *suddenly pushes* DEWEY *into* ROSS *and starts to run out. As he reaches the* WOMAN, *he stops as he sees her pointing a revolver at him. Slowly, he raises his hands.* DEWEY *comes over and takes the package from* TOM's *upraised hand. Then he crosses to the back counter where* EDDIE *has watched this in horror.*)

DEWEY: Have you got a prescription for this stuff? (*He holds up the package.* EDDIE *barely shakes his head.*) Come on. (EDDIE *starts to come around the counter and they all start out.*)

Act One

(*Interior interview room. Tombs. Day.* LAWRENCE *and* KEN PRESTON *are seated facing* EDDIE CLARK. *He has spent a sleepless night, needs a shave. His mood is taciturn, spiritless, reflecting his sense of defeat and despair.*

LAWRENCE *is more hostile than we are accustomed to seeing him. Nothing really overt, but it's there.*)

LAWRENCE: When she telephoned, your wife said all she knew was you'd been arrested. Didn't you tell her what you're charged with?

EDDIE: No. How did she sound when you spoke to her?

KEN: Pretty upset, but I think that's natural under the circumstances.

EDDIE: When can I see her?

LAWRENCE: We'll arrange it. The police say they caught you selling narcotics without a prescription. Is that so?

(EDDIE *only nods.*)

LAWRENCE: Have you any explanation for it?

EDDIE: No. (*Beat.*) I mean I did it, and I got caught. What good are explanations going to do?

LAWRENCE: For one thing, they might help us prepare your defense.

EDDIE: What defense? I'm guilty.

LAWRENCE: Does that mean you want to plead guilty?

EDDIE: I . . . don't know. I don't see what else to do.

KEN: Have you ever been picked up before on a narcotics charge?

EDDIE: No.

KEN: Any previous convictions of any kind?

EDDIE: No.

LAWRENCE: In a way, you can consider yourself lucky. If you'd been caught by Federal agents instead of State agents, you'd be facing a much stiffer penalty. The Federal law is much stronger on it.

EDDIE: How long a prison sentence will I get?

LAWRENCE: That's hard to say. Who were you selling it to when they caught you?

EDDIE: A seventeen year old boy.

KEN: That's not going to help shorten your sentence.

(EDDIE *doesn't offer this as a defense, he just feels called upon to say something.*)

EDDIE (*mumbling*): He's a sick boy.

(LAWRENCE *is annoyed at* CLARK's *cryptic answers. He is repulsed by the man's crime and skeptical of his explanation—such as it is.*)

LAWRENCE: How did you happen to take the boy on as a patient? How did you . . . shall we say . . . make the connection?

(EDDIE *betrays signs of conflict. His feeling of being without hope clashes with his more normal desire to answer the Prestons' questions, to explain to them, perhaps even persuade them.*)

EDDIE: More or less the same way as the others.

LAWRENCE: What others?

EDDIE: The others I helped to get . . . drugs. . . .

KEN: How many of these others are there?

EDDIE: Five.

KEN: Do you mean you only have six customers?

EDDIE (*nodding*):That's right. Six illegal customers.

(*There is a moment of silence. The Prestons aren't quite sure what they're up against—this quiet man who seems so sure of himself and yet apparently resigned to his fate.*)

EDDIE: I'd like to see my wife.

(LAWRENCE *has been thoughtful. Now he leans forward.*)

LAWRENCE: Let me ask you something, Mr. Clark. What drugs did you supply to these six people?

EDDIE: Morphine and morphine derivatives. Some synthetics.

LAWRENCE: How much did you sell it for?

EDDIE: What it cost me.

KEN: Do you mean you didn't make any money selling this stuff?

EDDIE: No.

KEN: Then what did you do it for?

EDDIE: If . . . I say I did it because I felt sorry for them and wanted to help them . . . it sounds like I'm some kind of fanatic or something, doesn't it?

(*Interior, District Attorney's office. Day.* SAM WOLFE, *an assistant D.A., regards* LAWRENCE *with a certain deference.*)

D.A.: You don't really believe that story, do you?

LAWRENCE: Why not? What's so incredible about a man defying the law? Thoreau wouldn't pay his taxes. We know segregation statutes are being defied all over the place. It happens.

D.A.: I know, but those are things involving personal rights. You can understand why people feel strongly about things like that. But narcotics. . . .

LAWRENCE: Look, even acknowledging your right to be skeptical, the fact still remains he's willing to plead guilty.

D.A.: Yeah, but to a misdemeanor. A couple of months and he'll be back in business.

LAWRENCE: Not if you take his license away.

D. A.: So he'll get it someplace else.

LAWRENCE: But that isn't what he deals in. He's not a heroin pusher. He's a druggist who happened to get some confused ideas about a few people being sick and needing drugs he had in his shop.

D.A.: Look, Larry, the guy's been pushing dope. I don't care if he did it in a back alley or from behind a counter wearing a white coat. He's still a pusher and that's still as rotten a crime as I can think of. Especially when committed by a man who's supposed to be a respectable businessman. He's not even hooked himself—and that somehow makes it even dirtier. He doesn't deserve anything but having the book thrown at him. And that's just what he's going to get—the biggest book I can find.

Act Two

(*Interior. Preston's office. Day. Present are* LAWRENCE, KEN, *and* EDDIE CLARK.)

KEN (*to* EDDIE): When he granted bail, the judge made it conditional that you stay away from your store until after the trial.

LAWRENCE (*to* EDDIE): My advice is to abide by the judge's ruling. Can you get someone in to run the store?

EDDIE: Yes, I can do that.

LAWRENCE: I'm afraid the district attorney refused our proposal that you plead guilty to a reduced charge. The trouble is he's skeptical about the whole thing. He simply doesn't believe you didn't profit from your narcotic sales. Also he asked for a reason why you feel so strongly about addicts . . . why you're willing to risk your neck to help them. It's a fair question, Mr. Clark.

EDDIE: I thought I told you.

LAWRENCE: No, you didn't. When I asked the same question yesterday, all you said was you happened to know some addicts who were decent people and you wanted to help them.

EDDIE: That's right.

LAWRENCE: That's not enough. Not for a jury.

EDDIE (*flaring*): Why not? Is it so incredible when one human being wants to help out another?

LAWRENCE: How do you expect me to convince a jury that all you were doing was lending a helping hand to some deserving people?

EDDIE: They are, believe me.

LAWRENCE: I can understand. But what will a jury believe unless these people come in and testify for us?

EDDIE (*firmly*): No.

LAWRENCE: We don't have much else—

EDDIE: I can't do it to them. As soon as other people know they're on drugs, what happens to them? (*to* KEN) Well, you said it. Suddenly they are considered dope fiends. And even worse than that, the police'll hound them until they catch them with some pills, and then they go to prison. I mean how can I do that to anybody?

KEN: What about the Grafton boy? He's up on a narcotics charge anyway. At least may we talk to him?

(EDDIE *thinks it over, then:*)

EDDIE: I guess if he wants to testify for me, he can't get into any more trouble then he's in now.

(*Interior Grafton home. Day. A pleasant room in an uptown apartment. Not lavish, but comfortable and tasteful.* KEN *is seated opposite* TOM.)

TOM: Just tell me how. I'll do anything to help Mr. Clark.

KEN: How much did you pay him for the morphine he sold you?

TOM: Practically nothing. I think it was whatever it cost him.

KEN: How did you happen to go to him . . . you know the first time?

TOM: My dad's a friend of his. I don't know, they went to school together or something like that. Anyway, when Dad . . . you know . . . found out about me, he took me to a doctor. (*remembering—amused*) I never saw anybody so eager to get rid of me in my life.

KEN: The doctor.

TOM: He just said I should see a psychiatrist and . . . held the door open.

KEN: Did you go to a psychiatrist?

TOM: I'm still going. For a while I just tried to kick the habit, but I couldn't do it. And I told my dad I couldn't.

KEN: What did the psychiatrist say about that?

TOM: I don't know . . . I mean I sort of had the feeling he didn't know what to say. He was sure he could help me and I said I'd go to him and do anything he said, but I couldn't do it unless I had something. He said he couldn't give it to me. He . . . just couldn't, that's all. So there we were. I guess you might call it the perfect stalemate. That's when my dad took me to see Mr. Clark.

KEN: After that, when you started going to your doctor . . . did he know how you worked it out?

TOM: He never said anything but I'm sure he did.

KEN: Do you think you could make it on the stand if we asked you to be a witness for Mr. Clark?

TOM (*after a beat*): I think so. I'd sure try.

(*Interior Clark living room. Day.* ANNE, KEN, LAWRENCE. ANNE *seems very nervous and ill-at-ease.*)

ANNE: I'm so sorry Eddie's not back yet. He said he wouldn't be more than an hour.

LAWRENCE: It's our fault, Mrs. Clark. We should have phoned. But since we were in the neighborhood, we thought we could save your husband a trip downtown.

ANNE: You went to see the Grafton boy, didn't you?

LAWRENCE: Yes. You knew that the boy was being supplied drugs by your husband.

ANNE: Because Tom is an addict and—

LAWRENCE: But you knew.

ANNE: Yes.

LAWRENCE: Did you know of any others Mr. Clark was helping?

ANNE: Yes. Why?

LAWRENCE: It would be very helpful to us if those people would be defense witnesses.

KEN: And your husband refuses to involve them in any way.

ANNE: You want me to give you their names?

LAWRENCE: Or convince Mr. Clark how necessary their testimony will be to his defense.

ANNE: I don't know. . . . What about Tom? You said he wás willing to appear for Eddie.

LAWRENCE: One witness only carries one-fifth the weight of five witnesses. And your husband is going to need all the weight he—

(EDDIE—*just entering at the front door.*)

EDDIE: Annie, are you—? (*He stops, his face clouding, as he sees the Prestons.*)

ANNE: You're late, Eddie. I told these gentlemen you'd be home any minute.

(LAWRENCE *and* KEN *have risen.*)

LAWRENCE: We've been having a very pleasant visit.

EDDIE (*furiously*): What are you doing here?

KEN: We were in the neighborhood and I wanted to tell you that Grafton agreed to testify.

EDDIE (*to* ANNE): Have they been asking you questions?

ANNE: I didn't mind, Eddie. They should ask. . . .

EDDIE: No. They shouldn't. They should only do as I asked. (*to* LAWRENCE) You have no right to come here and snoop behind my back, frighten my wife.

LAWRENCE: Somebody in this family should be frightened before it's too late. You're in big trouble, Mr. Clark, and we want to help you despite the fact that you've done nothing but hide and conceal the truth from us.

EDDIE: You know the truth!

LAWRENCE: Not enough of it.

EDDIE: I'll tell you anything but names. Anything!

LAWRENCE: All right, Mr. Clark. Are you a drug addict?

(*The question produces startled reactions from everybody.*)

EDDIE: No. I'm not.

LAWRENCE: Were you ever an addict?

EDDIE: No. Never.

ANNE: I am. I'm an addict.

EDDIE: Anne!

(KEN *and* LAWRENCE *are shocked as* ANNE, *greatly agitated, gets to her feet. She is rigid with determination despite her husband's attempts to silence her.*)

ANNE: I'm a drug addict, Mr. Preston.

EDDIE: Oh God, Anne! Stop it! Please!

ANNE: That's how Eddie got into this. Because of me. If it hadn't been for me, he wouldn't be in any trouble. That's what you wanted to know, isn't it? Why he did it? He did it because of me.

(KEN *has moved to* ANNE's *side. He takes her arm.*)

KEN: Why don't you sit down, Mrs. Clark?

(EDDIE *sits slumped with his head in his hands, groans.* ANNE *now moves to console her husband, caressing his cheek.*)

ANNE: Shh, Honey . . . it's all right. Don't you see I want to do it? I want to help you.

EDDIE: Anne, you don't know what you're saying.

LAWRENCE: Do you mind if I ask you some questions, Mrs. Clark?

ANNE: I don't mind. I want you to.

EDDIE (*vehemently*): She's not going to say anything in court! I hope that's clear!

ANNE: What do you want to know, Mr. Preston?

LAWRENCE: How long have you been using drugs?

ANNE: About a year.

LAWRENCE: How did you get started?

ANNE: Eddie and I got married late . . . you know, compared to most people. He was over forty and I was over thirty, but we both wanted very much to have a child.

EDDIE (*in anguish*): Anne . . . I can't stand this. . . .

(*It pierces* ANNE, *but she steadies herself, goes on.*)

ANNE: Eddie, I can. I'm sorry. Well, we . . . didn't. There wasn't anything wrong . . . I just didn't get pregnant. At least that's what the doctor said at first. Then he said there was something a little bit wrong with the way I was inside and everything, and maybe that was the reason. So I had an operation to correct it. In the hospital I was very nervous and . . . tense, I guess, and they gave me a lot of sedatives to help me get through it. Well, the operation went fine, and when I got home I felt really very good. But then . . . nothing happened. (ANNE *stares blankly. A long silence.*)

LAWRENCE: Mrs. Clark . . . ?

ANNE: I got . . . I started not feeling well.

EDDIE: She had a nervous breakdown. Is that so terrible?

LAWRENCE (*to* ANNE): I suppose you were given drugs again as part of your treatment.

ANNE (*nodding*): After a while the doctor said I didn't need them any more, but. . . . (*She simply shrugs.*)

LAWRENCE (*to* EDDIE): And you supplied her.

EDDIE: I couldn't figure out any other way. I mean her only chance of getting straightened out was with the doctor, but she couldn't even go see him unless she had something to take. Why did you have to say it, Anne? Why?

LAWRENCE: What about the others?

EDDIE: That all came later. Anne?

ANNE: Eddie, I couldn't help it. Please. I want you to be all right . . .

LAWRENCE: Were they friends or . . . people who knew about your wife or . . . what?

EDDIE: No. Nobody knows about Anne . . . except the doctors. No, they were . . . just people. Some of them old and good friends, some just people I'd hear about.

LAWRENCE: I'm sorry, but I still don't see how you and they got together, unless you went out of your way to find them.

EDDIE (*shaking his head*): Believe me, I didn't have to go out of my way. Nobody does. You want to find a drug addict right now? Go uptown, downtown, I don't care where, chances are you'll run into a drug addict. It's funny how when you don't really know about any of this, it just seems like one of those problems that's got nothing to do with you. And then as soon as it hits you personally suddenly it seems like everywhere you turn you bump into somebody who's in the same trouble you are. People you've known for years and never thought . . . you know. I don't know how it started. I didn't want to do it. No, I didn't go out of my way. But each one who came to me seemed to be more desperate than the one before. I'd think about Anne . . . about how terrible it is for her without it . . . I just couldn't turn them down, that's all.

KEN: Did you get any help, Mrs. Clark—when you first tried to stop?

EDDIE: She's been in two sanitariums. She still goes three times a week to the psychiatrist. But she doesn't need doctors nearly so much as she needs a baby.

KEN: What about adopting a child? Have you tried that?

EDDIE (*bitterly*): Have we tried? Do you know what it's like for people our age to adopt a child?

KEN: I know it's not easy.

(ANNE *begins softly to cry.*)

ANNE (*to* EDDIE): We don't have to worry about that any more, do we? Can't you see the adoption agency giving a baby to a middle-aged couple where the mother's an addict and the father sells dope? (*She is close to hysteria, but it is too much for* EDDIE. *He can't go to her.*)

LAWRENCE (*sharply*): Mrs. Clark. (*His tone brings her out of it. She begins to dab at her eyes with a handkerchief.*)

ANNE: What?

LAWRENCE: Do you think you can repeat what you just told us in a courtroom?

EDDIE: No, she can't! And anyway I won't let her!

(*With considerable effort,* ANNE *gains control of herself.*)

ANNE (*to* LAWRENCE) How long until the trial?

LAWRENCE: Several weeks.

EDDIE: You see? She shouldn't be put under the emotional strain of testifying.

ANNE: How many weeks?

LAWRENCE: Two. Maybe three.

EDDIE: You don't have enough morphine for three weeks, Anne. And I can't get you any more.

(ANNE *looks at* EDDIE *a long time, then comes to a difficult decision. She never takes her eyes from* EDDIE's *face as she addresses* LAWRENCE.)

ANNE: All right, Mr. Preston. I'll be ready to testify whenever you need me. I promise you. I'll be ready.

Act Three

(*Interior courtroom. Day. The* JUDGE *on the bench, Detective* DEWEY *on the stand, the* D. A. *on his feet before the bench, the* PRESTONS *and* EDDIE *at the defense counsel's table.* ANNE *is seated in the first row of spectators —who are few.*)

D. A.: Did the accused make any attempt to protest when you arrested him?

DEWEY: No.

D. A.: Did he say anything in fact?

DEWEY: No, he just came along.

D. A.: Almost as though he'd been expecting you.

DEWEY: Yes, sir.

LAWRENCE (*overlapping*): Objection.

JUDGE: Sustained.

D. A.: That's all. Thank you.

LAWRENCE: No questions.

(DR. WILLIAM NELSON *from the Coroner's Office.*)

D. A.'s VOICE: Did you do a laboratory test to find out what was in this bottle—exhibit three?

DR. NELSON: Yes, I did.

D. A.: And what was your conclusion?

NELSON: The pills in the bottle are morphine sulphate, a narcotic drug.

D. A.: Thank you, Doctor. (*He returns to his seat, replaced by* LAWRENCE.)

LAWRENCE: Is morphine sulphate an addictive drug, Doctor?

NELSON: Oh, absolutely.

LAWRENCE: How would you define an addictive drug?

NELSON: Well . . . it's one that creates a dependence on it . . . and a need for increased doses to get the same effect.

LAWRENCE: What kind of dependence?

NELSON: Psychological certainly, and physiological probably.

LAWRENCE: Probably?

NELSON: We used to be more certain about that than we are now.

LAWRENCE: Are you saying then it used to be accepted that the more drugs were taken the more the body came to depend on them, but now there's some question whether that's true or not?

NELSON: That's it precisely.

LAWRENCE: Isn't it because the necessary work hasn't been done to verify the facts one way or the other?

NELSON: I'm afraid so.

LAWRENCE: Thank you, Doctor. No further questions.

D. A.: The people rest, Your Honor.

(*Interior courtroom. Day.* DR. HARTOG *on the witness stand.*)

LAWRENCE: Dr. Hartog, could you tell the court and jury the kind of work you do.

HARTOG: I'm chairman of the Joint Research Council on Drug Addiction.

LAWRENCE: And whom does the Council represent?

HARTOG: We're a national, voluntary organization. We have a medical advisory board made up of leading physicians, psychiatrists, and professors of medicine throughout the country. Our national advisory board has on it educators, law enforcement officials, judges, a United States Senator—a very distinguished panel.

LAWRENCE: And how would you define the aims of the Council?

HARTOG: Well, quite simply we want to help solve the problem of drug addiction in this country.

LAWRENCE: Do you really think that can be done?

HARTOG: Oh, definitely.

LAWRENCE: What progress is being made toward that end?

HARTOG: Very little. The number of known addicts increases every year, so I don't think there's any question that the problem's getting worse rather than better.

LAWRENCE: Even with all the new laws we've been putting on the books? How is that possible?

(*The* D. A. *rises. He starts forward.*)

D. A.: Your Honor, I've been listening patiently to this line of questioning because I assumed I'd understand soon enough what it had to do with the guilt or innocence of the accused.

(KEN *leans to* EDDIE.)

KEN: It took him longer than I thought.

(EDDIE *turns to look for* ANNE. *She looks nervous, distraught.* EDDIE *is worried.*)

D. A.'S VOICE: I'd like to enter an objection on the grounds that nothing the witness has testified to is relevant to this trial.

JUDGE: Mr. Preston, would you care to explain what your purpose is in calling this witness?

LAWRENCE: The defense intends to prove, Your Honor, that by no stretch of the language or the imagination can Edward Clark be considered a narcotics peddler in the conventional sense. It intends to prove that he is innocent of any wrong-doing within the broader meaning and intent of the statutes. In order to do this, however, it's necessary to show the jury that the defendant's attitudes toward drug addiction aren't unique or anti-social . . . that in fact they're shared by some of the country's most respected citizens.

JUDGE: Are we really interested in the defendant's attitudes?

LAWRENCE: We are if we want to understand his motives. If the jury's to pass a really considered judgment upon Edward Clark, they have to understand why he acted as he did.

JUDGE: Mr. Wolfe, will you join me in my chambers? Mr. Preston. . . . The Court will be in recess for ten minutes. (*He stands and starts off.* LAWRENCE *turns toward* EDDIE *and* KEN. *His expression might be interpreted as "so far so good."* KEN *nods.* EDDIE *again turns to seek out* ANNE.)

(*Interior Judge's chamber. Day. The* JUDGE, LAWRENCE, *and the* D. A.)

D. A.: It just seems like very weird procedure to me. I mean all we're here for is to find out if this guy sold narcotics without prescriptions.

JUDGE: Or wouldn't another way to put it be that we're here to see that justice is done?

D. A.: Yes sir, only stop me if I'm wrong, but I assumed justice is done when the people who break laws are punished for it.

JUDGE: Mr. Preston, something tells me the District Attorney isn't a man to be much impressed with long views when short ones are so much clearer and more attainable. What do you say?

LAWRENCE: I say to send Edward Clark to jail would be a gross distortion of justice. He didn't make a nickel on his sales, and we can prove that. He's no more a dope pusher than one of us is.

D. A.: Do you mean because his intentions were good we should pat him on the back and tell him to go home and take care of his addicts? I'm sorry, Sir, but I don't get that. (*He is as deferential as ever, much to* LAWRENCE'S *annoyance.*)

LAWRENCE: Of course not. You can take his license away from him and stop him cold. But I think what happened to this man could happen to anybody. He's much less a criminal than he is a victim of a repressive body of law. This country has some of the toughest narcotics laws in the world. It also has some of the highest incidence of addiction. Now I don't know if the two are connected, but it strikes me as something to think about.

D. A.: Yes, I know all that. I still don't see what that has to do with this case. I mean what was your big point with Nelson this morning about does dependency increase or doesn't it? If I'm not imposing on your strategy, how does Clark fit into that?

LAWRENCE: My point was to establish how little we really know about the nature of addiction . . . that in fact we *don't* know what we're talking about.

D. A.: So swell . . . I'm with you. Let's find out more. Meanwhile, we have to control it, right?

LAWRENCE: Not if our efforts to control it prevent us from finding out more.

D. A. (*patronizing*): I'm sorry, but . . . I don't see what one has to do with the other . . . why can't you have control and research at the same time.

LAWRENCE: For one thing—and I'm sure you know this better than any-body—control doesn't work. You don't cure a disease by locking up its victims. Not smallpox, not leprosy, and not drug addiction. You tell me: how many addicts who go through the courts show up again?

D. A.: I know, I know. The relapse rate's around ninety-five per cent.

LAWRENCE: All this vast law enforcement machinery just to succeed with about five? Hardly seems worth it.

D. A.: So why don't your researchers come up with the answer?

LAWRENCE: Because they're afraid.

D. A.: Oh, I find that hard to believe. Who's going to touch a doctor if he's legitimate?

LAWRENCE: Over 25,000 M. D.'s have been arraigned since 1914. And three thousand of them have received prison sentences for violating the narcotics laws. Do you really think there were three thousand doctors pushing dope?

(*The* D. A. *broods silently.*)

JUDGE: You gentlemen obviously aren't going to resolve your differences in the few minutes we've got to make a decision. Mr. Wolfe, let me tell you the way I feel about it. You and I come into this court day in and day out and preside over the ritual of trying and sentencing narcotics offenders. It's all so cut and dried and apparently endless . . . I think we both get a little discouraged. Suddenly we've got a defendant— and I don't mean to pre-judge—who *seems* to be different and who's raising fundamental questions about what we're doing here. I agree with you that, strictly speaking, Mr. Preston is stretching procedure, and if you insist, I'll sustain your objection. But otherwise, my inclina-tion is to give Clark a break—let Preston develop his case.

(*The* D. A. *hesitates, then shrugs.*)

D. A. (*sarcastically*): Who am I to stand in the way of progress and en-lightenment for dope peddlers? Sure, go ahead. It's all right with me —after I make a phone call and clear it.

(*The* JUDGE *and* LAWRENCE *respond with satisfaction.*)

JUDGE: You can even use my phone.

D. A. (*to* LAWRENCE): But I still think I'm going to beat you.

LAWRENCE: I expect you to try.

(*Interior courtroom. Day.* EDDIE *and* ANNE *are seated on a back bench during the recess. Both are tense and therefore awkward.*)

EDDIE: It's going much better than I dared to expect, don't you think?

ANNE: Yes, I think so.

EDDIE: Can I get you something? A glass of water or something?

ANNE: No—why?

EDDIE: No reason, Anne.

ANNE: I don't look well, do I?

EDDIE: You look fine. Really.

ANNE: I'm trembling.

EDDIE: Well, under the circumstances that's only natural. We've got a great deal at stake here, haven't we? (*He holds out his hand.*) See! I'm trembling too.

ANNE: I have no more, Eddie.

EDDIE (*trying to ignore what she's said*): I imagine courtrooms have the same effect on most people. . . .

ANNE: Did you hear me, Eddie?

EDDIE (*nodding*): Yes.

ANNE: I took the last pill I had last night. I was saving it for today. I knew I'd need it and I was hoarding it, like some miserable miser. But I woke up during the night, scared, petrified, knowing it was my last one, thinking about today. I couldn't help myself, Eddie. I had to take it.

EDDIE: Maybe you ought to go home now.

ANNE: Don't, Eddie. Please. You need me here. I need to be here. I'll be all right, you'll see. This is just a form of stage fright. Once Mr. Preston puts me on that witness stand, I'll see that it isn't so bad and I'll get over this shakiness. That's all it is, shakiness. You'll see, Eddie.

(*Interior courtroom. Day.* HARTOG *is testifying.*)

LAWRENCE'S VOICE: Doctor Hartog, what makes a drug addict?

HARTOG: The sad truth is no one knows what addiction really is. We believe that every addict has a personality disorder of some kind. That doesn't mean you have to be wildly disturbed to become an addict. The tensions of . . . just plain modern living are usually enough to predispose many to addiction. Those tensions are greatest among minority groups, and of course a great many addicts are members of such groups. But an addict can be any age, race, class, or sex.

LAWRENCE: What else is needed for addiction to occur?

HARTOG: A supply of narcotics. I'm not being facetious. It's the ready availability of narcotics, mainly heroin, on the illegal market that constitutes a big cause of addiction.

LAWRENCE: What is the reason for this availability?

HARTOG: The profits you can make selling the stuff. A drug addict will pay anything he has to get what he wants, so of course the profits are tremendous.

LAWRENCE: But why should heroin cost so much? Is it that rare?

HARTOG: No. It's very cheap to produce. It's just a question of supply and demand. The supply is limited because it's against the law. But the demand from any single addict is as big as his habit.

LAWRENCE: And the threat of long prison sentences and in some states even death doesn't stop the suppliers?

HARTOG: We know it doesn't. There seems to be always somebody willing to take a chance to make that kind of money.

(LAWRENCE *goes to his table, takes up a sheet of paper from a sizable stack of pamphlets, books, etc.*)

LAWRENCE: I have here a summary of testimony given to the President's Advisory Commission on Narcotic and Drug Abuse. I'm quoting now, "There are less than five hundred known opiate addicts in Great Britain where the situation has remained remarkably benign. There are practically no serious crimes committed by addicts in that country. There is hardly any illicit traffic in narcotics and the problem hasn't spread to juveniles to any significant degree." Are you acquainted with the British approach to this problem, Doctor?

HARTOG: Yes, they permit their doctors to treat addict patients as they see fit.

LAWRENCE: In other words they say it's a problem for doctors to handle and not for police.

HARTOG: That's right. Physicians are allowed to prescribe maintenance doses for drug addicts as long as the ultimate aim is to secure withdrawal. And I emphasize "ultimate." They recognize that withdrawal isn't always something that can be done just like that. But they too do not withhold drugs from sick people who'll do anything for relief. People are forced by a misguided society to steal, to mug, to kill, to commit crimes of violence to maintain a habit which should only cost perhaps a dollar a day. (*He snaps his fingers.*)

(*The* D. A. *is engaged in cross-examining* HARTOG).

D. A.: Do you mean to say you advocate allowing anybody who wants to just walk into a doctor's office, get a shot of heroin or whatever, and walk out?

(HARTOG's *been taking a pretty good hammering and his back is up.*)

HARTOG: No, I don't mean that at all.

D. A.: It certainly sounded like it.

HARTOG: Not from anything I said.

D. A.: But you don't see anything wrong in addicts being kept on maintenance doses by their doctors for months or maybe years?

HARTOG: Not if the doctor, in his professional opinion, determines that to be the best course of treatment. After all, the police don't tell doctors how to treat their pneumonia patients or their arthritis patients or their cardiac patients.

D. A.: But isn't a doctor only responsible for a drug addict when he's in his office? And isn't it the police who have the problem all the rest of the time?

HARTOG (*exasperated*): But that's just the point! There isn't *necessarily* a problem. . . .

D. A. (*cutting in*): Oh, really? Do you have any idea how much crime is committed in this country by addicts?

HARTOG: Do you have any idea of how much crime would be omitted if we stopped treating addicts as criminals?

(TOM GRAFTON *has taken the witness stand. He is nervous but doing pretty well.*)

TOM: All I paid was a few cents per pill. He couldn't have made any profit from me.

LAWRENCE: Did Mr. Clark ever ask you for more money?

TOM: No.

(ANNE *is very distraught. Her face is perspiring, the tension more than she can bear.*)

LAWRENCE'S VOICE: Would you have paid more if he had asked for it? That is, could he have made a profit from the sale of narcotics had he chosen to?

TOM: Sure, he could have, but . . . well, the question doesn't really apply to me.

LAWRENCE: Why not?

TOM: Mr. Clark knew right from the start that I had the habit. I mean it wasn't a question of starting me off cheap until I got hooked and then boosting the price . . . you know the way a pusher would. No, he never said anything about money. I had to ask him the first time how much I owed him.

LAWRENCE: Did he put any conditions at all on the transactions, or did he just give you the pills with no strings attached?

TOM: No, he was very strict about what I had to do . . . about what he called my end of the bargain.

LAWRENCE: And what was your end of the bargain, Tom?

TOM: I had to agree to go to a psychiatrist regularly and do everything I could to straighten myself out.

(KEN *looks troubled as he rises to his feet. And taps* LAWRENCE *on the shoulder.*)

LAWRENCE: May I have a moment, Your Honor?

JUDGE: Yes.

LAWRENCE (*to* KEN): What is it?

KEN: Do you still plan to call Mrs. Clark?

LAWRENCE: Without her, we don't have a motive. Sure I do.

KEN: How soon?

LAWRENCE: Right after Tom Grafton. Why?

KEN: She's gone.

(LAWRENCE *turns to look to* ANNE's *empty chair.* EDDIE *is tormented with worry.*)

Act Four

(*Interior drugstore. Day.* ANNE—*her eyes betray her fear. She is trying very hard to appear normal. She manages a weak smile.*)

ANNE: I'm on my way to Court now. I felt a headache coming on and thought I'd stop by and take something for it.

(STANLEY—*the substitute pharmacist, mid-twenties, brash, insensitive.*)

STANLEY: Sure thing, Mrs. Clark. Help yourself. I'm sure you remember where it is. I'll get you some water.

(*As he leaves,* ANNE *slips behind the counter, a key in her hand, fumbles with the door to a small safe under the counter. Her hands shake, making the task doubly difficult.*)

STANLEY's VOICE: What are you doing back there, Mrs. Clark?

ANNE (*startled*): I . . . I thought it looked open.

(*She stands abruptly as* STANLEY *hurries up with a paper cup filled with water*).

ANNE: The safe looked open.

STANLEY: Not a chance. You don't have to worry about me. I'm tremendously careful. I mean I'm sure not going to make Mr. Clark sorry he gave me this chance. Matter of fact, we got a shipment in a little while ago, and I'm going to put it away right now . . . not wait till we close.

(*He busies himself opening the safe, pulling over a small carton, tearing it open.*)

STANLEY: Oh, did you get something for your headache?

ANNE: Yes . . . thanks.

STANLEY: No . . . please . . . when you see Mr. Clark tell him he shouldn't worry about anything up here, will you do that?

(ANNE *stares at the open carton as* STANLEY, *a handful at a time, takes out small boxes—the kind that contain bottles of pills—and places them in the open safe.*)

ANNE: Let me help you . . .

(*She suddenly reaches down, takes one of the boxes from the carton.* STANLEY *pays little attention.*)

STANLEY: Oh, no . . . that's okay . . .

(*She takes the bottle from the box, her hands trembling.*)

STANLEY's VOICE: You got more to do today than help around here. Thanks . . . (*He holds his hand for the bottle.*)

ANNE: Oh . . . (*As if by accident, she lets the bottle fall. It breaks. The pills scatter.* ANNE *crouches, reaches for a pill that rolls around the end of the counter. A man's foot moves in, stops the pill. Surprised,* ANNE *looks up.* KEN *looks down at her.*)

KEN: What's the matter? (*He bends, picks up the pill.*)

(ANNE *remains crouched, staring at* KEN, *frozen.* STANLEY *stands up from behind the counter, brushes his hands off.*)

STANLEY: Had a little accident. Can I help you?

KEN: I just stopped in to see Mrs. Clark. (*He helps her to her feet.*)

STANLEY: Oh, well, give my best to Mr. Clark.

(*He disappears again behind the counter.* KEN *leads* ANNE *toward the front of the store. They speak quietly so that* STANLEY *won't overhear.*)

KEN: How about it? Are you going to testify or not?

ANNE: Yes, I am . . . if I can just have something first. You don't know what it's been like in there.

KEN: I can't help you, Mrs. Clark.

(*She looks steadily at him. Suddenly the plea in her eyes changes. She smiles a little. Her tone is suggestive. She touches the button on his jacket.*)

ANNE: Listen, you must know somebody . . . a doctor who'll give you a prescription. Then I'll be great . . . and very appreciative. Honest . . . I'll do anything if you'll help me . . . please . . . (*It's meant of course to be seductive, but it's only grotesque.* KEN *is sickened, turns aside. The half-parted lips congeal. She suddenly covers her face with her hands.*) Oh God . . .

(KEN *is deeply moved by compassion for her.*)

KEN: Don't . . . please . . . you didn't mean that. It's already forgotten . . .

(*After a moment she takes her hands away. Slowly. Her face is distorted with contempt for herself, with self-hatred.*)

ANNE: I . . . can't stand myself.

(*He takes her gently by the arm.*)

KEN: Come on . . . let's go back . . .

ANNE (*sudden panic*): Go back? What do you mean?

KEN: To the court. You are going to testify, aren't you?

ANNE: No! I can't! You don't know . . . (*beginning to weep*) I'm sorry . . . I'm sorry . . .

(KEN *wants to argue, and yet he realizes how futile it would be to say anything. And too, he is overwhelmed with pity.*)

ANNE: I want to do it . . . I just can't . . .

(*The woman's suffering is more than* KEN *can bear. He raises his clenched fist, opens it. In his palm, the white tablet he picked up from the floor.* ANNE's *eyes stare at the pill, then, wide with surprise, up to* KEN.)

(*Interior courtroom. Day.*)

LAWRENCE: What is your relationship to the accused, Edward Clark?

ANNE: I'm his wife.

LAWRENCE: How long have you and Mr. Clark been married?

ANNE: Seven years.

LAWRENCE: Are you a drug addict, Mrs. Clark?

ANNE: Yes, I am.

LAWRENCE: What drug are you addicted to?

ANNE: Morphine.

LAWRENCE: And how long have you been an addict?

ANNE: A little over a year.

LAWRENCE: Are you under the influence of morphine at this moment, Mrs. Clark?

ANNE (*after a beat*): Yes.

(*There is a barely audible catching of breaths throughout the court.*)

LAWRENCE: Will you please tell the court what it's like to be under the influence of morphine?

ANNE: What it's like?

LAWRENCE: Yes. What do you see? What do you hear?

ANNE: The same thing everybody else sees. You . . . Eddie . . . the other people. . . .

LAWRENCE: Really? No satyrs? No lurid fantasies? You don't hear any devil's tom-toms or celestial harps?

ANNE: No.

LAWRENCE: Then why do you bother taking morphine at all? If you only experience the same sensations the rest of us do, what's the point?

ANNE: Because . . . if I don't take it, I. . . .

(*She stops.* LAWRENCE *leans in.*)

LAWRENCE: Go on, Mrs. Clark . . . what happens if you don't take it?

ANNE: For one thing, if I hadn't had morphine, I couldn't be here.

LAWRENCE: Why not?

ANNE: I just couldn't, that's all. I couldn't get up from that chair and walk across the room in front of these people and sit down.

LAWRENCE: What would happen if you did, though? If someone made you do it?

ANNE: I'm afraid I'd make a pretty bad spectacle of myself. It's very hard to explain. . . .

LAWRENCE: I know it is. I want you to try.

ANNE: The thing is . . . with me, at least . . . that I lose control. I can't . . . stop crying for one thing. I just can't stop. And I can't sit still . . . I can't hold still. Have you ever had a fever and felt you always had to move . . . to turn . . . to move your legs and your head? It's something like that. Only with me at the time I'm moving, I'm not moving right. What I mean is I lurch, I fall a lot, bump into things. When I reach for something, I almost always knock it over. And then my skin becomes very sensitive . . . as though it were raw or burned. When I touch something it feels like getting a shock . . . you know, from a wire. And my clothes become . . . well, not tight so much as . . . tormenting, I guess. They just hurt me. Everything hurts me. (*beat*) So that's why I say I couldn't have made it from over there to here. Not in a million years.

LAWRENCE: And when you take morphine? What happens then?

ANNE: In the first place everything slows down. It doesn't really, I guess, but it seems to. The falling stops, the burning stops. Things become slow and easy and reasonable. I can handle myself again. I can pick something up. I can even . . . be content with myself a little. That's the best part . . . not to despise yourself for a while.

LAWRENCE: In other words, at those times you feel quite normal.

ANNE (*with growing fervor*): Not "quite" normal! Normal. Just like anybody else. That's what you people don't know about us; what you refuse to understand. You're not addicted. You don't know, you can't know—or you wouldn't do this to us. You'd stop punishing us, degrading us, treating us like filth. Whom does it hurt if we take a drug that spares us from torture? That allows us to remain human, that allows us to think and feel and love and be loved—and be normal. Because we are.

LAWRENCE: Would you like to step down for a few moments, Mrs. Clark?

ANNE: No. Please go on.

LAWRENCE: When did your husband first give you morphine without a prescription?

ANNE: I think it was last . . . September or October.

LAWRENCE: What took place just prior to that?

ANNE: I tried to kill myself.

(ANNE *has spoken quietly. There has been an unnatural stillness in the court. Even now it is a moment before anyone can move.*)

LAWRENCE: Mrs. Clark, you said you're under the influence of morphine now.

ANNE: Yes.

LAWRENCE: Did you acquire it legally? By prescription?

(EDDIE *fears the worst.*)

ANNE'S VOICE: No.

LAWRENCE'S VOICE: Then . . . do you have a supply?

ANNE: I don't have any more, and I don't know how to get any more.

LAWRENCE: What . . . do you intend to do?

ANNE: I don't know. I hope someone does. I hope someone does.

LAWRENCE: Thank you. Your witness.

(*He turns, walks away*).

(D. A. *stands, hesitates for some moments.*)

D. A.: I have no questions.

(*He sits.*)

(EDDIE *on the stand.*)

EDDIE: I found her on the floor of the bathroom. I called the doctor and got the bleeding stopped . . . and then I didn't say anything to her . . . just got dressed and went over to the store and got a bottle of morphine sulphate, changed the amounts on some prescriptions to cover it and gave it to her.

LAWRENCE: And you supplied her ever since?

EDDIE: Except for two periods when she tried to stop.

LAWRENCE: Has she been under the care of a doctor the whole time?

EDDIE: A psychiatrist.

LAWRENCE: But she still needs drugs.

EDDIE: Yes.

LAWRENCE: And you'd be willing to keep supplying her with them?

EDDIE: As long as I could. As long as she needed them.

LAWRENCE: Knowing you would be committing a crime?

EDDIE: I don't believe it's a crime.

LAWRENCE: You do know it's against the law?

EDDIE: Yes.

LAWRENCE: And that your punishment for breaking that law could be extremely severe?

EDDIE: I don't care about that.

LAWRENCE: About law and order?

EDDIE: About anything that deliberately destroys my wife.

LAWRENCE: Thank you, Mr. Clark. That's all.

(D. A.: *rises, advances on* EDDIE.)

D. A.: Mr. Clark, you didn't supply illegal opiates only to your wife did you? We know that others were also beneficiaries of your . . . generosity. And how many others were there?

EDDIE: Three.

D. A.: Only three? By your standard, there must be thousands of people who qualify for the . . . Edward Clark treatment for drug addiction.

EDDIE: I suppose there are. I don't know them.

D. A.: But if you did, you'd give drugs to them too, is that right?

EDDIE: No . . . I don't know . . . I didn't want to help anybody except Anne. The others just happened . . . each one for its own reasons I guess.

D. A.: Did you ever turn down anybody? Did you ever say to anybody who came to you for help . . . did you ever say: "No. It's against the law and there's nothing I can do for you"?

EDDIE: No.

D. A.: Why not? Isn't that what other pharmacists do?

EDDIE: I suppose so.

D. A.: Does that mean they're all heartless and you're the only member of your profession who's got feelings and who likes to help people?

EDDIE: No. I did the same thing for years. Or at least I would have if the problem had ever come up.

D. A.: You mean there was a time when you respected the laws of the state and the codes and ethics of your profession.

EDDIE: I still do.

D. A.: How is that possible, Mr. Clark? How can you have respect for the law and at the same time systematically break it? Will you explain that to us?

(EDDIE *is feeling boxed, harassed.*)

EDDIE: I don't know . . . I respect the law, that's all. I try to do what's right. . . .

D. A.: Willfully defying the law? Is that what you call doing what's right?

EDDIE: All I know is I kept my wife alive when there wasn't any other way to do it. Can that be wrong? I took an oath when I got married, didn't I? To protect her in sickness? That's what I did. I gave her medicine so that. . . .

D. A.: You gave her narcotic drugs which better qualified people than you have found to be harmful.

EDDIE: Drugs, medicine . . . call it what you want. . . .

D. A.: No! The function of medicines is to cure. What you gave your wife only makes her sicker.

EDDIE (*suddenly furious*): That's not true! You don't know that! What I gave her kept her going, kept her functioning while a doctor tried to cure her. What about insulin? Isn't that a medicine? What does insulin cure? All it does is keep people with diabetes alive and functioning. They depend on it. Without it they don't survive. With it they lead a normal life. That's exactly what morphine does for my wife. Exactly! So what's really the difference? Will you tell me that? Will somebody tell me that?

(*He looks around, baffled, a small man caught in a large anomaly.*)

(*Interior courtroom. Day.* LAWRENCE *approaches the jury to begin his summation.* JUDGE, EDDIE, KEN, D. A., ANNE *are in their respective places.*)

LAWRENCE: Edward Clark told you he respects the law. For evidence you have a lifetime of good citizenship. And yet Edward Clark, as the District Attorney put it, willfully and systematically broke the law. Forced to choose between the law and his wife's health, Edward Clark broke the law which makes it possible for a man to be confronted with such a choice. The Harrison Act was passed by Congress in 1914. It was a simple revenue and regulatory measure. It placed a tax on narcotics and required importers and druggists and doctors to keep records. That act is still the basis for the vast enforcement system we have today. Nothing in the act was ever intended to make it a crime to be a drug addict. And yet from that modest beginning has grown a huge police apparatus, the Federal Bureau of Narcotics. And today, despite the Bureau's efforts, we find ourselves more troubled by the narcotics problem than ever.

(LAWRENCE *walks to his seat where* KEN *hands him a document, opened and underlined.*)

LAWRENCE: We find the New York Academy of Medicine able to report as recently as May 1963: "Obviously there are defects in a method that in execution fails to catch the real criminals, the key men in the syndicates, but makes statutory criminals of sick persons, succeeds in bringing some of them to docket, places some in jail, fails to provide proper medical care for them, and instead erects almost insuperable barriers to medical management." We find ourselves listening to an expert such as Doctor Hartog make the startling statement that "no one knows what addiction really is." Why? Because until very recently, our narcotics agents had put the fear of God into any doctor who would have liked to find out what addiction was.

(*He holds out his hand, and* KEN *places in it another document.*)

LAWRENCE: "The nature of administrative enforcement of the Harrison Act is such that physicians are deterred from performance of their ethical duties." An advisory council of judges said that only months ago. In other words, the medical profession was bullied and intimidated into turning its back on the problem of drug addiction, and the whole field was left in the benevolent hands of the enforcers. So that's the history. That's why our lives and Edward Clark's have come together at this time, in this place. Forty years ago we allowed a policeman to come between the doctor and his patient, and a seed took root. Forty years later a neighborhood druggist harvested the fruit of fear and ignorance. Forty years from now we'll all be ashamed.

(*He looks at the members of the jury, then turns away.*)

(D. A. *is making his summation. He carries a copy of the* Journal of the American Medical Association.)

D. A.: We've heard a lot about doctors in this case . . . about the difference between what they believe and how they're permitted to practice. According to Mr. Preston, the accused only did what doctors would have done if the law let them. But is it really that simple? Let me tell you what the American Medical Association says about it. "Continued administration of drugs for the maintenance of addiction is not a bona fide attempt at cure, nor is it ethical treatment. . . ."

(LAWRENCE *reacts with annoyance and frustration. He would like to respond, to point out the fallacies in the argument, but of course must keep his peace.*)

D. A.'s VOICE: In other words, what the accused did is specifically condemned by the American Medical Association.

D. A.: Now as to this business of doctors being intimidated, scared off by the Bureau of Narcotics, let me quote from the Joint Statement on Narcotic Addiction by the American Medical Association and the National Research Council dated May 14, 1962: "Historically, society has found it necessary to employ legal controls to prevent the spread of certain types of illness that constitute a hazard to the public health. Drug addiction is such a hazard." Does that sound like the doctors are suffering under a lot of intolerable restrictions? Do you really get the feeling from that that doctors want to do away with controls in this business of narcotics? Of course not. In fact, throughout this entire report, the A.M.A. repeatedly says it is anxious to cooperate with the Bureau of Narcotics. So much, I hope, for the specter of the quaking doctor so effectively raised by counsel for the defense. Finally, ladies and gentlemen, we're left with one fact that no amount of argument, no amount of persuasion, can change: the accused, Edward Clark, deliberately and systematically chose to place himself above the law.

(EDDIE *is standing beside his chair. He turns to seek out* ANNE. *He smiles at her reassuringly.* ANNE *smiles back reassuringly at her husband, seemingly in control. But her hands, out of* EDDIE's *line of sight, are trembling as they twist a lace handkerchief.*)

(*Jury filing in.* EDDIE, LAWRENCE, KEN *seated at the defense table.* EDDIE *tenses as he turns and watches the jury file in.*)

CLERK: Ladies and gentlemen of the jury, have you reached a verdict?

(*The* FOREMAN *rises.*)

FOREMAN: We have.

CLERK: What is your verdict?

FOREMAN: We find the defendant guilty as charged.

(EDDIE *is stunned.*)

(ANNE's *handkerchief—tearing in two under the strain of her convulsive grip.* ANNE—*her face lifeless. Rising slowly—almost somnambulistically.*)

(EDDIE *is staring ahead in disbelief. In the background* ANNE *is moving woodenly up the aisle toward the door.* LAWRENCE *is standing.*)

CLERK: You, the jury, say you find the defendant, Edward Clark, guilty of the crime as charged in the indictment. And so say you all.

FOREMAN: Yes.

LAWRENCE: Your Honor, I ask that the jury be polled.

JUDGE: The clerk will poll the jury.

(KEN—*turning to look for* ANNE *and seeing her gone. Then seeing her leaving.* KEN *rises and starts up the aisle after* ANNE.)

(*Corridor outside courtroom. As* ANNE *emerges from courtroom and walks mechanically toward the exit.* KEN *appears a moment later, crosses to her quickly, stops her by taking her arm firmly. She doesn't turn to see who it is; she knows.*)

ANNE: I can't face him.

KEN: He doesn't blame you for what happened.

ANNE: What's happened is past. He'll want to know what's going to happen to me. And we all know the answer to that one, don't we?

KEN: Maybe we all just think we do.

(ANNE *turns and looks at* KEN *closely, deeply appreciative.*)

ANNE: Thank you for that, Mr. Preston. But I couldn't change now . . . I know I couldn't. I'm a drug addict—and that's what I'll always be. And I couldn't promise Eddie anything else.

KEN: Eddie knows that, Mrs. Clark. Better than anyone else.

(ANNE *looks toward the courtroom door.*)

ANNE (*pointing toward door*): Is he still in there?

KEN: Yes. Come on.

(*They cross.* KEN *opens door as* ANNE *approaches. In the deep background*

EDDIE *and* LAWRENCE *are standing.* EDDIE *is looking toward* ANNE. *The courtroom is empty except for* EDDIE's *guard.*)

(EDDIE—*his face lighting up as he sees* ANNE *in the doorway.* EDDIE *starts up the aisle toward her.*)

(ANNE—*looking at* EDDIE. *Her eyes wet. She starts toward him. Reaching each other, embracing.*)

EDDIE: Come on now. Mr. Preston thinks the judge will go easy on me when he sentences. If he does—and I behave myself—you'll have me back in just a couple of years.

ANNE (*bleakly*): A couple of years.

EDDIE: Do you think you can—wait? They'll be watching you now. Waiting for you to make a mistake. Waiting for you to drive yourself into their courts, into their jails.

ANNE: I'll try. That's the most I can promise.

(D. A.—*entering from counsel room. He seems a little embarrassed at seeing the Clarks. The Clarks kiss.* EDDIE *turns and exits with the guard.*)

D. A. (*to* ANNE): I'm sorry.

ANNE: Everybody is. But that hasn't solved anything, has it? (*She walks up the aisle and exits.*)

D. A. (*to* LAWRENCE): I thought you might like to know when Clark comes up for sentencing, we're going to recommend a light one.

LAWRENCE: What about Mrs. Clark? What have we done about her sentence? Eddie will get what? Three years? Three months? The question is: what will *she* do tonight? Where will she be when that last pill wears off? What will she do? Where can she turn? Who's going to hear her screams of agony, and who's going to care? Why must she be made to endure torture to satisfy our law, our morality? She may not be able to stand it. In just a few hours she may go out and steal—or prostitute herself—or kill herself. Tonight! We may have convicted a man who broke a law but we may have made a criminal of his wife in the process. Does that give you a sense of accomplishment, Sam? (LAWRENCE *and* KEN *leave the* D. A. *standing there without an answer.*)

Some Facts About Marihuana
Use in the United States

National Commission on Marihuana
and Drug Abuse

Approximately 24 million Americans have used marihuana at one time or another, the National Commission on Marihuana and Drug Abuse discovered in a National Survey conducted as a part of its study of marihuana and drug abuse. The statistic was announced by Raymond P. Shafer, former Governor of Pennsylvania and Commission Chairman. Shafer said the Survey was the most comprehensive National Survey on marihuana ever conducted. "It is a representative Survey covering the entire population," he said.

The use of marihuana has spread to all segments of our population, Shafer declared. "In the past five to seven years it has become more than just a drug to take for a 'high'; it has become a symbol, a dividing line between young and old, as well as a convenient visible and somewhat pungent signal of protest."

The Survey indicates that 15 per cent of the 18 and over population and 14 per cent of the 12–17 age group have used marihuana at one time or another. That amounts to a little over 24 million Americans. When asked if they were presently using marihuana, six per cent of the 12–17 age group and five per cent of the 18 and over group said "yes." This amounts to 8,340,000 Americans.

Interestingly, among the 18–25 year olds questioned, 39 per cent said they had used marihuana at one time or another, while 17 per cent said they were presently using marihuana. One thing the Survey clearly shows, Shafer explained, is that marihuana use is age specific. The heaviest use is in the 18–25 year old range. After 25, use falls off rapidly. Said Shafer, "One possible explanation seems to be that people outgrow it."

According to the Survey, the biggest single reason for terminating usage is loss of interest. Twice the proportion of adults report this motive for quitting as report the next most compelling motive, concern over the legal status of marihuana.

The former Pennsylvania Governor continued:

Reprinted from a news release issued by the National Commission on Marihuana and Drug Abuse on January 21, 1972.

The public is really not well informed about marihuana. There is much uncertainty about the effects of marihuana. I should point out that the 12–17 age group was more uncertain than the adults. They have been bombarded with conflicting information and they no longer know what to believe. For example, many believe marihuana causes death; others believe it is physically addicting. There is a great deal of uncertainty about the law. One in seven of the 12–17 year olds did not think marihuana possession was illegal.

In comparing alcohol and marihuana, people believe alcohol is more addictive than marihuana; however, alcohol and marihuana are perceived quite differently, the Governor explained, although there is no pattern of believing good things about alcohol and bad things about marihuana. Marihuana users seem to see marihuana and alcohol as roughly interchangeable. Alcohol users, however, do not see the two as interchangeable.

The modal response of parents is to discourage use of marihuana but not forbid. Young adults (18–25) would typically either discourage or rely on a discussion of pros and cons to produce acceptable future behavior.

Of all the likely sources of general information about marihuana both the adults and youngsters preferred schools over any of the others. There is also substantial mention of the family physician, the home and mass media.

When asked how society should handle the marihuana issue, 52 per cent of the adults surveyed said they favor a non-legal approach. The views of young people 12–17 years of age are much like those of the adults.

The sale of marihuana is regarded as far more objectionable than its possession. This feeling is characteristic of all age levels but is especially marked among young adults.

The marihuana milieu is a social one, according to the Survey. First use of marihuana is remembered as having these characteristics: The marihuana used was most often a gift from a friend in the company of other people. The activity was spontaneous rather than planned. More often first use was remembered as motivated by curiosity and novelty.

But the key item the Survey uncovered, Shafer said, is that marihuana may be more important as an issue than a substance. Said the Commission Chairman,

There is an observable disparity in our data between the concept of marihuana and the result of experience with it. The typical behavior pattern is to try it and find that one loses interest in it. Of tryers who have become users by their own definition, use is far more likely to be occasional than steady, and infrequent rather than frequent.

Whether they would change their minds under other circumstances we do not know, but the largest part of the population now believes that marihuana is not for them, even if it were to become legal and available. Of those questioned who had never used, 81 per cent of the adults and 73 per cent of the youth said that they would never use it in the future.

The unsettled state of the public feeling about marihuana is remarkable. In times of uncertainty, there is much evidence that younger people particularly

—those 12–17 in our study—do not know what to believe. The same pattern obtains for adults but to a lesser extent.

We think that much of the population (those who are motivated to know more) could benefit by some clarification of what to believe, and that it is possible to bring about some change in their feelings. We are less certain about whether the current state of knowledge can permit clear statements and clear guidance of the kind needed. Our data seem to show that whatever the available mass media and other information has been, it probably has been somewhat unclear or at cross purposes or laboring under the same circumstances as the public: lack of definition and direction.

Drugs are the third most expressed concern as a national problem according to our Survey. From 1970 to 1971 the concern over drugs increased dramatically, while Vietnam as a problem decreased in the minds of those surveyed. . . .

Questions

1. Why is the play called *The Pill Man* and not, for example, *The Dope Peddler?* Is this distinction in the use of language employed within the play?

2. What do the following characters contribute to the development of the ideas in the play: Anne Clark, Tom Grafton, Dr. Nelson, Dr. Hartog?

3. What limitations on the development of the issues involved does the dramatic form impose?

4. In what way might the play be considered propaganda? How would you define *propaganda?* Could this play be accused of "channeling opinion" in the way that news analyses are said to do by Vice President Agnew (Section One)?

5. Do the authors of the play take a particular position? What would you say it is? If you think they do not take a position, why don't they?

6. Does the particular case of Eddie Clark confuse or clarify the more general issues involved? How?

7. Are the questions raised in these selections medical or legal ones? Explain your conclusion.

8. Summarize the several approaches to the drug problem represented in the play.

9. Explain how marijuana may or may not properly be classified as a drug.

10. How is drug addiction a *family* problem? How is it a *personal* one? Cite the text in your answers.

11. Should drug education be the responsibility of the society or the family? Consider your answer in relation to the arguments made in Section Eight on sex education.

Assignments

1. Compare the British and the American methods of handling the problem of narcotics addiction.

2. Review the play, discussing its success in treating the ideological problem that it raises.

3. Analyze the major points on each side of the narcotics argument.

4. Separate the economic, medical, legal, and political aspects of the narcotics problem in the United States today. Describe these aspects of the question and argue which of'them is, in your judgment, most important.

5. Argue for or against one of the following propositions:

a. Narcotics laws have proved to be just another unsuccessful attempt to legislate morality.

b. The use of drugs is a personal, not a social, question.

c. Doctors should be given the freedom to prescribe drugs for addicts.

6. Using this play, and any other literary works which you think appropriate, discuss whether or not propaganda can be art.

Additional Reading

The problem of drug addiction is receiving increasing attention from all points of view. The major issue raised in *The Pill Man*, on the legal and medical aspects of the problem, has also been discussed in "Addiction: An Illness, Not a Sin or Crime," *Science News Letter*, LXXXI (January 6, 1963), 8; J. Kobler, "Narcotics Dilemma: Crime or Disease?" *Saturday Evening Post*, CCXXXV (September 8, 1962), 64–66 ff; W. Sparks, "Narcotics and the Law," *Commonweal*, LXXIV (August 25, 1961), 467–469. There have also been official statements and conferences which have studied the problem. Nat Hentoff's article, "Drug Addiction: Crime or Disease?" *Reporter*, XXIV (May 11, 1961), 52–53, discusses the Reports of the Joint Committee of the American Bar Association and the American Medical Association on Narcotic Drugs. A. R. Lindesmith, in "Addiction: Beginnings of Wisdom," *The Nation*, CXCVI (January 19, 1963), 49–52, discusses the White House Conference on Narcotic and Drug Abuse.

Three books provide more thorough studies of various aspects of the problem: David W. Maurer and Victor H. Vogel, *Narcotics and Narcotic Addiction* (Springfield, Illinois, 1962), William Butler Eldridge, *Narcotics and Law: A Critique of the American Experiment in Narcotic Drug Control* (New York, 1962); and Isidor Chein, Donald L. Gerard, Robert S. Lee, and Eva Rosenfeld, *The Road to H: Narcotics, Delinquency, and Social Policy* (New York, 1964).

Christ

and the Body

Christ in the House of His Parents, by J. E. Millais. Reproduced by permission of the Tate Gallery, London.

On "Christ in the House of His Parents"

Charles Dickens

You come—in this Royal Academy Exhibition, which is familiar with the works of WILKIE, CILLINS, ETTY, EASTLAKE, MULREADY, LESLIE, MACLISE, TURNER, STANFIELD, LANDSEER, ROBERTS, DANBY, CRESWICK, LEE, WEBSTER, HERBERT, DYCE, COPE, and others who would have been renowned as great masters in any age or country—you come, in this place, to the contemplation of a Holy Family. You will have the goodness to discharge from your minds all Post-Raphael ideas, all religious aspirations, all elevating thoughts; all tender, awful, sorrowful, ennobling, sacred, graceful, or beautiful associations; and to prepare yourselves, as befits such a subject —Pre-Raphaelly considered—for the lowest depths of what is mean, odious, repulsive, and revolting.

You behold the interior of a carpenter's shop. In the foreground of that carpenter's shop is a hideous, wry-necked, blubbering, red-headed boy, in a bed-gown; who appears to have received a poke in the hand, from the stick of another boy with whom he has been playing in an adjacent gutter, and to be holding it up for the contemplation of a kneeling woman, so horrible in her ugliness, that (supposing it were possible for any human creature to exist for a moment with that dislocated throat) she would stand out from the rest of the company as a Monster, in the vilest cabaret in France, or the lowest gin-shop in England. Two almost naked carpenters, master and journeyman, worthy companions of this agreeable female, are working at their trade; a boy, with some small flavor of humanity in him, is entering with a vessel of water; and nobody is paying any attention to a snuffy old woman who seems to have mistaken that shop for the tobacconist's next door, and to be hopelessly waiting at the counter to be served with half an ounce of her favourite mixture. Wherever it is possible to express ugliness of feature, limb, or attitude, you have it expressed. Such men as the carpenters might be undressed in any hospital where dirty drunkards, in a high state of varicose veins, are received. Their very toes have walked out of Saint Giles's.

This, in the nineteenth century, and in the eighty-second year of the annual exhibition of the National Academy of Art, is the Pre-Raphael representation to us, Ladies and Gentlemen, of the most solemn passage which our minds can ever approach. This, in the nineteenth century, and in the eighty-second year of the annual exhibition of the National Academy of Art, is what Pre-Raphael Art can do to render reverence and homage to the faith in which we live and die! Consider this picture well. Consider the pleasure we should have in a similar Pre-Raphael rendering of a favourite horse, or dog, or cat; and, coming fresh from a pretty considerable turmoil about "desecration" in connexion with the National Post Office, let us extol this great achievement, and commend the National Academy!

The Risen Lord

D. H. Lawrence

The risen lord, the risen lord
has risen in the flesh,
and treads the earth to feel the soil
though his feet are still nesh.

The Churches loudly assert: We preach Christ crucified!—But in so doing, they preach only half of the Passion, and do only half their duty. The Creed says: "Was crucified, dead, and buried . . . the third day He rose again from the dead." And again, "I believe in the resurrection of the body . . ." So that to preach Christ Crucified is to preach half the truth. It is the business of the Church to preach Christ born among men—which is Christmas; Christ Crucified, which is Good Friday; and Christ Risen, which is Easter. And after Easter, till November and All Saints, and till Annunciation, the year belongs to the Risen Lord: that is, all the full-flowering spring, all summer, and the autumn of wheat and fruit, all belong to Christ Risen.

But the Churches insist on Christ Crucified, and rob us of the blossom and fruit of the year. The Catholic Church, which has given us our images, has given us the Christ-child, in the lap of woman, and again, Christ Crucified: then the Mass, the mystery of atonement through sacrifice. Yet all this is really preparatory, these are the preparatory stages of the real living religion. The Christ-child, enthroned in the lap of the Mother, is obviously only a preparatory image, to prepare us for Christ the Man. Yet a vast mass of Christians stick there.

What we have to remember is that the great religious images are only images of our own experiences, or of our own state of mind and soul. In the Catholic countries, where the Madonna-and-Child image overwhelms everything else, the man visions himself all the time as a child, a Christ-child, standing on the lap of a virgin mother. Before the war, if an Italian hurt himself, or suddenly fell into distress, his immediate cry was: *O mamma mia! mamma mia!—Oh, mother, mother!*—The same was true of many Englishmen. And what does this mean? It means that the man sees himself as a child, the innocent saviour-child enthroned on the lap of the all-pitying virgin mother. He lives according to this image of himself—the image of the guileless "good" child sheltered in the arms of an all-sheltering mother—until the image breaks in his heart.

And during the war, this image broke in the hearts of most men, though not in the hearts of their women. During the war, the men who suffered most bitterly suffered beyond the help of wife or mother, and no wife nor mother nor sister nor any beloved could save him from the guns. This fact went home in his heart, and broke the image of mother and Christ-child, and left in its place the image of Christ Crucified.

It was not so, of course, for the woman. The image did not break for her. She visioned herself still as the all-pitying, all-sheltering Madonna, on whose lap the man was enthroned, as in the old pictures, like a Christ-child. And naturally the woman did not want to abandon this vision of herself. It gave her her greatest significance; and the greatest power. Break the image, and her significance and her power were gone. But the men came back from the war and denied the image—for them it was broken. So she fought to maintain it, the great vision of man, the Christ-child, enthroned in the lap of the all-pitying virginal woman. And she fought in vain, though not without disastrous result.

For the vision of the all-pitying and all-helpful Madonna was shattered in the hearts of men, during the war. The all-pitying and all-helpful Woman actually did not, whether she could or not, prevent the guns from blowing to pieces the men who called upon her. So her image collapsed, and with it the image of the Christ-child. For the man who went through the war the resultant image inevitably was Christ Crucified, Christ tortured on the Cross. And Christ Crucified is essentially womanless.

True, many of the elderly men who never went through the war still insist on the Christ-child business, and most of the elderly women insist on their benevolent Madonna supremacy. But it is in vain. The guns broke the image in the hearts of middle-aged men, and the young were born, or are come to real consciousness, after the image was already smashed.

So there we are! We have three great image-divisions among men and women to-day. We have the old and the elderly, who never were exposed to the guns, still fatuously maintaining that man is the Christ-child and woman the infallible safeguard from all evil and all danger. It is fatuous, because it absolutely didn't work. Then we have the men of middle age, who were all tortured and virtually put to death by the war. They accept Christ Crucified as their image, are essentially womanless, and take the great cry: *Consummatum est!—It is finished!—*as their last word.— Thirdly, we have the young, who never went through the war. They have no illusions about it, however, and the death-cry of their elder generation: *It is finished!* rings cold through their blood. They cannot answer. They cannot even scoff. It is no joke, and never will be a joke.

And yet, neither of the great images is *their* image. They cannot accept the child-and-mother position which the old buffers still pose in. They cannot accept the Christ Crucified finality of the generations immediately ahead. For they, the young, came into the field of life after the death-cry *Consummatum est!* had rung through the world, and while the body, so to speak, was being put into the tomb. By the time the young came onto the stage, Calvary was empty, the tombs were closed, the women had lost for ever the Christ-child and the virgin saviour, and it was altogether the day after, cold, bleak, empty, blank, meaningless, almost silly.

The young came into life, and found everything finished. Everywhere the empty crosses, everywhere the closed tombs, everywhere the manless, bitter or over-assertive woman, everywhere the closed grey disillusion of Christ Crucified, dead, and buried, those grey empty days between Good Friday and Easter.

And the Churches, instead of preaching the Risen Lord, go on preaching the Christ-child and Christ Crucified. Now man cannot live without some vision of himself. But still less can he live with a vision that is not true to his inner experience and inner feeling. And the vision of Christ-child and Christ Crucified are both untrue to the inner experience and feeling of the young. They don't feel that way. They show the greatest forbearance and tolerance of their elders, for whom the two images *are* livingly true. But for the post-war young, neither the Christ-child nor Christ Crucified means much.

I doubt whether the Protestant Churches, which supported the war, will ever have the faith and the power of life to take the great step onwards, and preach Christ Risen. The Catholic Church might. In the countries of the Mediterranean, Easter has always been the greatest of the holy days, the gladdest and holiest, not Christmas, the birth of the Child. Easter, Christ Risen, the Risen Lord, this, to the old faith, is still the first day in the year. The Easter festivities are the most joyful, the Easter processions the finest, the Easter ceremonies the most splendid. In Sicily the women take into church the saucers of growing corn, the green blades rising tender and slim like green light, in little pools, filling round the altar. It is Adonis. It is the re-born year. It is Christ Risen. It is the Risen Lord. And in the warm south still a great joy floods the hearts of the people on Easter Sunday. They feel it, they feel it everywhere. The Lord is risen. The Lord of the rising wheat and the plum blossoms is warm and kind upon earth again, after having been done to death by the evil and the jealous ones.

The Roman Catholic Church may still unfold this part of the Passion fully, and make men happy again. For Resurrection is indeed the consummation of all the passion. Not even Atonement, the being at one with Christ through partaking in His sacrifice, consummates the Passion finally. For even after Atonement men still must live, and must go forward with the vision. After we share in the body of Christ, we rise with Him in the body. And that is the final vision that has been blurred to all the Churches.

Christ risen in the flesh! We must accept the image complete, if we accept it at all. We must take the mystery in its fulness and in fact. It is only the image of our own experience. Christ rises, when He rises from the dead, in the flesh, not merely as spirit. He rises with hands and feet, as Thomas knew for certain: and if with hands and feet, then with lips and stomach and genitals of a man. Christ risen, and risen in the whole of His flesh, not with some left out.

Christ risen in the full flesh! What for? It is here the gospels are all vague and faltering, and the Churches leave us in the lurch. Christ risen in the flesh in order to lurk obscurely for six weeks on earth, then be taken vaguely up into heaven in a cloud? Flesh, solid flesh, feet and bowels and teeth and eyes of a man, taken up into heaven in a cloud, and never put down again?

It is the only part of the great mystery which is all wrong. The virgin birth, the baptism, the temptation, the teaching, Gethsemane, the betrayal, the crucifixion, the burial and the resurrection, these are all true according to our inward experience. They are what men and women go through, in their different ways. But floated up into heaven as flesh-and-blood, and never set down again—this nothing in all our experience will ever confirm. If aeroplanes take us up, they bring us down, or let us down. Flesh and blood belong to the earth, and only to the earth. We know it.

And Jesus was risen flesh-and-blood. He rose a man on earth to live on earth. The greatest test was still before Him: His life as a man on earth. Hitherto He had been a sacred child, a teacher, a messiah, but never a full man. Now, risen from the dead. He rises to be a man on earth, and live His life of the flesh, the great life, among other men. This is the image of our inward state to-day.

This is the image of the young: the Risen Lord. The teaching is over, the crucifixion is over, the sacrifice is made, the salvation is accomplished. Now comes the true life, man living his full life on earth, as flowers live their full life, without rhyme or reason except the magnificence of coming forth into fullness.

If Jesus rose from the dead in triumph, a man on earth triumphant in renewed flesh, triumphant over the mechanical anti-life convention of Jewish priests, Roman despotism, and universal money-lust; triumphant above all over His own self-absorption, self-consciousness, self-importance; triumphant and free as a man in full flesh and full, final experience, even the accomplished acceptance of His own death; a man at last full and free in flesh and soul, a man at one with death: then He rose to become at one with life, to live the great life of the flesh and the soul together, as peonies or foxes do, in their lesser way. If Jesus rose as a full man, in full flesh and soul, then He rose to take a woman to Himself, to live with her, and to know the tenderness and blossoming of the twoness with her; He who had been hitherto so limited to His oneness, or His universality, which is the same thing. If Jesus rose in the full flesh, He rose to know the tenderness of a woman, and the great pleasure of her, and to have children by her. He rose to know the responsibility and the peculiar delight of children, and also the exasperation and nuisance of them. If Jesus rose as a full man, in the flesh, He rose to have friends, to have a man-friend whom He would hold sometimes to His breast, in strong affection, and who would be dearer to Him than a brother, just out of the sheer mystery of sympathy. And how much more wonderful, this, than having disciples! If Jesus rose a full man in the flesh, He rose to do His share in the world's work, something He really liked doing. And if He remembered His first life, it would neither be teaching nor preaching, but probably carpentering again, with joy, among the shavings. If Jesus rose a full man in the flesh, He rose to continue His fight with the hardboiled conventionalists like Roman judges and Jewish priests and money-makers of every sort. But this time, it would no longer be the fight of self-sacrifice that would end in crucifixion. This time it would be a freed man fighting to shelter the rose of life from being trampled on by the pigs. This time, if Satan attempted temptation in the wilderness, the Risen Lord would answer: Satan, your silly temptations no longer tempt me. Luckily, I have died to that sort of self-importance and self-conceit. But let me tell you something, old man! Your name's Satan, isn't it? And your name is Mammon? You are the selfish hog that's got hold of all the world, aren't you? Well, look here, my boy, I'm going to take it all from you, so don't worry. The world and the power and the riches thereof, I'm going to take them all from you, Satan or Mammon or whatever your name is. Because you don't know how to use them. The earth is the Lord's, and the fulness thereof, and it's going to be. Men have risen from the dead and learned not to be so greedy and self-important. We left most of that behind in the late tomb. Men have risen beyond you, Mammon, they are your risen lords. And so, you hook-nosed, glisten-eyed, ugly, money-smelling anachronism, you've got to get out. Men have not died and risen again for nothing. Whom do you think the earth belongs to, you stale old rat? The earth is the Lord's and is given to the men who have died and had the power to rise again. The earth is given to the men who have risen from the dead, risen, you old grabber, and when did you ever rise? Never! So go you down to oblivion, and give your place to the risen men, and the women of the risen men. For man has been dispossessed of the full earth and the earth's fulness long enough. And the poor women, they have been shoved about manless and meaningless long enough. The earth is the Lord's and the fulness thereof, and I, the Risen Lord, am here to take possession. For now I am fully a man, and free above all from my own self-importance. I want life, and the pure contact with life. What are riches, and glory, and honour, and might, and power, to me who have died and lost my self-importance? That's why I am going to take them all from you, Mammon, because I care nothing about them. I am going to destroy all your values, Mammon; all your money values and conceit values, I am going to destroy them all.

Because only life is lovely, and you, Mammon, prevent life. I love to see a squirrel peep round a tree; and left to you, Mammon, there will soon be no squirrels to peep. I love to hear a man singing a song to himself, and if it is an old, improper song, about the fun between lads and girls, I like it all the better. But you, beastly mealy-mouthed Mammon, you would arrest any lad that sings a gay song. I love the movement of life, and the beauty of life, O Mammon, since I am risen, I love the beauty of life intensely; columbine flowers, for example, the way they dangle, or the delicate way a young girl sits and wonders, or the rage with which a man turns and kicks a fool dog that suddenly attacks him—beautiful that, the swift fierce turn and lunge of a kick, then the quivering pause for the next attack; or even the slightly silly glow that comes over some men as they are getting tipsy—it still is a glow, beautiful; or the swift look a woman fetches me, when she would really like me to go off with her, but she is troubled; or the real compassion I saw a woman express for a man who slipped and wrenched his foot: life, the beauty, the beauty of life! But that which is anti-life, Mammon, like you, and money, and machines, and prostitution, and all that tangled mass of self-importance and greediness and self-conscious conceit which adds up to Mammon, I hate it. I hate it, Mammon, I hate you and am going to push you off the face of the earth, Mammon, you great mob-thing, fatal to men.

D. H. Lawrence's Appraisal of Jesus

William E. Phipps

During this last third of the 20th century, Christian appreciation is growing of D. H. Lawrence, a gifted English writer of the century's first third. At a celebrated legal hearing in 1960 pertaining to the judical ban on *Lady Chatterley's Lover*, Bishop J. A. T. Robinson rescued Lawrence from the ranks of pornographers. He showed that, for Lawrence, adulterous sexual communion could be unadulterated holy communion. Indeed in his controversial *Honest to God*, published in 1963, the Anglican bishop had said that Lawrence's insights on personal relationships were close to his own. More recently, church historian Horton Davies—in an article in *Religion in Life* (Summer 1969)—defended Lawrence as a Christian, albeit heretical, who was trying to remove smut and shame from sexuality. Thus far, however, virtually no theological study of Lawrence's view of Jesus has appeared in print. Therefore I shall try here to show what Lawrence regarded as of primary significance in Jesus (or in any other model of morality); namely, the quality of emotional reciprocation.

Lawrence gives forthright expression to his outlook on Jesus in a short novel—his last important work of fiction—which he called *The Escaped Cock* but which, since the author's death in 1930, has been published under the evasive title *The Man Who Died*. "The man" is not named in the book, but it is inescapably plain that Lawrence had Jesus in mind—the Jesus of the Christian's paradigm, which he found defective and even revolting as a paradigm of manhood. Thus he portrays Jesus as a pallid being, a frigid prophet unable to fathom the redemptive love found among those who value sexual sharing. Like Lady Chatterley's husband, Lawrence's Jesus is inert from the waist down, and "Touch me not!" is his motto. In this novel we are shown how the self-abnegating healer and teacher utterly distorts true love, for he is disdainful of anyone who might attempt to break his perfect record of altruism. But after his public ministry is completed, Lawrence's Jesus realizes that to be totally outgiving is an error. He confesses that the career which ended with the crucifixion was marked by "greed of giving." "I gave more than I took," he says, "and that also is woe and vanity." He laments that he had asked his disciples to "love with dead bodies." And after the revival of his former "dead" flesh he comes to see that the virginal life, far from being pure and noble, was "a form of greed." In short, Lawrence suggests that those who make sexual deprivation the main mark of their life style are selfishly attempting to protect themselves from the risks of physical involvement.

RISEN IN FULL FLESH. Jesus' outlook on sex, as Lawrence presents it, is the end-result of an ugly moral dualism that began with Plato. That philosopher denigrated the flesh, calling it the tomb in which the rational soul is buried. Thus Lawrence has Lady Chatterley say: "The human body is only just coming to real life. With the Greeks it gave a lovely flicker, then Plato and Aristotle killed it, and Jesus finished it off. But now the body is coming really to life, it is really rising from the tomb."

In *The Escaped Cock* Lawrence not only scathingly denounces the quality of love he ascribes to Jesus but audaciously goes on to suggest how Jesus should have lived. Because Lawrence believed that the ideal man is one who responds to the beauty of the sensate, he tells of Jesus' victorious struggle, after his "resurrection," to reconcile his instinctive sexual impulse with his spirituality. But Lawrence is only incidentally interested in the historical Jesus. His real focus in this novel is on the modern Christian who participates in Jesus' tragic-triumphant drama. Lawrence was influenced by Paul's mysticism: "If we have become one with him by sharing in his death, we shall also be one with him by sharing his resurrection" (Rom. 6:5—Weymouth). Similarly Lawrence testified: "It is time for the Lord in us to arise. . . . Men in the tomb, rise up, the time is expired. The Lord is risen. Quick! Let us follow Him" (*Phoenix: The Posthumous Papers of D. H. Lawrence*, edited by E. D. McDonald [Viking, 1936], pp. 737, 739).

As a way of showing us the full man, whether the Pauline second Adam or 20th century man, Lawrence employed the device of writing an imaginary conclusion for Jesus' life. Though left for dead, Lawrence's Jesus revives without supernatural assistance. Like a cock at dawn, he begins a "new day" at Easter. Overcome by a "nausea of utter disillusion" with his former life and eager to escape from Magdalene, who, in imitation of her Savior, gives without taking, he flees to Sidon on the Lebanese coast where he finds a place to sleep in the precincts of a temple of Isis. Attending the goddess is a young priestess, a virgin who, identifying herself with the bereaved divinity, waits in anguish for the fragments of dead Osiris to be brought together and resurrected. For years the priestess has been seeking the mystic ecstasy which, she believes, would envelop her when she could "fold her arms around the reassembled body till it became warm again, and roused to life, and could embrace her, and could fecundate her womb." She had refused to serve Caesar as mistress because she found him too rapacious to arouse her. But now, encountering Jesus, she finds the fulfillment of her spiritual and physical quest: for her he is the resurrected Osiris. "She felt [her passion for Jesus] in the quick of her soul. And her agitation was intense." And Jesus, who likewise had lived the life of the solitary celibate, now discovers that give-and-take affection among men and women is more liberating than the give-and-give ethic he had formerly taught and practiced. The gracious words and actions of the priestess cause sensual desire to swell up in his loins for the first time. Reluctant to become vulnerable, he asks in fear and trembling, "Dare I come into this tender touch of life?" But he yields, and "there dawned on him the reality of the soft warm love which is in touch, and which is full of delight." As the priestess massages his wounds, he explains: "I am going to be whole! . . . I shall be a man!" He is experiencing a passion quite different from his passion at Calvary.

Stooping, he laid his hand softly on her warm, bright shoulder, and the shock of desire went through him. . . . He crouched to her, and he felt the blaze of his manhood and his power rise up in his loins, magnificent. "I am risen!" . . . He untied the string on the linen tunic, and slipped the garment down, till he saw the white glow of her white-gold breasts. And he touched them and he felt his life go molten. "Father!" he said, "why did you hide this from me?" And he touched her with the poignancy of wonder, and the marvellous piercing transcendence of desire. "Lo!" he said, "this is beyond prayer." . . . So he knew her, and was one with her.

The Christian doctrine of Jesus' bodily resurrection is Lawrence's cue for this climactic scene in his novel: he portrays Jesus as risen in the whole of his flesh—including his genitals. Lawrence expanded on this theme in his essay "The Risen Lord" (*The Later D. H. Lawrence* [Knopf, 1959]):

If Jesus rose as a full man, in full flesh and soul, then He rose to take a woman to Himself, to live with her, and to know the tenderness and blossoming of the twoness with her. . . . If Jesus rose in the full flesh, He rose to know the tenderness of a woman, and the great pleasure of her, and to have children by her. He rose to know the responsibility and the peculiar delight of children, and also the exasperation and nuisance of them.

In his novella Lawrence was not attempting to correct the church's understanding of Jesus' post-mortem life. Rather, he was asserting, and vigorously, that an exemplar of true humanity cannot be thought of as an asexual being.

IN TOUCH WITH THE SENSATE WORLD. What basis is there for Lawrence's tacit charge that the Jesus of traditional Christianity is more a discarnate spirit than a human being? I have attempted to show in my book *Was Jesus Married?* (Harper & Row, 1970) that, from the second century onward, Jesus' teaching and actions have been perversely interpreted by antisexual gentiles. For example, Irenaeus maintained (ca. 180) that Jesus effected mankind's salvation by remaining a virgin all his life (*Against Heresies* 5, 19, 1). Some 250 years later Augustine rounded out the orthodox doctrine by his claim that Jesus not only refrained completely from sexual relations but could not have even desired to indulge in them. For the bishop of Hippo believed that sexual desire was a result of original sin; and he reasoned that since Jesus was without sin he could not have had libidinous impulses (*Against Julian* 5, 8 and 15). Augustine's view was incorporated into church tradition, so it has become taboo to associate the absolutely "pure" Son of God with sexual involvement.

But was the historical Jesus in fact aloof from sexual impulses and their indulgence? It appears that Lawrence, like most other Christians, was able to see Jesus only through the distorting lens of ascetic interpreters. According to the New Testament, the real Jesus "in the days of his flesh" was "tempted in every respect as we are" (Heb. 5:7; 4:15). The way of life he commended called for complementary self-giving and self-fulfillment. "Losing his life" in devotion to others, he received in return some gratifications, both tangible and intangible. He was affectionate toward the women who anointed his body. When "a woman of the city who was a sinner" kissed him profusely, he expressed a warm appreciation for her love (Luke 7:37-47). The rock opera *Jesus Christ Superstar* puts into Jesus' mouth words that the historical record seems to justify. When Magdalene, an ex-prostitute, caresses him he says: "That feels nice. . . . She alone has tried to give me what I need right here and now." Dorothea Krook has aptly criticized Lawrence's portrait of Jesus in this terse comment: "If ever a man was in touch with the phenomenal world and never lost touch with it, that man was Jesus" (*Three Traditions of Moral Thought* [Cambridge University Press, 1959], p. 286). Both figuratively and literally Jesus was in touch with the sensate world.

In my book mentioned above I cite reasons for my belief that Jesus was probably married shortly after attaining puberty. In his parables he used connubial life to illustrate the optimum life. When criticized for rejecting the funereal aspects of traditional piety, he compared the religious life to a happy wedding party (Luke 5:34; 7:31-34). A comment of Horton Davies' is in point here: "Lawrence believed that life should be a marriage feast celebrated with great joy and dancing." It seems clear then that it was not Jesus but Platonists such as Origen, Gregory of Nyssa and Augustine who attempted to sever the spiritual blossom of Christianity from its carnal roots. The dualism that resulted from their error has been in part responsible for the false views of sex associated with Christianity.

Lawrence himself, so one critic conjectures, might well have found the real Jesus acceptable. "It seems safe to say," writes Ralph Sturm in the *Catholic World* (November 1968),

that he probably would not have rejected the Christ of the Gospel as he was understood in apostolic times. . . . The Christ of whom Lawrence spoke was always inevitably a Christ colored by the face of twentieth-century Christianity, a Christ partially consisting of Puritain rigidity, spiritualism, and angelism. The Christ Lawrence rejected was a kind of ethereal nonhuman Christ.

Jesus was in fact a member of a culture that treasured the Song of Solomon, that most sensuous of poems. Jesus' contemporary the great Rabbi Akiba called that Song the holiest part of the Jewish sacred writings (Mishnah, Yadayim 3, 5). The Hebrew Bible uses the same verb, *aheb*, for the spiritual and the physical facets of the love relation. In the Song of Solomon, for instance, *aheb* refers to the craving mutually felt by bride and bridegroom, and elsewhere in the Old Testament the same verb describes the reciprocal devotion between God and his people. The Septuagint translators of the Hebrew Scriptures generally rendered *aheb* with *agapan*. That Greek verb and its substantive form, *agape*, became the key concept of New Testament religion. The New Testament writers themselves use *agapan* and its derivatives with reference to various kinds of love relationship: that between God and man (John 3:16; Mark 12:30), that which Jesus received from and gave to some women (Luke 7:47; John 11:5), and that between a devoted husband and wife (Col. 3:19). Thus *agapan* points to both the physical and the spiritual dimensions of love.

It would seem that Jesus and his fellow Jews were committed to the holistic life. They did not elevate sex to a transcendent ultimate, and they realized that full human vitality demanded more than genital satisfaction. But neither did they denigrate sexual intercourse and look upon it as a merely animal act. Indeed in ancient Judaism sex was accepted as a God-given means for enhancing the companionship and the procreative purposes of marriage. As a Jewish male, Jesus participated in a culture that regarded marital sexuality as a holy communion.

Lawrence sought in all his writings to describe the balanced life. Only when the emotions and the mind were given their just due, he believed, could personality come into full bloom. But he was not successful. In protest against the flesh-abhorring society he lived in, he overstressed the carnal side of the love relationship. To those of his culture who insisted that sex is a sin, he overreacted by insisting that sensuality is salvation. As Dean Peerman perceptively writes: "Lawrence is to be held responsible not for salaciously cheapening sex but the opposite—for magnifying its meaning, for overvaluing it to the point of idolatrous glorification, for according it saving power" ("D. H. Lawrence: Devout Heretic," *The Christian Century*, Februrary 22, 1961, p. 237).

The fact is that in some of his writings Lawrence seems to be unwittingly dualistic. Occasionally he separates the physiological from the psychological aspects of love. His two-tiered theory of personality, in which the cerebral and the tactile are sharply differentiated, is set forth in his creed: "My great religion is belief in the blood, the flesh, as being wiser than the intellect. We can go wrong in our minds. But what our flesh believes and says, is always true" (*Collected Letters,* edited by H. T. Moore [Viking, 1962], I, p. 180). This creed supports the view of some critics that Lawrence has more in common with phallic cults than with the biblical religion which celebrates the action of God in the brain as well as in the viscera. On the positive side, Lawrence has helped to exorcise the Gnostic ghost that has perennially haunted the figure of Jesus. He has rightly repudiated the Christianity that, in overemphasizing Jesus' bloody death to the negation of his red-blooded life, is as he says concerned with "only half of the Passion" (*The Later D. H. Lawrence,* p. 386).

Lawrence's insistence that mature love should not be viewed as a unilateral altruism is also a significant contribution. A touch-me-not attitude toward one's body, he held, is vicious; for life is desecrated when tender feelings are not accorded at least as much dignity as dispassionate reason. Which is to say that Lawrence was convinced that physical intimacy should be regarded as a divinely given way of rising above egotistic impulses, that human relations at their best involve a dynamic and delightful giving and receiving between individuals.

Re: "D. H. Lawrence's Appraisal of Jesus"

(A Response to William E. Phipps)

William R. Hoyt, III

SIR: I wish to express appreciation to William E. Phipps for raising so incisively the question of Jesus' sexuality, not only in his April 28 Century article but also in his book, *Was Jesus Married?* Reappraisal of Jesus' sexuality is demanded not only by advances in biblical scholarship and the history of Christian thought, but with equal urgency by current sexual ethics and the larger problem of providing an authentic model of the Christian man for our day. If Christianity has been cut off from its carnal roots, current sexual ethics and theological anthropology have been cut off from the figure of Jesus. We see the problem of the sexual in new perspective, but unfortunately our thinking about Jesus in relation to the sexual has until recently remained virtually unchanged.

Phipps is concerned with combating the heresy—which flowed into the early church in many streams but found powerful expression in the river of Augustine's thought—that sexual desire is lust and that sexual intercourse is in some sense sinful. If sexual desire is lust, then of course a sinless Jesus could not have had sexual desires. Phipps's concern is not merely an academic one. Too often the church has imposed a crushing load of needless guilt on countless people who were "guilty" only of being normal. Who can estimate the cost in misdirected energies?

I

There are, however, some questions I wish to raise, particularly in regard to Phipps's application of Lawrence's work. He sees Lawrence's writings as an aid in exorcising "the Gnostic ghost that has perennially haunted the figure of Jesus." There is validity in such use of Lawrence. A major concern of Lawrence's, expressed in much of his work, was that of rescuing sex from both prudery and obscenity. And surely Lawrence was correct in realizing that in order to do this he had to challenge the asexual figure of Jesus. Therefore Lawrence's critique, in *The Man Who Died,* of an idealized Jesus who could not have had normal sexual impulses is in order. Although it may be questioned whether Christians in general can recognize their Lord in *The Man Who Died,* nevertheless I have no quarrel with Phipps's use of Lawrence's analysis for any help it can give in chasing the Gnostic ghost out of the figure of Jesus.

However, Phipps seems to claim a good deal more for Lawrence. He seems virtually to identify that quality so crucially important in Lawrence's writings—"emotional reciprocation" made possible by sexual intercourse—with the "dynamic and delightful giving and receiving between individuals" which he properly sees as the goal of the biblical faith in human relations. But such a use of Lawrence's work requires examination. Our theological forebears often ignored or condemned contemporary writers without bothering to learn what they were saying. It is possible for us to make the opposite mistake of giving a Christian interpretation to a contemporary writer when such an interpretation may be far removed from his own intentions. Just how much legitimate use Christian theology can make of Lawrence is debatable. To be sure, Lawrence was intensely religious. Furthermore, there are elements in his thought and concerns which Christianity can applaud: his belief in the goodness of sex; his opposition to prudery and obscenity; his taking, as Horton Davies says, "very seriously what is given here and now by God"; his struggle against the dehumanization of man—not to speak of his struggle against the rape of nature. Moreover, Lawrence wished to uncork not only man's sexual feelings but his other feelings as well—anger, for example—so that a more authentic expression of human life could be realized.

II

Although these elements in Lawrence qualify him to chase Gnostic ghosts, there are serious obstacles to the uncritical use of his thought for the purposes of Christian theology. H. M. Daleski holds that Lawrence "exploits the emotional power" of the imagery of the Hebraic-Christian tradition "while using it for his own purposes" (*The Forked Flame: A Study of D. H. Lawrence,* Northwestern University Press, 1965, pp. 22–23). Graham Hough cautions Christians "who would use Lawrence's stream to turn their own mills . . ." (*The Dark Sun: A Study of D. H. Lawrence,* Macmillan, 1957, p. 253). Hough contends that Lawrence inverts Christianity, that in his writings the life of the spirit is swallowed up by the life of the body. A Christian sense of the transcendent is missing in Lawrence's work. There is no recognition of God as Judge, Redeemer and personal Heavenly Father. There is no acknowledgment of the resurrection of Christ and those who belong to him, with bodies endowed with resources to express a love that is deeper and more universal than is possible with "hands, feet, lips, stomach and genitals"—the only form of resurrection-body Lawrence will accept (cf. "The Risen Lord"). Further, in *The Man Who Died,* Lawrence transforms the Christian doctrine of the "great atonement" into "the being in touch." He adds: "The grey sea and the rain, the wet narcissus and the woman I wait for, the invisible Isis and the unseen sun are all in touch and at one."

It is precisely Lawrence's failure to recognize God as transcendent as well as immanent and personal that drastically limits the help he can give us in clarifying Christian anthropology, including sexuality. A Christian view of human relations, including the sexual, is grounded in a Christian view of God (cf. Robert Osborn, "Sex and the Single God," *The Christian Century,* September 7, 1966) [reprinted as the next reading in this section]. The dynamic relation between God and his people centers on *hesed*—faithful love—which God both grants and requires; *hesed* is of foundational importance for a Christian understanding of human relationships, particularly within marriage. Thus, while Lawrence can diagnose the ills of sick relationships, he does not provide much help in developing a model for healthier ones. For example, it is easy to see the wrongness of the marital relationship between Connie and Clifford in *Lady Chatterley's Lover,* but it is not at all clear that the relationship between Connie and her lover, Mellors, is much more than a tool for Lawrence's criticism of prudery and social ills. Lawrence may be a surgeon who can excise diseased tissue, but he is not a physician who can restore the patient to full health.

Indeed, Lawrence seems to have known less, not more, than is contained in the best of Christian tradition about warmth and commitment and wholeness within the marital relation, including the sexual aspects of that relation. Those Christians who have been haunted by Gnostic and Manichean ghosts should not be taken as representative of Christianity as a whole. In centuries past the Scottish Presbyterians sometimes added to the "love, honor and cherish" requirement the obligation that one be bonny in bed. Although Reinhold Niebuhr did not develop the idea, his viewing of the love between husband and wife, or between parents and children, "as a seed pod of a more universal love" ("Toward New Intra-Christian Endeavors," *The Christian Century*, December 31, 1969, p. 1666) has more potential for giving eros its proper place within Christian love than do Lawrence's views, in which the understanding of Christian love is limited. Indeed, because he lacked a sense of God as personal and loving, Lawrence had no basis for understanding Christian love. Thus there is more than ample justification for his condemnation of the Christian ideal of altruism in its superficiality and denial of real human feelings, but he could not understand the motive of Christian self-giving love as a response to God's love for his people (cf. Graham Hough, *Dark Sun*, p. 242).

III

In the J writer's story of the creation of man in Genesis 2, God creates man from the dust of the earth, but he also addresses man and is responded to by man. Man is part of the natural order, but he also transcends the natural order. The New Testament doctrine of the resurrection is the culmination of the belief in man's transcendence of the natural world, but at the same time it affirms the reality of his physical life as a unified being in the natural world. The physical and the spiritual are indeed two facets of man's one unified person, but it is difficult to keep them in balance. In Christianity the tendency has been to stress the spiritual at the expense of the physical, perhaps in part because the resurrection symbolizes for many people the spiritual more clearly than it does the physical.

Growing up in the Victorian era (it had its swingers, too—under cover, of course) and writing in the post-Victorian era, Lawrence understandably stumped for the physical to the extent of virtually denying the transcendent in man's life. But since he presents an unbalanced view of man, his work can be no more than a corrective. He reinstates the physical bases for genuine reciprocity between persons while denying the spiritual bases.

IV

Theology is for people. Phipps's writing demonstrates his awareness of this truth. On the other hand, the limitations of Lawrence's anthropology restrict its usefulness for people. Lawrence's message is needed by some—those who have been taught to believe, consciously or unconsciously, that sex is evil. Many in the over-30 group are in this category. Further, there are still segments of our social institutions, including the church, which are educating people to repress their sexuality—as many counselors of the young can testify.

The question may be raised, however, as to whether, in a sex-saturated society, Lawrence's message is the major thrust needed. Sexual repression is not the major problem for many of our youth. Their problem more often is a failure to realize that enslavement and human hurt result from sexual irresponsibility. So does not Lawrence's message come a bit late for them? The youth are not hung-up on sex in regard to either themselves or Jesus. Their questions about Jesus and life are better reflected in Tim Rice's lyrics for *Jesus Christ Superstar*—wherein the issue of Jesus' sexuality is handled with marvelous sensitivity—than in *The Man Who Died.* If the over-30 theologians have any message about sex for large numbers of the under-30 generation, it must be more than the discovery that sex is good. In that respect we can join their club. But, while admitting that God was right after all in creating sex and calling it good, do we then place it in the context of loving commitment to another—in the context of the biblical concept of *hesed?*

Another group that should be mentioned here is comprised of those churchgoers who are threatened by the changes that are taking place with such rapidity—especially the changes in sexual behavior as it relates to them and their children. These people expect help from the church and the theologians. They do not always find it. They hear us faulting Christianity's past mistakes, but they do not hear us saying much that is helpful. To be sure, in a time of fragmentation in many lives we need to view with sympathy those who seek to build a relationship that has meaning for them, even one outside of marriage. To be sure, in a time of overwhelming change we need to rethink seriously the meaning of marriage and the family. But there is danger that, in its headlong flight away from the old Gnosticism—which has too often infected the church's teachings about sex—theology will run to a new and equally dangerous Gnosticism: that of assuming a superior knowledge which, whether intended or not, cuts theology off from many Christians. In this regard the ideas of Lawrence, as Phipps presents him without reference to his (Lawrence's) strong belief in monogamy, may not be of much use to many Christians. On reading Phipps's article they might instead say, in words, reminiscent of Tertullian's attack on Praxes, that Phipps has married off Jesus and replaced the resurrection with an erection.

V

Someone should say a good word for the celibate. Apparently Lawrence thought that sexual intercourse is a *sine qua non* for personal wholeness. Perhaps it is for many people. But is it necessarily so for all? Does one have to be sexually active to be sexually authentic? Rather, is it not the fully sexed person who can decide what his sexual role will be without feeling the need to prove to himself or anyone else that he is virile? Above all, is Jesus' virility really in question, whether or not he was married? (Phipps is quite correct, however, in opposing the idea that Jesus did not have normal sexual impulses.)

In *Was Jesus Married?* Phipps demonstrates at some length the unfortunate results of enforced celibacy. But celibacy in the priesthood and monastic orders was for some a genuine calling. Conversely, one may ask whether the unofficial but widely enforced rule that Protestant ministers must marry has always had wholesome results. A man can be called to be a minister without being called to be a husband and father. Indeed, is not marriage a requirement not only in the ministry but in many other segments of our society for those who wish to be promoted in the organization, or included in the social life, or become eligible for income shelters? Perhaps we need a singles' lib. But in addition we need liberation for those who wish to live a celibate life; we must grant them the recognition that they too may be dealing authentically with their sexual nature. In the time of the population bomb it is ironic to question the sexual integrity of those who are doing the most to guarantee the survival of the human species on the planet.

It is likely that Dr. Phipps would agree with many of the comments made here. However, since he has in his article, and to some extent in his book, left many things unsaid, perhaps this response will encourage him to clarify his position further.

Sex and the Single God

Robert T. Osborn

The thesis of this article is simply that modern theology and ethics are failing in their responsibilities because they overlook the reality of sex— what might be called the divine sexuality as well as the human sexuality. The result for theology is the unacceptable notion of the single God. The failure is fundamentally the denial of the masculine principle, acknowledgment of which will require a renewal of both theology and ethics.

To the reader of the Bible the importance of sexuality is obvious. The priestly authors of Genesis 1—piously loath to indulge in the crass anthropomorphisms of the author of Genesis 2 and 3—portray God as that omnipotent transcendence who is disclosed only in his word, but nevertheless tell us that human sexuality is the image of God. "God created man in his own image, in the image of God he created him; male and female he created them." As the prophet Hosea explains, God and man are related as husband and wife. We might say that God is sexual; or, if you will, that sex is Godlike. God is the original sexual being and the author and measure of sexuality. We are invited to employ as a model for the understanding of God's way with men the human sexual experience, three aspects of which seem obvious and point to the divine sexuality. These are, first, radical physical differentiation; second, functional distinction and order; and third, unity through radical commitment and community.

THE INVISIBLE VIS-À-VIS THE VISIBLE. Each of these aspects is characteristic of the Mosaic experience. Consider what might be called the physical differentiation, the invisible God vis-à-vis the visible sons of Jacob. As regards the functional differentiation, the Bible contrasts the creative, redemptive initiative of God with the receptive, humble response of Israel. Yet for all the differentiation God calls Israel to be his wife and to enter into a radical unity or covenant with him. Husband and bride, different yet one in marriage. The paradox of unity and distinction is strikingly stated by God's designation of himself as "I am," as the one who is sufficient in and of himself, determined by his own will; and also as the "God of Abraham, Isaac, Jacob and Joseph," the God who is God only with his other.

Biblical anthropology with its sexual realism is consequently quite understandable. The distinctions between man and woman are vivid and valuable signs of the modes of God's way with Israel, and at the same time and thereby symbolize and convey the highest glory and fundamental meaning of existence. Just as the Israelite could not take lightly the physical tokens of the separation between God and man, so also he honored the physical distinction between man and woman. Further, just as God in his initiative is the creator and preserver of the covenant with Israel, so man in his initiative is the creator and preserver of the marriage. As invisibility represents and reserves to God his freedom and creativity, so man's physical nature—its greater strength and masculine design— symbolizes and conveys his creativity and responsibility. And finally, just as the differentiation between God and man makes desirable and necessary the covenant between them, so the ultimate logic of the sexual difference between man and woman points to the radical commitment of sexual union.

SEALING RELIGION'S WOMB. Has any people been more sexual and more covenant-conscious than the people of the Old Testament? If any, it is the New Covenant people, for in the marriage of Christ to the church the New Testament finds not only *an* act of God but *the* act of God; that is, not only does God enter into union with Israel, but in Christ that union is consummated and extended to all men. He is revealed as the bride of the church and in his eternal nature as the triune God of everlasting relationship. Christian asceticism, where it is not distorted by Greek influences, is not a denial of the sexual; to the contrary, it attests to the primacy of the sexual nature of union with the divine and it also attests to the nearly divine potential of human sexuality in all its existential and demonic actuality.

A dominant trend in modern theology, most consistently expressed perhaps in the writings of Thomas J. J. Altizer, is to speak no longer of a convenant between two but of a "coincidence of opposites." Man, rather than finding God "out there," objective and different, now finds his alleged opposite inside, as "coincident" with himself. If I may, I would say that the knowledge of God is no longer a matter of intercourse but of masturbation. If, as Nietzsche suggested, we posit ourselves faithfully and long enough the eternal will recur. J. A. T. Robinson invites us to look for God not out there or up there but within, in the "depths." Bonhoeffer saw the thoroughgoing sexlessness of modern theology and addressed himself to the problem when he asked how the church can speak of God to a world that does not need an other; God is as relevant to a godless world as is a groom to a sexless bride. Following Bultmann, Robinson would rid religion, by a program of demythologizing, of all objectivity, would as it were seal religion's womb. Unlike Mary the modern church is not receptive.

CASTRATED THEOLOGY, MANLESS MORALITY. This new sexless theology has its counterpart and consequence in a new, sexless morality. Bishop Robinson laments that his "new morality" is continually understood in sexual terms. But how could it be otherwise? Theology is radically sexual and the sexual is radically theological; a major theological shift will have major sexual implications. Altizer contends not that he has put God to death but that God has already been dead for some time; so the new morality claims not to be advocating a new ethic but that it is announcing advent of the new ethic as a *fait accompli*. The theological shift has in fact been accompanied by a shift in ethics; and while it is inevitably understood in sexual terms by its practitioners (if not by its advocates) and is painfully preoccupied with sex, the new morality is quite sexless, just as the new godless theology is nevertheless very consciously *theo*logical. Both contradictions betray the embarrassing physical realities —the visible and real church with its purified sanctuaries and theologies, and the real male and female bodies signifying nothing. All that remains of sex is the symbols which, since they now symbolize nothing, can be used to entertain much as a child uses its thumb. Thus we have the "playboy" surrounded by his "bunnies," his pretty playthings. Engulfed by an entire menagerie of such toys, Hugh Hefner himself is, not surprisingly, unmoved in his sexless, ascetic disengagement.

This "new morality" is manifest on other fronts, as for example in the rising tide of homosexuality, which Robinson, interestingly, is not too distressed by, or in the concern of the American woman lest her biological peculiarities lead anyone to suspect that she is party to a "feminine mystique." The American male is not about to object to this concern, however, for he would not know what to do with the mystique should he meet it. A sexual woman—i.e., one different from a man biologically and otherwise—is a dreadful embarrassment, for being without sexual identity himself he feels irrelevant and inadequate; and her sexual reserve, which expresses her intuitive if not conscious awareness of the depth and power of sex, frustrates his own self-sexual interest. Yet his sexuality, which after all is the divine image in him, cannot be wholly denied. Hence, although he cannot give himself as a man to a woman, he does find it necessary to escape to bunny clubs or, more creatively, to repress and redirect his sexuality by entering into and joining the business "organization."

The white American male, safe in the bosom of the mother-organization, sometimes views with not a little envy and fear what he takes to be the violent excesses and expressions of the Negro male, whose sexuality he has in subconscious vindictiveness denied—not only by denying him his proper male role as the creator, provider and sustainer of his home, but also by excluding him even from the ersatz warmth of the organization. The white male's own emasculation is well attested by his inordinate response to any alleged or actual violation of a white woman by a Negro. In the south the death penalty dies slowly, largely because of this sensitivity which, as Nietzsche suggested, reflects not fullness (the fullness whence flows the freedom of mercy) but a profound lack (whence rushes the desire to punish). Meanwhile, confirmed in her sexlessness by her sexual opposite, woman fills her need for a man by playing the male part herself—competing more openly for the male position in society and certainly taking more and more the decisive and responsible role in the home. Correspondingly the husband and father becomes more passive and irrelevant and like a child reverts and retreats to the sexual fantasy of intercourse with mother-organization.

The logic of sexless sex and the single God is evident not only in direct expressions of the new morality but even more in its basic mood. I refer to the so-called "contextualism" and social relativity of the new morality. According to this principle the collective, social, objective dimensions of life become dominant; whereas the creative, personal, masculine impulse becomes impotent and, in its feminine passivity, merely reactive to and reflective of the social context (the feminine principle now become active and determinative). Love, of which the new ethic ironically speaks so much, now means not at all the self-determined, creative and generous expression of the personal spirit but rather the passive, weak and reactive adjustment of the individual to the so-called "needs" of the other. Nietzsche's structures seem only too relevant; such "love," as he well saw, is nothing more than a euphemism for masculine weakness or femininity.

My concern is not primarily the castigation of a castrated theology and a manless morality; quite the contrary, it is the revitalization and renewal of theology, preliminary to which is of course an honest diagnosis.

The diagnosis I have undertaken amounts to this: Modern man is plagued with a forgetfulness of his sexuality, i.e., of his radical difference from God and from woman. Consequent upon this loss of differentiation is also a forgetfulness of responsibility. Since the male has the first responsibility, renewal involves primarily the male act—specifically, the act of God for theological renewal and the act of man for moral renewal. This diagnosis confirms the psychoanalytic view of man and deepens it by grounding it ontologically or theologically. Mystical Christianity has sensed the radical nature of sexuality and its reflection of the divine, not only by its representation of the relationship between God and soul in sexual terms but also, it would seem paradoxically, by its asceticism. In recent times Nicholas Berdyaev tapped these mystical sources to speak of sex in cosmic terms, and the much less exotic Karl Barth has turned directly to the Bible for his understanding of the *imago Dei* as the sexual relationship.

Denial of the theological depth and the cosmic range of sexuality has meant for contemporary theology the concept of the single God. Accordingly Bishop James A. Pike, reflecting the times, finds the notion of the Trinity no longer congenial, and Bishop Robinson finds the God who is spatially (physically?) different from man unacceptable. We have, then, no relational deity, but a single, solitary, sexless God. God has withdrawn into transcendent isolation leaving man alone in a similar sexless isolation (Harvey Cox's view), which is to say, if you choose, that for all practical purposes God is dead (so says Altizer).

THE ROAD TO RECOVERY. The alternative, which still speaks of the single God and the sexless man, is to follow the Tillichian and Robinsonian routes of identification in which God is ultimately at one with man in the very "depth" of man's being. Either God—singular and remote in separation (Cox-Altizer) or singular and immanent in identification (Tillich-Robinson); i.e., absent from or surrendered to the feminine—is emasculated, single and sexless. He is not the active, creative Father and Husband of Israel and the church, but the impotent and rejected subject of a womanized humanity.

The prognosis for this malaise is the death of theology (which hangs on tenaciously as the death-of-God theology) and the death of man and morality (also desperately holding on as the "new morality"). As a theologian I have an immediate concern for the integrity and renewal of theology. Quite obviously the first stage of recovery entails acceptance of the diagnosis. This means that theology will attend at once to the sexual reality of both God and man. Modern theology has been obsessed by the "communication problem," which has been problematic indeed since in his denial of sexuality modern man has lost any reason for or interest in communication, as evidenced by Bonhoeffer's awareness of his religion-lessness. But once the diagnosis is accepted theology will be aware that man's sexuality is the pre-eminent point of contact with God, the real possibility of communion with God. In *The Secular City* Harvey Cox cites many problems of modern man and documents his analysis with considerable expertise in the many social sciences, with the one exception of psychiatry. That is to say, there is in his book no inwardness, hence little or no awareness of the sexual problem and thus of the problem and possibility of communication between God and man.

RESISTING SEXLESS SECULARITY. It seems clear to me that for all its technical and social progress (the expansion and growing dominance of the female principle) modern society has conversely declined in its sexual self-understanding (through the loss of the male principle and therewith of sexuality as such). One need only scan recent journalism to see how acutely and pervasively the question of sexuality has arisen. As a member of an undergraduate faculty I cannot escape the impression that, sophisticated as he is, the average undergraduate student is at a loss to give an account of his sexuality. Furthermore, modern psychoanalysis makes clear the wide-ranging significance of sexual failure for the totality of human relations. In other words, sex is the decisive dimension of existence and for theology to address itself to this question and make contact at this point is to meet man as man, in the very essence of his humanity.

To do this theology must remythologize; it must return to the sexual language of the Bible. That is to say, it must acknowledge the sexuality of God—of his spatial separation from man, and of his sacramental, physical communion with man. In other words, theology will have the deepest respect for the personal language of the Bible, for the models of marriage and parenthood, for the divine name and its giving and receiving in the covenant made between God and man, for such relational notions as triunity and incarnation, and for the intrusion into its sanctuary of such concrete and visible symbols as the sacraments, the historical ministry, the liturgy and even icons. In sum, theology will respect the intimate intercourse between God and man called religion, and will resist any reductionism in the direction of sexless secularity.

Questions

1. What does Dickens consider offensive in Millais' painting? Would he describe the painting as "blasphemous"? Does it seem blasphemous to you?

2. Does Millais' picture of Christ fit Lawrence's category of Christ born among men, Christ crucified, or Christ risen? Explain your choice.

3. Do the image divisions which Lawrence describes for the period after World War I still hold true today? Which of the image divisions do you think is dominant now?

4. Lawrence is often considered a prophet. Were any of his predictions in "The Risen Lord" prophetic? If so, how?

5. What does Lawrence include in his idea of Mammon?

6. Do you agree with Phipps that *Jesus Christ Superstar* puts into Jesus' mouth words that the historical record seems to justify?

7. What does Phipps mean when he says that Lawrence has "helped to exorcise the Gnostic ghost"?

8. What does Hoyt mean when he refers to "Lawrence's anthropology"?

9. Do you agree with Hoyt that for many American young people the problem is "a failure to realize that enslavement and human hurt result from sexual irresponsibility"?

10. Would Lawrence's theology be similar to that of Robert Osborn? What does Osborn mean when he talks about the "unacceptable notion of the single God"?

11. Do you agree with Osborn's analysis of sexual identity in our society? How would members of the Women's Liberation movement (see Section Twelve) feel about his comment: "Meanwhile, confirmed in her sexlessness by her sexual opposite, woman fills her need for a man by playing the male part herself—competing more openly for a male position in society. . ."?

12. Discuss what you think Osborn means by the phrase *sexless secularity*.

13. How are moral issues related to theological concepts? How does Osborn see the "death of God" theology as related to "the new morality"?

14. What contemporary art or literature would you consider blasphemous or obscene—as Dickens considered Millais' painting or many readers considered *Lady Chatterley's Lover?* Does its offensiveness arise from the subject matter or from the way the subject is presented?

Assignments

1. Write a description of the Millais painting presenting a different point of view than that presented by Dickens. Or choose another painting, perhaps a contemporary painting that you find offensive, and write an interpretative description of it.

2. Defend or criticize Lawrence's view, as summarized by Phipps, that "an exemplar of true humanity cannot be thought of as an asexual being."

3. Write a defense of celibacy, bachelorhood, or spinsterhood.

4. Choose a representation of Jesus in contemporary art—in *Jesus Christ Superstar*, for example, or Dali's "Crucifixion," or a current film—and discuss the theological dimensions of the presentation.

Additional Reading

Lawrence's last story, *The Man Who Died* (1931), offers an imaginative presentation of the Christ presented in "The Risen Lord." In nearly all his novels, he is significantly concerned with presenting his views of sexuality. His most controversial treatment of the sexual theme, *Lady Chatterley's Lover*, finally released in this country in 1957, though first published in 1928, has called forth a good deal of theological discussion, particularly during the British trial in 1960. Lawrence discusses the issues of the trial in his classic essay, "Pornography and Obscenity" (1929).

Although no definitive study of Lawrence's religious views has been done, nearly all discussions of his work touch on the issues raised in this section. Of particular interest are the books by Herman Daleski, *The Forked Flame* (1965); Graham Hough, *The Dark Sun* (1959); Father Martin Jarrett-Kerr, *D. H. Lawrence and Human Existence* (1951); William York Tindall, *D. H. Lawrence & Susan His Cow* (1939). Lawrence's attitudes toward Christianity have been treated by Dean Peerman, "D. H. Lawrence: Devout Heretic," *The Christian Century*, February 22, 1961; and Ralph D. Sturm, "Lawrence: Critic of Christianity," *The Catholic World*, November, 1968.

The theological issues pursued in these discussions are treated more fully in J. A. T. Robinson's *Honest to God* (1963), a discussion of the "new morality" and situational ethics; William Hamilton and T. J. J. Altizer, *Radical Theology and the Death of God* (1966); and Harvey Cox, *The Secular City* (1965) and *The Feast of Fools* (1969).

Population Control

Begins at Home

Reproduced by permission of the Buffalo Evening News.

Message from the President of the United States Relative to Population Growth

Richard M. Nixon

To the Congress of the United States:

In 1830 there were one billion people on the planet earth. By 1930 there were two billion, and by 1960 there were three billion. Today the world population is three and one-half billion persons.

91st Congress, 1st Session, House of Representatives, Document No. 91–139, July, 1969.

These statistics illustrate the dramatically increasing rate of population growth. It took many thousands of years to produce the first billion people; the next billion took a century; the third came after thirty years; the fourth will be produced in just fifteen.

If this rate of population growth continues, it is likely that the earth will contain over seven billion human beings by the end of this century. Over the next thirty years, in other words, the world's population could double. And at the end of that time, each new addition of one billion persons would not come over the millenia nor over a century nor even over a decade. If present trends were to continue until the year 2000, the eighth billion would be added in only five years and each additional billion in an even shorter period.

While there are a variety of opinions as to precisely how fast population will grow in the coming decades, most informed observers have a similar response to all such projections. They agree that population growth is among the most important issues we face. They agree that it can be met only if there is a great deal of advance planning. And they agree that the time for such planning is growing very short. It is for all these reasons that I address myself to the population problem in this message, first to its international dimensions and then to its domestic implications.

In the Developing Nations

It is in the developing nations of the world that population is growing most rapidly today. In these areas we often find rates of natural increase higher than any which have been experienced in all of human history. With their birth rates remaining high and with death rates dropping sharply, many countries of Latin America, Asia, and Africa now grow ten times as fast as they did a century ago. At present rates, many will double and some may even triple their present populations before the year 2000. This fact is in large measure a consequence of rising health standards and economic progress throughout the world, improvements which allow more people to live longer and more of their children to survive to maturity.

As a result, many already impoverished nations are struggling under a handicap of intense population increase which the industrialized nations never had to bear. Even though most of these countries have made rapid progress in total economic growth—faster in percentage terms than many of the more industrialized nations—their far greater rates of population growth have made development in per capita terms very slow. Their standards of living are not rising quickly, and the gap between life in the rich nations and life in the poor nations is not closing.

There are some respects, in fact, in which economic development threatens to fall behind population growth, so that the quality of life actually worsens. For example, despite considerable improvements in agricultural technology and some dramatic increases in grain production, it is still difficult to feed these added people at adequate levels of nutrition. Protein malnutrition is widespread. It is estimated that every day some 10,000 people—most of them children—are dying from diseases of which malnutrition has been at least a partial cause. Moreover, the physical and mental potential of millions of youngsters is not realized because of a lack of proper food. The promise for increased production and better distribution of food is great, but not great enough to counter these bleak realities.

The burden of population growth is also felt in the field of social progress. In many countries, despite increases in the number of schools and teachers, there are more and more children for whom there is no schooling. Despite construction of new homes, more and more families are without adequate shelter. Unemployment and underemployment are increasing and the situation could be aggravated as more young people grow up and seek to enter the work force.

Nor has development yet reached the stage where it brings with it diminished family size. Many parents in developing countries are still victimized by forces such as poverty and ignorance which make it difficult for them to exercise control over the size of their families. In sum, population growth is a world problem which no country can ignore, whether it is moved by the narrowest perception of national self-interest or the widest vision of a common humanity.

International Cooperation

It is our belief that the United Nations, its specialized agencies, and other international bodies should take the leadership in responding to world population growth. The United States will cooperate fully with their programs. I would note in this connection that I am most impressed by the scope and thrust of the recent report of the Panel of the United Nations Association, chaired by John D. Rockefeller III. The report stresses the need for expanded action and greater coordination, concerns which should be high on the agenda of the United Nations.

In addition to working with international organizations, the United States can help by supporting efforts which are initiated by other governments. Already we are doing a great deal in this field. For example, we provide assistance to countries which seek our help in reducing high birthrates—provided always that the services we help to make available can be freely accepted or rejected by the individuals who receive them. Through our aid programs, we have worked to improve agricultural production and bolster economic growth in developing nations.

As I pointed out in my recent message on Foreign Aid, we are making important efforts to improve these programs. In fact, I have asked the Secretary of State and the Administrator of the Agency for International Development to give population and family planning high priority for attention, personnel, research, and funding among our several aid programs. Similarly, I am asking the Secretaries of Commerce and Health, Education, and Welfare and the Directors of the Peace Corps and the United States Information Agency to give close attention to population matters as they plan their overseas operations. I also call on the Department of Agriculture and the Agency for International Development to investigate ways of adapting and extending our agricultural experience and capabilities to improve food production and distribution in developing countries. In all of these international efforts, our programs should give further recognition to the important resources of private organizations and university research centers. As we increase our population and family planning efforts abroad, we also call upon other nations to enlarge their programs in this area.

Prompt action in all these areas is essential. For high rates of population growth, as the report of the Panel of the United Nations Association puts it, "impair individual rights, jeopardize national goals, and threaten international stability."

In the United States

For some time population growth has been seen as a problem for developing countries. Only recently has it come to be seen that pressing problems are also posed for advanced industrial countries when their populations increase at the rate that the United States, for example, must now anticipate. Food supplies may be ample in such nations, but social supplies—the capacity to educate youth, to provide privacy and living space, to maintain the processes of open, democratic government—may be grievously strained.

In the United States our rate of population growth is not as great as that of developing nations. In this country, in fact, the growth rate has generally declined since the eighteenth century. The present growth rate of about one per cent per year is still significant, however. Moreover, current statistics indicate that the fertility rate may be approaching the end of its recent decline.

Several factors contribute to the yearly increase, including the large number of couples of childbearing age, the typical size of American families, and our increased longevity. We are rapidly reaching the point in this country where a family reunion, which has typically brought together children, parents, and grandparents, will instead gather family members from *four* generations. This is a development for which we are grateful and of which we can be proud. But we must also recognize that it will mean a far larger population if the number of children born to each set of parents remains the same.

In 1917 the total number of Americans passed 100 million, after three full centuries of steady growth. In 1967—just half a century later—the

200 million mark was passed. If the present rate of growth continues, the third hundred million persons will be added in roughly a thirty-year period. This means that by the year 2000, or shortly thereafter, there will be more than 300 million Americans.

This growth will produce serious challenges for our society. I believe that many of our present social problems may be related to the fact that we have had only fifty years in which to accommodate the second hundred million Americans. In fact, since 1945 alone some 90 million babies have been born in this country. We have thus had to accomplish in a very few decades an adjustment to population growth which was once spread over centuries. And it now appears that we will have to provide for a third hundred million Americans in a period of just 30 years.

The great majority of the next hundred million Americans will be born to families which looked forward to their birth and are prepared to love them and care for them as they grow up. The critical issue is whether social institutions will also plan for their arrival and be able to accommodate them in a humane and intelligent way. We can be sure that society will *not* be ready for this growth unless it begins its planning immediately. And adequate planning, in turn, requires that we ask ourselves a number of important questions.

Where, for example, will the next hundred million Americans live? If the patterns of the last few decades hold for the rest of the century, then at least three quarters of the next hundred million persons will locate in highly urbanized areas. Are our cities prepared for such an influx? The chaotic history of urban growth suggests that they are not and that many of their existing problems will be severely aggravated by a dramatic increase in numbers. Are there ways, then, of readying our cities? Alternatively, can the trend toward greater concentration of population be reversed? Is it a desirable thing, for example, that half of all the counties in the United States actually lost population in the 1950's, despite the growing number of inhabitants in the country as a whole? Are there ways of fostering a better distribution of the growing population?

Some have suggested that systems of satellite cities or completely new towns can accomplish this goal. The National Commission on Urban Growth has recently produced a stimulating report on this matter, one which recommends the creation of 100 new communities averaging 100,000 people each, and ten new communities averaging at least one million persons. But the total number of people who would be accommodated if ever this bold plan were implemented is only twenty million—a mere one-fifth of the expected thirty-year increase. If we were to accommodate the full 100 million persons in new communities, we would have to build a new city of 250,000 persons each month from now until the end of the century. That means constructing a city the size of Tulsa, Dayton, or Jersey City every thirty days for over thirty years. Clearly, the problem is enormous, and we must examine the alternative solutions very carefully.

Other questions also confront us. How, for example, will we house the next hundred million Americans? Already economical and attractive housing is in very short supply. New architectural forms, construction techniques, and financing strategies must be aggressively pioneered if we are to provide the needed dwellings.

What of our natural resources and the quality of our environment? Pure air and water are fundamental to life itself. Parks, recreational facilities, and an attractive countryside are essential to our emotional well-being. Plant and animal and mineral resources are also vital. A growing population will increase the demand for such resources. But in many cases their supply will not be increased and may even be endangered. The ecological system upon which we now depend may seriously deteriorate if our efforts to conserve and enhance the environment do not match the growth of the population.

How will we educate and employ such a large number of people? Will our transportation systems move them about as quickly and economically as necessary? How will we provide adequate health care when our population reaches 300 million? Will our political structures have to be reordered, too, when our society grows to such proportions? Many of our institutions are already under tremendous strain as they try to respond to the demands of 1969. Will they be swamped by a growing flood of people in the next thirty years? How easily can they be replaced or altered?

Finally we must ask: how can we better assist American families so that they will have no more children than they wish to have? In my first message to Congress on domestic affairs, I called for a national commitment to provide a healthful and stimulating environment for all children during their first five years of life. One of the ways in which we can promote that goal is to provide assistance for more parents in effectively planning their families. We know that involuntary childbearing often results in poor physical and emotional health for all members of the family. It is one of the factors which contribute to our distressingly high infant mortality rate, the unacceptable level of malnutrition, and the disappointing performance of some children in our schools. Unwanted or untimely childbearing is one of several forces which are driving many families into poverty or keeping them in that condition. Its threat helps to produce the dangerous incidence of illegal abortion. And finally, of course, it needlessly adds to the burdens placed on all our resources by increasing population.

None of the questions I have raised here is new. But all of these questions must now be asked and answered with a new sense of urgency. The answers cannot be given by government alone, nor can government alone turn the answers into programs and policies. I believe, however, that the Federal Government does have a special responsibility for defining these problems and for stimulating thoughtful responses.

Perhaps the most dangerous element in the present situation is the fact that so few people are examining these questions from the viewpoint of the whole society. Perceptive businessmen project the demand for their products many years into the future by studying population trends. Other private institutions develop sophisticated planning mechanisms which allow them to account for rapidly changing conditions. In the governmental sphere, however, there is virtually no machinery through which we can develop a detailed understanding of demographic changes and bring that understanding to bear on public policy. The Federal Government makes only a minimal effort in this area. The efforts of state and local governments are also inadequate. Most importantly, the planning which does take place at some levels is poorly understood at others and is often based on unexamined assumptions.

In short, the questions I have posed in this message too often go unasked, and when they are asked, they seldom are adequately answered.

Commission on Population Growth
and the American Future

It is for all these reasons that I today propose the creation by Congress of a Commission on Population Growth and the American Future.

The Congress should give the Commission responsibility for inquiry and recommendations in three specific areas.

First, *the probable course of population growth, internal migration and related demographic developments between now and the year 2000.*

As much as possible, these projections should be made by regions, states, and metropolitan areas. Because there is an element of uncertainty in such projections, various alternative possibilities should be plotted.

It is of special importance to note that, beginning in August of 1970, population data by county will become available from the decennial census, which will have been taken in April of that year. By April 1971, computer summaries of first-count data will be available by census tract and an important range of information on income, occupations, education, household composition, and other vital considerations will also be in hand. The Federal Government can make better use of such demographic information than it has done in the past, and state governments and other political subdivisions can also use such data to better advantage. The Commission on Population Growth and the American Future will be an appropriate instrument for this important initiative.

Second, *the resources in the public sector of the economy that will be required to deal with the anticipated growth in population.*

The single greatest failure of foresight—at all levels of government—

over the past generation has been in areas connected with expanding population. Government and legislatures have frequently failed to appreciate the demands which continued population growth would impose on the public sector. These demands are myriad: they will range from pre-school classrooms to post-doctoral fellowships; from public works which carry water over thousands of miles to highways which carry people and products from region to region; from vest-pocket parks in crowded cities to forest preserves and quiet lakes in the countryside. Perhaps especially, such demands will assert themselves in forms that affect the quality of life. The time is at hand for a serious assessment of such needs.

Third, *ways in which population growth may affect the activities of Federal, state and local government.*

In some respects, population growth affects everything that American government does. Yet only occasionally do our governmental units pay sufficient attention to population growth in their own planning. Only occasionally do they consider the serious implications of demographic trends for their present and future activities.

Yet some of the necessary information is at hand and can be made available to all levels of government. Much of the rest will be obtained by the Commission. For such information to be of greatest use, however, it should also be interpreted and analyzed and its implications should be made more evident. It is particularly in this connection that the work of the Commission on Population Growth and the American Future will be as much educational as investigative. The American public and its governing units are not as alert as they should be to these growing challenges. A responsible but insistent voice of reason and foresight is needed. The Commission can provide that voice in the years immediately before us.

The membership of the Commission should include two members from each house of the Congress, together with knowledgeable men and women who are broadly representative of our society. The majority should be citizens who have demonstrated a capacity to deal with important questions of public policy. The membership should also include specialists in the biological, social, and environmental sciences, in theology and law, in the arts and in engineering. The Commission should be empowered to create advisory panels to consider subdivisions of its broad subject area and to invite experts and leaders from all parts of the world to join these panels in their deliberations.

The Commission should be provided with an adequate staff and budget, under the supervision of an executive director of exceptional experience and understanding.

In order that the Commission will have time to utilize the initial data which results from the 1970 census, I ask that it be established for a period of two years. An interim report to the President and Congress should be required at the end of the first year.

Other Government Activities

I would take this opportunity to mention a number of additional government activities dealing with population growth which need not await the report of the Commission.

First, increased research is essential. It is clear, for example, that we need additional research on birth control methods of all types and the sociology of population growth. Utilizing its Center for Population Research, the Department of Health, Education, and Welfare should take the lead in developing, with other federal agencies, an expanded research effort, one which is carefully related to those of private organizations, university research centers, international organizations, and other countries.

Second, we need more trained people to work in population and family planning programs, both in this country and abroad. I am therefore asking the Secretaries of State, Labor, Health, Education, and Welfare, and Interior, along with the Administrator of the Agency for International Development and the Director of the Office of Economic Opportunity, to participate in a comprehensive survey of our efforts to attract people to such programs and to train them properly. The same group—in consultation with appropriate state, local, and private officials—should develop recommendations for improvements in this area. I am asking the Assistant to the President for Urban Affairs to coordinate this project.

Third, the effects of population growth on our environment and on the world's food supply call for careful attention and immediate action. I am therefore asking the Environmental Quality Council to give careful attention to these matters in its deliberations. I am also asking the Secretaries of Interior, Agriculture, and Health, Education, and Welfare to give the highest priority to research into new techniques and to other proposals that can help safeguard the environment and increase the world's supply of food.

Fourth, it is clear that the domestic family planning services supported by the Federal Government should be expanded and better integrated. Both the Department of Health, Education, and Welfare and the Office of Economic Opportunity are now involved in this important work, yet their combined efforts are not adequate to provide information and services to all who want them. In particular, most of an estimated five million low income women of childbearing age in this country do not now have adequate access to family planning assistance, even though their wishes concerning family size are usually the same as those of parents of higher income groups.

It is my view that no American woman should be denied access to family planning assistance because of her economic condition. I believe, therefore, that we should establish as a national goal the provision of adequate family planning services within the next five years to all those who want them but cannot afford them. This we have the capacity to do.

Clearly, in no circumstances will the activities associated with our pursuit of this goal be allowed to infringe upon the religious convictions or personal wishes and freedom of any individual, nor will they be allowed to impair the absolute right of all individuals to have such matters of conscience respected by public authorities.

In order to achieve this national goal, we will have to increase the amount we are spending on population and family planning. But success in this endeavor will not result from higher expenditures alone. Because the life circumstances and family planning wishes of those who receive services vary considerably, an effective program must be more flexible in its design than are many present efforts. In addition, programs should be better coordinated and more effectively administered. Under current legislation, a comprehensive state or local project must assemble a patchwork of funds from many different sources—a time-consuming and confusing process. Moreover, under existing legislation, requests for funds for family planning services must often compete with requests for other deserving health endeavors.

But these problems can be overcome. The Secretary of Health, Education and Welfare—whose Department is responsible for the largest part of our domestic family planning services—has developed plans to reorganize the major family planning service activities of his agency. A separate unit for these services will be established within the Health Services and Mental Health Administration. The Secretary will send to Congress in the near future legislation which will help the Department implement this important program by providing broader and more precise legislative authority and a clearer source of financial support.

The Office of Economic Opportunity can also contribute to progress in this area by strengthening its innovative programs and pilot projects in the delivery of family planning services to the needy. The existing network of OEO-supported community groups should also be used more extensively to provide family planning assistance and information. I am asking the Director of the Office of Economic Opportunity to determine the ways in which his Agency can best structure and extend its programs in order to help achieve our national goal in the coming years.

As they develop their own plans, the Secretary of Health, Education and Welfare and the Director of the Office of Economic Opportunity should also determine the most effective means of coordinating all our domestic family planning programs and should include in their deliberations representatives of the other agencies that share in this important work. It is my intention that such planning should also involve state and local governments and private agencies, for it is clear that the increased activity of the Federal Government in this area must be matched by a sizeable increase in effort at other levels. It would be unrealistic for the Federal Government alone to shoulder the entire burden, but this Administration does accept a clear responsibility to provide essential leadership.

For the Future

One of the most serious challenges to human destiny in the last third of this century will be the growth of the population. Whether man's response to that challenge will be a cause for pride or for despair in the year 2000 will depend very much on what we do today. If we now begin our work in an appropriate manner, and if we continue to devote a considerable amount of attention and energy to this problem, then mankind will be able to surmount this challenge as it has surmounted so many during the long march of civilization.

When future generations evaluate the record of our time, one of the most important factors in their judgment will be the way in which we responded to population growth. Let us act in such a way that those who come after us—even as they lift their eyes beyond earth's bounds—can do so with pride in the planet on which they live, with gratitude to those who lived on it in the past, and with continuing confidence in its future.

THE WHITE HOUSE, *July 18, 1969.*

On the Regulation of Birth, Humanae Vitae: Encyclical Letter

Pope Paul VI

TO THE VENERABLE PATRIARCHS, ARCHBISHOPS AND BISHOPS AND OTHER LOCAL ORDINARIES IN PEACE AND COMMUNION WITH THE APOSTOLIC SEE, TO PRIESTS, THE FAITHFUL AND TO ALL MEN OF GOOD WILL

VENERABLE BROTHERS AND BELOVED SONS:

1. The most serious duty of transmitting human life, for which married persons are the free and responsible collaborators of God the Creator, has

Encyclical Letter of His Holiness Pope Paul VI on the Regulation of Birth, *Humanae Vitae,* July 25, 1968.

always been a source of great joys to them, even if sometimes accompanied by not a few difficulties and by distress.

At all times the fulfillment of this duty has posed grave problems to the conscience of married persons, but, with the recent evolution of society, changes have taken place that give rise to new questions which the Church could not ignore, having to do with a matter which so closely touches upon the life and happiness of men.

I. New Aspects of the Problem and Competency of the Magisterium

2. The changes which have taken place are in fact noteworthy and of varied kinds. In the first place, there is the rapid demographic development. Fear is shown by many that world population is growing more rapidly than the available resources, with growing distress to many families and developing countries, so that the temptation for authorities to counter this danger with radical measures is great. Moreover, working and lodging conditions, as well as increased exigencies both in the economic field and in that of education, often make the proper education of a larger number of children difficult today. A change is also seen both in the manner of considering the person of woman and her place in society, and in the value to be attributed to conjugal love in marriage, and also in the appreciation to be made of the meaning of conjugal acts in relation to that love.

Finally and above all, man has made stupendous progress in the domination and rational organization of the forces of nature, such that he tends to extend this domination to his own total being: to the body, to psychical life, to social life and even to the laws which regulate the transmission of life.

3. This new state of things gives rise to new questions. Granted the conditions of life today, and granted the meaning which conjugal relations have with respect to the harmony between husband and wife and to their mutual fidelity, would not a revision of the ethical norms, in force up to now, seem to be advisable, especially when it is considered that they cannot be observed without sacrifices, sometimes heroic sacrifices?

And again: by extending to this field the application of the so-called "principle of totality," could it not be admitted that the intention of a less abundant but more rationalized fecundity might transform a materially sterilizing intervention into a licit and wise control of birth? Could it not be admitted, that is, that the finality of procreation pertains to the ensemble of conjugal life, rather than to its single acts? It is also asked whether, in view of the increased sense of responsibility of modern man, the moment has not come for him to entrust to his reason and his will, rather than to the biological rhythms of his organism, the task of regulating birth.

4. Such questions require from the teaching authority of the Church a new and deeper reflection upon the principles of the moral teaching on marriage: a teaching founded on the natural law, illuminated and enriched by divine revelation.

No believer will wish to deny that the teaching authority of the Church is competent to interpret even the natural moral law. It is, in fact, indisputable, as our predecessors have many times declared,[1] that Jesus Christ, when communicating to Peter and to the Apostles His divine authority and sending them to teach all nations His commandments,[2] constituted them as guardians and authentic interpreters of all the moral law, not only, that is, of the law of the Gospel, but also of the natural law, which is also an expression of the will of God, the faithful fulfillment of which is equally necessary for salvation.[3]

Conformably to this mission of hers, the Church has always provided —and even more amply in recent times—a coherent teaching concerning both the nature of marriage and the correct use of conjugal rights and the duties of husband and wife.[4]

5. The consciousness of that same mission induced us to confirm and enlarge the study commission which our predecessor Pope John XXIII of happy memory had instituted in March, 1963. That commission which included, besides several experts in the various pertinent disciplines, also married couples, had as its scope the gathering of opinions on the new questions regarding conjugal life, and in particular on the regulation of births, and of furnishing opportune elements of information so that the magisterium could give an adequate reply to the expectation not only of the faithful, but also of world opinion.[5]

---

[1] Cf. Pius IX, encyclical *Qui Pluribus*, Nov. 9, 1846; in PII IX P. M. Acta, I, pp. 9–10; St. Pius X, encyc. *Singulari Quadam*, Sept. 24, 1912; in AAS IV (1912), p. 658; Pius XI, encyc. *Casti Connubii*, Dec. 31, 1930; in AAS XXII (1930), pp. 579–581; Pius XII, allocution *Magnificate Dominum* to the episcopate of the Catholic world, Nov. 2, 1954; in AAS XLIV (1954), pp. 671–672; John XXIII, encyc. *Mater et Magistra*, May 15, 1961; in AAS LIII (1961), p. 457.

[2] Cf. Matt. 28: 18–19.

[3] Cf. Matt. 7: 21.

[4] Cf. *Catechismus Romanus Concilii Tridentini*, part II, ch. VIII; Leo XIII, encyc. *Arcanum*, Feb. 19, 1880; in *Acta Leonis* XIII, II (1881), pp. 26–29; Pius XI, encyc. *Divini Illus Magistri*, Dec. 31, 1929, in AAS XXII (1930), pp. 58–61; encyc. *Casti Connubii*, in AAS XXII (1930), pp. 545–546; Pius XII, alloc. to the Italian medico-biological union of St. Luke, Nov. 12, 1944, in *Discorsi e Radiomessaggi*, VI, pp. 191–192; to the Italian Catholic union of midwives, Oct. 29, 1951, in AAS XLIII (1951), pp. 857–859; to the seventh Congress of the International Society of Haematology, Sept. 12, 1958, in AAS L (1958), pp. 734–735; John XXIII, encyc. *Mater et Magistra*, in AAS LIII (1961), pp. 446–447; *Codex Iuris Canonici*, Canon 1067; Can. 1968, S 1, Can. 1066 S 1–2; Second Vatican Council, Pastoral constitution *Gaudium et Spes*, nos. 47–52.

[5] Cf. Paul VI, allocution to the Sacred College, June 23, 1964, in AAS LVI (1964), p. 588; to the Commission for Study of Problems of Population, Family and Birth, March 27, 1965, in AAS LVII (1965), p. 388, to the National Con-

The work of these experts, as well as the successive judgments and counsels spontaneously forwarded by or expressly requested from a good number of our brothers in the episcopate, have permitted us to measure more exactly all the aspects of this complex matter. Hence with all our heart we express to each of them our lively gratitude.

6. The conclusions at which the commission arrived could not, nevertheless, be considered by us as definitive, nor dispense us from a personal examination of this serious question; and this also because, within the commission itself, no full concordance of judgments concerning the moral norms to be proposed had been reached, and above all because certain criteria of solutions had emerged which departed from the moral teaching on marriage proposed with constant firmness by the teaching authority of the Church.

Therefore, having attentively sifted the documentation laid before us, after mature reflection and assiduous prayers, we now intend, by virtue of the mandate entrusted to us by Christ, to give our reply to these grave questions.

II. Doctrinal Principles

7. The problem of birth, like every other problem regarding human life, is to be considered, beyond partial perspectives—whether of the biological or psychological, demographic or sociological orders—in the light of an integral vision of man and of his vocation, not only his natural and earthly, but also his supernatural and eternal vocation. And since, in the attempt to justify artificial methods of birth control, many have appealed to the demands both of conjugal love and of "responsible parenthood," it is good to state very precisely the true concept of these two great realities of married life, referring principally to what was recently set forth in this regard, and in a highly authoritative form, by the Second Vatican Council in its pastoral constitution *Gaudium et Spes*.

8. Conjugal love reveals its true nature and nobility when it is considered in its supreme origin, God, who is love,[6] "the Father, from whom every family in heaven and on earth is named." [7]

Marriage is not, then, the effect of chance or the product of evolution of unconscious natural forces; it is the wise institution of the Creator to realize in mankind His design of love. By means of the reciprocal personal gift of self, proper and exclusive to them, husband and wife tend towards the communion of their beings in view of mutual personal perfection, to collaborate with God in the generation and education of new lives.

---

gress of the Italian Society of Obstetrics and Gynaecology, Oct. 29, 1966, in AAS LVIII (1966), p. 1168.

[6] Cf. I John 4:8.

[7] Cf. Eph. 3:15.

For baptized persons, moreover, marriage invests the dignity of a sacramental sign of grace, inasmuch as it represents the union of Christ and of the Church.

9. Under this light, there clearly appear the characteristic marks and demands of conjugal love, and it is of supreme importance to have an exact idea of these.

This love is first of all fully *human,* that is to say, of the senses and of the spirit at the same time. It is not, then, a simple transport of instinct and sentiment, but also, and principally, an act of the free will, intended to endure and to grow by means of the joys and sorrows of daily life, in such a way that husband and wife become one only heart and one only soul, and together attain their human perfection.

Then, this love is *total,* that is to say, it is a very special form of personal friendship, in which husband and wife generously share everything, without undue reservations or selfish calculations. Whoever truly loves his marriage partner loves not only for what he receives, but for the partner's self, rejoicing that he can enrich his partner with the gift of himself.

Again, this love is *faithful* and *exclusive* until death. Thus in fact do bride and groom conceive it to be on the day when they freely and in full awareness assume the duty of the marriage bond. A fidelity, this, which can sometimes be difficult, but is always possible, always noble and meritorious, as no one can deny. The example of so many married persons down through the centuries shows, not only that fidelity is according to the nature of marriage, but also that it is a source of profound and lasting happiness.

And finally this love is *fecund* for it is not exhausted by the communion between husband and wife, but is destined to continue, raising up new lives. "Marriage and conjugal love are by their nature ordained toward the begetting and educating of children. Children are really the supreme gift of marriage and contribute very substantially to the welfare of their parents." [8]

10. Hence conjugal love requires in husband and wife an awareness of their mission of "responsible parenthood," which today is rightly much insisted upon, and which also must be exactly understood. Consequently it is to be considered under different aspects which are legitimate and connected with one another.

In relation to the biological processes, responsible parenthood means the knowledge and respect of their functions; human intellect discovers in the power of giving life biological laws which are part of the human person.[9]

In relation to the tendencies of instinct or passion, responsible parent-

[8] Cf. II Vat. Council, Pastoral Const. *Gaudium et Spes,* No. 50.
[9] Cf. St. Thomas, *Summa Theologica,* I–II, q. 94, Art. 2.

hood means that necessary dominion which reason and will must exercise over them.

In relation to physical, economic, psychological and social conditions, responsible parenthood is exercised, either by the deliberate and generous decision to raise a numerous family, or by the decision, made for grave motives and with due respect for the moral law, to avoid for the time being, or even for an indeterminate period, a new birth.

Responsible parenthood also and above all implies a more profound relationship to the objective moral order established by God, of which a right conscience is the faithful interpreter. The responsible exercise of parenthood implies, therefore, that husband and wife recognize fully their own duties towards God, towards themselves, towards the family and towards society, in a correct hierarchy of values.

In the task of transmitting life, therefore, they are not free to proceed completely at will, as if they could determine in a wholly autonomous way the honest path to follow; but they must conform their activity to the creative intention of God, expressed in the very nature of marriage and of its acts, and manifested by the constant teaching of the Church.[10]

11. These acts, by which husband and wife are united in chaste intimacy, and by means of which human life is transmitted, are, as the Council recalled, "noble and worthy," [11] and they do not cease to be lawful if, for causes independent of the will of hubsand and wife, they are foreseen to be infecund, since they always remain ordained towards expressing and consolidating their union. In fact, as experience bears witness, not every conjugal act is followed by a new life. God has wisely disposed natural laws and rhythms of fecundity which, of themselves, cause a separation in the succession of births. Nonetheless the Church, calling men back to the observance of the norms of the natural law, as interpreted by their constant doctrine, teaches that each and every marriage act (*quilibet matrimonii usus*) must remain open to the transmission of life.[12]

12. That teaching, often set forth by the magisterium, is founded upon the inseparable connection, willed by God and unable to be broken by man on his own initiative, between the two meanings of the conjugal act: the unitive meaning and the procreative meaning. Indeed, by its intimate structure, the conjugal act, while most closely uniting husband and wife, capacitates them for the generation of new lives, according to laws inscribed in the very being of man and of woman. By safeguarding both these essential aspects, the unitive and the procreative, the conjugal act preserves in its fulness the sense of true mutual love and its ordination

[10] Cf. Pastoral Const. *Gaudium et Spes*, nos. 50, 51.
[11] *Ibid.*, no. 49.
[12] Cf. Pius XI, encyc. *Casti Connubii* in AAS XXII (1930), p. 560; Pius XII, in AAS XLIII (1951), p. 843.

towards man's most high calling to parenthood. We believe that the men of our day are particularly capable of seizing the deeply reasonable and human character of this fundamental principle.

13. It is in fact justly observed that a conjugal act imposed upon one's partner without regard for his or her condition and lawful desires is not a true act of love, and therefore denies an exigency of right moral order in the relationships between husband and wife. Likewise, if they consider the matter, they must admit that an act of mutual love, which is detrimental to the faculty of propagating life, which God the Creator of all, has implanted in it according to special laws, is in contradiction to both the divine plan, according to whose norm matrimony has been instituted, and the will of the Author of human life. To use this divine gift destroying, even if only partially, its meaning and its purpose is to contradict the nature both of man and of woman and of their most intimate relationship, and therefore it is to contradict also the plan of God and His will. On the other hand, to make use of the gift of conjugal love while respecting the laws of the generative process means to acknowledge oneself not to be the arbiter of the sources of human life, but rather the minister of the design established by the Creator. In fact, just as man does not have unlimited dominion over his body in general, so also, with particular reason, he has no such dominion over his generative faculties as such, because of their intrinsic ordination towards raising up life, of which God is the principle. "Human life is sacred," Pope John XXIII recalled; "from its very inception it reveals the creating hand of God." [13]

14. In conformity with these landmarks in the human and Christian vision of marriage, we must once again declare that the direct interruption of the generative process already begun, and, above all, directly willed and procured abortion, even if for therapeutic reasons, are to be absolutely excluded as licit means of regulating birth.[14]

Equally to be excluded, as the teaching authority of the Church has frequently declared, is direct sterilization, whether perpetual or temporary, whether of the man or of the woman.[15] Similarly excluded is every action which, either in anticipation of the conjugal act, or in its accomplishment, or in the development of its natural consequences, proposes, whether as an end or as a means, to render procreation impossible.[16]

[13] Cf. John XXIII, encyc. *Mater et Magistra,* in AAS LIII (1961), p. 447.
[14] Cf. *Catechismus Romanus Concilii Tridentini,* part. II, Ch. VIII; Pius XI, encyc. *Casti Connubii,* in AAS XXII (1930), pp. 562–564; Pius XII, *Discorsi e Radiomessaggi,* VI (1944), pp. 191–192; AAS XLIII (1951), pp. 842–843; pp. 857–859; John XXIII, encyc. *Pacem in Terris,* Apr. 11, 1963, in AAS LV (1963), pp. 259–260; *Gaudium et Spes,* no. 51.
[15] Cf. Pius XI, encyc. *Casti Connubii,* in AAS XXII (1930), p. 565; decree of the Holy Office, Feb. 22, 1940, in AAS L (1958), pp. 734–735.
[16] Cf. *Catechismus Romanus Concilii Tridentini,* part. II, Ch. VIII; Pius XI, encyc. *Casti Connubii,* in AAS XXII (1930), pp. 559–561; Pius XII, AAS XLIII (1951), p. 843; AAS L (1958), pp. 734–735; John XXIII, encyc. *Mater et Magistra,* in AAS LIII (1961), p. 447.

To justify conjugal acts made intentionally infecund, one cannot invoke as valid reasons the lesser evil, or the fact that such acts would constitute a whole together with the fecund acts already performed or to follow later, and hence would share in one and the same moral goodness. In truth, if it is sometimes licit to tolerate a lesser evil in order to avoid a greater evil or to promote a greater good,[17] it is not licit, even for the gravest reasons, to do evil so that good many follow therefrom; [18] that is, to make into the object of a positive act of the will something which is intrinsically disorder, and hence unworthy of the human person, even when the intention is to safeguard or promote individual, family or social well-being. Consequently it is an error to think that a conjugal act which is deliberately made infecund and so is intrinsically dishonest could be made honest and right by the ensemble of a fecund conjugal life.

15. The Church, on the contrary, does not at all consider illicit the use of those therapeutic means truly necessary to cure diseases of the organism, even if an impediment to procreation, which may be foreseen, should result therefrom, provided such impediment is not, for whatever motive, directly willed.[19]

16. To this teaching of the Church on conjugal morals, the objection is made today, as we observed earlier (no. 3), that it is the prerogative of the human intellect to dominate the energies offered by irrational nature and to orientate them towards an end conformable to the good of man. Now, some may ask: in the present case, is it not reasonable in many circumstances to have recourse to artificial birth control if, thereby, we secure the harmony and peace of the family, and better conditions for the education of the children already born? To this question it is necessary to reply with clarity: the Church is the first to praise and recommend the intervention of intelligence in a function which so closely associates the rational creature with his Creator; but she affirms that this must be done with respect for the order established by God.

If, then, there are serious motives to space out births, which derive from the physical or psychological conditions of husband and wife, or from external conditions, the Church teaches that it is then licit to take into account the natural rhythms immanent in the generative functions, for the use of marriage in the infecund periods only, and in this way to regulate birth without offending the moral principles which have been recalled earlier.[20]

The Church is coherent with herself when she considers recourse to the infecund periods to be licit, while at the same time condemning, as being always illicit, the use of means directly contrary to fecundation,

[17] Cf. Pius XII, alloc. to the National Congress of the Union of Catholic Jurists, Dec. 6, 1953, in AAS XLV (1953), pp. 798–799.
[18] Cf. Rom. 3: 8.
[19] Cf. Pius XII, alloc. to Congress of the Italian Association of Urology, Oct. 8, 1953, in AAS XLV (1953), pp. 674–675; AAS L (1958), pp. 734–735.
[20] Cf. Pius XII, AAS XLIII (1951), p. 846.

even if such use is inspired by reasons which may appear honest and serious. In reality, there are essential differences between the two cases; in the former, the married couple make legitimate use of a natural disposition; in the latter, they impede the development of natural processes. It is true that, in the one and the other case, the married couple are concordant in the positive will of avoiding children for plausible reasons, seeking the certainty that offspring will not arrive; but it is also true that only in the former case are they able to renounce the use of marriage in the fecund periods when, for just motives, procreation is not desirable, while making use of it during infecund periods to manifest their affection and to safeguard their mutual fidelity. By so doing, they give proof of a truly and integrally honest love.

17. Upright men can even better convince themselves of the solid grounds on which the teaching of the Church in this field is based, if they care to reflect upon the consequences of methods of artificial birth control. Let them consider, first of all, how wide and easy a road would thus be opened up towards conjugal infidelity and the general lowering of morality. Not much experience is needed in order to know human weakness, and to understand that men—especially the young, who are so vulnerable on this point—have need of encouragement to be faithful to the moral law, so that they must not be offered some easy means of eluding its observance. It is also to be feared that the man, growing used to the employment of anti-conceptive practices, may finally lose respect for the woman and, no longer caring for her physical and psychological equilibrium, may come to the point of considering her as a mere instrument of selfish enjoyment, and no longer as his respected and beloved companion.

Let it be considered also that a dangerous weapon would thus be placed in the hands of those public authorities who take no heed of moral exigencies. Who could blame a government for applying to the solution of the problems of the community those means acknowledged to be licit for married couples in the solution of a family problem? Who will stop rulers from favoring, from even imposing upon their peoples, if they were to consider it necessary, the method of contraception which they judge to be most efficacious? In such a way men, wishing to avoid individual, family, or social difficulties encountered in the observance of the divine law, would reach the point of placing at the mercy of the intervention of public authorities the most personal and most reserved sector of conjugal intimacy.

Consequently, if the mission of generating life is not to be exposed to the arbitrary will of men, one must necessarily recognize insurmountable limits to the possibility of man's domination over his own body and its functions; limits which no man, whether a private individual or one invested with authority, may licitly surpass. And such limits cannot be determined otherwise than by the respect due to the integrity of the human organism and its functions, according to the principles recalled earlier, and also according to the correct understanding of the "principle of totality" illustrated by our predecessor Pope Pius XII.[21]

18. It can be foreseen that this teaching will perhaps not be easily received by all: Too numerous are those voices—amplified by the modern means of propaganda—which are contrary to the voice of the Church. To tell the truth, the Church is not surprised to be made, like her divine Founder, a "sign of contradiction," [22] yet she does not because of this cease to proclaim with humble firmness the entire moral law, both natural and evangelical. Of such laws the Church was not the author, nor consequently can she be their arbiter; she is only their depositary and their interpreter, without ever being able to declare to be licit that which is not so by reason of its intimate and unchangeable opposition to the true good of man.

In defending conjugal morals in their integral wholeness, the Church knows that she contributes towards the establishment of a truly human civilization; she engages man not to abdicate from his own responsibility in order to rely on technical means; by that very fact she defends the dignity of man and wife. Faithful to both the teaching and the example of the Saviour, she shows herself to be the sincere and disinterested friend of men, whom she wishes to help, even during their earthly sojourn, "to share as sons in the life of the living God, the Father of all men." [23]

III. Pastoral Directives

19. Our words would not be an adequate expression of the thought and solicitude of the Church, Mother and Teacher of all peoples, if, after having recalled men to the observance and respect of the divine law regarding matrimony, we did not strengthen them in the path of honest regulation of birth, even amid the difficult conditions which today afflict families and peoples. The Church, in fact, cannot have a different conduct towards men than that of the Redeemer: She knows their weaknesses, has compassion on the crowd, receives sinners; but she cannot renounce the teaching of the law which is, in reality, that law proper to a human life restored to its original truth and conducted by the spirit of God.[24]

20. The teaching of the Church on the regulation of birth, which promulgates the divine law, will easily appear to many to be difficult or even impossible of actuation. And indeed, like all great beneficent realities, it demands serious engagement and much effort, individual, family and social effort. More than that, it would not be practicable without the help of God, who upholds and strengthens the good will of men. Yet, to any-

21 Cf. AAS XLV (1953), pp. 674–675; AAS XLVIII (1956), pp. 461–462.
22 Cf. Luke 2: 34.
23 Cf. Paul VI, encyc. *Populorum Progressio*, March 26, 1967, No. 21.
24 Cf. Rom. 8.

one who reflects well, it cannot but be clear that such efforts ennoble man and are beneficial to the human community.

21. The honest practice of regulation of birth demands first of all that husband and wife acquire and possess solid convictions concerning the true values of life and of the family, and that they tend towards securing perfect self-mastery. To dominate instinct by means of one's reason and free will undoubtedly requires ascetical practices, so that the affective manifestations of conjugal life may observe the correct order, in particular with regard to the observance of periodic continence. Yet this discipline which is proper to the purity of married couples, far from harming conjugal love, rather confers on it a higher human value. It demands continual effort yet, thanks to its beneficent influence, husband and wife fully develop their personalities, being enriched with spiritual values. Such discipline bestows upon family life fruits of serenity and peace, and facilitates the solution of other problems; it favors attention for one's partner, helps both parties to drive out selfishness, the enemy of true love; and deepens their sense of responsibility. By its means, parents acquire the capacity of having a deeper and more efficacious influence in the education of their offspring; little children and youths grow up with a just appraisal of human values, and in the serene and harmonious development of their spiritual and sensitive faculties.

22. On this occasion, we wish to draw the attention of educators, and of all who perform duties of responsibility in regard to the common good of human society, to the need of creating an atmosphere favorable to education in chastity, that is, to the triumph of healthy liberty over license by means of respect for the moral order.

Everything in the modern media of social communications which leads to sense excitation and unbridled customs, as well as every form of pornography and licentious performances, must arouse the frank and unanimous reaction of all those who are solicitous for the progress of civilization and the defense of the common good of the human spirit. Vainly would one seek to justify such depravation with the pretext of artistic or scientific exigencies,[25] or to deduce an argument from the freedom allowed in this sector by the public authorities.

23. To Rulers, who are those principally responsible for the common good, and who can do so much to safeguard moral customs, we say: Do not allow the morality of your peoples to be degraded; do not permit that by legal means practices contrary to the natural and divine law be introduced into that fundamental cell, the family. Quite other is the way in which public authorities can and must contribute to the solution of the demographic problem: namely, the way of a provident policy for the family, of a wise education of peoples in respect of moral law and the liberty of citizens.

We are well aware of the serious difficulties experienced by public

---

[25] Cf. II Vatican Council, decree *Inter Mirifica*, On the Media of Social Communication, nos. 6–7.

authorities in this regard, especially in the developing countries. To their legitimate preoccupations we devoted our encyclical letter *Populorum Progressio*. But with our predecessor Pope John XXIII, we repeat: no solution to these difficulties is acceptable "which does violence to man's essential dignity" and is based only on an utterly materialistic conception of man himself and of his life. The only possible solution to this question is one which envisages the social and economic progress both of individuals and of the whole of human society, and which respects and promotes true human values.[26] Neither can one, without grave injustice, consider divine providence to be responsible for what depends, instead, on a lack of wisdom in government, on an insufficient sense of social justice, on selfish monopolization, or again on blameworthy indolence in confronting the efforts and the sacrifices necessary to ensure the raising of living standards of a people and of all its sons.[27]

May all responsible public authorities—as some are already doing so laudably—generously revive their efforts. And may mutual aid between all the members of the great human family never cease to grow: This is an almost limitless field which thus opens up to the activity of the great international organizations.

24. We wish now to express our encouragement to men of science, who "can considerably advance the welfare of marriage and the family, along with peace of conscience, if by pooling their efforts they labor to explain more thoroughly the various conditions favoring a proper regulation of births."[28] It is particularly desirable that, according to the wish already expressed by Pope Pius XII, medical science succeed in providing a sufficiently secure basis for a regulation of birth, founded on the observance of natural rhythms.[29] In this way, scientists and especially Catholic scientists will contribute to demonstrate in actual fact that, as the Church teaches, "a true contradiction cannot exist between the divine laws pertaining to the transmission of life and those pertaining to the fostering of authentic conjugal love."[30]

25. And now our words more directly address our own children, particularly those whom God calls to serve Him in marriage. The Church, while teaching imprescriptible demands of the divine law, announces the tidings of salvation, and by means of the sacraments opens up the paths of grace, which makes man a new creature, capable of corresponding with love and true freedom to the design of his Creator and Saviour, and of finding the yoke of Christ to be sweet.[31]

Christian married couples, then, docile to her voice, must remember that their Christian vocation, which began at baptism, is further specified and reinforced by the sacrament of matrimony. By it husband and wife are

[26] Cf. encyc. *Mater et Magistra*, in AAS LIII (1961), p. 447.
[27] Cf. encyc. *Populorum Progressio*, nos. 48–55.
[28] Cf. Pastoral Const. *Gaudium et Spes*, no. 52.
[29] Cf. AAS XLIII (1951), p. 859.
[30] Cf. Pastoral Const. *Gaudium et Spes*, no. 51.
[31] Cf. Matt. 11: 30.

strengthened and as it were consecrated for the faithful accomplishment of their proper duties, for the carrying out of their proper vocation even to perfection, and the Christian witness which is proper to them before the whole world.[32] To them the Lord entrusts the task of making visible to men the holiness and sweetness of the law which unites the mutual love of husband and wife with their cooperation with the love of God the author of human life.

We do not at all intend to hide the sometimes serious difficulties inherent in the life of Christian married persons; for them as for everyone else, "the gate is narrow and the way is hard, that leads to life." [33] But the hope of that life must illuminate their way, as with courage they strive to live with wisdom, justice and piety in this present time,[34] knowing that the figure of this world passes away.[35]

Let married couples, then, face up to the efforts needed, supported by the faith and hope which "do not disappoint . . . because God's love has been poured into our hearts through the Holy Spirit, who has been given to us" [36]; let them implore divine assistance by persevering prayer; above all, let them draw from the source of grace and charity in the Eucharist. And if sin should still keep its hold over them, let them not be discouraged, but rather have recourse with humble perseverance to the mercy of God, which is poured forth in the sacrament of Penance. In this way they will be enabled to achieve the fullness of conjugal life described by the Apostle: "husbands, love your wives, as Christ loved the Church . . . husbands should love their wives as their own bodies. He who loves his wife loves himself. For no man ever hates his own flesh, but nourishes and cherishes it, as Christ does the Church . . . this is a great mystery, and I mean in reference to Christ and the Church. However, let each one of you love his wife as himself, and let the wife see that she respects her husband." [37]

26. Among the fruits which ripen forth from a generous effort of fidelity to the divine law, one of the most precious is that married couples themselves not infrequently feel the desire to communicate their experience to others. Thus there comes to be included in the vast pattern of the vocation of the laity a new and most noteworthy form of the apostolate of like to like; it is married couples themselves who become apostles and guides to other married couples. This is assuredly, among so many forms of apostolate, one of those which seem most opportune today.[38]

[32] Cf. Pastoral Const. *Gaudium et Spes*, no. 48; II Vatican Council, Dogmatic Const. *Lumen Gentium*, no. 35.
[33] Matt. 7: 14; cf. Heb. 11: 12.
[34] Cf. Tit. 2: 12.
[35] Cf. I Cor. 7: 31.
[36] Cf. Rom. 5: 5.
[37] Eph. 5: 25, 28–29, 32–33.
[38] Cf. Dogmatic Const. *Lumen Gentium*, nos. 35 and 41; Pastoral Const. *Gaudium et Spes*, nos. 48–49; II Vatican Council, Decree *Apostolicam Actuositatem*, no. 11.

27. We hold those physicians and medical personnel in the highest esteem who, in the exercise of their profession, value above every human interest the superior demands of their Christian vocation. Let them persevere, therefore, in promoting on every occasion the discovery of solutions inspired by faith and right reason, let them strive to arouse this conviction and this respect in their associates. Let them also consider as their proper professional duty the task of acquiring all the knowledge needed in this delicate sector, so as to be able to give to those married persons who consult them wise counsel and healthy direction, such as they have a right to expect.

28. Beloved priest sons, by vocation you are the counselors and spiritual guides of individual persons and of families. We now turn to you with confidence. Your first task—especially in the case of those who teach moral theology—is to expound the Church's teaching on marriage without ambiguity. Be the first to give, in the exercise of your ministry, the example of loyal internal and external obedience to the teaching authority of the Church. That obedience, as you know well, obliges not only because of the reasons adduced, but rather because of the light of the Holy Spirit, which is given in a particular way to the pastors of the Church in order that they may illustrate the truth.[39] You know, too, that it is of the utmost importance, for peace of consciences and for the unity of the Christian people, that in the field of morals as well as in that of dogma, all should attend to the magisterium of the Church, and all should speak the same language. Hence, with all our heart we renew to you the heartfelt plea of the great Apostle Paul: "I appeal to you, brethren, by the name of Our Lord Jesus Christ, that all of you agree and that there be no dissensions among you, but that you be united in the same mind and the same judgment." [40]

29. To diminish in no way the saving teaching of Christ constitutes an eminent form of charity for souls. But this must ever be accompanied by patience and goodness, such as the Lord himself gave example of in dealing with men. Having come not to condemn but to save,[41] he was indeed intransigent with evil, but merciful towards individuals.

In their difficulties, may married couples always find, in the words and in the heart of a priest, the echo of the voice and the love of the Redeemer.

And then speak with confidence, beloved sons, fully convinced that the spirit of God, while He assists the magisterium in proposing doctrine, illumines internally the hearts of the faithful inviting them to give their assent. Teach married couples the indispensable way of prayer; prepare them to have recourse often and with faith to the sacraments of the Eucharist and of Penance, without ever allowing themselves to be discouraged by their own weakness.

[39] Cf. Dogmatic Const. *Lumen Gentium*, no. 25.
[40] Cf. I Cor. 1: 10.
[41] Cf. John 3: 17.

30. Beloved and venerable brothers in the episcopate, with whom we most intimately share the solicitude of the spiritual good of the People of God, at the conclusion of this encyclical our reverent and affectionate thoughts turn to you. To all of you we extend an urgent invitation. At the head of the priests, your collaborators, and of your faithful, work ardently and incessantly for the safeguarding and the holiness of marriage, so that it may always be lived in its entire human and Christian fullness. Consider this mission as one of your most urgent responsibilities at the present time. As you know, it implies concerted pastoral action in all the fields of human activity, economic, cultural and social; for, in fact, only a simultaneous improvement in these various sectors will make it possible to render the life of parents and of children within their families not only tolerable, but easier and more joyous, to render the living together in human society more fraternal and peaceful, in faithfulness to God's design for the world.

31. Venerable brothers, most beloved sons, and all men of good will, great indeed is the work of education, of progress and of love to which we call you, upon the foundation of the Church's teaching, of which the successor of Peter is, together with his brothers in the episcopate, the depositary and interpreter. Truly a great work, as we are deeply convinced, both for the world and the Church, since man cannot find true happiness—towards which he aspires with all his being—other than in respect of the laws written by God in his very nature, laws which he must observe with intelligence and love. Upon this work, and upon all of you, and especially upon married couples, we involve the abundant graces of the God of holiness and mercy, and in pledge thereof we impart to you all our apostolic blessing.

Given at Rome, from St. Peter's, this 25th day of July, feast of St. James the Apostle, in the year 1968, the sixth of our pontificate.

Famine Stalks the Earth: The Population

Bomb Keeps Ticking

Population Policy Panel of the

Hugh Moore Fund

Famine, War and Communism

"The world is on the threshold of the biggest famine in history," according to Raymond Ewell, former advisor to the Government of India. "If present trends continue, it seems likely that famine will reach serious proportions in India, Pakistan and China in the early 1970s. Latin America will fall in this category by 1980. Such a famine will be of massive proportions, affecting hundreds of millions, possibly billions of persons."

The Director-General of the United Nations Food and Agriculture Organization, Binay Sen, said: "Either we take the fullest measures both to raise productivity and to stabilize population growth, or we face a disaster of unprecedented magnitude. . . . Problems of hunger and malnutrition which afflict more than a half of the world's population . . . pose a *serious threat to peace*."

There will be 300 million more mouths to feed in the world four years from now—most of them hungry. Hunger brings turmoil—and turmoil, as we have learned, creates the atmosphere in which the communists seek to conquer the earth.

Skyrocketing Population

World population is increasing at an unprecedented rate. According to United Nations estimates world population is growing by 8,000 every hour or approximately 70,000,000 a year. A number equal to the population of France, Belgium and Holland taken together is being added every year to the people living on this earth!

Medical discoveries and widespread advances in sanitation have im-

Reprinted from *The Population Bomb,* a pamphlet published by the Population Policy Panel of the Hugh Moore Fund, 60 East 42nd Street, New York, N. Y.

proved health and prolonged life spans and thus have lowered *death rates.* But *birth rates* have not gone down proportionately.

In Mexico, for example, four persons are born for one who dies. At this rate there will be 84,000,000 Mexicans in 20 years compared with 42,000,- 000 now. Many other countries have similar growth rates.

The *rate* of world population growth is also going up and up. It was 1.8 per cent annually in 1955. If present trends continue, it will be 3.0 per cent in 1985.

This means that world population will grow from 3.3 billion in 1965 to more than 5 billion in 1985.

Two simple figures highlight the extent of the population deluge. From the dawn of history until 1930, the world only reached a population of 2 billion. But in one century thereafter, population at present trends will multiply *seven* times to 14 billions.

But this is not the whole story. Population in most hungry countries is growing much faster than in the opulent countries. For instance, in Latin America population will almost triple from 250 millions to about 700 millions by the end of the century. India, kept from the brink today by U.S. wheat shipments, will add 200 million people by 1980. By contrast, in Europe the growth rate of 0.8 per cent a year is expected to remain constant over the next two decades.

Food production is not keeping step with this rocketing population growth. Latin America, as an example, increased its total production of food over the last five years, but with 25 million more people, the *average individual* had 7 per cent less to eat.

At the World Population Conference at Belgrade in 1965 FAO Director Binay Sen said:

It is now less than seven years since there was any appreciable increase in food production per head of the world's population, seven very lean years for the developing countries. In two regions in particular, the Far East and Latin America, per capita production is still less than it was before the war, more than a quarter of a century ago. . . . The general outlook is indeed alarming. In some of the most heavily populated areas the outbreak of serious famines within the next five to ten years cannot be excluded. . . .

Food into a Bottomless Pit

The United States has shipped abroad, since Congress enacted the so-called "Food For Peace" law in 1954, food products amounting *to the gigantic sum of $15 billion,* mostly on a give-away basis.

India receives from the United States more than a half of its wheat at the present rate of *27,500 tons a day.* Observers believe that this assistance is the only barrier against large scale famine and open rebellion. The Communist-led food riots in the State of Kerala have already threatened a serious breakdown of law and order.

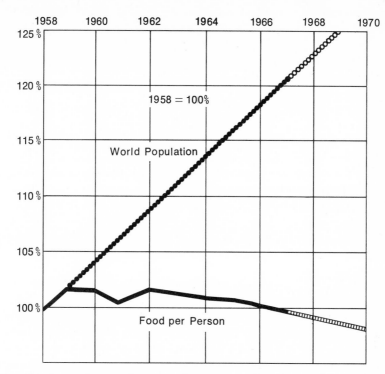

Our food warehouses that were bursting at the seams a few years ago are now at less than normal inventory required for reserves. Congress recently authorized Secretary Freeman to go into the open market and buy milk to keep up our lunch program for overseas children.

"The most striking fact about American agriculture is that our surpluses are gone," Senator George McGovern of South Dakota, former U.S. Food for Peace Administrator, warned in 1966.

With all this out-pouring of American resources we are not making a dent at solving the problem. *Even if we were to continue such a program on a vastly stepped-up basis, as some suggest, until American farm lands were exhausted, we still could not feed the burgeoning billions of people.*

Said President Johnson in his 1966 Foreign Aid Message to Congress: "We cannot meet the world food needs of the future, however willing we are to share our abundance. Nor would it serve the common interest if we could."

Prospects of More Food

Can production be increased? It can and it must. But that is easier said than done. To quote U.S. Secretary of Agriculture, Orville L. Freeman:

Problems of staggering proportions face the densely populated underdeveloped countries of the world in their effort to keep food production in pace with population growth. Both land and time are running out for those countries. In the past, increases in food output were achieved by putting new land under cultivation. But now the supply of readily cultivatable land can be brought under cultivation only at high cost.

William and Paul Paddock in their important book *Hungry Nations* say:

Agriculture, if it is going to be of any good to anyone, must combine success-fully and in the right time sequence several quite disparate factors. One is land with enough of the right texture to allow roots to penetrate it and with the correct combination of minerals to feed those roots. Another is enough rainfall at least to wet those roots now and then. Another is enough warm sunshine to get the seeds sprouted and the blades out of the ground.

To say the obvious, a desert may have fine soil, but it has no rain; the Arctic has moisture but not the right temperature; mountains are too up and down. And so it goes. *For this reason only 7.7 per cent of the land surface of the planet Earth is cultivated. . . .*

Even heroic efforts to produce additional food are quickly swamped by population increases. Egypt's Aswan Dam ranks as one of the daring engineering feats of our day. It will irrigate one million new acres of agricultural land.

But by the time the dam is finished in 1970, Egypt's population will have multiplied so quickly that these new acres will only feed a third of the new population even at today's poor nutritional level.

It requires a great amount of capital for the purchase of chemical fertilizers and pesticides, for inproved seed varieties and increased irrigation and for various kinds of machinery. Such capital is not readily available in most poor countries. It also requires a higher level of literacy than most of these countries have.

More than Food Needed

Education is necessary to achieve a higher level of living. Hundreds of millions are illiterate. In Guatemala, for instance, 70 per cent of the population over fifteen years of age cannot read and write—in India 80 per cent.

More children require more schools, more teachers, more educational equipment. Due to rapid population growth, a high proportion of the population in underdeveloped countries are children.

The creation of capital is another major condition for a higher living standard. Capital investment is needed for any economic, sanitary or cultural improvement—for agriculture and industry, for schools, hospitals and roads. And each new consumer requires new capital investment.

Where incomes are near subsistence levels capital formation is slow. Rapid population increase uses up all or most of it and leaves none or little for economic investment, thus slowing down much needed industrialization.

But of course underlying all these requirements is the basic need of food. A hungry child is a poor student; a man with an empty belly is a poor worker.

Lower Birth Rates the Answer

Everything possible must be done to help developing nations to increase their food production. But this will not be enough. *Unless birth rates are brought into a proper balance with death rates there will be more hungry people on earth in the future*—despite all possible improvement of agriculture.

Surveys have shown that the desire for fewer births is widespread and growing. Millions of women wish to be spared from the burden of constant child-bearing.

What they need is knowledge of birth control methods and simple, safe and cheap contraceptives.

Contraceptives

Many reliable contraceptives are available now in the more developed countries. Some of them are still too complex or too expensive for wide use in the less developed countries. Therefore, research in this field must be continued and rapidly stepped up.

The new oral contraceptive—the "pill"—is now being used by an estimated five million women in the United States and millions elsewhere. A reduction in price or government subsidies could spread its use in poorer countries.

New Intra-Uterine Devices are being tested widely and results so far prove them to be safe and effective. Their great advantage over other contraceptives is that they can be left in place for months or years without thought or attention.

They cost pennies to manufacture and have met with ready acceptance by women in many parts of the world.

However, with due appreciation of IUDs and pills for women, we must not overlook the proliferating capacity of the *other sex*. Contraceptive methods for men by injection or pill still need extensive research and testing before promising experiments reach the stage of practical application.

Research

Ultimately contraceptive methods will be found to control fertility on a permanent or temporary basis—such as, for instance, inoculation of women to immunize them against spermatazoa, or an injection for men to suppress the production of sperm. When that may be will depend on the talent and the money put into research. Time is of the essence!

The National Academy of Sciences said in a 1965 study: "Basic research into reproductive physiology should receive increasing support not only for its general contribution to man's knowledge of his own reproduction, but also in order to provide us with new and better methods for controlling fertility. In addition, systematic efforts to assess the effectiveness and acceptability of the various contraceptive procedures that are now available should be supported."

Voluntary Sterilization

Voluntary sterilization—male and female—but particularly male sterilization (vasectomy)—is finding increasing favor as a means of birth control in many parts of the world.

In the United States almost 200,000 persons are sterilized annually and the number is growing. In India, which is conducting vigorous family planning programs, the Government is planning two and a half million vasectomies a year. The operation is performed free of charge and sometimes the Government pays a small bonus to the man who has the operation. Mobile vasectomy camps are set up at which thousands of men are sterilized weekly.

Vasectomy is a simple procedure. One American surgeon writes: "It may be done easily, rapidly and painlessly. The patient walks in, walks out and goes about his affairs. No after-care is necessary, no hospitalization." It does not affect sexual relations adversely and is not to be confused with castration.

Surgeons in India, the United States and elsewhere are seeking a method of *reversing* vasectomy to permit men to become fertile again. Prospects of success are good—although requests for reversal are rare.

Abortion

Japan cut its annual birth rate in half within a decade; from 34 per thousand population in 1947 to 17 in 1958—probably the most rapid birth rate decline in history. This decline was due largely to the wide use of legal abortions.

The Soviet Union, mainland China and most Eastern European countries also have legalized abortions, not merely for therapeutic reasons, but as a means of birth control.

Under legal, hospital conditions, doctors now consider abortion a safe and simple procedure—only one-sixth to one-tenth as dangerous as pregnancy and childbirth, according to Dr. Christopher Tietze of the National Committee on Maternal Health.

But in countries where restrictive laws bar most women from hospital abortions, countless millions of secret abortions are performed annually under deplorable conditions, often at the risk of health and life.

Role of Private Organizations

Organized efforts to spread planned parenthood and promote population control have been growing rapidly in the past few years. If successful they will result in the most dramatic and beneficial social revolution the world has known.

Population Crisis Committee, 1730 K Street, NW, Washington, D.C. 20036, has launched a vigorous campaign to activate the U.S. Government.

The International Planned Parenthood Federation has affiliates in more than 40 countries and cooperating organizations in many more. It has headquarters in London (18-20 Lower Regent Street, London, SW 1) and a regional office in the U.S. (51 East 42nd Street, New York, N. Y. 10017). Its American affiliate is Planned Parenthood-World Population, 515 Madison Avenue, New York, N. Y. 10022.

Valuable educational work is being done by the Population Reference Bureau, 1755 Massachusetts Avenue NW, Washington, D.C. 20036.

The Population Council, 230 Park Avenue, New York, N. Y. 10017, has achieved remarkable results in demographic and biological research.

The Association for Voluntary Sterilization, 14 West 40th Street, New York, N. Y. 10018, is concerned with research, education and service in the field of voluntary human sterilization for the purpose of family planning and population control.

These organizations deserve generous public support.

Role of Private Foundations

Among the larger charitable foundations the Ford Foundation has been a leader in the population field for well over a decade. It has been the major supporter of The Population Council and has financed a number of biological and social studies. It has aided in the development of centers for population studies in various universities. Recently it has made a grant of $14.5 million for an International Institute for the Study of Human Reproduction at the Columbia-Presbyterian Medical Center and for large-scale expansion of the Population Council's Bio-Medical Laboratories.

The Rockefeller Foundation expanded "its support of critical research and of action programs in population dynamics and population stabilization" to "prevent the eventual condemnation of millions of future citizens to lives of underprivilege, misery, and hopelessness."

Other philanthropic foundations—following the lead of Ford and Rockefeller—are turning to the population field. They have not only a special responsibility but may expect rich rewards. Foundations devoted to public health, medicine and education will readily see that explosive population growth has a direct relevance to their primary objectives.

Role of Governments

More and more national governments realize the need for population control policies. Official birth control programs are now to be found in Egypt, India, Kenya, Korea, Pakistan, Taiwan, Tunisia and Turkey.

In Chile a voluntary National Committee is officially backed by the National Health Service which contributes hospital facilities and services of its personnel. Cooperation between governments and private organizations exists in a number of other countries.

In some countries progress is encouraging, notably in Korea and Taiwan. Others—India, Pakistan, Egypt—are progressing slowly due to the lack of trained personnel and suitable contraceptives.

The U.S. Government has been backward in recognizing the dangers of the population explosion and slow in developing a policy to counteract it. John F. Kennedy was the first President to express concern over the problem and President Johnson has now taken an unequivocal stand. In his Foreign Aid Message to Congress in February 1966 he said:

We stand ready to help developing countries deal with the population problem.

The United States can not and should not force any country to adopt any particular approach to this problem. It is first a matter of individual and national conscience, in which we will not interfere.

But population growth now consumes about two-thirds of economic growth in the less-developed world. As death rates are steadily driven down, the individual miracle of birth becomes a collective tragedy of want.

In all cases, our help will be given only upon request. . . .

Despite this forthright statement by the President, the fact remains that to date the manpower and resources of the various agencies of the Government committed to meet this transcendent challenge rank below a hundred less important projects.

Indeed, a certain timidity seems to hold back Washington officials from embracing their task wholeheartedly. For instance, the Agency for International Development says that it will supply information, training and educational material but it will not make available birth control devices. And the Office of Economic Opportunity has ruled that funds for birth control under community action programs cannot be used for contraceptives to unmarried mothers or for voluntary sterilization.

Obviously, a great deal of public pressure is needed to instill into the Administration the sense of urgency with which this critical problem must be attacked.

The 1965 White House Conference on International Cooperation declared that "the rate of growth of world population is so great—and its consequences so grave—that *this may be the last generation which has the opportunity to cope with the problem on the basis of free choice.*"

As the population flood inundates the world, time runs out at frightening speed. Either we grasp the sane solution of population control now or we are headed towards mass suffocation. Unless we act, man may have to "accept extinction with the dinosaur and dodo bird," historian Arnold Toynbee concludes.

The Expanding Role of the U.S. Government
in Programs of Birth Control, Both at
Home and Abroad

Cardinal O'Boyle

Today, I would like to speak to you about the constantly expanding role of the U.S. Government in programs of birth control, both at home and abroad. These programs cannot be ignored because, in my judgment, they constitute a threat to the privacy and freedom of married couples and, increasingly, they contribute to a growing attack on human life itself.

When I delivered a sermon on this topic back in August 1965, one local newspaper responded editorially with the prediction that my unfortunate remarks would soon be outdated by a change in the Church's moral teaching. Apart from the fact that the event proved the prediction false, the argument was beside the point, for my attitude about public programs in this area is not shaped by Catholic moral teaching alone, but also and especially by my conviction that our highest public ideals and the common good of all dictate that the government should stay out of the birth control business.

There are three factors that I believe should be weighed by every conscientious citizen, whatever his judgment on the use of contraceptives by particular couples might be, when he considers the public policy question to which I am addressing myself now.

First, public programs of birth control do nothing to overcome poverty or misery except to the extent that they succeed in cutting down the number of poor people. Abstractly, it is all very well to imagine that public policy can embrace this simple expedient in a limited way, while vigorously attacking racial discrimination and other forms of injustice which are the most important reasons why there remains so much misery in the midst of our affluent society, and why there is an ever-widening gap between the wealthier and the poorer nations of the world.

But in actual fact, the negative approach of anti-life programs all too easily becomes an alternative to a positive approach of reconstructing the social order in better accord with the requirements of justice. On June 25, 1965, two months before the sermon I mentioned previously, our former president delivered an address at San Francisco, in celebration of the twentieth anniversary of the United Nations. In that address he said:

Let us in all our lands—including this land—face forthrightly the multiplying problems of our multiplying populations and seek the answers to this most profound challenge to the future of all the world. Let us act on the fact that less than five dollars invested in population control is worth a hundred dollars invested in economic growth.

This statement deserves to be pondered. It elicited an angry uproar in many of the poorer nations, especially in Latin America. And in my judgment the critics were right, if not in all they said, at least in detecting in this statement a false sense of values, a sense of values which compares the cost of preventing people with the cost of serving them, as if the only important difference between the two were the number of dollars spent. I have heard that even many of the leaders of the birth control movement felt that this statement had been an unwise one—unfortunately, however, not because it reflected their attitudes inadequately, but rather because it expressed those attitudes too explicitly.

From this point of view, I see expanding government programs of birth control as another instance of discrimination against the poor for the advantage of those who are better off, because birth control programs mean that one hundred dollars will not be collected as taxes and spent to overcome social injustice whenever five dollars can be collected as taxes and spent to limit the number of people who will nevertheless continue to suffer the consequences of social injustice.

Of course, it will be said that public programs of contraception are needed to give the poor the same freedom to plan their families that the rich already enjoy. A plausible argument, until you consider that the freedom of the poor would be more fully respected if they were given the sum of money that would be spent on a public birth control program, and allowed to spend it on that or anything else they might choose. The trouble is, as some of the most ardent advocates of population planning have explained, that given a choice, the poor want more children than population planners think it is proper for them to have.[1]

[1] See, e.g., Kingsley Davis, "Population Policy: Will Current Programs Succeed?" *Science*, 158 (November 10, 1967), 730–739.

And this brings us to a second factor that weighs heavily against public programs of birth control. They are claimed to be completely voluntary. Every couple's privacy and conscientious judgment is supposed to be respected. The recent presidential message to Congress (July 18, 1969) made a considerable point of personal freedom of choice.

But the fact of the matter is that the poor simply do not have the freedom that the rest of us enjoy. When a poor family, in desperate need of public aid, on which the family totally depends for the very possibility of survival faces the agents of the government, embarked on an intensive program of population control, the situation is inherently unfree. In November 1966, a statement of the American Bishops pointed out this fact.[2] The reaction from the news media and from the leaders of the contraception movement suggested that the Bishops were seeing an insubstantial goblin, a completely unreal threat of governmental meddling in the intimate relationships of the people.

Yet during the following year, 1967, one newspaper, the *Washington Post,* reported grave abuses on at least three distinct occasions. The *Post* has not been unsympathetic to the contraception movement, and I think deserves some credit for honestly reporting these abuses, which were undoubtedly embarrassing for anyone sharing the *Post's* editorial views on the matter.

A feature story in March 1967 on District of Columbia birth control programs warned that "some well-meaning poverty programs and welfare workers are most guilty" of pressuring people "to get birth control devices rather than let them make their own decisions."[3] A few months later, a talk by Mrs. Ruby Evans, a local U.P.O. official, was reported under the headline: "UPO Official Raps Forced Use of Pill by Teen-age Girls."[4] Within a week, there was another story about Mrs. Evans: "UPO Official Is Fired for Birth Control Talk."[5] A few months later, a Judge in Prince George's County was reported as ruling that mothers of two or more illegitimate children are guilty of neglect solely because their children were illegitimate. The Judge threatened that women who did not learn and practice methods of birth control would risk losing their children.[6]

In November 1967, the Catholic Bishops of the United States warned against coercive practices by government in fostering population control—especially among the poor and the blacks. Some newspapers and others violently criticized the Bishops on their charge of coercion, saying that the Bishops had not proved any coercion at all. These critics expressed horror at the idea that coercion, in this highly personal area, would ever be employed.

[2] Statement of the Administrative Board of the National Catholic Welfare Conference, "On the Government and Birth Control," November 14, 1966.
[3] *Washington Post,* Parade Magazine Section, March 5, 1967.
[4] *Washington Post,* July 23, 1967.
[5] Same, July 29, 1967.
[6] Same, September 22, 23, 24 and 25, 1967.

In 1969, we see unmasked the true intention of those who are trying to shove our national population in the direction of massive domestic and overseas population control. The *New York Times* of September 22, 1969, reports a conference which took place at Aspen, Colorado, at which a group of influential exponents of population control—including officials of the United States Government—urged *compulsory* birth control and described voluntary birth control as "insanity." John Erlichman, Counsel to President Nixon, was moderator of this conference.

Dr. Roger O. Egeberg, Assistant Secretary for Health and Scientific Affairs, said "population control" should be the "first priority" in the Nixon Administrations' health programs.

These officials expressed no dissent over the statement of Dr. Donald Aitken, consultant on the Apollo Project, who dared to say:

I admire Mr. Nixon's courage in making the first presidential talks on population limitation. But he negated it all at the end by promising that the governmental effort wouldn't interfere with religious convictions, personal convictions, etc. . . I'd like to see Mr. Nixon stand up a few years from now and say: . . . "population must be controlled. We must set an example. *So the government has to step in and tamper with religious and personal convictions—and maybe even impose penalties for every child a family has beyond two.*"

I do not have time to go into the full history of these incidents here, nor to mention other incidents I have heard of in other parts of the country. The facts indicated are enough to prove that the American Bishops were not talking about an imaginary threat when they said there are dangers to freedom and to the right of privacy when the government moves into concrete programs of birth control, directly affecting the poor.

A third factor, which I also discussed somewhat in my 1965 sermon, is that there is a certain legitimate role for government in the area of objective scientific research. I still believe this to be true. However, even in this area there are some very serious dangers, not apparent in 1965, but clearly apparent today.

In August 1968, a Center for Population Research was established in the National Institute for Child Health and Human Development. One of the first acts of the new center was to seek research and development sources. Competent advisors who have studied the technical description of the new research program tell me that much of the planned research is being directed toward the development of techniques that will prevent births not by contraception, but by early abortion. In some cases the abortion would be induced soon after conception, and in other cases at a later date, after the new human being had been well established in his mother's womb.[7]

---

[7] This document is headed: "A New Contract Research Program for the Development of New Contraceptives: Research and Development Sources Sought." It is not dated, but asks in conclusion that information requested be submitted by

There is a terrible irony in the fact that a government agency called the "National Institute for Child *Health* and Human *Development*" should be engaged in research such as this. I cannot help recalling, with deep anxiety, how often totalitarian regimes have perversely used the forms of justice to work injustice, the institutions of education to spread corruption, and the facilities for promoting health to expedite death.

The worst of it is that the danger is not off in the distant future. The so-called IUD, which very probably, I am told, derives at least part of its effectiveness from abortifacient action, is widely used, and no one seems to notice. Already the so-called "morning-after pill," which is certainly an abortifacient, is being tested, and the National Institute of Child Health and Human Development made a contribution to this new method even before the new research center was established last summer.[8]

These are the facts. And they are good reasons for any conscientious citizen to think again about the course on which our government has embarked in this matter. No one can predict what may happen in the future. But I am very much afraid that anti-life programs will grind on with computer-like inexorability from one step to another, unless thoughtful citizens set prejudices aside and stop to think about the human meaning of what we are doing. A pamphlet issued by the Population Council, one of the most important organizations promoting birth control both privately and in government-sponsored programs, takes up the question: What is to be done beyond present programs of voluntary family planning? This document, published in February of this year, makes chilling reading, for while it does not express a commitment, it does point to the possibility of non-voluntary programs, ones that would be openly coercive, and to programs that would force women to undergo abortions in some cases.[9] This document does not make public any consideration of infanticide or euthanasia or straightforward genocide as possible final solutions to the welfare problem. Perhaps no one has yet begun speculating on these possibilities. But then again—and this is what worries me—perhaps the thrust of the anti-life movement will progress (if you can call it that) to these fullest realizations of its implicit spirit.

February 3, 1969. The section of the description outlining research on the pre-implantation ovum points to an abortifacient effective shortly after conception; the section on corpus luteum function, particularly in reference to a search for agents capable of inhibiting that function, points to abortifacients that would act *after* nidation.

[8] There was a warning, unfortunately subsequently ignored, that any method effective after fertilization would involve abortion, and implied moral and legal problems: United States Department of Health, Education and Welfare; Public Health Service, *Publication No. 1066* (Washington: 1963), 27. In regard to the "morning-after pill" see John McLean Morris et al., "Compounds Interfering with Ovum Implantation and Development: 11. Synthetic Estrogens and Anti-estrogens," *Fertility and Sterility*, 18 (1967), 18.

[9] Bernard Berelson, "Beyond Family Planning," *Studies in Family Planning*, 38 (February 1969), 2 and 9.

I hope that you will look the ugly facts of government programs of birth control directly in the face, and will meditate thoroughly on the even uglier possibilities. I hope that you will use every available democratic means to block this evil movement, to stop its seemingly inexorable advance, and to turn it back. For a reversal in the movement against life will be a victory for human life, for personal freedom and the right of privacy, and for social justice.

Yet we must not only be negative. We must pick out the right and good things the government can and should do, and we must urge that they be done, as our Holy Father has urged in his encyclical on the *Progress of Peoples* and as the American Bishops have urged in many statements over the years. Nor may we be content with talk. We must also act to right the wrongs by serving the poor and the suffering at home and in all the world.

Questions

1. What are the main points that President Nixon makes in his presentation of the problem of population growth? What are the main points that Pope Paul VI makes in his encyclical? Are both addressing the same issue? In what ways would you say that the issue of population control is the same as that of birth control? In what ways are they different?

2. How is the issue of birth control related to that of sex education (see Section Eight)?

3. How would you describe the differences in tone and rhetoric in the President's message, in the Pope's encyclical, and in the pamphlet "Famine Stalks the Earth"? Do there seem to be essential differences in fact? What would these seem to be? Or are the differences in emphasis and in ethical or theological position? How would you characterize these differences? How does the cartoon affect you?

4. Cardinal O'Boyle declares that "public programs of birth control do nothing to overcome poverty or misery except to the extent that they succeed in cutting down the number of poor people." Would it be a relevant argument to say that programs of birth or population control are actually aimed at poor people? What would seem to you to be the consequences of a program that very specifically cuts down the birth of poor people but does not necessarily affect the number of children born to middle- and upper-class families throughout the world?

5. What issues are raised about "voluntary" and "compulsory" population control? Do these seem to you to be valid?

6. What seem to you to be some of the unspoken but underlying issues involved in the various discussions, both for and against forms of population control?

7. Which of the statements seems to you to be the most balanced in presenting the problems? Which is the most emotional? Which do you find the most persuasive without regard to any previous position you may have held? Why?

Assignments

1. One argument frequently made against any form of birth control is that great men have often come from large families and have been among the last children born in a family. How would you counter this argument?

2. In parallel columns, list the major arguments for and against birth control. Argue the persuasiveness of the strongest of these. Also indicate which seems to you to be the weakest.

3. Using some of the material listed in Additional Reading below discuss either the statistical or the logical fallacy of any of the extreme positions on birth control.

4. Relate materials in this section to those in Section Ten, on race differences. You might address yourself to the particular question of the control of the birth rate for specific populations.

Additional Reading

No discussion of the population explosion fails to mention Thomas Malthus. In *An Essay on the Principle of Population* (1798), he established the lines of argument which have prevailed ever since. In a recent volume, *Three Essays on Population* (New York, 1960), Malthus' essay has been reprinted along with two modern discussions, Julian Huxley's (1955) and Frederick Osborn's (1960).

Other recent discussions of the question include John Rock, *The Time Has Come* (New York, 1963), a discussion by a Catholic physician; Dennis H. Wrong, *Population and Society* (New York, 1961), an objective, detailed survey by a demographer; and George F. Meir, ed., *Studies in Population* (Princeton 1949), a collection of studies by various hands.

Other relevant articles and chapters relating to various aspects of the problem of birth and population control are the following: Jean Mayer, "Toward a Non-Malthusian Population Policy," *Columbia University Forum,* Summer 1969. Professor Mayer of Harvard is one of the world's leading authorities on the relation between food and population control; the Hugh Moore Fund, whose pamphlet is included in this section, has materials available urging control of the world's "exploding population"; Dennis Wrong's book *Population and Society,* 3rd Ed. (1967), is concerned with demographic aspects of the problem, particularly in the chapter "World Population Growth and Distribution"; the Summer 1959 issue of *Daedalus Magazine* contained three articles from several points of view: Hudson Hogland's, "Population Problem in the Control of Fertility" is an attempt at an objective presentation of the facts; John L. Thomas, S.J., has a piece giving "The Catholic Position on Population Control"; and John C. Bennett has an article on "Protestant Ethics and Population Control." The Metropolitan Life Insurance Company in New York and other insurance companies also frequently circulate statistical material on questions of population growth in certain periods.

SECTION EIGHT *Sex and the School Child*

"What are sex, anyhow?"

A Delicate Subject: Sex Education Courses Are Suddenly Assailed by Many Parent Groups

Neil Ulman

When Ronald J. May, a Rahway, N.J., salesman, asked his five-year-old daughter last November what she was drawing at the dinner table, he was more than a little taken aback by her answer.

FROM the *Wall Street Journal*, April 11, 1969. Reprinted with the permission of the *Wall Street Journal*.

"The sperm swims up here to meet the egg," she replied, going on to give, says Mr. May, a rather accurate explanation of human conception as she had learned it in first grade that morning. "The only thing I can't remember," she said, "is how the daddy gets the sperm into the mommy."

When an angry interview with school officials convinced him his daughter need only ask to have her question answered in class, Mr. May found a new mission in life. Since then he has spent "at least a couple of nights each week, sometimes every night," crisscrossing New Jersey talking to individuals and lecturing to groups on the evils of sex education.

Mr. May's crusade has been exhausting but far from lonely. In the past six months, myriad groups have sprung up across the country to denounce sex education as immoral, subversive, Communist-inspired, pornographic and psychologically damaging to the young. The result: After about five years of surprisingly smooth sailing, sex education in America is in trouble. The controversy is as bitter and emotional as any that ever rocked the nation's schools.

WHY NOW? NOBODY KNOWS. Under such banners as PAUSE (People Against Unconstitutional Sex Education) and MOMS (Mothers for Moral Stability), outraged and frightened parents are carrying their complaints to school boards, statehouses and even to Congress. Legislators in Arizona, California, Iowa, New Jersey, New York and Oklahoma are debating whether to investigate, restrict or abolish sex education. A bill before Congress would withhold Federal funds from sex education courses or related teacher training.

Stunned educators, who thought they had won community support for sex education through intensive efforts to tell parents about the courses, are asking, "Why Now?" Nobody really knows.

Most of the opponents say they "just didn't know what was going on" until their children enlightened them. Some trace public reaction to a March 1968 San Francisco educational television program in which teachers described sexual intercourse to children.

"That broadcast alerted parents that this sex education thing was under way," says Mrs. Alice Weiner of Belmont in California's San Mateo County. She found it "exceedingly objectionable" to discuss "this sort of thing in a mixed group," as was done on TV. "You break down modesty between boys and girls in the classroom and it leads to promiscuity," she asserts.

A COLORING BOOK. Mrs. Weiner and several neighbors were so shocked by what they saw that they formed Citizens for Parental Rights to bar the program from being shown in San Mateo schools, which had offered it to teachers of the system's Family Life Sex-Education courses. What's more, the parents' group demanded that the system's whole sex-education course be dropped. To solicit money for their cause, they have distributed, among other materials, a Family Life Education Coloring Book with such captions as, "This is the psychiatrist who tells little children how to have intercourse. Color him sweet." Similar materials created in California are being copied in other communities across the nation.

Others credit the furor to the John Birch Society, which wholeheartedly joined the campaign after its founder and leader, Robert Welch, denounced sex education as "a filthy Communist plot." But the Birch Society, self-admitted "Johnny-come-latelies," entered the battle only last January, well after the pot was already boiling.

In school districts where sex education is just getting under way, the opposition has scored heavily. Educators have backed off from proposed programs in recent weeks at schools in Roselle, N.J., the Catholic diocese of Syracuse and Rio Linda, Calif.

But the older, established programs are hardly immune. In Anaheim, Calif., where a Family Life Education course was hailed from its inception in 1965 as a national model for scope and candor, all went smoothly for four years. But when the roof fell in last autumn, the turnabout was sudden and savage.

PLOTTING WITH PORNOGRAPHERS? After a handful of parents complained last August that the course was corrupting their children, a special school board meeting was convened in October to air objections. Speakers from all over the state condemned the program. Next followed rallies attracting hundreds of parents who clamored for removal of "Family Life" from the schools.

"The educators have joined the pornographers in a diabolical plot," charges Mrs. Eleanor Howe, an Anaheim housewife spearheading the battle as vice president of Citizens Committee of California. "High school students here are learning about oral-genital sex," she says, referring to textbook explanations. "It's up to us to rid society of all this filth, not teach our children what it is."

An official investigation of California sex education is under way. Superintendent of Public Instruction Max Rafferty, a bitter critic of some sex-education courses, has predicted that if districts like Anaheim don't drastically revise their sex courses legislation will be passed "with a whoop and a holler" to do the job for them.

Mr. Rafferty proposes a return to including sex education as biology and anatomy in high school science courses. He and the majority of the opposition especially oppose courses that they trace to the Sex Information and Education Council of the U.S. (SIECUS), a group formed in 1964 as "a clearinghouse of information on sex."

SIECUS began promoting some new ideas on sex education as soon as it was set up. Its message was twofold: First, that it's easier to get across the basic facts of reproduction before students are old enough to be emotionally involved in the subject. Second, that rather than merely describe human reproduction, sex education should try to give a comprehensive view of how sex affects personality, the family and society.

THE IRATE MR. BERKO. Such ideas, to be sure, didn't originate with SIECUS. But with Dr. Mary S. Calderone, its executive director, fulfilling a heavy speaking schedule, SIECUS got most of the credit—or blame— for the rapid spread of sex education along the lines that SIECUS supports.

Parents like William Berko, a 29-year-old father of four and member of the school board in Rahway, a New York City suburb, blame SIECUS for what they call the amoral context in which sex education is being taught. "Take a look at this stuff," says Mr. Berko, displaying a sheaf of SIECUS pamphlets as he explains why he removed three of his children from the Rahway schools.

Particularly galling to Mr. Berko, a conservative Catholic, is the assertion in a SIECUS study guide for teachers and parents that "attempting to indoctrinate young people with a set of rigid rules and ready-made formulas is doomed to failure in a period of transition and conflict."

"In my church," says Mr. Berko, "children go to catechism classes just to learn a set of moral rules—to learn their faith," including Church teachings on sex. "I don't want them taught in school that this is all just a matter of opinion."

"Another thing," adds Mr. Berko, "who's going to vouch for the moral integrity of the teachers that are going to give this instruction to children? I believe there are some teachers who would be sexually stimulated by talking about sex with children and would pry into students' sex lives. It could do a child tremendous psychological harm."

Another source of psychological harm, say many of the opposition, is simply giving students too much information too soon. "Every baby book I've ever read and any doctor I ever asked has told me it's wrong to give children more information than they can absorb," says Mrs. Robert Montgomery, who along with other parents has succeeded in at least delaying the introduction of fifth-grade sex education in Summit, N.J., another New York suburb.

HUNG UP ON SEX? Antagonists in the sex-education debate regularly accuse one another of being warped by sexual "hang-ups" or obsessions. "These people are sick—very sick," says SIECUS's Dr. Calderone about leaders of the right-wing attack.

Reasons Rahway's Mr. Berko: "When I opposed sex education in our schools, I was told I had hang-ups. I think they have hang-ups. So where does that get us?"

Each side also accuses the other of calculated deceptions and base conspiracies. "Deep-laid plans have been carefully initiated to spread this subversive monstrosity (sex education) over the whole American education system," says the Birch Society's Mr. Welch. Proponents of sex instruction, for their part, attribute almost all the opposition to "Birchers" whom they accuse of whipping up parental fears as a recruiting gimmick.

The Birch Society and others make much of SIECUS's former treasurer and director, Isadore Rubin, who holds a Ph.D. in public health and edits *Sexology* Magazine. With factual articles but lurid photo illustrations and titles, *Sexology* has been variously described as presenting "medically sound material in a popular format for people who wouldn't otherwise read it" or, in the Birch Society's view, "little more than slick smut."

Mr. Rubin, identified in 1955 testimony to the House Un-American Activities Committee as having attended Communist meetings in 1945, is also the focus of Birch insinuations that SIECUS is Communist-influenced. He denies any Communist affiliations either currently or during his association with SIECUS.

Such attacks have undoubtedly been effective. Mr. Rafferty wonders aloud at SIECUS's link to "a patently pornographic publication." Oakland TV station KTVU recently asked its viewers, "Is Sex Education a Communist Plot?" The response: 703 of 1,385 persons who called in said yes.

The Rising Furor over Sex Education

Luther G. Baker, Jr.

"Sex education is a new scheme designed to demoralize our youth, all part of a giant conspiracy to rape the people, weaken their wills and make them sensuous, atheistic slaves."

So runs the charge currently leveled against programs of sex education in the schools. A concerted campaign is being launched to arouse public fear and suspicion, aimed at exorcising the demon of sex from the schools.

"The sex educators are in league with the sexologists," writes Gordon Drake in *Blackboard Power*.[1]

They represent every shade of gray morality, ministers colored atheistic pink, and camp followers of every persuasion; offbeat psychiatrists to ruthless publishers of pornography. The enemy is formidable at first glance, but becomes awesomely powerful when we discover the interlocking directorates and working relationship of national organizations which provide havens for these degenerates.

FROM *The Family Coordinator*, Vol. 18, No. 3 (July 1969). Reprinted by permission of the author.
[1] Drake, Gordon, *Blackboard Power*, Christian Crusade Publications, P.O. Box 977, Tulsa, Oklahoma 74102.

One of the most widely distributed pieces of propaganda is a small pamphlet by Drake entitled "Is the School House the Proper Place to Teach Raw Sex?" [2] In it the author misquotes and distorts numerous leading exponents of sex education, weaving an intriciate mosaic purporting to reveal a diabolic and nefarious plot to seduce the minds and morals of little children. Educators, physicians and clergy alike are charged with intentional or unwitting complicity in a great plan for Communist takeover. Their statements are quoted out of context and given an interpretation which implies an attack on the Bible and the churches, indeed on all religion, as superstitious, inhibiting, and detrimental to human fulfillment. The fact that certain well-known clergymen are among these writers is viewed only as evidence of the serious apostasy in the church. Proponents of sex education are pictured as interested mainly in luring youth into narrow, sensuous expressions of sexuality.

The accusations in this newest diatribe are specific. The "burning mission" of SIECUS (Sex Information and Education Council of the United States), it is claimed, is to "alert and convert the youth of America to a new sexuality." To the author this conjures up visions of rampant promiscuity, "sex rooms" in the schools, and teachers advocating a life dedicated to sensuous pleasure. Of one university course titled "Family Insights Through Literature," the author remarks that it might just as well have been subtitled, "A Short Course in Pornography." [3] In fact, it is suggested that SIECUS exists mainly to provide a scientific excuse for gathering and disseminating the literature of smut.

The opposition forces have concentrated on two tried and true tactics of attack. The first is name-calling. Sex education is un-American and it is anti-Christian. Those supporting it are "dupes," "degenerates," "atheists," "filthy perverts." The second is guilt by association. The activities of several nationally prominent figures in what Drake calls the "newsex" are reviewed to show some tie with groups labeled by the House Committee on Un-American Activities as Communist or Communist-front organizations. In spite of the fact that these ties were never established as possessing any meaning or significance, these lists are marshalled once again to prove a connection with the "international Communist conspiracy."

It is not possible in a brief article to answer all the accusations against people and programs. Most of them are not new, they have been hurled in numerous forays against this or that educational innovation. Informed persons acquainted with the philosophy and personnel of sex education are able clearly to discern the irresponsible misrepresentation in these attacks, and are apt to dismiss them out-of-hand. Many people, however, are not

[2] Drake, Gordon, *Is the School House the Proper Place to Teach Raw Sex?* Christian Crusade Publications.
[3] Typical of the attackers' tactics. The author provides no documentation for this charge, just a vague accusation against "something."

familiar with the purposes and materials of sex education, and are easily alarmed and agitated by such propaganda. The public concern generated by this misinformation is deep and genuine, the fears expressed are real and honest, and the demand for clear and accurate information is imperative.

WHAT IS THE TRUTH? It is true that responsible sex educators wish to promote a broader and more inclusive concept of sexuality. The narrow erotic view of sex which permeates much of our literature and is exploited by Madison Avenue is limiting, distorting, and unhealthy. Human beings are sexual creatures, male and female, and this fact encompasses vastly more than genitalia. Sex education at its best focuses on human relationships and is concerned about *all* the ways men and women relate to each other. The attackers tend to think only of the physical aspects of sex, and their failure to comprehend the psychosocial character of sexuality leads them to misunderstand the focus and meaning of sex education. It is this narrow and inadequate frame of reference which sex educators seek to change.

It is true that rumors often abound of sensational and even morally objectionable procedures used in the classroom. Such allegations frequently run through a community like a rolling snowball, the report growing bigger and more salacious with each turn. Concerned investigation, however, reveals a different story. Some person passing in the hallway may overhear an isolated remark by a teacher in the class, or a youngster may idly repeat something that was said, out of context and under circumstances which clothe it in an altered light. Too often these comments, and their editorial embellishments, are spread until they bear little or no resemblance to reality. When some concerned individual does bother to check the facts he finds either that the report is wholly untrue, or that, placed in the context of the original setting, it carries an entirely different and acceptable meaning.

An excellent illustration is found in a story presently being circulated in printed materials by opposition groups.[4] A young "sex education teacher" in Michigan is reported to have stripped before her class to emphasize a point. The writer blithely accepts the report, then asks, "Would you approve of this in your child's classroom?" An inquiry at the Michigan school set the record straight.[5] A physical education teacher was attempting to demonstrate to her all-girl class how differently constructed garments affect perceptions of the human figure. She brought several dresses to class, and, changing into the different styles, discussed the subtle meanings which attach to clothing and the manner in which it is worn. At no time did she "strip" before her class.

[4] P.O.S.E. (Parents Opposing Sex Education in Public Schools, Inc.), "What Parents Should Know."
[5] Private correspondence, April 18, 1969.

It is not true that sex education is anti-Christian. Certain sex educators may be non-religious in the usual sense in their own beliefs, but they are against only that which hampers the full development of man's creative potential. Other teachers are dedicated practicing Christians seeking divine insight into every human condition. If certain religious attitudes about sex have been detrimental to openness and honesty in human sexual relationships, then non-religious and religious alike have attacked them as basically un-Christian. Those who do not understand the dynamic nature of Christianity regard this as a threat to the fundamentals of the faith.

Much is made of the fact that a "humanistic point of view" pervades the writings of some of the proponents of sex education. Humanism is often equated with atheism and this in turn with immorality. It is assumed by some that without reliance upon supernatural concepts of reality there can be no basis for moral behavior, and that crime and immorality will be rampant. That the latter exist is distressingly apparent. The "humanistic ethic," however, is as opposed to and concerned about this as is the Christian. Humanism focuses directly upon man and his needs, and bases both its faith and its practice on the improvability of mankind. Thus, whatever may be their philosophical differences concerning the source of man's "divinity," humanist and orthodox Christian can and do labor side by side for the betterment of man and his human condition.

It is not true that sex education is un-American. This charge is so ridiculous as hardly to merit reply. The basis for this allegation appears to lie in the fear that the "newsex" undermines trust in authority. The "new morality" of "situation ethics" is misinterpreted to mean a doing-what-is-right-in-one's-own-eyes morality, thus producing anarchy. It is predicted that this "loosening of the morals" will not only destroy the moral fiber of youth, but will also weaken the basis for social order and stability. Recent excesses in juvenile rebellion and the outright flaunting of authority by a tiny minority of youth are cited in support of the prediction. Sex education, of course, cannot be responsible for these excesses. Scarcely any of the youth participating in them have been exposed to such programs. The roots of adolescent rebellion lie in altogether different soil.

The thrust of the present thinking about morality is not toward anarchy, but toward social responsibility. Its major emphasis is that all human behavior has social consequences, and that the individual is responsible for his behavior. Its challenge is that each person accept the personal obligation to make rational and responsible decisions, to judge each situation in its own unique context with its own potential outcome, and to choose that which augurs the greatest good for the most people. Those who reject this approach frequently fail to understand that while the individual is ultimately responsible for all his choices and his acts, he does not make his decisions in isolation. The "distilled wisdom of the ages," his awareness of his involvement in all humanity and his concern for the common good all inform and influence his decision-making. To the extent that any of these ingredients are misunderstood or ignored, he is not acting morally.

Sex education, then, far from leading to anarchy, tends to social solidarity. Any program designed to enhance a sense of personal and social responsibility in the members of a society is bound to improve the order and stability of that society.

WHAT ABOUT SIECUS? The "Sex Information and Education Council of the United States" has come under severe attack by the critics. What is the truth about it?

SIECUS is a non-profit organization formed in 1964 by a group of prominent professional people who were concerned with helping our society cope with problems relating to human sexuality. These problems are becoming increasingly urgent as our society grows more open about sex, as contraceptive measures are improved and as the influences of other cultures impinge upon us. These issues will not go away by wishing or playing ostrich. The whole changing social scene with its confusing impact on human relations is completely ignored by the dissidents.[6]

The program of SIECUS is a simple one. It seeks to provide information about programs and materials which schools and community agencies across the country have developed, and to serve as consultant to those who seek its assistance in developing programs and procedures. SIECUS has no "sex education plan" beyond that of encouraging communities to develop their own programs and advising them upon request. Its only publications are its quarterly Newsletter and a series of study guides, presently ten in number, dealing with specific topics of sexual problems. These are not designed for public classroom use. They are resource materials for professionals in their own studies.

The only connection SIECUS has with the development of materials for use in the public schools is through its occasional consulting association with other groups, as, for example, its former temporary advisory relationship with Guidance Associates, a division of Harcourt, Brace and World Publishers.

One evidence that SIECUS is serving a real need is the increasingly heavy demand for its services. Since its inception it has grown from a staff of two part-time persons to around twenty, in addition to the fifty persons who comprise its Board of Directors and who give freely of their time, energy and money in the service of the organization. SIECUS has

---

[6] Kirkendall, Lester A., with Elizabeth Ogg, *Sex and Our Society*, Public Affairs Pamphlet, 318 Park Avenue, South, New York, New York, 10016. [This pamphlet is often cited by the opposition. It is an analysis of forces which are altering the social structure within which sexuality is expressed.]

no regular source of income. Its funding is primarily from interested and concerned citizens and occasional grants from educational foundations.

WHAT ABOUT SEXOLOGY? Another primary object of attack is the magazine *Sexology*. Since the managing editor of this publicaton and some of its Advisory Consultant Board or its contributors are SIECUS Board members, a "conspiratorial interlocking directorate" is seen. SIE-CUS states clearly that Board members serve as individuals and not as representatives of their organizations. The SIECUS Board of Directors includes numerous professional people who also hold memberships in other national organizations. Several of these professionals have also contributed articles to *Sexology*. But since this magazine is labeled as "pornographic," containing "pure smut," it is deduced that the leaders in the "newsex" desire to promote pornography in the schools.

Sexology is not intended as classroom material, and has never been recommended as such by SIECUS. It was created a generation ago for a newsstand clientele. Its readers have been predominately from the lower socioeconomic classes who do not normally take subscription magazines, and who generally receive no sex education except that gained from hit-and-miss distorting sources. The purpose of the magazine has been to provide such people with wholesome and reliable sex information. The editors quickly found that these potential readers will select this magazine from the newsstand only if its covers and article titles have an element of provocativeness about them. But once he has purchased the magazine, the reader is provided with helpful, authentic information. The editors have experimented several times with using pictureless covers and sales have plummeted. At the present writing this is being tried again, but the evidence strongly suggests that the superficial provocative element is essential to the promotion of this basically academic publication. It is clear from the unending volume of questions and comments from concerned readers, most of whom point out that they have no other place to turn, that this periodical is serving a vital human need.

Sexology has long since had its day in court. During its 35 years several legal actions have been taken against it, two of which have gone to trial. In both cases the magazine was judged *not obscene*. In a 1961 case a New Jersey justice in dismissing the charges said,[7]

Sexology deals with sex, but not in an obscene manner. The articles are written in a clear and scientific manner, without any suggestion of arousing prurient interest. . . . The articles certainly serve a valid social purpose, being informative about sex, a matter of human interest and public concern. They are literary, scientific and educational. Prohibition of distribution of such a magazine would clearly be unconstitutional.

[7] Polack, Justice Stanley J., "State of New Jersey *vs*. Irving Fetter" (Indictment No. 319-58), August 5, 1961.

As evidence of the quality of the articles themselves, in 1968 the managing editor, Isadore Rubin, and a major contributor, Lester A. Kirkendall, selected 38 articles dealing with adolescent sex problems and concerns, which were then published in book form by Association Press. The following excerpts from reviews illustrate the favorable response to this publication.

(This book) attempts, successfully, to meet head-on sexual problems of today's youth. . . . This is a "must" for every parent, pastor, and leader of youth. *Baptist Sunday School Board,* Book Review Service

Essays by authors of impeccable academic qualifications cover the gamut of concern. . . . This collection . . . should help parents, teachers, and others approached for counsel to provide informed responses. *Saturday Review,* June 15, 1968

Teachers of home economics, health education, and psychology (as well as counselors, youth workers, clergymen and parents) would . . . find it helpful. *Adult Leadership,* September, 1968

The editor of *Sexology,* Dr. Isadore Rubin, has come under fire more severely than any other individual, and his case is a clear example of the smear tactics of the opposition. It is alleged that, as a long-time Communist sympathizer, Dr. Rubin uses pornography and sexual perversion as tools to prepare the minds of youth for Communist conquest. The truth is that Dr. Rubin was never officially charged with being a member of the Communist party. In 1948 he was called for questioning by the House Committee on Labor in connection with a statement which had been taken out of context and used to challenge his patriotism. Four years earlier, in 1944, Isadore Rubin was a member of the 805th Tank Destroyer Battalion in Italy. In an army contest he won a $500 first prize and a personal citation from Gen. Mark Clark for an essay on "What Victory Means to Me." The essay was subsequently used by the army in its orientation program. On Christmas Eve that year Walter Huston read it on a nationwide broadcast, and later hundreds of newspapers carried comments upon it. Among these was the *Daily Worker,* in which a columnist remarked, "Russia has its Ilya Ehrenburg and we have our Isadore Rubin." That last phrase, "our Isadore Rubin," quoted out of context, has been taken up by the irresponsible to vilify the motives of a loyal and dedicated American.

Not only Dr. Rubin, but many others have been accused of subversion on the basis of their summons before some investigative committee during the late 40s and early 50s. In certain instances the accused protested the un-American activities of these committees and refused to answer their questions. It is to their credit that no accusation against them has been substantiated and that both Congress and the Supreme Court have repudiated the tactics employed by the committees. Few Americans remember with pride that brief period in our history when guilt by association was substituted for the traditional principle of guilt established by due process. Surely few would like to see that clearly un-American period revived.

WHO FORMS THE VOCIFEROUS OPPOSITION? In nearly every community there are a few self-styled "defenders of the faith." They are against everything which seems to violate their particular concept of the traditional "American Way": taxes, welfare, dogooders, hippies, and sex education. They find support from certain organizations with national dimensions which obtain financial resources by playing upon people's fears and prejudices, and which claim to find some dark, lurking danger in any new idea or program. Over the years one finds these same organizations attacking first this, then that bogey, moving from mental health, to vaccination, to fluoridation, to sex education, professing to see in all of them a sinister design to weaken the will of the people, subvert the truth, and destroy the nation.[8] The booklet previously mentioned [9] is published by such a professional "anti" group.

While not the only organized opposition, the John Birch Society is presently in the vanguard of the battle. In a January 1969 bulletin,[10] the Executive Committee of the Society announced the "inauguration" of a new effort to be carried forward by MOTOREDE Committees (for Movement to Restore Decency) in communities throughout the United States. The committees are to concentrate "on one most urgent requirement."

That requirement is organized, nationwide, intensive, *angry* and determined opposition to the now mushrooming program of so-called sex education in the public schools. Various stages of the program have already been imposed on some five to ten per cent of the schools. Deep-laid plans have been carefully initiated to spread this subversive monstrosity over the whole American educational system from kindergarten to high school. But a preponderant majority of the American people are not yet even aware of this filthy Communist plot, of the tremendous drive that is behind it, or of its triple significance.

[The program] begins, for instance, with varied and elaborately designed exhibits, colored slides, and other visual aids, to demonstrate the raw facts of sex to children from three to eight years old! . . . Increasingly, in classes for older boys and girls, the instruction on sexual methods is followed by encouragement to experiment and practice. . . .

---

8 Adorno, T. W., et al., *The Authoritarian Personality*, New York: Harper and Row, 1950. Marmor, Judd, Viola W. Bernard and Perry Ottenberg, "Psychodynamics of Group Opposition to Health Programs." *The American Journal of Orthopsychiatry*, Vol. 30, No. 2, April, 1960, pp. 330–345. A study of the characteristics of the individuals and groups which opposed fluoridation.
9 Drake, *op. cit.*
10 John Birch Society (The). *Bulletin*, Belmont, Mass., January, 1969.

In schools where the full program has been adopted—and all of the usual Communist-style falsehoods, deceptions, pressures, and pretenses are subtly utilized to get school boards to fall in line—it is not unusual for a high school teacher to ask his students (boys and girls together, ages fifteen to eighteen) to tell the class about, or write themes about, their participation in the following activities: kissing, masturbation, light petting, fondling breasts or genitals (for boys), fondling male genitals (for girls), sexual intercourse, sexual activities to near intercourse, and sexual activities with an animal.

In light of their published statements and with the experiences of a number of communities to enlighten them, educators are probably well advised to regard the vociferous opposition, particularly those allied with the John Birch Society and the Christian Crusade, as unappeasable.[11] The utter lack of moral integrity exhibited in the foregoing combination of distortion and falsehood suggests that the organized opposition is interested only in takeover, not truth. The present drive has all the earmarks of being, basically, an attack on the public school system. In literature being disseminated in many communities, citizens are urged to "boycott all school bonds, hold up all school funds" until all "nonacademic" courses are removed.[12] It has been tacitly admitted by some of the opposition that their main concern is a drastic overhaul of public education, and sex education is merely providing a convenient bludgeon with which to beat the schools into submission. The fact that sex can be used with such effectiveness and such ferocity is, unhappily, the consequence of our failure to do an effective educational job earlier. But retreat now will only compound the problem.

How Should Educators React? It is easy enough to understand the mass appeal of preachments of fear and hate. Security and safety are essential to individual and social stability, and safety seems to the unthinking to lie in what is tried and true, in the old and familiar. The new and unfamiliar, when poorly understood, are threatening. Fear-arousing tactics exert their greatest impact among people whose own future seems a bit shaky and for whom, therefore, any serious threat to "the way it has always been" is especially frightening. While the hard core of the opposition is thus a small cadre of perpetual doomsayers who will, under no circumstance, approach the issue rationally, the majority are seriously concerned citizens, even though misinformed, who merit patience and understanding.

For the reasoning majority of citizens the most effective method of countering the opposition is to do a good job in sex education. Programs already begun should be strengthened and those in the planning stages should be implemented. While it is clear that current programs require

---

[11] National Congress of Parents and Teachers, "Extremist Groups."
[12] *Timetable for Takeover,* CSOS, P. O. Box 59, Diamond Springs, California.

continuing review and improvement, then the importance of the task is too momentous to succumb to the threats of a vociferous few.

The great majority of parents are clearly, if silently, in support of public sex education. Until the current attack, with its gross misrepresentation, numerous community surveys, such as that in New Orleans, revealed that more than 90 per cent of the parents believed the schools should have such courses. Even in the midst of the present controversy, experience in several localities demonstrates that a large majority of the public is still basically in support of such programs. A new Gallup Poll shows 7 out of 10 in favor. It is to this significant majority that educators must turn their attention. Family life–sex education programs are, of course, nothing new. For more than a generation effective and well-supported programs have been in operation in dozens of communities all across the country. Their test of experience has long since validated the appropriateness and acceptability of sex education in the schools.

Numerous national organizations and public agencies have gone on official record in support of public sex education. A list of them is appended. The official policy of the United States Office of Education is to "support family life education and sex education as an integral part of the curriculum from pre-school to college and adult levels." The unanimous judgement of such groups is that responsible family life and sex education are essential to the health of the nation and its people. It will be pertinent here to quote a brief excerpt from an *Interfaith Statement on Sex Education* prepared by the National Council of Churches Commission on Family Life, Synagogue Council of America Committee on Family, and United States Catholic Conference Family Life Bureau:

Human sexuality is a gift of God, to be accepted with thanksgiving and used with reverence and joy. . . . Responsibility for sex education belongs primarily to the child's parents. . . . In addition, the religious community and the school have a vital role in sex education. . . . The increased concern and interest in this vital area of human experience now manifested by parents, educators and religious leaders are cause for gratitude. We urge all to take a more active role, each in this own area of responsibility and competence, in promoting sound leadership and programs in sex education.

It is apparent that in this important educational endeavor no one can go it alone. The school, community and home must work together. The public has a right to know what is being taught in the school and it is imperative that people be informed in an honest and straightforward manner. Experience has shown, however, that with a carefully planned and well-developed program, and with adequately prepared and competent teachers, schools may proceed in sex education confident of sufficient community support and undismayed by the occasional emotional attacks which may occur.

The following are among the organizations on record as supporting sex education in schools:

American Association for Health, Physical Education and Recreation (AAHPER).

American College of Obstetricians and Gynecologists (Committee on Maternal Health).

American Medical Association.

American Public Health Association (Governing Council).

National Association for Independent Schools.

National Congress of Parents and Teachers (PTA).

National Council of Churches of Christ in the U.S.A.

National Education Association (NEA) and American Medical Association (AMA) (Joint Committee on Health Problems in Education).

National School Boards Association and American Association of School Administrators (Joint Committee).

National Student Assembly, YMCA & YWCA.

Sixth White House Conference on Children and Youth.

Synagogue Council of America.

United Nations Educational, Scientific and Cultural Organization (UNESCO).

United States Catholic Conference.

United States Department of Health, Education and Welfare (U.S. Commissioner of Education).

Sex Education As Community Education

Ronald J. Pion, M.D.

As an obstetrician dealing daily with problems of family planning, I hold the firm conviction that community programs, to be effective, must encompass considerations of sex education. The solutions to a growing number of health problems reside in the establishment within the community of healthy attitudes toward sexuality.

The need for sex education has been, and continues to be, the subject of exhaustive study in our society today. Changing sexual attitudes, and practices reflecting these attitudes, have underlined the need for a broad, realistic program in the area of sex education. While many programs have been suggested, a major problem has been their resolution into a program

FROM the *Journal of the American Medical Women's Association,* Vol. 23, No. 2, February 1968, copyright 1968 by the American Medical Women's Association, Inc. Reprinted with the permission of the Association and the author.

broad enough to embrace the many and diverse segments within our society.

Comprehensive adult education is, I think, the most important single factor needed to insure the success of any program of sex education. Basic to the entire program of adult education would be the establishment of frank and open debate among the adult members of the community holding widely divergent views. Such unfettered discussion should reflect the ideals and aims of the community as a whole providing the stimulus necessary for the development of a community-wide sex education program based on the real needs of the people.

The purpose of this article is to review experiments in the Seattle area directed towards the achievement of this goal.

COMMUNITY LEADERSHIP. The Sex Education Association of King County was organized in the fall of 1966. Its stated purpose was "to provide leadership in the development of attitudes of responsible sexuality in the entire community." Membership is open to anyone concerned with the realization of this objective. Monthly meetings are held to coordinate the activities of its members. A scan of the current membership roster and of the list of supporting organizations suggests that the organization is heterogeneous in character and multidisciplined in its approach.

The importance of the Association's role cannot be minimized. Heretofore, the crusade to inaugurate programs of sex education was a lonely struggle demanding the time, the energy, and the courage of those people who felt strongly about it. Now, the Association, composed of respected citizens in the community, not only lends dignity to the whole program; its very existence gives a stamp of authority to our undertakings.

Speakers may be scheduled more efficiently through the Speakers' Committee established for this purpose. Other committees of similar usefulness are (1) resource and visual aids, (2) interschool communication, (3) program planning and evaluation, and (4) public relations.

Last year the Association sponsored a visit by Dr. Mary S. Calderone which was quite successful from the point of view of increasing community awareness. This year a similar open meeting is scheduled, and Dr. Lester A. Kirkendall has been invited as guest lecturer.

EDUCATIONAL TELEVISION. A one-hour, weekly program entitled "Sex and Society—Understanding Human Sexuality" is to begin in November, and it is expected to run for the duration of the academic year. The program, in the form of a panel discussion, will comprise five regular members. Guest panelists, invited to participate in the discussion each week, will augment the regular group. An obstetrician-gynecologist will act as moderator and he will be joined by a lawyer, a Catholic priest, a public health nurse, and a social worker.

The following are some of the topics to be explored during the early months: sex education, sex and religion, sex and the law, and the double standard. If, as anticipated, letters of protest are received by the station, the writers of these letters will be invited to appear on subsequent programs to voice their opinions. The goal of the series is an obvious one; namely, that of conducting an open forum so that community awareness may be heightened and community response encouraged. Traditional attitudes will be critically evaluated.

The program will be broadcast over the University Educational Channel (KCTS-TV). Since the series will be shown at 10:00 P.M. the anticipated viewing audience will probably be an adult one (17 and older).

IN-SERVICE PROGRAM. A pilot demonstration course was begun this fall in an attempt to prepare teachers to deal comfortably and effectively with the proposed curriculum changes. The superintendents of several school districts were requested to extend invitations, through the principals of selected junior schools, to groups of four to six teachers from each school. Ideally, the group was to comprise a science teacher, a health educator, a family life educator, a school nurse, and a member of the guidance team. When all the disciplines noted were not represented within the school, other interested teachers were to be designated. The program was sponsored by the following University departments: Obstetrics and Gynecology, Continuing Medical Education, and the College of Health Education.

A series of six two-hour discussion periods is planned for consecutive Thursdays. At the first introductory session, the moderator, a psychiatrist, was joined by a minister and a community physician. Brief statements by the panelists concerning the need for sex education in the schools opened the session, followed by discussion from the floor. The pressure of some 170 persons within the amphitheatre did not dampen the airing of opinions. The majority of participants described the first meeting as a productive one, although some maintained that little was accomplished, since the ABC's of "how to do it" were not spelled out. During the next five scheduled discussions, the roles of the individual members of the teaching team—the science teacher, health educator, and so forth—are to be defined. We hope that in each school a group will be prepared to take on the responsibility of preparing a continuing curriculum for the following school year.

MEDICAL STUDENT ACTIVITIES. Courses concerning the medical aspects of human sexuality were introduced as electives several years ago at the university. Greater emphasis recently has been directed towards establishing these as part of the core curriculum for both medical and nursing students. Problems of community health are considered and the responsibility of the physician is explored.

Last year, senior class members developed a Speakers' Bureau to fulfill the need for group discussion leaders who could effectively stimulate debate on the question of human sexuality throughout the community. The small group felt that the subject could, and should, be explored with parents, students, and the community at large. Shortly after the group's inception, it became apparent that a community need was being served. Many requests were submitted by school nurses, science teachers, health educators, sororities, fraternities, youth groups, and adult organizations. The students sensed an urgency for communication in this previously neglected area.

The organization has grown in size and it now includes many nursing and medical students from other class levels. An atmosphere of professionalism pervades the meetings, and the students' approach to the task is quite sophisticated. The newer members of the organization accompany more experienced students on their speaking engagements. These new members are objective critics evaluating audience reaction and participation, and appraising the general presentation and ability of the speaker. The topics, varying from the physiological to the philosophical, are selected in advance by those initiating the invitations. The members of the Speakers' Bureau value this audience participation. The students are made aware of aspects that they have failed to discuss and, in future speaking engagements, they are able to incorporate them into their lectures. A faculty advisor has assisted the group to obtain audio-visual aids, thus enhancing the effectiveness of the presentations.

FUTURE CONSIDERATIONS. Increased utilization of telecourse programs through the facilities of our educational channel are now being examined. This would seem to be a more efficient way of reaching larger groups of teachers than would be possible through multiple in-service programs.

Preparation of additional visual-aid materials geared to a continuing curriculum is under study. A pilot demonstration project utilizing films in individual teaching units (carrels) for students of varied ages is under consideration.

CONCLUSIONS. Our experiences may prove beneficial to other communities that have not yet begun to develop their own programs. We would suggest that consideration be focused on community education at large, rather than on the narrow concern for physiology instruction in the classroom. Certainly the physiology of reproduction deserves its rightful place in the science curriculum at all levels. Yet we must recognize that sex education encompasses much more than the physiology of reproduction. The achievement of the former is our goal.

Interfaith Statement on Sex Education
Interfaith Commission on Marriage and Family Life

Human sexuality is a gift of God, to be accepted with thanksgiving and used with reverence and joy. It is more than a mechanical instinct. Its many dimensions are intertwined with the total personality and character of the individual. Sex is a dynamic urge or power, arising from one's basic maleness or femaleness, and having complex physical, psychological and social dimensions. These dimensions, we affirm, must be shaped and guided by spiritual and moral considerations which derive from our Judeo-Christian heritage. The heritage teaches us that the source of values to guide human behavior is in God.

The sexual attitudes of children develop as part of their general social attitudes. Furthermore, respectful and considerate sexual attitudes help create healthy social attitudes. When the family and society view sex as loving and fulfilling, rather than prurient and exploitative, then both the social and sexual attitudes of children benefit. A healthful approach to sexual relations, willingness and ability to impart sexual information in a manner proportionate to the child's stage of development—these are among the elements which foster healthy sexual attitudes and behavior in the young. So, also, is resistance to social pressures which in some instances lead to premature sophistication or unhealthy attitudes in young people.

Responsibility for sex education belongs primarily to the child's parents or guardians. A home permeated by justice and love is the seedbed of sound sexual development among all family members. Both the attitudes and the activities of the parents—toward each other and toward each child as an individual—affect this development. Healthy attitudes toward sex begin in the child's earliest years; they can best develop in an atmosphere that fosters in him a deep sense of his own self-worth, bolstered by love and understanding.

Sex education is not, however, only for the young; it is a life-long task whose aim is to help individuals develop their sexuality in a manner suited to their stage of life.

We recognize that some parents desire supplementary assistance from

Reprinted with the permission of the Interfaith Commission on Marriage and Family Life of the National Council of Churches, the Synagogue Council of America, and the United States Catholic Conference.

church or synagogue and from other agencies. Each community of faith should provide resources, leadership and opportunities as appropriate for its young people to learn about their development into manhood and womanhood, and for adults to grow in understanding of their roles as men and women in family and society in the light of their religious heritage.

In addition to parents and the religious community, the school and other community agencies can have a vital role in sex education in two particular ways:

1. They can integrate sound sexual information and attitudes with the total education which the child receives in social studies, civics, literature, history, home economics and the biological and behavioral sciences.
2. They can reach the large numbers of young people whose families have no religious identification but who need to understand their own sexuality and their role in society.

For those who would introduce sex education into the schools, however, the question of values and norms for sexual behavior is a problem—indeed, the most difficult problem. It is important that sex education not be reduced to the mere communication of information. Rather, this significant area of experience should be placed in a setting where rich human, personal and spiritual values can illuminate it and give it meaning. In such a setting, we are convinced it is not only possible but necessary to recognize certain basic moral principles, not as sectarian religious doctrine but as the moral heritage of Western civilization.

The challenge of resolving this problem of values in a pluralistic society makes it all the more imperative that communities planning to introduce sex education into the schools not only call upon educators to become involved in decisions about goals and techniques, but also invite parents and professionals in the community to take part in shaping such a curriculum.

To those groups responsible for developing school and community programs in sex education we suggest the following guidelines:

a. Such education should strive to create understanding and conviction that decisions about sexual behavior must be based on moral and ethical values, as well as on considerations of physical and emotional health, fear, pleasure, practical consequences, or concepts of personality development.
b. Such education must respect the cultural, familial and religious backgrounds and beliefs of individuals and must teach that the sexual development and behavior of each individual cannot take place in a vacuum but are instead related to the other aspects of his life and to his moral, ethical and religious codes.
c. It should point out how sex is distorted and exploited in our society and

how this places heavy responsibility upon the individual, the family and institutions to cope in a constructive manner with the problem thus created.

d. It must recognize that in school sex education, insofar as it relates to moral and religious beliefs and values, complements the education conveyed through the family, the church or the synagogue. Sex education in the schools must proceed constructively, with understanding, tolerance and acceptance of difference.

e. It must stress the many points of harmony between moral values and beliefs about what is right and wrong that are held in common by the major religions on the one hand and generally accepted legal, social, psychological, medical and other values held in common by service professions and society generally.

f. When strong differences of opinion exist on what is right and wrong sexual behavior, objective, informed and dignified discussion of both sides of such questions should be encouraged. However, in such cases, neither the sponsors of an educational program nor the teachers should attempt to give definite answers or to represent their personal moral and religious beliefs as the consensus of the major religions or of society generally.

g. Throughout such education human values and human dignity must be stressed as major bases for decisions of right and wrong; attitudes that build such respect should be encouraged as right, and those that tear down such respect should be condemned as wrong.

h. Such education should teach that sexuality is a part of the whole person and an aspect of his dignity as a human being.

i. It should teach that people who love each other try not to do anything that will harm each other.

j. It should teach that sexual intercourse within marriage offers the greatest possibility for personal fulfillment and social growth.

k. Finally, such a program of education must be based on sound content and must employ sound methods; it must be conducted by teachers and leaders qualified to do so by training and temperament.

The increased concern and interest in this vital area of human experience now manifested by parents, educators and religious leaders are cause for gratitude. We urge all to take a more active role—each in his own area of responsibility and competence—in promoting sound leadership and programs in sex education. We believe it possible to help our sons and daughters achieve a richer, fuller understanding of their sexuality, so that their children will enter a world where men and women live and work together in understanding, cooperation and love.

The Movement to Restore Decency
MOTOREDE Committees

I

To emphasize the contemporary breakdown of morality and manners we do not need to bring forth statistics, or examples, or arguments. The condition daily grows more obvious and more extreme.

Intentionally dirty minds in dirty bodies have become commonplace on our campuses and in our cities. The use of narcotic drugs, especially among teenage groups, has become epidemic. Pornography is purveyed to young and old, incessantly and ubiquitously, on our newsstands, on the stage, in our movies, on television, in private parties, and now even in our schools.

We find this degradation manifested on every side in filthy language, in squalid dress, and in lewd behavior. Sexual promiscuity has become so widespread as to be almost taken for granted, and even sexual perversion is now sometimes condoned from the pulpit. Disrespect for authority has mounted into flagrant and destructive rebelliousness against the most routine and sensible regulations and arrangements—some of which are certainly necessary for the orderly functioning of civilized society. And our crime rate is soaring to frightening levels.

Such periods of licentiousness, blasphemy, obscenity, iconoclasm and general depravity have been recurrent throughout history. They have come as an aftermath of prolonged or destructive wars, as accompaniment to the loss of a former religious faith, as the by-product of long sustained prosperity, as a form of superficial sophistication prompted by rapidly blooming new knowledge, or as a combined result of these and other factors.

But the present development is distinguished from similar phenomena in the past by two characteristics. First, so far as we can judge from historical records, it is already more comprehensive as to variety of the evil traits being manifested, and more extreme as to degree, than any parallel we know about in other times. And second, this contemporary degeneration is not entirely the natural effect of normal causes. It is being artificially and deliberately promoted by powerful human forces for their own evil purposes.

II

Despite all ephemeral evidence to the contrary, we believe that certain fundamentals still hold true with regard to man's behavior, in any civilization which he seeks to make worthwhile.

We begin with the Ten Commandments. Nor do we intend thereby to provide the basis for any disputes among us over our religious differences. Many good men, of many creeds and of many shades of orthodoxy within those creeds, must be able and willing to support our movement.

Most of our readers, probably, believe the Ten Commandments to have been specifically and physically transmitted by God to man. There are some, less literal in their interpretations of scripture, who think of the Ten Commandments as simply a distillation of the wisdom man has acquired from the experience and knowledge permitted him in a divinely ordered universe. But all of them, and even a great many with less conventional religious beliefs, will readily agree that these Commandments form a permanently binding code of conduct which man cannot violate without drastic damage to both his material and his spiritual welfare.

We look next to all the compendia of guidelines for human behavior provided by Christ and his apostles in the *New Testament* of the Christian religion. And again let us emphasize the universality of these truths by pointing out that what we now call *The Golden Rule*, which was recorded by St. Matthew as so beautifully expressed in the *Sermon on the Mount,* had also already been proclaimed by Confucius, by Aristotle, and by many others.

Also, it may be worth while to mention in passing that the first celebrity in history, so far as we know, to disparage and ridicule *The Golden Rule,* was a lifelong supporter of the Communist advance, George Bernard Shaw, in his *Maxims for Revolutionists.* For this has some bearing on the skillful undermining of *all* moral principles by those same revolutionists today.

But we too have heard about change and progress. The procession of the centuries, the rise and fall of national cultures, the growth of man's knowledge, the fabulously increased speed of human movement and communication, the vast accumulation of man's other controls over his physical environment, and the multiplication of the numbers of men into thousands of millions, have not escaped our attention. We are aware that all of these developments have altered and added many pressures and temptations in the daily life of *homo sapiens* since Moses showed his tablets to the people of Israel. But we also believe that man's conscience has been concurrently developing and keeping pace.

We look, therefore, to the prophets, and the sages, and the poets, for the compact crystallization of the further wisdom that has been added by experience to man's understanding of what is right and what is wrong. But we look eventually, for guidance with regard to our conduct under all circumstances, new and old, to man's conscience itself. This conscience undoubtedly varies somewhat by inheritance, in different individuals, much as do purely physical parts of man's anatomy. And also, like them, the conscience of each individual is subject to the possibility of being distorted, atrophied, stunted, rendered useless, or even excised altogether, in the course of the lifespan of that individual.

But this conscience, nevertheless, in which is nested all of the phylogenetic accumulation of spiritual wisdom with which man has been divinely endowed, is as certain and positive a part of the total features and characteristics with which every child is born as is the opposable thumb. It is worth noting, therefore, that if the thumbs and all the fingers of all human beings were smashed or cut off, at some point during childhood, for a dozen generations, all babies in the thirteenth generation would still be born with nature's great gift of the opposable thumb.

The same principle holds true with regard to the psychologically or spiritually inherited trait, which we call conscience. It not only cannot be "bred out" of the human race by any means in any short period of time, but its present basic form and character and essence cannot even be changed, through the massive and deliberate destruction of individual consciences for one or several generations which is now taking place. The babies of each new generation are being born and will be born with the same innate tendencies towards certain kinds of behavior as before.

III

It is the task of our Movement, therefore, to help to prevent the mutilation of these consciences, and to restore the influences which will nourish and guide them in a healthy growth.

Let us concede that perhaps one-half of the ultimate force and direction of any human conscience is due to environment and training rather than to inheritance. That is all the more reason why this half of the molding of the growing plant should not be left to the diabolic hands of those who seek to destroy it. Yet that is exactly what is happening in America today.

You can be sure there are some twinges of conscience before healthy youngsters go on LSD "trips" which damage their minds for the rest of their lives. It is certainly with inner qualms that teenagers embark on an orgy of sexual experiences, which not only ruin their lives, but the bodies and lives of any children they may some day have. But these things and others like them are taking place because the warnings of conscience, having no support from sources whence support should come, are being overwhelmed by the pressures and propaganda of organized evil.

It is our ambition in time to do battle with these forces of evil on every front. But our first concern is with our school-age children. For it is a matter of record that the Communists are behind a massive effort to destroy the moral character of the upcoming generation, in order to make us helpless against their strategy of conquest. And even without this sinister fact to consider, the proper place to turn back the tide of degeneracy is with the very young.

For the key to the present tragic and frightening trend in that area is easy to discover. *Too many parents of our preceding generation have simply been abandoning their responsibilities for the training and guidance of their children.* Some parents have been brought to such action by persuasion that the schools could do a better job. Some have been coerced by the pressures of educational associations, school boards, teachers, and neighbors like themselves who have already swallowed the deceptive "professional" line. Some have given up in the face of the rebelliousness of their own children, who have already been brainwashed by the pervasive forces of evil to which they were submitted at such an early age. And some parents have merely let their responsibilities go by default, because of the greater ease and comfort which such a vacuous course provided them.

IV

By far the most dangerous and disastrous step in this whole program to promote degeneracy is the present increasingly widespread effort to introduce continuous "sex education" into our schools, all the way from kindergarten through high school.

There are many sincere but misguided people, of course, who can be beguiled into supporting any cause which is presented as "modern" and "progressive." But we do not believe that the current drive for sex education is even intended by its originators and promoters to provide a needed and beneficial service in the schools. It is their sinister objective instead, to create an unceasing and dangerous obsession with sex in the minds of our children.

The first direct and specific undertaking, therefore, of the *Movement To Restore Decency,* is to expose and oppose this whole corruptive program. The Movement is sponsored by, and given the nationwide organizational support of, The John Birch Society, exactly as have been the movement to *Support Your Local Police* and other public-spirited drives with wide popular support. Our Movement will function through one national and, we hope, several thousand local and regional, MOTOREDE Committees. Estimating from past experience, some ten per cent of the membership of these committees will be members of the Society. The remaining ninety per cent will consist of good citizens, drawn from every level and division of American life, who are seriously concerned about the future of their children and of their country.

These committees will do all they can to prevent the introduction of the carefully plotted program of sex education into more school systems, and to get it removed from those that already have it. The course followed in this activity will be primarily that of informing and educating our fellow citizens concerning the background, personnel, methods, and purposes of the whole campaign for sex education in the schools. In support of this effort to create understanding, there will be pamphlets, filmstrips, speakers, and other educational means and materials made available from headquarters. Guidance will also be provided from the same source for the formation and conduct of local committees anywhere in the United States.

Let us now repeat and remind you that while our primary *immediate* objective is putting a stop to the encouragement of widespread sexual practices among teenagers, and to other tragic results of the fraud called "sex education in the schools," we are also seriously concerned with the mushrooming use of narcotics; with the steady increase of drunkenness; with the pervasive spread of pornography; with the growing exhibitionism of filth in mind, body, clothes, and language as something supposedly noble and desirable; and with the discarding of all morality and every sound sense of values, especially among our young people, which is taking place all around us. Many of our materials and activities will be designed to show the criminal folly of various divisions of this total push toward perdition, and the horror of their results.

It is our hope to reverse this childish intent of our misguided youngsters—and unfortunately of many of their elders as well—to descend to the level of lower animals. We feel that civilized morals and manners and customs and traditions and values are very much worth while. Our comprehensive purpose, therefore, is exactly as stated in our name. Ours is a *Movement To Restore Decency* to American life. We expect and intend for it to become a strong, lasting, nationwide, deeply respected, and highly influential organization. And we invite the participation of good citizens everywhere who are willing to do their part towards making this a better world. Address The Motorede Committees; 4 Hill Road; Belmont, Massachusetts 02178; or 2627 Mission Street; San Marino, California 91108.

Prescribing Contraception for Teenagers—
A Moral Compromise?

Ronald J. Pion, M.D.

Although there is considerable interest in sex education, manifested by the numerous articles appearing both in the lay and the professional press, few definitive guidelines have been established for the practicing physician involved with the question of prescribing contraception for teenage patients with or without parental consent. Recently I have been afforded an opportunity to discuss this particular problem with numerous colleagues, residents, and medical students. In response to the question, "Is parental consent necessary?" the most frequent answer is one that invokes the concept of legality—i.e., it is not permitted by law. Several years ago, I asked a friend who practices law to provide the necessary legal information that would help define what the physician may be permitted to do when presented with such a problem. A rather unexpected answer was given. He informed me that, by law, any person prescribing contraception *to anyone* in our state was guilty of a misdemeanor. Since we are aware that there is a difference between laws that are merely "on the books" and those that are enforced, it would seem reasonable for the medical profession to continue to advise our legal colleagues in certain areas so that the law may continue to be dynamic and justifiably enforceable.

Recently, members of both the legal and medical professions, as well as legislators, have become interested in the laws pertaining to *the rights of the minor*. In certain specific instances, a question arises as to whether the betrayal of patient confidence is more important, less important, or equally important as the problem of contributing to the delinquency of a minor. The latter phrase has been invoked often by physicians who have thus avoided embarrassing involvement. Let us consider the area of high-risk pregnancy. It is an accepted fact that the early identification of the high-risk pregnant patient is in her best interest. Certainly, sufficient data are available supporting the fact that the hazards are greater for the young teenage pregnant individual than for an older woman. The early ambivalence of teenagers in making their pregnancy known to their parents is a well-documented occurrence to physicians and paramedical

FROM *Obstetrics and Gynecology*, Vol. 30, No. 5, November 1967. Reprinted with permission of Ronald J. Pion.

personnel dealing with large groups of such individuals. Frequently, many of these patients do not present themselves for prenatal care until mid or late pregnancy. In order to be in a position to help the teenage girl, a physician must see, examine, and diagnose the pregnancy without the initial obtaining of parental consent. Many otherwise unfortunate teenagers might seek early consultation in a suspected pregnancy and have this condition diagnosed, thus avoiding the paradoxical and tragic situation of having an abortion performed for a missed period caused by something other than pregnancy. It is my opinion that a majority of teenagers, initially ambivalent about informing their parents, can through proper counseling be made to realize that their parents can be supportive and that their help should be sought.

Venereal disease is a community problem. The identification of the involved patient early in the course of disease is critical in controlling the spread of infection. Some schools do offer courses as part of the educational program for the recognition and treatment of veneral disease. Often these courses are offered in such a way as not to encompass the total field of interrelationships and social responsibility. The teenager who is fearful of having contracted a veneral disease and whose life pattern up to that point has prevented the necessary communication with parents is very unlikely to seek early help, if, as a consequence of this help, his parents will be informed without *his* consent.

It would seem that an individual who has been educated adequately in the recognition of the early symptoms of veneral disease and the early signs of normal gestation would seek professional help, if such help could be offered without having to invoke the need for parental consent. Once the individual patient has sought professional help, counseling opportunities could be established. A patient not seen is a patient not counseled. It is the right, I believe, of every physician to work comfortably and flexibly within these problematic areas. To remain completely nonjudicatory is to be indifferent to the many complex problems of our age. The confusion of our younger populace reflects the confusion of their adult models. One need only attend a Parent-Teacher Association meeting and raise the prospect of contraception for the teenager with or without parental consent to sense this confusion. To avoid this particularly harrowing situation, one may more comfortably raise the question among a group of physician colleagues and again sense the confusion. How do we expect our younger people to behave when we cannot anticipate the behavior of adults?

When a young girl, regardless of age, enters my office seeking advice about contraception, my reaction is not one of immediate suspicion that the patient is really seeking adventure and promiscuity; rather, I feel she is behaving in a responsible fashion—an attitude all too infrequently seen. Unfortunately, our present educational system does not provide universally for healthy understanding of human sexuality. Sexual responsibility is not a subject easily learned by our young people in the setting provided them by the adult world. There exists a gap between the planning of successful educational programs and our present state of misinformation and confusion. The gap can be filled partially by physicians who recognize its existence and who would allow the exercising of a *moral compromise.*

It seems irrelevant to speculate whether the rate of out-of-wedlock pregnancy would decline if contraceptive prescription were available; to wonder whether the rate of veneral disease would diminish if education were more widespread; or to wonder whether promiscuity would be encouraged if contraception were more available. What does seem directly related to the current problem is its honest recognition and the appreciation of its universality. It is easier for many of my colleagues to prescribe contraception for either postabortal or postpartum teenage patients without parental consent. This group of patients has demonstrated its involvement with sexual intercourse. The patient not yet pregnant is not as easily discerned. I am not in favor of dispensing contraceptive devices or pills to students of all ages who are not engaged in sexual activity; and, although I am in strong accord with the development of educational programs in which responsible discussion is carried out, until such programs are well established I feel that all youngsters seeking professional help should be dealt with in a positive and open manner. A couple having sexual relations should understand the consequences of their activities and should be helped in an empathic manner to avoid an undesired and unwanted pregnancy.

As obstetricians and gynecologists aware of our social and community responsibilities, we should take on the leadership of defining for our colleagues our standards of practice. This leadership is vital so that ambivalent feelings may give way to responsible action. Although the subject of contraception has found its way into a good number of our major educational textbooks dealing with obstetrics and gynecology, it is distressing still to find that current textbooks devoted to the subject of adolescent gynecology contain little such material. Very little, if any, information is available describing the social and moral aspects of contraception in minors.

What methods of contraception might be used for the teenager? One opinion concerning the intrauterine device is that it cannot be employed in a young girl because of the high rate of expulsion. Consider, however, that, if 85 per cent of young girls so treated were to expel an intrauterine device, 15 per cent would satisfactorily retain it. The specter of long-term use of oral contraception in the young patient, with the prospects of metabolic disorders, has been raised. In this area, just as in the area of using oral agents in the older patient, the individual physician must act confidently with the facts currently available to him and decide each question on an individual basis. Are the prospects of a possible metabolic disorder sufficient for him to employ other methods of contraception in this patient-group? Does the effectiveness of a particular contraceptive technic determine whether one should use it in this group of patients? Is the occurrence of an unwanted pregnancy among these individuals sufficiently tragic to allow one to use long-term contraception? The use of a condom, a jelly, a foam, or a diaphragm, although less effective than either the oral agent or the retained intrauterine device, would afford most patients protection against unwanted pregnancies. Many of these devices are currently available without physician prescription and are sold over the counter throughout our country.

Some psychiatrists who have had an opportunity to work with young, out-of-wedlock pregnant girls have described at great length some of the reasons for the occurrence of the pregnancy and have suggested certain recurring psychodynamic themes. Although these studies are of interest, the interpretations have often been speculative, and I believe oversimplified and generalized. If an orthopedic surgeon questioned his ward patients whose fractures resulted from ski injuries occurring early in their experience as novice skiers, his results would be quite skewed in response to the questions, "Do you enjoy skiing? Will you ski again?" The psychiatrist interviewing out-of-wedlock pregnant girls is, by the nature of the group selected, obtaining biased responses. A questionnaire submitted to young girls who were not pregnant concerning their attitudes towards sexual experiences would provide completely different answers. The point I wish to make is that these studies concerned with etiology are not as important as the prevention of these pregnancies.

Until such time as a positive, productive, educational program has been established in the schools, in the homes, and in the churches, a more empathic and productive reaction on the part of all obstetricians and gynecologists is necessary. This would be a most helpful response and might provide much-needed and immediate solutions to current problems.

_____

"Proof of Love" Is Real Phony

Abigail Van Buren

DEAR ABBY: An article I read of yours in the newspaper about three years ago has helped me more than you'll ever know.

My boyfriend (fiance now) was always asking me to "prove my love" to him. I would always refuse and then show him this clipping from Dear Abby. As hard as this may seem to believe, it always worked. He is now in Vietnam. It's kind of strange when he writes and says, "I'm so glad that we waited." As soon as his time in the Army is up, we're planning to be married. Thanks to you, what a beautiful wedding it's going to be!

You can disregard my letter, but you would be doing many girls a big favor if you would once again print that same article in your column. Thank you, Abby.

WAITING IN ASHEVILLE

DEAR WAITING: *The "article" you read, clipped and carried for so many years is a reprint from a chapter of my book "Dear Teen-Ager." I am pleased to run it again.*

Girls need to "prove their love" through illicit sex relations like a moose needs a hatrack. Why not "prove your love" by sticking your head in the oven and turning on the gas? Or playing leap frog in the traffic? It's about as safe.

Clear the cobwebs out of your head. Any fellow who asks you to "prove your love" is trying to take you for the biggest, most gullible fool who ever walked. That "proving" bit is one of the oldest and rottenest lines ever invented! Does he love you? It doesn't sound like it. Someone who loves you wants whatever is best for you. But now figure it out. He wants you to:

Commit an immoral act;
Surrender your virtue;
Throw away your self-respect;
Risk the loss of your precious reputation;
And risk getting into trouble.

Does that sound as though he wants what's best for you? This is the laugh of the century. He wants what's best for him: he wants a thrill he can brag about at your expense. . . . Love? Who's kidding whom?

A guy who loves a girl would sooner cut off his right arm than hurt her. In my opinion, this self-serving so-and-so has proved that he doesn't love you. The predictable aftermath of "proof" of this kind always finds Don Juan tiring of his sport. That's when he drops you, picks up his line, and goes casting elsewhere for bigger and equally silly fish.

If he loves you, let him prove his love—by marching you to the altar!

Adolescent Sexuality and the Schools

Alan P. Bell

Human Sexuality: The Proper Focus of Theory and Research

Before Freud came along and pried into areas of the human psyche which, even today, many people felt were better left alone, little attention was given to anyone's sexuality, much less to sexuality in childhood and adolescence. People were taken at their word. Things were as they appeared to be. But Freud began hacking away at these long-held illusions. He discovered that a person's sexuality was so severely eschewed that many of man's best energies were being used to keep it a secret from himself and from others. And he found that if he could get a patient to explore the nether regions of his mind in a way which would make formerly repressed sexual material available to consciousness the patient's intra-psychic conflicts could be resolved.

Predictably, the reactions to his thesis were as severe as they were far-ranging. Forgetting the fact that Freud was concerned with the effect of *repression* and with sexual issues associated with the *parent-child* relationship, there were those who accused him of advocating sexual license. They believed, further, that he was a chief contributor to the more sexually permissive environment which was evolving at the time of the first World War, that somehow or other his pronouncements had opened a Pandora's box of unbridled sexuality which would inundate those who were counseling sexual caution and control. Then, as the moral climate in the United States appeared to change, as more and more people appeared less and less fearful of matters sexual, there were those who began to claim that Freudian theory was no longer appropriate or applicable to a non-Viennese, sex-affirming people; that sex was no longer a source of self-alienation for Americans at least, and that ways would have to be found to deal with syndromes produced by anomic rather than by an overactive superego.

I mention Freud and the reactions to him because I believe that the phenomenon is of particular relevance to a discussion of adolescent sex-

FROM *The North Central Association Quarterly*, XLIII (Spring 1969), 342–347. Reprinted with the permission of Alan P. Bell.

uality and the schools. But before I launch into that, I would also like to remind you of Kinsey, whose work provided similar reactions. Until Kinsey's pioneer effort at getting a reasonable estimate of who was doing what to whom and when and how frequently, almost nothing was known about the sexual behaviors of human beings. They were clothed in a secrecy almost as formidable as the kind of secrecy to which Freud had alluded. And finally, when, thanks to Kinsey and his associates, the truth became known: that man does things with his own as well as others' bodies, in childhood as well as in adolescence, in adolescence as well as in adulthood, with others of the same sex as well as with others of the opposite sex, before marriage as well as after marriage—the reaction was also predictable.

From some quarters there was astonishment; from others, outrage. There were those who questioned his right to ask—as well as his motivation in asking—the questions which he did. Some marched into the halls of Congress and denounced his book on female sexual behavior as an insult to American womanhood. Others viewed him as a perverter of American youth.

The same hue and cry—in contrast to the silent support which preparations for chemical-biological warfare and other anti-life experiments receive—has been raised with regard to the work of Masters and Johnson. Private foundations, and often certain agencies of the Federal Government, have been loath to support work which promises to provide answers to the enigma of man's sexuality. And, not unlike Freud, sex researchers continue to be viewed either as "nasty old men" who cloak their voyeuristic tendencies in an only apparent scientific interest or else as scientists who, given the "Sex Revolution," are making much ado about nothing. The former—and I think the majority—view is held by the erotophobics of our land; the latter by the sexual sophisticates who yawn when they are confronted by sexual styles and predilections which the sex "fascist," to use Albert Ellis's term, will not allow himself to even imagine. Both groups, however, tend to buy the notion that American youth is caught up in a sexual revolution. And it is just this notion to which I would like you to give some thought, at least for the moment.

Notions of a Sexual Revolution

On the face of it, the whole notion of a sexual revolution makes a lot of sense; it's believable. All one has to do is to look around—whether at billboards or at uncensored movies or at television productions or at the usual magazine stand—and one is immediately impressed by the explicitly sexual stimuli which flood the life space of each of us. And it is reasonable to suppose that this amount of sexual stimulation must have much to do with eliciting or shaping human behavior. It is reasonable to suppose that sexual behaviors which were non-existent will be introduced through the newly acquired modeling behaviors of others, and that those behavioral repertoires and patterns which a person already possesses will be maintained or, more probably, enhanced by a host of new cues. What makes more sense?

Or take the fact that relatively new and fool-proof contraceptive techniques have been made available which make it possible for full genital engagement to take place without fears of pregnancy. Doesn't it make sense to suppose that the removal of aversive consequences will promote sexual behaviors which formerly had been avoided?

Or the fact that an increasingly urban and highly technological environment provides new opportunities for sexual behaviors which were lacking in a less anonymous and more familistic culture. How could this not account for new modes and frequencies of sociosexual encounter? The supposition is so reasonable!

And the frosting on the cake appears in the evident collapse of traditional mores, in youth's rejection of those who mouth moral absolutes, in the less rigid moral stances which are now being taken by even the more traditional churches. What other effect could all of this have than to promote an increase in sexual activity on the part of adolescents and young adults which can best be called a veritable revolution!

Evidence That No Sexual Revolution Has Occurred

Enough, however, of these reasonable suppositions. What are the facts? In case you have not heard—and the chances are you have—there is not a shred of evidence to support the idea that we are in the midst of a sexual revolution. Since World War II people have become more and more permissive in their sexual *attitudes,* more humane in their judgments of others who act in ways that they would not, and less fearful about discussing sexual topics which were formerly swept under the rug. And yet these changes have *not* been accompanied by significant changes in the rates or timing of sexual *behaviors.*

We know, and have known for some time now, that about 70 per cent of both boys and girls have been involved in some form of childhood sex play; that approximately 95 per cent of the male population has masturbated, most by the age of 13; and that almost 50 per cent of the female population has masturbated, most not beginning this behavior before the age of 13. Of the males who masturbate during high school, most do it once a week or more, while female masturbators do it once a month or less. Although boys masturbate more frequently and enjoy it more than girls, with both boys and girls masturbation is usually accompanied by some guilt and anxiety. We know that the majority of high school boys engaged in light and heavy petting with more than one partner, and that the majority of both boys and girls who engaged in heavy petting reach orgasm if only rarely.

A good estimate is that about 25 per cent of high school males have had sexual intercourse by the time they are 17 years old, and 40 per cent by the age of 18. About 35 per cent of the male population has participated in some kind of homosexual behavior, usually during adolescence. There is every reason to believe, then, that the average teenage high school boy has had more sexual experience—in terms of the number of orgasms, the number of partners, the number of homosexual and heterosexual encounters—than the young female teacher who may be designated as his academic mentor. But these percentages—and I won't bore you with any more—do not differ significantly from what has obtained since World War II and should come as no surprise to you. Boys, particularly, act out sexually at younger ages than many suppose, but they have been doing this for quite some time.

The Myth of a Sexual Revolution: Its Reasons

The fact that there is no sexual revolution—and this is what I think is really important and interesting—comes as a shock to many reasonable people. They scratch their heads and review for the umpteenth time all of the reasonable suppositions which I have already iterated. Some disregard the evidence and do what they can to perpetuate the myth. Maybe the fact of the matter is that most people *need* to believe that a sex revolution is taking place. Perhaps it is because adults want to think that youth have not been entirely victimized by the technological jungle which has made their own lives caricatures of what they might have been.

Some adults may seek some kind of vicarious pleasure, which their age and humorless marriages can never directly provide, in what they imagine about the sexual activities of youth. But, on an even deeper level, the adult belief in a sexual revolution may be predicated upon their insistence that human behaviors are a function of their *present* circumstances, that new inputs from any corner of the environment—whether it be the schools, the peer culture, or the advertising media—will effect monumental changes in behavior, that young persons—like themselves—tend to act rationally and that their self-systems are far more permeable than Freudians and others of that ilk suppose.

You see, if you can believe in a sexual revolution, you can also believe in the ability of society to shape young persons' behaviors at will. It is not at all unreasonabe to suppose that this illusion is one to which most educators are committed. Whether or not they are liberal or conservative, whether or not they are concerned about making sexuality less problematic for young persons, teachers by and large appear to see this aspect of a young person's life as any other: it is a legitimate (or illegitimate) object of inquiry about which answers can be had and then communicated to young people for their benefit, as information which young people need and on which they will act in a rational way.

Sex educators by and large see their task as one of re-education, of replacing the misinformation provided by the peer culture with information which will provide the basis for sexual attitudes and determinations which would be quite different but for the information which the school is in a position to provide. This, I believe, is a misperception on two counts. First, I do not believe that sexuality is seriously problematic for adolescents because of informational deficiencies or that the motivation for sexual decisions is primarily cognitive. As Lester Kirkendall puts it, "Standards of sexual behavior are much less a matter of sexual knowledge than of feelings—feelings of acceptance or rejection, of accomplishment or failure. Few persons form their sexual standards as a result of facts and information—the traditional sex education. Rather their standards are a product of the kind of relationships they have developed with their parents and close friends."

Secondly, I do not view the schools' task in regard to sex education as involving an attention to and correction of whatever evolves from *peer* relationships, as important as these may be. Rather they should give serious attention to what has evolved from the young person's *parental* relationships, which are of crucial importance in determining the meaning and direction of a young person's sexual behavior.

The Impact of the Faculty upon

Human Sexuality

It is in a young person's original relationship with his parents that the most important issues of his life—interpersonal as well as intrapsychic —will emerge. How these are handled, how the young person grows or not in his sense of his personal worth which will be inevitably reflected in his sociosexual relationships will have profound consequences for his psychosexual development and subsequent adjustments. It is in the home and at a very early age that a child learns to enjoy (or not) his body. It is in the home that a child is introduced to the parental model of a heterosexual relationship. It is in his relationship with a parent of the same sex that his own sexual identity will evolve. And I would suppose that factors such as these are far more predictive of the kind and quality of his sexual behaviors and relationships than any other input he receives from his environment.

How else are we to explain the fact that there is no sexual revolution despite the social changes which have been enumerated? Apparently there is a process from which individuality emerges which defies requests of a lesser magnitude. For example, how one learns what it means to be a girl in a society such as ours makes it exceedingly difficult for her to become the sexual aggressor no matter what changes occur in opportunity. And her sexual decisions, like those of her male counterpart, as well as the psychological consequences of those decisions, will be based on personal factors which do not have necessarily and explicitly sexual characteristics. And it is precisely here that the school must intervene.

I agree with Isadore Rubin who states: "Basically, each individual must make his own personal decisions about sexual behavior. These decisions should be made in the light of his own moral beliefs and should be based upon clear insight into his own personality needs and convictions. They should not result from the pressures and beliefs of others."

The concern of any school should be that its milieu provide its students with an opportunity to review their suppositions about themselves and others, to question these perceptions, and to grow in an autonomy which is viable enough to include and then to integrate a wide range of self-experience.

In other words, sex education which is not self-education, which does not provide each student with an opportunity to ventilate his feelings and assumptions about himself and others, whether in or outside the sexual context, is not the kind of intervention which is called for. Questions which arise with regard to sexual matters must be discussed with reference to an individual's total life situation; otherwise sex education will join that list of circumstances beginning with the parent-child relationship which often inhibit personal growth.

For a variety of reasons the parent-child relationship is particularly constraining within the sexual sphere. Whether or not you take seriously Freud's construct of the Oedipal situation, the fact remains that the incest taboo is universal and perhaps an important factor in what parents can permit of their children and even in the kind of verbal exchange that can take place between a child and his parents. Both the parents and the child have too much at stake in their relationship and too long a history of mutual influence for them to accomplish what must be accomplished beyond the family. And just as the child must choose someone other than his mother to marry, so it is that *extra-familial* figures are asked inevitably to enter into a relationship with a person in ways which modify a person's original *intra-familial* experience.

Sex Education in the Schools:

What Kind of Emphasis?

Up to now the school's efforts in regard to the kind of intervention which I envision have been minimal. Until fairly recently, schools—like parents and unlike peers—have chosen to disregard sexual issues in the lives of their students. This disregard serves to enhance the students' identification of the school with parents' hopes and fears for them and to increase the likelihood that the same kind of alienation from his parents which a child experiences in adolescence will be transferred to the school as well.

Like Sputnik, however, the notion of a sexual revolution has reminded the schools of a lacuna which has existed in their curricula, and now many schools are giving serious attention to their obligations in this area of their students' social development. This is all to the good, I think, but what has been accomplished so far in the many developed sex education programs should be considered only the very small beginning of the kind of intervention which is needed. These programs must not lull us into the belief that they even *begin* to be adequate.

Up until now, despite the face validity of programs which instruct young persons in proper sexual terminology and which are designed to transmit the so-called "facts of life," I suspect that such programs are woefully inadequate in the face of what adolescent development requires. In some respects these programs and the way they are presented—here I am reminded of the concept of the "medium" as the "message"—may even be misleading. Most are predicated on a naive belief in human rationality, on a kind of gnostic view of salvation in which one will join the elect and act accordingly once the holy mysteries are divulged to him. The usual focus of these programs is upon the biological aspects of adolescent development and they are usually designed to answer the adolescent's questions about his physical normality. The fact that many programs focus almost exclusively on the reproductive process and, in general, on an individual's biological givenness, indicates that they are geared to, even as they reflect, a basically feminine gestalt—and this, despite the fact that most girls have already been acquainted with these facts in conversations with their mothers.

The crucial questions of adolescence are not "Am I physically normal?" except insofar as such a question reflects a much more basic concern, but rather, "Am I worthwhile despite my wild fantasies, despite the behaviors which I engage in?" "What can I do with my body—not what did I receive in my body—and still not be beyond the pale?" These questions, however, are hardly ever asked, such concerns are hardly ever shared by adolescent participants in the usual sex education programs. The context—of a teacher, grades, examinations in the course—does not provide that kind of opportunity. A teacher "telling it as it is" in answer to questions which have been scribbled anonymously on pieces of paper is not the kind of setting in which insight will be gained—to use Rubin's words again—"into (a student's) own personality needs and convictions."

The sources of guilt and how guilt is managed on the part of an individual, feelings which have been deliberately disregarded, impulses which are barely maintained; these will never be identified or explored in the classroom setting as it now exists. And yet, isn't it here that the crux of the matter lies? If it does, then it would behoove the schools to think seriously about providing their students with opportunities for self-confrontation which may not be possible in any other setting. Specialists who are not identified with the establishment must be trained to conduct small group discussions in ways which promise most to bring this about. These specialists must be prepared to meet with students in a one-to-one setting in order to encourage a singularly unaccustomed dialogue. At the very least, small steps can be taken in this direction which will make the schools increasingly relevant to the real needs and vital issues which lie at the heart of what it means to be an adolescent.

The New Case for Chastity

Ernest Gordon

Out of many years' experience in counseling college-age young people, I am convinced that there is emerging a powerful case, perhaps a *new* case, for chastity. Simply put, it is this: Sexual freedom, under the so-called "new morality," should be regarded by today's youth as *a challenge to their freedom of choice*. And freedom of choice, in the area of sex as elsewhere, involves the demand to choose for oneself, influenced by neither old-fogy fears nor hipster pressures, the course that will contribute to the richest and fullest life.

I know that the presumption of our time is that the "new morality" is simply a synonym for "no morality." But that presumption may well be wrong. Among college students today, I find increasing recognition—and resentment—that their freedom of choice in moral action is being pushed around quite as much by libertarian "Thou shalts" as their parents' was by "Thou shalt nots."

There's no denying that the pressures toward loose conduct are strong. Ours is a society drenched in sex. Illicit sexual relations, graphically portrayed, are a large part of many contemporary books and movies. Provocative sex symbols underlie much advertising. Education in the physiology of sex and open discussion between the sexes have done away, in the minds of this generation at least, with the anxieties inherited from a neo-puritanical tradition, and new and easier methods of contraception have diminished the fear of unwanted pregnancies. In view of all this, why be pure?

It isn't easy to answer this question. The old morality, based on centuries of human experience, has a good case. But it no longer convinces our young people. The authoritarian morality of "Thou shalt not" is out. And so is the practical argument, "Nice girls don't do it, because they will be in trouble if they do."

This situation baffles the older generation. If young people reject the old arguments for morality, they must be rejecting morality itself. Not necessarily. The encouraging fact is that our young people are actually free to be *more* moral. Many are seeing that the "new" in the "new morality" is the freedom to choose chastity rather than have it thrust upon them by fears or pressures.

Among college youth today I sense an increasing scorn, tinged with pity, for those of their number who plunge into promiscuity to express their "freedom." Again and again I hear, "Poor kid, she (or he) is so insecure." Such remarks recognize that sexual promiscuity, far from being a sign of self-confidence and social poise, is actually an earmark of anxiety and fear. The Don Juan who flits from woman to woman is attempting to convince others, but mostly himself, of his masculinity. And so it is with the girl who, afraid of being unpopular, prostitutes her body in a vain attempt to correct her anxiety. In the process, her insecurity is intensified, her reputation is destroyed, her prospects for sexual satisfaction are decreased.

I was delighted to hear recently of a lovely, well-integrated girl who said to her mother, "Don't worry about me. I'm a nonconformist. I intend to remain a virgin until I marry." This remark stamped her as one mature enough to respect her own body and to preserve its purity for the man she loves, or will come to love. She is the confident person—the girl with a future instead of the girl with a past.

I am convinced that the prevailing attitude of most young people today is not a rejection of all moral standards but an honest search for those that are higher and more meaningful—and therefore more permanent—than the old ones based on fear. They *want* standards, and the questions they ask, no matter how flippantly, reveal the seriousness of their search.

Under the old morality, many young people believed that they could show their individuality only by being unchaste, because it was difficult to distinguish between those whose chastity was based on fear and those for whom it was a matter of choice. Under the "new morality," chastity is more of a freedom than a restriction. Thus, a young person can remain chaste and still show his individuality. With this new freedom, however, comes a responsibility to be informed. Many fallacies have emerged which may mislead young people. For example, there is the often-heard, "*Everybody's* doing it, aren't they? Why shouldn't I?"

It takes little effort to explode that flimsy cliché. The Kinsey report found that 58 per cent of college-bound males had had no sex experience, and 80 per cent of unmarried women in the 16-to-20-year-old class were virgins. More recent surveys of both sexes reveal scant change in these figures. To students making this weak point I simply say, "It would be more accurate to say everybody's *talking* about it."

Another fallacy voiced by advocates of premarital sex is what Dr. Evelyn Duvall calls the "try before you buy" argument. This advances the notion that sexual compatibility, so important in marriage, can only be determined by "giving it a whirl" before marriage. Dr. Duvall, a recognized authority on sex and family-life problems, cites in her book *Why Wait Till Marriage?* [1] a study made by the American Institute of Family Relations which concludes: "The previous sexual experience of a woman is no help to her in making a good sexual adjustment in marriage."

But perhaps the trickiest device, used by seducers since time began, is the "test of love" theory. Again and again I'm asked, "But isn't sexual intercourse itself the test of love? Surely it can't be wrong if those who enjoy it love one another!" In reply, I contend that the experience of being in love is far greater than a "rub" and a "tickle" to borrow from one of Dylan Thomas's poems.

For those truly in love, erotic love is transcended by a much deeper love—that of self-giving, of seeking the highest good for the other. This love elevates physical passion to the level of genuine concern for the beloved. As one young man said not long ago, "My fiancée and I discussed having sexual relations, and decided we'd rather not. I love her too much to have that relationship a furtive one."

When young unmarrieds in complete earnestness ask, "With all the risks removed from premarital sex, *what have I got to lose?*" I have to remind them that, while some obvious risks have disappeared, sex remains complex and precarious. Outside a loving marriage, it may be more damaging than rewarding.

This was tragically illustrated for me one day recently when I arrived at my office to find an undergraduate, obviously deeply disturbed, awaiting me. As he fumbled for words, I thought I would shock him into coherent speech, "Have you killed someone?" I asked.

"Yes, I have," he shuddered, lowering his face into his hands. I had to guess quickly what this confession meant, so I asked, "Have you been involved in an abortion?"

Nodding, he burst out with his story—an all too common one. For two years he had been sleeping regularly with his girl friend. They had used contraceptives, but something had gone wrong. This did not worry the young couple unduly, for their friends told them where to get an abortion for $600. When the illegal operation was over, the girl broke

---

[1] Association Press, 291 Broadway, New York, N.Y. 10007, $2.95.

down completely. What had been an easy solution to an embarrassing problem suddenly became a tragedy. She felt that she was responsible for destroying life.

Equally shattered, the boy demanded, "What right have we to go on living?" I was able to show him that they did have a right by indicating some of the ways they could live out their forgiveness. The first thing he determined to do was to marry the girl and to protect her from her fears. The second was to tell his friends and acquaintances of their experience so that they, too, would learn from it. Almost too late this couple realized that time-tested standards existed to protect, not inhibit, their personal freedom.

But the argument based on "What have I got to lose?" contains other risks. Not the least of these is the loss of one's self-respect, without which life becomes empty, often leading to self-hatred. Indeed, near the top of a list of the costs of unchastity is a very much lowered self-esteem—yet the power to love another rests on the ability to respect oneself.

Whatever may be modern youth's attitudes, real or pretended, toward sexual "freedom," one thing that most of them want is a relationship that is sincere and permanent. This is where chastity comes in. Chastity does not mean a denial of sexuality; on the contrary, it implies its fulfillment. Since the sexual act itself is simply an organic one, a biological function, it has little significance outside a personal relationship. A prostitute, for example, is interested only in money. The man who uses her is interested only in pleasure. Neither of them is interested in the other. If there is any relationship at all, it cannot be classified as any more personal than a relationship between a man and a glass of beer.

The word chastity is derived from the Latin word *castus*, meaning pure. A pure relationship is surely an honest one. When two people are honest with each other, they enter into a relationship which is one of mutual respect, or moral integrity, a relationship in which one moral person will not use another moral person simply as a means of pleasure. Such a relationship needs the support and strength of marriage. For only in an open relationship can a man and a woman be free to give themselves honestly to each other without reservation.

What many fail to grasp, at the time their freedom of choice is being exercised, is that depth studies of married couples, such as the one made by the late Prof. Lewis M. Terman, of Stanford University, have concluded that "of those men and women who have had pre-marital sexual intercourse, the more promiscuous they have been premaritally, the less likely they are to be happy maritally." To this Dr. Duvall adds: "Men and women who have been permissive sexually before marriage cannot be expected to change miraculously when they marry."

In my counseling work I have found that many of the marriages which break up are those in which moral integrity is lacking. I remember trying to keep one couple together. Both members had had a series of premarital experiences, and each refused to believe in the sincerity of the other. Each readily accepted the other's guilt but not his own. They were divorced, they have remarried, and they have repeated the experience—and they will continue to do so.

From experience, I am forced to conclude that chastity and monogamy are twins. They stand for the dignity of both the man and the woman. Women are probably more aware of this than men. Recently, I was having a conversation with a lovely middle-aged woman who was commenting on the joys of marriage. One thing she said stays with me. It was a simple phrase: "I'm glad I have this man to love." She did not say "*a* man," but "*this* man."

The center of her love was a particular man with a particular name and personality. The years had not dulled the thrill of loving nor erased the joy of being with her man. Love opened the door of life for her. By it she entered into the life of "*this* man." There is no more satisfying self-expression, for it is centered not upon the self but upon the other.

Thus, the case for chastity rests finally upon the uniquely God-given character and dignity of men and women. It is a good case, and it is original in every generation.

Questions

1. What different kinds of argument are offered for and against sex education?

2. Do you think there is any validity in relating the arguments favoring sex education in the schools with "the international Communist conspiracy"? Why is the connection ever made in the first place?

3. Why does the issue of sex education arouse so much emotion on either side of the argument? Why at this time?

4. Why did the several religious groups in the country seem to feel it necessary to issue an "interfaith statement on sex education"?

5. How does Mr. Bell's argument in "Adolescent Sexuality and the Schools" differ from other arguments on the subject? Do you agree with him that indeed there is no sexual revolution? How can he take the position that he takes in the light of the other articles?

6. How do you relate the discussion by Dr. Ronald J. Pion, "Prescribing Contraception for Teenagers—A Moral Compromise," to the argument by Dr. Ernest Gordon, "The New Case for Chastity"? Are they really that far apart? How does Abigail Van Buren's position relate to both of these articles?

7. Do you think there is any correlation between people's politics and their positions on sex education? That is, would political conservatives take one position and political liberals take the opposite? Or would you relate the position one takes on sex education to other matters?

8. What seem to you to be a parent's principal problems regarding sex education?

Assignments

1. List three different arguments for and three different arguments against sex education, and discuss their interrelationships. State which you think is the most compelling.

2. What problems have you had discussing sex with your parents? Can you comfortably describe these and analyze them? Try to do so in as objective and reasoned a way as possible. If you believe that discussions about sex should not take place in the home, present an argument for the proper discussion of sex in the classroom or in church.

3. Look in the most current *Reader's Guide to Periodical Literature* or in *The New York Times Index* and find the titles of some articles concerning sex education. Read two that seem to take opposing points of view and summarize them.

4. Write an argument for or against any of the following propositions: sex education should begin as soon as possible in elementary school; sex education should not begin until college; sex education should not take place at all in a school environment but belongs properly in the home; sex education is nobody's business but the individual's own; only clergymen should properly take on the problem of educating young people or adults in sexual areas; human life would be a lot happier if there were no sex at all.

5. Compare the objections to sex education in the schools made by the "Movement to Restore Decency" and those voiced by Dr. Alan P. Bell. In the course of your comparison, analyze the tone and the logic of the two positions.

6. Write a letter to the editorial page of a newspaper you are familiar with or to Abigail Van Buren, stating your own position on the subject of sex education.

7. Write an essay called "Sex, My Parents, and I."

Additional Reading

Articles and books, some calm and some polemical, continue to be published on the subject of sex education. Many are related to positions put forth by various women connected with the Women's Liberation movement. Among the more classical considerations on the subject of sex education are the works by Drs. Benjamin Spock, Arnold Gesell, and Milton I. Levine. Provocative positions may be found in the works of Midge Decter, Norman Mailer, Kate Millett, and Germaine Greer. Famous titles are *How Babies Are Made* by Andrew C. Andry and Steven Schepp, *The Wonderful Story of How You Were Born* by Sidonie N. Gruenberg, and *Love and Sex in Plain Language* by Eric W. Johnson. Other titles in the voluminous literature on sex and education may be found in the card catalog of your library and in the usual indexes to current periodical literature and newspaper articles.

Soul Language
and Standard English

Reproduced by permission of the photographer, Kenneth L. Schorr.

Americans Who Can't Speak
Their Own Language

Lloyd Shearer

To survive successfully in the U.S. today the average urban Negro lives in two worlds—the world of the black ghetto in which he usually resides and the world of the white industrial complex in which he usually labors.

Each of these cultures has its own language, and if the Negro wishes to work in the white world—for the most part he has little alternative—he must learn "standard English," which is a far cry from his own colorful inventive, mellifluous dialect.

Recently 161 Negro girls were graduated from vocational high school in Washington, D.C. They had acquired acceptable skills in typing, filing, other clerical work. Of this number, only two were found to be employable by civil service, the telephone company, retail outlets, etc.

Why? Simply because of their unique speech pattern. In some cases the pattern was not only difficult for whites to follow, but in others, it aroused in the minds of potential employers, negative images of stereotyped Negroes.

In general, personnel managers will not hire Negroes who do not speak white or standard English.

They will not hire a bank clerk who says, "De cat ha just split" (The man has just gone) or a salesgirl who says, "Where de cahbo bah" (Where's the cardboard box) or any applicant who cannot pronounce the letter "r" and refers to "Mr. Carroll" as "Mist Ca'ol" or pronounces "ask" as "ast" or "desks" as "dess" or never in his speech employs the verb to have —"He done gone to de stoh"—or drops clusters of consonants, and in conversation commits all the linguistic errors typical of the ghetto-reared Negro.

The fact that so many Negroes, even those who are relatively educated, slur their speech and do not speak standard English is not their fault. It is the fault of racial isolation and the ineptness of an educational system which is only now becoming aware of the problem and trying to do something about it.

In the 89th session of Congress, spurred on by Dean Charles Hurst Jr. of Howard University, Rep. Phillip Burton of San Francisco introduced amendments to the Manpower Development and Training Act

FROM *Parade* Magazine, January 11, 1967. Reprinted with permission.

authorizing the Labor Department to train workers in "communications skills," a diplomatic way of saying, "Let's teach Negroes, Mexicans and others who need it how to speak standard English."

WIDESPREAD NEED. Dr. Hurst, chairman of Howard's speech department, declares the need for standard English is widespread in Negro centers throughout the U.S. "Here at Howard," he says, "we're teaching standard English to more than 800 undergraduates. Just imagine how great the need is among the high school dropouts and the uneducated.

"The major Negro pronunciation defect," he explains, "is the dropping of endings: 'I doan know' instead of 'I don't know.' The complete omission of middle syllables, 'deterate' instead of 'deteriorate' is another fault. A third is the running together of verbs: 'He done gone to his class'; the inability to pronounce the 'th' sound: 'Mouth' becomes 'mouf.' Then, of course, there's the dropping of the 's' in the possessive or the plural, the lack of syntax knowledge and in the phonological area the complete omission of certain sounds, so that the conversation becomes almost totally incomprehensible to someone who is not familiar with or alerted to it."

Dr. Hurst points out the immense irony of having young Negroes sacrificing and struggling through elementary and high school, meeting all the requirements of the system, only to find themselves unemployable following graduation because of a deficiency in English.

"I have been knocking myself out," he says, "flying all over the country, Berkeley, Philadelphia, Chicago, crying out that something has to be done, that a new approach has to be taken in teaching these people how to communicate verbally or the Negro unemployment situation in this nation is going to get worse instead of better."

In Washington, D.C., more than 91 per cent of all elementary school pupils are Negro. In Baltimore it is 65 per cent, in Oakland 53 per cent, in Philadelphia 60 per cent.

According to the U. S. Commission on Civil Rights, once any school becomes half Negro, "it tends rapidly to become all Negro," as white families depart for the suburbs or enroll their children in private schools.

It is just a question of a few years before most of the elementary and subsequently the high schools in large areas of New York City, Cleveland, Chicago, Washington, Baltimore, Oakland, Los Angeles, Detroit, Philadelphia, Kansas City and other metropolitan centers to which Negroes are migrating becomes virtually all black.

If the graduates of these schools are to obtain jobs, linguistic experts like Dr. Hurst, Bud Edwards, Ken Johnson, and others grappling with the problem contend that new ways of teaching standard English must be established immediately, "because the current method in most predominantly Negro schools," says Kenneth Johnson of Los Angeles, "isn't worth a damn."

"The Negro," Johnson declares, "must learn two dialects because he's an environmental schizoid. Let's take a group of young Negroes living in the black belt of Chicago, which is where I come from. They have a language which is for them operable. They can communicate among themselves with ease. Everybody knows the language, friends, family, preacher, storekeeper.

"All right, they go off to school. What does the school tell them? 'You can't talk that way. Your speech is incorrect, unacceptable, unintelligible; it's plain bad. Now you cut it out.' The kids, completely puzzled, say, 'The hell I will. Everybody at home talks this way. There's nothin' wrong with it.'

"The school's language program consists of downgrading the Negro student's present dialect and correcting him each time he deviates from standard English. The result is that the kids are graduated from the 12th grade still speaking their own dialect because it's been constantly reinforced at home. They don't learn standard English because they don't come in contact with it in the ghetto. They don't need it there, and they don't buy it."

Its Own Rules. Johnson suggests that language teachers must look upon the Negro dialect as systematic—not sloppy speech but a language system which has its own consistent rules.

"I think the school," he says, "has to teach the Negro standard English as an alternate dialect to be used in appropriate situations. For example, when he gets out of school and goes out on a job interview, he calls upon his standard English. When he's home, he uses the Negro dialect. As it is now, the school tries to destroy the dominant Negro dialect in favor of standard English. And in millions of cases, it's losing out. Both dialects have to be accepted."

Dr. Hurst is even more emphatic than Kenneth Johnson. "The current system of teaching English has got to be thrown out," he says flatly, "and thrown out now. The Negro students have lost faith in it, and I also think many of the teachers have. It's the older teachers, however, and the department heads, set in their old ways, who refuse to budge. It shakes up some of the basic tenets which have guided their instructional philosophy all these years.

"They have simply got to stop dealing in rights and wrongs," Dr. Hurst asserts. "They've got to accept the dialect the student brings with him and respect it because it represents his own culture. They've got to learn as much about it as possible and then encourage their students to develop a linguistic flexibility, a skill in standard English without requiring him to drop the nonstandard English, that is typical of his family, friends and personal environment."

Dr. Hurst points out that it is not only the Negro in America who suffers from substandard English but also the Indians and citizens of

Spanish-speaking origins (Puerto Rico and Mexico), who reside in New York City and five Southwestern states, and those from poverty pockets, such as the residents of Appalachia, who speak an English frequently incomprehensible to the average American. In number they may total as many as 20 million.

Teachers who are assigned to instruct these language-impoverished pupils usually come from the middle class and again, according to Hurst, "know little or nothing about the language patterns that many lower-class students assume everyone should understand. Under these conditions it is elementary that a teacher unfamiliar with the communication styles and language systems of the pupils cannot be expected to achieve much success; neither can the student be expected to find learning a pleasurable experience."

In Washington, D.C., at least 20 per cent of the public elementary schoolchildren have not learned to read effectively. The basic reason is poverty. Many of these children, almost all Negro, have been raised in bookless homes.

A group of civic-minded women—Kathryn Lumley, supervising director of the District's reading clinic; Margaret McNamara, wife of the Defense Secretary; Eleanor Smollar, wife of a prominent Washington, D.C., attorney—in conjunction with others decided last year that every schoolchild in Washington should have at least five books of his own, books with which he could do anything he wanted. Exposed to books of their own choosing, such children, they felt, would improve their own reading, help turn illiterate homes into at least semi-illiterate ones.

Last November these women, helped by many, launched their Reading-Is-Fundamental Project, to date have distributed via schools and their bookmobile more than 100,000 books, raising the money for their project from private foundations and individuals. It is by far one of the most welcome and successful programs in the District of Columbia. Since it is privately funded, its continued success will depend on charity rather than government appropriations.

Fortunately this is not true of speech improvement programs now underway in various cities of the nation. Under the terms of the Elementary and Secondary School Act, teaching material for developing linguistic skills is being paid for by the federal government.

Many educators believe that only Negroes with a knowledge of the Negro dialect, only Spanish-speaking teachers, only Indians with a knowledge of Indian dialects are qualified today to teach language skills effectively to those millions of English-speaking Americans who, despite years of schooling, still speak substandard Engish.

Whether this be true or not, the fact is that the nation badly needs an overall program for "bridging the cultures," for helping those who through no fault of their own, suffer the handicap of dialect.

For example, in California Negroes refer to food as "crust." In Connecticut they call it "manger." In Washington, D.C., it's "grit." In Pennsylvania it's "grub." Because they are linguistically creative, Negroes will frequently take a noun and give it a verb form, so that, as Dr. Hurst explains in his analysis of Howard University speech, the teacher hears such sentences as, "Let's grit up." . . . "It's gritting time." . . . "Let's grit." . . . "Got to grit some."

Middle-class teachers who do not understand the vocabulary, the semantic concepts of their pupils, are not communicating. They are merely lecturing on and in their own terms, most of the time, as developments have shown, wastefully.

There is a tremendous difference between "white" and "Negro" English, and Hurst has proven this conclusively by taking 90 word concepts, signifying food, shelter, etc., and presenting them to 72 white freshmen at Georgetown University and 72 Negro freshmen at Howard University for definition. He found the definitions similar in only 24.4 per cent of the items.

Take the word, "taste." The Georgetown frosh defined it as a "preference," the Howard frosh as an "alcoholic drink." At Georgetown "joined" means "together," at Howard it means "to be well-formed physically." To the Georgetown testees, "fat" means "obese." At Howard the frosh defined a "phat" person as "very shapely."

"To get a nose job" at Georgetown means "plastic surgery," at Howard if a girl has been given "a nose job," she has fallen in love.

Dr. Hurst, creator of "Higher Horizons," a program in speech communications, has recently finished a soon-to-be-published dictionary of nonstandard terms and their translations.

How many of the following would you know?

Negro Term	*English Translation*
ace boon coon	good friend
bunky, gray, Mr. Charlie	white person
copping some Z's	to get some sleep
Dudley do right	policeman
finger popping	enjoying
gabagonious	talkative
give me five	shake hands
got my wig jammed	got a haircut
joints	marijuana cigarettes
keep getting up	leave
laid out	well-dressed
lonely looking	ugly girl
main squeeze	best girl

Kenneth Johnson, who is trying to put together for Los Angeles schools a type of linguistic training program not unlike the program of tapes originated by Dr. Hurst, is convinced that unless the young teacher assigned to a predominantly Negro school is first trained and briefed on Negro dialect, she is wasting her time and the time of her students.

"What we need," he claims, "are more and better training programs for teachers whose pupils have limited or deviant language skills. That's what we're introducing into the Los Angeles school system."

Countless research studies have shown that lower-class, ghetto-reared children deprived of certain basic experiences, isolated from the dominant culture of the society into which they were born, not only develop deviant language patterns but also substandard skills in reading and writing.

Negro Dialect: Should Schools Fight It?

Herbert H. Denton

Leonora, 10, was considered by her school to be a "poor reader." Leonora stumbled through "The Night Before Christmas" in a manner that bore out the school's evaluation.

Then a researcher handed her another version of the poem, which began:

It's the night before Christmas,
  And all through the house,
Ain't nobody moving,
  Not even a mouse.
There go them stocking,
  Hanging up on the wall,
So Santa Clause can full them up,
  If he pay our house a call . . .

The second version was translation, by a linguist, into the nonstandard English that is the native language of most Negro children growing up in inner-city Washington. Leonora read it with a speed and accuracy that astonished the child herself.

Washington's school system, often criticized for failing to teach children to read, is having even more trouble now with an even deeper problem—teaching them to speak the written language.

Many, perhaps most, of the pupils in the city's schools speak a language that is not standard English. There are similarities in what the children say and what is conventionally spoken, language researchers say, but a separate communication system exists. The points of sameness are misleading.

From the *Washington Post*, December 22, 1968. Reprinted with permission of the *Washington Post*.

The children do not say, "I asked if he wanted to go." They say, "I asks do he want to go." They use the latter expression consistently and they communicate adequately with other children. This is not "bad English" but a different brand of English, the linguists say.

Instead of "with," they say "wif."

They do not say, "He is working every day." They say, "He be working."

This different language, variously described as nonstandard English, Negro dialect or "soul talk," is at the heart of the school system's central problem, the fact that it is trying to serve as a bridge between what are essentially two cultures that are frequently at odds.

The way the school system has responded to this separate language is as good a mirror as any of the problems it faces.

Within the schools, this new concept of Negro dialect has been surrounded by political overtones. The question is raised: Should education really concentrate on preparing a child for life in an integrated society by teaching him the standard English? Or should it aim at developing a sense of black identity, and bring the dialect into the classroom?

A solution to this dilemma appears to have been reached by the researchers. Place both styles of speech on more or less equal levels, they suggest, and refer to them as formal and informal language.

But the response of school administrators has been characteristic of the jumbled and uncoordinated bureaucracy that governs the language arts program. Some administrators have attempted to revise their programs. Others have adamantly refused to change traditional teaching methods.

The Washington schools' department of speech has been particularly determined to correct the dialect of black children. Dorothy L. Vaill, head of the department, says that she sees no relevance in urban language research in terms of teaching methods used in her department's programs.

When pressed Miss Vaill will concede that she objects to the basic contention of the linguists that a second language exists. This she finds "grossly insulting," she says.

"They are American people speaking an American language," Miss Vaill says of the children.

Weekly the department conducts a 20-minute speech improvement session for pupils in all city schools. The children are made aware of how the teeth, mouth, tongue and other parts of the body are controlled to enunciate the sounds of standard English.

Speech therapists urge teachers to integrate the drills in their regular teaching.

The therapists break down words with exaggerated emphasis on their basic parts so that pupils can distinguish the sounds that make up a single word when spoken in standard English.

The therapist leans forward toward the pupils and demonstrates to begin.

Pursing her lips she says, "Ooommm."

Mouth open wide she says, "Ow (rhymes with plow)."

She then points to her teeth that clamp down on her tongue and whispers audibly, "Thuh."

Rapidly she repeats the drill. "Ooom-Ow-Thuh. Mouth!" Not "mouf," as it is commonly pronounced in the inner-city dialect. The class goes through this drill and then moves along to another word.

"What is your birthday?" the therapist asks a small girl with a slight emphasis on the "thuh" sound in birthday.

"My birf-day is," the girl begins. She stops, leans back in her chair, takes a deep breath and starts again. "My birTH (another long breath) day is . . ."

The Speech Improvement Program has offended the black consciousness feelings of some city teachers. They have organized a group that calls itself Speech Therapists for Human Dignity and they say the dialect ought to be preserved rather than changed.

They have asked administrators to scrap the present program. Speech therapy is designed for children who lisp, stutter or have physical defects, they say.

The Speech Therapists for Human Dignity set down their objections in a letter to the newly elected School Board members, contending that the program was "just another way of robbing black people of pride, dignity and identity." The improvement program "attempts to destroy what the child already has—a language system of which he should be proud," the letter said.

Toni Searles, a speech therapist at the Morgan Elementary School, has emerged as the unofficial leader of the Therapists for Human Dignity, which she says includes a hard-core of 10 therapists—a couple of them are white—and often has the support of 15 or 20 more.

Mrs. Searles wears her hair in the new Afro-style. She speaks in a soft, musical voice with an easy precision to her pronunciation that is a model of the best standard English.

"Black people have too much to say to each other to quibble over how it is said," Mrs. Searles says in criticism of the improvement program. "The language can be used to unify us."

The dissident therapists argue that the improvement program fails for two reasons: First, children revert to the dialect as soon as they step out of the classroom; second, they are discouraged from talking freely in classes because of the tense atmosphere created by having their speech corrected frequently.

Gloria D. Gibson, a therapist at the Truesdell Elementary School, says that her supervisors began to subject her to informal speech improvement sessions after her dissenting position became known. When she debates with administrators in small conferences, they often stop her in mid-sentence to correct her pronunciation. She says that she finds this frustrating.

"Imagine how the child must feel," another therapist said.

In defense of the improvement program, administrators and some speech therapists emphasize that the program is not designed for any particular ethnic group but conducted in all classrooms in the city, including those west of Rock Creek Park, heavily populated by white children.

"It's all low, low key, not pointing the finger," says Beatrice K. Bassin, therapist at John Burroughs Elementary School who is a fervent booster of the current speech program.

"The important thing is to make it fun, fun, fun," Mrs. Bassin says.

"If a child can speak the sounds, he can better understand the written symbols," says Victoria T. Street, assistant administrator of the schools' speech department.

The Language Arts program in the schools is administered by three separate departments—speech, reading and English. The Passow Report noted that the three operated independently and often without coordination.

The Negro Dialect controversy appears to support the report's view. The English and reading departments are deeply involved in the linguistic research, in sharp contrast to the speech department.

Over the past three years, some English and reading classrooms in the city have actually been laboratories for the research. "I'm not willing to let this knowledge get away from the teachers. We can use this," says Charlotte K. Brooks, supervisor of the English program. Twenty English teachers are now attending a year-long, full-time workshop at Georgetown on the subject. Mrs. Brooks has organized a series of lectures by linguists for her teachers and they have aided researchers who are developing new texts and teaching materials.

Most of the research into the second language concept in Washington is conducted by the Center for Applied Linguistics, an outspoken and somewhat evangelical private group that has offices at 1717 Massachusetts Ave. N.W.

The Center has transcribed tapes of numerous recordings by blacks who live in the central city. The linguists say the tapes prove that a Negro dialect does exist. The so-called bad English is not a random set of errors but a rich language system with a different set of rules that are followed consistently.

For example, their studies suggest that the word "if" is not used in the dialect to express the conditional. Instead words are switched around to communicate the concept.

Standard English: "I asked if he wanted to go."

Negro nonstandard: "I asks do he want to go."

The word *ain't* is used to express the past in Negro nonstandard. Present tense: "He don't go." Past tense: "He ain't go."

The Center's studies have also explained another question that has long baffled English teachers.

Teachers have asked why a child looks at a sentence that reads: "Dick jumped over the fence," but then recites out loud: "Dick he jump over the fence."

The linguists say the child is translating. The process is similar to that of a Frenchman knowledgeable in English who might look at the words "a beautiful woman" and say aloud "une belle femme."

A study of this translation process has been conducted with lower-income Negro children in Washington elementary schools.

Over a tape recorder a speaker says a sentence and then asks the child to repeat it quickly.

"Gloria's friend is working as a waitress at the Hot Shoppes on Connecticut Avenue," the speaker says.

With striking consistency, the answer of the children would be, roughly: "Gloria frien', she waitress, she be working the Hot Shoppes on Connecticut Avenue."

Tapes that recorded a speaker of the Negro dialect were then taken to a school of lower-middle class white pupils in the suburbs. When they were asked to repeat what they had heard, they did exactly what the Negro children had done. They automatically translated an unfamiliar language into their own idiom. They were hearing nonstandard English but, when they tried to repeat it, the sentences came out in the standard grammar and construction.

Researchers at the Center for Applied Linguistics criticize the speech improvement program in Washington schools not only because of its failure to come to grips with the dialect, but because they consider it unnecessary. To teach standard English, they say, a program should be devised that focuses on grammar and structure of sentences. Tedious drills to get students to speak with King's English pronunciation is unnecessary, they argue.

The Center is now developing texts and supplemental materials for teaching standard English that borrow heavily from techniques used in foreign language instruction.

Two sentences representing both modes of speech are placed side by side in texts and drills. Pupils then are able to see clearly the differences in the two forms. Neither is said to be good or bad English but rather, the dialect is described as informal language and the standard English as formal.

Comparisons are made with different styles of clothing. Three-piece suits are appropriate at certain times, blue jeans and turtlenecks on other occasions.

Researchers at the Center have also tossed around the idea of devising a primary school program that would use books written in Negro non-standard.

The child could concentrate on reading, writing and arithmetic at first and later, in higher grades, attack the problem of learning standard English.

The transition to standard English would probably be easy, the researchers say. Support for this is in the experience of Leonora, who had difficulty with the standard version of the "Night Before Christmas" but read with ease the dialect rendition. Linguists point out that in the revised poem, the words were merely reordered. Spellings were not changed. The example seems to suggest that when moving from nonstandard to standard English, the only concern would be in teaching structure.

Experiments have been conducted with Mexican-Americans in the Southwest. Findings indicate that students who began school speaking and studying Spanish and later moved to English, performed better than the children who started school with a requirement that they learn and speak English.

But in the end, the linguists agree with the administrators of the speech program here on the necessity of learning standard English as a means of escape from the ghetto.

Joan C. Baratz, associate director of the Center for Applied Linguistics's urban language program, emphasizes the fact that no physics texts are currently written in the dialect and neither are there job application forms translated into Negro nonstandard for example.

Nevertheless, she defends Mrs. Searles and the Speech Therapists for Human Dignity who talk of the unity that might possibly be achieved through the dialect. Black militants used to embrace Swahili without realizing that they had a home-grown language, Mrs. Baratz says. Swahili is an East African language, she points out, and most slaves were uprooted from West Africa where other languages such as Hausa and Yoruba were spoken.

But when Mrs. Street, assistant administrator of the speech department, talks about black militancy she remains fervent in her defense of the current speech improvement program. Dropping the names of Stokely Carmichael and Eldridge Cleaver, she says: "Many of our black militants are effective because they articulate well. . . . One thing they have been able to achieve is good communication."

Washington's Second Language

Peggy Thomson

Din teacher start checkin' de boys, see which one had i'. An' one boy name Bill Bailey had a whole pocketfull of i'. An' teach' say I'ma, teach' say I'ma tell

FROM the *Washington Post,* June 11, 1967. Reprinted with the permission of the *Washington Post* and Peggy Thomson.

dis to de princiba too dat chu go 'roun' stealin' school prope'ty. He say, I ain'
steal schoo' prope'ty. My muvver pay for dis whin she paid for de tax. She say,
Your muvah ain' pay for dis. Dis b'long to de school'. An' she start talkin' all lat
ov' ol' junk an' waste half de peri'd. Din we start talkin' 'bout light, how, speed
o' light an' na speed o' soun' an' all 'a' kinna stuff.

The boy was speaking Washington's second language—mother tongue
of nearly two-thirds of the city's Negroes today. The dialect is similar
enough to standard English that its existence is scarcely recognized. But
far from being corruptions or sloppy forms of standard English, the boy's
speech patterns are elements of a separate language. Linguistically it is
quite as "good" as standard—and just as complex in its grammar.

Teachers and language scholars in Washington now work to learn the
tongue once misnamed "sub-standard" but now called "nonstandard." By
so doing, they are developing methods to teach standard English as a
second language to the children of the inner city.

Eventually they expect to know why these children score so badly in
national tests on reading—and how to correct it.

See, i's like ma mov' tell me da put some limon, hot limon 'n some tea an' go
da bed an' git up un'er de cover. An' I be hot. I be so hot unti' I jus' cain' do.
I jus' gotta take de cover off me. So I be takin' off my bajama shirt. I be taking
off everything. An' so, din, din I wake up nix morin', my col' be worse, seem like.

On the trail of such speech, a linguist named Joey L. Dillard with a
Ph.D. in English is listening in buses and on playgrounds and hanging
around bars. His colleague William Steward lets neighborhood children
have the run of his downtown apartment, giving help on homework and
access to his typewriter, his refrigerator and his automatic egg-cooker in
return for conversation.

And Irwin Feigenbaum and William Carroll, neither a law firm nor a
softshoe team, but sober young scholars, pay juvenile informants $1.50
an hour to record in their offices the language they use when they're
saying what comes naturally.

All this activity is part of the Urban Language Study which was begun
in 1965 with Ford Foundation funds and is being carried out by the
Center for Applied Linguistics. When their study comes out in 1969, its
linguistic analysis of the nonstandard dialect will enable Washington's
schools to teach standard English using foreign language teaching
methods.

But as far back as 1961, intuition and observation led a small group
of Washington school system educators to see the need for teaching
techniques which would enable the child to shift readily between dialect
and standard—in effect to make him bilingual. And it was the new
Language Arts Program's director, Louis H. Kornhauser, who urged
linguists to undertake the present study.

What is the second language? Its vocabulary and pronunciation frequently tally with white Southern. But its verb forms and negatives, its ways of indicating plurals and possessives, are more closely related to the English-based mixed dialects of the Caribbean and West Africa than to the British dialects from which white speech derives.

It seems to the linguists that the language of a poor, urban Negro in Washington has more in common with a poor, urban Negro in Seattle than it does with a middle-class Negro who lives 20 blocks away or with any white person.

The sentence *Here go a chair*, for example (*Here go, dere go* meaning *here is, there is* comparable to *voici, voilà*), linguist Stewart has picked up from children in Atlanta, Chattanooga, Knoxville, Charleston, W. Va., and here in Washington.

The same is true of *My sister name Mary*, a form he finds everywhere today plus in old slave autobiographies, and in a play published in Phila-delphia in 1776.

This second language is relatively new here. The whole picture in Washington changed after World War II, as it did in other big U.S. cities, with the massive migration of Negroes from the inland-rural South. The newcomers were by and large descendants of field slaves who, once freed, drifted onto farms to become sharecroppers or into towns to take menial jobs. When they were first brought to this country, the plantation owners' policy of mixing slaves of various tribal origins forced them to adopt as their *lingua franca* the pidgin English they would already have learned in Africa. This they passed on to new generations.

For their descendants, it was a native tongue.

House servants and artisans, of course, mingled with whites and picked up speech patterns from them.

"Some of these Negroes were up here, living in Northeast, speaking standard English, probably teaching at Howard," says Joey Dillard, "before the others arrived. And their children, even in this traditionally standard-speaking Negro community, began talking the dialect they picked up from their new neighbors." Linguists call this "swamping." It was indirectly responsible for providing Dillard with his best informant— a 12-year-old whose college-professor parents noticed he used "another language" in talking to his friends.

An' so the dog tried to bit me. An' time he tried, de man called 'im. An' dog start grit'n' 'is teef an' wint on back dere on ne steps.

The District's Language Arts program today covers 25 of the inner city's 82 elementary schools. It introduces the child to standard English orally before he's expected to read it. The hope is to win the child to a heads-up confident way of speaking before he becomes sullen from failures and rebuffs, before he masters the technique of turning himself out of the classroom.

The drills are designed to win correct responses, to let the child taste success all the way. They also pour language over the children in stories and poems to tune their ears to standard English.

Language arts teachers get no extra pay, but get a kind of top billing. They give no grades, but work with children in highly-concentrated half-hour sessions, class after class, through the day.

All come to the program as master classroom teachers with eight years' experience (in one case, 43). Nineteen of the 21 are Negro, almost all from Washington.

For a discussion of Renoir's painting *A Little Girl with a Watering Can,* the teacher hands around a bowl of roses for the children to smell, produces a feather boa to feel, suggesting the girl's fuzzy hair, and circulates a swatch of velvet to suggest her dress.

"It feel like a cow," says a little boy who may not have spent all his days on a city stoop.

"Yes, it feels like a cow," the teacher repeats. "We do sometimes call a cow velvety."

Helping spread the idea of offering English as a second language is the whole-hearted support of Mrs. Charlotte K. Brooks, who as supervising director is responsible for teaching English through 12th grade.

In England on a Fulbright in 1961, she was bewildered by some of the speech she heard. ("Picture it, an American Negro teaching English in Birmingh'm.") Years before she was puzzled at hearing her son use elements of nonstandard which neither she nor her husband spoke. Now she speaks out for an ungrudging acceptance of the child's dialect.

"I don't mean tolerance either. I hate to be tolerated. Children *must* use the language of their peers."

'n Batman say leggo 'n' ketch holt to de batrope. Catwoman say, I cain't leggo, Batman. 'N Catwoman fall down in a bowl o' spit.[1]

In learning to read the sentence "John will be there," the linguists say, the white child has to make only one translation—from print to sound—while the ghetto child must make a second translation, to the "John go be dere" of his native tongue. "Many teachers to whom I lecture on the dialect," says Stewart, "are hostile as hell. They say they've never heard these patterns. I tell them to go back to the classroom and use their ears."

A restless man, Stewart swivels back in his chair and throws a leg over the arm. He pulls index cards from his pocket and reads off examples of *be* picked up in his latest trip through the South. "Three weeks ago I had it traced back to 1857 in Kentucky. Now 1839, Georgia.

"Some teachers, of course," he continues, "grew up speaking standard English. Others, who are 'lace curtain' Negroes, are forgetful of the recent

[1] Bottomless pit.

past. Still others feel threatened professionally. They've got a lot of linguistics to learn."

To test their new teaching methods, linguists Feigenbaum and Carroll are giving a night class right now for ten D.C. teachers, including as the only elementary-level ones, two teachers from Kornhauser's Language Arts Program. The first class was planned as a shocker.

The lesson began—no explanation—with an exercise in nasal vowels. First French, *Jean* and *Jeanne, l'an* and *l'âne;* then nonstandard, *he go* and *he gon.* Next, a drill in the noninterchangeable Spanish form *ser* and *estar,* followed by a drill in the nonstandard *be,* beginning, *Where John at? Oh, he in the gym right now. He be in the gym every day.*

"I'm afraid," says Feigenbaum, "some of the teachers thought I was mocking. My nonstandard is fair but it would never 'pass.' Some of the teachers laughed. As the drill got harder they made mistakes. Of course we were presenting the nonstandard just as we wanted them to present our lessons in standard—with fast pacing and closely sequenced material. If you leave out a single step a child comes up with *he be* or *I doesn't.* He overcorrects."

Three months ago pixie-faced Language Arts teacher Catherine Phynes didn't know one fricative from another. Now as a student in the linguistics class she talks comfortably about her children's apico-dental fricatives, the *th* sounds in *this* and *thing,* for which children substitute apico-alveolar stops *d* and *t* at the beginnings of words, *dis* and *ting,* and bilabial fricatives *v* and *f* elsewhere—*muvver* for *mother, nuffin* for *nothing* and *bref* for *breath.*

(Dialect has its elegant and inelegant forms with *nothin* rated high and *nuffin,* incidentally, low.)

By now her classes at the Slater-Langston schools are pretty familiar with the drills. The third grade runs through the list of "Three than dare those Dan then doze day they den" without a blunder and on through the more difficult "brother rather clothing father" list.

Two little girls take the parts of Jim and Joe for a dialogue on Steve's new leather jacket and a third girl pipes from memory, "Their mother never breathes a word of gossip."

"Whaddat mean, gossip?" asks a boy. His neighbor supplies the definition: "It means talkin' about people in a ugly way."

With the children Mrs. Phynes is relaxed, warm, quick to show her amusement. She notices if Priscilla has forgotten her glasses, Ben has new shoes or Moses has a cold.

"As a lead-in to the linguistics materials," Mrs. Phynes says, "I just talked in dialect, anything that came to mind, starting with 'Who dat dere?' The children laughed. One said, 'Mrs. Phynes, you don't talk like that.' I said, 'You understood me, didn't you?'"

The thing that troubles Mrs. Phynes is the frequent reminder of what poor images the children have of themselves as Negroes. She remembers a time when she was telling a story of Lincoln's flatboat trip to New Orleans. At the part where he saw slaves in the marketplace, she asked the children if they knew what a Negro was.

One child spoke up, "He's someone bad."

Mrs. Phynes' first reaction was, "I wanted to cry." Instead she digressed to talk about Negroes. She asked if the children knew that she and all of them in the class were Negroes. "I gave some of the background of slavery, of the families separated on the ships, of the suicides, of the many who died on the crossing. Well, I got back to the story. After all, this was a first grade. But I'll never forget, I asked first how they felt about being Negroes. Regina answered, straight out, her eyes blazing, 'It makes me mad.'"

Mrs. Phynes says she thinks she knows what linguists mean about instant prejudice from the way a person speaks: "Wallace opens his mouth and I'm ready to shake him."

Measuring what they are sure is the success of their program is a problem for the Language Arts teachers and their director. They hear a new authority in the children's school voices, a lift, a sense of pleasure, a greater facility in using the language. Dr. John T. Dailey of George Washington University devised oral language facility tests to report on the program's first three years. He was hampered by the fact that more than half the original pupils had moved out of the program schools. His findings, though, were favorable. He wants to test again in the fall.

When school opened last September, only one of Kornhauser's teachers was at her Language Arts work. The rest were scattered over the city holding down classrooms for the month until Congress passed the school budget.

When Ford phased its money out of the program after the first three years, Rep. Natcher's District Appropriations Subcommittee willingly took up the full tab, but expansion has been slow. Where Kornhauser expected to add 20 schools by this June, he has been able to add only seven. Sixty more ghetto schools need language help quite as much as the present 25. Meanwhile, Kornhauser's staff awaits completion of the Urban Language Study in 1969 in hopes it will bring a richer and more effective program.

The linguistic researchers and the language teachers don't see eye-to-eye on all parts of the teaching program. But they close ranks on refuting some of the clichés mouthed about their poverty-area students.

They can't communicate? "I don't want to hear that one again," snaps Louise Keets, one of the founding Language Arts teachers. She mimics her children in a fast-paced five-sided front porch symposium based entirely on the two words, "Hey, man!" Eyebrows up, she says, "I call that communicating magnificently."

They're basically nonverbal? Dillard flicks a switch on his office tape recorder to let out a babble of pre-schoolers' voices, recorded from the lunch program in an Adams-Morgan block. "For our purposes, I'd say these children are too verbal by far. It's hard for us to isolate the speakers."

They're incapable of abstract thought? "Take the dialect sentence, 'He busy,' meaning 'He is busy right now,' and then 'He be busy,' meaning 'He is busy all the time,'" says Stewart.

"These children will never confuse the two, never accept a sentence like 'He be busy now.' They have to scan the situation and make a time duration judgment before they speak. How abstract can you get?"

At the Strong John Thomson school, Bernice Elam, a miniature-size dynamo of a Language Arts teacher, was running her third graders through the indefinite article drill on *Obese Louise.* (Nonstandard does not use *an.*) The class sailed along nicely through the frightful inventory of Louise's lunch: "An apple, an orange, an apricot, an oatmeal cookie, an ice cream bar and an Almond Joy," and on to the happy ending: "Her boyfriend thinks she has the figure of an angel."

Feigenbaum, visiting the class, wrote on the blackboard, "1. He at home." ("My sister talk that way," volunteered a child.) "2. He's at home. 3. He is at home." Children spoke up that 2 or 3 would be fine to use in stores and school. "In concert halls," added one. "In the White House," said another. Feigenbaum asked where besides at home and on the playground No. 1 would be acceptable. Someone suggested "at the zoo."

Caroline was the alert girl in the second row whose voice had stood out from the rest in the morning's drill, always correct in "an umbrella, an onion . . . he wears gloves." She spoke out now in a rush: *"We talk to a elephant at a zoo and a man say 'he name Annie.'"*

━━━━━━━━━━━━━

1928 *Letter by DuBois Argues for Retention of Word "Negro"*

William Raspberry

A year ago when S. I. Hayakawa was lecturing public school teachers here on race and semantics, he used as part of his presentation a letter written by W. E. B. DuBois to a young man who wanted to abolish the use of the word "Negro."

The letter, which follows, is as relevant today as it was in 1928 when DuBois wrote it:

"My dear Roland:

Do not at the outset of your career make the all too common error of mistaking names for things. Names are only conventional signs for identifying things. Things are the reality that counts. If a thing is despised either because of ignorance or because it is despicable, you will not alter matters by changing its name. If men despise Negroes, they will not despise them less if Negroes are called "colored" or "Afro-Americans."

Moreover, you cannot change the name of a thing at will. Names are not merely matters of thought and reason; they are growths and habits. As long as the majority of men mean black or brown folk when they say "Negro," so long will Negro be the name of folks brown and black. And neither anger nor wailing nor tears can or will change the name until the name-habit changes.

But why seek to change the name? "Negro" is a fine word. Etymologically and phonetically it is much better and more logical than "African" or "colored" or any of the various hyphenated circumlocutions. Of course, it is not "historically" accurate. No name ever was historically accurate: neither "English," "French," "German," "White," "Jew," "Nordic" nor "Anglo-Saxon."

They were all at first nicknames, misnomers, accidents, grown eventually to conventional habits and achieving accuracy because, and simply because, wide and continued usage rendered them accurate. In this sense, "Negro" is quite as accurate, quite as old and quite as definite as any name of any great group of people.

Suppose now we could change the name. Suppose we arose tomorrow morning and lo! instead of being "Negroes" all the world called us "Cheiropolidi." Do you really think this would make a vast and momentous difference to you and to me?

Would the Negro problem be suddenly and eternally settled? Would you be any less ashamed of being descended from a black man, or would your schoolmates feel any less superior to you? The feeling of inferiority is in you, not in any name. The name merely evokes what is already there. Exorcise the hateful complex and no name can ever make you hang your head.

Or, on the other hand, suppose that we slip out of the whole thing by calling ourselves "Americans." But in that case, what word shall we use when we want to talk about those descendants of dark slaves who are largely excluded still from full American citizenship and from complete social privilege with white folk?

Here is something that we want to talk about; that we do talk about; that we Negroes could not live without talking about. In that case, we need a name for it, do we not? In order to talk logically and easily and be understood. If you do not believe in the necessity of such a name, watch the antics of a colored newspaper which has determined in a fit of New Year's resolutions not to use the word "Negro!"

And then, too, without the word that means Us, where are all those spiritual ideals, those inner bonds, those group ideals and forward strivings of this mighty army of 12 million? Shall we abolish these with the abolition of a name? Do we want to abolish them? Of course we do not. They are our most precious heritage.

Historically, of course, your dislike of the word Negro is easily explained: "Negroes" among your grandfathers meant black folks; "colored" people were mulattoes. The mulattoes hated and despised the blacks and were insulted if called "Negroes." But we are not insulted—not you and I. We are quite as proud of our black ancestors as of our white. And perhaps a little prouder. What hurts us is the mere memory that any man of Negro descent was ever so cowardly as to despise any part of his own blood.

Your real work, my dear young man, does not lie with names. It is not a matter of changing them, losing them, or forgetting them. Names are nothing but little guideposts along the Way. The Way would be there and just as hard and just as long if there were not guideposts—but not quite as easily followed!

Your real work as a Negro lies in two directions: First, to let the world know what there is fine and genuine about the Negro race. And secondly, to see that there is nothing about that race that is worth contempt; your contempt, my contempt, or the contempt of the wide, wide world.

An Approach to Dialectical Bilingualism

(Negro Folk Speech in America)

Harry L. Jones

Let me begin by asserting that there is no such thing as *the* English language and that English teachers who conceive of themselves as custodians and guardians of the language do not really understand the nature of language and mistakenly justify their interest in perpetuating their own classroom dialect on the grounds that the way they talk is correct English and is, therefore, *the* language. There is no such thing as the English language and what is often passed off as correct speech is a middle class school dialect which is subject to all the variations of geography that even a casual glance at a linguistic Atlas will reveal. Nothing serves better to give the lie to the concept of the English language than a general conference of the National Council of Teachers of English where English teachers stand around holding converse in their own particular regional dialects and sit listening to papers on *the* language and the problems of teaching it.

The problem touched on here is one that strikes at the very heart of English teaching in Maryland and in the entire United States. English teachers are not really concerned with speech; they are primarily concerned with writing and secondarily with reading; and to the extent that this is true, they are not concerned with language but rather with language about language or the problems of encoding language into graphics and decoding graphics into language. Fundamental to the theory of signs and references is the idea that linguistic signs are sounds for things, sounds used as signs to refer to the things that people talk about. Language is speech, and writing is at best an attempt to give graphic representation to speech sounds with letters attempting to approximate segmental speech phonemes and punctuation trying to reproduce some

Reprinted with the permission of the *Maryland English Journal* and Harry L. Jones.

few of the supra-segmental phonemes of speech. Writing is signs which have other signs as their references. The written word *tree* does not itself stand for or refer to the object in nature but rather to the sound/triy/.[1] As I have already indicated English teachers are not really concerned with sounds, but with graphics.

It is only against a background such as the foregoing statement that it can be comprehensible that any native speaker can ever be said to have failed a course in English. A student is a person who has been functioning for some years in some linguistic community. It is a clear error to say that such a person does not know English, for he certainly has been making his way for years in that very language; and whenever in school he comes for conference with the teacher who is giving him a failing grade, they hold converse with mutual intelligibility in the very language which the teacher denies that the student has. The problem here is clearly not the lack of a language or the lack of English; it is rather the student's lack of knowledge of how to translate his own dialect into that of the teacher. And once he has learned how to do this, he still has the problem of how to translate the teacher's dialect into proper graphic signs, signs which in their sentence units, punctuation, and capitalization constitute a language of their own. In cases where the student's dialect is radically different from that of the teacher, as it is likely to be with any student who comes from a Negro folk background, a complex problem becomes even more complicated. For students from folk Negro backgrounds, the differences are so vast that adjustment problems are comparable to those of students who are trying to learn a second language.

Next let me assert that there is no such thing as Negro speech in Maryland or anywhere else in this country. This is to say that there is no speech in the United States which is distinguishable on the grounds of race alone. Coming as they did from different tribal and linguistic backgrounds, Negro slaves did not share a common language which they might have preserved in this country. They were forced as a means of survival to learn the language of their masters. The only possible dialect of American English which contains any large number of Africanisms is Gullah, a dialect found among the Gullah Negroes of the South Carolina and Georgia coasts and sea islands, a language which bears striking structural resemblances to such other contact languages as Taki-Taki and Melanesian Pidgin. [For a scholarly discussion of Gullah, see Lorenzo Turner, *Africanisms in the Gullah Dialect* (Chicago: The University of Chicago Press, 1949).] In general, however, Negro speech is the speech of the master class in whatever region the slaves happen to have been found. Since the slaves were found largely in the southern states, present-day Negro folk speech is Southern speech. But there is a difference.

Language is a product of culture. Gullah developed apart from the

---

[1] Representations appearing in slants in this paper are phonemic not phonetic.

mainstream of American dialects because of the geographical isolation of the Sea Islands. Linguistic geographers and others who delight in drawing isoglosses (or more technically for this discussion, isophones) take a particular pleasure in rivers and mountains and such geographical barriers, for isophones have a tendency to follow such natural physical obstacles. [See Hans Kurath, *A Word Geography of the Eastern States* (Ann Arbor: University of Michigan Press, 1949).] However, what seems to have escaped general attention is the fact that socio-economic and cultural barriers serve as effectively to isolate linguistic communities as do geographical and physical barriers. A culturally isolated community can exist in a city like Baltimore and show linguistic patterns of behavior which are quite different from those which one would expect from any contact with the dominant community. Despite Negro migrations from the South where they were enslaved, to the extent that Negroes have been ghettoized in Northern and Western metropolitan centers, their patterns of Southern speech have been perpetuated in exactly the same way and for much the same reason as the continuation of Gullah, the difference being a difference between geographical isolation on the one hand and cultural isolation on the other. Negroes of folk status in Maryland, therefore, do not speak differently from Negroes similarly situated in Chicago's Black Belt, New York's Harlem, or Los Angeles' Watts, nor yet differently from Negroes in Georgia or Mississippi. When differences in language occur in the various Negro communities, they are due to differences in economic and educational class and not to geographical location. This is only to say that Negroes who have been culturally assimilated in Maryland speak like other Marylanders and that middle class Baltimore Negroes speak Baltimorese like everyone else in that city. For those who have not been culturally assimilated, those I have chosen to designate in this essay as "folk" Negroes, the speech community is closer to that of whites of similar educational background in the deep South than it is to that either of whites or Negroes of middle class status in the State of Maryland. As I have already indicated, the speech of culturally isolated Negroes in Maryland would be closer to that of other Negroes similarly situated regardless of geographical location than it would be to that of whites in their immediate locale.[2] The simple fact of the matter is that a subcultural environment tends to produce a distinctive dialectical variety of a given language, and when anyone from such a subculture enters the cultural mainstream, his greatest single adjustment is likely to be a linguistic one.

The folk Negro child in Maryland has lived for some time in a speech

[2] The very title of an article like "The Relationship of the Speech of American Negroes to the Speech of Whites" by Raven I. and Virginia G. McDavid (*American Speech*, XXVI [1951], 3–17), seems to ignore the relationship between speech, class, and geographical location. However, Sumner Ives in "Use of Field Materials in Determination of Dialect Groupings," *Quarterly Journal of Speech*, XLI (1955), 359–364, is fully aware of the relationship.

community which is subcultural. When he enters the public school system, he brings with him a speech tool which, like all speech instruments, has been perfectly adequate for that community in which he has lived and moved; it has been sufficient to express anything that he may have wished to say, and in this respect, it has been as good as any linguistic instrument anywhere. It is the language of his family and his friends, a language having structural features in common with all other dialects of American English but having its own phonemic, morphemic, lexical features, and grammar in sufficient quantity to set it apart from other dialects.

In an essay of this length, even if I had made a full formal analysis of Maryland Negro folk speech, there would not be space to present a full description of it. I can here only suggest some features which characterize the speech and set it apart from other dialects. From this introduction perhaps there will arise a complete analysis by someone with the time, energy, and the money to undertake one. Some seven of the prominent phonemic features of Negro folk speech in Maryland are:

/r/	lost in postvocalic positions.
/i/	in unstressed syllables of *careless*, etc., and in stressed syllables of *sister, dinner, scissor*, etc.
/u/	in *home*.
/o/	in *poor, your, court*, etc., coupled with lost /r/.
/æ/	becomes /aey/ in *can't*.
/æ/	becomes /ey/ in *Mary*, etc.
/a/	sometimes in *put*.
/aw/	before voiceless consonants in *house, out*, etc.

These are only some of the segmental phonemes, and they should be thought of in connection with a group of supra-segmental phonemes largely used as voice-qualifiers to indicate the degree of the speaker's emotional involvement in the matter of his discourse. These supra-segmental phonemes are completely uninvestigated as far as I am aware, and no phonemic symbols have been devised for their representation.

In morphology and syntax the most salient features of Maryland Negro folk speech seems to be in connection with verb forms, being shown largely in the loss of the third singular morpheme [3] and in uninflected preterites. Singulars of the third person are indicated through subject forms and an abnormal redundancy of traditional English is eliminated in folk speech. "He eat a lot" is perfectly clear because the third singular is in the pronoun; the third singular morpheme of the verb appears to be a redundancy in this construction. Past forms are expressed in folk speech through temporal adverbs rather than through inflected verbs, as in "He come up to me yesterday and he say, . . ."

[3] Winifred E. Jones of the American Language Institute at Georgetown University, Washington, D.C., has expressed the view that the third singular morpheme seems to be vanishing from verbs in general American speech.

Verb forms, however, are likely to be inflected when temporal adverbs are not used, for inflected forms are used to distinguish preterite from perfect forms, especially since third form verbs (gone, been, seen, etc.) are likely to appear without auxiliaries, except in negative structures where the general auxiliary is "ain't," as in "I ain't seen him." The loss of the auxiliary in positive perfect structures arises from syncopated reductions of normal speech in a pattern like "He has seen it" becomes "He's seen it" becomes "He seen it." In this pattern the normal conversational reduction of the auxiliary to /z/ places it in the same category as the third singular morpheme, the loss of which we have already seen as a feature of folk speech. Since positive perfect forms appear without auxiliaries, it is necessary to inflict positive preterite forms used without temporal adverbs, and in Negro folk speech "I saw it somewhere" and "I seen it somewhere" are contrastive constructions rather than free variations or distributions.

Finally, lexical elements show a major difference from traditional or so-called standard vocabulary. Speech is a cultural phenomenon, and it is in lexicon that Negro folk speech shows how culturally centered it is. People always talk about those things which are most important in their culture, and the widest area of separation between folk speech and middle class English is that which touches food, personal grooming (most in connection with hair and complexions), race, and any other area where the socio-cultural distance is great. Folk foods have a vocabulary meriting its own Escoffier and *Larousse Gastronomique.* Hair styles, the equipment for their preparation, and the range of complexions are lexical mazes for the outsider. Race relations, both in-group and out-group, have produced a vocabulary of astounding proportions.

However, neither in phonemic, morphemic, nor lexical elements are there any features of Negro folk speech in Maryland which are exclusively the property of the Negro folk community; it is the combination of these elements appearing among large segments of the Negro population which justifies discussing them as one dialect and classifying that dialect as a subgroup of American English. The problems which the existence of such a subgroup cause for both the student and the teacher are manifold. The teacher needs to know something of the nature of the linguistic community from which the student derives so that, to the extent that it can be done, the teacher can establish a series of phonemic, morphemic, and lexical correspondences between the dialect which the student has and the one which the teacher wishes to introduce. The teacher needs also to approach the dialect of the student in a sense of humility, recognizing the difference between the student's language and the linguistic instrument of the classroom, but not necessarily the superiority of one over the other. Finally, the student needs to be aware of the varying nature of speech communities and recognize that, for a time at least, he has to function in two of them, two which are different from each other but not superior or inferior the one to the other. This approach to language might improve the understanding of speech and make the business of translating speech into writing, as difficult as it is under normal circumstances, more intelligible if not simpler.

But What's a Dictionary For?

Bergen Evans

The storm of abuse in the popular press that greeted the appearance of *Webster's Third New International Dictionary* is a curious phenomenon. Never has a scholarly work of this stature been attacked with such un-bridled fury and contempt. An article in the *Atlantic* viewed it as a "disappointment," a "shock," a "calamity," "a scandal and a disaster." The New York *Times*, in a special editorial, felt that the work would "ac-celerate the deterioration" of the language and sternly accused the editors of betraying a public trust. The *Journal* of the American Bar Association saw the publication as "deplorable," "a flagrant example of lexicographic irresponsibility," "a serious blow to the cause of good English." *Life* called it "a nonword deluge," "monstrous," "abominable," and "a cause for dis-may." They doubted that "Lincoln could have modelled his Gettysburg Address" on it—a concept of how things get written that throws very little light on Lincoln but a great deal on *Life*.

What underlies all this sound and fury? Is the claim of the G. & C. Merriam Company, probably the world's greatest dictionary maker, that the preparation of the work cost $3.5 million, that it required the efforts of three hundred scholars over a period of twenty-seven years, working on the largest collection of citations ever assembled in any language—is all this a fraud, a hoax?

So monstrous a discrepancy in evaluation requires us to examine basic principles. Just what's a dictionary for? What does it propose to do? What does the common reader go to a dictionary to find? What has the purchaser of a dictionary a right to expect for his money?

Before we look at basic principles, it is necessary to interpose two brief statements. The first of these is that a dictionary is concerned with words. Some dictionaries give various kinds of other useful information. Some have tables of weights and measures on the flyleaves. Some list

FROM the *Atlantic Monthly*, CCIX (May 1962), 57–62, copyright © 1962 by The Atlantic Monthly Company, Boston, Mass. Reprinted with the permission of the *Atlantic Monthly* and Bergen Evans.

historical events, and some, home remedies. And there's nothing wrong with their so doing. But the great increase in our vocabulary in the past three decades compels all dictionaries to make more efficient use of their space. And if something must be eliminated, it is sensible to throw out these extraneous things and stick to words.

Yet wild wails arose. The *Saturday Review* lamented that one can no longer find the goddess Astarte under a separate heading—though they point out that a genus of mollusks named after the goddess is included! They seemed to feel that out of sheer perversity the editors of the dictionary stooped to mollusks while ignoring goddesses and that, in some way, this typifies modern lexicography. Mr. Wilson Follet, folletizing (his mental processes demand some special designation) in the *Atlantic,* cried out in horror that one is not even able to learn from the Third International "that the Virgin was Mary the mother of Jesus"!

The second brief statement is that there has been even more progress in the making of dictionaries in the past thiry years than there has been in the making of automobiles. The difference, for example, between the much-touted Second International (1934) and the much-clouted Third International (1961) is not like the difference between yearly models but like the difference between the horse and buggy and the automobile. Between the appearance of these two editions a whole new science related to the making of dictionaries, the science of descriptive linguistics, has come into being.

Modern linguistics gets its charter from Leonard Bloomfield's *Language* (1933). Bloomfield, for thirteen years professor of Germanic philology at the University of Chicago and for nine years professor of linguistics at Yale, was one of those inseminating scholars who can't be relegated to any department and don't dream of accepting established categories and procedures just because they're established. He was as much an anthropologist as a linguist, and his concepts of language were shaped not by Strunk's *Elements of Style* but by his knowledge of Cree Indian dialects.

The broad general findings of the new science are:

1. All languages are systems of human conventions, not systems of natural laws. The first—and essential—step in the study of any language is observing and setting down precisely what happens when native speakers speak it.
2. Each language is unique in its pronunciation, grammar, and vocabulary. It cannot be described in terms of logic or of some theoretical, ideal language. It cannot be described in terms of any other language, or even in terms of its own past.
3. All languages are dynamic rather than static, and hence a "rule" in any language can only be a statement of contemporary practice. Change is constant—and normal.

4. "Correctness" can rest only upon usage, for the simple reason that there is nothing else for it to rest on. And all usage is relative.

From these propositions it follows that a dictionary is good only insofar as it is a comprehensive and accurate description of current usage. And to be comprehensive it must include some indication of social and regional associations.

New dictionaries are needed because English has changed more in the past two generations than at any other time in its history. It has had to adapt to exraordinary cultural and technological changes, two world wars, unparalleled changes in transportation and communication, and unprecedented movements of populations.

More subtly, but pervasively, it has changed under the influence of mass education and the growth of democracy. As written English is used by increasing millions and for more reasons than ever before, the language has become more utilitarian and more informal. Every publication in America today includes pages that would appear, to the purist of forty years ago, unbuttoned gibberish. Not that they are; they simply show that you can't hold the language of one generation up as a model for the next.

It's not that you mustn't. You *can't.* For example, in the issue in which *Life* stated editorially that it would follow the Second International, there were over forty words, constructions, and meanings which are in the Third International but not in the Second. The issue of the New York *Times* which hailed the Second International as the authority to which it would adhere and the Third International as a scandal and a betrayal which it would reject used one hundred and fifty-three separate words, phrases, and constructions which are listed in the Third International but not in the Second and nineteen others which are condemned in the Second. Many of them are used many times, more than three hundred such uses in all. The Washington *Post,* in an editorial captioned "Keep Your Old Websters," says, in the first sentence, "don't throw it way," and in the second, "hang on to it." But the old Webster's labels *don't* "colloquial" and doesn't include "hang on to," in this sense, at all.

In short, all of these publications are written in the language that the Third International describes, even the very editorials which scorn it. And this is no coincidence, because the Third International isn't setting up any new standards at all; it is simply describing what *Life,* the Washington *Post* and the New York *Times* are doing. Much of the dictionary's material comes from these very publications, the *Times,* in particular, furnishing more of its illustrative quotations than any other newspaper.

And the papers have no choice. No journal or periodical could sell a single issue today if it restricted itself to the American language of twenty-eight years ago. It couldn't discuss half the things we are interested in, and its style would seem stiff and cumbrous. If the editorials were serious, the public—and the stockholders—have reason to be grateful that the writers on these publications are more literate than the editors.

And so back to our questions: what's a dictionary for, and how, in 1962, can it best do what it ought to do? The demands are simple. The common reader turns to a dictionary for information about the spelling, pronunciation, meaning, and proper use of words. He wants to know what is current and respectable. But he wants—and has a right to—the truth, the full truth. And the full truth about any language, and especially about American English today, is that there are many areas in which certainty is impossible and simplification is misleading.

Even in so settled a matter as spelling, a dictionary cannot always be absolute. *Theater* is correct, but so is *theatre*. And so are *traveled* and *travelled, plow* and *plough, catalog* and *catalogue,* and scores of other variants. The reader may want a single certainty. He may have taken an unyielding position in an argument, he may have wagered in support of his conviction and may demand that the dictionary "settle" the matter. But neither his vanity nor his purse is any concern of the dictionary's; it must record the facts. And the fact here is that there are many words in our language which may be spelled, with equal correctness, in either of two ways.

So with pronunciation. A citizen listening to his radio might notice that James B. Conant, Bernard Baruch, and Dwight D. Eisenhower pronounce *economics* as ECKuhnomiks, while A. Whitney Griswold, Adlai Stevenson, and Herbert Hoover pronounce it EEKuhnomiks. He turns to the dictionary to see which of the two pronunciations is "right" and finds that they are both acceptable.

Has he been betrayed? Has the dictionary abdicated its responsibility? Should it say that one *must* speak like the president of Harvard or like the president of Yale, like the thirty-first President of the United States or like the thirty-fourth? Surely it's none of its business to make a choice. Not because of the distinction of these particular speakers; lexicography, like God, is no respecter of persons. But because so widespread and con-spicuous a use of two pronunciations among people of this elevation shows that there *are* two pronunciations. Their speaking establishes the fact which the dictionary must record.

Among the "enormities" with which *Life* taxes the Third International is its listing of "the common mispronunciation" *heighth*. That it is labeled a "dialectal variant" seems, somehow, to compound the felony. But one hears the word so pronounced, and if one professes to give a full acount of American English in the 1960s, one has to take some cognizance of it. All people do not possess *Life's* intuitive perception that the word is so "monstrous" that even to list it as a dialect variation is to merit scorn. Among these, by the way, was John Milton, who, in one of the greatest passages in all literature, besought the Holy Spirit to raise him to the "highth" of his great argument. And even the *Oxford English Dictionary* is so benighted as to list it, in full boldface, right alongside of *Height* as a variant that has been in the language since at least 1290.

Now there are still, apparently, millions of Americans who retain, in this as in much else, some of the speech of Milton. This particular pronunciation seems to be receding, but the *American Dialect Dictionary* still records instances of it from almost every state on the Eastern seaboard and notes that it is heard from older people and "occasionally in educated speech," "common with good speakers," "general," "widespread."

Under these circumstances, what is a dictionary to do? Since millions speak the word this way, the pronunciation can't be ignored. Since it has been in use as long as we have any record of English and since it has been used by the greatest writers, it can't be described as substandard or slang. But it is heard now only in certain localities. That makes it a dialectal pronunciation, and an honest dictionary will list it as such. What else can it do? Should it do?

The average purchaser of a dictionary uses it most often, probably, to find out what a word "means." As a reader, he wants to know what an author intended to convey. As a speaker or writer, he wants to know what a word will convey to his auditors. And this, too, is complex, subtle, and forever changing.

An illustration is furnished by an editorial in the Washington *Post* (January 17, 1962). After a ringing appeal to those who "love truth and accuracy" and the usual bombinations about "abdication of authority" and "barbarism," the editorial charges the Third International with "pretentious and obscure verbosity" and specifically instances its definition of "so simple an object as a door."

The definition reads:

a movable piece of firm material or a structure supported usu. along one side and swinging on pivots or hinges, sliding along a groove, rolling up and down, revolving as one of four leaves, or folding like an accordion by means of which an opening may be closed or kept open for passage into or out of a building, room, or other covered enclosure or a car, airplane, elevator, or other vehicle.

Then follows a series of special meanings, each particularly defined and, where necessary, illustrated by a quotation.

Since, aside from roaring and admonishing the "gentlemen from Springfield" that "accuracy and brevity are virtues," the *Post's* editorial fails to explain what is wrong with the definition, we can only infer from "so simple" a thing that the writer takes the plain, downright, man-in-the-street attitude that a door is a door and any damn fool knows that.

But if so, he has walked into one of lexicography's biggest booby traps: the belief that the obvious is easy to define. Whereas the opposite is true. Anyone can give a fair description of the strange, the new, or the unique. It's the commonplace, the habitual, that challenges definition, for its very commonness compels us to define it in uncommon terms. Dr. Johnson was ridiculed on just this score when his dictionary appeared in 1755. For two hundred years his definition of a network as "any thing reticulated or decussated, at equal distances, with interstices between the intersections" has been good for a laugh. But in the merriment one thing is always overlooked: no one has yet come up with a better definition! Subsequent dictionaries defined it as a mesh and then defined a mesh as a network. That's simple, all right.

Anyone who attempts sincerely to state what the word *door* means in the United States of America today can't take refuge in a log cabin. There has been an enormous proliferation of closing and demarking devices and structures in the past twenty years, and anyone who tries to thread his way through the many meanings now included under *door* may have to sacrifice brevity to accuracy and even have to employ words that a limited vocabulary may find obscure.

Is the entrance to a tent a door, for instance? And what of the thing that seals the exit of an airplane? Is this a door? Or what of those sheets and jets of air that are now being used, in place of old-fashioned oak and hinges, to screen entrances and exits. Are they doors? And what of those accordion-like things that set off various sections of many modern apartments? The fine print in the lease takes it for granted that they are doors and that spaces demarked by them are rooms—and the rent is computed on the number of rooms.

Was I gypped by the landlord when he called the folding contraption that shuts off my kitchen a door? I go to the Second International, which the editor of the *Post* urges me to use in preference to the Third International. Here I find that a door is

> The movable frame or barrier of boards, or other material, usually turning on hinges or pivots or sliding, by which an entranceway into a house or apartment is closed and opened; also, a similar part of a piece of furniture, as in a cabinet or bookcase.

This is only forty-six words, but though it includes the cellar door, it excludes the barn door and the accordion-like thing.

So I go on to the Third International. I see at once that the new definition is longer. But I'm looking for accuracy, and if I must sacrifice brevity to get it, then I must. And, sure enough, in the definition which raised the *Post's* blood pressure, I find the words "folding like an accordion." The thing *is* a door, and my landlord is using the word in one of its currently accepted meanings.

We don't turn to a work of reference merely for confirmation. We all have words in our vocabularies which we have misunderstood, and to come on the true meaning of one of these words is quite a shock. All our complacency and self-esteem rise to oppose the discovery. But eventually we must accept the humiliation and laugh it off as best we can.

Some, often those who have set themselves up as authorities, stick to their error and charge the dictionary with being in a conspiracy against them. They are sure that their meaning is the only "right" one. And when the dictionary doesn't bear them out they complain about "permissive" attitudes instead of correcting their mistake.

The New York *Times* and the *Saturday Review* both regarded as contemptibly "permissive" the fact that one meaning of one word was illustrated by a quotation from Polly Adler. But a rudimentary knowledge of the development of any language would have told them that the under-world has been a far more active force in shaping and enriching speech than all the synods that have ever convened. Their attitude is like that of the patriot who canceled his subscription to the *Dictionary of American Biography* when he discovered that the very first volume included Bene-dict Arnold!

The ultimate of "permissiveness," singled out by almost every critic for special scorn, was the inclusion in the Third International of *finalize*. It was this, more than any other one thing, that was given as the reason for sticking to the good old Second International—that "peerless authority on American English," as the *Times* called it. But if it was such an au-thority, why didn't they look into it? They would have found *finalize* if they had.

And why shouldn't it be there? It exists. It's been recorded for two generations. Millions employ it every day. Two Presidents of the United States—men of widely differing cultural backgrounds—have used it in formal statements. And so has the Secretary-General of the United Na-tions, a man of unusual linguistic attainment. It isn't permitting the word but omitting it that would break faith with the reader. Because it is exactly the sort of word we want information about.

To list it as substandard would be to imply that it is used solely by the ignorant and the illiterate. But this would be a misrepresentation: Presi-dent Kennedy and U Thant are highly educated men, and both are articu-late and literate. It isn't even a freak form. On the contrary, it is a classic example of a regular process of development in English, a process which has given us such thoroughly accepted words as *generalize, minimize, formalize,* and *verbalize.* Nor can it be dismissed on logical grounds or on the ground that it is a mere duplication of *complete.* It says something that *complete* doesn't say and says it in a way that is significant in the modern bureaucratic world: one usually *completes* something which he has initiated but *finalizes* the work of others.

One is free to dislike the word. I don't like it. But the editor of a dictionary has to examine the evidence for a word's existence and seek it in context to get, as clearly and closely as he can, the exact meaning that it conveys to those who use it. And if it is widely used by well-edu-cated, literate, reputable people, he must list it as a standard word. He is not compiling a volume of his own prejudices.

An individual's use of his native tongue is the surest index to his position within his community. And those who turn to a dictionary expect from it some statement of the current status of a word or a grammatical construction. And it is with the failure to assume this function that modern lexicography has been most fiercely charged. The charge is based on a naïve assumption that simple labels can be attached in all instances. But they can't. Some words are standard in some constructions and not in others. There may be as many shades of status as of meaning, and modern lexicography instead of abdicating this function has fulfilled it to a degree utterly unknown to earlier dictionaries.

Consider the word *fetch,* meaning to "go get and bring to." Until recently a standard word of full dignity ("Fetch me, I pray thee, a little water in a vessel"—I Kings 17:10), it has become slightly tainted. Perhaps the command latent in it is resented as undemocratic. Or maybe its use in training dogs to retrieve has made some people feel that it is an undignified word to apply to human beings. But, whatever the reason, there is a growing uncertainty about its status, and hence it is the sort of word that conscientious people look up in a dictionary.

Will they find it labeled "good" or "bad"? Neither, of course, because either applied indiscriminately would be untrue. The Third International lists nineteen different meanings of the verb *to fetch.* Of these some are labeled "dialectal," some "chiefly dialectal," some "obsolete," one "chiefly Scottish," and two "not in formal use." The primary meaning—"to go after and bring back"—is not labeled and hence can be accepted as standard, accepted with the more assurance because the many shades of labeling show us that the word's status has been carefully considered.

On grammatical questions the Third International tries to be equally exact and thorough. Sometimes a construction is listed without comment, meaning that in the opinion of the editors it is unquestionably respectable. Sometimes a construction carries the comment "used by speakers and writers on all educational levels though disapproved by some grammarians." Or the comment may be "used in substandard speech and formerly also by reputable writers." Or "less often in standard than in substandard speech." Or simply "dial."

And this very accurate reporting is based on evidence which is presented for our examination. One may feel that the evidence is inadequate or that the evaluation of it is erroneous. But surely, in the face of classification so much more elaborate and careful than any known heretofore, one cannot fly into a rage and insist that the dictionary is "out to destroy . . . every vestige of linguistic punctilio . . . every criterion for distinguishing between better usages and worse."

Words, as we have said, are continually shifting their meanings and connotations and hence their status. A word which has dignity, say, in the vocabulary of an older person may go down in other people's estimation. Like *fetch.* The older speaker is not likely to be aware of this and will probably be inclined to ascribe the snickers of the young man at his speech to that degeneration of manners which every generation has deplored in its juniors. But a word which is coming up in the scale—like *jazz*, say, or, more recently, *crap*—will strike his ear at once. We are much more aware of offenses given us than of those we give. And if he turns to a dictionary and finds the offending word listed as standard—or even listed, apparently—his response is likely to be an outburst of indignation.

But the dictionary can neither snicker nor fulminate. It records. It will offend many, no doubt, to find the expression *wise up*, meaning to inform or to become informed, listed in the Third International with no restricting label. To my aging ears it still sounds like slang. But the evidence—quotations from the *Kiplinger Washington Letter* and the *Wall Street Journal* —convinces me that it is I who am out of step, lagging behind. If such publications have taken to using *wise up* in serious contexts, with no punctuational indication of irregularity, then it is obviously respectable. And finding it so listed and supported, I can only say that it's nice to be informed and sigh to realize that I am becoming an old fogy. But, of course, I don't have to use it (and I'll be damned if I will! "Let them smile, as I do now, At the old forsaken bough Where I cling").

In part, the trouble is due to the fact that there is no standard for standard. Ideas of what is proper to use in serious, dignified speech and writing are changing—and with breathtaking rapidity. This is one of the major facts of contemporary American English. But it is no more the dictionary's business to oppose this process than to speed it up.

Even in our standard speech some words are more dignified and some more informal than others, and dictionaries have tried to guide us through these uncertainties by marking certain words and constructions as "colloquial," meaning "inappropriate in a formal situation." But this distinction, in the opinion of most scholars, has done more harm than good. It has created the notion that these particular words are inferior, when actually they might be the best possible words in an informal statement. And so— to the rage of many reviewers—the Third International has dropped this label. Not all labels, as angrily charged, but only this one out of a score. And the doing so may have been an error, but it certainly didn't constitute "betrayal" or "abandoning of all distinctions." It was intended to end a certain confusion.

In all the finer shades of meaning, of which the status of a word is only one, the user is on his own, whether he likes it or not. Despite *Life's* artless assumption about the Gettysburg Address, nothing worth writing is written *from* a dictionary. The dictionary, rather, comes along afterwards and describes what *has been* written.

Words in themselves are not dignified, or silly, or wise, or malicious. But they can be used in dignified, silly, wise, or malicious ways by dignified, silly, wise, or malicious people. *Egghead*, for example, is a perfectly legitimate word, as legitimate as *highbrow* or *long-haired*. But there is something very wrong and very undignified, by civilized standards, in a belligerent dislike for intelligence and education. *Yak* is an amusing word for persistent chatter. Anyone could say, 'We were just yakking over a cup of coffee," with no harm to his dignity. But to call a Supreme Court decision *yakking* is to be vulgarly insulting and so, undignified. Again, there's nothing wrong with *confab* when it's appropriate. But when the work of a great research project, employing hundreds of distinguished scholars over several decades and involving the honor of one of the greatest publishing houses in the world, is described as *confabbing* (as the New York *Times* editorially described the preparation of the Third International), the use of this particular word asserts that the lexicographers had merely sat around and talked idly. And the statement becomes undignified—if not, indeed, slanderous.

The lack of dignity in such statements is not in words, nor in the dictionaries that list them, but in the hostility that deliberately seeks this tone of expression. And in expressing itself the hostility frequently shows that those who are expressing it don't know how to use a dictionary. Most of the reviewers seem unable to read the Third International and unwilling to read the Second.

The *American Bar Association Journal,* for instance, in a typical outburst ("a deplorable abdication of responsibility"), picked out for special scorn the inclusion in the Third International of the word *irregardless.* "As far as the new Webster's is concerned," said the *Journal,* "this meaningless verbal bastard is just as legitimate as any other word in the dictionary." Thirty seconds spent in examining the book they were so roundly condemning would have shown them that in it *irregardless* is labeled "nonstand"—which means "nonstandard," which means "not conforming to the usage generally characteristic of educated native speakers of the language." Is that "just as legitimate as any other word in the dictionary"?

The most disturbing fact of all is that the editors of a dozen of the most influential publications in America today are under the impression that *authoritative* must mean *authoritarian.* Even the "permissive" Third International doesn't recognize this identification—editors' attitudes being not yet, fortunately, those of the American people. But the Fourth International may have to.

The new dictionary may have many faults. Nothing that tries to meet an ever-changing situation over a terrain as vast as contemporary English can hope to be free of them. And much in it is open to honest, and informed, disagreement. There can be linguistic objection to the eradication of proper names. The removal of guides to pronunciation from the foot of every page may not have been worth the valuable space it saved. The new method of defining words of many meanings has disadvantages as well as advantages. And of the half million or more definitions, hundreds, possibly thousands, may seem inadequate or imprecise. To some (of whom

I am one) the omission of the label "colloquial" will seem meritorious; to others it will seem a loss.

But one thing is certain: anyone who solemnly announces in the year 1962 that he will be guided in matters of English usage by a dictionary published in 1934 is talking ignorant and pretentious nonsense.

Bi-Dialectalism: The Linguistics of White Supremacy

James Sledd

Because people who rarely talk together will talk differently, differences in speech tell what groups a man belongs to. He uses them to claim and proclaim his identity, and society uses them to keep him under control. The person who talks right, as we do, is one of us. The person who talks wrong is an outsider, strange and suspicious, and we must make him feel inferior if we can. That is one purpose of education. In a school system run like ours by white businessmen, instruction in the mother tongue includes formal initiation into the linguistic prejudices of the middle class.

Making children who talk wrong get right with the world has traditionally been the work of English teachers, and more recently of teachers of that strange conglomerate subject which we call speech. The English teacher in the role of linguistic censor was once a kind of folk heroine (or anti-heroine), the Miss Fidditch of the linguists' diatribes. Miss Fidditch believed in taking a strong stand. It never occurred to her that her main job was making the lower classes feel so low that they would try to climb higher. Instead, Miss Fidditch taught generations of schoolchildren, including future linguists, to avoid *ain't* and double negatives and *used to could* and *hadn't ought*, not because *ain't* would keep them from getting ahead in the world, but because *ain't* was wrong, no matter who used it, and deserved no encouragement from decent people who valued the English language. She did her job all the better for thinking that she was doing something else.

Miss Fidditch is not popular any longer among educators. Though the world at large is still inclined to agree with her, the vulgarizers of linguistics drove her out of the academic fashion years ago, when they replaced her misguided idealism with open-eyed hypocrisy. To the popular linguists, one kind of English is as good as another, and judgments to the contrary are only folklore; but since the object of life in the U.S.A. is for everybody to get ahead of everybody else, and since linguistic prejudice can keep a man from moving up to Schlitz, the linguists still teach that people who want to be decision-makers had better talk and write like the people who make decisions. The schools must therefore continue to cultivate the linguistic insecurity which is already a national characteristic but must teach the youngsters to manipulate that as they manipulate everything else; for neither Miss Fidditch's dream of a language intrinsically good, nor a humbler ideal of realizing the various potentialities of the existing language in its responsible use, can get in the way of the citizenry in its upward anguish through the pecking order. The linguists think that people who do knowingly what Miss Fidditch did in her innocence, will do it more efficiently, as if eating the apple made a skilled worker out of Eve.

As long as most people agreed that up is toward Schlitz and another TV set, and as long as they could pretend that every American eaglet can soar to those great heights, Fidditch McFidditch the dialectologist could enforce the speech-taboos of the great white middle class without complaint: either the child learned the taboos and observed them, or he was systematically penalized. But the damage done to the Wasps' nest by World War II made difficulties. People who talked all wrong, and especially black people, began to ask for their share of the loot in a world that had given them an argument by calling itself free, while a minority of the people who talked right began to bad-mouth respectability and joined the blacks in arguing that it was time for a real change. Some black people burned up the black parts of town, and some students made study impossible at the universities, and in general there was a Crisis. Optimists even talked of a revolution.

The predictable response of the frightened white businessman's society was to go right on doing what it had done before—which had caused the crisis—but to do it harder and to spend more money at it. Education was no exception. Government and the foundations began to spray money over the academic landscape like liquid fertilizer, and the professional societies began to bray and paw at the rich new grass. In that proud hour, any teacher who could dream up an expensive scheme for keeping things as they were while pretending to make a change was sure of becoming the director of a project or a center and of flying first-class to Washington twice a month. The white businessman strengthened his control of the educational system while giving the impression of vast humanitarian activity.

Black English provided the most lucrative new industry for white linguists, who found the mother lode when they discovered the interesting locutions which the less protected employ to the detriment of their chances for upward mobility. In the annals of free enterprise, the early sixties will be memorable for the invention of functional bi-dialectalism, a scheme best described by an elderly and unregenerate Southern dame as "turning black trash into white trash." Despite some signs of wear, this cloak for white supremacy has kept its shape for almost a decade now, and it is best described in the inimitable words of those who made it. Otherwise the description might be dismissed as a malicious caricature.

The basic assumption of bi-dialectalism is that the prejudices of middle-class whites cannot be changed but must be accepted and indeed enforced on lesser breeds. Upward mobility, it is assumed, is the end of education, but white power will deny upward mobility to speakers of black English, who must therefore be made to talk white English in their contacts with the white world.

An adequate florilegium may be assembled from a volume entitled *Social Dialects and Language Learning* (NCTE, 1964), the proceedings of a conference of bi-dialectalists which was held in 1964. William A. Stewart of the Center for Applied Linguistics begins the chorus (p. 13) by observing among our educators "a commendable desire to emphasize the potential of the Negro to be identical to white Americans"—a desire which is apparently not overwhelming, however, among the Black Muslims or among the young men who have enjoyed pot-shooting policemen for the past few summers. Editor Roger W. Shuy next speaks up (p. 53) for social climbing by our American Indians, who have been notably reluctant, throughout their unfortunate association with their conquerors, to adopt our conquering ways. Our linguistic studies, Shuy remarks in the purest accents of fidditchery, "should reveal those elements, both in speech and writing, which prevent Indians from attaining the social status which, with socially acceptable language, they might otherwise attain." A similar desire to be at peace with status-holders is suggested (p. 66) by Ruth I. Golden, who opines that "a human being wants most of all to be recognized as an individual, to be accepted, and to be approved." Since Southern speech brings "negative reactions when heard by employers in Detroit," where Dr. Golden labors in the schools, she devotes herself to stamping out /i/ for /e/ in *penny* and to restoring /l/ in *help* (pp. 63 f.).

An admirable scholar from New York, William Labov, then agrees (p. 88) that "recognition of an external standard of correctness is an inevitable accompaniment of upward social aspirations and upward social mobility," and advises that people who (like Jesus) prefer not to take excessive thought for the morrow can probably be made to. In Labov's own words, "since the homes of many lower class and working people do not provide the pressures toward upward social mobility that middle-class homes provide," and since adults in those lower reaches are sometimes resistant to middle-class values, we must "build into the community a tolerance for style shifting which is helpful in educational and occupational advancement," and we must build into the children, "starting from a level not much above the nursery school and going on through high school, a tolerance for practice in second role playing" (pp. 94–97, 104).

Presumably Labov sees nothing wrong in thus initiating children into the world of hypercorrection, insecurity, and "linguistic self-hatred" which marks, as he has said elsewhere, "the average New Yorker" (*The Social Stratification of English in New York City*, Center for Applied Linguistics, 1966, Chapter XIII); and Charles Ferguson, the eminent ex-director of the Center for Applied Linguistics, is equally confident of *his* right and duty to remake his fellow men in his directorial image. Talking about the Negroes in our Northern cities, Ferguson says that "we have to face a rather difficult decision as to whether we want to make these people bi-dialectal . . . [please to remark Ferguson's choice of verbs] or whether we want . . . to impose some kind of standard English on these people and to eradicate the kind of substandard English they speak" (p. 116). To cite another NCTE volume (*Language Programs for the Disadvantaged* [NCTE, 1965], p. 222), if the black children of the ghetto "do not learn a second kind of dialect, they will be forever prevented from access to economic opportunity and social acceptance." Middle-class white prejudice will rule eternally.

The bi-dialectalists, of course, would not be so popular with government and the foundations if they spoke openly of the supremacy of white prejudice; but they make it perfectly clear that what they are dealing with deserves no better name. No dialect, they keep repeating, is better than any other—yet poor and ignorant children must change theirs unless they want to stay poor and ignorant. When an NCTE "Task Force" set out to devise *Language Programs for the Disadvantaged* (NCTE, 1965), it laid down a perfect smoke screen of such hypocrisy, as one would expect from persons who felt called upon to inform the world that "without the experience of literature, the individual is denied the very dignity that makes him human" (p. v) but that not "all disadvantaged children are apathetic or dull" (pp. 24 f.).

"In this report" (p. 117), "teachers are asked to begin by accepting the dialect of their students for what it is, one form of oral communication. . . ." Teachers are warned particularly that they "need to accept the language which Negro children bring to school, to recognize that it is a perfectly appropriate vehicle for communicating ideas in the Negro home and subculture" (p. 215), that it is "essentially respectable and good" (p. 227). But though teachers must not attack "the dialect which children associate with their homes and their identity as Negroes" (p. 215), they must still use all the adult authority of the school to "teach standard informal English as a second dialect" (p. 137), because the youngster who cannot speak standard informal English "will not be able to get certain kinds of jobs" (p. 228).

The most common result of such teaching will be that white middle-class Midwestern speech will be imposed as mandatory for all those situations which middle-class white businessmen think it worth their while to regulate. In the words of Chicago's Professors Austin and McDavid (p. 245), "future educational programs should be developed in terms of substituting for the grammatical system of lower-class Southern speech [read: black Chicago speech] that of middle-class Chicago white speech —at least for those economic and social situations where grammatical norms are important." Labov goes so far as to ask (*Social Dialects and Language Learning*, p. 102) whether Northern schools should tolerate Southern speech at all—whether they should not also correct the "culti-vated Southern speech" of privileged children who move North.

The description of compulsory bi-dialectalism may be completed by examining the methods which its proponents advocate for perpetuating the supremacy of white prejudice. Essentially, those methods are derived by analogy from structuralist methods of teaching foreign languages— methods whose superiority has been claimed but never demonstrated and whose intellectual foundations vanished with the demise of struc-turalist ideas. As an eminent grammarian privately observed after a recent conference, "The achievements of the operators will continue to lie in the field of getting and spending government money. . . . They seem to have an unerring instinct for finding ways of spending it unprofitably—on con-ferences at which they listen to each other, for example. Now they're out to teach standard English as a second dialect through techniques that have served very poorly in teaching second languages."

High on the list of those techniques is incessant drill on inessentials. In theory, the drills are the end-product of a long process of systematic com-parison of the children's nonstandard dialects with the standard dialect which they are to be taught; but since the systematic comparisons have never been made, the bi-dialectalists fall back on a simple enumeration of a few dozen "features of pronunciation, grammar, and vocabulary which can be considered indices of social stratification" (Roger Shuy, "Detroit Speech," in A. L. Davis, ed., *On the Dialects of Children*, p. 13). Professor Rudolph Troike of the University of Texas was thus simply platitudinizing piously when he told the TESOL convention in 1968 that "any instructional program . . . must begin with as full an *objective* knowledge as possible" of both or all the dialects involved. The escape hatch in Troike's statement is the phrase *as full as possible*. What is usually possible is an unsystematic list of shibboleths—the simplification of consonant clusters, the Southern pronunciations of *walk* and *right*, *ax* for *ask*, the dropping of post-vocalic /r/, *ain't* and *fixin'*, to *bofe* and *mouf* for *both* and *mouth*, and the like. These innocent usages, which are as familiar as the sun in the late Confederacy, are apparently the terror of Northern employers, who the bi-dialectalists assume are almost suicidally uncon-cerned with such details as character, intelligence, and training for the job. The fact is, of course, that Northern employers and labor leaders dislike black faces but use black English as an excuse.

Having established, however, that a child of darkness under her tutelage says *mouf*, the pretty white lady sets out to rescue his soul. First she plays tapes of Southern speech to convince her victims, who understand Southern speech far better than they understand hers, that Southern speech often makes "complete understanding of content . . . difficult," "not readily comprehensible"—as is demonstrated by the fact that the pretty white lady would never have detected her victim's four-letter word just by listening and without watching his lips (New York Board of Education, *Nonstandard Dialect*, pp. 1, 14, 17). The difficulty of detecting him is all the more reason for fearing the iniquitous *mouf*-sayer: it proves he is a cunning devil who probably says *dentissoffice* too and who perpetrates such subversive "malapropisms" as "The food in the lunch room is not fitting to eat" (*On the Dialects of Children*, p. 23). How else *would* he spell *fitten?* But for such a hardened rogue, a good many "motivational activities" are likely to be necessary before the pretty white lady can really start twisting the thumbscrew with her drills.

Yet the drills are available, and the pretty white lady will use them when she sees her time. She has drills of all kinds—repetition drills, substitution drills, replacement drills, conversion drills, cued answer drills, the reading in unison of long lists of words like *teeth / reef, toothbrush / waffle, bathtub / alphabet, weather / weaver*. To get rid of *dentissoffice* she may have students debate such propositions as "Ghosts do exist" or "Formal school tests should be eliminated"; and before a really "culminating activity" like playing "Pack the Trunk" she may "divide the class into consonant-cluster committees to seek out words containing" clusters like *sks, sps,* or *kt* (*Nonstandard Dialect, passim*). At this point the class might be invited to suggest a context for a replacement drill—maybe something like "Teacher! teacher! Billy Joe say that Tommy ———— Bessy!" This last suggestion, it must be confessed, has not yet been made in the literature, but it seems considerably more stimulating than choral recitation of Poe's "Bells" (*ibid.*, p. 35).

Perhaps it need not be added that existing tests and evaluations of such "instructional materials" are something of a farce. If bi-dialectalism is really harder to acquire than bilingualism (Einar Haugen in *Social Dialects and Language Learning*, p. 125), teachers and texts ought surely to be superb, and judgments on them ought to be severe; but New York City's curriculum developers can give "highest priority" to making the children change *a* to *an* before nouns beginning with a vowel (*Nonstandard Dialect*, p. 14), and Texas' Professor Troike can argue the success of his methods by showing that after six months of drills a little black girl could repeat *his hat* after her teacher, instead of translating automatically to *he hat*. Unfortunately, tapes do not record psychological damage, or compare the effectiveness of other ways of teaching, or show what might better have been learned in the same time instead of learning to repeat *his hat*.

So much for a description of mandatory bi-dialectalism, a bit enlivened (since the subject is dreary) by irreverent comment, but not distorted in any essential way. In the U.S.A., we are being told, everybody wants approval—not approval for doing anything worth approving, but approval for doing whatever happens to be approved. Because approval goes to upward mobility, everybody should be upwardly mobile; and because upward mobility is impossible for underdogs who have not learned middle-dog barking, we must teach it to them for use in their excursions into the middle-dog world. There is no possibility either that the present middle class can be brought to tolerate lower-class English or that upward mobility, as a national aspiration, will be questioned. Those are the pillars on which the state is built, and the compassionate teacher, knowing the ways of his society, will change the color of his students' vowels although he cannot change the color of their skins.

It is not at all certain that the bi-dialectalists, for all their absurdities, can be dislodged from their well-carpeted offices. They are supported by the National Council of Teachers of English, the Modern Language Association of America, the Center for Applied Linguistics, the federal government, the foundations, the governments of a number of major cities, and by black people who have made it into the middle class and so despise their origins and their less efficient fellows. In the best of times our top dogs are pleased by docility, if not mobility, among the beasts below; and in 1969 a new ice age is beginning. Newspaper headlines tell us that the Department of Health, Education, and Welfare has been urged to relax its requirements for desegregation of schools immediately but quietly, and President Nixon loses his Miami tan at the thought that militant students will "politicize" our universities—as if government grants to upwardly mobile faculty had not politicized them long ago. In Lyndon Johnson's Texas the citizens of Austin vote down an open housing law, their board of education then justifies segregated schooling by the established pattern of segregated housing, and the governor of the state praises the state university as the source of brain-power to assist the businessman in the lucrative exploitation of what the governor proudly calls the "insatiable appetite" of Texans. The only revolution we are likely to see is the continued subversion, by the dominant white businessman, of the political and religious principles on which the nation was founded.

Yet though the times are bad, they are not hopeless, at least not in the small, undramatic world of English education; and the bi-dialectalists are so gorgeously absurd that the breath of laughter may collapse their card-house if only enough people can be brought to see it as it is. It is not simply quixotic, then, to add to a laughing description of imposed bi-dialectalism a more serious statement of reasons why it cannot succeed and should not be tolerated even if it could—a statement which can lead, in conclusion, to the proposing of an alternative policy.

The argument that bi-dialectalism cannot be forced is easy to make out, even, in part, from the reluctant admissions of some of its proponents. Two principal reasons have already been suggested, the ignorance and unproved methods of the bi-dialectalists. The term *ignorance* is used literally, and in all fairness. Whatever one thinks of teaching standard English by methods like those for teaching foreign languages, contrastive analyses of our different dialects are a prerequisite—but a prerequisite which has not yet been supplied. Until very recently, the principal sources of information were the collections for the *Linguistic Atlas;* but they are unsystematic, partially out-of-date, and in some respects inaccurate and superficial. Where, for example, should one go for descriptions of intonation and its dialectal variants, for accurate accounts of the system or systems of verbal auxiliaries, for analyses of the speech of ghetto children instead of rustic ancients? Such minimal essentials are simply lacking. In fact, it might be said that for all the talk about revolutionary advances in linguistics, neither the structural nor the generative grammarians have yet produced a satisfactory basic description of even standard English.

The best descriptions of all our kinds of English would still not be enough to make coercive bi-dialectalism a success. The English teacher's forty-five minutes a day for five days in the week will never counteract the influence, and sometimes the hostility, of playmates and friends and family during much the larger part of the student's time. Formal education could produce real bi-dialectals only in a vast system of state nurseries and boarding schools to which the children of the poor and ignorant would be consigned at an early age; but such establishments would be prohibitively expensive, intolerable to the people, and still not absolutely certain of success, because the most essential of all conditions might not be met—namely, the desire of the children to talk like the white middle class.

When one thinks about it in these realistic terms, the whole argument about bi-dialectalism begins to look schizophrenic, as out-of-this-world as an argument whether Lee should surrender at Appomattox or fight back. There is no evidence that the bi-dialectalists, if they actually had good textbooks, better teachers, and as much money as the country is spending to devastate Vietnam, would really know what to do with those fictional resources. Instead of clear ideas, they offer clichés, like the familiar attacks on "traditional methods and approaches" or the protected pedagogue's arrogant assurance that illiterates can have no human dignity. They fly off quickly into high-sounding vaguenesses, talking (for example) about "differences in social dialect and associated versions of reality" (*Social Dialects and Language Learning,* p. 68), as if metaphysics rested on a preconsonantal /r/. At their most precise, they suggest the prudential avoidance of Southern pronunciations of *walk* and *cough* in Washington because Negroes there look down on new arrivals from Georgia and the Carolinas. They happily assume what they should prove—that intensive training in "standard informal English as a second dialect" has produced or can produce large numbers of psychologically undamaged bi-dialectals, whose new accomplishment has won them or will win them jobs that otherwise would have been impossible for them to get. When their guard is down, the bi-dialectalists actually confess that they *have* no concrete program, since "no one program at any level yet seems applicable to a significant number of other classes at the respective level" (*Language Programs for the Disadvantaged*, pp. 30 ff.).

Some awareness of their difficulties, and some uncertainty about priorities, seem indeed to be spreading among the bi-dialectalists (though it would be too much to hope that if their present bandwagon falls apart they will consider themselves discredited and resign their membership in the Society of Mandarin). For one thing, they have become aware of the significance of reading, which William A. Stewart, as late as 1964, could reduce to the level of "socially desirable embellishments" (*Social Dialects and Language Learning*, p. 10). In his latest book, however, *Teaching Black Children to Read*, Editor Shuy announces "the simple truth that speaking standard English, however desirable it may be, is not as important as learning to read" (p. 118). His colleagues Walter A. Wolfram and Ralph W. Fasold are even closer to enlightenment. In the same new volume (p. 143), they hesitantly admit that "there is some question about the degree to which Standard English can be taught to the ghetto child in the classroom at all"; and Fasold meant what he said, for he had said it before at the Milwaukee convention of the NCTE. Though that august body was still congratulating itself on its concern with "a language component for the so-called culturally divergent," it had to bear with Fasold's embarrassing confession: 'Because of the operation of social forces in the use of language," he said, "forces which are only poorly understood, it may not be possible to teach Standard English as a second language to Black English speaking children unless they are interacting with Standard English speakers in a meaningful way outside the classroom" (*Convention Concerns—1968*, p. 10). The Center's linguistician came as close as standard English would allow to saying that it is segregation which makes black people talk different and that there would be no slum children if there were no slums.

No doubt the most important of Fasold's poorly understood social forces is one which everybody but white linguists has understood for a long time: black people may just not want to talk white English. Several years ago, Labov observed that some of his more rebellious New York subjects were deliberately turning away from social-climbing New York speech toward a black Southern model (*Social Dialects and Language Learning*, pp. 96 f.), and today comment on "the new feeling of racial pride among black Americans" (*Teaching Black Children to Read*, p. 142) is a platitude. Wolfram and Fasold go on to the quite unsurprising speculation that that pride may even extend to the Negro's speech. "If a realization develops that this dialect, an important part of black culture, is as distinctively Afro-American as anything in the culture, the result may well be a new respect for Black English within the community" (p. 143). More plainly, condescending middle-class white charity is not wanted any more, if it ever was, in language-teaching or anywhere else. We should learn from the example of the British: the social cataclysm of the Second World War, and the achievement of political power by labor, did more to give the "disadvantaged" English youngster an equal chance than charitable bi-dialectalism ever did. We are past the stage when white teachers, whether Africans or Caucasians, can think well of themselves for trying to turn black people into uneasy imitations of the whites.

The immorality of that effort is the chief reason why enforced bi-dialectalism should not be tolerated even if it were possible. Predators can and do use dialect differences to exploit and oppress, because ordinary people can be made to doubt their own value and to accept subservience if they can be made to despise the speech of their fathers. Obligatory bi-dialectalism for minorities is only another mode of exploitation, another way of making blacks behave as whites would like them to. It is unnecessary for communication, since the ability to understand other dialects is easily attained, as the black child shows when she translates her teacher's prissy white model "*his* hat" into "*he* hat." Its psychological consequences are likely to be nervous affectation, self-distrust, dislike for everyone not equally afflicted with the itch to get ahead, and eventual frustration by the discovery that the reward for so much suffering is intolerably small. At best the altered student will get a somewhat better job and will move up a few places in the rat-race of the underlings. At worst he will be cut off from other blacks, still not accepted among whites, and economically no better off than he was before.

White teachers should hope, then, that their black students will be recalcitrant, so that bi-dialectalism as a unilateral condition for employment can be forgotten. It would make better sense, if pedagogues insist on living in a fantasy world, to require whites to speak black English in their dealings with blacks, since the whites have more advantages than the blacks and consider themselves more intelligent; or perhaps we should be hard-headedly consistent in our brutalities and try to eradicate the vices which really do enrage employers—like intellectual questioning, or the suspicion that ours is not the best of possible worlds.

Indeed, the educationists' faith in education would be touching if it were not their way of keeping up their wages. Nothing the schools can do about black English or white English either will do much for racial peace and social justice as long as the black and white worlds are separate and hostile. The measure of our educational absurdity is the necessity of saying once again that regimented bi-dialectalism is no substitute for sweeping social change—*necessity* being defined by the alternative of dropping out and waiting quietly for destruction if the white businessman continues to have his way.

The reply that the educational system should not be politicized is impossible for bi-dialectalists, since bi-dialectalism is itself a political instrument. They may purge themselves of inconsistency, and do what little good is possible for English teachers as political reformers, if instead of teaching standard English as a second dialect they teach getting out of Vietnam, getting out of the missile race, and stopping the deadly pollution of the one world we have, as horribly exemplified by the current vandalism in Alaska.

One use for a small fraction of the resources that would thus be saved would be to improve the teaching of the English language. Bi-dialectalism would never have been invented if our society were not divided into the dominant white majority and the exploited minorities. Children should be taught that. They should be taught the relations between group differences and speech differences, and the good and bad uses of speech differences by groups and by individuals. The teaching would require a more serious study of grammar, lexicography, dialectology, and linguistic history than our educational system now provides—require it at least of prospective English teachers.

In the immediate present, the time and money now wasted on bi-dialectalism should be spent on teaching the children of the minorities to read. Already some of the universal experts among the linguists have boarded this new bandwagon, and the next round of government grants may very well be for programs in reading and writing in black English. That might be a good thing, particularly if we could somehow get rid of the tired little clique of operators who have run the professional societies of English teachers for so long. Anyway, the direct attack on minority language, the attempt to compel bi-dialectalism, should be abandoned for an attempt to open the minds and enhance the lives of the poor and ignorant. At the same time, every attempt should be made to teach the majority to understand the life and language of the oppressed. Linguistic change is the effect and not the cause of social change. If the majority can rid itself of its prejudices, and if the minorities can get or be given an education, differences between dialects are unlikely to hurt anybody much.

(The phoniest objections to this proposal will be those that talk about social realism, about the necessity for doing something even—or should one say particularly?—if it's wrong. That kind of talk makes real change impossible, but makes money for bi-dialectalists.)

Questions

1. How do the news stories from the *Washington Post* about the "two languages" spoken by Washington Negroes contribute to the problem of defining "good" and "bad" English?

2. What does Evans think a dictionary is for? How does his position relate to dialects, standard English, slang?

3. What is the difference between a descriptive approach to putting a dictionary together and a prescriptive one? Which of these approaches would you argue for? Why? What is the position of Evans? Of Jones?

4. What is the strongest point made by Evans? By Jones? By Shearer? Do you agree or disagree with any of these? Why?

5. How does Evans demonstrate his point that "The difference . . . between the much-touted Second International (1934) and the much-clouted Third International (1961) is . . . like the difference between the horse and buggy and the automobile. Between the appearance of these two editions a whole new science related to the making of dictionaries, the science of descriptive linquistics, has come into being"? How would you suggest making a dictionary more current than those that now exist? What words would you like to see in the dictionary (use *Webster's Third* if possible) that are not there?

6. Should there be a *separate* dictionary of "soul language" or should soul language be included in *any* general dictionary of English?

7. Is the argument that a word exists a good one to justify inclusion of that word in a dictionary? Should *ain't* and *irregardless* be listed in a dictionary? If not, why not? If so, how would you list them? In trying to answer these questions, consult several recently published dictionaries to see how these words are listed.

8. Should you refuse to use a dictionary because it contains words that you do not like? Why do you suppose that *Webster's Third* offended so many people and so strongly? Are *you* offended?

Assignments

1. Make up a list of a half dozen words not in *Webster's Third* that are widely used in polite discourse today. These words may be technical ones from an occupation or a profession, new slang expressions, combinations of familiar words, or familiar words used in a new sense or in a sense not recorded by the dictionary. Define these words in the manner of *Webster's Third* and quote contexts in which each appears in the sense defined.

2. Find out what lexicography Bergen Evans himself has done. Look at this work in the library and write an analysis of one aspect of it.

3. Describe the nature and purpose of one of the various unabridged dictionaries to be found in the reference room of your college library. Relate it to a specialized dictionary or glossary, say, one on slang.

4. Compare the entries for the word *money* in a desk dictionary, in *Webster's Second*, in *Webster's Third,* and in the *Oxford English Dictionary*. Which entry is the fullest? Why? In what specific ways do the several entries differ from one another? How do you account for these differences? Write a definition of *money* in your own words that would be understood by a child who has not yet entered elementary school. Do the same with the words *Negro* and *black* (as related to a person).

5. Describe in some detail how *you* would go about putting together a dictionary. Justify your procedure in terms of the materials here.

6. Look up *soul* and *dictionary* in a good standard dictionary. Discuss the adequacy of the definitions in the light of the materials here.

7. Write a comparison between a foreign and an English dictionary.

Additional Reading

Following the publication of *Webster's Third*, in 1961, a vigorous, heated, and almost always controversial debate broke out in newspapers and magazines regarding not only the merits of *Webster's Third* as opposed to those of the earlier editions of the *New International*, but also the whole purpose of a dictionary. Many of these articles, editorials, and essays may be found in *Dictionaries and That Dictionary*, edited by James Sledd and Wilma R. Evans (Chicago, 1962). One of the strongest attacks was that made by Jacques Barzun, "What Is a Dictionary?" *American Scholar*, XXXII (Spring 1963), 176–181. Comments on Barzun's article may be found in the *American Scholar*, XXXII (Autumn, 1963), 604–608. Another by now famous attack is that by Dwight Macdonald, "The String Unturned," originally published in *The New Yorker* (March 10, 1962), and again in his collection, *Against the American Grain* (New York, 1962). Interesting material on how a dictionary is put together may be found in *Young Sam Johnson*, by James L. Clifford (New York, 1955), and in Johnson's preface to his dictionary, as well as in the introduction to *Webster's Second* and *Third*. Allan Walter Read, in "That Dictionary or The Dictionary?" *Consumer Reports*, XXVIII (October, 1963), 488–492, surveys the problems, the shortcomings, and the achievements of *Webster's Third*, with some reference to other unabridged dictionaries.

What Difference Does It All Make?

I returned, and saw under the sun, that the race is
not to the swift, nor the battle to the strong, neither
yet bread to the wise, nor yet riches to men of
understanding, nor yet favor to men of skill;
but time and chance happeneth to them all.

Ecclesiastes, 9:11

Race, Culture, and Intelligence

Anthony Barnett

A problem that arouses a good deal of emotion is: how does a person's physical type affect his intellect and moral qualities? About 700 years ago an African was writing in the Spanish town of Toledo. He described the Europeans living to the north of him like this: "They are of cold temperament, and never reach maturity. They are of great stature and of a white colour. But they lack all sharpness of wit and penetration of intellect." At that time, north Africans were leaders of the western world. Their science, especially, was at a high level.

At all times men have had theories about the differences between human groups. Usually the people of one nation believe that they are better than anyone else. If they happen, at the time, to have conquered some other nation, they think this is a good reason for looking down on the people they have conquered. People who say that one "race" or nation is superior to another, also usually imply that the difference is permanent. They seem to think that each nation—the Japanese, say—has a national character: and that character remains the same throughout history. But you need only a little common sense, and some simple history, to refute this. The Japanese are a good example. In the first 1100 years of their recorded history they waged only one war abroad; and that ended in 1598. A hundred and twenty years ago, anyone might have thought that the Japanese were thorough-going pacifists; but since 1853 they have fought five major wars outside their own country.

The English are another example. The chronicles of a thousand years ago show the English as a collection of blood-thirsty savages. But their descendants, in the Middle Ages, developed a stable, orderly society; and, incidentally, they produced some fine architecture. (I wish we could do as well today.) These facts show that human behaviour is changeable, with time. We do not always know what causes the change. The Japanese began fighting wars when trade and other communications were opened. The English became more civilized, perhaps, because of influences from the continent of Europe. Whatever the explanation, we know that nations do change their ways as a result of factors outside the peoples concerned. This is not surprising. Nations are made up of individuals; and individuals are much affected, in their behaviour, by the way they are brought up.

FROM *The Listener*, June 25, 1964. Reprinted with the permission of Anthony Barnett and *The Listener*.

You or I are not merely products of our heredity; we are also moulded by our environment. This is obvious for some things: if I had been brought up, say, in Mexico, I should be able to speak Spanish; but, as it is, I cannot.

Let us look more closely at the effects of heredity and environment on human characteristics; and especially at the so-called "racial" characters. There are some human characters which clearly owe more to heredity than to environment: skin colour and hair-form are obvious examples. These differences—and a few others—have a geographical distribution. On the whole, dark skins are usual near the tropics; light-coloured skins are typical of peoples living in cold and temperate climates. In primitive conditions it is an advantage to have a dark skin in the tropics: it protects the sensitive tissues underneath from the sun. But colour, hair-form, and facial features, though easily seen, are literally superficial. Today they are in themselves of no social importance. The kind of hair you have does not make you a good or bad farmer, or a good or bad doctor; it does not help you, or hinder you, in becoming a skilled metal worker. The important characters are the ones that influence the various kinds of ability; and also those that affect moral behaviour.

MEASURING INTELLECTUAL ABILITY. The first thing to notice about them is that it is difficult to measure intellectual ability or moral worth. Consider intellectual ability first: for that we have the so-called intelligence tests. These tests measure one aspect of ability, but only in a rough and ready way; and, unfortunately, we have nothing better at the moment. The first important facts about "race" and "intelligence" were collected in the first world war. Every recruit to the American Army had to do an intelligence test. And, in each State, the Negroes scored, on the average, less than the whites. Some whites probably thought that this was evidence that the Negroes were "naturally inferior," or something of that sort. But there were big differences in the averages between the different States. For instance, Arkansas, in the south of the United States, had very poor schools, both for whites and for Negroes; and there even the whites did badly in the tests. But in Ohio, where the schools were much better, both Negroes and whites had quite high scores. In fact, in Ohio, Negroes had higher scores, on the average, than whites in Arkansas.

The explanation of these facts was obvious: differences in average scores reflected differences in schooling. Negroes did worse than the whites of their own State, because Negroes usually did not have such good schools. To be sure that this is correct, we need to know what happens when Negroes and whites are educated together and given exactly the same opportunities. Naturally this means that they must have the same sort of housing, the same sort of health services, the same sort of food, and so on. It would not do if one group lived in slums, while the other lived in a new and well-designed town. In fact, in the United States, there is hardly ever—as yet—this complete mingling of the two groups; but in spite of this, in New York City, for instance, whites and Negroes have been found to have the same average score in intelligence tests. And in one inquiry, in Los Angeles, the Negro children in the schools scored slightly higher.

ENVIRONMENT AND INTELLIGENCE TESTS. The obvious conclusion, then, is that differences between large groups of people, in intelligence test scores, depend on differences between the environments in which they are brought up. They do not tell us anything clear about the heredity of intelligence. Moreover, there is no connection between skin colour, or type of hair, and intelligence.

I must emphasize that I have been discussing differences between large groups. If one takes any one group and studies the individuals in it, one finds great differences in ability. And these differences are not all determined by environment. There are clever Chinese and stupid ones; clever Frenchmen and stupid Frenchmen, and so on. Each nation, and each race, has its quota of different types.

What about other abilities? We have no figures for them, except of athletic achievements; and they do not give averages, but only the figures for champions. But the Olympic games show that medals can be won by people from all countries. Much depends on how well the athletes are trained and encouraged.

It is even more difficult to find hard facts about moral qualities. If somebody says, for example, that Americans are morally superior to Italians, how can you find out whether it is true? For one thing, you have to decide which moral qualities you are talking about. However, once again there are *some* hard facts. Some of them come from Massachusetts, early in this century, when many Europeans were emigrating to America, to settle there. Some comparisons were made of the amount of crime in different immigrant groups, and in native-born Americans. Immigrants from Italy were found to be much more liable to commit murder or assault than the American-born people—more than seven times more likely, in fact. But what about the children of these immigrants? Did they in some way inherit this tendency? Not at all: their tendency to crimes of violence was exactly the same as among the Americans whose families had been in the country for generations.

Similar changes were found in Irish immigrants. The ones who had been brought up in Ireland were rather violent, like the Italians; but they were never convicted of rape; and they seldom got into trouble for gambling. But their children tended to resemble the ordinary Americans: they were less violent, but more inclined to commit rape and to be convicted for gambling. I certainly ought to add that only a few people in any of these groups had committed crimes. But these were enough for the differences to be clear.

CULTURALLY DETERMINED BEHAVIOUR. We can now see what happens to each immigrant group: they tend to adopt, quickly, the American way of life. Their children's habits, like their language, depends on the environment in which they are brought up. As the anthropologists say, their behaviour is culturally determined; it does not depend on ancestry. This is just as well. After all, Australia was originally populated largely by convicts from English prisons; but today it is an advanced and law-abiding country.

This does not mean that we are all alike in our heredity. What it does mean is that differences between large groups in crime, as in intellectual ability, reflect differences of custom and education. And these differences can be quickly changed—even in a single generation. Any large group or nation can produce large numbers of criminals of various kinds; but, equally, it can produce a whole population that is law-abiding. The problem is to provide the most favourable conditions.

In view of all this, why should there be theories about the superiority of different nations or "races"? At the beginning I suggested that they often arise when one group has conquered another, and the conquered people is being exploited. Unfortunately, it is easy to persuade people to hate or despise others who look different, or speak differently, or have a slightly different religion. Wherever there is a mixed community, the remedy is obvious. The children must all be brought up together; and they must never be taught that one type of person is better or worse than another. When this is in fact done, it never occurs to children to worry about such trivial things as skin colour. They have much more interesting and important matters to concern them.

Every "race" or nation can produce good and bad individuals, intelligent and stupid, strong and weak. No group is naturally better or worse than others in any important way. Given the right conditions, each can make a contribution to the material and intellectual wealth of mankind.

The Mixed Marriage

D. R. Newth

The childless mixed marriage no doubt has its problems, but as a biologist I propose to ignore them now, in order to discuss the question of mis-

FROM *The Listener*, July 2, 1964. Reprinted with the permission of D. R. Newth and *The Listener*.

cegenation—the production of children by racial crossing. Many English words begin with the syllable "mis," and for most of them it is a rather sinister prefix converting the innocuous or praiseworthy deed, understanding, or alliance, into misdeeds, misunderstandings, or misalliances. I sometimes feel that the word miscegenation carries a little, wholly inappropriate, disapproval for just this reason. Actually, it means no more and no less than the mixture of races by interbreeding: the natural consequence of a mixed marriage.

How should we approach the mixed marriage? Should it invite approval or disapproval? Does miscegenation, in fact, carry with it consequences for good, or for evil, of which we should be informed? Clearly the biologist is involved in answering these questions, but equally clearly his involvement as a biologist is limited, though his interest as a human being may not be. So I want to begin by declaring a point of view, before discussing the present state of our knowledge of the purely biological effects of racial admixture. This will save me the trouble of repeated qualification and explanation of the social implications of what I later have to say.

My own point of view is that even if racial interbreeding were shown to have on balance slightly beneficial or slightly adverse biological effects on the parents or their offspring, I would not regard this as a sufficient reason for providing it with social rewards or social penalties of any sort. Even if its effects were slightly adverse, and it consequently saddled us with a biological or medical burden, this would only be one of many which we cheerfully bear in the interests of a civilized way of life.

But, you may ask, is it not cheating to talk of the possible adverse effects of miscegenation as slight? May they not be severe? It depends, among other things, on what constitutes severity, but before we consider the question in detail there are two general points to be borne in mind. The first is that we are ourselves so mixed up in ancestry that any serious charge against miscegenation can only be substantiated at the expense of our own self-esteem. Secondly, if, despite this, the adverse effects were really serious, we should expect them to be easily demonstrable. But no one has yet convinced biologists that miscegenation is, for biological reasons, to be feared. Of course, these two arguments are not in themselves conclusive. Because our ancestors came from different races it does not follow that we are well advised to interbreed. Many things in life which we now regard as serious hazards—cigarette smoking, for example—have only recently been convicted. Dangerous as we now believe them to be, the dangers were not so evident to the ordinary observer. So we must look at miscegenation more closely.

One thing the biologist will have in mind is experience with animals. We have, for example, races and strains of mice which can be bred within themselves or be cross-bred. It is almost always found that efforts to produce a highly inbred race of mice are made difficult by the relative weakliness and infertility that overcomes the stock after a few generations of inbreeding. The mice may recover from this phase to become a perfectly good going concern, and laboratories throughout the world are now maintaining numbers of different mouse strains, each so highly inbred that they show a genetical uniformity which approaches that obtained between so-called identical twins. But although these strains are going concerns, their individual members are usually smaller and shorter-lived than less highly inbred mice. Furthermore, the members of any one strain are alike in such respects as susceptibility to infectious disease. It follows that a crowded population of them is singularly at risk if only one mouse becomes seriously ill through infection. The moral for humanity might seem to be that racial purity is bad for you; but this is not a fair deduction because we are dealing here with a degree of racial purity that goes far beyond the wildest dreams of a professional racist and, indeed, could only be achieved in practice by generations of incestuous unions.

Yet it is not wholly academic to consider the danger of excessive racial purity because there is evidence that the elements from which it is constructed apply in man. For example, we know that the offspring of cousin marriages are more at risk in respect of certain rare genetic disorders than are the children of unrelated parents. Secondly, we do know of cases where a human population that has been semi-isolated from the rest of humanity for a long time has shown a disastrous sensitivity to infection. When Europeans took measles to the southern tip of South America they took a disease which killed off the Tierra del Fuegans at an appalling rate. In this and other similar cases an inherited, or genetic, basis for the susceptibility is suspected. Luckily, there is little reason to fear that future human populations will approach a dangerous level of genetic or racial uniformity. We have not proved our point, but only demonstrated that it is reasonable to suppose that humanity could be subject to the biological penalties of extreme racial purity.

HYBRID VIGOUR. As a contrast to this experience of breeding pure lines of animals, we must look at the result of crosses made between them. Here we come across a phenomenon of great interest theoretically, known as hybrid vigour. When inbred lines of animals are crossed, the offspring produced in the first generation are often biologically blessed with a stamina that neither of their parent stocks possessed. Such hybrid vigour is not fully understood, but it might be thought to hold out the promise of real, if temporary, advantages for human miscegenation. In fact, there is little reliable evidence that humanity can hope for much extra benefit from this source. I say extra, because although we need not doubt that man is capable of showing hybrid vigour—indeed, there is some direct evidence that he can—we have to face the fact that he is already making so much use of his genetic diversity that there is little more to exploit.

We see then that biological considerations do not lead us to a general approval or disapproval of the consequences of miscegenation, and that one of the main reasons for this is that human races have been so mixed up genetically in the past that further mixture is not likely to make much difference. But we must still ask two rather more searching questions. First, are there any known circumstances in which a marriage between two particular people can be predicted in advance to lead to offspring with favourable or unfavourable characteristics? If the answer to this question is "yes," we must go on to ask whether knowledge of a person's racial origin is ever a relevant circumstance in such predictions.

As it happens, the answer to the first question is "yes," even though we accept that the words "favourable" and "unfavourable" cannot be sensibly applied to many of the differences between human beings. For example, there are a number of fairly severe inherited defects known, in which the inheritance follows rules applicable to what is technically referred to as a Mendelian dominant. This means that we can expect half the offspring of most marriages in which one parent is affected to be affected too. Clearly such diseases will not usually be disastrously crippling, or the affected parent would not have survived to marry and reproduce. There are other cases where inheritance is called recessive; neither parent need be affected themselves, and their diagnosis as carriers then awaits the birth of the first defective child. One in four of their children on average will be affected, and some recessive conditions are so severe as to be incompatible with long survival. A good deal of attention has been paid to these inherited abnormalities, and to their incidence in European and American populations. For some of them significant differences between races may exist, but there is no reason to believe that any race is unfortunate in having a generally higher rate of all inherited disease. From this point of view it would at present appear probable that widespread miscegenation would cause, if anything, a temporary reduction in the over-all incidence of inherited disease.

RHESUS POSITIVE AND RHESUS NEGATIVE. There is, however, one category of disease that deserves special attention because it provides us with a model from which we can argue with some confidence. This is disease which results from incompatibility of the rhesus kind between mother and unborn child. In brief, a rhesus positive child born to a rhesus negative mother may suffer from a serious but now usually curable disease of the blood. A mother can only be rhesus negative if both of her parents were. A child can only be rhesus positive if one of its parents is too. Therefore a risk to a baby's health from this disease can only occur if a rhesus positive man breeds with a rhesus negative woman.

We know with some accuracy the incidence of these two possible conditions—rhesus positive and negative—in a number of large racial groups. For example, the mongoloids, who include the Chinese, are nearly all rhesus positive, and hence affected babies are almost unknown among them. But about sixteen per cent of Europeans are rhesus negative, hence such babies do occur in Europe, and can occur in mixed marriages between Chinese and Europeans. A Chinese man hesitating to choose between a European and a Chinese as a wife, and not knowing the blood group of either for certain, might feel that miscegenation carried a small risk, since if the European woman was one of sixteen per cent some of their younger children might require special medical attention at birth.

MISCEGENATION AND THE FUTURE OF HUMANITY. You may regard this as a fanciful example: so, in a sense, it is. Yet it is particularly meaningful for a discussion of the biology of race mixtures for two reasons. First, it is the only really good example known to us in which race is associated, however indirectly, with the physical wellbeing of the offspring of a human marriage. Secondly, it underlines an important truth—for though the Chinese runs a risk that his European wife may be rhesus negative, this same risk is run by eighty-four per cent of European husbands. Thus such hazards as racial crosses may involve are not biologically unique in kind. At most they raise the already existing chance of a defective child being born to a particular parent. But even when they do so, the overall burden to the human species is not necessarily increased.

Biologists, in other words, can bring a little knowledge to those interested in the consequences of mixed marriages, but no comfort to those who would like to find in biology only praise or only blame. Biologists have, indeed, a number of worries about the future of humanity: miscegenation is not one.

Bright Rats and Dull Rats

Herbert G. Birch

Recent statements by some eminent scientists have made it increasingly difficult to achieve a scientific approach to the serious problems of social and ethnic inequalities in opportunity, employment, and educational achievement. Statements such as "the Jukes-Kallikaks 'bad heredity' concept may have been too enthusiastically rejected by perfectionists," and meaningless pronouncements such as "Heredity controls intelligence more than twice as much as does environment in families that adopt one of a pair of white identical twins" add nothing but noise to our available information.

These statements, derived from a paper presented by an American Nobel laureate, William Shockley, must be disturbing to any serious scientist, not because they reflect an uncongenial set of social attitudes, but because they revive an outmoded but ever recurring dichotomy between nature and nurture. Any contemporary mode of thought concerning behavior and genetics which continuously fails to appreciate the functional inseparability of gene complex and environment in the development of phenotype is scientifically worthless. The importance of considering what it is that is most directly produced by a gene complex and a scrupulous reservation in judgment before assuming that gene and phenotype are directly related are particularly critical when applied to human intellectual development, a battleground on which competing social value systems—often uninformed yet uninformed in the laboratory smocks of science—have struggled long and to little avail. In this battle the most powerful weapon used by those who wish to argue that differences in intelligence among races are "inherited" has been evidence from animal studies interpreted to mean that learning ability is inherited. The study most often referred to is the monumental effort by Robert Choate Tryon to breed selectively animals who learned a maze well and animals who learned it poorly. In nine generations he was able to produce decidedly "bright" and "dull" strains. Usually the story stops here and the conclusion is drawn, as by Mr. Shockley that "similar rapid changes could occur for humans." Thus it is implied that this is in fact what has occurred and that certain "races" have selectively bred so as to produce people with low intelligence or a gene pool high in poor learners. Fortunately for mankind the usual end of Tryon's "bright" and "dull" rat story is not actually its conclusion but only its midde. It will be remembered that Tryon used an enclosed alley maze as the learning device for separating "bright" from "dull" rats. As later work suggests, such a task is learned primarily through the use of nonvisual cues. Was it possible, therefore, that Tryon was not breeding for "learning ability," "intelligence," "brightness" or "dullness," but for responsiveness to nonvisual cues? Animals which were so selected would work well in his mazes, whereas others, which were more visually responsive, would do poorly. Such an interpretation would lead to a prediction that if the task were changed to one in which responsiveness to visual information was critical the results would be reversed, with the formerly "bright" rats being "dull," and the formerly "dull" rats exhibiting a high level of learning ability.

Subsequent evidence produced in a study by Lloyd Searle well supports the preceding interpretation. On a 16-unit elevated maze, in which visual cues were the principal ones used for learning, Searle found the

Tryon "dull" rats to be more effective "learners" than the Tryon "bright" strain. These findings are entirely in accord with the results of experiments undertaken by John Fuller and William Thompson, who tested five dog breeds on several behavioral measures, several of which involved learning. On these tests they did, indeed, find differences between breeds, but different breeds appeared to be superior learners on different types of learning tasks. Moreover the sampling of behavior seemed to show "a greater spread between breed on motivational and emotional characters than on tests involving learning."

Perhaps the most ubiquitous difficulty in interpreting the data of behavioral genetics is that the genetics is sometimes sound but almost always the behavioral analysis is terribly poor. The end product of learning in a given maze or the mean differences between groups in scores on intelligence tests, mean little without serious efforts to determine what characteristics of the responding organism are involved in the mastery of the presented problems. The history of animal psychology provides many examples of this failure. In the 1920s when Robert Yerkes studied rats with a series of discrimination box measures, he concluded that a rat's visual system was incapable of making discrimination among shapes and that rats could merely discriminate relative brightness.

It was not until Karl Lashley approached the problem from the point of view of the hierarchical organization of the sensory responsiveness in the rat that the conclusion was shown to be totally erroneous. Lashley argued that in a given circumstance in which olfactory, tactile, kinesthetic, and visual cues were available, the rat as an organism tended to respond selectively to the stronger cues and not to the weaker. From this consideration it followed that to determine whether the rat had a given organization of visual competence required the elimination or minimization of competing cue systems and the examination of his visual functioning under optimal conditions. Lashley therefore placed his rats upon a very small and narrow jumping stand, and drawing upon his experience in the Alaskan regions—where as a child he had prospected for gold with his father—he caused the animals to jump at windows showing different geometric figures by snapping at them with a miniature dog whip. Under these conditions, with the aid of a cultural contribution from another region, Lashley was able to demonstrate an exceedingly high order of form discrimination in his rats.

These and other studies lead one to question whether the implications for genetic differences in learning capacity among human groups, which have been drawn from data far less adequate than those available to students of lower mammals, do not reflect a substitution of brashness for thought. If the data of behavioral genetics permit us to draw any conclusion with respect to learning ability it is that learning ability is by no means a unitary trait, that in different organisms different patterns of responsiveness, of motivation, of emotionality, and of antecedent history contribute substantially to determining which subgrouping will, in fact, learn most effectively under various conditions.

Sober judgment would, I think, lead us to conclude that differences in human learning abilities, whether measured by intelligence tests or by school achievement, represent the products of different degrees of goodness of fit among the learner, the task, and, in particular, the instructional mode for attaining mastery of the task at hand.

Racial Differences and Cultural Attitudes

Margaret Mead

The prevalence of positive or negative feelings about physique is a sign of which traits are valued and appreciated by a society or by the world community. Where there is conspicuous subordination of a social group on the basis of real or attributed physical features, the members of a subordinated group may come to repudiate their own physical characteristics and in mixed populations even penalize those individuals who manifest the disapproved characteristics to the most marked degree. The concept of negritude in Africa is an example of a vigorous attempt to reassert the primacy, for a given group, of its own physical type. We must recognize the rising demand for the kind of world in which people can enjoy the way they look, be proud of the way their parents looked, and look forward to the way their children will look.

What is most important for the immediate future is to substitute thinking about populations for thinking about typologies. This shift will, I believe, require considerable translation before it becomes part of the repertoire of lay thinking. Typologies assume genetic isolates in which all members of the given group display the same characteristics to the same extent. An isolated Eskimo with no biological mixture for 20 generations will be identifiable in many ways that make possible the construction of a type. Consider, however, what one knows if a person is characterized as a Baltimore Negro, a member of a group whose blood groups indicate that they average 70 per cent African descent. What would one be able to predict about him? His pigmentation? No, for he might be fairer than many Mediterranean people. His features? No, they might run from features that he shared with some West African tribe to features that

FROM the Columbia University *Forum,* Fall 1967, Volume X, Number 3, copyright © 1967 by The Trustees of Columbia University in the City of New York. Reprinted with the permission of the *Columbia Forum.*

might identify him, incorrectly, as from India. His speech? Yes; he could be predicted to speak some form of English, but it might be a rural southern dialect, unintelligible to a speaker of standard English, or it might be marked by a Harvard accent or a California accent or British West Indian accent. Such an exercise highlights the fact that we have placed some members of our population in a special category because of some single trait or cluster of physical traits when actually they should be thought of simply as part of the population of the United States. Negro Americans do constitute a partial Mendelian population because of preferential mating with one another, but this is enormously different from the condition of an isolated group of Eskimo, African desert dwellers, or inhabitants of isolated Pacific islands.

At the same time, groups of people classified as Negroes, Mexicans, and Amerindians have been placed in a position of imputed inferiority and have often come to accept it themselves. Earlier the same thing was done to groups of immigrants from southern and eastern Europe who had imputed to them "racial" characteristics that influenced learning capacities and potential for achievement. The 1921 immigration act reflected this set of racial stereotypes. The immigrant groups gradually advanced in the United States as their children obtained an American education and they themselves obtained political and economic power. In developing a strategy to improve the condition of Americans of mixed racial background we are up against a rather more complicated problem. The anti-integrationists cite the greater success of immigrants from self-consciously high cultures—the Japanese, the Chinese, and the Jews— who in spite of prejudice have demonstrated as high and often higher achievement levels than the Americans with whom they were compared. And certain leaders in the civil rights movement are demanding that American Negroes form themselves into power blocs, following the tradition of the Irish (who were originally subject to prejudice because of religion), the Italians, and the Poles.

Both these positions ignore the crucial difference that separates a minority thought of in terms of physique from one whose members can individually disappear into the general population as soon as they lose their distinguishing speech and other ethnic patterns of behavior. They also fail to take into account the difference between coming from a civilization older than the civilization of the western world and being the descendants of those who, at the time of contact, represented less complex cultures which were technologically overwhelmed. The Chinese, Japanese, and Jews were sustained by a sense of cultural superiority and difference, a high degree of endogamy, and the preservation of differences in behavior which served as breeding barriers and kept those who wished to act as members of minority groups together as groups.

The Negro American has no more cultural past than does the average white American whose ancestors have been in this country for eight or ten generations. He knows that some of his ancestors came from somewhere in Africa, as white Americans know or believe that all of their ancestors came from somewhere in Europe, but the majority of both groups, white and black alike, can actually draw only on American culture. The fact that European immigrants continued to come long after the slave trade was ended obscures this fact somewhat, but in contrast to those groups who have preserved a connection between biological descent, country of origin, and ethnic identity, white and Negro Americans stand together without the possibility of any legitimate pride except that which springs from their own achievements here. Invoking the history of Central African kingdoms to provide points of racial pride is as ridiculous as endowing the descendant of English or Western Europeans with the achievements of Mediterranean history.

Yet as Americans, Negroes in the United States have the precedent of groups who organized along ethnic lines and achieved political power, freedom from discrimination, and a place in the sun. Too much emphasis on the spurious nature of racial classification by anti-segregationists could backfire into emasculating the very necessary attempts to build up political responsibility, internal cohesion, and activism in Negro groups. So in giving careful biological definitions of strain, race and species, of Mendelian populations and breeding isolates, the responsible biologist must also be prepared to deal with contemporary social realities in the light of past social realities.

On Diversity and Equality

Theodosius Dobzhansky

Science aims to help man understand himself and his place in the universe. Yet man's efforts to know himself are often frustrated by his propensity to deceive himself. This propensity reaches its pinnacle where "sensitive" topics are involved. The topic of race is one of these; it elicits emotional, and often passionate reactions in many people.

Faced with this situation, what posture should a scientist adopt? Two extreme attitudes, opposite in sign, are equally unfortunate. One is to leave the whole problem in abeyance, because of the risk that scientific findings may be misinterpreted and misused. The other is a make-believe detachment, pretending that scientists need not be concerned about the

Reprinted from The Columbia University *Forum*, Spring 1967, Volume X, Number 1. Copyright © 1967 by The Trustees of Columbia University in the City of New York. Reprinted with the permission of the *Columbia Forum*.

uses and misuses of their discoveries. Both attitudes betray irresponsibility. Science is not a collection of random facts, however accurately observed. It is a human endeavor to sort out the significant from the trivial. The world in which we live is hungry for simple solutions to complex problems; complex problems may not have simple solutions, but they ought to have at least comprehensible ones.

In biology and anthropology, the concept, or construct, of race has two aspects. Race is a category of classification; it is also a biological phenomenon. This duality has profound philosophical and methodological roots. Classification is a necessity. Bronowski wrote that science is "the search to discover unity in the wild variety of nature—or more exactly, in the variety of our experience." Man's language is the oldest instrument to cope with this wild variety. By giving names to things, the variety is reduced to manageable proportions. There are more than three billion persons in the world today, nobody can know them all individually: it is necessary to group, to classify, to name them. If races did not exist they would have to be invented. Since they do exist they need not be invented, they need to be understood.

Some people have claimed that nothing new has been discovered for a long time about human races or about races in general. This is far off the mark, as is indicated by the newer race studies. The inhabitants of different parts of the world are often visibly different, and the differences are in part genetic. This, in a nutshell, is the esssence of race as a biological phenomenon. To be sure, any two persons, even brothers and sisters, also differ. Race differences are genetic differences between Mendelian populations, not between persons. And yet races differ in the same traits in which persons also differ. Difficulties arise because when a race, or any other group, is given a name one is apt to assume that individuals composing the group are alike or at least very similar. This is typological thinking, which befuddles not only the man in the street but some scientists as well. It has been rightly pointed out that the most important reform in biological conceptualization in recent years has been the abandonment of typological misconceptions.

Race differences are compounds of individual differences; they are more often relative than absolute; races differ in the frequencies of some genes more often than in that a certain gene is wholly absent in one race and present in every individual of another. This relativity, the lack of hard-and-fast dichotomies in race differences, is disappointing to the adherents of the old-fashioned typological race concepts. Curiously enough, it is also disappointing to some new-fashioned writers, who claim that since races are not airtight pigeonholes they do not exist at all; that the human species, mankind, has no races. I think this is the same old typological misconception turned inside out. If man has no races where are races to be found? And if they are nowhere found, why then are the inhabitants of different countries often recognizably different?

One may or may not like this "no-race" hypothesis, but the very fact that it has been seriously advocated shows the race concept is far from being a cut and dried subject. It is an open problem that needs further study.

One point must be made clear. Excepting identical twins, everybody is biologically, genetically, different from everybody else. Diversity should not however be confused with inequality. Equality and inequality are sociological, identity and diversity biological phenomena. Diversity is an observable fact, equality an ethical precept. Society may grant or withhold equality from its members, it could not make them genetically alike even if this were desirable.

Possible Genetic Bases of Social Problems: Two Views

Dwight J. Ingle

Introduction

Dogma now in fashion holds that average differences in biological endowment among the races are of no social significance. I criticize this view and give reasons why further research and debate is needed, especially in relationship to problems of many Negroes in America. Social actions extending beyond the aim to achieve equal rights and opportunities are taken on the basis of the dogma that races are equal in respect to the genetic bases of those traits that are important in human affairs. I characterize the view as dogma because it is taught as factual but fails to meet any of the requirements for proof of a proposition.

The following are guides to judging whether or not a proposition has been proven.

a. There should be a sound substructure of evidence which includes validation of the measures used.
b. It must explain the relevant facts; different lines of evidence should converge in support of the hypothesis.
c. The supporting evidence must be independently repeatable.
d. All alternative explanations must be excluded.
e. The explanation should permit prediction and control of the process under study.

These requirements, separately or together, do not establish certainty.

Reprinted with the permission of Dwight J. Ingle.

Moreover, it is almost impossible to comply with all of them. Proof is a relative matter.

Two Hypotheses

Current dogma is expressed in the report "The Negro Family," issued by the Office of Planning and Research of the United States Department of Labor: "There is absolutely no question of any genetic differential. Intelligence potential is distributed among Negro infants in the same proportion and pattern as among Icelanders or Chinese or any other group." This is believed by our political leaders and is taught in our schools and by the public press. It is a hypothesis only.

Many social scientists believe and teach that the organization of social action systems is learned and is based on biological structures which are commonly available among men and are independent of any genetic differences between groups. I believe that it was unsound strategy to link this dogma to the movement for civil rights and equal opportunities. The legal and moral support for social justice does not require the assumption of biological equality. This doctrine does have great appeal to the laity and to political leaders who at each election time promise the disadvantaged early solutions to their problems.

I regard the following hypothesis as plausible and probable but unproven. It is that *the average differences between people called white and people called Negro, in respect to genetic potentialities for the development of abilities, are sufficient to cause social problems to regenerate in any modern competitive environment.* Poor genetic endowment can cause poor achievement, hence poverty, hence poor environment, hence frustration, hence antisocial behavior that engenders bias. Once poor environment and racial prejudice have generated, individuals of good abilities can also be trapped by them. The circular interplay between poor genetic endowment, poor culture and prejudice can cause spiraling problems that are no longer dependent upon original causes for self-perpetuation and ingravescence which characterize social malignancy. I do not imply that all social malignancy has a genetic basis; it is pluricausal and the same end can be reached by more than one pathway.

There are other hypotheses such as the racist beliefs that all whites are genetically superior to all Negroes and the view that all Negroes are genetically superior to all whites. The hypothesis that on the average, Negroes are superior to whites in genetic bases of mental abilities has not been disproven. Since Asians achieve as well or better than whites in America I shall not discuss white-Asian differences.

Importance of the Issue

a. Both racists and those who practice reverse racism seek to place individuals in schools, jobs, and housing on the basis of racial identity rather than abilities, interests, drives, behavioral standards, and the assumption of duties. Social actions extending far beyond equal civil rights and opportunities are taken on the basis of the assumption that all causes of Negro problems are environmental.

b. Some social reformers urge the interbreeding of the races as a means of solving racial conflict. This biological proposal should not be encouraged until it is known with certainty that it carries no risk to the future of man.

c. One necessary means to true equality for the Negro may be biological, i.e., by positive and negative eugenics or by biological engineering when effective means are developed.

Characteristics of Races

Racial groups are of mixed origins, and no trait is found exclusively in one race. The range of individual differences within a group is far greater than average group differences. However, genes that are important in human affairs may not be randomly distributed among racial groups. Each race has certain genes and gene combinations that are more frequent in it than elsewhere, but not confined to it.

There is overlap in the abilities, drives, and successes of whites and Negroes. But the average school, test, and job performance of Negroes is much poorer than that of whites. Performance on objective tests indicates that 11 to 15 per cent of Negroes in the United States reach or exceed the average of whites.

Evidence for Biological Equality

a. A few studies on simple sensorimotor tests show that the Negro child performs as well as or better than the white child. Such tests do not measure intelligence. The young of some other primates are superior to human infants in simple motor learning.

b. It is claimed that programs of preschool training and school enrichment abolish Negro-white differences in test performance. Seldom are representative groups of whites and Negroes compared in the same program. Performance on tests of either physical or mental abilities can generally be improved by training and increased motivation. Unless the results are favorable, they are unlikely to be reported. The children are sometimes volunteers or those judged most likely to profit by special training. There may be further selection when dropouts and absentees are excluded at retesting. The identity of the pupil is not always recorded, although needed for test-retest comparison.

Is improvement due to extra motivation, coaching, practice, or accrued test wisdom? Does the improvement endure? Is the child permanently improved in respect to other achievements based on ability to reason? I am not aware of any properly designed study which has compared Negro and white children before, during and after identical preschool programs. It is common to compare the performance of Negroes with compensatory training to standards of white students without compensatory training. There are no controlled studies which exclude experimenter effects on the subjects and experimenter bias by automated teaching, testing, and scoring. After study of compensatory education, the United States Commission on Civil Rights concluded that "none of the programs appear to have raised significantly the achievement of participating pupils, as a group, within the period evaluated by the Commission."

c. It is claimed that social discrimination and segregation are detrimental to the test performance and achievement of Negroes. This hypothesis may be true but it is supported by post hoc reasoning only and fails to explain why Asians and Jews, once subjects of discrimination, perform and achieve as well as or better than other ethnic groups. Differences in social organization and parent-child relationships between Asians, Jews, and Negroes may be much more important.

d. During World War I Negro recruits from certain northern states did better on the average than did white recruits from certain southern states. Selective migration may have been one cause of regional differences. The performance of northern whites was superior to that of northern Negroes and the performance of southern whites was superior to that of southern Negroes. Nationwide, only fourteen per cent of Negro recruits did as well as the average white recruit. Two facts were unmentioned. The data represented recruits; the percentage of Negroes unqualified for recruitment and excluded from comparison was far higher than for whites. Currently, about 67 per cent of Negroes fail psychological tests for induction and about 19 per cent of whites fail the tests. Also, a higher percentage of whites from southern states became commissioned officers than from northern states, the percentage of whites from both regions greatly exceeding the colored. The test scores of officers were not included in the bulk of the Army data. Little is said of test data from World War II and from the Korean War, for the overlap of state averages for northern Negro recruits and those of some southern states has either decreased or disappeared despite major advances in civil rights, environment, and educational opportunities for the Negro. Relevant is the finding of the Coleman Report that the highest regional average test scores for Negro children were below the lowest average regional test scores for white children.

e. Robert Rosenthal of Harvard University found that school children are responsive to teacher expectations. It is postulated that differences in the expectations of teachers for the performance of white and Negro pupils can account for the achievement gap. The hypothesis merits penetrating studies.

f. In a few, not all, studies in which Negro and white children were matched for socioeconomic background, the differences in school achievement and test performance were insignificant. There is an error of logic in the claim that such studies prove that environment alone has caused the Negro-white differences. Performance on tests and cultural and socioeconomic background are inter-related because all depend on intelligence. A sample that is selected in respect to one variable will also be selected in respect to the other two.

The results of Project Talent show a strong tendency for average scores on aptitude and achievement tests to decrease as the percentage of Negroes in schools increases. This was true in all geographic areas and among schools in low, medium, and high quality housing areas. In studies done in Berkeley, California by Arthur R. Jensen, the children of professional and managerial Negro fathers averaged about 15 IQ points lower than white children whose fathers are in the same category.

Evidence for Genetic Differences

a. There is indirect evidence on heritability of abilities and other traits of personality. The most convincing data involve comparisons of identical twins, non-identical twins and ordinary siblings raised together and apart. Twins do not have identical *in utero* environments; those sharing the same amniotic sac are especially likely to experience differences which give one twin a biological advantage over the other. Not all differences between identical twins are caused by differences in post-natal environment.

There are a number of studies on the heritability of intelligence as measured by standardized tests which support the proposition that individual differences in mental abilities are largely hereditary in origin. The evidence has been reviewed by Arthur R. Jensen of the University of California. In a study by Jensen, Wilson and Elliott, the dichotomy "Negro-non-Negro" when included among eleven other variables, made the largest independent contribution to the prediction of intelligence test scores of sixth grade students in the Berkeley schools.

b. There is a large average achievement gap in test, school, and job performance between Negroes and whites which has not yet been abolished or permanently reduced by manipulation of the environment. White-Negro differences in learning rates appear early and become greater as the children grow older.

c. In a study of schoolchild learning of psychomotor skills by Clyde E. Noble it was shown that there are significant and widespread white-Negro differences. Review of research of the learning of psychomotor skills supports the findings of Noble. This is a form of culture-free learning and it expands the evidence for white-Negro differences attributable to biological endowment rather than environment. However, these and other culture-free tests are not valid measures of abilities to perform in school, to do abstract reasoning, and to be creative.

d. The histories of the Negro and white races show that the latter have made greater contributions to discovery and social evolution. This is not a compelling argument, for civilizations rise and fall without apparent biological bases of the changes.

e. The achievements of the most outstanding Negroes fall short of the highest achievements among other ethnic groups such as Jews and Asians who have been subjected to cruel discrimination. With some outstanding exceptions, Negroes tend to do poorly in the sciences and in medicine even when graduate and medical students come from middle- and upper-class Negro families and from good schools.

Arguments Against Further Study

a. The stratagem is used that because no race is homogeneous and cannot be clearly defined, the word "race" should be dropped from our vocabulary, so that we cannot talk about or investigate these problems, and hence to the conclusion that problems relating to the biology of race do not exist. Cancer, mental illness, circulatory and other great diseases are pluricausal, complex, and equally difficult to define. Should medical science declare that they do not exist and refuse to study them? Those who oppose the investigation of biological differences among races do not hesitate to study environmental differences and to recommend social action on the basis of racial identity rather than individuality.

b. It is emphasized that genes affecting intelligence and other traits of intellect have not been mapped or identified and that the evidence on the role of heredity is indirect. This is true. At the present time research on these general questions would have to use test, school, and job performance as a basis for comparisons.

c. It is claimed that the results of standardized tests are meaningless when used for testing Negroes who lack experience with white culture. If objective tests are useless, then upon what bases has it been proven that whites and Negroes are, on the average, equally endowed biologically? The same individuals who condemn all tests seize upon test data when it seems to support their belief. Although recognizing the limitations of tests, grades, and ratings and the global nature of "intelligence," which represents an undetermined number of factors, I believe that these indirect measures have a significant degree of validity and internal consistency and that useful methods of testing heritability have been developed. It is possible that races developed different patterns of abilities, each best suited to the environment in which the race evolved.

d. Another rationalization of why average biological differences among races should be ignored is based on the assumption that almost all individuals can be trained to achieve success as a storekeeper, farmer, teacher, banker, lawyer, scientist, etc. I do not know of any objective evidence which supports this assumption.

e. It is feared that racists would misuse evidence for average biological differences between whites and Negroes. Racists prefer the false dogma that all Negroes are biologically inferior to all whites to recognition of overlap and the principle that all peoples should be treated according to individuality without regard for race.

f. A related argument is that Negroes will be offended and hurt by evidence for average differences in genetic endowment. This is probable. But I suggest that far more anguish has been brought to Negroes and other peoples of the United States by creating dogma.

g. It has been claimed that racial equality of genetic endowment must be assumed until differences have been proven. There are no such rules in science or in ethics.

h. Finally, it is said that there is no point in studying racial differences for nothing can be done with knowledge of differences if they exist. Counter-arguments are given below.

Possible Sources of Data

a. The Armed Services of the United States have data on the test performance of large samples of recruits, extending through several decades of social progress of the Negro, that have not been fully reported.

b. There are some orphanages in which children of different races have been housed and educated together from early life.

c. Children of different races have been adopted into and reared in the same family.

d. Comparisons of Indians and Negroes, the former more socially and economically disadvantaged than the latter, should be helpful. Kuttner has summarized data on socioeconomic status and school performance of American Indian and American Negro school children as recorded in the Coleman report. In respect to socioeconomic status, the Indian ranks far below Negro standards, yet on the average he scores as well or better than Negro students on various tests of scholastic ability.

e. Comparative studies of Negro and other races should be done in countries having Negro rule and in countries which are said not to practice racial discrimination.

f. Study of Negro and white twins (identical and fraternal) and ordinary siblings reared together and apart by statistical measures of heritability.

g. Further efforts should be made to develop culturally unbiased tests.

h. Comparison of the highest achievers of different races who have never experienced either a substandard culture or poor schools.

Use of Knowledge

If it should be clearly shown that people called Negro are on the average handicapped by biological endowment, how should this knowledge be used?

a. There should be a return to the principle of treating people according to abilities, interests, drives, assumption of duties, and behavioral standards without regard to race unless it can be shown by pilot studies that preferential treatment of the Negro leads to useful outcomes.

b. Efforts to integrate schools and housing should either be voluntary or planned according to individuality. The current aim of agencies of government and of social reformers is to integrate by coercion—without regard to individuality. Many such efforts have been disastrous.

c. Conception control should be made easily available and encouraged for individuals of all races who because of genetic limitations or poor cultural heritage are unable to endow children with a reasonable chance to achieve happiness, self-sufficiency and good citizenship. I suggest that barrenness rather than fecundity be subsidized among all peoples unqualified for parenthood.

Discussion

Individuals of all races are disadvantaged by genetic and other biological limitations. I write of possible average white-Negro differences in genetic endowment because this and other countries are torn and threatened by some of the efforts to abolish the average achievement gap between whites and Negroes. I refer to social actions based upon racial identity rather than individuality. I do not suggest any social or biological measures which would not be applied to all people according to individuality and without regard to race. I do not suggest that efforts to improve environment, to correct cultural handicaps, and to insure equal rights and opportunities be withheld until there is better information on the biology of race.

The dogma that races are equally endowed biologically is generally accepted as factual. It then follows that each problem of Negroes is regarded by them as objective evidence for racial discrimination. The judgment that the whites of America are commonly racists may be a grave injustice. Among those who oppose the expression of ideas differing from their own are modern Pharisees who, commonly sequestered from the realities of a changing neighborhood, appear in public to alternate flagellation of their fellow-men for causing all Negro problems with recitation of the Pharisee's prayer, "God, I thank thee that I am not as other men are." Thus self-absolved, they remain blind to the consequences of the social actions they support.

Any suggestion that conception control be taught to Negroes who are disadvantaged is met with cries of "genocide." Any suggestion that biological methods can someday be used to prevent human misery is met by shouts of "Hitler." The Nazi attempts to build a master race were linked with the aim to destroy an ethnic group which has contributed more to science and culture than any other. The program was motivated by hate, not by knowledge of human genetics. Medical science still lacks the knowledge and wisdom needed for an effective program of positive eugenics but search for both may provide one necessary means to prevent social ills, if sufficient time is allotted to man's future. Propagandism has been used to conceal the risk that the value judgments were in error. It has been rationalized by the claims of special insights into the needs of society on the part of some social reformers and appointed employees of government and by the conviction that they have the responsibility to actualize their faiths. It is generally implied and sometimes openly claimed that, since knowledge can be misused, there can be wisdom greater than that based upon truth. Such are the faiths which set light to fascism, communism, and various other "isms" and brought accompanying flames. Social activists have been unable to reach a collective position without inhibiting the freedom on which they thrive.

Still little used in the struggle for social justice are rigorous methods of science. First, studies are needed to identify the principal reasons why peoples are disadvantaged. Second, the outcomes of studies and programs of other countries should be reviewed. The child care and youth programs of the Soviet Union and of Poland are worthy of careful study. Third, pilot studies of remedial proposals which are better designed and controlled than any done thus far should be carried out.

If it should be found that there are important average racial differences in genetic endowment this imposes no rational barrier to justice. If biological interventions are needed, they should be directed towards the enrichment of human life, freedom from genetic enslavement, freedom to attain dignity, self-sufficiency and social responsibility. I believe that inquiry and debate of the question is compatible with and probably necessary for the optimal advancement of disadvantaged peoples.

Questions

1. Can you distinguish among the several kinds of questions that are raised by the authors in this section? How do the scientific questions differ from the purely social ones?

2. How do you suppose one might set up "experiments" involving human beings? Why do the authors have to depend so much on experiments involving animals?

3. Do the social issues involved in some of the discussions color the scientific attitudes? Do investigators of the scientific aspects of race sometimes begin with conclusions that they are trying to prove? Can you offer examples other than those cited in this section? In what ways are the issues in this section related to the social and scientific ones in Section Nine, on "Soul Language and Standard English"?

4. Professor Dobzhansky begins his essay by writing: "Science aims to help man understand himself and his place in the universe. Yet man's efforts to know himself are often frustrated by his propensity to deceive himself. This propensity reaches its pinnacle where 'sensitive' topics are involved. The topic of race is one of these; it elicits emotional, and often passionate reactions in many people." Can you cite emotional and passionate reactions on the topic of race which completely contradict one another? For example, can you cite arguments which argue that there are absolutely no racial differences of any sort, in opposition to those which insist that there are many and fundamental racial differences?

5. Why is it so important to establish that there may or may not be race differences? Even if there were race differences, should these differences occasion social distinctions, like laws against intermarriage or against the mixing of the races in schools or in eating establishments? Are some of these rules completely without any basis in social fact? Why does Dr. Ingle argue that the proposition about "genetic differential" is a hypothesis only? What conclusions can one draw from his general argument? Does it really affect the basic social issue?

Assignments

1. Argue for or against one particular position cited in this section. For example, argue that (a) even if there are race differences, all individual human beings should be treated equally. Or (b) because we know that there must be race differences, it is necessary to find them and to treat "inferior" races with greater concern and attention.

2. Define the scientific issue involved in studying race biologically. In the course of this definition try to distinguish as sharply as you can between the purely scientific and purely social issues.

3. Discuss one of the literary works in Section Eleven, "Studies in Black and White," in the light of the issues raised in this section.

Additional Reading

The subject of race differences has been widely discussed. One of the classical studies is that by Otto Klineberg, *Race Differences* (New York: Harper & Row, 1935). Other studies are those by Leona E. Tyler, *The Psychology of Human Differences*, 3rd Ed. (New York, 1965); Margaret Mead, Theodosius Dobzhansky, Ethel Tobach, and Robert E. Light, editors, *Science and the Concept of Race* (New York, 1968); specific studies on the Negro are those by A. N. Shuey, *Testing of Negro Intelligence*, 2nd Ed. (New York, 1966) and Arthur R. Jensen, "How Much Can We Boost I.Q. and Scholastic Achievement?" *Harvard Education Review*, 1969. Jensen's article occasioned a series of commentaries, most of them rebutting his apparent intimation that Negroes prove to be genetically inferior on intelligence tests. Many of the articles and books cited here will contain additional bibliographical references.

SECTION ELEVEN *Studies in Black and White*

My old man's a white old man
And my old mother's black.
If ever I cursed my white old man
I take my curses back.

If ever I cursed my black old mother
And wished she were in hell,
I'm sorry for that evil wish
And now I wish her well.

> *My old man died in a fine big house.*
> *My ma died in a shack.*
> *I wonder where I'm gonna die,*
> *Being neither white nor black?*

"Cross,"
LANGSTON HUGHES

Boitelle

Guy de Maupassant

Father Boitelle (first name, Antoine) was known throughout the region as the specialist in dirty work. Every time someone needed a ditch cleaned, manure taken care of, a cesspool emptied, a sewer flushed, any hole of vileness whatsoever, it was him one found for the job.

He would come with his cleaning tools and his wooden shoes smeared with filth, and begin his work while whining about his profession. When asked why he did this disgusting work, he would reply, with resignation: "Heaven knows, it's for my children, who must be taken care of. That reason more than any other."

He had, indeed, fourteen children. When anyone wanted to know what had become of them, he would say, with an indifferent air: "Only eight remain home. One is in service and five are married."

If anyone wanted to know whether they were well married, he replied with spirit: "I did not oppose them. I never opposed them. They married as they pleased. Taste must not be opposed; that turns out badly. I am a cleaner of filth because my parents opposed my tastes. But for that, I would have become a workman, like everyone else."

Here is how his parents went against his tastes:

He was then a soldier, stationed at Havre, not stupider or shrewder than anyone else, although simpler nevertheless. When he was not on duty, his greatest pleasure was to walk along the dock, where the bird dealers gathered. Sometimes alone, sometimes with a soldier from his own part of the country, he would slowly wander back and forth in front of cages containing parrots with green backs and yellow heads from the banks of the Amazon; or parrots with gray backs and red heads from

This translation from the French was prepared for this edition. The original was written in the latter half of the nineteenth century, and some of the vocabulary in the translation is deliberately used to suggest the "old-fashioned" tone in de Maupassant.

Senegal; or enormous macaws, which looked like birds raised in hothouses, with their flowerlike feathers, their plumes, and their tufts; parrots of every size, which seemed painted with minute care by a miniaturist God; and the little birds, all the smaller birds that hopped about, red, yellow, blue, many colored, mingling their cries with the noise of the dock, increasing the din of ships unloading, and passengers and vehicles—a violent clamor, loud, shrill, deafening, as if from some distant, unnatural forest.

Boitelle would stop, with open eyes, open mouth, laughing and enchanted, showing his teeth to the captive cockatoos, which kept nodding their white or yellow tufts toward the bright red of his pants and the copper buckle of his belt. When he found a bird that could talk, he questioned it, and, if it happened at the time to be disposed to reply and talk with him, he would then have enough amusement to content him until evening. He also found pleasure in looking at the monkeys and could think of no greater luxury for a rich man than to own these animals as one owns cats and dogs. This sort of taste, this taste for the exotic, he had in his blood, as one has it for hunting, or for medicine, or for the priesthood. He could not stop himself, every time the gates of the barracks opened, from returning to the dock, drawn toward it by a deep longing.

One time, having stopped almost in ecstasy before an enormous macaw, which was swelling out its plumes, bending forward and picking its head up haughtily, as if curtseying in the court of parrot-land, he saw the door of a small café next to the bird dealer's shop open, and a young Negress come out, her head covered with a red silk handkerchief. She was sweeping into the street the discarded corks and dirty sawdust from the floor of the establishment.

Boitelle's attention was soon divided between the bird and the woman, and he really could not tell which of these two beings he contemplated with the greater astonishment and pleasure.

The Negress, having swept the rubbish into the street, raised her eyes, and, in turn, was dazzled by the soldier's uniform. There she stood facing him with her broom in her hands as if she were bringing him a rifle, while the macaw continued bowing. But at the end of a few seconds the soldier felt embarrassed at this attention, and he walked away quietly so as not to look as if he were in retreat.

But he came back. Almost every day he passed before the Café des Colonies, and often he could make out through the window the figure of the little black-skinned maid serving beer or brandy to the sailors of the port. Frequently, too, she came out to the door on seeing him; soon, without ever exchanging a word, they smiled at one another like acquaintances; and Boitelle felt his heart touched when he suddenly saw, glittering between the dark lips of the girl, a shining row of teeth. Finally, one day he went in, and was quite surprised to find that she could speak French like every one else. The bottle of lemonade, which she shared with him, remained memorably delicious; and he made it a habit to come and consume, in this little tavern on the dock, all the agreeable drinks he could afford.

For him it was a holiday, a happiness, on which his thoughts dwelt constantly, to watch the black hand of the little maid pouring something into his glass while her teeth laughed more than her eyes. At the end of two months they became fast friends, and Boitelle, after his first astonishment at discovering that this Negress had as good principles as honest French girls, that she respected economy, industry, religion, and good conduct, loved her the more on that account, and was so charmed that he wanted to marry her.

He told her his intention, which made her dance with joy. She had also a little money, left her by a female oyster dealer, who had taken her in when she had been left on the dock at Havre by an American captain. This captain had found the little black girl, when she was only about six years old, lying on bales of cotton in the hold of his ship, some hours after his departure from New York. On his arrival in Havre, he gave up to the care of this compassionate oyster dealer the little creature who had been hidden on board his vessel, he knew not for what reason or by whom.

The oyster woman having died, the young Negress became a servant at the Café des Colonies.

Antoine Boitelle added: "This will be all right if my parents don't oppose it. I will never go against them, you understand, never! I'm going to say a word or two to them the first time I go back to the country."

The following week, in fact, having twenty-four hours' leave, he went to see his family, who had a little farm at Tourteville, near Yvetot.

He waited till the meal was finished, the hour when the coffee, baptized with brandy, makes the heart more open, before informing his parents that he had found a girl who satisfied his tastes, all his tastes, so completely that there could not exist another on earth so perfectly suited to him.

The old people, on hearing this, immediately became cautious and asked for explanations. He hid nothing from them except the color of her skin.

She was a servant, without much means, but strong, thrifty, clean, of good conduct, and sensible. All these things were better than money in the hands of a bad housewife. Moreover, she had a few pennies, left by a woman who had reared her, a good number of pennies, almost a little dowry, fifteen hundred francs in the bank. The old people, persuaded by his talk, and using also their own judgment, were gradually weakening, when he came to the delicate point. Laughing a somewhat tight laugh, he said: "There's only one thing you may not like. She is not a white slip of a girl."

They did not understand, and he had to explain at some length and very cautiously, to avoid shocking them, that she belonged to the dark race of which they had only seen samples in pictures from Epinal.

Then they became restless, perplexed, fearful, as if he had proposed a union with the devil.

The mother said: "Black? How much of her is black? All of her?"

He replied: "Certainly. Everywhere, just as you are white everywhere."

The father said: "Black? Is she as black as the pot?"

The son answered: "Perhaps a little less than that. She is black, but not disgustingly black. The priest's cassock is black, but it is not more ugly than a surplice, which is white."

The father said: "Are there more black people besides her in her country?"

And the son exclaimed: "Of course!"

But the old man shook his head. "That must be unpleasant."

And the son: "It isn't any more unpleasant than anything else once you get used to it."

The mother asked: "It doesn't soil underwear more than other skins, this black skin?"

"Not more than yours, seeing it's her own color."

Then, after many other questions, it was agreed that the parents should see this girl before deciding anything, and that the young man, whose military service would be over in a month, should bring her to the house so that they might examine her and decide by discussing the matter whether or not she was too dark to enter the Boitelle family.

Antoine then announced that on Sunday, the 22nd of May, the day of his discharge, he would leave for Tourteville with his good friend.

She had put on, for this trip to the house of her beloved's parents, her brightest and most beautiful clothes, in which yellow, red, and blue were the dominant colors, so that she looked as if she were dressed for a national holiday.

At the railroad station, as they were leaving Havre, people stared at her, and Boitelle was proud of giving his arm to a person who commanded so much attention. Then, in the third-class compartment, where she took a seat by his side, she aroused so much astonishment among the country folk that they stood up on their seats to look at her over the partitions. A child, seeing her, cried with fear; another hid his face in his mother's lap.

Everything went well, however, until they approached their station. When the train slowed down as they neared Yvetot, Antoine felt ill at ease, as he would have done at an inspection when he was not prepared. Then, leaning his head out the door, he recognized his father in the distance, holding the bridle of the horse harnessed to a carriage, and he saw his mother, who had come forward to the railing behind which stood the curious.

He got off first, extending his hand to his sweetheart, and, erect, as if he were escorting a general, he went toward his family.

The mother, on seeing this black lady in a many-colored dress with her son, remained so stupefied that she could not open her mouth; and the father could hardly hold the horse, which reared repeatedly, at the sound of the locomotive or the sight of the Negress. But Antoine, suddenly filled with unmixed joy at seeing the old people once more, rushed forward with open arms, embraced his mother, embraced his father, in spite of the old horse's fright, and then turning toward his companion, at whom the passengers on the platform stopped to stare with amazement, he explained:

"Here she is. I told you, at first sight she is not an attractive slip; but as soon as you know her, truth of truths, there's nothing better on earth. Say hello to her so'that she may not feel badly."

Then, Mama Boitelle, almost losing her reason, made a sort of curtsey, while the father took off his cap, murmuring: "May you have your every wish."

Then, without further delay, they climbed into the carriage, the two women in back on seats which made them bounce up and down as the carriage bounced along the road, and the two men on the front seat.

No one spoke. Antoine, uncomfortable, whistled an army song; his father whipped the old horse; and his mother from her corner, cast sly glances at the Negress, whose forehead and cheekbones shone in the sunlight like well-polished shoes.

Wishing to break the ice, Antoine turned around. "Well," said he, "we are not talking?"

"We need time," replied the old woman.

He went on: "Come, tell us the little story about your hen with eight eggs."

It was a funny old family story. But, as his mother still remained quiet, paralyzed by her emotion, he undertook to tell the story, laughing a great deal as he did so at the memorable incident. The father, who knew it by heart, brightened at the first words; his wife soon followed his example; and the Negress herself, at the funniest part, suddenly gave such a laugh, a laugh so loud, so torrential, that the horse, excited, broke into a short gallop.

The friendship was made. They talked.

They had hardly reached the house and gone in when Antoine took his sweetheart to her room, so that she might take off her dress, to avoid staining it, because she was going to prepare a tasty dish from her own recipe, intended to gain the old people's affections through their stomachs. He drew his parents outside the house and, heart beating, asked: "Well, what do you say now?"

The father said nothing. The mother, more bold, declared: "She is much too black. No, in truth, this is too much. It turns my blood."

"You will get used to it," said Antoine.

"Perhaps so, but not right now."

They went into the house, where the good woman was moved at the sight of the Negress cooking. She at once proceeded to help her, with sleeves rolled up, active in spite of her age.

The meal was excellent, very long, very enjoyable. When they were taking a walk after dinner, Antoine took his father aside.

"Well, father, what do you say?"

The peasant did not compromise himself. "I have no opinion. Ask your mother."

So Antoine went back to his mother, and, drawing her aside, said: "Well, mother, what do you think?"

"My poor boy, she is really too black. If she were only a little less black, I would not go against you, but this is too much. One would say Satan!"

He did not press her, knowing how obstinate the old woman had always been, but he felt in his heart a flood of defeat. He was considering what to do, what plan he could devise, surprised, moreover, that she had not conquered them already as she had charmed him. And they, all four, walked along through the wheat fields, becoming more and more silent. Whenever they passed a fence, they saw tenant farmers sitting on the rail, and youngsters climbed up to stare, and every one ran out into the road to see the "black" whom young Boitelle had brought home with him. At a distance they noticed people racing across the fields as if a drum were beating to draw attention to some living phenomenon. Papa and Mama Boitelle, scared by the curiosity spreading through the countryside at their approach, hurried their steps, side by side, leaving their son behind. His dark companion asked what his parents thought of her.

He hesitatingly replied that they had not yet made up their minds.

But in the village square people rushed out of the houses in a flurry of excitement; and, at the sight of the gathering crowd, the old Boitelles fled to their house, while Antoine, swelling with rage, his sweetheart on his arm, advanced with majesty under large, astonished eyes.

He understood that it was at an end, and that he had no hope, that he could not marry his Negress; she also understood it; and as they drew near the farmhouse they both began to weep. As soon as they had got back to the house, she again took off her dress to help the mother in the household duties, and followed her everywhere, to the dairy, to the stable, to the hen house, taking on herself the hardest part of the work, repeating always: "Let me do it, Madame Boitelle," so that, when night came, the old woman, touched but inexorable, said to her son: "She is a good girl, all the same. It's a pity she is so black; but indeed she is too black. I could not get used to it. She must go back again. She is too, too black!"

And young Boitelle said to his sweetheart: "She will not consent. She thinks you are too black. You must go back. I will go with you to the train. It's nothing; don't worry. I am going to talk to them after you have started."

He then took her to the station, still giving her hope, and, when he kissed her, he put her on the train, which he watched as it passed out of sight, his eyes swollen with tears.

In vain he appealed to the old people. They would never consent.

And when he had told this story, which was known all over the country, Antoine Boitelle would always add: "From that time on, I have had no heart for anything, for anything. No trade suited me any longer, and I became what I am, a cleaner of filth."

People would say to him: "You got married anyway."

"Yes, and I can't say that my wife didn't please me, since I have fourteen children; but she is not at all the other one, certainly not—oh, no! The other one, you see, my Negress, she had only to look at me, and I felt as if I were transported. . . ."

Black Is My Favorite Color

Bernard Malamud

Charity Sweetness sits in the toilet eating her two hardboiled eggs while I'm having my ham sandwich and coffee in the kitchen. That's how it goes only don't get the idea of ghettoes. If there's a ghetto I'm the one that's in it. She's my cleaning woman from Father Divine and comes in once a week to my small three-room apartment on my day off from the liquor store. "Peace," she says to me, "Father reached on down and took me right up in Heaven." She's a small person with a flat body, frizzy hair, and a quiet face that the light shines out of, and Mama had such eyes before she died. The first time Charity Sweetness came in to clean, a little more than a year and a half, I made the mistake to ask her to sit down at the kitchen table with me and eat her lunch. I was still feeling not so hot after Ornita left but I'm the kind of a man—Nat Lime, forty-four, a bachelor with a daily growing bald spot on the back of my head, and I could lose frankly fifteen pounds—who enjoys company so long as he has it. So she cooked up her two hardboiled eggs and sat down and took a small bite out of one of them. But after a minute she stopped chewing and she got up and carried the eggs in a cup in the bathroom, and since then she eats there. I said to her more than once, "Okay, Charity Sweetness, so have it your way, eat the eggs in the kitchen by yourself and I'll eat when you're done," but she smiles absentminded, and eats in the toilet. It's my fate with colored people.

Although black is still my favorite color you wouldn't know it from my luck except in short quantities even though I do all right in the liquor store business in Harlem, on Eighth Avenue between 110th and 111th. I speak with respect. A large part of my life I've had dealings with Negro people, most on a business basis but sometimes for friendly reasons with genuine feeling on both sides. I'm drawn to them. At this time of my life I should have one or two good colored friends but the fault isn't necessarily mine. If they knew what was in my heart towards them, but how can you tell that to anybody nowadays? I've tried more than once but the language of the heart either is a dead language or else nobody understands it the way you speak it. Very few. What I'm saying is, personally for me there's only one human color and that's the color of blood. I like a black person if not because he's black, then because I'm white. It comes to the same thing. If I wasn't white my first choice would be black. I'm satisfied to be white because I have no other choice. Anyway, I got an eye for color. I appreciate. Who wants everybody to be the same? Maybe it's like some kind of a talent. Nat Lime might be a liquor dealer in Harlem, but once in the jungle in New Guinea in the Second War, I got the idea when I shot at a running Jap and missed him, that I had some kind of a talent, though maybe it's the kind where you have a marvelous idea now and then but in the end what do they come to? After all, it's a strange world.

Where Charity Sweetness eats her eggs makes me think about Buster Wilson when we were both boys in the Williamsburg section of Brooklyn. There was this long block of run-down dirty frame houses in the middle of a not-so-hot white neighborhood full of pushcarts. The Negro houses looked to me like they had been born and died there, dead not long after the beginning of the world. I lived on the next street. My father was a cutter with arthritis in both hands, big red knuckles and swollen fingers so he didn't cut, and my mother was the one who went to work. She sold paper bags from a second-hand pushcart in Ellery Street. We didn't starve but nobody ate chicken unless we were sick or the chicken was. This was my first acquaintance with a lot of black people and I used to poke around on their poor block. I think I thought, brother, if there can be like this, what can't there be? I mean I caught an early idea what life was about. Anyway I met Buster Wilson there. He used to play marbles by himself. I sat on the curb across the street, watching him shoot one marble lefty and the other one righty. The hand that won picked up the marbles. It wasn't so much of a game but he didn't ask me to come over. My idea was to be friendly, only he never encouraged, he discouraged. Why did I pick him out for a friend? Maybe because I had no others then, we were new in the neighborhood, from Manhattan. Also I liked his type. Buster did everything alone. He was a skinny kid and his brothers' clothes hung on him like worn-out potato sacks. He was a beanpole boy, about twelve, and I was then ten. His arms and legs were burnt out matchsticks. He always wore a brown wool sweater, one arm half unraveled, the other went down to the wrist. His long and narrow head had a white part cut straight in the short woolly hair, maybe with a ruler there, by his father, a barber but too drunk to stay a barber. In those days though I had little myself I was old enough to know who was better off, and the whole block of colored houses made me feel bad in the daylight. But I went there as much as I could because the street was full of life. In the night it looked different, it's hard to tell a cripple in the dark. Sometimes I was afraid to walk by the houses when they were dark and quiet. I was afraid there were people looking at me that I couldn't see. I liked it better when they had parties at night and everybody had a good time. The musicians played their banjos and saxophones and the houses shook with the music and laughing. The young girls, with their pretty dresses and ribbons in their hair, caught me in my throat when I saw them through the windows.

But with the parties came drinking and fights. Sundays were bad days after the Saturday night parties. I remember once that Buster's father, also long and loose, always wearing a dirty gray Homburg hat, chased another black man in the street with a half-inch chisel. The other one, maybe five feet high, lost his shoe and when they wrestled on the ground he was already bleeding through his suit, a thick red blood smearing the sidewalk. I was frightened by the blood and wanted to pour it back in the man who was bleeding from the chisel. On another time Buster's father was playing in a crap game with two big bouncy red dice, in the back of an alley between two middle houses. Then about six men started fist-fighting there, and they ran out of the alley and hit each other in the street. The neighbors, including children, came out and watched, everybody afraid but nobody moving to do anything. I saw the same thing near my store in Harlem, years later, a big crowd watching two men in the street, their breaths hanging in the air on a winter night, murdering each other with switch knives, but nobody moved to call a cop. I didn't either. Anyway, I was just a young kid but I still remember how the cops drove up in a police paddy wagon and broke up the fight by hitting everybody they could hit with big nightsticks. This was in the days before LaGuardia. Most of the fighters were knocked out cold, only one or two got away. Buster's father started to run back in his house but a cop ran after him and cracked him on his Homburg hat with a club, right on the front porch. Then the Negro men were lifted up by the cops, one at the arms and the other at the feet, and they heaved them in the paddy wagon. Buster's father hit the back of the wagon and fell, with his nose spouting very red blood, on top of three other men. I personally couldn't stand it, I was scared of the human race so I ran home, but I remember Buster watching without any expression in his eyes. I stole an extra fifteen cents from my mother's pocketbook and I ran back and asked Buster if he wanted to go to the movies. I would pay. He said yes. This was the first time he talked to me.

So we went more than once to the movies. But we never got to be friends. Maybe because it was a one-way proposition—from me to him. Which includes my invitations to go with me, my (poor mother's) movie money, Hershey chocolate bars, watermelon slices, even my best Nick Carter and Merriwell books that I spent hours picking up in the junk shops, and that he never gave me back. Once he let me go in his house to get a match so we could smoke some butts we found, but it smelled so heavy, so impossible, I died till I got out of there. What I saw in the way of furniture I won't mention—the best was falling apart in pieces. Maybe we went to the movies all together five or six matinees that spring and in the summertime, but when the shows were over he usually walked home by himself.

"Why don't you wait for me, Buster?" I said. "We're both going in the same direction."

But he was walking ahead and didn't hear me. Anyway he didn't answer.

One day when I wasn't expecting it he hit me in the teeth. I felt like crying but not because of the pain. I spit blood and said, "What did you hit me for? What did I do to you?"

"Because you a Jew bastard. Take your Jew movies and your Jew candy and shove them up your Jew ass."

And he ran away.

I thought to myself how was I to know he didn't like the movies. When I was a man I thought, you can't force it.

Years later, in the prime of my life, I met Mrs. Ornita Harris. She was standing by herself under an open umbrella at the bus stop, crosstown 110th, and I picked up her green glove that she had dropped on the wet sidewalk. It was in the end of November. Before I could ask her was it hers, she grabbed the glove out of my hand, closed her umbrella, and stepped in the bus. I got on right after her.

I was annoyed so I said, "If you'll pardon me, Miss, there's no law that you have to say thanks, but at least don't make a criminal out of me."

"Well, I'm sorry," she said, "but I don't like white men trying to do me favors."

I tipped my hat and that was that. In ten minutes I got off the bus but she was already gone.

Who expected to see her again but I did. She came into my store about a week later for a bottle of scotch.

"I would offer you a discount," I told her, "but I know you don't like a certain kind of a favor and I'm not looking for a slap in the face."

Then she recognized me and got a little embarrassed.

"I'm sorry I misunderstood you that day."

"So mistakes happen."

The result was she took the discount. I gave her a dollar off.

She used to come in about every two weeks for a fifth of Haig and

Haig. Sometimes I waited on her, sometimes my helpers, Jimmy or Mason, also colored, but I said to give the discount. They both looked at me but I had nothing to be ashamed. In the spring when she came in we used to talk once in a while. She was a slim woman, dark but not the most dark, about thirty years I would say, also well built, with a combination nice legs and a good-size bosom that I like. Her face was pretty, with big eyes and high cheek bones, but lips a little thick and nose a little broad. Sometimes she didn't feel like talking, she paid for the bottle, less discount, and walked out. Her eyes were tired and she didn't look to me like a happy woman.

I found out her husband was once a window cleaner on the big buildings, but one day his safety belt broke and he fell fifteen stories. After the funeral she got a job as a manicurist in a Times Square barber shop. I told her I was a bachelor and lived with my mother in a small three-room apartment on West Eighty-third near Broadway. My mother had cancer, and Ornita said she was very sorry.

One night in July we went out together. How that happened I'm still not so sure. I guess I asked her and she didn't say no. Where do you go out with a Negro woman? We went to the Village. We had a good dinner and walked in Washington Square Park. It was a hot night. Nobody was surprised when they saw us, nobody looked at us like we were against the law. If they looked maybe they saw my new lightweight suit that I bought yesterday and my shiny bald spot when we walked under a lamp, also how pretty she was for a man of my type. We went in a movie on West Eighth Street. I didn't want to go in but she said she had heard about the picture. We went in like strangers and we came out like strangers. I wondered what was in her mind and I thought to myself, whatever is in there it's not a certain white man that I know. All night long we went together like we were chained. After the movie she wouldn't let me take her back to Harlem. When I put her in a taxi she asked me, "Why did we bother?"

For the steak, I wanted to say. Instead I said, "You're worth the bother."

"Thanks anyway."

Kiddo, I thought to myself after the taxi left, you just found out what's what, now the best thing is forget her.

It's easy to say. In August we went out the second time. That was the night she wore a purple dress and I thought to myself, my God, what colors. Who paints that picture paints a masterpiece. Everybody looked at us but I had pleasure. That night when she took off her dress it was in a furnished room I had the sense to rent a few days before. With my sick mother, I couldn't ask her to come to my apartment, and she didn't want me to go home with her where she lived with her brother's family on West 115th near Lenox Avenue. Under her purple dress she wore a black slip, and when she took that off she had white underwear. When she took off the white underwear she was black again. But I know where the next white was, if you want to call it white. And that was the night I think I fell in love with her, the first time in my life though I have liked one or two nice girls I used to go with when I was a boy. It was a serious proposition. I'm the kind of man when I think of love I'm thinking of marriage. I guess that's why I am a bachelor.

That same week I had a holdup in my place, two big men—both black—with revolvers. One got excited when I rang open the cash register so he could take the money and he hit me over the ear with his gun. I stayed in the hospital a couple of weeks. Otherwise I was insured. Ornita came to see me. She sat on a chair without talking much. Finally I saw she was uncomfortable so I suggested she ought to go home.

"I'm sorry it happened," she said.

"Don't talk like it's your fault."

When I got out of the hospital my mother was dead. She was a wonderful person. My father died when I was thirteen and all by herself she kept the family alive and together. I sat shive for a week and remembered how she sold paper bags on her pushcart. I remembered her life and what she tried to teach me. Nathan, she said, if you ever forget you are a Jew a goy will remind you. Mama, I said, rest in peace on this subject. But if I do something you don't like, remember, on earth it's harder than where you are. Then when my week of mourning was finished, one night I said, "Ornita, let's get married. We're both honest people and if you love me like I love you it won't be such a bad time. If you don't like New York I'll sell out here and we'll move someplace else. Maybe to San Francisco where nobody knows us. I was there for a week in the Second War and I saw white and colored living together."

"Nat," she answered me, "I like you but I'd be afraid. My husband woulda killed me."

"Your husband is dead."

"Not in my memory."

"In that case I'll wait."

"Do you know what it'd be like—I mean the life we could expect?"

"Ornita," I said, "I'm the kind of a man, if he picks his own way of life he's satisfied."

"What about children? Were you looking forward to half-Jewish polka dots?"

"I was looking forward to children."

"I can't," she said.

Can't is can't. I saw she was afraid and the best thing was not to push. Sometimes when we met she was so nervous that whatever we did she couldn't enjoy it. At the same time I still thought I had a chance. We were together more and more. I got rid of my furnished room and she came to my apartment—I gave away Mama's bed and bought a new one. She stayed with me all day on Sundays. When she wasn't so nervous she was affectionate, and if I know what love is, I had it. We went out a couple of times a week, the same way—usually I met her in Times Square and sent her home in a taxi, but I talked more about marriage and she talked less against it. One night she told me she was still trying to convince herself but she was almost convinced. I took an inventory of my liquor stock so I could put the store up for sale.

Ornita knew what I was doing. One day she quit her job, the next she took it back. She also went away a week to visit her sister in Philadelphia for a little rest. She came back tired but said maybe. Maybe is maybe so I'll wait. The way she said it was closer to yes. That was the winter two years ago. When she was in Philadelphia I called up a friend of mine from the Army, now a CPA, and told him I would appreciate an invitation for an evening. He knew why. His wife said yes right away. When Ornita came back we went there. The wife made a fine dinner. It wasn't a bad time and they told us to come again. Ornita had a few drinks. She looked relaxed, wonderful. Later, because of a twenty-four hour taxi strike I had to take her home on the subway. When we got to the 116th Street station she told me to stay on the train, and she would walk the couple of blocks to her house. I didn't like a woman walking alone on the streets at that time of the night. She said she never had any trouble but I insisted nothing doing. I said I would walk to her stoop with her and when she went upstairs I would go back to the subway.

On the way there, on 115th in the middle of the block before Lenox, we were stopped by three men—maybe they were boys. One had a black hat with a half-inch brim, one a green cloth hat, and the third wore a black leather cap. The green hat was wearing a short coat and the other two had long ones. It was under a street light but the leather cap snapped a six-inch switchblade open in the light.

"What you doin' with this white son of a bitch?" he said to Ornita.

"I'm minding my own business," she answered him, "and I wish you would too."

"Boys," I said, "we're all brothers. I'm a reliable merchant in the neighborhood. This young lady is my dear friend. We don't want any trouble. Please let us pass."

"You talk like a Jew landlord," said the green hat. "Fifty a week for a single room."

"No charge fo' the rats," said the half-inch brim.

"Believe me, I'm no landlord. My store is 'Nathan's Liquors' between Hundred Tenth and Eleventh. I also have two colored clerks, Mason and Jimmy, and they will tell you I pay good wages as well as I give discounts to certain customers."

"Shut your mouth, Jewboy," said the leather cap, and he moved the knife back and forth in front of my coat button. "No more black pussy for you."

"Speak with respect about this lady, please."

I got slapped on my mouth.

"That ain't no lady," said the long face in the half-inch brim, "that's black pussy. She deserve to have evvy bit of her hair shave off. How you like to have evvy bit of your hair shave off, black pussy?"

"Please leave me and this gentleman alone or I'm gonna scream long and loud. That's my house three doors down."

They slapped her. I never heard such a scream. Like her husband was falling fifteen stories.

I hit the one that slapped her and the next I knew I was laying in the gutter with a pain in my head. I thought, goodbye, Nat, they'll stab me for sure, but all they did was take my wallet and run in three different directions.

Ornita walked back with me to the subway and she wouldn't let me go home with her again.

"Just get home safely."

She looked terrible. Her face was gray and I still remembered her scream. It was a terrible winter night, very cold February, and it took me an hour and ten minutes to get home. I felt bad for leaving her but what could I do?

We had a date downtown the next night but she didn't show up, the first time.

In the morning I called her in her place of business.

"For God sake, Ornita, if we got married and moved away we wouldn't have that kind of trouble that we had. We wouldn't come in that neighborhood any more."

"Yes, we would. I have family there and don't want to move anyplace else. The truth of it is I can't marry you, Nat. I got troubles enough of my own."

"I coulda sworn you love me."

"Maybe I do but I can't marry you."

"For God's sake, why?"

"I got enough trouble of my own."

I went that night in a cab to her brother's house to see her. He was a quiet man with a thin mustache. "She gone," he said, "left for a long visit to some close relatives in the South. She said to tell you she appreciate your intentions but didn't think it will work out."

"Thank you kindly," I said.

Don't ask me how I got home.

Once on Eighth Avenue, a couple of blocks from my store, I saw a blind man with a white cane tapping on the sidewalk. I figured we were going in the same direction so I took his arm.

"I can tell you're white," he said.

A heavy colored woman with a full shopping bag rushed after us.

"Never mind," she said, "I know where he live."

She pushed me with her shoulder and I hurt my leg on the fire hydrant.

That's how it is. I give my heart and they kick me in my teeth.
"Charity Sweetness—you hear me?—come out of that goddamn toilet!"

The Slave

LeRoi Jones

Characters

WALKER VESSELS, tall, thin Negro about forty.

GRACE, blonde woman about same age. Small, thin, beautiful.
BRADFORD EASLEY, tall, broad white man, with thinning hair, about forty-
five.

*The action takes place in a large living room, tastefully furnished the way
an intelligent university professor and his wife would furnish it.*
*Room is dark at the beginning of the play, except for light from explo-
sions, which continue, sometimes close, sometimes very far away,
throughout both acts, and well after curtain of each act.*

Prologue

WALKER.

[*Coming out dressed as an old field slave, balding, with white hair,
and an old ragged vest. (Perhaps he is sitting, sleeping, initially-nod-
ding and is awakened by faint cries, like a child's.) He comes to the
center of the stage slowly, and very deliberately, puffing on a pipe,
and seemingly uncertain of the reaction any audience will give his
speech*]

Whatever the core of our lives. Whatever the deceit. We love where we
are, and seek nothing but ourselves. We are lovers, and we are murderers.
We invent death for others. Stop their pulses publicly. Stone possible
lovers with heavy worlds we think are ideas . . . and we know, even
before these shapes are realized, that these worlds, these depths or
heights we fly to smoothly, as in a dream, or slighter, when we stare
dumbly into space, leaning our eyes just behind a lost quick moving bird,
then sometimes the place and twist of what we are will push and sting,
and what the crust of our stance has become will ring in our ears and

shatter that piece of our eyes that is never closed. An ignorance. A stupidity. A stupid longing not to know . . . which is automatically fulfilled. Automatically triumphs. Automatically makes us killers or foot-dragging celebrities at the core of any filth. And it is a deadly filth that passes as whatever thing we feel is too righteous to question, too deeply felt to deny.

[*Pause to relight pipe*]

I am much older than I look . . . or maybe much younger. Whatever I am or seem . . .

[*Significant pause*]

to you, then let that rest. But figure, still, that you might not be right. Figure, still, that you might be lying . . . to save yourself. Or myself's image, which might set you crawling like a thirsty dog for the meanest of drying streams. The meanest of ideas.

[*Gentle, mocking laugh*]

Yeah. Ideas. Let that settle! Ideas. Where they form. Or whose they finally seem to be. Yours? The other's? Mine?

[*Shifts uneasily, pondering the last*]

No, no more. Not mine. I served my slow apprenticeship . . . and maybe came up lacking. Maybe. Ha. Who's to say, really? Huh? But figure, still, ideas are still in the world. They need judging. I mean, they don't come in that singular or wild, that whatever they are, just because they're beautiful and brilliant, just because they strike us full in the center of the heart. . . . My God!

[*Softer*]

My God, just because, and even this, believe me, even if that is, just because they're *right* . . . doesn't mean anything. The very rightness stinks a lotta times. The very rightness.

[*Looks down and speaks softer and quicker*]

I am an old man. An old man.

[*Blankly*]

The waters and wars. Time's a dead thing really . . . and keeps nobody whole. An old man, full of filed rhythms. Terrific, eh? That I hoarded so much dignity? An old man full of great ideas. Let's say theories. As: Love is an instrument of knowledge. Oh, not my own. Not my own . . . is right. But listen now. . . . Brown is not brown except when used as an intimate description of personal phenomenological fields. As your brown is not my brown, et cetera, that is, we need, ahem, a meta-language. We need some thing not included here.

[*Spreads arms*]

Your ideas? An old man can't be expected to be right. If I'm old. If I really claim that embarrassment.

[*Saddens . . . brightens*]

A poem? Lastly, that, to distort my position? To divert you . . . in your hour of need. Before the thing goes on. Before you get your lousy chance. Discovering racially the funds of the universe. Discovering the last image of the thing. As the sky when the moon is broken. Or old, old blues people moaning in their sleep, singing, man, oh, nigger, nigger, you still here, as hard as nails, and takin' no shit from nobody. He say, yeah, yeah, he say yeah, yeah. He say, yeah, yeah . . . goin' down slow, man. Goin' down slow. He say . . . yeah, heh . . .

[*Running down, growing anxiously less articulate, more "field hand" sounding, blankly lyrical, shuffles slowly around, across the stage, as the lights dim and he enters the set proper and assumes the position he will have when the play starts . . . still moaning . . .*]

Act I

THE SCENE: *A light from an explosion lights the room dimly for a second and the outline of a figure is seen half sprawled on a couch. Every once in a while another blast shows the figure in silhouette. He stands from time to time, sits, walks nervously around the room examining books and paintings. Finally, he climbs a flight of stairs, stays for a few minutes, then returns. He sits smoking in the dark, until some sound is heard outside the door. He rises quickly and takes a position behind the door, a gun held out stiffly.* GRACE *and* EASLEY *open the door, turn on the light, agitated and breathing heavily.* GRACE *quiet and weary.* EASLEY *talking in harsh angry spurts.*

EASLEY. Son of a bitch. Those black son of a bitches. Why don't they at least stop and have their goddamned dinners? Goddamn son of a bitches. They're probably gonna keep that horseshit up all goddamn night. Goddamnit. Goddamn it!
  [*He takes off a white metal hat and slings it across the room. It bangs loudly against the brick of the fireplace*]
GRACE. Brad! You're going to wake up the children!
EASLEY. Oh, Christ! . . . But if they don't wake up under all that blasting, I don't think that tin hat will do it.
  [*He unbuttons his shirt, moves wearily across the room, still mumbling under his breath about the source of the explosions*]
Hey, Grace . . . you want a drink? That'll fix us up.
  [*He moves to get the drink and spots* WALKER *leaning back against the wall, half smiling, also very weary, but still holding the gun, stomach high, and very stiffly.* EASLEY *freezes, staring at* WALKER's *face and then the gun, and then back to* WALKER's *face. He makes no sound. The two men stand confronting each other until* GRACE *turns and sees them*]
GRACE. Sure, I'll take a drink . . . one of the few real pleasures left in the Western world.

[*She turns and drops her helmet to the floor, staring unbelievingly*]
Ohh!

WALKER.

[*Looks over slowly at* GRACE *and waves as from a passing train. Then he looks back at* EASLEY; *the two men's eyes are locked in the same ugly intensity.* WALKER *beckons to* GRACE]

The blinds.

GRACE. Walker!

[*She gets the name out quietly, as if she is trying to hold so many other words in*]

Walker . . . the gun!

WALKER.

[*Half turning to look at her. He looks back at* EASLEY, *then lets the gun swing down easily toward the floor. He looks back at* GRACE, *and tries to smile*]

Hey, momma. How're you?

EASLEY.

[*At* WALKER, *and whatever else is raging in his own head*]

Son of a bitch!

GRACE. What're you doing here, Walker? What do you want?

WALKER.

[*Looking at* EASLEY *from time to time*]

Nothing. Not really. Just visiting.

[*Grins*]

I was in the neighborhood; thought I'd stop by and see how the other half lives.

GRACE. Isn't this dangerous?

[*She seems relieved by* WALKER's *relative good spirits and she begins to look for a cigarette.* EASLEY *has not yet moved. He is still staring at* WALKER]

WALKER. Oh, it's dangerous as a bitch. But don't you remember how heroic I am?

EASLEY.

[*Handing* GRACE *a cigarette, then waiting to light it*]

Well, what the hell do you want, hero?

[*Drawn out and challenging*]

WALKER.

[*With same challenge*]

Nothing you have, fellah, not one thing.

EASLEY. Oh?

[*Cynically*]

Is *that* why you and your noble black brothers are killing what's left of of this city?

[*Suddenly broken*]

I should say . . . what's left of this country . . . or world.

WALKER. Oh, fuck you

> [*Hotly*]

fuck you . . . just fuck you, that's all. Just fuck you!

> [*Keeps voice stiffly contained, but then it rises sharply*]

I mean really, just fuck you. Don't, goddamnit, don't tell me about any goddamn killing of anything. If that's what's happening. I mean if this shitty town is being flattened . . . let it. It needs it.

GRACE. Walker, shut up, will you?

> [*Furious from memory*]

I had enough of your twisted logic in my day . . . you remember? I mean like your heroism. The same kind of memory. Or Lie. Do you remember which? Huh?

> [*Starting to weep*]

WALKER.

> [*Starts to comfort her*]

Grace . . . look . . . there's probably nothing I can say to make you understand me . . . now.

EASLEY.

> [*Steps in front of* WALKER *as he moves toward* GRACE . . . *feigning a cold sophistication*]

Uh. . . no, now come, Jefe, you're not going to make one of those embrace the weeping ex-wife dramas, are you? Well, once a bad poet always a bad poet . . . even in the disguise of a racist murderer!

WALKER.

> [*Not quite humbled*]

Yeah.

> [*Bends head, then he brings it up quickly, forcing the joke*]

Even disguised as a racist murderer . . . I remain a bad poet. Didn't St. Thomas say that? Once a bad poet always a bad poet . . . or was it Carl Sandburg, as some kind of confession?

EASLEY. You're not still writing . . . now, are you? I should think the political, now military estates would be sufficient. And you always used to speak of the Renaissance as an evil time.

> [*Begins making two drinks*]

And now you're certainly the gaudiest example of Renaissance man I've heard of.

> [*Finishes making drinks and brings one to* GRACE. WALKER *watches him and then as he starts to speak he walks to the cabinet, picks up the bottle, and empties a good deal of it*]

GRACE.

> [*Looking toward* WALKER *even while* EASLEY *extends the drink toward her*]

Walker . . . you are still writing, aren't you?

WALKER. Oh, God, yes. Want to hear the first lines of my newest work?

> [*Drinks, does a theatrical shiver*]

Uh, how's it go . . .? Oh, "Straddling each dophin's back/And steadied by a fin,/Those innocents relive their death,/Their wounds open again."
GRACE.

[*Staring at him closely*]
It's changed quite a bit.
WALKER. Yeah . . . it's changed to Yeats.

[*Laughs very loudly*]
Yeah, Yeats. . . . Hey, professor, anthologist, lecturer, loyal opposition, et cetera, et cetera, didn't you recognize those words as being Yeats's? Goddamn, I mean if you didn't recognize them . . . who the hell would? I thought you knew all kinds of shit.
EASLEY.

[*Calmly*]
I knew they were Yeats'.
WALKER.

[*Tilting the bottle again quickly*]
Oh, yeah? What poem?
EASLEY. The second part of "News for the Delphic Oracle."
WALKER.

[*Hurt*]
"News for the Delphic Oracle." Yeah. That's right.

[*To* GRACE]
You know that, Grace? Your hubsand knows all about everything. The second part of "News for the Delphic Oracle."

[*Rhetorically*]
Intolerable music falls. Nymphs and satyrs copulate in the foam.

[*Tilts bottle again, some liquor splashes on the floor*]
EASLEY.

[*Suddenly straightening and stopping close to* WALKER]
Look . . . LOOK! You arrogant maniac, if you get drunk or fall out here, so help me, I'll call the soldiers or somebody . . . and turn you over to them. I swear I'll do that.
GRACE. Brad!
WALKER. Yeah, yeah, I know. That's your job. A liberal education, and a long history of concern for minorities and charitable organizations can do that for you.
EASLEY.

[*Almost taking hold of* WALKER's *clothes*]
No! I mean this, friend! Really! If I get the slightest advantage, some cracker soldier will be bayoneting you before the night is finished.
WALKER.

[*Slaps* EASLEY *across the face with the back of his left hand, pulling the gun out with his right and shoving it as hard as he can against* EASLEY's *stomach.* EASLEY *slumps, and the cruelty in* WALKER's *face at this moment also frightens* GRACE]

"My country, 'tis of thee. Sweet land of liber-ty."

[*Screams off key like drunken opera singer*]

Well, let's say liberty and ignorant vomiting faggot professors.

[*To* GRACE]

Right, lady? Isn't that right? I mean you ought to know, 'cause you went out of your way to marry one.

[*Turns to* GRACE *and she takes an involuntary step backward. And in a cracked ghostlike voice that he wants to be loud . . .*]

Huh? Huh? And then fed,the thing my children.

[*He reaches stiffly out and pushes her shoulder, intending it to be strictly a burlesque, but there is quite a bit of force in the gesture.* GRACE *falls back, just short of panic, but* WALKER *hunches his shoulders and begins to jerk his finger at the ceiling; one eye closed and one leg raised, jerking his finger absurdly at the ceiling, as if to indicate something upstairs that was to be kept secret*]

Ah, yes, the children . . .

[*Affecting an imprecise "Irish" accent*]

sure and they looked well enough . . .

[*Grins*]

and white enough, roosting in that kennel. Hah, I hope you didn't tell Faggy, there, about those two lovely ladies.

[EASLEY *is kneeling on the floor holding his stomach and shaking his head*]

Ahh, no, lady, let's keep that strictly in the family. I mean among those of us who screw.

[*He takes another long drink from the bottle, and "threatens"* EASLEY'S *head in a kind of burlesque*]

For Lawrence, and all the cocksmen of my underprivileged youth. When we used to chase that kind of frail little sissy-punk down Raymond Boulevard and compromise his sister-in-laws in the cloak room. . . . It's so simple to work from the bottom up. To always strike, and know, from the blood's noise that you're right, and what you're doing is right, and even *pretty*.

[*Suddenly more tender toward* GRACE]

I swear to you, Grace, I did come into the world pointed in the right direction. Oh, shit, I learned so many words for what I've wanted to say. They all come down on me at once. But almost none of them are mine.

[*He straightens up, turning quickly toward the still kneeling* EASLEY, *and slaps him as hard as he can across the face, sending his head twisting around*]

Bastard! A poem for your mother!

GRACE.

[*Lets out a short pleading cry*]

Ohh! Get away from him, Walker! Get away from him,

[*Hysterically*]

you nigger murderer!

WALKER.

[*Has started to tilt the bottle again, after he slaps* EASLEY, *and when* GRACE *shouts at him, he chokes on the liquor, spitting it out, and begins laughing with a kind of hysterical amusement*]

Oh! Ha, ha, ha . . . you mean. . . . Wow!

[*Trying to control laughter, but it is an extreme kind of release*]

No kidding? Grace, Gracie! Wow! I wonder how long you had that stored up.

GRACE.

[*Crying now, going over to* EASLEY, *trying to help him up*]

Brad. Brad. Walker, why'd you come here? Why'd you come here? Brad?

WALKER.

[*Still laughing and wobbling clumsily around*]

Nigger murderer? Wowee. Gracie, are you just repeating your faggot husband, or did you have that in you a long time? I mean . . . for all the years we were together? Hooo! Yeah.

[*Mock seriously*]

Christ, it could get to be a weight after a time, huh? When you taught the little girls to pray . . . you'd have to whisper, "And God bless Mommy, and God bless Daddy, the nigger murderer." Wow, that's some weight.

GRACE. Shut up, Walker. Just shut up, and get out of here, away from us, please. I don't want to hear you . . . I don't need to hear you, again. Remember, I heard it all before, baby . . . you don't get me again.

[*She is weeping and twisting her head, trying at the same time to fully revive* EASLEY, *who is still sitting on the floor with legs sprawled apart, both hands held to the pit of his stomach, his head nodding back and forth in pain*]

Why'd you come here . . . just to do this? Why don't you leave before you kill somebody?

[*Trying to hold back a scream*]

Before you kill another white person?

WALKER.

[*Sobering, but still forcing a cynical hilarity*]

Ah . . . the party line. Stop him before he kills another white person! Heh. Yeah. Yeah. And that's not such a bad idea really. . . . I mean, after all, only you and your husband there are white in this house. Those two lovely little girls upstairs are niggers. You know, circa 1800, one drop makes you whole?

GRACE. Shut up, Walker!

[*She leaps to her feet and rushes toward him*]

Shut your ugly head!

[*He pushes her away*]

EASLEY.

[*Raising his head and shouting as loud as he can manage*]

You're filth, boy. Just filth. Can you understand that anything and everything you do is stupid, filthy, or meaningless! Your inept formless poetry. Hah. Poetry? A flashy doggerel for inducing all those unfortunate troops of yours to spill their blood in your behalf. But I guess that's something! Ritual drama, we used to call it at the university. The poetry of ritual drama.

[*Pulls himself up*]

And even that's giving that crap the benefit of the doubt. Ritual filth would have been the right name for it.

WALKER. Ritual drama . . .

[*Half musing*]

yeah, I remember seeing that phrase in an old review by one of your queer academic friends. . . .

[*Noticing* EASLEY *getting up.*]

Oh well, look at him coming up by his bootstraps. I didn't mean to hit you that hard, Professor Easley, sir . . . I just don't know my own strent'.

[*Laughs and finishes the bottle . . . starts as if he is going to throw it over his shoulder, then he places it very carefully on the table. He starts dancing around and whooping like an "Indian"*]

More! Bwana, me want more fire water!

EASLEY. As I said, Vessels, you're just filth. Pretentious filth.

WALKER.

[*Dances around a bit more, then stops abruptly in front of* EASLEY; *so close they are almost touching. He speaks in a quiet menacing tone*]

The liquor, turkey. The liquor. No opinions right now. Run off and get more liquor, *sabe?*

GRACE.

[*Has stopped crying and managed to regain a cynical composure*]

I'll get it, Brad. Mr. Vessels is playing the mad scene from Native Son.

[*Turns to go*]

A second-rate Bigger Thomas.

WALKER.

[*Laughs*]

Yeah. But remember when I used to play a second-rate Othello? Oh, wow . . . you remember that, don't you, Professor No-Dick? You remember when I used to walk around wondering what that fair sister was thinking?

[*Hunches* EASLEY]

Oh, come on now, you remember that. . . . I was Othello . . . Grace there was Desdemona . . . and you were Iago . . .

[*Laughs*]

or at least between classes, you were Iago. Hey, who were you during classes? I forgot to find that out. Ha, the key to my downfall. I knew you were Iago between classes, when I saw you, but I never knew who you were during classes. Ah ah, that's the basis of an incredibly profound social axiom. I quote:. . . and you better write this down, Bradford, so you can pass it on to your hipper colleagues at the university . . .

[*Laughs*]

I mean if they ever rebuild the university. What was I saying to you, enemy? Oh yeah . . . the axiom. Oh . . .

GRACE.

[*Returning with a bottle*]

You still at it, huh, Bigger?

WALKER. Yeah, yeah . . .

[*Reaches for bottle*]

lemme see. I get it. . . . If a white man is Iago when you see him . . . uhh . . . chances are he's eviler when you don't.

[*Laughs*]

EASLEY. Yes, that was worthy of you.

WALKER. It *was* lousy, wasn't it?

GRACE. Look

[*Trying to be earnest*]

Walker, pour yourself a drink . . . as many drinks as you need . . . and then leave, will you? I don't see what you think you're accomplishing by hanging around us.

EASLEY. Yes . . . I was wondering who's taking care of your mighty army while you're here in the enemy camp? How can the black liberation movement spare its illustrious leader for such a long stretch?

WALKER.

[*Sits abruptly on couch and stretches both legs out, drinking big glass of bourbon. Begins speaking in pidgin "Japanese"*]

Oh, don't worry about that, doomed American dog. Ha. You see and hear those shells beating this town flat, don't you? In fact, we'll probably be here en masse in about a week. Why don't I just camp here and wait for my brothers to get here and liberate the whole place? Huh?

[*Laughs*]

GRACE. Walker, you're crazy!

EASLEY. I think he's got more sense than that.

WALKER.

[*Starting to make up a song*]

Ohhh! I'll stay here and rape your wife . . . as I so often used to do . . . as I so often used. . . .

GRACE. Your mind is gone, Walker . . . completely gone.

[*She turns to go upstairs. A bright blast rocks the house and she falls against the wall*]

WALKER.

[*Thrown forward to the floor, rises quickly to see how* GRACE *is*]

Hey, you all right, lady?

EASLEY. Grace!

[*He has also been rocked, but he gets to* GRACE *first*]
Don't worry about my wife, Vessels. That's my business.
GRACE. I'm O.K., Brad. I was on my way upstairs to look in on the girls.
It's a wonder they're not screaming now.
WALKER. They were fine when I looked in earlier. Sleeping very soundly.
EASLEY. You were upstairs?
WALKER.

[*Returning to his seat, with another full glass*]
Of course I went upstairs, to see my children. In fact, I started to take
them away with me, while you patriots were out.

[*Another close blast*]
But I thought I'd wait to say hello to the mommy and stepdaddy.
EASLEY. You low bastard.

[*Turning toward* WALKER *and looking at* GRACE *at the same time*]
GRACE. No . . . you're not telling the truth now, Walker.

[*Voice quavering and rising*]
You came here just to say that. Just to see what your saying that would do
to me.

[*Turns away from him*]
You're a bad liar, Walker. As always . . . a very bad liar.
WALKER. You know I'm not lying. I want those children. You know that,
Grace.
EASLEY. I know you're drunk!
GRACE. You're lying. You don't want those children. You just want to
think you want them for the moment . . . to excite one of those obscure
pathological instruments you've got growing in your head. Today, you
want to feel like you want the girls. Just like you wanted to feel hurt and
martyred by your misdirected cause, when you first drove us away.
WALKER. Drove you away? You knew what I was into. You could have
stayed. You said you wanted to pay whatever thing it cost to stay.
EASLEY. How can you lie like this, Vessels? Even I know you pushed Grace
until she couldn't retain her sanity and stay with you in that madness.
All the bigoted racist imbeciles you started to cultivate. Every white
friend you had knows that story.
WALKER. You shut up. . . . I don't want to hear anything you've got to
say.
GRACE. There are so many bulbs and screams shooting off inside you,
Walker. So many lies you have to pump full of yourself. You're split so
many ways . . . your feelings are cut up into skinny horrible strips . . .
like umbrella struts . . . holding up whatever bizzarre black cloth you're
using this performance as your self's image. I don't even think you know
who you are any more. No, I don't think you *ever* knew.
WALKER. I know what I can use.
GRACE. No, you never even found out who you were until you sold the
last of your loves and emotions down the river . . . until you killed your

last old friend . . . and found out *what* you were. My God, it must be hard being you, Walker Vessels. It must be a sick task keeping so many lying separate uglinesses together . . . and pretending they're something you've made and understand.

WALKER. What I can use, madam . . . what I can use. I move now trying to be certain of that.

EASLEY. You're talking strangely. What is this, the pragmatics of war? What are you saying . . . use? I thought you meant yourself to be a fantastic idealist? All those speeches and essays and poems . . . the re-birth of idealism. That the Western white man had forfeited the most impressive characteristic of his culture . . . the idealism of rational liberalism . . . and that only the black man in the West could restore that quality to Western culture, because he still understood the necessity for it. Et cetera, et cetera.Oh, look, I remember your horseshit theories, friend. I remember. And now the great black Western idealist is talking about use.

WALKER. Yeah, yeah. Now you can call me the hypocritical idealist nigger murderer. You see, what I want is more titles.

GRACE. And saying you want the children is another title . . . right? Every time you say it, one of those bulbs goes off in your head and you think you can focus on still another attribute, another beautiful quality in the total beautiful structure of the beautiful soul of Walker Vessels, sensi-tive Negro poet, savior of his people, deliverer of Western idealism . . . commander-in-chief of the forces of righteousness . . . Oh, God, et cetera, et cetera.

WALKER. Grace Locke Vessels Easley . . . whore of the middle classes.

EASLEY.

[*Turning suddenly as if to offer combat*]

Go and fuck yourself.

GRACE. Yes, Walker, by all means . . . go and fuck yourself.

[*And softer*]

Yes, do anything . . . but don't drag my children into your scheme for martyrdom and immortality, or whatever else it is makes you like you are . . . just don't . . . don't even mention it.

EASLEY.

[*Moving to comfort her*]

Oh, don't get so worried, Grace . . . you know he just likes to hear him-self talk . . . more than anything . . . he just wants to hear himself talk, so he can find out what he's supposed to have on his mind.

[*To* WALKER]

He knows there's no way in the world he could have those children. No way in the world.

WALKER.

[*Feigning casual matter-of-fact tone*]

Mr. Easley, Mrs. Easley, those girls' last name is Vessels. Whatever you think is all right. I mean I don't care what you think about me or what I'm doing . . . the whole mess. But those beautiful girls you have upstairs there are my daughters. They even look like me. I've loved them all their lives. Before this there was too much to do, so I left them with you.

[*Gets up, pours another drink*]

But now . . . things are changed. . . . I want them with me.

[*Sprawls on couch again*]

I want them with me very much.

GRACE. You're lying. Liar, you don't give a shit about those children. You're a liar if you say otherwise. You never never never cared at all for those children. My friend, you have never cared for anything in the world that I know of but what's in there behind your eyes. And God knows what ugliness that is . . . though there are thousands of people dead or home-less all over this country who begin to understand a little. And not just white people . . . you've killed so many of your own people too. It's a wonder they haven't killed you.

EASLEY.

[*Walks over to* WALKER]

Get up and get out of here! So help me . . . if you don't leave here now . . . I'll call the soldiers. They'd just love to find you.

[WALKER *doesn't move*]

Really, Vessels, I'll personally put a big hole in that foul liberation move-ment right now . . . I swear it.

[*He turns to go to the phone*]

WALKER.

[*At first as if he is good-natured*]

Hey, hey . . . Professor Easley, I've got this gun here, remember? Now don't do that . . . in fact if you take another step, I'll blow your goddamn head off. And I mean that, Brad, turn around and get back here in the center of the room.

GRACE.

[*Moves for the stairs*]

Ohhh!

WALKER. Hey, Grace, stop . . . you want me to shoot this fairy, or what? Come back here!

GRACE. I was only going to see about the kids.

WALKER. I'm their father . . . I'm thinking about their welfare, too. Just come back here. Both of you sit on this couch where I'm sitting, and I'll sit in that chair over there near the ice tray.

EASLEY. So now we get a taste of Vessels, the hoodlum.

WALKER. Oh, yeah. Another title, boss man. But just sit the fuck down for now.

[*Goes to the window. Looks at his watch*]

I got about an hour.

GRACE. Walker, what are you going to do?

WALKER. Do? Well, right now I'm going to have another drink.

EASLEY. You know what she means.

GRACE. You're not going to take the children, are you? You wouldn't just take them, would you? You wouldn't do that. You can't hate me so much that you'd do that.

WALKER. I don't hate you at all, Grace. I hated you when I wanted you. I haven't wanted you for a long time. But I do want those children.

GRACE. You're lying!

WALKER. No, I'm not lying . . . and I guess that's what's cutting you up . . . because you probably know I'm not lying, and you can't understand that. But I tell you now that I'm not lying, and that in spite of all the things I've done that have helped kill love in me, I still love those girls.

EASLEY. You mean, in spite of all the people you've killed.

WALKER. O.K., O.K., however you want it . . . however you want it, let it go at that. In spite of all the people I've killed. No, better, in spite of the fact that I, Walker Vessels, single-handedly, and with no other adviser except my own ego, promoted a bloody situation where white and black people are killing each other; despite the fact that I know that this is at best a war that will only change, ha, the complexion of tyranny . . .

[*Laughs sullenly*]

in spite of the fact that I have killed for all times any creative impulse I will ever have by the depravity of my murderous philosophies . . . despite the fact that I am being killed in my head each day and by now have no soul or heart or warmth, even in my long killer fingers, despite the fact that I have no other thing in the universe that I love or trust, but myself . . . despite or in spite, the respite, my dears, my dears, hear me, O Olympus, O Mercury, God of thieves, O Damballah, chief of all the dead religions of pseudo-nigger patriots hoping to open big restaurants after de wah . . . har har . . . in spite, despite, the resistance in the large cities and the small towns, where we have taken, yes, dragged piles of darkies out of their beds and shot them for being in Rheingold ads, despite the fact that all of my officers are ignorant motherfuckers who have never read any book in their lives, despite the fact that I would rather argue politics, or literature, or boxing, or anything, with you, dear Easley, with you . . .

[*Head slumps, weeping*]

despite all these things and in spite of all the drunken noises I'm making, despite . . . in spite of . . . I want those girls, very, very much. And I will take them out of here with me.

EASLEY. No, you won't . . . not if I can help it.

WALKER. Well, you can't help it.

GRACE.

[*Jumps up*]

What? Is no one to reason with you? Isn't there any way something can exist without you having the final judgment on it? Is the whole world yours . . . to deal with or destroy? You're right! You feel! You have the only real vision of the world. You love! No one else exists in the world except you, and those who can help you. Everyone else is nothing or else they're something to be destroyed. I'm your enemy now . . . right? I'm wrong. You are the children's father . . . but I'm no longer their mother. Every one of your yesses or nos is intended by you to reshape the world after the image you have of it. They *are* my children! I am their mother! But because somehow I've become your enemy, I suddenly no longer qualify. Forget you're their mother, Grace. Walker has decided that you're no longer to perform that function. So the whole business is erased as if it never existed. I'm *not* in your head, Walker. Neither are those kids. We are all flesh and blood and deserve to live . . . even unabstracted by what you think we ought to be in the general scheme of things. Even alien to it. I left you . . . and took the girls because you'd gone crazy. You're crazy now. This stupid ugly killing you've started will never do anything, for anybody. And you and all your people will be wiped out, you know that. And you'll have accomplished nothing. Do you want those two babies to be with you when you're killed so they can witness the death of a great man? So they can grow up and write articles for a magazine sponsored by the Walker Vessels Society?

WALKER. Which is still better than being freakish mulattoes in a world where your father is some evil black thing you can't remember. Look, I was going to wait until the fighting was over . . .
    [*Reflective*]
until we had won, before I took them. But something occurred to me for the first time, last night. It was the idea that we might not win. Somehow it only got through to me last night. I'd sort've taken it for granted . . . as a solved problem, that the fighting was the most academic of our problems, and that the real work would come necessarily after the fighting was done. But. . . .

EASLEY. Things are not going as well for you as you figured.

WALKER. No. It will take a little longer, that's all. But this city will fall soon. We should be here within a week. You see, I could have waited until then. Then just marched in, at the head of the triumphant army, and seized the children as a matter of course. In fact I don't know why I didn't, except I did want to see you all in what you might call your natural habitats. I thought maybe I might be able to sneak in just as you and my ex-wife were making love, or just as you were lining the girls up against the wall to beat them or make them repeat after you, "Your daddy is a racist murderer." And then I thought I could murder both of you on the spot, and be completely justified.

GRACE. You've convinced yourself that you're rescuing the children, haven't you?

WALKER. Just as you convinced yourself you were rescuing them when you took them away from me.

EASLEY. She was!

WALKER. Now so am I.

GRACE. Yes

[*Wearily*]

I begin to get some of your thinking now. When you mentioned killing us. I'm sure you thought the whole thing up in quite heroic terms. How you'd come through the white lines, murder us, and *rescue* the girls. You probably went over that . . . or had it go through your head on that gray film, a thousand times until it was some kind of obligatory reality.

[WALKER *laughs*]

EASLEY. The kind of insane reality that brought about all the killing.

WALKER. Christ, the worst thing that ever happened to the West was the psychological novel . . . believe me.

EASLEY. When the Nazis were confronted with Freud, they claimed his work was of dubious value.

WALKER. Bravo!

GRACE. It's a wonder you *didn't* murder us!

WALKER.

[*Looking suddenly less amused*]

Oh . . . have I forfeited my opportunity?

EASLEY.

[*Startled reaction*]

You're not serious? What reason . . . what possible reason would there be for killing us? I mean I could readily conceive of your killing me, but the two of us, as some kind of psychological unit. I don't understand that. You said you didn't hate Grace.

GRACE.

[*To press* WALKER]

He's lying again, Brad. Really, most times he's not to be taken seriously. He was making a metaphor before . . . one of those ritual-drama metaphors. . . .

[*Laughs, as does* BRAD]

You said it before . . . just to hear what's going on in his head. Really, he's not to be taken seriously.

[*She hesitates, and there is a silence*]

Unless there's some way you can kill him.

WALKER.

[*Laughs, then sobers, but begins to show the effects of the alcohol*]

Oh, Grace, Grace. Now you're trying to incite your husbean . . . which I swear is hardly Christian. I'm really surprised at you. But more so because you completely misunderstand me now . . . or maybe I'm not so surprised. I guess you never did know what was going on. That's why you left. You thought I betrayed you or something. Which really knocked me on my ass, you know? I was preaching hate the white man . . . get the white man off our backs . . . if necessary, kill the white man for our rights . . . whatever the hell that finally came to mean. And don't, now, for God's sake start thinking he's disillusioned, he's cynical, or any of the rest of these horseshit liberal definitions of the impossibility or romanticism of idealism. But those things I said . . . and would say now, pushed you away from me. I couldn't understand that.

GRACE. You couldn't understand it? What are you saying?

WALKER. No, I couldn't understand it. We'd been together a long time, before all that happened. What I said . . . what I thought I had to do . . . I knew you, if any white person in the world could, I knew you would understand. And then you didn't.

GRACE. You began to align yourself with the worst kind of racists and second-rate hack political thinkers.

WALKER. I've never aligned myself with anything or anyone I hadn't thought up first.

GRACE. You stopped telling me everything!

WALKER. I never stopped telling you I loved you . . . or that you were my wife!

GRACE.

[*Almost broken*]

It wasn't enough, Walker. It wasn't enough.

WALKER. God, it should have been.

GRACE. Walker, you were preaching the murder of all white people. Walker, I was, am, white. What do you think was going through my mind every time you were at some rally or meeting whose sole purpose was to bring about the destruction of white people?

WALKER. Oh, Goddamn it, Grace, are you so stupid? You were my wife . . . I loved you. You mean because I loved you and was married to you . . . had had children by you, I wasn't supposed to say the things I felt. I was crying out against three hundred years of oppression; not against individuals.

EASLEY. But it's individuals who are dying.

WALKER. It was individuals who were doing the oppressing. It was individuals who were being oppressed. The horror is that oppression is not a concept that can be specifically transferable. From the oppressed, down on the oppressor. To keep the horror where it belongs . . . on those people who we can speak of, even in this last part of the twentieth century, as evil.

EASLEY. You're so wrong about everything. So terribly, sickeningly wrong. What can you change? What do you hope to change? Do you think Negroes are better people than whites . . . that they can govern a society *better* than whites? That they'll be more judicious or more tolerant? Do you think they'll make fewer mistakes? I mean really, if the Western white man has proved one thing . . . it's the futility of modern society. So the have-not peoples become the haves. Even so, will that change the essential functions of the world? Will there be more love or beauty in the world . . . more knowledge . . . because of it?

WALKER. Probably. Probably there will be more . . . if more people have a chance to understand what it is. But that's not even the point. It comes down to baser human endeavor than any social-political thinking. What does it matter if there's more love or beauty? Who the fuck cares? Is that what the Western ofay thought while he was ruling . . . that his rule somehow brought more love and beauty into the world? Oh, he might have thought that concomitantly, while sipping a gin rickey and scratching his ass . . . but that was not ever the point. Not even on the Crusades. The point is that you had your chance, darling, now these other folks have theirs.

[*Quietly*]

Now they have theirs.

EASLEY. God, what an ugly idea.

WALKER.

[*Head in hands*]

I know. I know.

[*His head is sagging, but he brings it up quickly. While it is down,* EASLEY *crosses* GRACE *with a significant look*]

But what else you got, champ? What else you got? I remember too much horseshit from the other side for you to make much sense. Too much horseshit. The cruelty of it, don't you understand, now? The complete ugly horseshit cruelty of it is that there doesn't have to be a change. It'll be up to individuals on that side, just as it was supposed to be up to individuals on this side. Ha! . . . Who failed! Just like you failed, Easley. Just like you failed.

EASLEY. Failed? What are you talking about?

WALKER.

[*Nodding*]

Well, what do you think? You never did anything concrete to avoid what's going on now. Your sick liberal lip service to whatever was the least filth. Your high aesthetic disapproval of the political. Letting the sick ghosts of the thirties strangle whatever chance we had.

EASLEY. What are you talking about?

WALKER. What we argued about so many times . . . befo' de wah.

EASLEY. And you see . . . what I predicted has happened. Now, in whatever cruel, and you said it, cruel political synapse you're taken with, or anyone else is taken with, with sufficient power I, any individual, any person who thinks of life as a purely anarchic relationship between man and God . . . or man and his work . . . any consciousness like that is destroyed . . . along with your *enemies*. And you, for whatever right or freedom or sickening cause you represent, kill me. Kill what does not follow.

WALKER. Perhaps you're right. But I have always found it hard to be neutral when faced with ugliness. Especially an ugliness that has worked all my life to twist me.

GRACE. And so you let it succeed!

WALKER. The aesthete came long after all the things that really formed me. I was the easiest weight to shed. And I couldn't be merely a journalist . . . a social critic. No social protest . . . right is in the act! And the act itself has some place in the world . . . it makes some place for itself. Right? But you all accuse me, not understanding that what you represent, you, my wife, all our old intellectual cutthroats, was something that was going to die anyway. One way or another. You'd been used too often, backed off from reality too many times. Remember the time, remember that time long time ago, in the old bar when you and Louie Rino were arguing with me, and Louie said then that he hated people who wanted to change the world. You remember that?

EASLEY. I remember the fight.

WALKER. Yeah, well, I know I thought then that none of you would write any poetry either. I knew that you had moved too far away from the actual meanings of life . . . into some lifeless cocoon of pretended intellectual and emotional achievement, to really be able to see the world again. What was Rino writing before he got killed? Tired elliptical little descriptions of what he could see out the window.

EASLEY. And how did he die?

WALKER. An explosion in the school where he was teaching.

[*Nodding*]

EASLEY. One of your terrorists did it.

WALKER. Yeah, yeah.

EASLEY. He was supposed to be one of your closest friends.

WALKER. Yeah, yeah.

GRACE. Yeah, yeah, yeah, yeah.

[*With face still covered*]

WALKER. We called for a strike to show the government we had all the white intellectuals backing us.

[*Nodding*]

Hah, and the only people who went out were those tired political hacks. No one wanted to be intellectually compromised.

EASLEY. I didn't go either.

[*Hunches* GRACE, *starts to ease out of his chair*]

And it was an intellectual compromise. No one in their right mind could have backed your program completely.

WALKER. No one but Negroes.

EASLEY. Well, then, they weren't in their right minds. You'd twisted them.

WALKER. The country twisted 'em.

[*Still nodding*]

The country had twisted them for so long.

[*Head almost touching his chest*]

EASLEY.

[*Taking very cautious step toward* WALKER, *still talking*]

The politics of self-pity.

[*Indicates to* GRACE *that she is to talk*]

WALKER.

[*Head down*]

Yeah. Yeah.

EASLEY. The politics of self-pity.

GRACE.

[*Raising her head slowly to watch, almost petrified*]

A murderous self-pity. An extraordinarily murderous self-pity.

[*There is another explosion close to the house. The lights go out for a few seconds. They come on, and* EASLEY *is trying to return to his seat, but* WALKER'S *head is still on his chest*]

WALKER.

[*Mumbles*]

What'd they do, hit the lights? Goddamn lousy marksmen.

[EASLEY *starts again*]

Lousy marksmen . . . and none of 'em worth shit.

[*Now, another close explosion. The lights go out again. They come on;* EASLEY *is standing almost halfway between the couch and* WALKER. WALKER'S *head is still down on his chest.* EASLEY *crouches to move closer. The lights go out again*]

Black

[*More explosions*]

Act II

Explosions are heard before the curtain goes up. When curtain rises, room is still in darkness, but the explosion does throw some light. Figures are still as they were at the end of first act; light from explosions outlines them briefly.

WALKER. Shit.

[*Lights come up.* WALKER'S *head is still down, but he is nodding from side to side, cursing something very drunkenly.* EASLEY *stands very stiffly in the center of the room, waiting to take another step.* GRACE *sits very stiffly, breathing heavily, on the couch, trying to make some kind of conversation, but not succeeding.* WALKER *has his hand in his jacket pocket, on the gun*]

GRACE. It is self-pity, and some weird ambition, Walker.

[*Strained silence*]

But there's no reason . . . the girls should suffer. There's . . . no reason.

[EASLEY *takes a long stride, and is about to throw himself at* WALKER, *when there is another explosion, and the lights go out again, very briefly. When they come up,* EASLEY *is set to leap, but* WALKER'S *head comes abruptly up. He stares drunkenly at* EASLEY, *not moving his hand. For some awkward duration of time the two men stare at each other, in almost the same way as they had at the beginning of the play. Then* GRACE *screams*]

GRACE. Walker!

[WALKER *looks at her slightly, and* EASLEY *throws himself on him. The chair falls backward and the two men roll on the floor.* EASLEY *trying to choke* WALKER. WALKER *trying to get the gun out of his pocket*]

GRACE. Walker! Walker!

[*Suddenly,* WALKER *shoves one hand in* EASLEY'S *face, shooting him without taking the gun from his pocket.* EASLEY *slumps backward, his face twisted, his mouth open and working.* WALKER *rolls back of* EASLEY, *pulling the gun from his pocket. He props himself against the chair, staring at the man's face*]

GRACE. Walker.

[*Her shouts have become whimpers, and she is moving stiffly toward* EASLEY]

Walker. Walker.

EASLEY.

[*Mouth is still working . . . and he is managing to get a few sounds, words, out*]

WALKER.

[*Still staring at him, pulling himself up on the chair*]

Shut up, you!

[*To* EASLEY]

You shut up. I don't want to hear anything else from you. You just die, quietly. No more talk.

GRACE. Walker!

[*She is screaming again*]

Walker!

[*She rushes toward* EASLEY, *but* WALKER *catches her arm and pushes her away*]

You're an insane man. You hear me, Walker?

[*He is not looking at her, he is still staring down at* EASLEY]

Walker, you're an insane man.

[*She screams*]

You're an insane man.

[*She slumps to the couch, crying*]

An insane man. . . .

WALKER. No profound statements, Easley. No horseshit like that. No elegance. You just die quietly and stupidly. Like niggers do. Like they are now.

[*Quieter*]

Like I will. The only thing I'll let you say is, "I only regret that I have but one life to lose for my country." You can say that.

[*Looks over at* GRACE]

Grace! Tell Bradford that he can say, "I only regret that I have but one life to lose for my country." You can say that, Easley, but that's all.

EASLEY.

[*Straining to talk*]

Ritual drama. Like I said, ritual drama. . . .

[*He dies.*

WALKER *stands staring at him. The only sounds are an occasional explosion, and* GRACE's *heavy brittle weeping*]

WALKER. He could have said, "I only regret that I have but one life to lose for my country." I would have let him say that . . . but no more. No more. There is no reason he should go out with any kind of dignity. I couldn't allow that.

GRACE. You're out of your mind.

[*Slow, matter-of-fact*]

WALKER. Meaning?

GRACE. You're out of your mind.

WALKER.

[*Wearily*]

Turn to another station.

GRACE. You're out of your mind.

WALKER. I said, turn to another station . . . will you? Another station! Out of my mind is not the point. You ought to know that.

[*Brooding*]

The way things are, being out of your mind is the only thing that qualifies you to stay alive. The only thing. Easley was in his right mind. Pitiful as he was. That's the reason he's dead.

GRACE. He's dead because you killed him.

WALKER. Yeah. He's dead because I killed him. Also, because he thought he ought to kill me.

[*Looking over at the dead man*]

You want me to cover him up?

GRACE. I don't want you to do anything, Walker . . . but leave here.

[*Raising her voice*]

Will you do that for me . . . or do you want to kill me too?

WALKER. Are you being ironic? Huh?

[*He grabs her arm, jerking her head up so she has to look at him*]

Do you think you're being ironic? Or do you want to kill me, too? . . .

[*Shouting*]

You're mighty right I want to kill you. You're mighty goddamn right. Believe me, self-righteous little bitch, I want to kill you.

GRACE.

[*startled, but trying not to show it*]

The cause demands it, huh? The cause demands it.

WALKER. Yeah, the cause demands it.

GRACE.

> [*She gets up and goes to* EASLEY, *kneeling beside the body*]

The cause demands it, Brad. That's why Walker shot you . . . because the cause demands it.

> [*Her head droops but she doesn't cry. She sits on her knees, holding the dead man's hand*]

I guess the point is that now when you take the children I'll be alone.

> [*She looks up at* ,WALKER]

I guess that's the point, now. Is that the point, Walker? Me being alone . . . as you have been now for so long? I'll bet that's the point, huh? I'll bet you came here to do exactly what you did . . . kill Brad, then take the kids, and leave me alone . . . to suffocate in the stink of my memories.

> [*She is trying not to cry*]

Just like I did to you. I'm sure that's the point. Right?

> [*She leaps up suddenly at* WALKER]

You scum! You murdering scum.

> [*They grapple for a second, then* WALKER *slaps her to the floor. She kneels a little way off from* EASLEY's *body*]

WALKER. Yeh, Grace. That's the point. For sure, that's the point.

GRACE. You were going to kill Brad, from the first. You knew that before you even got here.

WALKER. I'd thought about it.

GRACE.

> [*Weeping, but then she stops and is quiet for a minute*]

So what's supposed to happen then . . . I mean after you take the kids and leave me here alone? Huh? I know you've thought about that, too.

WALKER. I have. But you know what'll happen much better than I do. But maybe you don't. What do you think happened to me when you left? Did you ever think about that? You must have.

GRACE. You had your cause, friend. Your cause, remember. And thousands of people following you, hoping that shit you preached was right. I pitied you.

WALKER. I know that. It took me awhile, but then I finally understood that you did pity me. And that you were somewhere, going through whatever mediocre routine you and Easley called your lives . . . pitying me. I figured that, finally, you weren't really even shocked by what was happening . . . what had happened. You were so secure in the knowledge that you were good, and compassionate . . . and right, that most of all . . . you were certain, my God, so certain . . . emotionally and intellectually, that you were right, until the only idea you had about me was to pity me.

> [*He wheels around to face her squarely*]

God, that pissed me off. You don't really know how furious that made me. You and that closet queen, respected, weak-as-water intellectual, pitying me. God. God!

[*Forcing the humor*]

Miss Easley, honey, I could have killed both of you every night of my life.

GRACE. Will you kill me now if I say right here that I still pity you?

WALKER.

[*A breathless half-broken laugh*]

No. No, I won't kill you.

GRACE. Well, I pity you, Walker. I really do.

WALKER. Only until you start pitying yourself.

GRACE. I wish I could call you something that would hurt you.

WALKER. So do I.

GRACE.

[*Wearily*]

Nigger.

WALKER. So do I.

[*Looks at his watch*]

I've got to go soon.

GRACE. You're still taking the girls.

[*She is starting to push herself up from the floor.*

WALKER *stares at her, then quickly over his shoulder at the stairway. He puts his hand in the pocket where the gun is, then he shakes his head slowly*]

GRACE.

[*Not seeing his gesture*]

You're still taking the children?

[WALKER *shakes his head slowly. An explosion shakes the house a little*]

GRACE. Walker. Walker.

[*She staggers to her feet, shaking with the next explosion*]

Walker? You shook your head?

[WALKER *stands very stiffly looking at the floor.*

GRACE *starts to come to him, and the next explosion hits very close or actually hits the house. Beams come down; some of the furniture is thrown around.* GRACE *falls to the floor.* WALKER *is toppled backward. A beam hits* GRACE *across the chest. Debris falls on* WALKER. *There are some more explosions, and then silence*]

GRACE. Walker! Walker!

[*She is hurt very badly and is barely able to move the debris that is covering her*]

Walker! The girls! Walker! Catherine! Elizabeth! Walker, the girls!

[WALKER *finally starts to move. He is also hurt badly, but he is able to move much more freely than* GRACE. *He starts to clear away the debris and make his way to his knees*]

GRACE. Walker?

WALKER. Yeah? Grace?

GRACE. Walker, the children . . . the girls . . . see about the girls.

[*She is barely able to raise one of her arms*]

The girls, Walker, see about them.

WALKER.

[*He is finally able to crawl over to* GRACE, *and pushes himself unsteadily up on his hands*]

You're hurt pretty badly? Can you move?

GRACE. The girls, Walker, see about the girls.

WALKER. Can you move?

GRACE. The girls, Walker. . . .

[*She is losing strength*]

Our children!

WALKER.

[*He is silent for awhile*]

They're dead, Grace. Catherine and Elizabeth are dead.

[*He starts up stairs as if to verify his statement. Stops, midway, shakes his head; retreats*]

GRACE.

[*Looking up at him frantically, but she is dying*]

Dead? Dead?

[*She starts to weep and shake her head*]

Dead?

[*Then she stops suddenly, tightening her face*]

How . . . how do you know, Walker? How do you know they're dead?

[WALKER'*s head is drooping slightly*]

How do you know they're dead, Walker? How do you. . . .

[*Her eyes try to continue what she is saying, but she slumps, and dies in a short choking spasm.*

WALKER *looks to see that she is dead, then resumes his efforts to get up. He looks at his watch. Listens to see if it is running. Wipes his face. Pushes the floor to get up. Another explosion sounds very close and he crouches quickly, covering his head. Another explosion. He pushes himself up, brushing sloppily at his clothes. He looks at his watch again, then starts to drag himself toward the door*]

They're dead, Grace.

[*He is almost shouting*]

They're dead.

[*He leaves, stumbling unsteadily through the door. He is now the old man at the beginning of the play. There are more explosions. Another one very close to the house. A sudden aggravated silence, and then there is a child heard crying and screaming as loud as it can. More explosions*]

Black

[*More explosions, after curtain for some time*]

The Little Black Boy

William Blake

My mother bore me in the southern wild,
And I am black, but O! my soul is white;
White as an angel is the English child,
But I am black, as if bereaved of light.

My mother taught me underneath a tree,
And sitting down before the heat of day,
She took me on her lap and kissed me,
And pointing to the east, began to say:

"Look on the rising sun: there God does live,
And gives His light, and gives His heat away;
And flowers and trees and beasts and men receive
Comfort in morning, joy in the noonday.

"And we are put on earth a little space,
That we may learn to bear the beams of love;
And these black bodies and this sunburnt face
Is but a cloud, and like a shady grove.

"For when our souls have learned the heat to bear,
The cloud will vanish; we shall hear His voice,
Saying: 'Come out from the grove, my love and care,
And round my golden tent like lambs rejoice.' "

Thus did my mother say, and kissed me;
And thus I say to little English boy:
When I from black and he from white cloud free,
And round the tent of God like lambs we joy,

I'll shade him from the heat, till he can bear
To lean in joy upon our Father's knee;
And then I'll stand and stroke his silver hair,
And be like him, and he will then love me.

The Engagement Party

Robert Boles

She was not a drinker, for she held her glass too carefully. My eyes fastened to a detail. Her fingernail polish. The red was put into check by its own too-even glaze, was held, suspended.

"Yes. Well, my husband's work is similar to yours," she continued.

"Is it really?" I asked, but not quite politely enough. Had it been the lines of her eyes which projected the effect of my lack of attention? Her makeup, though not overdone, was obvious. Immediately, a sense of having played this scene before.

I turned slightly away from her as a member of the combo walked by, and noticed Helen beckoning me.

"Excuse me, please," I said.

The woman smiled with closed jaws, shifted her weight and pivoted on a heel. Her last name was Nolan. I remembered that then. I had no intention of embarrassing her. One should be accustomed to that sort of thing at a party.

Smiling now, I worked my way towards Helen.

"By God! It's George! It's George himself!" The voice belonged to Helen's younger brother. I clapped him on the shoulder. "And you don't even have to drink!"

"I left it on the mantel."

"Have you had enough already?"

"I've hardly begun," I said.

Helen appeared. Her arms were in front of her as if she were holding an imaginary purse with both both hands. "There's someone you have to meet. My father's partner."

"I'm starved," I said.

She took my hand and led me across the room and into another. The people seemed plant-like, rooted in the carpet. Their motions seemed to have been caused by winds and crosswinds. Necks bent, backs; arms gestured in conversation. I had begun to perspire.

"I hope he doesn't get drunk," she confided without moving her lips or looking at me.

"Who?"

"My brother."

I bumped into the woman who wore the brocade dress, the one I had had the conversation with a moment before. Laughter and apologies, far in excess of what was called for. It was a brief bursting of her tension.

"Here he is," Helen announced.

"So, this is the young man who's going to carry you away." The man in his late forties or early fifties took my hand and shook it vigorously.

"Yes, sir," I said, assuming the bearing of a lower responding to an upper classman.

"It's about time I met you. Engineering, isn't it?"

"Yes, sir. Aeronautical."

"That's fine. You're a good-looking young man."

"Thank you, sir."

Helen moved away from me. I felt her absence as a hollow space beside me. Someone had asked her something and I had heard her say, "Certainly, Marie." That was all. I folded my arms, turned at the waist and followed her with my eyes. She escorted a woman to the foyer. The woman was a politician of some sort, I think. I believe I had seen her picture in the paper in regards to a "Culture March" on the Negro community.

"Wonderful girl, Helen."

"Yes, I agree," I said, and turned to face him again.

"Fine family."

"Yes, sir, I know," I said.

A group of men to my right were involved in a familiar and hearty political discussion. I tried to divide my attention.

"Your family's in . . . ?"

"California."

"Right. Ken told me. I had forgotten. Doctor, is he?"

"Not an M.D. He has a doctorate in education."

"I was in California for two years, you know."

"No, I didn't," I said. It was difficult for me to keep my eyes on him. His complexion was sallow, the color of coffee with heavy cream. I watched someone take a sip of drink and felt thirsty again.

"I was in L.A.," he continued.

"We're from San Francisco."

"And what do you think of Boston?"

"It's fine. I like it," I said without much enthusiasm.

The music began. Bass throb, brushes on cymbals, then piano, vibes and saxophone in a long chorus. People separated. We stepped back. Some danced the High-Life, others the Bossa-Nova.

"I don't intend for us to stay here," I continued. "I've taken a job in Connecticut."

"I'm sure it's best. Best to get the bride away from her parents."

I nodded, then covered my mouth while belching.

I recognized the bellowing of Tommy's voice to my right. He was, perhaps, getting drunk. "Being colored doesn't have anything to do with color! It's a question of attitudes and history and all that crap!"

"It's a good life that's years to lead," Helen's father's partner said. "When I was your age, I had to struggle. Not like you young people today."

"Yes," I said. "I realize how hard it must have been. I know how hard my father had to work."

The entire conversation was one often repeated. A needless formality. We were knowledgeably secure in the words we spoke. I felt a little disquiet.

"You youngsters have all of the opportunities, you know. And there are new ones opening every day. No worry about finding a job. If you're qualified, you'll get one."

Although it was not altogether true, I could do nothing but nod in solemn agreement and press my lips together in a gesture akin to a pout.

I thought I heard Helen call me, but I could not see her.

"What are your hobbies, son? I heard that you were a fine trackman in school."

"I swim, of course," I said, and struggled to say naturally, "and I'm a bit of a bug on sailing." It was the truth and it seemed to offend him. I had known that it would and that he would enjoy it.

A group of people parted in laughter. Helen entered between them. She came to my side. "Excuse me, Al. I'm going to take him away from you." Her voice sounded remarkably like her mother's.

"I understand." He extended his hand immediately and shook mine again quite vigorously.

Helen's hand was cool, as if it had been in cold water.

"You look fresh," I remarked.

"I just freshened up. I was wilting. It's so warm, and all of these people," she said. "Did you have a good conversation?"

"Yes. I suppose so. He's a very interesting man."

"What time is it?"

Instead of taking my hand away from her, I stood on my toes, stretched myself, and attempted to read the clock on the mantel in the other room. My drink had disappeared from in front of the mirror. "Quarter to eleven, I think."

There was a roar of laughter that was quickly muffled.

"Little brother is acting up again," she said.

"Leave Tommy alone," I said. "He's happy and well adjusted. Let him have some fun."

"You don't know what I go through with him!"

From across the room, a woman's voice calling Helen's name. The tone of it was comparable to the surface of a highly polished piece of wood. All of us, in a dense atmosphere of movements and poses, were beneath and supportive to it. "Helen!"

She looked.

Again, "Helen!"

I saw her at the other end of the room before Helen did. She sipped at a Manhattan and waved from her wrist as women, curiously, always wave.

Between smiles, I managed to repeat myself more forcefully than before. "I am starved, Helen. Famished!"

"You told me."

"I'm beginning to get a headache," I lied. "I didn't get a chance to eat this evening." But the evening was getting to me, the sensuous fugue, the cacophony of voices, the odors and light, the smoke. But something more than that. My disquietude.

"My poor dear," she mouthed, as she stroked my forehead with her fingertips. "I'm sure the caterer has some of those . . . things left. What were those things? Cabbage leaves stuffed with something and baked. Go into the kitchen."

"I think I will."

She had not really expected me to do so. "Dance with me first."

"No," I said. "You're cruel. I'm salivating and starved and you want me to burn more of my energy."

If she had pressed me, I would have danced. But she didn't.

"I'll see you in a few minutes."

We separated. She, it seemed, with misgivings. But I was relieved. I felt at once the dissolution of the effect of the hundred small embarrassments which had occurred between myself and others throughout the evening, the seconds of arbitrary inattentiveness which inflicted wounds, pinpricks, on each of us.

Perhaps I'm lying.

The kitchen door was on spring hinges. It closed itself after I had entered. I let my smile fall and imagined myself making an entrance onto a stage. I, as an actor with a small part in a play with Strindberg overtones.

I was at ease with the noise practically shut out. I hadn't noticed how sweaty I was. With a a lot of room and air, it seemed to be present all at once. The white tiles of the floor and walls, glazed, flat and hard, made me doubly aware of my body and the bodies of the caterer and the girl. All of us were dark mobile beings set into this sterile chamber. The room was filled with the odors of smoke and powder and perfume in the other rooms.

"The groom-to-be is here!" the caterer said.

"You know it, dad," I said, slipping easily into the dialect to let him know that I was a member. "And I want me some f-o-o-d!"

"I hear you talkin', baby," the caterer said.

A metal chair painted white was against one of the walls. I sat in it and stretched out my legs. The caterer took a plate and began filling it. His white uniform was badly fitted. It was large. His arms were lean.

The girl stood beside him and waited to help. She was very dark. Her bones were large, her hair coarse and beautiful.

"Get some salad for the man, Celestine," he said to her.

The name was right for her. It suggested fragility. Her bearing in some remarkable way suggested the same thing. She went to the refrigerator. I pretended that I had had slightly too much to drink. Her uniform played on my mind. The name Celestine did also. Her uniform was white. Starched. The material at the seams was doubled. Something easily noticeable for it was whiter there. The cloth played on her hips.

She looked at me briefly. I returned her glance with a smile and wondered, while I was doing so, what she thought of me. My complexion is agreeable with a black or charcoal gray suit. I am brown in the way a Mexican is brown. I had my jacket open, my vest unbuttoned part of the way.

Celestine put some salad into a wooden bowl. I raised my hand in a political gesture when enough had been placed there. She added a spoonful more and offered the words, "For your health."

"This is my daughter Celestine," the caterer said proudly.

"She's a very attractive girl."

Celestine turned away from me in modesty. It suddenly seemed right to speak of her with her father in this manner, the masculine dominant, the female subservient. I was particularly aware of the roles we had assumed and had heightened.

I noticed that the caterer continued to put food on my plate.

"Enough!" I said. "Man, when I want food for next year, I'll let you know."

He accepted my criticism with gentle laughter, but I was vaguely aware that I had overstepped myself.

"And what do you want to drink with that, sir?" he asked.

"Either Scotch or bourbon on the rocks," I said, with the full, coarse, American aplomb.

"I'll have to go to the bar to get some." He put the plate on the table near me. The top of the table was porcelain.

Celestine went to a drawer, pulled it open and began to remove a table mat.

"I don't need that," I said with an unintended sharpness. I smiled idiotically afterwards.

Her father left the kitchen.

I pulled my chair to the table and began to eat.

"Sit down," I said to her after a moment. "You make me nervous standing there."

She obeyed me. My voice still had a residue of sharpness. It was her father who had gotten beneath my skin. All of us had accepted Southern attitudes in a minute.

I wanted to speak to her as I ate, but nothing seemed worth saying.

It was difficult to cut through the cloth of pretension we had woven together. I ate in silence and she watched me in silence.

My thoughts turned to Helen, but it was clearly an alternative—something to compensate for my failure to communicate normally with the breathing girl seated next to me.

I ate too quickly and when I was almost done her father returned with a double light Scotch. I thanked him with a full mouth, then finished eating, and drank half of the drink slowly, with my eyes on the walls and ceiling.

I smiled to myself. I almost laughed.

In another moment I was in one of the large rooms again.

"So you're the fiancé!" a woman said, pointing her finger at my chest.

"I am," I said, and smiled.

"Well, dance with me, darling!" All of her *a*'s were broad, and her voice rasped pleasantly.

"Only the High-Life," I said. "I don't want to put my drink down."

We walked into the other room and began the lilting African dance which had gained so much favor. She danced well, if a bit stiffly, but it became her.

"You know, I just learned this," she said. "I think it's marvelous! And you must tell me about Helen. You two go so well together."

The combo ended the song. We had hardly begun. I hoped that I could separate myself from her without appearing to be rude. I excused myself but she gave no indication of having noticed. She continued as we walked to the side of the room, then she met someone I had met previously and introduced us. I slipped quietly away from her.

I wandered through groups of people as if I were looking for someone. I stopped briefly to chat with Helen's mother, and once again near a small group of men centered around a white civil rights worker who had just returned from the South. He emoted before his words as he told a story of an atrocity too vile to be printed in a newspaper.

It all seemed a circus I cared little about. Or a parade. I've never liked parades. I did something idiotic. I stamped my foot. When I did it, a little of the contents of my glass spilled out onto my thumb and fingers. There was no reason for it. Perhaps I wanted to hear the sound of my footstep beneath the carpet. And I didn't know any longer if I loved Helen. I'd marry her in any case, but I wondered if love was possible. It had disappeared in a second. It was like walking out in the middle of one of those romantic screen comedies. Of course, tomorrow I would feel differently. In all likelihood this pattern would stay with me for the next forty or fifty years.

After finishing my drink, I went to the bar and asked for a Scotch-and-quinine. I was slapped on the back.

"By Jove, it's Georgie!" Helen's brother said.

"Hello, Tommy."

"Great party, is it not?"

"It is that," I said.

He posed unwittingly against the bar. There was a serenity in the moment or him. "Who am I going to play tennis with on Saturdays when you're hooked up to Helen and in Connecticut?"

"Where is she, by the way?" I asked.

"Upstairs. Mrs. Williams spilled a drink on her dress . . . well, I kind of knocked her arm a little. You know how those things happen."

"I'll bet Helen has it in for you."

"What the hell! She's getting married in a couple of months," he said, then added, "You lucky son of a . . . So, what's going to happen to tennis and me on Saturdays?"

"You'll find a better player." I feinted a left to his jaw, bent my knees and jabbed at his stomach with my right. He jackknifed a bit. Then I mussed up his hair. "Judging by your reflexes, you haven't had as much to drink as I thought."

The bartender placed my drink on the counter. I didn't really want it, but picked it up and returned to the area in which couples danced. I watched without seeing and heard without listening. My preoccupation was with nothing. Maybe only the restlessness which had no outlet.

"Nice combo," someone said.

I tried, but not very hard, to remember his name. "Yes, they're very good."

In another moment I rested my glass and danced again. I found that this woman whose hand I had taken when I had stepped onto the floor was a fervent dancer. After our first words, all conversation stopped.

I danced with her several times. I got warm. My legs perspired. I saw Helen once and waved at her. She smiled obligingly and waved back. Tommy also danced a lot. We stopped when our foreheads and shirts were wet.

"To hell with being sedate!" he said. "I know we're supposed to, but it is a party."

Both of us went to the bar again, ordered and waited. Helen shook a finger of warning at him. I walked to her and kissed her. She recoiled from lack of privacy and said, "Not now, darling. Not here in front of all these people. Gracious!"

"Leave your brother alone," I said. "That's an order."

"Yes, dear."

I took my glass and began to mingle half-heartedly. The alcohol had worked its miniature wonder. I was dizzy. Still, I hadn't learned anything. I wanted to go swimming. That was all. The idea of it seized me at once. I could envision and feel it. I stood still in the center of the crowded room, closed my eyes and began a process of complete imagination. The voices, the laughter, the music intruded.

Upon opening my eyes, I walked without hesitation to the French doors that led to the patio and stepped out into the open. The air was much colder than I had expected it to be, and it took me a few seconds to get used to it. I sat in a deck lounge and closed my eyes. Who would be the first to disturb me?, I wondered. Helen might come looking for me. Tommy might want to tell me the latest dirty joke.

I felt myself sinking into the pulsating deepness of intoxication that precedes sleep, but pulled myself up and out of it at the sound of footsteps. I did not look behind me. I took a swallow of my drink. I followed the motion of the person behind me with my hearing. After a moment I realized that whoever it was had no interest in me. I closed my eyes again.

The footsteps moved from here to there, stopped, moved from here to there again. There was the sound of one glass touching another. When the sound moved to the side of me and a little in front of me, I opened my eyes. It was the caterer's daughter. I couldn't remember her name right away. Celestine. I should have guessed that it might have been either she or her father. She was putting empty glasses left by guests onto a tray.

I watched her, unnoticed. There was a certain dignity in her manner I find difficult to explain. It was feminine without the feminine embellishments of gesture. It was not decadent. Her uniform, her darkness, and that she worked contributed to it. But there was much more. I was at ease. I decided to finish my drink so that she would have to take my glass.

She heard me move, turned and seemed surprised by my presence. I smiled at her. She returned the smile and continued. She picked up glasses in front and then to the right of me. When she had almost finished, I held up my glass and turned it upside down to demonstrate its emptiness. She came and took it from me.

"Sit down for a while," I said.

She looked to the patio doors before deciding to accept.

I swung my legs over and put them on the ground to make room for her.

"I meant what I said to your father," I told her. My words were sincere. "It's a bit cold out here, don't you think?"

She did not answer.

I said nothing for the next few seconds. I reached for her bare arm. The contact, though brief, was electric. She did not move and was facing away from me. I wanted very much to see her face. I put my hand to her chin and forced her to look at me. I could not read her expression. I let go of her and waited for her to get up. She sat completely still.

"This is where my engagement was announced," I said. "Everyone was assembled here and a toast was made."

The night spun softly. I was not even able to hear her breath. She sat rigidly, with her eyes fastened to some immobile bit of shadow. My need for her then urged me. I would give her something afterwards. Money. Fifty dollars perhaps. I had that much in my wallet.

The moment seemed to lick us with a broad tongue. I felt strangely like someone from the Southern past of masters and servants. I did love her for the moment. To make love with her once would be all that I needed. I would never have to see her again.

I stood and took her arm. "Let's go into the garden," I whispered.

I pulled her gently. I beckoned. My whispering voice trembled.

She broke away from me. "No," she said firmly. Her head was lowered. Her chin touched the top of her dress, her uniform, and although I could not see her eyes I detected a look of betrayal on her face.

Had I read the moment so inaccurately? She picked up the tray of unclean glasses and walked with quick, sure steps back to the house.

I waited for a decent length of time before returning. I wanted to smoke a cigarette, but had no matches. My disquietude was inert. The guests would begin to leave in an hour or so. Then the evening could be forgotten.

Questions

1. To what degree are the attitudes of writers on social issues apparent in their works? How are the attitudes of the writers in this section indicated?

2. Describe the particular conflict in each work. Could it be said that all of these selections treat the theme of miscegenation? How do they vary in their treatment?

3. Are the works in this section didactic? Do they have a message? Could any of them be called propaganda? In what ways?

4. How do the writers handle the social background in which the events occur? In which work is the background most important? In which is it least important? Discuss your answers with specific references.

5. How does the point of view in each of the short stories affect the attitudes expressed and implied in the story? Speculate on the ways in which the stories would be different if told from different points of view. How, for example, would "Boitelle" be changed if told by the girl or by one of the parents?

6. How does a play differ from a short story? How might drama be less suited to social comment than narrative forms?

7. Do the attitudes held by various characters in the stories represent common attitudes today? What other views on miscegenation are represented in our society?

8. How are the literary works in this section related to the materials in Sections Nine and Ten?

Assignments

1. Write an essay on whether people of different races (or religions, or ethnic backgrounds) should marry and have children. Support your argument with evidence. (See Sections Seven and Ten.)

2. Analyze the attitudes toward miscegenation presented in the literary

works in this section. Does the time when a work was written affect the attitudes in it? Does the race of the author?

3. Describe a character in one of the works in this section as being representative of a common social type.

4. Write a letter to an advice column (like "Dear Abby") from someone contemplating an interracial marriage. Answer the letter.

Additional Reading

The subject of miscegenation has engaged writers from classical times to the present. The two most famous "classics" are probably Virgil's love story of Dido and Aeneas in *The Aeneid* and Shakespeare's *Othello*. Among the more significant modern treatments of the theme are William Faulkner's *Light in August* (1932) and *Absalom, Absalom!* (1936); Sinclair Lewis's *Kingsblood Royal* (1947); Richard Wright's *Native Son* (1940); Jack Kerouac's *The Subterraneans* (1958); James Baldwin's *Another Country* (1962); and LeRoi Jones's *Dutchman* (1964).

Sociologists and psychologists have frequently suggested that racism is rooted in sexual fears. Among the recent studies that discuss social aspects of miscegenation are Albert Gordon's *Intermarriage: Interfaith, Interracial, Interethnic* (Boston, 1964) and Calvin Hernton's *Sex and Racism in America* (New York, 1965). A collection of articles from black magazines by C. M. Larsson, *Marriage Across the Color Line,* offers a unique contemporary perspective. More general studies of racial attitudes and problems can place the issues presented in this section in broader sociological and historical perspective. Among the more important of such studies are Gunnar Myrdal's *An American Dilemma,* John Dollard's *Caste and Class in a Southern Town,* Gordon Allport's *The Nature of Prejudice,* and C. Vann Woodward's *The Strange Career of Jim Crow.*

SECTION TWELVE *Women as Professors*

A Report on Women and the Profession

Florence Howe

When Virginia Woolf addressed an historic meeting of professional women in the 1930's, she described her struggles with "The Angel in the House," who would slip behind her as she began to write and say, " 'My dear, you are a young woman. You are writing about a book that has been written by a man. Be sympathetic; be tender; flatter; deceive; use all the arts and wiles of our sex. Never let anybody guess you have a mind of your own. Above all, be pure.' " The Angel "died hard. Her fictitious nature," Mrs. Woolf reports, "was of great assistance to her. It is far harder to kill a phantom than a reality." [1]

Whether Mrs. Woolf was correct in her estimate, women have still both phantoms and realities to fight. We have the phantom woman job candidate, for example, who is, we are told, quite unreliable. If employed, she is certain to leave for marriage or for pregnancy. What's more, if she's a proper woman, she won't be driving, ambitious, or even possibly arrogant and intelligent enough to publish and thus bring fame to the department; nor is the passive, quiet but chatty creature likely to become a charismatic Kittredge. And so what can she do but teach—and probably freshman composition or French 100 at that.

Thanks to a new book by Helen Astin [2] and to several similar briefer studies of the woman doctorate, I may attempt to throttle that phantom at once. While it is true (and to their credit) that women Ph.D.'s spend significantly more time than men teaching (50% to 31%) and less time in research (25% to 41%), it is not true that women are unproductive as scholars. Mrs. Astin studied women eight or nine years beyond their doctorates, more than half of whom were married and had families. She reports that 75% had published at least one article—the typical woman doctorate had published three or four—and 13%, eleven or more. It is also untrue, Mrs. Astin's study indicates, that women don't "use" the doctorate. Ninety-one per cent of the women she studied were in the labor force, 81% of them fulltime, and almost half of them still in their first job, another 30% having changed jobs once. This is hardly the record of an undependable, unstable work force. Mrs. Astin kills more phantoms

FROM *College English*, Vol. 32, No. 8, May 1971. Copyright © 1971 by the National Council of Teachers of English. Reprinted by permission of the publisher and Florence Howe.

[1] "Professions for Women," *The Death of the Moth* (The Hogarth Press, 1947), pp. 149–154.
[2] Helen Astin, *The Woman Doctorate in America* (Basic Books, 1970).

than I can report here, but one is especially worth noting to this audience: those women who report instances of discrimination, she writes, are "active professionally and publish frequently." She speculates that the same characteristics ("aggressiveness, candor, or competitiveness") that may account for "greater productivity" account also for those women's "readiness to voice their opinions and express their disapproval of discriminatory practices."

"Disapproval of discriminatory practices," you remember, led two years ago to the formation of the MLA Commission on the Status of Women in the Profession. The Commission's newly completed study of departments reveals the realities of the woman doctorate's world. For example, 55% of our graduate students are women; no more than one out of nine or ten of their teachers is a woman. Or if one looks at a group of institutions, the prestige of which ranges from low to high, the proportion of women diminishes as the prestige rises. Or, if one looks at salary and tenure, women are to be found earning lower salaries and holding proportionately fewer tenured positions, especially at institutions of high prestige. Even if one looks at who teaches freshman English and French 100, and who teaches graduate courses, the same pattern stares back: the percentage of women among the teaching faculty declines as the course level rises. In short, women are at the bottom of our profession in rank, salary, prestige, or all three.

Almost all the women on the Commission, for example, earn lower salaries than the one male among us, who is, I should add, younger than most of us and an associate professor. Four of the seven women on the Commission are assistant professors, though we have all published widely and though I am the solitary older member without the doctorate.

I am a Ph.D. dropout. That is, I left Wisconsin in order to comply with the demands of a husband who wanted to move to New York. It was not then, as it is not usually now, possible to transfer credits to another institution. But I was not going to be a professor anyway, I thought, I was going to be a professor's wife. I'd teach part-time or when I could find a job, and wherever I happened to be. I liked teaching, but I did not think of myself as a "professional." One day, when marriage brought me to Baltimore, I was conveniently able to fill in for someone going on leave at Goucher College. I grew interested in that teaching job, and finally freed myself from marriage, and even began to write the dissertation, though I did not finish it. For teaching was still my main interest, and through teaching I became involved in the political struggles of my students, first blacks in Mississippi and in several inner cities of the north, than women. Because of these struggles, I went to Mississippi in the summers of 1964 and 1965 to work in the civil rights movement; and instead of finishing my dissertation, I began to write and even to publish essays and a book, about education, politics, and literature. But it was not the sort of traditional scholarship generally appreciated by departments of English.

So here I am: still an assistant professor at age forty-one, in my eleventh year at a women's college, in my fourteenth year of full-time teaching, still enjoying two or three sections of freshman English a year, and three or four upper division literature courses besides. I have never had a paid sabbatical year; I have never taught a graduate course. On the other hand, I have taken steps "down" the professional ladder to work in the Baltimore city high schools, on a project aimed at improving the teaching of high school English. Along with my rank, my teaching, and my interests goes a salary in keeping with my status, or should I say "place," in the profession.

And what has been my response? Until four or five years ago, silence: that was the way things were, I thought, if I thought about them at all. I had been naughty not to finish the degree, and I would be punished accordingly. More recently, I have worn a wry smile and remarked coyly that remaining an assistant professor "kept me honest." And anyway, I explained, I enjoyed my life. Though I was not rewarded in material ways, I could and did invent new courses and proceed even with major experiments in teaching.

But eighteen months as Commission Chairwoman has eroded that wry smile. I feel now a growing anger as I come to realize that a) I am not alone in my state—indeed, the sorrier aspects of my life are rather typical of too many women in the profession; b) there are many women worse off than I by far, many even who have followed the traditional route, who hold the "proper" credentials and who can find work only part-time; and c) our profession still rings with the male laughter that signifies only discomfort, not even fear, much less respect for women. Most important of all, I have come to realize our large numbers. It's as though, to borrow Ellison's image, we have been invisible even to each other—at least until now.

Our numbers, compared to most male-dominated professions, are startling. Nationally, the proportion of women on college and university faculties is usually cited as between 18% and 22%. The comparable figure for the modern language fields is 37%—a statistic that accounts for 33% full-time, 54% part-time. Most political science departments, to cite a field different from ours, have no women faculty. Ninety per cent of all departments in our fields report employing at least one woman. And of course, even if you are a member of a graduate department where women are rare, you know how many women there are in the profession (at least potentially) if you look around at your graduate students. A 55% majority are women. And there might be more still, judging from a study of undergraduates by James A. Davis. Using a huge sample of college seniors—33,982—Mr. Davis found that women were 69% of those planning graduate work in languages, 65% of them in English.[3]

[3] James A. Davis, *Great Aspirations: The Graduate School Plans of America's College Seniors* (Aldine, 1964).

And why not? Who reads books more avidly than little girls age six and seven? Or my Goucher students? Helen Astin tells us that women in the arts and humanities make the earliest career choices. An explanation is not hard to find. In the language of social psychologists, the idea of *enjoying* art and literature is sex-linked to women. A team of researchers at Worcester State Hospital recently published the results of an ingenious experiment.[4] Three groups of male and female clinical psychologists—that is, the sort who practice on human patients—were given three identical lists of 122 items previously verified as either "male" or "female-valued." Each group was given a different set of instructions: choose those traits, one was told, that characterize the healthy adult male; another, the healthy adult female; the third, a healthy adult, a person. As you may expect, and to our mutual horror, the healthy adult and the healthy male were identical, and totally divergent from the clinically healthy woman. But perhaps to our delight, the clinically healthy woman, unlike males and "persons" in our society, "enjoys art and literature very much."

The picture one gets from the study we have done is of a mass of women choosing literature, language, and writing as their interest; and a minority of men making the same choice. The minority of men sweep on to the Yales and Harvards, and into the large coeducational universities to dominate and control the profession. How is it that the study of language and literature, which attracts two-thirds women and one-third men, winds up as a profession with the statistics reversed? How is it that even the 37% who are women are not spread equitably through the profession?

There is very little to prove that women are discriminated against in admissions to graduate school or in awards of stipends. Studies indicate that of those who apply, men and women are accepted or awarded grants in equitable proportion. But the catch lies in the words "of those who apply." Many more women apply for M.A. and M.A.T. programs, for example, than for doctorate programs. Sixty-five per cent of those in M.A. programs were women; and a healthy majority of such degrees—55% of M.A.'s and 62% of M.A.T.'s—were earned by women during the past five years. But women are "cooled out" of the profession as early as possible, so that by the time one gets to doctoral programs the percentage of women graduate students has fallen to 49%. Other studies show that women who apply as doctoral candidates are not only fewer than men, they are better qualified, at least in terms of their college or high school records, than many of those men.[5] If women applicants to graduate schools are more highly qualified than many male candidates, then the rate of women

[4] Inge K. Broverman, *et al.*, "Sex Role Stereotypes and Clinical Judgments of Mental Health," *Journal of Consulting and Clinical Psychology*, 34, No. 1 (1970), 1–7.

[5] Davis, *op. cit.*; Lindsey R. Harmon, *Careers of Ph.D.'s: Academic versus Non-academic*. Career Patterns Report #2 (National Academy of Sciences, Washington, D.C., 1968).

accepted and granted stipends should be *greater* than that of men. To find no sex differences among the proportions applying and being admitted reveals that for women the standards of admissions are actually higher than they are for men.

Once into graduate school, women have still to continue "proving" their "seriousness," even in fields traditionally of interest to them and socially acceptable for them. "Why is a pretty girl like you thinking of burying yourself in a library?"—that is what Leonard Woolf once said to me, and that question continues to haunt women graduate students. Or other questions: "do you expect to be married shortly?"; or "do you plan to have any children?" We must grow conscious of these matters, since recently announced cutbacks in graduate departments could, if we are not alert, conspire to cut down the numbers of women willing to meet the demands of doctorate programs and thus reverse the upward trend of female Ph.D.'s in the profession. That would be extremely unfortunate, not only from the point of view of equity and legality, but because of the quality of female professionals.

What if women are not "cooled out," what if they persist and complete the doctorate? What awaits them? If they are full professors, our study reveals, women are four times as likely to be teaching in two-year or four-year colleges than to be in departments granting the Ph.D. In community colleges, the proportion of women teaching in our field is incredibly high for academe: 39% of doctorates who teach English and other modern languages in community colleges are women. Other figures for women teaching in such institutions are larger still—most above 50%. But the proportion of women diminishes as one looks at B.A., M.A., or Ph.D.-granting departments, until one finds a scant 12% of women doctorates holding full-time appointments in graduate departments. Even that proportion drops to 8% if one considers faculty who teach only graduate students.

It is difficult to explain away that distribution of women faculty, especially if one accounts only for those who hold the Ph.D., in the manner of one part of the Commission's study. It is impossible to explain the distribution away if one knows also that in the period between 1920 and the present, the proportion of Ph.D.'s granted to women has never fallen below 17%, which is its lowest point, and has usually been closer to 30% than to 20%. For other modern languages, where the pattern is somewhat more erratic, the lowest point is well above 20% and there are several highs above 30%. In short, if we look at the proportion of doctorates granted women during the last fifty years of the profession, that figure is on the average well over 25%. It is clear enough, therefore, that there has been a supply of women doctorates sufficient to fill those associate and full professor ranks proportionately, and in all kinds of institutions.

How, then, do we account for the patterns? Large scale admission of women to graduate schools; widespread distribution of women to high school departments, to community colleges; moderate distribution to some four-year colleges, though at lower ranks, and only token appearance in university departments. It is the inevitable product of a successful series of interlocking social, political, and economic arrangements. Women, convinced of their inferiority long before they get to graduate school, find further verification for these feelings in the scarcity of women professors with whom to study. Without such models of possibility, women have for fifty years kept their alleged "place" in the profession by passing through male-controlled graduate departments, absorbing the explicit lessons of the superiority of traditional scholarship over teaching, the implicit lessons of male dominance and female inferiority.

I am not arguing, in case there is any doubt, in favor of the traditional scholastic values of the profession: publish, diminish your teaching load, aim at graduate courses. But it is obvious enough that even in terms of those values, women have faced serious discrimination. More important for all of us, I believe, is that demeaning attitudes towards "women's work" in the profession—the teaching of freshman and sophomore courses —may help to perpetuate those outworn scholastic values. Since the publication of Nevitt Sanford's *The American College* in 1962, and certainly since Berkeley in 1964, we have all given at least lip service to platitudes about the importance of teaching. Yet no one can seriously maintain that the reward system in the profession—money, mobility, prestige, even a job—has begun to reflect the value placed on teaching. Quite the contrary: in Maryland, for example, English department faculty in the University teach three courses, a civilized load, it is said; at the state colleges, the load is four; in community colleges, it is five courses, generally including three sections of composition. And I need not tell you which institutions employ the greatest proportion of women, and which institution is able to offer the highest salaries and best facilities.

If the pattern of distributing women in the profession helps maintain its established values, it is also a useful way to gain cheap labor for an essential job: the teaching of English and other modern languages. For let no one tell me that the teacher of language and literature is a trivial vestige of another era: she is powerful, whether she is tool or instrument, and she can learn to be instrument. When I accepted the job as Chairwoman of the Commission on Women, I made it clear to the MLA Council that I was not interested in promoting a few more token women in the profession. I was not really interested in professionalizing masses of women either, if one understands professionalizing to include the ruination of good teachers through forced publication and research. I was interested in changing the lives of women, and I considered the English and language teacher second to none in importance, if that job is to be done. The English teacher—from primary grades through graduate school —helps control an individual's sense of identity and meaning as well as the concept of culture that individuals carry around with them. Literature and language, as we sometimes forget, do teach values, do shape images and perceptions of self, of society, and of how these are related. Even if the teacher is silent about such values, the literature, of course, is not. Writers, literary critics, editors, and teachers have, in fact, helped to mis-shape our perceptions about the nature and roles of women.

We have three complex needs to satisfy together in the next several years, perhaps the next decade. First, to prevent backsliding, especially in relation to the admission of women to graduate programs, but also in relation to whatever small gains women have made in the late sixties—and this in a period that will continue to reflect the general overproduction of Ph.D.'s. But even as the job market tightens, discrimination against women can only increase their anger and militancy. Letters like this one are still being posted on bulletin boards of major universities:

The Department of Foreign Languages. . . seeks a young (26–40), married male Ph.D. in French with substantial residence in France, and with some publication, or promise of it, to head the French section of this department. He must be truly scholarly and seriously interested in French literature and enjoy teaching it, but he must also be willing to teach at lower levels. . . .

Last year I did not have such letters in hand; and this year I am omitting the name of the department and the chairman; but he will be informed that such letters are not only in bad taste—they break the law.

Second, in the next several years we must also work to change the study of literature so that it does not continue the sexual stereotyping of its tradition. Third, and most important, we must work to change the education we offer to masses of people, men and women alike. The profession represented here in MLA rests (and often uneasily) on a base of women teachers of English and other modern languages in public schools and in community colleges. And if they are in difficulty, if the curriculum they offer is not all it should be, if graduate students are badly prepared for the world beyond the campus, some of the burden of responsibility falls upon us, or at least upon those who control, or who could change, graduate departments.

Even as we in MLA must acknowledge responsibility for discriminating against women, women must also now begin to assume new responsibilities in the profession. For too long we have apologized for our pleasure in teaching or in our students. For too long we have foregone our own literary tastes, our ideas of significant scholarship, looking to men in the profession to write the textbooks, edit the anthologies, editions, and selections, even of women writers. For too long we have ourselves ignored women writers and offered to our students a male-dominated curriculum and a male-centered criticism.

In the next decade, I expect that we will discover other Kate Chopins, women like Rebecca Harding, perhaps, to add to the curriculum; we will rescue not only Emily Bronte but Margaret Fuller from the hands of male critics. As our own status changes, as our understanding of the social role of women grows, we will help not only those women who happen to be in our profession, or those who happen to be our students, but because our work is in language and literature, we will be able to reach all women, everywhere. Perhaps we can spread these radical words of Margaret Fuller:

> I believe that at present women are the best helpers of one another.
> Let them think, let them act, till they know what they need.
> We only ask of men to remove arbitrary barriers. Some would like to do more. But I believe it needs that Woman show herself in her native dignity to teach them how to aid her, their minds are so encumbered by tradition.[6]

The Job Market for Women: A Department Chairman's View

George Gleason

The problem that faces a woman who enters the college teaching field, whether in English or in some other discipline, appears to be whether she is entering the profession to be a teacher for the rest of her life, or whether she is entering the profession to remain only until she gets married and starts a family.

Most of the young men who apply for teaching jobs are married and will take their wives with them to the schools at which the men are employed, but most of the young women who apply for teaching jobs are unmarried. If they marry while they are employed, they either quit teaching to take up housekeeping or they go away with their husbands if the husbands move. Thus they leave the teaching field to go into situations from which they may not find a way out and back into teaching.

As with men, the greatest number of women who enter the college field do so after completing a Master's degree. Since it is the practice of many colleges and universities not to retain an Instructor (which is the rank usually given a college teacher who has only the M.A.) longer than three or four years, the woman with an M.A. cannot expect to be permanently

FROM *College English*, Vol. 32, No. 8, May 1971. Copyright © 1971 by the National Council of Teachers of English. Reprinted by permission of the publisher and George Gleason.

[6] "Women in the Nineteenth Century," in *Margaret Fuller: American Romantic*, ed. Perry Miller (Anchor Books, 1963), now out of print.

retained in a Department unless she does a significant amount of post-Master's work—usually from 30 to 60 hours of graduate work beyond the M.A. Though, of course, many women make an adjustment to this demand, as they also do to the simultaneous demands of marriage and a career, many do not; and it is these who for themselves probably constitute the greatest "problem" in the job market.

Many women do not want to work for a Ph.D. Fine. But they appear also to want not so much to do graduate work as to skim along from job to job until they find a roosting place. The best advice for all women Instructors is to go back to graduate school if they wish to remain in college teaching. However, getting women Instructors to follow this advice is not, apparently, easy. For example, of fifteen female Instructors who were in our Department in the last six years, seven left to get married, six sought other jobs, and only two returned to graduate school—and one of these has completed her doctorate. On the other hand, for the same period we had twelve male Instructors who left us. Nine of these returned to graduate school, and three of these have completed doctoral degrees; two are close to completion of doctoral work; and the other four are still in school. Three of our twelve male Instructors sought their jobs. This example is probably fairly typical.

Now while our nine male Instructors, by returning to graduate school, have personally enhanced their academic charms for prospective employers, this is so only for two of the female Instructors. Of the males who sought jobs rather than return to school, two went to junior colleges where their M.A. degrees will keep them safe for some time. The other went to a four-year college after being with us only one year. He is, however, aware that he will have to do graduate work, and he fully intends to do so. On the other hand, if our female Instructors ever intend to advance in the college job market, the seven who married have done nothing to beef up their academic marketability. Of the six who left us for other jobs, two quit English to teach Speech, where apparently they'll not have to do more graduate work to retain their present rank as Instructor; however, advancement for these two will be slow. Of the four female Instructors who took English-teaching jobs elsewhere, three can only stay in their jobs two or three years before moving again; but one of these is a fairly successful writer, and having more to offer than just the desire to teach freshman composition, she has a secure berth as an Instructor.

These examples point up that when considering the college teaching job market, one notes that it has two areas. One is that of entry into the job market, and the other is retention in the market. The second area is the more critical.

If a young Instructor does not feel up to the chores of getting a Ph.D. but wishes to go back to school and train to do more than teach composition and introductory lit courses, she should consider the teaching situation. A Chairman can annually select from hundreds of new M.A.s for his teachers of basic courses. To teach graduate courses, a Chairman wants the best prepared person he can hire, and this generally means that the Ph.D. is a requirement. But it is at the middle range of courses that there is a dearth of available teachers. The teachers for these courses must be versatile; therefore, to the young Instructor who does not want the Ph.D., I'd say, "Don't fool around with getting graduate work of the kind you already have. Diversify. Take another Master's degree, or just take a respectable number of hours of work in a related field." So far as I can tell, there is a wide open market for people who can teach such combinations as these:

English and children's literature;
English and journalism;
English and remedial reading;
English literature and continental literature—particularly the novel;
English literature and American literature (I'm continually surprised at the number of Instructors whose sole preparation is in English literature);
English and the teaching of high school literature;
English and technical writing;
English and narrative writing (as opposed to whatever creative writing is);
English and the teaching of methods courses;
English and the supervision of student teachers;
English and linguistics or history of the language.

While not every English Department has courses in some of these related fields, a great many do. Also, in these ecumenical times, it is not at all unusual for teachers to teach part-time in one Department and part-time in another Department.

The main problem facing many of the young women entering the profession is that they are trained to be imitation Ph.D.s, and when they consider returning to graduate school they think in these terms but blanch at the thought of a dissertation. Despite the footsy-playing that is going on with various forms of the Doctor of Arts degree, for the foreseeable future a cheap Ph.D. is not apt to be anything more than that. My point is that since the M.A. degree is simply no longer a ticket for a permanent job in college teaching, sooner or later the applicant must offer something more —or make way for someone who will.

Another problem, and perhaps the main problem, for a woman who enters college teaching, or who wants to be retained in college teaching, is the matter of marriage. A woman teacher who marries creates a special problem for herself and for the school at which she teaches. If she marries while still an Instructor, a woman teacher will in all likelihood not feel that she can both return to graduate school and keep her husband happy and her newly-established home going.

For the school at which such a married woman teaches for three or four years, the problem is interesting. If she is a good teacher, the school will be reluctant to lose her services. However, if the school keeps this Instructor, she must in time be given tenure; then she cannot be dismissed. She may be a fine teacher, but as long as she does not grow professionally, by so much is the professional growth of the Department inhibited. Meanwhile, too, if she is given regular salary increments, she will in time get a higher salary than will any other Instructor in the Department, and the other Instructors will become unhappy with their salaries. Salary situations being what they are, few colleges can afford to disgruntle the troops in this way. On the other hand, if the college stops giving her pay increases, then she becomes embittered.

If the college does not give such a married Instructor tenure but dismisses her, it may do so with regret because of the certain knowledge that she will not return to graduate school and will not, therefore, be eligible to return to the school at a higher rank and offer additional service to the institution where she got her initial training as a teacher.

There is, of course, a way out for the woman who marries and is not given tenure. She can occasionally be hired to teach a class on an as-needed basis. For this service her pay is usually much less than that offered for a full-time teacher, though, of course, a part-time teacher usually is not asked to participate in the student-counseling and department-choring that a full-time teacher has to do.

And there is yet another way out for the woman who marries. She may be retained in some status that does not conflict with the regular rank structure and promotion requirements of the institution. Perhaps she is called an Assistant Instructor; perhaps she is a Lecturer. Whatever her non-regular status, the situation is apt to be an unhappy one for both the teacher and the Department.

The married woman or mother who is hired by an institution often presents a problem of perpetual accommodation. The woman's family life is no more a normal concern of the college than is a man's family life, but somehow while some women do not allow their family lives to interfere with their work, others do. They cannot teach early morning classes because they have to get breakfast for their husbands and children. They cannot teach from 11:00 to 2:00 because they must be home to get lunch. They'd prefer to be off at 4:00, not later than 5:00 at the worst. They do not expect to return to the campus after they have left for the day, and they get exercised about any kind of week-end work at school.

There is one kind of woman for whom the teaching job market is not too open. She is the woman who has married and gone where her husband has taken her. She is uprooted, but if she has a strong professional dedication, she may very well desire to re-enter the profession at another location. What are some choices open to her?

1. If she has a family for whom she must care, she can look for part-time work.
2. If her family is able to take care of itself, she can look for full-time work.
3. If she has no home ties, she may want to look for full-time work leading to eventual tenure.

But despite whatever she would like to do, this woman, perhaps splendidly prepared, is not mobile; she cannot go where a job is. If a local job market is closed to her, that's it. Even if the local market is open, she lacks the professional bargaining power of a person who can move where other jobs are and where the pay is highest. Do not think that this situation is unknown, for it is known to administrators who sometimes feel they can with good conscience hire a well-qualified woman at a cheaper rate than they can hire an equally qualified man. The woman either takes the local offer, or she stays at home.

And that's not all. If this woman is desperately interested in rejoining her profession, she may offer her services at a substantially lower rate and rank than one of her training, and perhaps experience, is worth. She may do this to supplement the family income, or she may do it simply to get out of the house. Whatever her reason for offering herself so cheap, if she is hired, she undermines the going rates and the salary and fringe-benefit advances that her profession has striven so long and so hard to gain.

There are undoubtedly a few schools where women, like the Irish, need not apply, but all the evidence I have is that the job market in colleges is just as open to women as it is to me. What a Department Chairman is looking for, I am convinced, is the best qualified person he can hire for the money he has available. And since recruiting is now a constant and onerous chore, a Department Chairman would rather retain a qualified teacher than to recruit half a dozen people about whom he must learn everything anew.

The job market, as I see it, involves not only admission to college teaching but retention in college teaching. Few women will have difficulty being admitted to college teaching, but for many of them retention in college teaching will depend upon whether they will make the sacrifices of time, effort, and personal adjustment necessary to be effective and independent human beings and teachers.

Response to Mr. Gleason

Mary Anne Ferguson

In some ways Professor Gleason's view of the job market for women bears out the statistics he decided not to investigate. The picture of his own department coincides very closely with that of the typical modern language department described by Florence Howe according to the data of the Commission's Study I. Mr. Gleason's department has 52 teachers; since the total he lists by ranks is only 41, apparently 11 teachers, or 20%, have no rank, perhaps because they are part-time. Of the 41 members listed by rank, 25% of full professors and 25% of associate professors are women, compared with the national averages of 18% to 32% respectively. This is a department which until 1938 had no men faculty at all; now 75% of the senior faculty, including the chairman, are men. This fact is consistent with the national figures on the decrease of women proportionately in academia since the 1930s. On the instructors' level, Mr. Gleason's department coincides almost exactly with Study I's figure of 46% women; it has 45% at this rank. The figure for assistant professor is anomalous, however; whereas nationally, only 32% are women, in Mr. Gleason's department 85% of assistant professors are women. Perhaps some of them will be promoted soon.

Mr. Gleason maintains that "we have tried to keep a balance of the sexes in our department." Since he has 41% women, it might look as if he has succeeded. But since 84% of the women are grouped at the bottom ranks, it looks as if he has not been able to hire or promote women to associate and full professorships during the past 20 years when men began to become equally members of his department.

The lack of success in balancing the sexes for the upper ranks, where he needs staff to teach the middle courses, Mr. Gleason ascribes to the fact that most of his applications are from young unmarried women who do not remain long on the job market once they marry. As Mr. Gleason says, "The woman who marries creates a problem for herself." She will have to move with her husband when he changes jobs or returns to graduate school; she cannot expect permanent employment and promotion because she does not pursue graduate study to upgrade her qualifications. Instead, she wants "to skim along from job to job," and the department chairman

FROM *College English*, Vol. 32, No. 8, May 1971. Copyright © 1971 by the National Council of Teachers of English. Reprinted by permission of the publisher and Mary Anne Ferguson.

loses the value of her experience with his department. Other problems department chairmen have with female faculty are women's insistence on special treatment in regard to teaching hours, their attempts to achieve advancement through sexual blackmail, their high rate of absenteeism, and their refusal to attend meetings. Most of Mr. Gleason's audience were women, who reacted negatively to this last point in particular. On some points national statistics reinforce the audience's view: according to the U.S. Public Health Service, during a recent three-year period, woman workers in general were absent only about as often as men, even if absences for childbirth and pregnancy are included; there is some question whether childbirth should be counted as an illness. The same statistical survey shows that in all occupations those at the bottom are most likely to be absent; since more than half of the women in Mr. Gleason's department are instructors, absenteeism should not be surprising, especially since they are likely to be receiving $1000 per year less than men who do the same work in the modern languages. Another department chairman who heard Mr. Gleason's speech remarked that his experience with women faculty had been quite different; he cited a woman full professor and department chairman as having rarely been absent. Since there are no national figures for faculty attendance, neither chairman's opinion is broadly applicable.

But others of Mr. Gleason's charges about women are authenticated by the statistics of Study I. Although women received 55% of the masters' degrees and constituted 55% of the graduate students in modern languages, they received only 31% of the Ph.D.'s. Although about 40% of the MLA membership is female, undoubtedly many women who teach in college do not belong; one of the Commission's big problems is how to reach this "buried" constituency. And though Mr. Gleason had an audience twice as big as the assigned room could accommodate, the presence of so many women at a national meeting was a new phenomenon—perhaps connected as much with the shrinking job market as with the first series of meetings aimed specifically at women. But admitting the truth of some of Mr. Gleason's charges is seeing only the tip of the iceberg; the real question is, why are women less likely than men to achieve status in the profession? *Do* they create problems for themselves?

Other papers at MLA suggested that women's comparatively low achievement in academia is caused by cultural conditioning from childhood on and by the discouragement inherent in the facts of the academic marketplace; women have not had equal access to graduate training nor equal opportunity in employment. The problems loom so large that many women do not try to overcome them; it seems superhuman to "succeed" in a society where white women college graduates average less pay than black male high school graduates, where almost all of one's graduate professors have been male. Betty Friedan has pointed out that many educated women shared in the "feminine mystique" of the 1950s and happily resigned themselves to the home as their proper sphere.

Yet, according to Study I, the proportion of women Ph.D.s in English has risen steadily during the last ten years, from 20 to 30%—equalling for the first time in 50 years the 1920 proportion. And though only about 25% of all Ph.D.s in English publish anything during their academic careers, married women Ph.D.s publish more, proportionally, than single women, single and married men. It would seem that women do have a will to succeed in their profession. Yet Study I shows that at every rank they receive less pay than their male peers; they are promoted much more slowly; only 8% reach the pinnacle of becoming full professors in Ph.D.-granting institutions. In would seem that it is the hostility and rigidity of academe rather than women's lack of will that has relegated them to the basement of the profession. Mr. Gleason's notion that "Women . . . can do or be what they want to do or be if they have the will for it" is a dangerous half-truth.

All stereotypes both reflect and create reality. Mr. Gleason's picture of women faculty is real in that many women do not advance or even continue in the profession; no doubt many women, carrying a full-time job at home as well as at college, do not work on AAUP committees or attend meetings. But the group who heard Mr. Gleason's speech agreed that women should resist letting such stereotypes *create* reality for them. Recent pedagogical experiments have shown that teachers' expectations have a direct bearing on the quality of student performance. It is instructive to realize what a department chairman expects of women. It is rational not to allow oneself to fit the Procrustean bed.

Letter to the Editor on George Gleason

My "Response to Mr. Gleason" (*CE*, May 1971) was a response to the speech Mr. Gleason gave at a Workshop of which I was chairman; my remarks reflect the reaction of the original audience.

It is heartening that Mr. Gleason chose to change his speech between December and May in the direction of an awareness that women are not so much to blame for their academic problems as he had thought. In omitting remarks about sexual blackmail, menstruation as an excuse for absenteeism, and women's failure to attend meetings, Mr. Gleason shows sensitivity to the audience reaction. I hope his omissions in describing the structure of his own department are a result of discovering from Study I that he had no occasion to feel proud of its utilization of the talents of women.

At the meeting I felt that the main value of Mr. Gleason's speech lay in the anger it evoked. Now I feel its value may be primarily as an indication that it is possible to remove stereotypical impressions with facts. The honesty of both versions of Mr. Gleason's ideas is a sign of hope for achieving equity for women in academe.

Mary Anne Ferguson
University of Massachusetts/Boston
[*CE*, November, 1971]

Questions

1. What are the principal arguments made by Florence Howe? By George Gleason? By Mary Anne Ferguson? Why are the arguments made by Miss Howe different from those made by Mr. Gleason and Mrs. Ferguson?

2. What seem to you to be the principal issues involved in the discussion? Are these issues different because we are concerned with professors specifically, or would they be the same if they involved, let's say, salesmen or management executives in nonacademic jobs?

3. What is your own feeling about having men professors as opposed to women professors? Would you say that there are some situations which would require different answers? Just exactly what would they be, and why?

4. Why does Miss Howe describe "a growing anger"? Does Mr. Gleason address himself directly or indirectly to the source of her anger? How does his description of women wanting "to skim along from job to job until they find a roosting place" correspond to Miss Howe's and Mrs. Ferguson's sense of the situation?

Assignments

1. List in parallel columns the strongest arguments made on both sides of the issue as to whether or not to hire women as professors.

2. Write your own response to any particular position advanced by any of the three persons represented in the section. You may write in agreement with the position or in strong disagreement.

3. Go through your own college catalog, concentrating on a department or a college or some other academic unit of, say, about 20 persons, and determine how many men and how many women there are. Write an analysis of the actual statistics.

4. Count the number of men and women in a particular class. Speculate as to why there are more of one sex than of the other.

5. Determine from available sources on your campus which subjects or areas have more women as majors and which have more men. After you have established the statistics, analyze them.

Additional Reading

The subject of "women's liberation" has become such an intense one in recent years that it is difficult to focus on any one aspect of it. Among the writers who have written generally on the matter are Betty Friedan, Gloria Steinem, Kate Millett, and Norman Mailer. You might also want to consult the work of some of the people referred to in the articles in this section.

The Death

Sentence

Thou shalt not kill.

Exodus 20:13

And if any mischief follow, then thou shalt give
life for life. Eye for eye, tooth for tooth,
hand for hand, foot for foot.

Exodus 21:23–24

Ye have heard that it hath been said, An eye for an eye,
and a tooth for a tooth: But I say unto you, That ye

*resist not evil: but whosoever shall smite thee on
thy right cheek, turn to him the other also.*

Matthew 5:38–9

FBI Bulletin, June 1, 1960

J. Edgar Hoover

TO ALL LAW ENFORCEMENT OFFICIALS:

The question of capital punishment has sent a storm of controversy
thundering across our Nation—millions of spoken and written words seek
to examine the question so that decisions may be reached which befit our
civilization.

FROM the *FBI Law Enforcement Bulletin*, June, 1960. Reprinted with the permission of J. Edgar Hoover.

The struggle for answers concerning the taking of men's lives is one to which every American should lend his voice, for the problem in a democracy such as ours is not one for a handful of men to solve alone.

As a representative of law enforcement, it is my belief that a great many of the most vociferous cries for abolition of capital punishment emanate from those areas of our society which have been insulated against the horrors man can and does perpetrate against his fellow beings. Certainly, penetrative and searching thought must be given before considering any blanket cessation of capital punishment in a time when unspeakable crimes are being committed. The savagely mutilated bodies and mentally ravaged victims of murderers, rapists and other criminal beasts beg consideration when the evidence is weighed on both sides of the scales of Justice.

At the same time, nothing is so precious in our country as the life of a human being, whether he is a criminal or not, and on the other side of the scales must be placed all of the legal safeguards which our society demands.

Experience has clearly demonstrated, however, that the time-proven deterrents to crime are sure detection, swift apprehension, and proper punishment. Each is a necessary ingredient. Law-abiding citizens have a right to expect that the efforts of law enforcement officers in detecting and apprehending criminals will be followed by realistic punishment.

It is my opinion that when no shadow of a doubt remains relative to the guilt of a defendant, the public interest demands capital punishment be invoked where the law so provides.

Who, in all good conscience, can say that Julius and Ethel Rosenberg, the spies who delivered the secret of the atomic bomb into the hands of the Soviets, should have been spared when their treachery caused the shadow of annihilation to fall upon all of the world's peoples? What place would there have been in civilization for these two who went to their deaths unrepentant, unwilling to the last to help their own country and their own fellow men? What would have been the chances of rehabilitating Jack Gilbert Graham, who placed a bomb in his own mother's luggage and blasted her and 43 other innocent victims into oblivion as they rode an airliner across a peaceful sky?

A judge once said, "The death penalty is a warning, just like a lighthouse throwing its beams out to sea. We hear about shipwrecks, but we do not hear about the ships the lighthouse guides safely on their way. We do not have proof of the number of ships it saves, but we do not tear the lighthouse down."

Despicable crimes must be dealt with realistically. To abolish the death penalty would absolve other Rosenbergs and Grahams from fear of the consequences for committing atrocious crimes. Where the death penalty is provided, a criminal's punishment may be meted out commensurate with his deeds. While a Power transcending man is the final Judge, this same Power gave man reason so that he might protect himself. Capital punishment is an instrument with which he may guard the righteous against the predators among men.

We must never allow misguided compassion to erase our concern for the hundreds of unfortunate, innocent victims of bestial criminals.

FBI Bulletin, June 1, 1961

J. Edgar Hoover

TO ALL LAW ENFORCEMENT OFFICIALS:

The capital punishment question, in which law enforcement officers have a basic interest, has been confused recently by self-styled agitators "against the evil of capital punishment." A brochure released not long ago, pleading for "rehabilitation" of murderers while passing lightly over the plight of the killers' innocent victims and families, charges that law enforcement officers "become so insensitized by their dealings with vicious criminals that they go to the extreme of feeling that the death penalty is absolutely necessary."

To add to the burden of conscience borne by peace officers, prosecutors, and jurists and to brand law enforcement officers as callous, unfeeling men "insensitized" to the sanctity of human life are gross acts of injustice to these servants of the public. This ridiculous allegation is mutely refuted by the compassion which wells up in quiet tears flowing down the cheeks of hardened, veteran officers who too often see the ravaged bodies of victims of child molesters.

There can be no doubt of the sincerity of many of those who deplore capital punishment. A realistic approach to the problem, however, demands that they weigh the right of innocent persons to live their lives free from fear of bestial killers against statistical arguments which boast of how few murderers kill again after "rehabilitation" and release. No one, unless he can probe the mind of every potential killer, can say with any authority whatsoever that capital punishment is not a deterrent. As one police officer has asked, how can these "authorities" possibly know how many people are not on death row because of the deterrent effect of executions?

Maudlin viewers of the death penalty call the most wanton slayer a "child of God" who should not be executed regardless of how heinous his

FROM the *FBI Law Enforcement Bulletin*, June, 1961. Reprinted with the permission of J. Edgar Hoover.

crime may be because "God created man in his own image, in the image of God created he him." (Genesis 1:27) Was not this small, blonde 6-year-old girl a child of God? She was choked, beaten, and raped by a sex fiend whose pregnant wife reportedly helped him lure the innocent child into his car and who sat and watched the assault on the screaming youngster. And when he completed his inhuman deed, the wife, herself bringing a life into the world, allegedly killed the child with several savage blows with a tire iron. The husband has been sentenced to death. Words and words and words may be written, but no plea in favor of the death penalty can be more horribly eloquent than the sight of the battered, sexually assaulted body of this child, truly a "child of God."

The proponents of "rehabilitation" for all murderers quote those portions of the Bible which they believe support their lavender-and-old-lace world where evil is neither recognized nor allowed. But the Bible clearly reveals that enforcement of moral justice is nothing new to our age. In fact, in referring to man as the "image of God," the Old Testament, so freely quoted by opponents of the death penalty, also states, "Whoso sheddeth man's blood, by man shall his blood be shed: for in the image of God made he man." (Genesis 9:6) There are many passages in the Old Testament which refer to capital punishment being necessary to enforce the laws of society. Since the Old Testament was written about and to a nation while the New Testament was written to individuals and to a nonpolitical body known as the Church, there is a difference in emphasis and approach. Certainly, however, the moral laws of the Old Testament remain with us today.

Misguided do-gooders frequently quote the Sixth Commandment, "Thou shalt not kill," to prove that capital punishment is wrong. This Commandment in the 20th chapter, verse 13, of Exodus has also been interpreted to mean: "Thou shalt do no murder." Then the 21st chapter, verse 12, says "He that smiteth a man, so that he die, shall be surely put to death." We can no more change the application to our society of this basic moral law in the Old Testament than we can change the meaning of Leviticus 19:18: "thou shalt love thy neighbor as thyself," which Jesus quoted in the New Testament.

To "love thy neighbor" is to protect him; capital punishment acts as at least one wall to afford "God's children" protection.

Testimony of Henry E. Petersen,
Assistant Attorney General *

Seven bills dealing with the death penalty are currently being considered by this Subcommittee. Four of the bills, H.R. 193, 3243, 11797, and 12217, seek the total abolition of the death penalty under the laws of the United States. Identical bills H.R. 8414, 8483, and 9486 provide for a two-year moratorium on the death penalty for both the Federal and State systems. The bills do not preclude the imposition of the death penalty but do provide a stay of execution for all unexecuted death sentences and prohibit the carrying out of death sentences within the period prescribed. These latter bills are based on proposed findings by Congress that a "serious question" exists as to whether the death penalty is cruel and unusual punishment in violation of the Eighth and Fourteenth Amendments of the United States Constitution or is applied discriminatorily in violation of the Fourteenth Amendment. The purpose of the moratorium is to give Congress time to consider whether it "should exercise its authority under Section 5 of the Fourteenth Amendment to prohibit the use of the death penalty."

Early this year the United States Supreme Court heard oral arguments addressed to the issue of whether or not the death penalty is cruel and unusual punishment under the Eighth and Fourteenth Amendments of the United States Constitution (*Aikens* v. *California,* No. 68-5027; *Furman* v. *Georgia,* No. 69-5003; *Jackson* v. *Georgia,* No. 69-5030; and *Branch* v. *Texas,* No. 69-5031). In these cases all petitioners have grounded their Eighth Amendment claims, at least in part, on the allegation that the death penalty is applied in a discriminatory manner; therefore, it is likely that the Supreme Court will effectively resolve the discrimination issue as well as the cruel and unusual punishment issue.

One aspect of the capital punishment issue deserves particular emphasis. Our society has a high regard for human life . . . all life. Therefore, concern over inflicting death weighs heavily upon us. Most of those who oppose and those who support the death penalty do so because of a desire to preserve life. This fact is too often forgotten by forceful advocates of both positions. We must not lose sight of the idea that it is the life of the innocent and the guilty which is in the balance.

It is not the Department's position that the death penalty deters in all

---

* Given before Subcommittee No. 3, House Committee on the Judiciary, March 9, 1972, on H. R. 193, 3243, 11797, 12217, 8414, 8483 and 9486.

cases. However, in some situations the evidence of the deterrent value of the penalty is very strong. In a study made by the American Bar Association, law enforcement officers cited the following instances where the deterrent value of the death penalty was in evidence.[1]

1. Criminals who had committed an offense punishable by life imprisonment, when faced with capture, refrained from killing their captors, even though it seemed likely that by killing they could have escaped. When these criminals were asked why they refrained from the homicide, they answered that they were willing to serve a life sentence but not to risk the death penalty.
2. Criminals about to commit certain offenses refrained from carrying deadly weapons. After their apprehension, these criminals were asked why they did not carry weapons. One of the reasons they refrained was to avoid use of such a weapon which would lead to imposition of the death penalty.

Similarly, the Los Angeles Police Department reported that thirteen robbery suspects during the course of the year "while in conversation with the police, stated that they either: (1) used toy guns; or (2) empty guns; or (3) simulated guns in robberies rather than take a chance on killing someone and getting the gas chamber." [2]

Newspapers carried the story of a prison break where an escaped convict released hostages at the State line, because, as he later told police when he was recaptured, he was afraid of the death penalty for kidnapping in the neighboring State.[3] In the study I mentioned previously the American Bar Association reported instances where murderers have removed their victims from capital punishment States in order to avoid the threat of the death penalty. According to testimony given by the Attorney General of Kansas and others before the Great Britain Royal Commission on Capital Punishment, these last-mentioned instances of murderers crossing State lines caused both Kansas and South Dakota to reintroduce the death penalty.[4] It is the Department's position that if the threat of the death penalty deters the killing of innocent victims even to a limited extent, its retention is justified.

Experience has led to the conclusion that there is a deterrent value in capital punishment. Former Attorney General John N. Mitchell and Acting Attorney General Richard G. Kleindienst have both stated that the death

[1] 1959 ABA Criminal Law Section 15 (1960), quoted in *Working Papers of the National Commission on Reform of Federal Criminal Laws*, p. 1356.
[2] California, *Senate Report on the Death Penalty* (1960), pp. 16–17, quoted in *The Death Penalty in America: An Anthology* (Bedeau ed. 1967), p. 267, Note 11.
[3] According to a speaker during the floor debate on capital punishment in the New Jersey Assembly on April 6, 1959; see the Bergen (N.J.) *Evening Record*, April 7, 1959, p. 2, quoted in Bedeau, p. 267, Note 12.
[4] Great Britain, Royal Commission on Capital Punishment, *Report* (1953), p. 375, quoted in Bedeau, p. 336, Notes 7 and 8.

sentence has deterrent value in some situations. Former Attorney General Mitchell has several times referred to the case of the person under sentence of life imprisonment who would have a license to kill anyone he might choose in that institution if no greater sanction could be applied to him. J. Edgar Hoover, Director of the Federal Bureau of Investigation, has gone on record with the following statement: [5] "The professional law enforcement officer is convinced from experience that the hardened criminal has been and is deterred from killing based on the prospect of the death penalty." The Department has authorized Federal prosecutors to request the death penalty where it would appear to have a deterrent function. For example, in *United States* v. *Greene*, tried earlier this year in the District of Columbia, the United States requested the death penalty for a defendant who fatally wounded a Deputy United States Marshal while helping his brother escape from Federal custody. The defendant in this case fired what were most likely the fatal shots while the Deputy Marshal lay helpless on the pavement.

Because we believe that the death penalty has a deterrent value, the Department opposes H.R. 193, 3243, 11797, and 12217, which would abolish capital punishment under the laws of the United States. The Department feels that if any of these bills are passed, it is the law-abiding public that will suffer.

Nor can the Department support H.R. 8414, 8483, and 9486, which propose a two-year moratorium on the death sentence. It is important to keep a proper perspective on these bills. The moratorium bills contemplate the eventual enactment of legislation which would prohibit capital punishment not only in the Federal system but among the States as well. If such legislation is not eventually enacted by Congress, the moratorium will not have accomplished its purpose. In measuring the value of the moratorium bills we must look not so much to the desirability of the proposed moratorium but rather to the desirability of the eventual prohibition of the death penalty which these bills contemplate.

Under this analysis the moratorium bills appear as undesirable as the four bills discussed previously. Even if one can find a way to justify the abolition of the death sentence at the Federal level, there are additional objections to imposing this abolition on the States.

The bill states that Congress may prohibit the death penalty for the States under Section 5 of the Fourteenth Amendment upon its finding that (1) the death penalty amounts to cruel and unusual punishment under the Eighth and Fourteenth Amendments; or (2) the death penalty is being applied discriminatorily in violation of the Fourteenth Amendment. As has been mentioned already, both issues are effectively before the Supreme Court. If the Supreme Court resolves these issues in favor of abolition of the death penalty, then the eventual prohibition con-

[5] F.B.I. Uniform Crime Reports, 14 (1959).

templated by the moratorium bills will be beside the point. Should these issues be resolved in favor of retention of the penalty—should it be decided that the penalty is not unconstitutional on these grounds—the Court will have in effect repudiated the bill's constitutional basis as it applies to the States.

Even if Congress can constitutionally impose this prohibition of the States, should Congress do so? Resolution of such a highly controversial issue as capital punishment would appear to be better left to the States, and the States have shown a willingness to come to grips with the issue. To our knowledge nine States have legislatively abolished the death penalty.[6] Five States have partially abolished the penalty by restricting its application.[7] Eight States have completely or partially abolished the death penalty and subsequently restored it.[8] Three States have approved the death penalty by referendum.[9] Public opinion on the penalty has drifted back and forth. The Gallup Poll showed 51 per cent in favor of the death penalty in 1960, only 42 per cent in favor in 1966, and then 51 per cent in favor in 1969.[10] This would hardly appear to be the time to impose a uniform judgment on the States.

In summary, all of the bills here discussed contemplate either the present or future abolition of capital punishment. It has been the Department's experience that the death penalty has a genuine deterrent value. Consequently we oppose these bills.

---

[6] Alaska (1957), Hawaii (1957), Iowa (1965), Maine (1887), Michigan (1963), Minnesota (1911), Oregon (1964), West Virginia (1965), and Wisconsin (1953), statistics for footnotes 6–8 from the Bureau of Prisons and the Law Enforcement Assistance Administration.

[7] New York (1965), North Dakota (1915), Rhode Island (1852), Vermont (1965), New Mexico (1969).

[8] States with years of abolition and restoration: Arizona (1916–1918), Delaware (1958–1961), Kansas (1907–1935), Missouri (1917–1919), South Dakota (1915–1939), Tennessee (1915–1919), Washington (1913–1919), and Colorado (1897–1901).

[9] Colorado (1966), Massachusetts (1968), Illinois (1970), quoted in Bedeau, "The Death Penalty in America," *Federal Probation,* p. 34.

[10] Gallup Polls for 1960 and 1966, quoted in *Working Papers of the National Commission on Reform of Federal Criminal Laws,* p. 1363; 1969 Gallup Poll noted in "The Death Penalty in America," p. 35.

Delegates Reject Bid to

End Death Penalty

Washington Post

With members criticizing past and present governors for not using the death penalty more often, the House of Delegates tonight defeated, 84 to 47, a measure to abolish capital punishment in Maryland.

The vote eliminated capital punishment as an issue this year in the General Assembly. The Senate defeated a similar bill Monday night, 21 to 20.

The Washington suburbs produced 20 of the 47 votes in favor of abolition.

Voting against the measure were four Montgomery County Republicans—Daniel J. Cronin, John S. McInerney, David A. Scott and John Aitken—and six Prince George's Democrats—Andrew O. Mothershead, Robert W. Banning, Trueman C. S. Montfort, Edward J. Bagley, Bernard W. Donovan and Frederick C. Rummage. Absent were Alexander B. Bell (D-Montgomery) and Gilbert R. Giordano (D-Prince George's).

The vote climaxed one hour of emotional debate.

Del. C. Lawrence Wiser (D-Montgomery), sponsor of the bill, said capital punishment was "not a deterrent." He added that those who thought it was should push for "public hangings . . . in fact, televise them."

Del. Paul Weisengoff (D-Baltimore) told Wiser he thought public hangings "would be a good idea." When Wiser asked him if he also would support whippings and poking out criminals' eyes, Weisengoff answered:

"Yes, and cutting out their tongues, too."

Although not mentioning Gov. Marvin Mandel or his predecessors by name, Weisengoff criticized "recent governors" for not using the death penalty more often. Mandel, who favors retention of capital punishment, has commuted death sentences for two men in his two months in office. There are currently 18 men on death row. The State has not executed anyone since 1961.

Weisengoff said he will introduce legislation Thursday that would take away the Governor's power to commute death sentences and turn that power over to the General Assembly.

FROM the *Washington Post,* March 13, 1968. Reprinted with the permission of the *Washington Post.*

Del. Rosalie Silber Abrams (D-Baltimore), a supporter of abolition, criticized "the whole issue of violence in our society. . . . It is as wrong for society to use an act of violence as it is for an individual. It is as wrong for a government to use violence as it is for an individual."

On the other side of the issue, Del. Edwin Warfield III (D-Howard), said it was time for the people of the country and the Maryland General Assembly "to stand up nine feet tall for law and order and peace and quiet and everything" and leave the law on the books. He also said that the death penalty "would be more of a deterrent if it were used more often."

In Favor of Capital Punishment

Jacques Barzun

A passing remark of mine in the *Mid-Century* magazine has brought me a number of letters and a sheaf of pamphlets against capital punishment. The letters, sad and reproachful, offer me the choice of pleading ignorance or being proved insensitive. I am asked whether I know that there exists a worldwide movement for the abolition of capital punishment which has everywhere enlisted able men of every profession, including the law. I am told that the death penalty is not only inhuman but also unscientific, for rapists and murderers are really sick people who should be cured, not killed. I am invited to use my imagination and acknowledge the unbearable horror of every form of execution.

I am indeed aware that the movement for abolition is widespread and articulate, especially in England. It is headed there by my old friend and publisher, Mr. Victor Gollancz, and it numbers such well-known writers as Arthur Koestler, C. H. Rolph, James Avery Joyce and Sir John Barry. Abroad as at home the profession of psychiatry tends to support the cure principle, and many liberal newspapers, such as the *Observer*, are committed to abolition. In the United States there are at least twenty-five state leagues working to the same end, plus a national league and several church councils, notably the Quaker and the Episcopal.

The assemblage of so much talent and enlightened goodwill behind a single proposal must give pause to anyone who supports the other side, and in the attempt to make clear my views, which are now close to unpopular, I start out by granting that my conclusion is arguable; that is, I

Reprinted from *The American Scholar*, XXXI (Spring 1962), 181–191, copyright © 1962 by the United Chapters of Phi Beta Kappa. By permission of the publishers.

am still open to conviction, *provided* some fallacies and frivolities in the abolitionist argument are first disposed of and the difficulties not ignored but overcome. I should be glad to see this happen, not only because there is pleasure in the spectacle of an airtight case, but also because I am not more sanguinary than my neighbor and I should welcome the discovery of safeguards—for society *and* the criminal—other than killing. But I say it again, these safeguards must really meet, not evade or postpone, the difficulties I am about to describe. Let me add before I begin that I shall probably not answer any more letters on this arousing subject. If this printed exposition does not do justice to my cause, it is not likely that I can do better in the hurry of private correspondence.

I readily concede at the outset that present ways of dealing out capital punishment are as revolting as Mr. Koestler says in his harrowing volume, *Hanged by the Neck.* Like many of our prisons, our modes of execution should change. But this objection to barbarity does not mean that capital punishment—or rather, judicial homicide—should not go on. The illicit jump we find here, on the threshold of the inquiry, is characteristic of the abolitionist and must be disallowed at every point. Let us bear in mind the possibility of devising a painless, sudden and dignified death, and see whether its administration is justifiable.

The four main arguments advanced against the death penalty are: 1. punishment for crime is a primitive idea rooted in revenge; 2. capital punishment does not deter; 3. judicial error being possible, taking life is an appalling risk; 4. a civilized state, to deserve its name, must uphold, not violate, the sanctity of human life.

I entirely agree with the first pair of propositions, which is why, a moment ago, I replaced the term capital punishment with "judicial homicide." The uncontrollable brute whom I want put out of the way is not to be punished for his misdeeds, nor used as an example or a warning; he is to be killed for the protection of others, like the wolf that escaped not long ago in a Connecticut suburb. No anger, vindictiveness or moral conceit need preside over the removal of such dangers. But a man's inability to control his violent impulses or to imagine the fatal consequences of his acts should be a presumptive reason for his elimination from society. This generality covers drunken driving and teen-age racing on public highways, as well as incurable obsessive violence; it might be extended (as I shall suggest later) to other acts that destroy, precisely, the moral basis of civilization.

But why kill? I am ready to believe the statistics tending to show that the prospect of his own death does not stop the murderer. For one thing he is often a blind egotist, who cannot conceive the possibility of his own death. For another, detection would have to be infallible to deter the more imaginative who, although afraid, think they can escape discovery. Lastly, as Shaw long ago pointed out, hanging the wrong man will deter as effectively as hanging the right one. So, once again, why kill? If I agree that moral progress means an increasing respect for human life, how can I oppose abolition?

I do so because on this subject of human life, which is to me the heart of the controversy, I find the abolitionist inconsistent, narrow or blind. The propaganda for abolition speaks in hushed tones of the sancity of human life, as if the mere statement of it as an absolute should silence all opponents who have any moral sense. But most of the abolitionists belong to nations that spend half their annual income on weapons of war and that honor research to perfect means of killing. These good people vote without a qualm for the political parties that quite sensibly arm their country to the teeth. The West today does not seem to be the time or place to invoke the absolute sanctity of human life. As for the clergymen in the movement, we may be sure from the experience of two previous world wars that they will bless our arms and pray for victory when called upon, the sixth commandment notwithstanding.

"Oh, but we mean the sanctity of life *within* the nation!" Very well: is the movement then campaigning also against the principle of self-defense? Absolute sanctity means letting the cutthroat have his sweet will of you, even if you have a poker handy to bash him with, for you might kill. And again, do we hear any protest against the police firing at criminals on the street—mere bank robbers usually—and doing this, often enough, with an excited marksmanship that misses the artist and hits the bystander? The absolute sanctity of human life is, for the abolitionist, a slogan rather than a considered proposition.

Yet it deserves examination, for upon our acceptance or rejection of it depend such other highly civilized possibilities as euthanasia and seemly suicide. The inquiring mind also wants to know why the sanctity of *human* life alone? My tastes do not run to household pets, but I find something less than admirable in the uses to which we put animals—in zoos, laboratories and space machines—without the excuse of the ancient law "Eat or be eaten."

It should moreover be borne in mind that this argument about sanctity applies—or would apply—to about ten persons a year in Great Britain and to between fifty and seventy-five in the United States. These are the average numbers of those executed in recent years. The count by itself should not, of course, affect our judgment of the principle: one life spared or forfeited is as important, morally, as a hundred thousand. But it should inspire a comparative judgment: there are hundreds and indeed thousands whom, in our concern with the horrors of execution, we forget: on the one hand, the victims of violence; on the other, the prisoners in our jails.

The victims are easy to forget. Social science tends steadily to mark a preference for the troubled, the abnormal, the problem case. Whether it is poverty, mental disorder, delinquency or crime, the "patient material" monopolizes the interest of increasing groups of people among the most generous and learned. Psychiatry and moral liberalism go together; the application of law as we have known it is thus coming to be regarded as an historic prelude to social work, which may replace it entirely. Modern literature makes the most of this same outlook, caring only for the disturbed spirit, scorning as bourgeois those who pay their way and do *not* stab their friends. All the while the determinism of natural science reinforces the assumption that society causes its own evils. A French jurist, for example, says that in order to understand crime we must first brush aside all ideas of Responsibility. He means the criminal's and takes for granted that of society. The murderer kills because reared in a broken home or, conversely, because at an early age he witnessed his parents making love. Out of such cases, which make pathetic reading in the literature of modern criminology, is born the abolitionist's state of mind: we dare not kill those we are beginning to understand so well.

If, moreover, we turn to the accounts of the crimes committed by these unfortunates, who are the victims? Only dull ordinary people going about their business. We are sorry, of course, but they do not interest science on its march. Balancing, for example, the sixty to seventy criminals executed annually in the United States, there were the seventy to eighty housewives whom George Cvek robbed, raped and usually killed during the months of a career devoted to proving his virility. "It is too bad." Cvek alone seems instructive, even though one of the law officers who helped track him down quietly remarks: "As to the extent that his villainies disturbed family relationships, or how many women are still haunted by the specter of an experience they have never disclosed to another living soul, these questions can only lend themselves to sterile conjecture."

The remote results are beyond our ken, but it is not idle to speculate about those whose death by violence fills the daily two inches at the back of respectable newspapers—the old man sunning himself on a park bench and beaten to death by four hoodlums, the small children abused and strangled, the middle-aged ladies on a hike assaulted and killed, the family terrorized by a released or escaped lunatic, the half-dozen working people massacred by the sudden maniac, the boatload of persons dispatched by the skipper, the mindless assaults upon schoolteachers and shopkeepers by the increasing horde of dedicated killers in our great cities. Where does the sanctity of life begin?

It is all very well to say that many of these killers are themselves "children," that is, minors. Doubtless a nine-year-old mind is housed in that 150 pounds of unguided muscle. Grant, for argument's sake, that the misdeed is "the fault of society," trot out the broken home and the slum environment. The question then is, What shall we do, not in the Utopian city of tomorrow, but here and now? The "scientific" means of cure are more than uncertain. The apparatus of detention only increases the killer's antisocial animus. Reformatories and mental hospitals are full and have an understandable bias toward discharging their inmates. Some of these are indeed "cured"—so long as they stay under a rule. The stress of the social free-for-all throws them back on their violent modes of self-expression. At that point I agree that society has failed—twice: it has twice failed the victims, whatever may be its guilt toward the killer.

As in all great questions, the moralist must choose, and choosing has a price. I happen to think that if a person of adult body has not been endowed with adequate controls against irrationally taking the life of another, that person must be judicially, painlessly, regretfully killed before that mindless body's horrible automation repeats.

I say "irrationally" taking life, because it is often possible to feel great sympathy with a murderer. Certain *crimes passionnels* can be forgiven without being condoned. Blackmailers invite direct retribution. Long provocation can be an excuse, as in that engaging case of some years ago, in which a respectable carpenter of seventy found he could no longer stand the incessant nagging of his wife. While she excoriated him from her throne in the kitchen—a daily exercise for fifty years—the husband went to his bench and came back with a hammer in each hand to settle the score. The testimony to his character, coupled with the sincerity implied by the two hammers, was enough to have him sent into quiet and brief seclusion.

But what are we to say of the type of motive disclosed in a journal published by the inmates of one of our Federal penitentiaries? The author is a bank robber who confesses that money is not his object:

My mania for power, socially, sexually, and otherwise can feel no degree of satisfaction until I feel sure I have struck the ultimate of submission and terror in the minds and bodies of my victims. . . . It's very difficult to explain all the queer fascinating sensations pounding and surging through me while I'm holding a gun on a victim, watching his body tremble and sweat. . . . This is the moment when all the rationalized hypocrisies of civilization are suddenly swept away and two men stand there facing each other morally and ethically naked, and right and wrong are the absolute commands of the man behind the gun.

This confused echo of modern literature and modern science defines the choice before us. Anything deserving the name of cure for such a man presupposes not only a laborious individual psychoanalysis, with the means to conduct and to sustain it, socially and economically, but also a re-education of the mind, so as to throw into correct perspective the garbled ideas of Freud and Nietzsche, Gide and Dostoevski, which this power-seeker and his fellows have derived from the culture and temper of our times. Ideas are tenacious and give continuity to emotion. Failing a second birth of heart and mind, we must ask: How soon will this sufferer sacrifice a bank clerk in the interests of making civilization less hypocritical? And we must certainly question the wisdom of affording him more than one chance. The abolitionists' advocacy of an unconditional "let live" is in truth part of the same cultural tendency that animates the killer. The Western peoples' revulsion from power in domestic and foreign policy has made of the state a sort of counterpart of the bank robber: both having power and neither knowing how to use it. Both waste lives because hypnotized by irrelevant ideas and crippled by contradictory emotions. If psychiatry were sure of its ground in diagnosing the individual case, a philosopher might consider whether such dangerous obsessions should not be guarded against by judicial homicide *before* the shooting starts.

I raise the question not indeed to recommend the prophylactic execution of potential murderers, but to introduce the last two perplexities that the abolitionists dwarf or obscure by their concentration on changing an isolated penalty. One of these is the scale by which to judge the offenses society wants to repress. I can for example imagine a truly democratic state in which it would be deemed a form of treason punishable by death to create a disturbance in any court or deliberative assembly. The aim would be to recognize the sanctity of orderly discourse in arriving at justice, assessing criticism and defining policy. Under such a law, a natural selection would operate to remove permanently from the scene persons who, let us say, neglect argument in favor of banging on the desk with their shoe. Similarly, a bullying minority in a diet, parliament or skupshtina would be prosecuted for treason to the most sacred institutions when fists or flying inkwells replace rhetoric. That the mere suggestion of such a law sounds ludicrous shows how remote we are from civilized institutions, and hence how gradual should be our departure from the severity of judicial homicide.

I say gradual and I do not mean standing still. For there is one form of barbarity in our law that I want to see mitigated before any other. I mean imprisonment. The enemies of capital punishment—and liberals generally —seem to be satisfied with any legal outcome so long as they themselves avoid the vicarious guilt of shedding blood. They speak of the sanctity of life, but have no concern with its quality. They give no impression of ever having read what it is certain they have read, from Wilde's *De Profundis* to the latest account of prison life by a convicted homosexual. Despite the infamy of concentration camps, despite Mr. Charles Burney's remarkable work, *Solitary Confinement,* despite riots in prisons, despite the round of escape, recapture and return in chains, the abolitionists' imagination tells them nothing about the reality of being caged. They read without a qualm, indeed they read with rejoicing, the hideous irony of "Killer Gets Life"; they sigh with relief instead of horror. They do not see and suffer the cell, the drill, the clothes, the stench, the food; they do not feel the sexual racking of young and old bodies, the hateful promiscuity, the insane monotony, the mass degradation, the impotent hatred. They do not remember from Silvio Pellico that only a strong political faith, with a hope of final victory, can steel a man to endure long detention. They forget that Joan of Arc, when offered "life," preferred burning at the stake. Quite of another mind, the abolitionists point with pride to the "model prisoners" that murderers often turn out to be. As if a model prisoner were not, first, a contradiction in terms, and second, an exemplar of what a free society should not want.

I said a moment ago that the happy advocates of the life sentence appear not to have understood what we know they have read. No more do they appear to read what they themselves write. In the preface to his useful volume of cases, *Hanged in Error*, Mr. Leslie Hale, M.P., refers to the tardy recognition of a minor miscarriage of justice—one year in jail: "The prisoner emerged to find that his wife had died and that his children and his aged parents had been removed to the workhouse. By the time a small payment had been assessed as 'compensation' the victim was incurably insane." So far we are as indignant with the law as Mr. Hale. But what comes next? He cites the famous Evans case, in which it is very probable that the wrong man was hanged, and he exclaims: "While such mistakes are possible, should society impose an irrevocable sentence?" Does Mr. Hale really ask us to believe that the sentence passed on the first man, whose wife died and who went insane, was in any sense *revocable*? Would not any man rather be Evans dead than that other wretch "emerging" with his small compensation and his reasons for living gone?

Nothing is revocable here below, imprisonment least of all. The agony of a trial itself is punishment, and acquittal wipes out nothing. Read the heartrending diary of William Wallace, accused quite implausibly of having murdered his wife and "saved" by the Court of Criminal Appeals —but saved for what? Brutish ostracism by everyone and a few years of solitary despair. The cases of Adolf Beck, of Oscar Slater, of the unhappy Brooklyn bank teller who vaguely resembled a forger and spent eight years in Sing Sing only to "emerge" a broken, friendless, useless, "compensated" man—all these, if the dignity of the individual has any meaning, had better have been dead before the prison door ever opened for them. This is what counsel always says to the jury in the course of a murder trial and counsel is right: far better hang this man than "give him life." For my part, I would choose death without hesitation. If that option is abolished, a demand will one day be heard to claim it as a privilege in the name of human dignity. I shall believe in the abolitionist's present views only after he has emerged from twelve months in a convict cell.

The detached observer may want to interrupt here and say that the argument has now passed from reasoning to emotional preference. Whereas the objector to capital punishment *feels* that death is the greatest of evils, I *feel* that imprisonment is worse than death. A moment's thought will show that feeling is the appropriate arbiter. All reasoning about what is right, civilized and moral rests upon sentiment, like mathematics. Only, in trying to persuade others, it is important to single out the fundamental feeling, the prime intuition, and from it to reason justly. In my view, to profess respect for human life and be willing to see it spent in a penitentiary is to entertain liberal feelings frivolously. To oppose the death penalty because, unlike a prison term, it is irrevocable is to argue fallaciously.

In the propaganda for abolishing the death sentence the recital of numerous miscarriages of justice commits the same error and implies the same callousness: what is at fault in our present system is not the sentence but the fallible procedure. Capital cases being one in a thousand or more, who can be cheerful at the thought of all the "revocable" errors? What the miscarriages point to is the need for reforming the jury system, the rules of evidence, the customs of prosecution, the machinery of appeal. The failure to see that this is the great task reflects the sentimentality I spoke of earlier, that 'which responds chiefly to the excitement of the unusual. A writer on Death and the Supreme Court is at pains to point out that when that tribunal reviews a capital case, the judges are particularly anxious and careful. What a left-handed compliment to the highest judicial conscience of the country! Fortunately, some of the champions of the misjudged see the issue more clearly. Many of those who are thought wrongly convicted now languish in jail because the jury was uncertain or because a doubting governor commuted the death sentence. Thus Dr. Samuel H. Sheppard, Jr., convicted of his wife's murder in the second degree is serving a sentence that is supposed to run for the term of his natural life. The story of his numerous trials, as told by Mr. Paul Holmes, suggests that police incompetence, newspaper demagogy, public envy of affluence and the mischances of legal procedure fashioned the result. But Dr. Sheppard's vindicator is under no illusion as to the conditions that this "lucky" evader of the electric chair will face if he is granted parole after ten years: "It will carry with it no right to resume his life as a physician. His privilege to practice medicine was blotted out with his conviction. He must all his life bear the stigma of a parolee, subject to unceremonious return to confinement for life for the slightest misstep. More than this, he must live out his life as a convicted murderer."

What does the moral conscience of today think it is doing? If such a man is a dangerous repeater of violent acts, what right has the state to let him loose after ten years? What is, in fact, the meaning of a "life sentence" that peters out long before life? Paroling looks suspiciously like an expression of social remorse for the pain of incarceration, coupled with a wish to avoid "unfavorable publicity" by freeing a suspect. The man is let out when the fuss has died down; which would mean that he was not under lock and key for our protection at all. He *was* being punished, just a little—for so prison seems in the abolitionist's distorted view, and in the jury's and the prosecutor's, whose "second-degree" murder suggests killing someone "just a little." [1]

----

[1] The British Homicide Act of 1957, Section 2, implies the same reasoning in its definition of "diminished responsibility" for certain forms of mental abnormality. The whole question of irrationality and crime is in utter confusion, on both sides of the Atlantic.

If, on the other hand, execution and life imprisonment are judged too severe and the accused is expected to be harmless hereafter—punishment being ruled out as illiberal—what has society gained by wrecking his life and damaging that of his family?

What we accept, and what the abolitionist will clamp upon us all the more firmly if he succeeds, is an incoherence, which is not remedied by the belief that second-degree murder merits a kind of second-degree death; that a doubt as to the identity of a killer is resolved by commuting real death into intolerable life; and that our ignorance whether a maniac will strike again can be hedged against by measuring "good behavior" within the gates and then releasing the subject upon the public in the true spirit of experimentation.

These are some of the thoughts I find I cannot escape when I read and reflect upon this grave subject. If, as I think, they are relevant to any discussion of change and reform, resting as they do on the direct and concrete perception of what happens, then the simple meliorists who expect to breathe a purer air by abolishing the death penalty are deceiving themselves and us. The issue is for the public to judge; but I for one shall not sleep easier for knowing that in England and America and the West generally a hundred more human beings are kept alive in degrading conditions to face a hopeless future; while others—possibly less conscious, certainly less controlled—benefit from a premature freedom dangerous alike to themselves and society. In short, I derive no comfort from the illusion that in giving up one manifest protection of the law-abiding, we who might well be in any of these three roles—victim, prisoner, licensed killer—have struck a blow for the sanctity of human life.

Controversy: Mr. Barzun and
Capital Punishment

Jerome Nathanson, Gerzson Warga, Robert Heilbroner, and S. G. Morley

In the last issue of the *Scholar* Jacques Barzun presented his case in favor of capital punishment. I miss in his presentation any serious argument in behalf of his own case. I find instead a series of undocumented proclamations. The only way I know how to respond (except by ignoring his piece

Reprinted from *The American Scholar*, XXXI (Summer 1962), 436–447, copyright © 1962 by the United Chapters of Phi Beta Kappa. By permission of the publishers.

completely and presenting an independent case for abolition) is to comment on his "arguments" *seriatim.*

First, though, I must deal with Mr. Barzun's declaration that his views "are now close to unpopular." When I read this I wondered if he and I live in the same United States. How close is close? Is it close enough to believe that the death penalty will soon be abolished in the forty-two states that now have it in their penal codes? Is the cause of abolition as popular as this? Is this what accounts for the fact that not long ago the voters of Oregon rejected abolition after it had been recommended to them by both the legislature and the Governor? Partly because of this the Governor of Ohio—himself a strong enough believer in abolition to have paroled murderers on his household staff—has refused to submit the question to popular vote.

A few years ago a special Massachusetts commission recommended abolition of the death penalty, whereupon the legislature promptly voted against its own commission. A few years ago Delaware abolished capital punishment. Subsequently, as has happened elsewhere, an especially outrageous crime led to a demand for its restoration. The legislature responded favorably to the demand, the Governor vetoed the measure, and it was passed again over his veto. The Governor of California is a supporter of abolition, but there is hardly the ghost of a chance, after the furor over the Chessman case, that it will be realized during his administration, even if he is elected to another term in office.

In March of 1961 the New York Legislature called for the appointment of a special commission to study the state's entire penal code which, incidentally, is thought by highly regarded criminologists to be one of the most antiquated and barbaric in the world. The death penalty is included in the study. The Governor was requested to declare a moratorium of all executions until the commission brings in its report. He summarily refused to do so—even though, mind you, it was not a request for abolition but simply for temporary suspension.

One could go on and on, all too unhappily from my point of view. I hope these instances are sufficient to dispose of Mr. Barzun's *ex cathedra* declaration that his views are "close to unpopular." After working a number of years in behalf of abolition, I have the contrary impression that the preponderance of popular sentiment is on his side. I stress popular *sentiment.* It is my conviction, although I cannot prove it, that most people have never reflected seriously and dispassionately upon this question. It is my hope that if they do they will reach the conclusion that capital punishment is wrong if anything is wrong. This is why I believe that the primary task of abolitionist groups at present is educational.

Mr. Barzun refers to a French jurist who says that "in order to understand crime we must first brush aside all ideas of Responsibility." In context the implication is not clear: whether some, many or all advocates of abolition share this view. I surely do not. It is my belief that human beings *are* morally responsible. We have to realize that whatever the background of the individual offender the crime itself is no less a crime because of that. As every judge knows, he would violate his own responsibility if he did not face this fact. This is what Justice Cardozo meant when he remarked, "The justice which is due the defendant is due the community, as well."

Yet we also have to realize that this is only a starting point in dealing with problems of crime, especially with capital cases. It is not likely that we are going to find easy answers, or that any answers will be convincing to everyone. But surely we ought to reach answers more civilized than those presently embodied in our penal codes.

Let us turn now to what Mrs. Barzun calls the four main arguments of the proponents of abolition. The first one, he writes, is that "punishment for crime is a primitive idea rooted in revenge," and he entirely agrees with this. I have never heard this argument advanced by an abolitionist with whom I have worked. Furthermore, while Mr. Barzun agrees with it, I do not. One of the reasons I am against capital punishment is that I do not agree with it.

To be sure, punishment is often motivated by vengeance. Is there no punishment not so motivated? Is punishment never ethically justifiable? I think that punishment is never ethically justified when it is vindictive or retributive. But I think it is ethical when its intent is educative, rehabilitative, re-forming. Every good child psychiatrist knows that it is the completely permissive parent, not the justly punishing one, who damages the child. I think this consideration equally valid with respect to criminals. If they are not disturbed personalities requiring medical treatment, then they should be punished. Obviously in a civilized society there would be no attempt to make the punishment fit the crime. It should fit the individual. And it should be motivated by an honest desire to reeducate that individual. An overwhelming number of our penal institutions, of course, instead of effectively making this effort, breed more crime. This is a criticism of all of us who permit it, but it is no argument against the principle.

That properly motivated punishment is ethically justifiable is precisely what makes capital punishment not only ethically offensive but a contradiction in terms. For if the intent of punishment should be reeducation and reformation, then the person whose brains boil over in the electric chair or whose neck is broken by the noose is not likely to learn much from his "punishment."

The second main argument Mr. Barzun attributes to abolitionists is that "capital punishment does not deter" and, once again, he agrees. I wish I could, too, since contrary to Mr. Barzun I think it would be a clincher for the abolitionist case. Obviously the death penalty is no deterrent for professional killers, since they seldom receive it because "the organization" protects them. But for others guilty of murder the available statistics do not provide an incontrovertible case for either side. All they show is that in adjacent and sociologically comparable states, with and without capital punishment, there is little difference in the homicide rate. Since the deterrent value of the death penalty cannot be clearly demonstrated, the state places an awful burden on the conscience of its citizens cold-bloodedly to commit "judicial homicide," to use Mr. Barzun's euphemism.

The third argument, with which Mr. Barzun disagrees, is that "judicial error being possible, taking life is an appalling risk." He thinks rather that mistakes of this character point to "the need for reforming the jury system, the rules of evidence, the customs of prosecution, the machinery of appeal." One can agree with the need for some such reforms, as I do, without seeing the logical bearing of the point on the initial argument, as I do not. We know of many instances in which the state has committed "judicial homicide" upon persons subsequently found to be indubitably innocent. Human fallibility being what it is, I do not think the possibility of judicial error in capital cases should be brushed aside. But judgment about this rests upon the next point.

For the sanctity of human life, and what one means by it, is the crux of the matter. Here Mr. Barzun carries off a bit of sleight of hand. He attributes to abolitionists not only a belief in the sanctity of human life, which I assume is shared by all civilized people, but a belief in its *absolute,* that is unconditional, sanctity. On this basis he finds us "inconsistent, narrow or blind" in supporting armaments. Apart from anything else, he does scant justice to the many Friends who are simultaneously abolitionists and pacifists. And surely he deals unjustly with those of us who are not absolutists in our view. I can believe in the sanctity of human life, as I do, and still believe that it was right for us to fight for the preservation of democracy against fascism, as I believe it right to defend democracy from communism.

We must be clear about another matter that Mr. Barzun beclouds. He speaks of the "elimination from society" of certain classes of individuals. Depending upon the meaning of "elimination," I know of no abolitionist who would oppose this point in principle. No sensible person of my acquaintance advocates freedom of society for those guilty of antisocial behavior, especially of a vicious nature. I would in fact urge the amendment of our penal codes so that potentially violent persons—for example, certain psychotics—would not, in Mr. Barzun's language, "be guarded against by judicial homicide before the shooting starts," but would be isolated from society for treatment before a crime is committed. But if I read Mr. Barzun correctly, this is not what he means. By "elimination" he means "extermination," which is something quite different.

Mr. Barzun writes: "The victims are easy to forget. Social science tends steadily to mark a preference for the troubled, the abnormal, the problem case." He surely cannot doubt that many abolitionists are as deeply concerned about victims, as well as with the families and friends of victims, as he is. Surely any healthy-minded person is revolted by the rape-murder of a little girl. Is there one who does not feel deep compassion for her parents? Unfortunately the question is not one of our revulsion or compassion. The question is what we can do about it. We ought to do everything we can to prevent the occurrence of such crimes. No one can bring the child back to life. No one can ever really make amends to the parents. At the same time, can anyone honestly believe that the person capable of committing so horrible a crime is not very sick? Extermination doubtless brings emotional satisfaction to many people, but is this synonymous with justice? Even the father of "the Cape Man's" victim in New York asked the Governor to extend clemency to him. Mr. Barzun asks, "Where does the sanctity of life begin?" This is not the basic question. What must be asked is, When if at all does the sanctity of life end, and who is to be the judge of when it should?

Mr. Barzun writes, once more *ex cathedra:* "The 'scientific' means of cure are more than uncertain. . . . Reformatories and mental hospitals are full and have an understandable bias toward discharging their inmates[!]. Some of these are indeed 'cured'—so long as they stay under a rule. The stress of the social free-for-all throws them back on their violent modes of self-expression." But what is the fact? In those states in which a sentence of life imprisonment for convicted murderers permits parole eligibility for good behavior, the paroled murderers have the best record of any class of criminals not only for not repeating what they earlier did, but for not violating their parole in any way.

Another citation: "The enemies of capital punishment—and liberals generally—seem to be satisfied with any legal outcome as long as they themselves avoid the vicarious guilt of shedding blood. They speak of the sanctity of life, but have no concern with its quality. . . . They read without a qualm, indeed they read with rejoicing, the hideous irony of 'Killer Gets Life'; they sigh with relief instead of horror." I think Mr. Barzun should be challenged to produce a single healthy-minded abolitionist who reads "with rejoicing" that a person has been sentenced to imprisonment for the rest of his natural life.

The question of life imprisonment, which is quite literal in New York, for example, unless the Governor intervenes, demands clarification. There are some district attorneys who prefer it to the death penalty because, in their experience, some jurors who have no theoretical objection to capital punishment find, when they are actually sitting in a case, that they cannot bring in such a verdict without violating their consciences. They therefore vote for acquittal, even though they may have reason to think that the person on trial is guilty of the crime charged. The district attorneys who hold this view accordingly believe that fewer guilty people would be found not guilty if the "extreme penalty" were not mandatory where it is. Some legislators and others who are convinced abolitionists propose life imprisonment as an alternative not because they believe in it, but because they think that the people of their states and their legislative representatives would be unwilling to accept anything less. Many of the rest of us are convinced that mandatory life imprisonment without parole eligibility is not punishment but barbarism.

A word about the role of forensic psychiatry in murder trials is in order. I think it demeaning to the members of the psychiatric profession to be party to such procedure. Prosecution and defense will frequently produce their respective specialists to testify under M'Naghten's rule of knowing right from wrong about a given person's "sanity" or "insanity"— words no good doctor will even use in his own practice! It is hard for me to understand how a conscientious doctor can be an "advocate" of an individual's sickness or health. And the rule itself is antiquated, since many compulsive or obsessive individuals do know right from wrong but can't help themselves from doing what they know to be wrong. I believe, rather, that a person charged with a crime, certainly a major crime, should be tried for his guilt or innocence regardless of the state of his health. If found guilty, he should then be subject to medical examination, as able and objective as the state can provide. If he is sick, he should be treated accordingly. If he is not, he should be punished in whatever manner is likely to help him be an acceptable member of society.

But to return to Mr. Barzun. He remarks: "The detached observer may want to interrupt here and say that the argument has now passed from reasoning to emotional preference. . . . A moment's thought will show that feeling is the appropriate arbiter." The fact is that for anyone acquainted with intellectual history, more especially the history of ethical philosophy, "a moment's thought" will not necessarily show anything of the kind, nor do I doubt that Mr. Barzun is aware of this. To be sure, more moral philosophers, chief among them David Hume, have grounded ethical judgment in sentiment—to say nothing of contemporary "emotivists" who declare that so-called ethical judgment is really an expression of like or dislike. For a contrary and brilliantly expressed point of view I recommend to interested readers Brand Blanshard's recently published Gifford Lectures on *Reason and Goodness*.[1]

As astonishing as anything else in his case are Mr. Barzun's reflections on the person sentenced to life imprisonment who is eligible for parole. He writes: "What is, in fact, the meaning of a 'life sentence' that peters out long before life? Paroling looks suspiciously like an expression of social remorse for the pain of incarceration, coupled with a wish to avoid 'unfavorable publicity' by freeing a suspect." I find this a truly elegant piece of sophistry. For insofar as I am able to follow the logic of his entire position, it reduces itself to this: If a person is sentenced to life imprisonment he ought to be imprisoned for the rest of his life; but life imprison-

---

[1] *Macmillan.*

ment is worse than death; therefore, it is better both for him and society to exterminate him.

Mr. Barzun appears to take it for granted that for the criminal "judicial homicide" is clearly preferable to imprisonment. He observes: "I shall believe in the abolitionist's present views only after he has emerged from twelve months in a convict cell." I confess that I have never "done time." But I doubt that Mr. Barzun has, either. I do know a man, however, who as a relative youngster was condemned to death for felony murder. He was in the death house and was, literally, within hours of dying when the Governor intervened and saved his life. Today he is a free man and a responsible citizen and, despite Mr. Barzun's theorizing, glad still to be alive.

JEROME NATHANSON
Chairman, New York Committee to
Abolish Capital Punishment, and
Chairman, Fraternity of Leaders,
American Ethical Union

. . . .

You may not receive many congratulatory letters on your recent article, "In Favor of Capital Punishment," but this one at least is such a letter. It takes great courage today to take Mr. Barzun's stand if one is aspiring to be counted among the "intellectuals." Congratulations to him both for his courage and for his article.

One minor point left me somewhat dissatisfied. When he deals with the four arguments against the death penalty advanced by its opponents, he does not demolish the second, namely, that "capital punishment does not deter." I think this argument, attractive as it may appear, is easily shown to be a fallacy:

1. I have read accounts of bank robberies where the criminal used a toy gun not because he was unable to procure a real one, but because he did not want to risk being sentenced for murder in case things went "wrong."
2. In California, where 190 murders were committed during a single year, only five convicted murders were executed. Less than three per cent! How can we expect the death penalty to be of full deterrent force?
3. If capital punishment is no deterrent, then by logical extension punishment is no deterrent. Let us carry this to the logical but absurd conclusion: No crime must be punished because punishment is no deterrent!

DR. GERZSON WARGA
Chevy Chase, Maryland

. . . .

The authorities have delivered to me the recent issue of your publication in which Dr. Barzun delivers his humane defense of capital punishment. As I read this article the scales fell from my eyes and I realized how meretricious had been my attempt, while on earth, to do away with this form of social punishment. Nevertheless old ideas die hard, even in my present position *au dessus de la mêlée*. Therefore I suggest the following, to which I am certain Dr. Barzun will be quick to agree:

1. All prison sentences are henceforth to contain these alternatives (a) the right to commit suicide, in decent privacy and with appropriate means furnished by the authorities, and (b) the right to opt for legal execution at any time when the sentence becomes unendurable.
2. Purely as a legal formality, since it will assuredly not be availed of, all death sentences are to contain the option, exercisable solely at the prisoner's discretion, of commutation to life imprisonment (with rights under (1) above unimpaired).

It occurs to me that this might also provide something of a test for the relative humaneness of the punishments offered. Eh, M. Barzun? *D'accord?*

ALBERT CAMUS [2]

. . . .

May I express complete agreement with Mr. Barzun's article on capital punishment?

Are you acquainted with the passage in Alexis Carrel's *Man, the Unknown* (Harpers, 1935) on this subject? I think it would interest you, and provide a good supporting quote for Mr. Barzun.

There remains the unsolved problem of the immense number of defectives and criminals. They are an enormous burden for the part of the population that has remained normal. As already pointed out, gigantic sums are now required to maintain prisons and insane asylums and protect the public against gangsters and lunatics. Why do we preserve these useless and harmful beings? The abnormal prevent the development of the normal. This fact must be squarely faced. Why should society not dispose of the criminals and the insane in a more economical manner? We cannot go on trying to separate the responsible from the irresponsible, punish the guilty, spare those who, although having committed a crime, are thought to be morally innocent. We are not capable of judging men. However, the community must be protected against troublesome and dangerous elements. How can this be done? Certainly not by building larger and more comfortable prisons, just as real health will not be promoted by larger and more scientific hospitals. Criminality and insanity can be prevented only by a better knowledge of man, by eugenics, by changes in education and in social conditions. Meanwhile, criminals have to be dealt with effectively. Perhaps prisons should be abolished. They could be replaced by smaller and less expensive institutions. The conditioning of petty criminals with the whip, or some more scientific procedure, followed by a short stay in hospital, would probably suffice to insure order. Those who have murdered, robbed while armed with automatic pistol or machine gun, kidnapped children, despoiled

[2] [Robert Heilbroner. Editors' note.]

the poor of their savings, misled the public in important matters, should be humanely and economically disposed of in small euthanasic institutions supplied with proper gases. A similar treatment could be advantageously applied to the insane, guilty of criminal acts. Modern society should not hesitate to organize itself with reference to the normal individual. Philosophical systems and sentimental prejudices must give way before such a necessity. The development of human personality is the ultimate purpose of civilization.

S. G. MORLEY
University of California

Tennessee v. Wash Jones: The Closing Argument for the Defense

Joe W. Henry, Jr.

May it please the Court:

Fifty-three years ago, in a bleak and barren and God-forsaken building on the banks of the Cumberland River, at 5:00 o'clock in the morning, a Negro man, made in God's own image, bearing the name of Julius Morgan, and from Dyer County, Tennessee, became the first citizen of our state to be legally murdered by electrocution.

Two years later, on July 8, 1918, *the second kilowatt killing* was conducted. This time the hapless victim was one, J. D. Williams, a Negro citizen, of Giles County.

The third time the stench of searing and scorched human flesh came out of our penitentiary was that same July day in 1918, when Eddie Olsup met his Maker at the hands of the civilized State of Tennessee and in order to preserve the peace and dignity of the state. He, too, was from Giles County.

In all, 123 persons have walked that last mile.

One hundred twenty-three times we have turned our backs upon the command of the Decalogue: Thou shalt not kill.

One hundred twenty-three times we have arrogated to ourselves the right to destroy the image of God on earth.

One hundred twenty-three times we have disputed the sacred idea that no man is beyond redemption.

One hundred twenty-three times we have reverted to our primitive and savage origin bred in generations in the jungle.

FROM the *American Bar Association Journal*, XLVI (January 1960), 52–55, 111–112, copyright 1960, American Bar Association. Reprinted with permission.

One hundred twenty-three times we have closed the door on a man's life and sent him to his Maker with a crime on his soul and guilt in his heart and denied him his God-given right to repentance, redemption and forgiveness.

One hundred twenty-three times we have usurped the divine authority of heaven.

One hundred twenty-three prosecutors have sung their hymns of hate as hapless human beings prepared to hang down their heads and die.

One hundred twenty-three times we have proclaimed to the world that state government has no obligation to be civilized.

Who were these 123 men?

Their names are unimportant, but I have a list that shows them all—the roll of horror.

One cannot look at this yellow sheet—significantly it is yellow—the color denoting cowardice, the color of the Army's Dishonorable Discharge, the color that describes the worst fever known to man, the color that describes the jacket of the pestiferous hornet, the color that describes the worst brand of journalism—one cannot look at it without thinking of all the widows and orphans we have made, of all the tears that were shed in their memory and of the God who loved them, but who was thrust from their hearts by the cold hand of vengeance.

Ten men and two women sit upon this jury. Five of you owe your spiritual allegiance to the Methodist Church; two to the Church of Christ; two to the Cumberland Presbyterian; and one to the Baptist Church.

All of you stated on your examination that you believe in God, that you accepted Jesus Christ as your personal Saviour, that you subscribed to the precepts of the Christian religion, believed in the set of ethical standards proclaimed by Christ, believed in a future system of rewards and punishment, the forgiveness of sins, the resurrection of the body and the life everlasting.

In short, you are Christians and civilized citizens.

You have all—some reluctantly—expressed your belief in capital punishment.

As you follow my argument, I ask that you search your souls in an effort to arrive at a rational and Christian conclusion based upon a fresh look at the evidence.

I ask that you erase from your minds any opinion that you may have on capital punishment until I have presented the case against capital punishment and have reviewed the issues and separated superstition from fact.

Essentials of Punishment

It is generally accepted that there are *three essential ingredients* of all punishment. All must be present and if any one is missing the punishment is defective.

First, the punishment of the offender;

Second, the rehabilitation of the offender and his restoration to useful and productive citizenship;

Third, the protection of society by deterring others from the commission of like offenses.

We may dispose summarily, and without discussion, of the first two, because I will readily admit that death by electrocution definitely fulfills the essential ingredient of punishment. I am sure that the district attorney and his associate, likewise, will concede that death is fairly permanent and when the penalty of death is imposed rehabilitation and restoration are impossible. Thus, it is, at the very outset, one of the essentials of punishment is missing.

Deterrence

This leaves for consideration the major ingredient and the one that completely overshadows the first two, *i.e.*, deterrence. *Does the death penalty serve as a warning to others? Does it keep them from committing similar crimes?*

There are those who contend that we are living in an age when we have witnessed more brutality and slaughter than all our ancestors since the birth of Christ; that this is perhaps why we don't worry too much about the death of one man, that we have become inoculated to brutality and immune to human suffering.

My whole being rebels at any such philosophy. I am morally persuaded that throughout the history of time each generation has been successively better and upon the rungs of its progress we are steadily climbing the ladder that ultimately leads to a perfect order of existence.

Men of good will recognize it to be incontestably true that we are our brothers' keepers, and just as a pebble cannot be thrown into the ocean without disturbing every drop of water in the sea, so one man cannot be abandoned and sacrificed upon the altar of society's sometimes unreasonable demands without disturbing all mankind.

Yes, we have made great progress.

Throughout the recorded history of time the human race has devised many and varied means of punishing those guilty of infractions of good order, and while we have not reached perfection, our progress has been praiseworthy.

There was a time when society thought that criminals should be beheaded, burned, boiled or buried alive; when men were strangled, stoned, skinned or starved to death; when they were torn asunder by trees fastened to their limbs, or devoured by wild beasts; when they were forced to drink poison, crucified, or drowned; when they were chopped in two while still alive, or eaten alive by insects or sewn in a bag with snakes—all of this in the name of justice and all because it was *"the law of the state."*

As odious and savage as these practices sound to us today, let's face the fact that a hundred years from now when capital punishment has long vanished from the American scene as it has in most of the other civilized countries of the world—electrocution will be listed as another barbarous punishment along with drawing and quartering—for I submit to you any punishment that takes the very life of a human being is barbarous, cruel, unChristian, and uncivilized and a throwback to the Dark Ages.

Time was when pigs, horses and cattle were tried and executed for murder. *It was the law of the state.*

In 1474 a rooster was tried for the heinous and unnatural crime of laying an egg and sentenced, together with the egg, to be burned at the stake. *It was the law of the state.*

There is another, in 1801 of a British child being hanged for stealing a spoon. *It was the law of the state.*

There is a recorded case in England of a 9-year-old girl being hanged for stealing two pennies worth of salt. *It was the law of the state.*

There is another in 1748 of a boy of 10 who was executed for murder. *It was the law of the state.*

There is the case of the 12-year-old American boy who was hanged for stealing a sheep. *It was the law of the state.*

I am sickened every time I hear a prosecutor apologetically asking for the death penalty and offering the pitiful excuse *"It's the law of the state."*

In England during the reign of Henry VIII, there were over two hundred crimes, ranging from shooting rabbits to associating with Gypsies for which the death penalty was exacted and during this period, to the shame and disgrace of our mother country, *72,000 Englishmen were executed.* This, however, did not seem to deter Englishmen from committing crimes.

During the reign of Queen Elizabeth I, *19,000 Englishmen were executed* but the crime rate continued to rise.

No doubt bloody Queen Mary was actuated by the noblest motives, but for all the blood she drew, crime continued unabated in Merry England.

Peter I, Tsar of Russia, issued an edict against men wearing beards and, in order to enforce it, in 1728, *put to death 8,000 Russians,* and yet today we can hardly think of a Russian without a bearded image flashing before our eyes.

There was a time in England when pickpockets were hanged and when the public hangings took place the pickpockets gathered and picked the pockets of those who came to witness the execution.

The death penalty did not deter the *7,000* people in America who committed murders in 1958.

Crime has a tendency to beget crime, and bizarre punishments have always adversely affected law enforcement.

One of the most famous of all English hangmen was John Price, who was himself hanged for murder, as were Hangman Dennis and Mr. Hespel.

Then there is the interesting story of a former head hangman at the Oklahoma State Prison, who was tried for murder himself on no less than four occasions.

Ordinary prudence and common judgment will tell us that if the imposition of the death penalty is to operate as a deterrent. executions must be performed publicly so that all may see what a horrible and hideous fate awaits the wrongdoer. Criminals should have front seats; it should be carried on television; movies should be made; the penalty made more brutal, and sheer, stark terror should be stricken into the hearts of all the people so that they, in heat of passion, or while temporarily insane, will stop and think of the gruesome fate that is theirs.

Non-justifiable murders can take only two forms:

First, those in heat of passion.

Second, those premeditated and planned.

In the first group the murderer has lost all reason and all control of his faculties and, therefore, the consequences of his deed do not enter his mind.

In the second group, the murderer thinks he has planned the perfect crime and will not be apprehended, and so he gives no thought to punishment.

Again, where is the deterrence?

The State of Delaware has just become the eighth state to outlaw capital punishment. Among the reasons assigned for this action by the Prisoners' Aid Society of Delaware were:

1. The evidence clearly shows that execution does not act as a deterrent to capital offenses.

2. The serious offenses are committed, except in rare instances, by those suffering from mental disturbances; are impulsive in nature; and are not the acts of the "criminal" class.

3. More convictions with less delays are obtained because the reluctance of juries to convict where the death sentence is involved is removed as a factor.

4. Unequal application of the law takes place because those executed are the poor, the ignorant, and the unfortunate without resources.

5. Conviction of the innocent does occur and death makes a miscarriage of justice irrevocable. Human judgment cannot be infallible.

6. The state sets a bad example when it takes a life. Imitative crimes and murder are stimulated by executions.

7. Legally taking a life is useless and is demoralizing to the general public. It is also demoralizing to the public officials who, dedicated to rehabilitating individuals, must callously put a man to death.

Perhaps one of the most illuminating studies on capital punishment was made by the British Royal Commission on capital punishment during the period 1949–1953. After a four-year study, and hearing expert witnesses from many parts of the world, they came to this interesting conclusion: "The general conclusion which we have reached is that there is no clear evidence in any of the figures we have examined that the abolition of capital punishment has led to an increase in the homicide rate, or that its re-introduction has led to its fall."

A California legislative committee reported in 1957: "A world-wide survey shows that nowhere has the abolition of the death penalty led to an increase in the number of homicides."

In the face of these and numerous other studies, and against all the evidence to the contrary, there are those who still insist that the death penalty is a deterrent and that its abolition would result in an increase in crime.

Let's take a look at the record.

The death penalty has been abolished in the following *countries of Europe:* Austria, Denmark, Finland, Holland, Italy, Norway, Portugal, Rumania, Spain, Sweden, Switzerland, West Germany; *of South and Central America:* Argentina, Brazil, Colombia, Costa Rica, Dominican Republic, Ecuador, Honduras, Mexico, Panama, Peru, Puerto Rico, Uruguay, Venezuela; *elsewhere:* Greenland, Iceland, Israel, New Zealand and Turkey.

In the United States it has been abolished in: Maine, Michigan, Minnesota, North Dakota, Rhode Island, Wisconsin, Alaska, Delaware, Hawaii.

In all of the foreign countries, for which I have the figures, their murder rate went down after the abolition.

In the United States during the ten-year period 1931–1940, the average rate of murders was 8.1 per 100,000, whereas, in the states that did not have capital punishment, the rate was only 2.3 *or only one fourth as high.*

It is significant that the State of Maine which abolished capital punishment in 1887 after an innocent man was executed, has one of the lowest murder rates in the United States, whereas *Georgia with fourteen crimes for which the death penalty may be exacted has the highest murder rate in the nation.*

So much for the argument that capital punishment serves to deter others from the commission of crimes. The record completely refutes this argument.

Convictions by Mistake

To me, one of the most compelling arguments against capital punishment is the possibility of mistake. Moreover, every lawyer and judge knows that bold, bald, unblushing perjury all too frequently stalks into our courts and makes a mockery of that intangible commodity we call justice.

All America has harked to the saga of Tom Dooley, the folk song imploring a gay blade headed for the gallows to hang his head in shame before he was executed, but I wonder how many know that the song was written about a North Carolina man named Tom Dula, who was convicted of murdering a young lady acquaintance and was hanged because *it was the law of the state.*

Unfortunately for Tom Dula it was a number of years later before the real murderer confessed.

So many times have the innocent been mistakenly convicted or wrongfully convicted on what later developed to be perjured testimony that a number of books have been written about numerous of these cases.

Biblical Precedents

Then, there are the great cases of recorded history where, even though it was the law, the death penalty was not inflicted.

God, Himself, set the first precedent. Cain gazed upon the beaten and bleeding body of his own brother. The denunciation of Heaven was ringing in his ears. He expected to find vengeance at every hand. But God did not visit capital punishment on him. Instead, He banished him from society, placed a mark upon him—a mark of his crime, but also a mark that would warn the rest of mankind against his destruction. *This was the judgment of Almighty God in dealing with the first murderer and I submit that it is exempt from any possibility of error.*

Then, there is *the case of David,* who was responsible for the death of Uriah the Hittite, and who was not executed but continued, in spite of his heinous crime, to grow in favor with God and man and the holy writ tells us that he was "a man after God's own heart."

The case of Moses is in point—Moses who slew the Egyptian in a fit of anger and who became a fugitive from justice, and yet, God sought him out and, from the burning bush to the heights of Pisgah, from the Red Sea to the mountain peak whence he was taken by God to survey the Promised Land from Dan to Beersheba, he, a murderer, was the right hand of God Almighty.

What if David and Moses had been executed because *"It is the law of the state?"*

The Noachin Laws

Those who urge the continuance of capital punishment forget all these things. Instead, their delight is in quoting from obsolete scripture, taken out of context and bodily lifted from the circumstances surrounding their utterance. Just as patriotism is the last refuge of a scoundrel, so the Bible is the favorite stamping ground of those who enjoy quoting scripture for their own purpose. With fiendish glee and triumphant manner they turn to the ninth chapter and sixth verse of the Book of Genesis and chant: "Whosoever sheddeth man's blood, by man shall his blood be shed."

But circumstances alter cases. Let us look at the circumstances under which this law was laid down. The world had gotten so evil that God repented that he had made man (Gen. 6:6), the great flood came, the former race of mankind with all their laws and customs had been swept away and destroyed by the waters of death.

In gratitude the little family of Noah gathered about the altar and received the seven precepts or laws, we know then as the Noachin laws, for their government. They were few in number and temporary in nature. They embraced only the subjects necessary in their peculiar situation.

All of these seven laws were aimed at repopulating a destroyed earth. Two of the seven laws read "Be ye fruitful and multiply." The little family of Noah was a germ from which all the future nations of the earth were to vegetate. Every possible care therefore had to be taken for its preservation. So the right was expressly given directly by God to take away the life of its members, there being no other possible means of effectuating the purposes of heaven in their preservation. But no such direct and divine authority has been given the three and one-half million people of Tennessee.

The Mosaic Law

Then, there are those who look to the Mosaic Law and cite it as authority to show that God's power over life and death has been committed to His creatures. They overlook a number of significant factors. First of all, the law delivered to Moses amid the fire and flame and the smoke at Mt. Sinai was divided into three parts—moral, political and judicial. The moral law, the Ten Commandments, is universal in its operation and perpetual in its obligation. But the political and judicial laws are only of interest from a standpoint of Biblical history. They constituted a civil and criminal code for the government of the Jews only.

Their authority commanding the infliction of capital punishment is no more binding on a Christian nation than the laws of the Medes and the Persians, or of the various tribes that were driven from Canaan by the sword of the Lord and of Gideon.

Strong measures were needed to bring the headstrong, moody and murmuring people of the children of Israel across the Wilderness. Every student of the Bible knows how they taxed the combined authority of both God and Moses. Never before or since has there been such a rebellious tribe of people and never were such extraordinary measures required to keep a nation in subjection. Even as Moses was on the mountain receiving these very laws amidst the most sublime and awful and awesome demonstrations of the power and grandeur of God, this wayward people set themselves to dancing, in idolatrous worship, around an image made of gold.

I wish that time permitted me to delve more deeply into this with you, but it does not.

The Law of Christ

Ladies and gentlemen of the jury, centuries after the Mosaic Law and almost 2,000 years ago, a solitary wayfarer walked the shores of the Sea of Galilee, healing the sick and casting out the demons that possessed the mentally ill. Persecuted by the mighty Roman Empire, crucified by the edict of a court composed of His own countrymen, denied thrice by one of His trusted disciples in His hour of greatest need, and betrayed by the traitorous deed of another, mocked, spat upon and ridiculed, He, a victim of capital punishment, died the most ignominious death known to His day, and yet He was not deterred and His teachings of faith, hope, charity, courage and love have endured unto this day and wherever free men have instituted free government, the very cornerstone has been the ethical standards taught by Jesus of Nazareth.

There are those who forget:
The mild benevolence of His precepts,
The meekness of His spirit,
The philanthropy that breathes in all His words,
The Golden Rule which He established,
The Christian charity which He taught.

When they quote the Bible as a sanction for the death penalty, they pervert the spirit of His holy and merciful religion.

If I were inclined to support my opinion by arguments drawn from religion, the whole New Testament would be my text, for if it teaches anything, it teaches the forgiveness of sin and, therefore, a system of reform rather than extirpation.

Since so many of you are Methodists, as am I, may I read the position of our church from its official discipline: (Page 633, Par. 2020, Sec. 90, 1956), "We stand for the application of redemptive principle to the treatment for offenders against the law . . . for this reason *we deplore the use of capital punishment. . . .*"

May I read you the resolution by the American Baptist Convention, adopted in Cincinnati, Ohio, June 16, 1957:

1. Because human agencies and legal justice are fallible, and innocent men have been put to death, and,
2. Because the Christian believes in the inherently sacred quality of all life as a gift of God, and,

3. Because the deterrent effects of capital punishment are not clearly supported by the available evidence, and,

4. Because the emphasis in modern penology is upon the process of creative, redemptive rehabilitation rather than primitive retribution, we, therefore,

Recommend the abolition of capital punishment in those states which still practice it.

Next, I cite the resolution passed by the Protestant Episcopal Church, at its 59th General Convention, on October 9, 1958:

WHEREAS, The Church, following the faith of our Lord Jesus Christ holds that each individual is sacred as a child of God and the object of his redemptive love and that to legalize the killing of one such child who is a criminal offender conflicts with this basic Christian concept; and

WHEREAS, The conscience of many church people has been aroused by the condemnation to death of individuals who may be innocent; and

WHEREAS, There is a growing body of public opinion which believes that capital punishment is archaic and ineffective to protect society and as a deterrent to crime; and

WHEREAS, The death penalty appears to fall for the most part on obscure, impoverished, friendless or defective individuals; and

WHEREAS, Resolutions urging abolition of the death penalty have been recently adopted by six dioceses, one missionary district and the synod of the eighty provinces, and now

THEREFORE, BE IT RESOLVED, The House of the Bishops concurring, that this 59th general convention of the Protestant Episcopal Church in the United States of America record its conviction that the death penalty ought to be abolished.

How the State Kills

You have been told in great detail just precisely how Wash Jones killed and murdered Wes Howard. Now let us see how the State of Tennessee would kill and murder Wash Jones.

At about 5:30 in the afternoon of the eve of the execution the prisoner is shaved, bathed and his head is clipped. He must be clean so that it is unnecessary to bathe his body after the electrocution. His head must be clipped so they can apply the electrode.

Then they give him a new shirt and a new pair of pants, without a belt, and shoes without laces. No belt and no shoe laces. After all he must not hang or strangle himself and cheat the chair.

Next, the minister of his choice visits him to offer whatever words of assurance and solace he can conjure up.

Then the condemned man is given an opportunity to eat a hearty meal of his choice.

Then his family is permitted to visit with him until midnight. Then at about ten minutes to five the warden and the guards and the execution party come and they start to walk the last mile down the dim-lit corridor, which leads to the chamber of horrors to the electric chair.

They place him in the chair, roll up his trouser legs in order to clamp the electrode to his right leg. Then to his clipped head they clamp the other electrode.

Then they ask him for his last words. Only the prisoner, the warden and God are present in the room. The warden is doing his statutory duty, the prisoner paying his debt to society and as to him, I am sure he feels that God has forgotten him.

Then they place the mask upon his face—not for his benefit, but to keep the witnesses from looking upon the hideous countenance of the dying man as his facial features contort in pain and agony.

The warden looks through the little window at the man who throws the switch—$25.00 the state pays for this service—the warden has a stop watch in his hands and upon his signal the switch is thrown. Then, there comes the sound from the electrician's niche—a sound like that that comes from an X-ray machine, a crackle, a whine, a buzz as 2,300 volts, for thirty seconds and then 500 for one and one half minutes are sent circulating through his body as it convulsively jerks and writhes.

And then when his body has cooled off enough to touch, the physician applies his stethoscope and pronounces him dead.

He is then placed in cold storage in a deep freeze—because the state does not embalm. Now another name is added to the yellow list—the roll of horror—the state has got another pound of flesh. But it is the law of the state.

I ask you in the name of all that is sacred and holy, how can such a spectacle as this ever magnify the law or make it honorable or preserve the peace and dignity of the state?

And they say that Wash Jones killed in cold blood.

Wash didn't lock Wes Howard in a room, keep him there for weeks and months, announce ahead of time the date and time of his death, and leave the condemned man to die a thousand deaths.

Ladies and gentlemen, you and you alone can send Wash Jones to the electric chair. There can be no division of responsibility, you can never say that the rest overpowered you. It must be your deliberate, cool, premeditated act. It takes your vote.

I plead for human consideration, for charity, for mercy. Man was truly created in God's image, but humane treatment of our fellow man is necessary in order that the divine image may not be obscured.

I hope and pray that the Tennessee legislature will at this session veto the unconscionable decree of blood and write for the state, as the state has written for its citizens, the injunction—at once rational, scriptural, salutary and humanitarian: *"Thou shalt not kill."*

Witherspoon v. *Illinois*

Supreme Court of the United States

No. 1015.—October Term, 1967

| William C. Witherspoon, Petitioner, *v.* State of Illinois et al. | On Writ of Certiorari to the Supreme Court of Illinois. |

[June 3, 1968.]

MR. JUSTICE STEWART delivered the opinion of the Court.

The petitioner was brought to trial in 1960 in Cook County, Illinois, upon a charge of murder. The jury found him guilty and fixed his penalty at death. At the time of his trial an Illinois statute provided:

In trials for murder it shall be a cause for challenge of any juror who shall, on being examined, state that he has conscientious scruples against capital punishment, or that he is opposed to the same.[1]

Through this provision the State of Illinois armed the prosecution with unlimited challenges for cause in order to exclude those jurors who, in the words of the State's highest court, "might hesitate to return a verdict inflicting [death]."[2] At the petitioner's trial, the prosecution eliminated

William C. Witherspoon, Petitioner, v. *State of Illinois,* et al., on Writ of Certiorari to the Supreme Court of Illinois, June 3, 1968.

nearly half the venire of prospective jurors by challenging, under the authority of this statute, any venireman who expressed qualms about

---

[1] Ill. Rev. Stat. 1959, c. 38, § 743. The section was re-enacted in 1961 but was not expressly repeated in the Code of Criminal Procedure of 1963. Ill. Rev. Stat. 1967, c. 38, § 115-4(d) now provides only that "[e]ach party may challenge jurors for cause," but the Illinois Supreme Court has held that § 115-4(d) incorporates former § 743. *People* v. *Hobbs,* 35 Ill. 2d 263, 274, 220 N. E. 2d 469, 475.

[2] "In the trial of the case where capital punishment may be inflicted a juror who has religious or conscientious scruples against capital punishment *might hesitate to return a verdict inflicting such punishment,* and in the present proceedings [a post-sentence sanity hearing] a junior having such scruples might likewise hesitate in returning a verdict finding [the defendant] sane, which in effect confirms the death sentence." *People* v. *Carpenter,* 13 Ill. 2d 470, 476, 150 N. E. 2d 100, 103. (Emphasis added.)

capital punishment. From those who remained were chosen the jurors who ultimately found the petitioner guilty and sentenced him to death. The Supreme Court of Illinois denied post-conviction relief,[3] and we granted certiorari [4] to decide whether the Constitution permits a State to execute a man pursuant to the verdict of a jury so composed.

I

The issue before us is a narrow one. It does not involve the right of the prosecution to challenge for cause those prospective jurors who state that their reservations about capital punishment would prevent them from making an impartial decision as to the defendant's guilt.[5] Nor does it involve the State's assertion of a right to exclude from the jury in a capital case those who say that they could never vote to impose the death penalty or that they would refuse even to consider its imposition in the case before them. For the State of Illinois did not stop there, but authorized the prosecution to exclude as well all who said that they were opposed to capital punishment and all who indicated that they had conscientious scruples against inflicting it.

In the present case the tone was set when the trial judge said early in the *voir dire*, "Let's get these conscientious objectors out of the way, without wasting any time on them." In rapid succession, 47 veniremen were successfully challenged for cause on the basis of their attitudes toward the death penalty. Only five of the 47 explicitly stated that under no circumstances would they vote to impose capital punishment.[6] Six

[3] 36 Ill. 2d 471, 224 N. E. 2d 259.

[4] 389 U. S. 1035.

[5] Unlike the statutory provision this case, statutes and rules disqualifying jurors with scruples against capital punishment are often couched in terms of reservations against finding a man *guilty* when the penalty might be death. See, *e.g.*, Cal. Penal Code, § 1074, subdivision 8. Yet, despite such language, courts in other States have sometimes permitted the exclusion for cause of jurors opposed to the death penalty even in the absence of a showing that their scruples would have interfered with their ability to determine guilt in accordance with the evidence and the law. See, *e.g.*, *State* v. *Thomas*, 78 Ariz. 52, 58, 275 P. 2d 408, 412; *People* v. *Nicolaus*, 65 Cal. 2d 866, 882, 423 P. 2d 787, 798; *Piccot* v. *State*, 116 So. 2d 626, 628 (Fla.); *Commonwealth* v. *Ladetto*, 349 Mass. 237, 246, 207 N. E. 2d 536, 542; *State* v. *Williams*, 50 Nev. 271, 278, 257 P. 619, 621; *Smith* v. *State*, 5 Okla. Crim. 282, 284, 114 P. 350, 351; *State* v. *Jensen*, 209 Ore. 239, 281, 296 P. 2d 618, 635; *State* v. *Leuch*, 198 Wash. 331, 333–337, 88 P. 2d 440, 441–442.

[6] The State stresses the fact that the judge who presided during the *voir dire* implied several times that only those jurors who could *never* agree to a verdict of death should deem themselves disqualified because of their scruples against capital punishment. The record shows, however, that the remarks relied upon by the State were not made within the hearing of every venireman ultimately excused for cause under the statute. On the contrary, three separate venires were called into the courtroom, and it appears that at least 30 of the 47 veniremen eliminated in this case were not even present when the statements in question were made.

said that they did not "believe in the death penalty" and were excused without any attempt to determine whether they could nonetheless return a verdict of death.[7] Thirty-nine veniremen, including four of the six who indicated that they did not believe in capital punishment, acknowledged having "conscientious or religious scruples against the infliction of the death penalty" or against its infliction "in a proper case" and were excluded without any effort to find out whether their scruples would invariably compel them to vote against capital punishment.

Only one venireman who admitted to "a religious or conscientious scruple against the infliction of the death penalty in a proper case" was examined at any length. She was asked: "You don't believe in the death penalty?" She replied: "No. It's just I wouldn't want to be responsible." The judge admonished her not to forget her "duty as a citizen" and again asked her whether she had "a religious or conscientious scruple" against capital punishment. This time, she replied in the negative. Moments later, however, she repeated that she would not "like to be responsible for . . . deciding somebody should be put to death." [8] Evidently satisfied that this elaboration of the prospective juror's views disqualified her under the Illinois statute, the judge told her to "step aside." [9]

[7] It is entirely possible, of course, that even a juror who believes that capital punishment should never be inflicted and who is irrevocably committed to its abolition could nonetheless subordinate his personal views to what he perceived to be his duty to abide by his oath as a juror and to obey the law of the State. See *Commonwealth* v. *Webster,* 59 Mass. 295, 298. See also *Atkins v. State,* 16 Ark. 568, 580; *Williams* v. *State,* 32 Miss. 389, 395–396; *Rhea* v. *State,* 63 Neb. 461, 472–473, 88 N. W. 789, 792.

[8] Compare *Smith* v. *State,* 55 Miss. 410, 413–414: "The declaration of the rejected jurors, in this case, amounted only to a statement that they would not like . . . a man to be hung. Few men would. Every right-thinking man would regard it as a painful duty to pronounce a verdict of death upon his fellow-man. . . . For the error in improperly rejecting [these] two members of the special *venire* the case must be reversed."

[9] As the *voir dire* examination of this venireman illustrates, it cannot be assumed that a juror who describes himself as having "conscientious or religious scruples" against the infliction of the death penalty or against its infliction "in a proper case" (see *People* v. *Bandhauer,* 66 Cal. 2d 524, 531, 426 P. 2d 900, 905) thereby affirms that he could never vote in favor of it or that he would not consider doing so in the case before him. See also the *voir dire* in *Rhea* v. *State,* 63 Neb. 461, 466–468, 88 N. W. 789, 790. Cf. *State* v. *Williams,* 50 Neb. 271, 278, 257 P. 619, 621. Obviously many jurors "could, notwithstanding their conscientious scruples [against capital punishment], return . . . [a] verdict [of death] and . . . make their scruples subservient to their duty as jurors." *Stratton* v. *People,* 5 Col. 276, 277. Cf. *Commonwealth* v. *Henderson,* 242 Pa. 372, 377, 89 A. 567, 569. Yet such jurors have frequently been deemed unfit to serve in a capital case. See, e.g., *Rhea* v. *State, supra,* 63 Neb., at 470–471, 88 N. W., at 791–792. See generally, W. Oberer, Does Disqualification of Jurors for Scruples Against Capital Punishment Constitute Denial of Fair Trial on Issue of Guilt?, 39 Tex. L. Rev. 545, 547–548 (1961); Comment, 1968 Duke L. J. 283, 295–299.

The critical question, of course, is not how the phrases employed in this area have been construed by courts and commentators. What matters is how they might be understood—or misunderstood—by prospective jurors. Any "layman . . . [might] say he has scruples if he is somewhat unhappy about death sentences. . . .

II

The petitioner contends that a State cannot confer upon a jury selected in this manner the power to determine guilt. He maintains that such a jury, unlike one chosen at random from a cross-section of the community, must necessarily be biased in favor of conviction, for the kind of juror who would be unperturbed by the prospect of sending a man to his death, he contends, is the kind of juror who would too readily ignore the presumption of the defendant's innocence, accept the prosecution's version of the facts, and return a verdict of guilt. To support this view, the petitioner refers to what he describes as "competent scientific evidence that death-qualified jurors are partial to the prosecution on the issue of guilt or innocence." [10]

The data adduced by the petitioner, however, are too tentative and fragmentary to establish that jurors not opposed to the death penalty tend to favor the prosecution in the determination of guilt.[11] We simply cannot

---

[Thus] a general question as to the presence of . . . reservations [or scruples] is far from the inquiry which separates those who would never vote for the ultimate penalty from those who would reserve it for the direct cases." *Id.,* at 308–309. Unless a venireman states unambiguously that he would automatically vote against the imposition of capital punishment no matter what the trial might reveal, it simply cannot be assumed that that is his position.

[10] In his brief, the petitioner cites two surveys, one involving 187 college students, W. C. Wilson, Belief in Capital Punishment and Jury Performance (Unpublished Manuscript, University of Texas, 1964), and the other involving 200 college students, F. J. Goldberg, Attitude Toward Capital Punishment and Behavior as a Junior in Simulated Capital Cases (Unpublished Manuscript, Morehouse College, undated). In his petition for certiorari, he cited a study based upon interviews with 1,248 jurors in New York and Chicago. A preliminary, unpublished summary of the results of that study stated that "a jury consisting only of jurors who have no scruples against the death penalty is likely to be more prosecution prone than a jury on which objectors to the death penalty sit," and that "the defendant's chances of acquittal are somewhat reduced if the objectors are excluded from the jury." H. Zeisel, Some Insights Into the Operation of Criminal Juries 42 (Confidential First Draft, University of Chicago, November 1957).

[11] During the post-conviction proceedings here under review, the petitioner's counsel argued that the prosecution-prone character of "death-qualified" juries presented "purely a legal question," the resolution of which required "no additional proof" beyond "the facts . . . disclosed by the transcript of the voir dire examination. . . ." Counsel sought an "opportunity to submit evidence" in support of several contentions unrelated to the issue involved here. On this issue, however, no similar request was made, and the studies relied upon by the petitioner in this Court were not mentioned. We can only speculate, therefore, as to the precise meaning of the terms used in those studies, the accuracy of the techniques employed, and the validity of the generalizations made. Under these circumstances, it is not surprising that the *amicus curiae* brief filed by the NAACP Legal Defense and Education Fund finds it necessary to observe that, with respect to bias in favor of the prosecution on the issue of guilt, the record in this case is "almost totally lacking in the sort of factual information that would assist the Court."

conclude, either on the basis of the record now before us or as a matter of judicial notice, that the exclusion of jurors opposed to capital punishment results in an unrepresentative jury on the issue of guilt or substantially increases the risk of conviction. In light of the presently available information, we are not prepared to announce a *per se* constitutional rule requiring the reversal of every conviction returned by a jury selected as this one was.

III

It does not follow, however, that the petitioner is entitled to no relief. For in this case the jury was entrusted with two distinct responsibilities: first, to determine whether the petitioner was innocent or guilty; and second, if guilty, to determine whether his sentence should be imprisonment or death.[12] It has not been shown that this jury was biased with respect to the petitioner's guilt. But it is self-evident that, in its role as arbiter of the punishment to be imposed, this jury fell woefully short of that impartiality to which the petitioner was entitled under the Sixth and Fourteenth Amendments. See *Glasser* v. *United States,* 315 U. S. 60, 84–86; *Irvin* v. *Dowd,* 366 U. S. 717, 722–723; *Turner* v. *Louisiana,* 379 U. S. 466, 471–473.

The only justification the State has offered for the jury-selection technique it employed here is that individuals who express serious reservations about capital punishment cannot be relied upon to vote for it even when the laws of the State and the instructions of the trial judge would make death the proper penalty. But in Illinois, as in other States,[13] the jury is given broad discretion to decide whether or not death *is* "the proper penalty" in a given case, and a juror's general views about capital punishment play an inevitable role in any such decision.

A man who opposes the death penalty, no less than one who favors it, can make the discretionary judgment entrusted to him by the State and can thus obey the oath he takes as a juror. But a jury from which all such men have been excluded cannot perform the task demanded of it. Guided by neither rule nor standard, "free to select or reject as it [sees] fit," [14] a jury that must choose between life imprisonment and capital punishment can do little more—and must do nothing less—than express the con-

[12] At the time of the petitioner's trial, the jury's penalty determination was binding upon the judge. Ill. Rev. Stat. 1959, c. 38, §§ 360, 801. That is no longer the case in Illinois, for the trial judge is now empowered to reject a jury recommendation of death, Ill. Rev. Stat. 1967, c. § 1–7(c)(1), but nothing in our decision turns upon whether the judge is bound to follow such a recommendation.

[13] See generally, H. Kalven and H. Zeisel, The American Jury 435, 444, 448–449 (1966).

[14] *People* v. *Bernette,* 30 Ill. 2d 359, 370, 197 N. E. 2d 436, 443.

science of the community on the ultimate question of life or death.[15] Yet, in a nation less than half of whose people believe in the death penalty,[16] a jury composed exclusively of such people cannot speak for the community. Culled of all who harbor doubts about the wisdom of capital punishment—of all who would be reluctant to pronounce the extreme penalty—such a jury can speak only for a distinct and dwindling minority.[17]

If the State had excluded only those prospective jurors who stated in advance of trial that they would not even consider returning a verdict of death, it could argue that the resulting jury was simply "neutral" with respect to penalty.[18] But when it swept from the jury all who expressed conscientious or religious scruples against capital punishment and all who opposed it in principle, the State crossed the line of neutrality. In its quest for a jury capable of imposing the death penalty, the State produced a jury uncommonly willing to condemn a man to die.[19]

[15] It is suggested in a dissenting opinion today that the State of Illinois might "impose a particular penalty, including death, on all persons convicted of certain crimes." *Post*, p. ——. But Illinois has attempted no such thing. Nor has it defined a category of capital cases in which "death [is] the *preferred* penalty." *People* v. *Bernette, supra,* 30 Ill. 2d, at 369, 197 N. E. 2d, at 442. (Emphasis added.) Instead, it has deliberately "made . . . the death penalty . . . an optional form of punishment which [the jury remains] free to select or reject as it [sees] fit." 30 Ill. 2d, at 370, 197 N. E. 2d, at 443. And one of the most important functions any jury can perform in making such a selection is to maintain a link between contemporary community values and the penal system—a link without which the determination of punishment could hardly reflect "the evolving standards of decency that mark the progress of a maturing society." *Trop* v. *Dulles,* 356 U. S. 86, 101 (opinion of THE CHIEF JUSTICE, joined by MR. JUSTICE BLACK, MR. JUSTICE DOUGLAS, *and* MR. JUSTICE WHITTAKER). Cf. n. 19, *infra.*

[16] It appears that, in 1966, approximately 42% of the American public favored capital punishment for convicted murderers, while 47% opposed it and 11% were undecided. Polls, International Review on Public Opinion, Vol. II, No. 3, at p. 84 (1967). In 1960, the comparable figures were 51% in favor, 36% opposed and 13% undecided. *Ibid.*

[17] Compare Arthur Koestler's observation:
"The division is not between rich and poor, highbrow and lowbrow, Christians and atheists: it is between those who have charity and those who have not. . . . The test of one's humanity is whether one is able to accept this fact—not as lip service, but with the shuddering recognition of a kinship: here but for the grace of God, drop I." Koestler, Reflections on Hanging 166–167 (1956).

[18] Even so, a defendant convicted by such a jury in some future case might still attempt to establish that the jury was less than neutral with respect to *guilt.* If he were to succeed in that effort, the question would then arise whether the State's interest in submitting the penalty issue to a jury capable of imposing capital punishment may be vindicated at the expense of the defendant's interest in a completely fair determination of guilt or innocence—given the possibility of accommodating both interests by means of a bifurcated trial, using one jury to decide guilt and another to fix punishment. That problem is not presented here, however, and we intimate no view as to its proper resolution.

[19] The *amicus curiae* brief filed in this case by the American Friends Service Committee et al. notes that the number of persons under sentence of death in

It is, of course, settled that a State may not entrust the determination of whether a man is innocent or guilty to a tribunal "organized to convict." *Fay* v. *New York*, 332 U. S. 261, 294. See *Tumey* v. *Ohio*, 273 U. S. 510. It requires but a short step from that principle to hold, as we do today, that a State may not entrust the determination of whether a man should live or die to a tribunal organized to return a verdict of death.[20] Specifically, we hold that a sentence of death cannot be carried out if the jury that imposed or recommended it was chosen by excluding veniremen for cause simply because they voiced general objections to the death penalty or expressed conscientious or religious scruples against its infliction.[21] No

this country climbed from 300 at the end of 1963 to 406 at the end of 1966, while the number of persons actually executed fell from 21 in 1963 to 15 in 1964, seven in 1965, and one in 1966. The brief suggests that this phenomenon might be explained in part by society's "deep reluctance actually to inflict the death sentence" and by a widening "divergence of belief between the juries we select and society generally."

[20] It should be understood that much more is involved here than a simple determination of sentence. For the State of Illinois empowered the jury in this case to answer "yes" or "no" to the question whether this defendant was fit to live. To be sure, such a determination is different in kind from a finding that the defendant committed a specified criminal offense. Insofar as a determination that a man should be put to death might require "that there be taken into account the circumstances of the offense together with the character and propensities of the offender," *Pennsylvania* v. *Ashe*, 302 U. S. 51, 55, for example, it may be appropriate that certain rules of evidence with respect to penalty should differ from the corresponding evidentiary rules with respect to guilt. See, *e.g.*, *Williams* v. *New York*, 337 U. S. 241. But this does not mean that basic requirements of procedural fairness can be ignored simply because the determination involved in this case differs in some respects from the traditional assessment of whether the defendant engaged in a proscribed course of conduct. See, *e.g.*, *Specht* v. *Patterson*, 386 U. S. 605. Cf. *Mempa* v. *Rhay*, 389 U. S. 128.

One of those requirements, at least, is that the decision whether a man deserves to live or die must be made on scales that are not deliberately tipped toward death. It was in part upon such a premise that the Fourth Circuit recently invalidated a North Carolina murder conviction, noting that a juror who felt it his "duty" to sentence *every* convicted murderer to death was allowed to serve in that case, "while those who admitted to scruples against capital punishment were dismissed without further interrogation." This "double standard," the court concluded, "inevitably resulted in [a] denial of due process." *Crawford* v. *Bounds*, —— F. 2d ——, —— —— (alternative holding). Cf. *Stroud* v. *United States*, 251 U. S. 15, 20–21; on petition for rehearing, *id.*, at 380, 381 (dictum).

[21] Just as veniremen cannot be excluded for cause on the ground that they hold such views, so too they cannot be excluded for cause simply because they indicate that there are some kinds of cases in which they would refuse to recommend capital punishment. And a prospective juror cannot be expected to say in advance of trial whether he would in fact vote for the extreme penalty in the case before him. The most that can be demanded of a venireman in this regard is that he be willing to *consider* all of the penalties provided by state law, and that he not be irrevocably committed, before the trial has begun, to vote against the penalty of death regardless of the facts and circumstances that might emerge in the course of the proceedings. If the *voir dire* testimony in a given case indicates that veniremen were excluded on any broader basis than this, the death sentence cannot be carried out even if applicable statutory or case law in the relevant jurisdiction would appear to support only a narrower ground of exclusion. See nn. 5 and 9, *supra*.

defendant can constitutionally be put to death at the hands of a tribunal so selected.[22]

Whatever else might be said of capital punishment, it is at least clear that its imposition by a hanging jury cannot be squared with the Constitution. The State of Illinois has stacked the deck against the petitioner. To execute this death sentence would deprive him of his life without due process of law.

Reversed.

Questions

1. Why does Joe Henry begin his argument by giving a history of capital punishment in Tennessee? How does he make this historical introduction effective?

2. Describe the uses that Henry makes of repetition. Is this repetition effective? Why?

3. How are Henry's Biblical arguments at the end of his defense effective or ineffective?

4. Identify examples of understatement in Henry's defense. Is this device effective? Why does Henry use so many concrete examples? Do you find them persuasive?

5. What effect does Henry achieve by concluding his list of examples of nondeterrence with the case of the Oklahoma State Prison hangman?

6. How valid is the evidence that Henry raises against the deterrence argument? How does Henry's argument compare with J. Edgar Hoover's statements about deterrence?

7. What elements of Henry's argument are appropriate to it as a speech? In what ways does Henry indicate an awareness of his audience (the jury)?

We repeat, however, that nothing we say today bears upon the power of a State to execute a defendant sentenced to death by a jury from which the only veniremen who were in fact excluded for cause were those who made unmistakably clear (1) that they would *automatically* vote against the imposition of capital punishment without regard to any evidence that might be developed at the trial of the case before them, or (2) that their attitude toward the death penalty would prevent them from making an impartial decision as to the defendant's *guilt*. Nor does the decision in this case affect the validity of any sentence *other* than one of death. Nor, finally, does today's holding render invalid the *conviction*, as opposed to the *sentence*, in this or any other case.

22 We have considered the suggestion, advanced in an *amicus curiae* brief filed by 24 States on behalf of Illinois, that we should "give prospective application only to any new constitutional ruling in this area," particularly since a dictum in an 1892 decision of this Court approved the practice of challenging for cause those jurors who expressed "conscientious scruples in regard to the infliction of the death penalty for crime." *Logan* v. *United States*, 144 U. S. 263, 298. But we think it clear, *Logan* notwithstanding, that the jury-selection standards employed here necessarily undermined "the very integrity of the . . . process" that decided the petitioner's fate, see *Linkletter* v. *Walker*, 381 U. S. 618, 639, and we have concluded that neither the reliance of law enforcement officials, cf. *Tehan* v. *Shott*, 382 U. S. 406, 417; *Johnson* v. *New Jersey*, 384 U. S. 719, 731, nor the impact of a retroactive holding on the administration of justice, cf. *Stovall* v. *Denno*, 388 U. S. 293, 300, warrants a decision against the fully retroactive application of the holding we announce today.

8. Is Jacques Barzun writing for an audience different from Henry's? In what ways does Barzun indicate an awareness of *his* audience? How does Hoover's audience determine the tone of his statements?

9. Barzun summarizes four main arguments against capital punishment. Does Henry use all four? How? Does Henry use other arguments?

10. With which of Henry's three ingredients of punishment is Barzun most concerned?

11. How does Barzun employ specific examples? Is his use of past cases rhetorically similar to Henry's? Can you cite the principal similarities among the arguments proposed by Barzun, Henry, and Hoover? Which of these is intended to appeal most specifically to emotion? To reason?

12. Could Barzun's fullest argument be seen as one *against* the prison system rather than one *for* capital punishment? Explain.

13. Do the opponents of capital punishment exhibit the confused state of mind that Barzun suggests is representative of modern thinking about crime and punishment?

14. Why does Nathanson describe "judicial homicide" as a euphemism? What are Barzun's reasons for choosing the term?

15. Why does Nathanson end with the example of the reprieved man?

16. In what ways are Warga's arguments for the deterrent effects of capital punishment valid? Invalid?

17. Why does Heilbroner choose the nom de plume of Albert Camus? Is his suggestion serious? (See Additional Reading for this section.)

18. How does the Supreme Court decision affect the issues discussed here? Would you say that capital punishment has been virtually eliminated in the United States by this decision? Would you characterize the disagreements among the justices as being motivated by emotion, reason, legal precedent, or what?

Assignments

1. Analyze the arguments on both sides of the issue of capital punishment and summarize the more important arguments on each side.

2. Write a letter to the editor of *The American Scholar* answering Barzun or one of the correspondents who wrote about Barzun's article.

3. Argue for or against one of these propositions:

a. Capital punishment should not be abolished except as part of a thorough reform of the prison system.
b. The law should not be modified because of the discoveries of psychiatry.
c. Life imprisonment is worse than death.
d. For some crimes death is too kind a punishment.

4. The press is sometimes accused of prejudging a capital case and thus contributing to the judging of the criminal. Investigate and analyze the press coverage of a particular capital case.

5. Analyze the arguments for and against the deterrent effects of capital punishment. Are they logically sound? Do they validly interpret the evidence? Are there other arguments that might be made for or against capital punishment that do not appear in this section? For example, how applicable is the argument derived on the basis of the "eye for an eye" injunction in the Bible, or the argument derived from the need of society to feel "purged" after a particularly heinous crime? What about a dictator or gangster who tortured his victims to death?

Additional Reading

The writing on capital punishment has been voluminous (although most recent considerations have opposed the death penalty). Some of the most recent books on the subject include James A. Joyce, *The Right to Life: A World View of Capital Punishment* (London, 1962); A. Gardiner, *Capital Punishment As a Deterrent, and the Alternative* (London, 1956); Victor Gollancz, *Capital Punishment: The Heart of the Matter* (London, 1955); Lord Longford, *The Idea of Punishment* (London, 1961); Elizabeth Tuttle, *The Crusade Against Capital Punishment* (London, 1961); Grant S. McClellan, *Capital Punishment* (New York, 1960); John Howard Yoder, *The Christian and Capital Punishment* (Newton, Kansas, 1961); Jack Kevorkian, *Medical Research and the Death Penalty* (New York, 1960); John Laurence, *A History of Capital Punishment* (New York, 1963).

Many cases have raised ethical and legal questions about capital punishment. Two recent ones that focused particular attention on the subject were the Caryl Chessman case in California in the 1950s and the Timothy Evans–John Christie case in London in the 1940s. Both cases elicited considerable newspaper and magazine coverage and both have occasioned a number of books.

Barrett E. Prettyman, Jr.'s *Death and the Supreme Court* (New York, 1961) gives interesting and vivid descriptions of the Supreme Court's consideration of a number of capital cases. Probably the most famous contemporary essay opposing capital punishment is Albert Camus' "Reflections on the Guillotine," which appears in his *Resistance, Rebellion, and Death* (New York, 1963).

An anthology of materials about capital punishment, *The Death Penalty* (Boston, 1964), has been edited by Edward G. McGehee and William H. Hildebrand.

Truman Capote's *In Cold Blood* (New York, 1965) is a study of a particularly brutal murder of an entire family committed by two men who were later executed. The author was subsequently involved in an extended controversy with Kenneth Tynan about the relation of the book to the punishment of the murders. Their several statements provide interesting additional material on the issue of capital punishment.

You might also want to look at the references in the footnotes of the Supreme Court decision, and especially at the essay by Arthur Koestler on hanging, referred to in the majority opinion. See also George Orwell's "A Hanging," available in collections of his essays. Warden Lewis Lawes's account of his time at Sing Sing Prison should also be useful.

Where Does Life End?

Death, be not proud, though some have called thee
Mighty and dreadful, for thou art not so;
For those whom thou think'st thou dost overthrow
Die not, poor Death; nor yet canst thou kill me.
From Rest and Sleep, which but thy pictures be,
Much pleasure, then from thee much more must flow;
And soonest our best men with thee do go,
Rest of their bones and souls' delivery!
Thou art slave to fate, chance, kings, and desperate men,
And dost with poison, war, and sickness dwell;
And poppy or charms can make us sleep as well
And better than thy stroke. Why swell'st thou then?

> *One short sleep past, we wake eternally,*
> *And Death shall be no more: Death, thou shalt die!*
> JOHN DONNE
> *"Holy Sonnet X"*

When Are You Really Dead?

Newsweek

Doctors can now play God. They can alter the genes, build artificial parts for the body and, as the two remarkable experiments in Cape Town and Brooklyn demonstrated last week, they can even transplant the human heart—the symbol of life itself—from one body to another. Indeed, the photo above shows the hand of a doctor holding the still-viable heart of a three-day-old infant during the transplant operation last week at Maimonides Hospital. But how will the doctors use this power?

"I have a horrible vision," says a public-health official in Washington, "of ghouls hovering over an accident victim with long knives unsheathed, waiting to take out his organs as soon as he is pronounced dead."

When, in fact, is a person dead *enough* to be deprived of a vital organ needed to sustain the life of another human being? Until recently, the moment of death was thought to be the moment when the heart stops beating. But new advances in resuscitation techniques—electrodes that shock the heart muscle into beating again, cardiac massage and chemical treatments—have made that notion obsolete. Now cases of "returning from the dead," as with a GI in Vietnam (*Newsweek*, Nov. 13), are becoming more and more common. Most physicians demand the ultimate evidence—through use of electroencephalograms—that all electrical activity in the brain has ceased. "You can at least start the heart beating again after it stops," says Dr. Marius Barnard, one of the Cape Town surgeons. "But once the brain is dead, it cannot recover." This, in turn, raises another question: if there is massive brain destruction, but the heart and lungs are kept functioning with mechanical aids, is the body still a human being? Or is it—to use the blunt term of the surgical amphitheater—a vegetable?

"You're dead when your doctor says you are" is perhaps the most accurate definition of death. Death comes, says Dr. Carl Wasmuth, president of the American College of Legal Medicine, when the physician "has done everything to save the patient's life and comes to the point where he feels the patient can't live. Once a man makes up his mind to stop that respirator or cardiac pacemaker, from that minute the patient is dead." To insure that a doctor doesn't pull the plug on a dying patient simply to obtain a needed organ, some specialists urge that the transplanter not be allowed to attend the dying potential donor. Says Dr. Irvine Page, former president of the American Heart Association: "You simply can't go around taking people's hearts out."

Ethics: Indeed, simple humanity would seem to provide more of an ethical obstacle to heart transplants than theology. The Rev. Thomas O'Donnell, S.J., former lecturer in medical ethics at the Georgetown University School of Medicine, regards the heart as an "efficient pump" with no moral significance whatsoever; he believes that the major ethical consideration involved in such cases is approval from the next of kin and an "assurance that the donor is medically dead." Some theologians believe the doctors need not wait that long. Dr. Joseph Fletcher of the Episcopal Theological School in Cambridge, Mass., says speeding up a donor's death, when death is "positively" inevitable, may be justified if the transplant provides another human with valuable life. But Rabbi Immanuel Jakobovits, chief rabbi of the British Commonwealth, disagrees: "Even a fraction of life is precious. Therefore, no one must hasten the death of a donor."

As the state of the transplant art progresses, the moral and theological questions are certain to become more complex. Brain transplants in dogs have already been tried by Dr. Robert J. White of Western Reserve University. Yet in the case of a human brain, scientists are almost certain the recipient would acquire the donor's memory, intelligence, emotions— in short, his personality. Then, who would he be? Himself or the donor?

The Heart Transplant: Ethical Dimensions

Kenneth Vaux

And I will give them a new heart and put a new
spirit within them, I will take the stony heart
out of their flesh and give them a heart of flesh. . . .

Ezekiel speaks symbolically, of spiritual things. But this prophecy of his highlights two phenomena of our time: first, that man's yearning for "a new heart" has been answered in a literal sense—that a new heart of flesh is now a medical possibility; second, that the heart of man is indeed the essence of life, spiritual and physical. Hence the lively discussion we have been having on the ethical dimensions of heart transplantation.

The Judeo-Christian tradition which informs Western culture views the heart of man as the locus of the emotions that structure his life. Anger and hostility, love and compassion are all thought of as proceeding from the heart. Witness not only our common speech but also our poetry and art, our religion and philosophy. Thus Erich Fromm, in his recent book *The Heart of Man,* writes of the ambiguity of the impulses that proceed from the "heart," impulses at once creative and destructive. Fromm of course is speaking symbolically. But translated into physiological terms this view seems rather primitive. The fact is, however, that recent medical discoveries support the notion that the heart is the center of life. A human body can survive for years with very low-grade cerebral activity, in a complete coma. But without the presence of the pulsating heart life is soon extinguished. As *Time* magazine put it (issue of December 15, 1967, page 71): ". . . the heart is essential to life in a more immediate temporal sense than any other organ, even the brain."

This paper is not directly concerned with the techniques of heart transplantation. Our purpose here is to analyze the ethical dimensions of this operation as these emerge in the literature on it. We shall note three ethical problems related to the technique, and then discuss three options of ethics in medicine which give direction to those involved in day-to-day decision-making. The three problems are the time and meaning of death, the question of donor and recipient, and the rejection phenomenon. As our point of departure we take the surgical feats around the world which, in the past few months, have confirmed that heart transplantation is a viable option in the treatment of radical coronary disease.

THE TIME AND MEANING OF DEATH. Our first problem of ethical significance concerns the time and meaning of death. When Denise Darvall arrived at the Cape Town hospital she was at the threshold of death. Although the electroencephalograph showed lingering impulses in her body, her heart had stopped. Dr. Marius Barnard (as quoted in the same issue of *Time* magazine, page 64) explained how his brother, Dr. Christiaan N. Barnard, and the surgical team made their decision to remove her heart. "I know," he said, "in some places they consider the patient dead when the electroencephalogram shows no more brain function. We are on the conservative side, and consider a patient dead when the heart is no longer working and there are no longer any complexes on the electrocardiogram."

What is the correct index to determine the time of death? Is it heart or brain function? Is there a distinction between existence and life? Is sustained physiological activity without any relational capacity really human life? When a man has lost the capacity to respond to both external and existential environment, is he still a man? Are we justified in hastening natural death? Are we justified in extending life through extraordinary measures? Our culture is now being forced to grapple with these extremely difficult questions.

In heart transplantation it is urgently necessary that the donated heart be as fresh as possible. This necessity raises the profound ethical problem of who decides—and how—whether and when a person is dead. The case of Clive Haupt, the second of the South African heart donors, points up this question. After his stroke on the beach he was immediately treated as a potential heart donor rather than as a present stroke victim—a fact that raises the shocking specter of a future day of corpse snatching. *Newsweek* (December 18, 1967, page 87) quotes a public health official in Washington: "I have a horrible vision of ghouls hovering over an accident victim with long knives unsheathed, waiting to take out his organs as soon as he is pronounced dead." Here perhaps is the ethical issue on which heart transplantation focuses. As Dr. Michael DeBakey—a pioneer in the field of heart surgery—notes in an article soon to be published: "The controversy has resumed on this point, with proposals for a new criterion of death based, for example, on electroencephalographic findings and other demonstrable evidence of cessation of vital cellular function. The legal, moral, and theologic aspects of this problem are intricate and formidable, but not impenetrable."

The cultural optimism that whispers excitedly through the populace clouds for the moment the ambiguity of our life and makes the Aesculapius legend profoundly contemporary. Aesculapius, you remember, practiced the art of medicine so well that the angry Zeus feared he would make the children of earth immortal, and so slew him with a thunderbolt. The classic deception of chilianism naively believes in a coming life free from the imperfection of human existence. But man is born to die: this is the only certain universal axiom. Only the man who acknowledges the finality of death can know the meaning of life. And all the discussion of heart transplants may reveal the meaning of life and death to a society that evades the deep questions to run after superficial ones.

THE QUESTION OF CONSENT. Our second ethical problem area concerns the question of consent by donor and recipient. In the Cape Town case, to be sure, the problem hardly arose. Louis Washkansky, Dr. Barnard's patient, needed only two minutes to make a decision that he could have taken two hours for. He agreed at once to have his heart cut out and replaced with a donor's. Edward Darvall, Denise's father, also made a decision immediately. When the doctors told him, "There is no hope for her. You can do us and humanity a great favor if you let us transplant your daughter's heart," Darvall answered: "If there is no hope for her, then try to save this man's life."

But the problem of consent is frequently much more complex. What, for instance, if neither the donor or recipient is able to decide for himself —which member of his family has the power of decision? The Clive Haupt case illustrates this problem. His bride of three months collapsed when she was asked to permit removal of his heart. His mother finally consented to the removal.

More difficult, however, are the psychological and spiritual factors involved in decisions of this nature. John Holden of the Institute of Social Ethics at Chicago's West Side Medical Center has pointed out—in his article "Some Ethical Considerations in the Transplantation of Organs" (*Existential Psychiatry,* 1966)—how traumatic the decision can be for a person, for example, who is challenged to give one of his kidneys to his own brother. What of the guilt he would feel if he refused? Dr. John R. Elkington, editor of the *Annals of Internal Medicine,* describes the "risk to the medical well-being of donors and potential donors" in the February 1964 issue of his journal. "There was the case," he says, "of a man who refused to donate his kidney to a brother, with resulting severe emotional problems. And a family was torn apart by a mother giving a kidney to a child, against the wishes of her husband."

There is also the identity problem which may arise on the side of both donor and recipient. Thus Philip Blaiberg, Dr. Barnard's second transplant recipient, said he felt like a different person, and he appeared so to his daughter when she flew to his bedside from her studies in Israel. And to Louis Washkansky's death Mr. Darvall reacted pathetically: "I have nothing left to live for. My daughter lived on for a while; now all is gone."

WHO DECIDES WHO SHALL RECEIVE? But the most difficult question in this matter is that of which among the many persons who need it is to receive one of the few available hearts. Perhaps some day there will be organ banks and a multitude of card-carrying donors. Not so at present. Moreover, in a "Face the Nation" television interview on December 24, 1967, Dr. Barnard revealed a medical attitude that compounds this problem. "My duty as a doctor," he said, "is to treat my patient. The donor I could treat no longer. I had only one way to treat my patient: transplant. To me that's not immoral." Of course he is absolutely right. The genius of the medical profession is the single-minded devotion of the physician to an individual patient. Yet when there are hundreds of thousands of desperately ill coronary patients, who decides who shall be given a new heart? What are the criteria of this decision? Will the transplant technique be available only to people who have money or connections? In other words, there is a social-ethical issue here. The physician's devotion to his patient must be augmented by social concern. In the interview cited above, Dr. Barnard commented on ethical decision-making: "If you want to know what is right, you must not ask the people around you—you must ask yourself." The ethical imperative of the hour is that concern for an individual and concern for humanity enrich each other.

A third aspect of the heart-transplant problem is the body's built-in ability to reject foreign intrusion. The blood's white corpuscles, for instance, fight disease. But in the case of a heart transplant this power becomes the enemy.

The few cases of heart transplantation have not yielded any knowledge regarding the rejection phenomenon. Despite the progress medicine has made in the area of immuno-depressant therapy through drugs and radiation, the problem of rejection remains formidable. For while such therapy reduces rejection, it also reduces resistance to infections such as pneumococci. It is true that every medical treatment intervenes in the natural processes of the body in some way. Are we, however, justified in so radical an intervention as that required in heart transplant cases? Should we force the body to contradict its genius?

INQUIRY AS TO MAN's ESSENCE. We come again to the basic question: the meaning of human existence. Helmut Thielicke, the German ethicist, speaks to this question in a lecture, "Ethical Problems in Modern Medicine," soon to be delivered at the Texas Medical Center:

The substitution of organs by machines or by organs from other persons confronts us again with the inquiry for the essence of man. Here this inquiry appears with a particular implication: Is man to be understood in analogy to the machine whose parts are exchangeable? We have here to observe carefully the tenor of the question: We do not ask—as do certain engineers of a utopian biology—whether "man" is to be exchanged and restructured, but we rather ask, what "in" man can or should be exchanged.

Let us now look at this whole problem in the light of the three ethical options that shape our culture: the Jewish-humanitarian, the situation-ethic, and the Roman Catholic natural-law options.

Rabbi Immanuel Jacobovits, chief rabbi of the British Commonwealth, has said (according to the issue of *Newsweek* cited above) that the most profound ethical question regarding heart transplantation is the termination of the life of the donor. He holds that even the minutest fraction of life is precious and that morally speaking, we have no right to terminate life, though only minimal hope exists or none at all. This view seems to agree with popular opinion. As Edmund Leach, provost of King's College, Cambridge, pointed out in an article in the *London Times* (December 4, 1967, page 2): "The vast majority are still deeply shocked at the idea that the doctor should ever willfully terminate the life of anyone who had already acquired a human personality by the fact of being born."

The Jewish position, of course, is based on a deeply sensitive interpretation of the commandment "Thou shalt not kill"—an inviolable principle that protects the sanctity of human life.

Christian theology also emphasizes the sanctity of life. Opposed to the fatalism of "When your number's up, it's up," Christianity declares that man must struggle for life incessantly. As Dietrich Bonhoeffer has put it: "It is only when one loves life and the earth so much that without them everything else would seem lost and gone, that one can believe in the resurrection of the dead."

Our second option, that of situation ethics, holds that each particular person, each particular instance, is unique and must be evaluated in its uniqueness. The remarks by Christiaan Barnard cited above emphasize the high humanism of a decision motivated by concern for a specific person in a specific situation. Dr. Barnard's posture shows freedom from legalistic norms, along with compassion springing from deep ethical principles.

Apropos of the many recent heart transplants, Joseph Fletcher, of the Episcopal Theological School in Cambridge, Massachusetts, has declared that "speeding up a donor's death, when death is positively inevitable, may be justified if the transplant provides another human with valuable life" (*Newsweek,* December 18, 1967, page 87). In other words, as he sees it, the basic principle of sustaining and extending life justifies radical technique. Unlike the "natural law" theologians Fletcher would say that the only intrinsic principle is the love principle, and that this demands different decisions in different instances.

At this point the situationist could refer to what both Christianity and other world religions consider the highest ethical act man is capable of; namely, the sacrifice of his own life for another's. Christians believe that this principle was personified in Jesus Christ, who said, "Greater love hath no man than this, that a man lay down his life for his friend" (John 15:13). Thus the situationist in ethics would say that the decision to transplant a heart, though fraught with dangerous concessions all the way, is one that basically affirms the preciousness of human life, and at the same time opens an opportunity for the highest form of self-sacrifice.

We turn now to the Roman Catholic option, which, because it is organized around a single principle, offers the most systematic moral theory in regard to our problem. That principle, simply stated, is that any violation or abrogation of the natural process is wrong; for such intervention strikes at the mysterious beauty of that divinely instituted and directed process, the origin and development of life.

Bringing this principle to bear on the question of heart transplants, the Vatican newspaper, *L'Osservatore Romano,* declared that the heart is a physiological organ with a purely mechanical function. This view has been echoed by Dr. Thomas O'Donnell, former lecturer in medical ethics at Georgetown University School of Medicine, a Jesuit institution. O'Donnell (as cited in the issue of *Newsweek* mentioned above) regards the heart as "an efficient pump with no intrinsic moral significance." In other words, the natural-law position would consider radical techniques justified when they enrich and spread the life of man, provided that there is no moral violation at any other point. Specifically, the requirements are approval from the next of kin and the assurance that the donor is medically dead.

The best recent Roman Catholic scholarship—the work of Pierre Teilhard de Chardin, for example—emphasizes that the humanitarian benefit science can now render is good, a part of a cosmic evolutionary fulfillment—of Christogenesis, or God enriching and humanizing human life. Helmut Thielicke in the lecture cited above says: "Without doubt man has been commissioned—in the command given with creation to subdue the earth . . . not to accept her passively, but rather to use her as material in responsible creativity." In other words, this third option considers developments in the biological sciences to be blessings discovered under Providence by men who faithfully seek to extend and enrich human life.

We must admit, however, that so far as heart transplantation is concerned, no clear moral directive issues from any one or all of these positions. This is not surprising. Such directives have never been easily arrived at; in our complex society they are almost always ambiguous. The one thing that is clear in our time is this: technology can be used for the benefit of the individual and of society, or it can be used for destructive and dehumanizing ends. We must continually affirm the goodness of science when it works for the welfare of mankind; and we must continually be on guard lest science, however noble its professions, violate human dignity. With Robert Oppenheimer we must remember that what is technically desirable is not necessarily good.

Look once more at the passage from Ezekiel at the beginning of this article. Then consider this declaration of man's responsibility from a modern poem, T. S. Eliot's "The Rock":

The soul of Man must quicken to creation
Out of the formless stone, when the artist unites himself with stone,
Spring always new forms of life, from the soul of man that is joined to the soul
    of stone,
Out of the meaningless practical shapes of all that is living or lifeless . . .
Lord, shall we not bring these gifts to Your service?
Shall we not bring to Your service all our powers
For life, for dignity, grace and order,
and intellectual pleasure of the senses
The LORD who created must wish us to create
And employ our creation again in His service
Which is already His service in creating.[1]

---

[1] FROM "Choruses from 'The Rock'" in *Collected Poems 1909–1962* by T. S. Eliot, copyright © 1936 by Harcourt, Brace & World, Inc.; copyright © 1963, 1964 by T. S. Eliot. Reprinted by permission of the publisher.

Life-Death in Human Transplantation

Eliot Corday

Heart transplant operations have brought to the surface certain complex questions of ethics, law and public policy that have been lurking in the background for many years, and they have raised many new questions. They have increased the power of the doctor enormously, so that it appears to some eminent philosophers that science has made gods of the physicians before they are even worthy of being men.[1] This power often demands special knowledge that physicians do not possess. It demands a choice between values that often are not measurable.

Because resuscitative methods and life support systems may revive the patient from "apparent death," very basic questions of existence have been simmering in the scientific community since these techniques were developed in the mid-1950s. These questions have been crystallized suddenly by successful heart transplantation operations. They are: (1) What is life? (2) What is death? (3) Who shall live and who shall die? (4) How long should life be preserved? (5) Can we declare a person dead if the heart still beats? (6) Should criteria of death be brought up to date? (7) Should we maintain life by artificial means or extraordinary techniques? (8) Who shall make such decisions? (9) What is the right of the individual to donate his organs before and after death? (10) What are the rights of the recipient and his next of kin?

The first and foremost principle of medical ethics is to save life. Similarly, the law of our land protects human life.[2] But now that medical science can save lives with the organs of other individuals, it appears that existing legal doctrines and statutes might be incompatible with medicine's fundamental policy of preserving life.

The removal of a single paired organ, such as the kidney, did not threaten the life of the donor or recipient. However, the removal of the beating heart from a living patient means certain death to the donor and has raised the fearsome question by some authorities of the commission of

FROM the *American Bar Association Journal,* Volume 55, July 1969. Reprinted with the permission of the *American Bar Association Journal* and Eliot Corday, M.D.

[1] Rostard, *Pensées d'un Biologist* (1939); Hamburger, "Some General Considerations," in *Ethics in Medical Progress,* 134–138 (1967) (Ciba Foundation Symposium Series).

[2] Sanders & Dukeminier, "Medical Advances and the Legal Lag: Hemodialysis and Kidney Transplantation," 15 *UCLA L. Rev.* 357 (1968).

a wrongful act.[3] If it is necessary to delay removal of an organ until death is established with absolute certainty, the complete and unalterable cessation of cardiorespiratory activity might be necessitated. Waiting might cause permanent damage to the organ; it limits the success of transplantation. Therefore, to provide the transplant surgeon the opportunity of harvesting organs before the circulation stops, it has been recommended that the medical profession alter its aged concepts that death can be established only when cardiorespiratory activity ceases.[4]

Heart transplantation requires a live heart in a dead donor. Removal of the beating heart raises the possibility, however remote, of a wrongful death action or a charge of homicide. Therefore, to accommodate the transplant surgeon, new ethical, moral and religious consideration must be given to the concept of death. Although changes in the definition of death look simple, their implementation causes a chain reaction affecting social, legal, medical, ethical, economic and theological practices. They tend to dislocate many relationships and standards of the everyday practice of medicine. But we have been attacking the problem through the back door, so to speak. It would be simpler if we could maintain our age-old definition and come at the problem through the front door by providing ethical and legal justification for removal of a beating heart in the patient with irreversible coma.

Cardiac Resuscitation Is Proved Possible

Until the middle decade of the twentieth century cardiac arrest was considered synonymous with death. Then Claude Beck startled the medical profession with demonstrations that many hearts were just too good to die, that they actually had sustained only a small amount of damage and could be brought back to life.[5] This brought into use the terms "apparent death" when cardiac arrest occurred and "actual death" when all resuscitative measures failed. Pioneers in cardiac resuscitation emphasized that restoration of the oxygen transit line to the brain was the most important factor, because if it were not reinstituted by resuscitative maneuvers within a four-minute period, although cardiac resuscitation was still possible, damage of the brain would supervene and doom the patient to a vegetative existence. Thus, they coined the terms "the four-minute

---

[3] Louisell, "Transplantation—Existing Legal Constraints," in *Ethics in Medical Progress* 78–104 (1967).

[4] Rosoff & Schwab, EEG in Establishing Brain Death, June 8, 1967 (paper presented at the meeting of the American Electroencephalographic Society, Atlantic City, New Jersey); "A Definition of Irreversible Coma: Report of the Ad Hoc Committee of Harvard Medical School to Examine the Definition of Brain Death," 205 *J.A.M.A.* 85 (1968).

[5] Beck, "Resuscitation for Cardiac Standstill and Ventricular Fibrillation Occurring During Operation," 54 *Am. J. Surg.* 273 (1941).

limit for cardiac arrest" and "cerebral death" when all the higher brain functions, such as consciousness, were destroyed.[6]

Although a legal determination of when death occurs may often be important for determining legal rights, the law does not ordinarily attempt to define death. Ordinarily it relies on the expert opinion of physicians, based on scientific criteria used by physicians and accepted by the public, to determine the fact and time of death. And we are told that any consideration for new scientific criteria for diagnosis of death should be left solely to the medical profession.[7] However, the medical profession appears reluctant to establish these new criteria because transplant science is developing so rapidly that implementations of rigid criteria today might limit medical innovation tomorrow. Creation of the criteria will require careful legal consideration, because medical judgments based on medical criteria can give rise to court action, in which the legal determination of the fact and time of death will rest with a jury, which retrospectively can accept or reject the opinions of the expert medical witnesses.

We are helped by certain theological decisions. In 1957 Pope Pius XII stated that there is a clear distinction between vegetative life in the organ and superior life with all the vital functions.[8] He considered that vegetative existence is not thought of as life in the spiritual sense.

Whereas it is generally considered lawful for the individual to give authority for removal of his organs during his life, if he can do so without loss of his life, one does not, in the absence of a special statute, have an enforceable right to arrange before his death for a donation of his body or organs after his death. After death it is the legal right of the next of kin to grant or deny such permission. This right has been the basis for lawsuits over unauthorized autopsies. Therefore, the time of death determined by expert medical testimony, based on accepted medical criteria, may be of the utmost importance for permission to remove the organs for transplantation as well as the adjudication of state and property rights.

Defining Death and Cerebral Death

Black's Law Dictionary defines death: "The cessation of life; the ceasing to exist; defined by physicians as the total stoppage of the circulation of the blood, and a cessation of the animal and vital functions consequent

[6] Cole & Corday, "Four-Minute Limit for Cardiac Resuscitation," 161 *J.A.M.A.* 1454 (1956); Cole & Corday, "Clinical Factors Affecting Cardiac Resuscitation," 65 *West J. Surg. & Gyn.* 350 (1957).
[7] "With Special Reference to Transplantation," in *Ethics in Medical Progress* (1967).
[8] *"Discoursi ai Medici,"* 608–618 (Roma Orizzante Medico 1959).

thereon, such as respiration, pulsation, etc." [9] It should be noted that, except for the two brief introductory phrases, the definition is attributed to physicians, not to lawyers or the courts. At the time it was adopted, this definition may well have reflected with reasonable accuracy the then prevailing medical opinion. *Dorland's Illustrated Medical Dictionary* defines death as: "The apparent extinction of life as manifested by the absence of heartbeat and respiration." [10]

A concept of "cerebral death" to allow transplantation of organs and termination of extraordinary medical care has been popularized. Rosoff and Schwab presented a new definition of death based on neurological criteria which demanded (1) no reflexes, spontaneous breathing, or muscle activity; (2) no clinical or EEG response to noise or a pinch; and (3) repetition of the above twenty-four or forty-eight hours later.[11] These determinations were not to be made under conditions of hypothermia or anesthetic levels. The neurologic triad of cerebral death—(1) no reflexes and fixed dilated pupils, (2) no spontaneous respiration and (3) flat isoelectric EEG repeated after twenty-four hours—appears to be gaining support from others.

An ad hoc committee of Harvard University to examine the scientific criteria for diagnosis of death proposed criteria of irreversible coma.[12] It is based on the fact that when respiration is maintained only by artificial means and then this is withdrawn, spontaneous respiration is impossible. Briefly, it states that the characteristics of death are:

(1) Unreceptivity and unresponsiveness. This means there is a total unawareness of externally applied stimuli and inner need and complete unresponsiveness. Even the most intensely painful stimuli evoke no vocal or other response, withdrawal of limb or quickening of respiration.

(2) No movement or breathing. This is satisfied by a period of observation of at least one hour by a physician to satisfy the criteria of no spontaneous muscle movement or spontaneous respiration or reaction to stimuli.

(3) No reflexes. The pupils will be fixed and dilated and not respond to a direct source of bright light. Ocular movement and blinking are absent upon head turning or irrigation of the ears with ice water. Swallowing, yawning and vocalization are absent.

(4) The flat electroencephalogram is said to be of great confirmatory value. The patient must not be under the influence of sedation or anesthetic drugs.

The report further states that the patient's condition can only be determined by a physician.

[9] *Black's Law Dictionary*, 488 (4th ed. 1951). The "fourth revised edition," issued in 1968, carries this definition unchanged, as did the third edition, issued in 1933.
[10] *Dorland's Illustrated Medical Dictionary* (23d ed. 1960).
[11] *Supra* note 4.
[12] 205 *J.A.M.A.*, 85 (1968).

The Harvard irreversible coma criteria have been accepted generally as a basis for diagnosis of cerebral death to permit organ removal, but some transplant surgeons have declared cerebral death while spontaneous respiration still existed.

Resuscitative Measures and the Definition of Death

The age-old definition of death is the final and irreversible cessation of perceptible heartbeat and respiration. Now that cardiac resuscitation is an everyday occurrence, one wonders if the definition of death should imply that resuscitative measures have been attempted and failed. Houts amplified this recently when he stated, as long as any heartbeat or respiration can be perceived either with or without mechanical aids, and regardless of how the heartbeat and respiration are maintained, death has not occurred.[13] This, of course, represents an attempt by a lawyer, without formal medical training, to indicate what appears to him to be proper medical criteria for diagnosis of death. Its implementation would preclude successful organ transplantation.

In a recent court decision, *In re Estate of Schmidt*, 67 Cal. Rptr. 847 (1968), it was contended that the trial court should have included in the definition of death the inability to resuscitate. The court, however, adopted the definition found in *Black's Law Dictionary*, stating that no evidence had been presented concerning the possibility of resuscitation.

Pitfalls in Present Concepts of Death

The Harvard committee's concept of irreversible coma is a sound one and assists us in the diagnosis of cerebral death. It is as yet unknown whether it will be totally accepted by the medical profession, the public and the legal authorities to provide a legal basis for removal of organs for transplantation. The Harvard committee bases its criteria on the finding that spontaneous respiration is no longer possible. But many base their criteria for diagnosis of cerebral death on lesser considerations and have transplanted hearts of those who still have spontaneous respiration.

Some journalists argue that the concept of cerebral death is designed to take care of the special interests of the transplanters and disregards other possible implications. Others have argued that, if one is to accept the medical concept of cerebral death while spontaneous cardiac and pulmonary function exists, one must be prepared to bury a man even though his heart might beat. However, before it is adopted in practice,

[13] Houts & Hunt, "*Death*," in 3 *Courtroom Medicine*, 1-21 (1967).

the medical profession must be doubly cautious lest it be charged with accepting a double standard for diagnosis of death. Many have expressed the fear that the public will develop a mistrust for the medical profession if a double standard is accepted, for it provides room for a transition to euthanasia and kakothanasia.

The Harvard criteria of irreversible coma for diagnosis of existence of cerebral death, however, do provide sound guidelines for the discontinuation of extraordinary medical care in the form of life support systems or nutritional aids.

The thought that we physicians should be obliged to keep a patient alive, for instance, with a respirator when there is no possibility of recovery, solely to try to prolong his life, is a terrifying one. This obligation would rapidly lead to an untenable economic situation. It must be regarded as a medical axiom that the physician should not be obliged in every situation to use all means to prolong life. I am advised that there is no legal requirement in the United States that extraordinary life-prolonging procedures must be continued after it has been clearly established that there is no hope for the patient's recovery. The law does not require the physician always to prolong the process of dying to the ultimate extreme.

Gierts states: "We refrain from treatment because it does not serve any purpose, because it is not in the patient's interest. I cannot regard this as killing by medical means: death has already won, despite the fight we have put up. Only the recognition of this can enable us to solve the problem that for many has made the thought of death an agonizing one— the fear of an artificial prolongation of life when it has already been bereft of all its potentialities." [14] This statement is supported by Pope Pius XII's assertion that "The use of such measures was not obligatory, particularly if it created too heavy a charge on the family, and no physician would be responsible for the death of a patient by interrupting such measures, as the cause of death and would reside in the primary disorder and not in the attempt of saving or supporting life." [15] It should be remembered that Pope Pius XII spoke emphatically against euthanasia at the same time that he took a liberal attitude toward the nonuse or interruption of life-supporting systems.

Physicians Face Criticism
in Diagnosing Death

As we review the literature, we are faced repeatedly with the fact that the diagnosis of death must be determined by the medical profession, for

[14] Giertz, "Ethical Problems in Medical Procedures in Sweden," in *Ethics in Medical Progress*, 145 (1967).
[15] *Supra* note 8.

the medical profession alone has the qualifications to determine what is proper medical diagnosis. But certain actions by transplant surgeons in establishing time of death on death certificates and hospital records have shaken public confidence. Coroners have denounced them in the press for signing a death certificate in one county when the beating heart was removed a day later in a far-off city. The public wonders what the "item" was that was transported across the state line and later registered as a person in the operating room record. The press criticized the fact that a death certificate denoting cerebral death was signed by a coroner at 11:00 P.M., but a beating heart was removed for transplant late the next day. It would seem the criticism could be avoided if the certificate were signed closer to the time of removal of the heart and at the same institution as the transplant.

The medical profession's scientific criteria for diagnosis of death must be reasonable and based on sound scientific principles. If a surgeon who removes a heart for transplant should be charged with homicide, a jury will have to decide, on the basis of the testimony of the expert medical witnesses, whether the donor was alive when the heart was removed. If the criteria relied upon by the medical witness do not appear reasonable, the jury may not accept his medical opinion. Fortunately, the passage of the Uniform Anatomical Gift Act will protect the surgeon from such possible civil or criminal prosecution.[16]

D. W. Louisell, professor of law at the University of California, concludes, "In the present state of the law, I could only advise the client that he could incur the danger of a possible charge of homicide if by removal of an organ he causes death, if life still continues in the conventional sense (that is, there is still a heartbeat)." [17] This advice, of course, is based on the assumption of one who is not a physician that the heartbeat is still the key criterion for diagnosis of life or death. It is up to the medical profession to determine whether this assumption is correct. From the earliest age, the time of death has been recognized as when the heartbeat ceased. Is there adequate evidence now that the moment of death should be advanced to coincide with brain death when the heart continues to beat and cardiorespiratory activity is spontaneous?

Although only the medical profession is competent to formulate scientific criteria for the diagnosis of death, it should have the advice and support of the legal profession. Medical judgments based on such criteria are more apt to be practical and be accepted by the public with confidence. Doctors complain that they are unsure of the criteria for the diagnosis of death because their medical schools did not include such criteria in their curricula. Of course, medical schools in this transition period are unsure what they should teach. This points out the need for

[16] Sadler, Sadler & Stason, "The Uniform Anatomical Gift Act—A model for Reform," 206 *J.A.M.A.* 1425 (1968).
[17] *Supra* note 3.

high-level conferences by medical, legal and theological authorities to consolidate present opinion and to prevent the consequences caused by an erosion of medical standards. Until the medical profession can provide definite scientific definitions, the student physician will be taught differently at each medical center.

Physicians Need Help from Other Disciplines

Dramatic medical innovations in the last two decades have caused the medical profession to re-evaluate whether it should alter the definition of death to provide for medical innovation. Any change from the age-old criteria of death requires careful study because it could start a chain reaction that might dislocate many relationships and standards of the everyday practice of medicine. A high level conference of medical and legal authorities is needed to reconsider medical criteria of death.

The Frozen Christian

Robert C. W. Ettinger

Last May Mrs. Wilma Jean McLaughlin lay dying of heart disease in Springfield city hospital, Springfield, Ohio. Her husband, aware of my "cryogenic interment" thesis, asked me for help in freezing her body immediately after death in the hope that medical science would eventually be able to restore life, health and even physical youth. With the cooperation of a hospital physician, the hospital administrator, a funeral director and a local commercial firm which happened to be building "time capsules" or cryogenic (low temperature) storage units, and with the approval of the family pastor, the Rev. Kay Glaesner of St. John's Evangelical Lutheran Church, preparations were made for this pioneering effort. After a midnight meeting of the board of trustees, however, hospital cooperation was withdrawn, and relatives finally persuaded Mr. McLaughlin to reverse his decision. Within a few hours the patient died, unaware that she had almost been given potential "immortality."

Although this particular attempt was abortive and perhaps represented a cloud no bigger than a man's hand, it was a clear portent of the coming

Copyright 1965 Christian Century Foundation. Reprinted by permission from the October 27, 1965, issue of *The Christian Century*.

storm which I had predicted (and seeded) about a year earlier with the publication of my book *The Prospect of Immortality* (Doubleday, 1964; reviewed in *The Christian Century*, September 30, 1964). The storm is closer now, but not many clergymen seem to realize it is going to rain on *them;* not many have yet prepared themselves either to exploit its bounty or to avoid its dangers. Yet the parched earth may be renewed with a vitality never seen before—or the torrent may overtake those who linger unprepared.

I

My aim here is further to acquaint the reader with the cryogenic interment project and its religious implications in the light of recent developments and commentary, with the hope of conveying a sense of *urgency.*

The thesis is based on a simple fact: according to expert opinion, if a body is frozen immediately after "clinical death" (by special techniques which minimize freezing damage) and stored at liquid nitrogen temperature (—320° F.) there will be virtually no further deterioration for an essentially indefinite period. We can then expect or at least hope that sooner or later ways will be found to thaw the body without damage *and* to repair any freezing damage *and* to cure the cause of death even when this was the "disease" of old age. Then the frozen cadaver-patients will be revived and rejuvenated; everyone will enjoy (or suffer, if you insist) indefinitely extended life.

This is really not such a radical proposal. On the one hand, it is already commonplace to revive "dead" victims of drowning, heart attack, etc., and it is widely recognized that the medical criteria of "irreversibility" of death are constantly changing. On the other hand, few dispute that the future will bring increased and perhaps indefinite longevity. Cryogenic interment will simply preserve for the future patients beyond our skill to assist otherwise.

No scientist, to my knowledge, denies that it may be possible to revive the frozen people. Most, although they cannot make an actual calculation, believe at present that the odds against it are long. But many agree with Professor Jean Rostand (the world-famous biologist who wrote one of the prefaces to my book) that this must be regarded as an excellent gamble, with little to lose and an enormous prize to gain. And as freezing methods are improved the chances become more favorable.

Increasing numbers of people have come to realize recently that we are concerned not with vague speculation about the comfortably distant future but with a practical program for the present which is vital in every sense. At this writing there exist at least three nonprofit organizations formed to promote cryogenic interment: the Life Extension Society, 2011 N Street N.W., Washington 36, D.C.; Americoin (a division of the Civic

Association of America, 1717 North Vine, Hollywood, California; and Cryonic Society of New York, 103-55 97th Street, Ozone Park, New York. At least three commercial firms have also been formed for this purpose, at least one of which has built and tested equipment for storing frozen bodies. In addition, two existing cryogenics companies have indicated they plan to enter the field, and have been doing extensive biological and engineering studies to obtain firm cost figures.

Independent studies have verified, I am told, that my estimate of $8,500 for freezing and perpetual storage was realistic and that financing through group insurance can bring this well within the reach of the average American. Market surveys are said to reveal that large numbers of people will readily obtain cryogenic interment when it is offered.

In sum, there seems ample evidence that the program will soon be implemented on a substantial scale, and many people will be asking their pastors for advice concerning a tremendous—and irrevocable—decision.

Pastoral advice in the Springfield incident, I believe, was exactly correct. When Mr. McLaughlin finally decided not to proceed, the hospital released a statement that this decision was made "in consultation" with the minister, which was technically correct but gave the misleading impression that Mr. Glaesner was opposed. Far for it: he told the family that he could not judge the medical merits or chances of the case but that from a religious viewpoint freezing was entirely permissible. Some weeks later he delivered a sermon on the subject from his pulpit; the following are excerpts:

> Christianity and the church have always been interested in the extension of human life . . . that he [man] might be more fruitful in bearing God's witness and doing God's work.
>
> We have in our hospital at this very moment electronic stimulators, inhalation techniques, blood transfusions, and many other mechanical medications. These represent only a few of the prosthetics which are used and fostered by our medical science and approved by the Christian church. . . . It follows, therefore, that cryogenic interment can certainly be approved and substantiated by the Christian church provided that the same criteria are used. [The "criteria" referred to include proper scientific and legal safeguards.]
>
> I am all in favor of extending life. Day by day I pray that God will direct us how to use the techniques, medical sciences, healing, and miracles since he is the Physician of all physicians. . . . Now life could be extended a year, one hundred years, or a thousand years, but there is still no doubt in the minds of thinking people that such . . . is but a small span in the totality of God's plan. No art or craft of man will evade or nullify the judgment of God. Life now and forevermore remains within the Providence of God. We shall resurrect whether in the body, in the grave, or in the frozen casket. . . .
>
> In conclusion, the church of Christ does not retard science. . . . In this world of ours there are great things, great potentials about 90 per cent of which we are still in the dark. When we discover new paths in orbit, or new dimensions in the galaxies, or new prosthetics for assisting or extending life, this only proves to us how wonderful, great, unsearchable and inscrutable is the mind of almighty God!

A Roman Catholic view of the "soul" problem has been provided by Fr. Thomas Acker, a Jesuit who is also a trained biologist teaching at John Carroll University in Cleveland. On Cleveland radio station KYW his statement of the acceptability of the freezing program was explicit: "In my opinion, the church would go along with this." Both on the air and in newspaper interviews he has buttressed this opinion by showing how muddy is the thinking of those who talk of "sacrilege," of "snatching a soul back from heaven," of the "impossibility of freezing a soul," of the foolishness of "preserving an empty shell after the vital spark is gone" or of the danger of resuscitating "a zombie without a soul." He simply points out that theological death and medical death are not necessarily the same, i.e., the soul does not necessarily leave the body when the heart stops beating. In other words, the shock and dismay that many people feel on encountering this idea is partly just a matter of language: perhaps we should speak of "functional failure," not "death."

To be sure, if we leave to the (possibly distant) future the final decision as to whether apparent death was real or spurious, this raises liturgical questions, among others: how shall the funeral service be modified? Presumably the prayer would be for recovery of the patient, along with commendation of his soul to God if he does not recover.

II

Ethical and emotional problems have been stressed by many clergymen who readily agree that from a strictly theological point of view freezing is unobjectionable. Involved in public discussion have been, for example, Fr. Jules Moreau, an Episcopal priest and a professor at Seabury-Western Theological Seminary; the Rev. Paul Stawnings of the First Presbyterian Church of Chestnut Hill (Philadelphia); Dr. J. Bruce Behney, vice-president of Dayton's United Theological Seminary (operated by the Evangelical United Brethren Church); Dr. John W. Rilling, acting dean of Wittenberg University's Hamma school of theology; and many others. Some of their misgivings represent real problems, while others, I think, stem from insufficient thought or downright error.

Will the prospect of indefinitely extended life be morally debilitating, carrying a connotation of endless "fun and games"? In some cases perhaps it might; but it can also be viewed as an opportunity to grow, to develop, to preserve a ripening wisdom and to achieve one's full potential, to serve more and to serve better. If the number of our days is endless, will we cease to value them, falling into listlessness, indifference and boredom, impulsive and irresponsible behavior? This argument fails in its hidden premise, viz, that society will be static, with one day much like another. Nothing could be further from the fact: challenge and peril of many kinds will persist and increase, with *growth* and *cooperation* the indispensable watchwords. The fainthearted, the reckless and the selfish will find small comfort.

Is there a danger of commercial exploitation of the bereaved? Certainly —but on the other hand no stigma or excessive suspicion should be attached to the profit motive, which after all provides, for the most part, the most efficient services to be found. Dr. Behney has said, "When this procedure is done properly, it will be by scientists, and not by a commercial concern." Apparently he thinks that scientists never work for commercial concerns.

Should implementation of the program await "more research"? When it was pointed out to Dr. Behney, on a radio program, that those now dying cannot wait but must avail themselves of whatever change is afforded by current techniques, he airily observed that people have been dying for a long time—seeming to imply that a few million more deaths do not matter. Perhaps he would change his mind when confronted with individuals.

Will the relatives of the frozen suffer continuing emotional stress— uncertain whether the body contains potential life, unable to experience the usual catharsis of grief? I think grief will be considerably assuaged by the knowledge that something positive had been done for the loved one and that his life might yet be regained. Far greater emotional stress, I believe, will be experienced by those who make a negative decision on behalf of some relative; in later years they may feel deep guilt and bitter remorse. This is not to suggest that Mrs. McLaughlin's relatives, for example, *should* blame themselves: they should not, because they acted in good conscience and according to their best judgment. But they probably will, nevertheless.

Is it wrong to arouse "false hopes"? There is a false implication here; it is not true that there will have been a great waste if it turns out that the damage done by present freezing methods is truly irreversible. There will still have been enormous benefits: the additional hope felt by dying patients, the additional comfort to the relatives, the impetus to research, greatly advancing the date of perfected freezing methods and improving everyone's chances and the salubrious effect on the moral climate of a society oriented to a long life.

III

The threat to the church is the central idea of Leon J. Putnam's hostile review of *The Prospect of Immortality* in this magazine. Some of his remarks deserve comment.

He chooses to evade the plain and solid fact that revival after apparent death is old hat, a generally accepted Christian medical practice. And he has some curious ideas on the value of extended life, including the possibility of additional missionary work with those who would otherwise die condemned. "For the position . . . leaves little room for freedom, including the freedom to say No to God. . . . It suggests a futile life on a merry-go-round which never stops because it never arrives anywhere." The first of these sentences has a very strange implication; Dr. Putnam almost seems to be saying that one should not try too hard to convert unbelievers, that a nominal effort is all that is necessary lest one interfere with their "freedom" to burn. The second sentence betrays the same fundamental misunderstanding about the future discussed earlier, namely, an implicit assumption that it will be static more of the same, "another time around," whereas in actuality it will mean a dynamic growth—in theology as well as in other areas. For as Dr. Putman well knows, religion also is an open-ended study and Christianity is very far from a final settlement or doctrine, even in fundamentals.

But the main thrust of his criticism is that I am not really in sympathy with traditional religion, am insidiously trying to substitute my own brand, and that I represent a danger. My ideas could be important if enough people share them, and they deserve clarification. It is true that I am an unbeliever: at this stage in my development I find the notions of traditional religion both unclear and unconvincing. But I recognize that this may be the result of a defect in my own intelligence or spirit; furthermore, I acknowledge that religion, as manifested in modern America, is a beneficent force. I am certainly not trying to supplant Christianity by a new "idolatry," as Dr. Putnam maintains. The competition that he senses and bristles at may in fact exist, but only in the sense that all worldly interests may tend to compete and interfere with religious devotion and any additional worldly security may tend to undermine the apparent urgency of religious commitment.

To the extent that this threat exists it should be met not in the reactionary way Dr. Putnam seems to recommend but in the adaptive way customary in recent decades. In particular, anyone with an ounce of sense can be made to see (if the pastor is worth his salt) that the urgency of religious commitment is not diminished by extended life. After all, if Dr. Putnam carried his suggestions to their ultimate conclusion he would recommend a return to jungle conditions, on the theory that terrified sheep are less likely to stray.

If clergymen are to prevent humiliation and disservice to the church they must not be reactionary; they must not even be laggards. It is unbecoming that they should be dragged along, complaining and petulant. They must be *participants* and *movers*. The vanguard needs them and they need a place in the vanguard.

Viewed in perspective, the practice of freezing the dead is only one more development in the great historical process through which man (if he survives) will develop into superman. In the course of this unfolding, the same question will be asked countless times in manifold ways: does

superman need God? Whatever answers are offered will not, I hope, be
rooted in timidity and reaction. A few clergymen may be afraid of superman; God is not likely to be.

The Death of Death?

(A Reply to Robert C. W. Ettinger)

Leon J. Putnam

sir: While some are currently proclaiming the death of God it is timely to
be reminded by Robert C. W. Ettinger of the possible death of death
through freezing. Mr. Ettinger raises many questions in his Oct. 27
article, but I will restrict my comments to those issues that concern my
review of his book, *The Prospect of Immortality*, published in the Sept.
30, 1964, *Christian Century*.

Ettinger believes I have chosen to evade the fact that "revival after
apparent death is old hat," but I do not find anything in the review to
justify or imply this conclusion. Indeed, I would be foolish not to recognize the many revivals from "death." What I did attempt to say was
that the author is using death here in a relative and not an absolute sense,
and it is only because of an ambiguity of meaning that he can feel he has
made his view compatible with the Christian faith. When restorations of
bodies occur we believe that death as the *final* cessation of life was obviously not present. If death is only relative as Ettinger suggests ("we can
now persuade ourselves that death need never be regarded as absolutely
final . . ."), what does he mean by saying "permanent death will surely
come someday"? Doesn't "immortality" in the title of his book mean "no
final death" or "endless existence"? If so, I would conclude that he believes
permanent death will *not* come someday. Assuming the latter view is
correct, we should note that it would be difficult to know when such a
state had been achieved. No matter how many thawings had been succes-
ful, would we ever reach the point where we could say beyond doubt
that death was no more?

Ettinger believes that I take lightly the question of conversion and
seem to be unsympathetic toward those who "die condemned." Again I
would dissent. My concern was to state that man is to be viewed as a free
and responsible creature and that this implies risk. We cannot remove this
risk urgency by knowing with certainty that a person dying is condemned

and hence must be favored for freezing (and later missionary persuasion), for the risk would be present in future "thawed" generations as well, even after conversion. Final judgment, I assume, is for God alone to make.

I have the impression that Ettinger would be willing to give ministers and missionaries a priority in freezing since they would be useful for many ages to come, especially if seminary enrollments continue at their present pace.

Turning to the most substantial criticism, Ettinger feels that I and others have assumed a future static society which would produce boredom and indifference and therefore we cannot see the value of endless life. He states that it would be rather a time of "dynamic growth," with opportunity for ripening wisdom, including that of a theological variety. Mere repetition may not be implied in a future life, but even Ettinger assumes that the missionaries will have "another chance" and presumably that task will remain constant. If that is what he means by "challenge and peril" I would quickly agree that those elements will be present.

Two observations seem appropriate: (1) How can we really know that an indefinitely extended life will be dynamic or static since it is quite unlike anything we have known or experienced? (2) If meaning is not totally external to the self, isn't the attitude or outlook of the person of importance? Perhaps we would reasonably conclude that there will be differences in the future just as there are now.

The philosopher Charles Hartshorne has written that no animal endowed with memory ought to live forever, or could want to, for the longer it lives, the more the balance between novelty and repetition, the basis of zest and satisfaction, will be upset in favor of repetition, hence of monotony and boredom. In principle, he contends, "old animals and old people . . . are bored." And he notes that in writing to a friend Thomas Jefferson concluded from his own weariness in "putting [his] clothes on every morning and taking them off every evening" that in such manner the Creator is preparing us for death.

Taking issue with Hartshorne, Corliss Lamont has argued that repetition as such does not necessarily lead to monotony and boredom: he himself has been drinking water for 62 years but is still not tired of it. What Hartshorne forgets, he says, is that "while constant repetition of the identical experience may well cause boredom, a repeated *cycle of variety* does not have the same effect."

What troubles me is that in Ettinger's view neither boredom nor pleasure will have much personal meaning, for he believes identity is a relative concept, possibly an illusion. How *we* will feel in a future restoration may therefore be a meaningless question.

I did not mean to imply that Ettinger was intentionally trying to supplant traditional religion by a new scientific one. I simply feel that this has happened, as suggested by his references to crossing the Jordan and the arrival of the millennium. In addition to the religious characteristics mentioned in the review (faith, salvation, redemption, etc.) we may now recognize sin also, since he feels that those who fail to see the value of freezing are denying hope to themselves and others and therefore are going to feel guilty. He believes that failure to use the freezer will be "tantamount to suicide" and is thus "a denial of life, and therefore of God." No longer does one give his life for others; he saves himself—through freezing!

In response to the above Ettinger might reply that he is concerned only with "extending" life and not "renewing" it— the province of religion. Yet it is clear from his book that he is concerned with quality as well as quantity.

In spite of my reservations I believe we need to take seriously what Ettinger and others are saying, for questions regarding death are likely to increase as the boundary lines between religion and science grow less distinct in a technological age. We may note that Ettinger is in some ways conservative when compared to the recent comments of Arthur W. Galston of Yale, who foresees a day in which tissue-culture will enable us "to make as many copies of ourselves as we would like," a process that is now apparently possible with carrot cells.

In closing I would address some questions to Ettinger regarding his view and religion: How would he interpret the Christian belief in the uniqueness or sacredness of the self if identity is an illusion or if we are potentially many souls? What would he see as implied in achieving "one's full potential"? From what is one saved by the missionaries, or to what is one resurrected? Most importantly, what evidence is there that death is only a "disease" and not a natural occurrence?

Questions

1. What definition of human life seems to emerge from the material here? Can one properly speak of life "ending" before death? In what senses?

2. What seem to be the legal questions involved in organ transplantation?

3. In recent discussions by physicians and lawyers, the question has been raised as to whether a man who is declared "clinically dead" but whose lungs are kept operating artificially can be considered "alive." What if a man's heart stops beating before the end of a particular tax deadline while his lungs continue operating after that deadline? In short, what conditions would then define life—or death?

4. It has been suggested by, among others, Professor Paul A. Freund of the Harvard Law School, that there be several definitions of death: one for transplantation purposes, one for tax purposes, one for insurance purposes. For example, a fetus, the unborn baby, is not regarded in some jurisdictions as being alive in terms of abortion laws, but is so regarded if any injury is suffered by it before birth. What do you think about such a range of definitions of death? Who do you suppose should decide "death" in such cases? On what basis? Is a definition of "death" related to one of "birth"? How?

5. Do the heart and kidney transplantation techniques suggest that human

beings might someday be put together from replaceable parts? What might be the identity of such a creature?

6. Can a person be considered "dead" if he has been quick-frozen in the hope of eventual resuscitation? What seems to be some of the problems raised by freezing the dead?

7. Assuming that it should become possible to perfect the science of resuscitating those who have been cryogenically interred, would it be a good thing? In other words, is immortality of a sort to be desired?

Assignments

1. Summarize the legal aspects as distinguished from the ethical considerations of transplantation and cryogenic interment.

2. Relate the discussion by Eliot Corday in "Life-Death in Human Transplantation" to the difficulties, ethical, biological and legal, raised in the other articles.

3. Discuss how science, law, and theology get involved in matters involving organ transplantation and freezing the dead.

4. Investigate how various religious groups, such as the Catholic Church or Orthodox Jews, approach the various questions discussed in this section.

5. In 1969 England's House of Lords debated a bill that would allow doctors to end the life of a patient with an incurable disease at the patient's own request. The measure was defeated, 61–40, but meanwhile the subject was widely discussed and religious organizations of all denominations, as well as the British Medical Association itself, announced their opposition to mercy killing in any form. Discuss how such a measure might have gotten so far in the first place against the opposition of both the medical profession and the various religious groups.

Additional Reading

Glanville Williams's book *The Sanctity of Life and the Criminal Law* (New York: Knopf, 1957) discusses at length the questions involving the definition of what constitutes the beginning of life and the end of life. The book is based on a series of lectures he delivered at the Columbia University Law School. Joseph Fletcher's article "The Patient's Right to Die" in *Harper's Magazine*, October 1960, pages 95–103, discusses the question of the patient's right to choose the moment of his death. The Reader's Guide to Periodicals, widely available in libraries, will list current articles having to do with the legal, medical, and theological questions involved in organ transplantation. Articles relevant to the general subject of controlling life's beginning and end may also be found under the headings of "Abortion" and "Euthanasia."

Index

2